The Book of

Inventions

and

Discoveries

1992

The Book of

Inventions

and

Discoveries

1992

Associate Editor
Valérie-Anne Giscard d'Estaing

Macdonald
Queen Anne Press

A QUEEN ANNE PRESS BOOK

© Compagnie 1212 1991
English translation © Queen Anne Press 1991
First published in Great Britain in 1991 by Queen Anne Press, a division of
Macdonald & Co (Publishers) Ltd

165 Great Dover Street
London SE1 4YA

A member of the Maxwell Macmillan Publishing Corporation

A CIP catalogue record for this book is available from the British Library

ISBN 0–356–20274–7

Typeset by Rowland Phototypesetting Ltd, Bury St Edmunds, Suffolk

Printed and bound in Great Britain by BPCC Hazell Books, Paulton and Aylesbury

Editors: Ian Marshall, Janet Ravenscroft
Design: Anne Samuel, Peter Champion
Cover design: Roger Abraham at the Creative Space
Production: Oscar Heini
Picture research: Donna Thynne, Angela Anderson
Translator: Ros Schwartz
Indexer: David Linton

Acknowledgements

The following have also helped in the production of this edition of *The Book of
Inventions and Discoveries*:

Russell Ash, Audi, Dr Rowan Connell MB BS, Steve Dobell, Alan Freeman, Sally
Green, ICI, Jeremy Lord BSc AFIMA, the Nobel Foundation and Kate Truman.

If you have invented or discovered anything which you feel could be suitable for
inclusion in future editions of the book, then please write, giving details, to: The
Editor, Book of Inventions and Discoveries, Queen Anne Press, 165 Great Dover
Street, London, SE1 4YA.

CONTENTS

WARFARE

POWER AND INDUSTRY

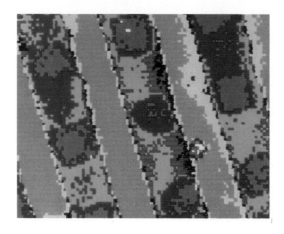

SCIENCE

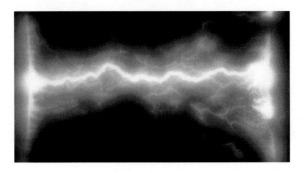

SPACE

MEDIA AND COMMUNICATIONS

INFORMATION TECHNOLOGY

EVERYDAY LIFE

LEISURE

Games and toys **245**

Sport **247**

THE BIZARRE

MEDICINE

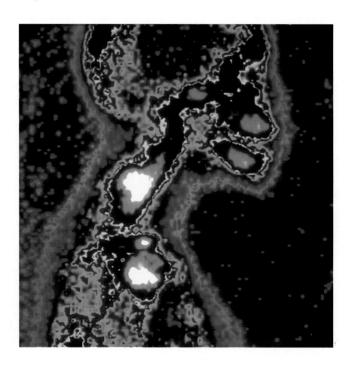

AGRICULTURE

ECOLOGY AND THE ENVIRONMENT

THE ARTS

TRANSPORT

By land

The motorcar

Origins

The idea of a self-propelling vehicle for road transport dates back to antiquity. It reappeared again during the Renaissance especially in Leonardo da Vinci's work. The first 'automobiles' were built in the 18th century. Varied and ingenious devices were used to drive the wheels: coil spring (Jacques de Vaucanson, 1740), wind-engine (J. H. Genevois, 1760), compressed air (W. Medhurst, 1799). Nevertheless, the car could not be born without the engine.

First cars

It was the steam engine that made it possible to produce the first truly usable cars. In fact, the 'truck' built by **Nicolas Cugnot** in **1771** is generally considered to be the first motor vehicle.

On Christmas Eve 1801 Cornishman Richard Trevithick ran his steam car on a stretch of road near Camborne where it reached a speed of 13 to 14.5km/h *8 to 9mph*.

Up to the end of the 19th century, with a few minor exceptions, all motor vehicles were powered by steam. The first attempts at propulsion by an internal combustion engine were made by the Swiss Isaac de Rivaz as early as 1807. His example was followed at distant intervals in England (Samuel Brown, 1826) and in France (Etienne Lenoir, 1862).

The petrol engine only came into its own after 1876, when the four-stroke cycle started to be used. It was in 1883 that the Frenchmen Malandin and Delamare-Deboutteville fitted a road vehicle with a four-stroke engine for the first time. But it was the Germans **Karl Benz** from **1885**, and **Gottlieb Daimler** and **Wilhelm Maybach** in **1889**, who built what can be considered to be the first true modern motorcar.

The first American petrol-driven motorcars were built by the brothers Charles and Frank Duryea in 1892.

Mercedes (1901)

Built in **1901**, the Mercedes was a much-improved version of the first car, invented by **Gottlieb Daimler** (1834–1900) and **Wilhelm Maybach** (1846–1929) in 1889. It was named after the daughter of their sponsor, E. Jellinek.

This car caused a sensation at the time, as much because of its appearance – it was the first car that didn't look like a horse-drawn carriage – as its technical qualities. Its top speed was 86km/h *53mph*.

After the merger of the Daimler and Benz companies in 1926, the make became known as Mercedes-Benz.

Model T Ford (1908)

Built at Detroit in **1908** by the American **Henry Ford** (1863–1947), the Model T Ford was put into mass production on the assembly line in 1908. It was a far cry from the hand-crafted automobile built by Henry Ford at Detroit in 1896, with its four-stoke engine and Kane Pennington cylinders. Assembly-line production, a Ford innovation for the car industry, was an application of the principles of Frederick W Taylor, the creator of Scientific Management, who stressed strict specialisation, elimination of all superfluous motion, and maximum utilisation of plant and equipment. It was this system that made it possible for 15 million Model Ts to roll out of the Ford factories between 1908 and 1927.

The Beetle (1936)

The Volkswagen VW 1936, better known as the Beetle, is the longest-lasting model. The prototype was devised by **Ferdinand Porsche** between 1934 and **1936**. About 30 vehicles were produced by Daimler-Benz in 1937 and the first stone of the Wolfsburg factory, where the car was to be mass-produced, was laid by Hitler in 1938.

About 23 million Beetles have been produced to date, and the model is still being manufactured in Mexico.

Assembly-line production brought the Model T within the price range of large numbers of people.

2 TRANSPORT

The 2 CV (1948)

It was **Pierre Boulanger**, Citroën's managing director, who conceived the 2 CV in 1935. He wanted to build an economical and practical car which would be high enough for someone to get in without removing their hat.

André Lefèbvre (1894–1963), father of the front-wheel drive car, worked on the prototype. The first trials were held in 1938, but were interrupted by the war. The official launch was in **1948**. As early as 1949, the model was so popular that prospective buyers had to submit a written application and faced a two-year wait when successful! The last car rolled off the production line in July 1990.

Austin Mini (1959)

Its British inventor, **Sir Alec Issigonis**, died in 1988, 29 years after the launch of the first model. With this engineer, born in Smyrna in 1906 of a Greek father and a Bavarian mother, died the last man of ideas who, on his own, was able to create a car and impose it on the market. Vital statistics: 998cc, 3m *9ft 10in* long, 1.4m *4ft 7in* wide, almost 6 million models sold.

Its success probably stemmed from the Mini being so amazingly modern and ahead of its time. As opposed to the 2 CV and the Beetle, it changed names along the way: BMC 850 in **1959**, then Morris and Austin Mini, and now just Mini.

Electric car (1891)

The first electric cars were developed in the United States in **1891**. The Electrobat, manufactured by the **Morris** and **Salom** firm of Philadelphia, was only produced in a small series.

In 1892 the Morrison, manufactured by William Morrison of Des Moines, Iowa, was launched.

A new boom (1990s)

The problem of pollution has brought the concept of the electric car back to the fore-front and big car manufacturers worldwide are currently developing electric engines for their utility (town use) vehicles: C15, J5 and 205 Citroën vans, Peugeot Miracle and Renault's Master. Around ten have been tested over the last three years and they will probably be on the market in 1991.

Fiat presented its first electric model in 1990: the two-seater Panda Elettra, designed for city use, and General Motors produced the prototype of a small high-powered racing car, with lightning acceleration (100km/h *62mph* in eight seconds). Not to be outdone, Japan has come up with a four-seater capable of 110km/h *68mph* designed by Nippon Steel and the National Institute for Environmental Studies. The first trials took place in 1990.

Reva (1990)

According to its inventor, the Frenchman **Raoul Parienti** from Nice, this is the first means of public transport designed for the individual. Reva, 2.2m *7ft 3in* long, is driven by an electric engine. The user inserts an electronic card into a slot, the car opens and is ready to go. When the user has finished with it, he parks it so that somebody else can use it. The batteries have to be recharged at special car parks.

Gas turbine car (1950)

The first car to be powered by a gas turbine was built by **Rover** in 1950. On 26 June 1952 one of these vehicles reached a speed of 242km/h *150mph*. Other manufacturers have since taken up the process: General Motors, Chrysler, Boeing, Fiat and Renault, whose *Etoile Filante* (Shooting Star) attained a speed of 308.9km/h *192mph* in 1956.

Twin-engined vehicle (1990)

Constructed in collaboration with the German company **Pöhlman**, and based on the Audi 100, the Audi Duo has two engines: the first, a combustion engine (petrol or diesel), drives the front wheels and the second, which is electric, drives the rear wheels. The driver chooses one or the other depending on his priorities: the electric engine saves energy, is very quiet and causes no pollution while the traditional engine provides greater power.

THE SELF-PARKING CAR

The prototype Futura, presented by Volkswagen at the 1989 Frankfurt Motor Show, is innovative in more ways than one. It has access through vertically opening doors, thermal shield windows, a variable powered direct injection engine, a new anti-lock braking system. But what is more extraordinary is that Futura is self-parking. After selecting a parking space, the driver simply presses a button and the laser sensors, four guiding wheels, electronic accelerator, automatic gearbox and power steering do the rest. It is hoped that it will be on the market soon.

The revolutionary Rover gas turbine engine is revealed.

Two vehicles in one, that's Voyager, launched by Chrysler in January 1990.

Voyager III (1990)

Launched by **Chrysler** at the **1990** Detroit Auto Show, the prototype Voyager III offers two cars in one. A three-seater shuttle driven by a 1.6 litre propane engine can be electronically linked to a five-seater rear section. This has a 2.2 litre petrol engine which can be used either instead of the first engine or to give it a boost, according to the needs of the user. It thus becomes a 4 × 4 vehicle capable of transporting eight people.

SOLAR-POWERED CAR

Kyocera has just brought out the first Japanese car which runs purely on solar energy. The SCV-O is covered with 640 solar cells and can reach a speed of 60km/h *37mph*. It even works when it is raining!

A CAR IN A SUITCASE

A favourite subject with inventors is the collapsible car that fits into a suitcase. In January 1990 Jacques Calvel, a French inventor from the Aveyron, presented a vehicle called Golfe (Golf) which folds up like a briefcase and can be transformed into a parallelepiped 1.75m *5ft 9in* long and 1.1m *3ft 7in* wide. Weighing 60kg *132lb*, it is driven by a bicycle motor and is capable of 30km/h *18½mph*. It was originally designed to be used on golf courses, hence its name. There is also the Minicady, invented in 1985 by another Frenchman, Jean Dumoulin, which again fits into a suitcase and is portable as well.

Mechanics

ABS (1972)

The Anti-Blocking System (ABS) perfected by the German firm **Bosch** has been mass-produced since 1978. The ABS allows the driver, by slamming on the brakes, to stop the car in the shortest possible time, be it on a straight road or on a bend, whether the road is wet, gravelled, icy or dry. This system, according to the specialists, represents the greatest step forward in safety since the invention of disc brakes and seat belts.

About a million cars had been fitted with ABS by 1988 and it is thought that that figure will have increased to 5 million by 1995.

Anti-skid system (1985)

Introduced in **1985** by the Swedish company **Volvo**, on its latest top of the line models, the ETC (Electronic Traction Control) system intervenes in case of skidding during acceleration. As soon as a drive wheel turns more quickly than a front wheel, this control device reduces the supply of petrol little by little until all four wheels are turning at the same speed. It thus considerably reduces the risk of loss of adhesion on a slippery road, even if the driver accelerates strongly. The driver is warned of the danger by means of a small light on the dashboard.

Back axle with integral trailing arm (1974)

First seen in **1974** on the Scirocco, the back axle with integral trailing arm, invented by the **Volkswagen** engineers, is fitted on all the new generation VWs. It was largely responsible for the Golf's popularity.

The brake (1895)

Automobile braking was first ensured by means of brake shoes such as were used in carts (**1895**). In 1899 the transmission shaft band and wheel brake appeared. These were commanded by a hand lever (brake drum).

The combined hydraulic (foot brake) and mechanical (hand brake) controls formed the subject of the 1924 Perrot-Lockheed patent. The American Chrysler Corporation was the first company to utilise this patented system.

Disc brake (1902)

The disc brake, invented by an Englishman, **Dr Lanchester**, was primarily used to equip military vehicles. The victory of Jaguar at the Le Mans 24-hour race in 1953 with a vehicle equipped with Dunlop disc brakes, which had been patented in 1945 and used in aeronautics, led to the spread of the invention.

Ecological brake pads (1990)

Said to be 'ecological' because other fibres and materials are used in their manufacture instead of asbestos, Valéo brake pads are already fitted to several vehicles, including the Citroën XM. Controlled by ultrasound, these pads, according to the manufacturer, have a life of between 25000km and 30000km *15500* and *18500 miles* as opposed to 15000km *9300 miles* for traditional models.

FOUR TIMES AS MUCH ELECTRICITY

The British group Chloride has begun manufacturing sulphur and sodium fondus-based accumulators. These two components are heated to 300°C *572°F* and react through a ceramic partition to generate electricity. According to the first trials, these accumulators would generate four times as much electricity as acid-lead batteries of the same weight.

AN ELECTRONIC ROAD MAP IN YOUR CAR

In 1981 Ron Dork, an engineer at General Motors, fitted the first prototype of the electronic road map, the Loran, on his Buick. It consisted of a computer system receiving data on the position of the car via navigation satellites identical to those used by ships. The computer instantly translated the information onto a screen on which the position of the car is displayed on a memorised road map.

The European project Carminat, on which Philips and Renault are working, aims to obtain concrete and marketable results in the near future. Carminat combined three previous projects.

Carin, introduced in 1985 by Philips, is based on the storage of an enormous library of maps on a CD-ROM compact disc. Using this data bank, Carin can indicate to the driver the best route between two points (in town or on the road) and then guide him along. Data about the vehicle's route are obtained by a tachometer and a compass. A different version proposed by Bosch uses the ABS sensors to work out the journey.

Atlas is designed to give the car all the necessary data about traffic and road conditions. Minerva is an in-car computer that deals with data about the state of the tyres, petrol consumption, fault-finding, etc. These three systems should soon be ready and so it is hoped that Carminat will be operational within five years.

More ambitious still, the Prometheus system, launched under Daimler-Benz's initiative, is intended to give complete driving assistance. At present, 11 manufacturers and more than 100 companies are collaborating on this project with a view to realising it early in the next century.

Kégresse's patents into practice to produce vehicles with caterpillar tracks and driven front wheels.

In 1937 Mercedes introduced its G5 (G for *Gelände*, land) which was capable of remarkable performances. With its 45hp fuel injection engine it could climb 55 percent ramps with a load of 770kg *1700lb* and turn in a 7m *23ft* diameter circle.

The Jeep (1940)

The Jeep was born on **10 June 1940**, the brainchild of three American military engineers who imposed a crazy deadline on the presentation of projects: 75 days! The model selected was that designed by the **Willys-Overland** engineers, and intensive production started in 1941 in association with Ford. More than 585 000 vehicles were built during the war. The origin of its name is rather mysterious: it could have come from the name of one of Popeye's friends, Jeep; or from the letters GP, meaning General Purpose, that Ford put on its model; or perhaps from the initials of the American military police units, GIP, who used them for the American landing in North Africa.

Differential (1827)

The differential was invented by the Frenchman **Onésiphore Pecqueur** in November **1827** for a steam engine. In a motorcar, the differential is the device which transmits the power from the engine to the wheels while allowing them to turn at different speeds as the car goes round bends. Then, the outside wheel has to turn faster than the inside wheel.

Electronic clutch (1988)

Officially introduced at the *Mondial de l'Automobile* in Paris, the Valéo electronic clutch couples the advantages of both the manual and the automatic gearboxes. By doing away with the third pedal, it frees the driver from having to operate the clutch while giving him complete freedom of choice when it comes to ratio, gear shifting, level of acceleration and down-shifting with or without acceleration.

Electronically variable shock-absorbers (1987)

Created by the German company **Boge**, they were first fitted on the 1988 model of the BMW M3, which was launched in **February 1987**. Today, they are an option on the BMW 635 and 750 as well as on the Lancia Thema 832. With the help of sensors and microcomputers, the shock-absorbers adjust to road conditions in a thousandth of a second.

Four-wheel drive

The last phase of the 1914–18 war created the need for an all-terrain vehicle. Therefore, in the early 1920s, French and German manufacturers tackled the problem. In 1926 **Georges Latil** introduced his T.L. tractor with four driving and directional wheels. The road model was soon adapted by foresters. For their part, Citroën and Unic were putting **Adolphe**

Four-wheel drive saloon (1983)

The first mass-produced all-weather (as opposed to all-purpose) saloon was the **Audi 80 Quattro**. Today most manufacturers have started to produce their own versions.

Four-wheel steering (1986)

This will be the next major revolution in the car industry. The four-wheel steering system (4WS) gives greatly increased comfort and safety. The ancestor of cars with four directional wheels is Amédée Bollée's steam car of 1876. After that, the same formula was used on a few prototypes. In 1967 an American, Mickey Thompson, raced a four-wheel steering car at Indianapolis. In 1965 the Japanese firm Mazda took out its first patents. But it was in **1986** that the first commercial model was introduced: the Skyline from **Nissan**. In 1987 Honda offered the system as an option on its sports model Prelude XX. The Japanese are

The latest Lamborghini thoroughbred, the Diablo, was designed by Marcello Gandini. It has an outstanding performance, with a top speed of 325km/h 202mph.

investing considerable sums of money to develop this system and are well ahead of the rest of the field.

Front-wheel drive

Hooke-type universal joint (1926)

The invention of the Hooke-type universal joint Tracta by the French engineers **Pierre Fenaille** and **Jean Grégoire** in 1926 made front-wheel drive cars possible. This joint allows transmission of the engine power to the front wheels.

The Citroën 7 (1934)

The true father of front-wheel drive is the French engineer **André Lefèbvre**. Hired by André Citroën on 1 March 1933, he managed to perfect and build, in only one year, the first front-wheel drive car. The Model 7 was officially introduced to Citroën agents on **24 March** 1934. After the bodywork and the accessories were further improved, it won universal acclaim at the 1934 Paris Motor Show. The system has so many advantages that most cars now have front-wheel drive.

Gearbox

Direct transmission (1899)

In 1899 **Louis Renault** (1877–1944) equipped his first car, completed in 1898, with a transmission coupled directly to the engine, and gear-shifting by selector rod. The transmission on the 1899 Renault had three speeds and a reverse gear. The fastest speed, third gear, was reached directly, the primary and secondary propeller shafts turning at the same speed.

Automatic gearbox (1910)

The automatic gearbox invented by the German **Föttinger** in 1910 was nothing more than a torque converter.

Preselector gearbox (1917)

In 1917 **Wilson**, a major in the British Army, invented the preselector gearbox for use in the battle tanks that had just been developed. After the war the box was fitted to all Armstrong-Siddeleys and, later on, to some Talbots in France. However, it was mainly used in large industrial vehicles and buses.

Fully automatic transmission (1971–90)

A belt-driven system called Variomatic, which provides fully automatic variations of gear ratio, appeared in 1971 on the Dutch car Daf before being fitted to the bottom of the range Volvos and being tested at Fiat.

In 1987, after several Japanese cars were fitted with a CVT transmission derived from the Daf system, a Selecta version of the Fiat Uno range appeared in which the V belts of the old Van Doorne system were replaced by a continuous metal transmission. The Ford Fiestamatic is also fitted with this system.

In 1990 the Fiat Group, in association with the Japanese Fugi, transformed CVT transmission into ECVT (electromagnetic) transmission, which is lighter and more compact. Introduced at the beginning of the year on the Lancia Y10 Selectronic, it will be fitted to other Fiat models as well as to the Ford Fiesta and Escort.

Volunteers to have their car crushed by the Robosaurus can receive a BMW in exchange.

All-electronic gearbox (1989)

The 1989 version of the Ferrari Formula 1 cars have a revolutionary gearbox. Fitted on John Barnard's instigation, it is a completely electronic box. The gear lever is fitted on the steering wheel and the driver has only to press a tab with the index finger to change the ratio.

Suspension

Hydropneumatic suspension (1924)

The first hydraulic suspension system was that of the French engineer **Georges Messier** who, in 1924, made an 'oleopneumatic suspension with position adjustment' (patented in 1920). It was fitted in 1926 on Messier cars without springs. It was in 1953 (20 years after Messier's death) that Citroën perfected its famous hydropneumatic suspension (combining a gas and an oil-based liquid) which was fitted first on 3000 of their 15 CV front-wheel drive cars before being extended to their other models from 1955 onwards.

Volvo CCS suspension (1986)

Launched in Turin in 1986 the CCS suspension, created by **Volvo**, is controlled by a microprocessor which enables it to react 3000 times per second transmitting each impulse to the wheels thus allowing them to adapt to the road. This new suspension keeps the vehicle steady in any conditions.

Hydroactive suspension (1989)

The hydroactive suspension of the **Citroën XM**, on the market since spring 1989, is controlled by an electronic calculator which instantaneously changes its setting to suit the road and the style of driving, using data provided by five sensors. Representing a new concept in active safety, this suspension automatically becomes firm before the driver suffers the drawbacks of too much softness, intelligently anticipating the car's reactions.

Transmission (1900)

It was in 1900 that a Frenchman, **Louis Bonneville**, perfected the first 'automatic transmission by epicyclic train', an invention which was mentioned in the 18 August 1900 issue of the American magazine *The Motor Car Journal*.

In 1950 another Frenchman, **Gaston Fleischel**, invented and patented a complete range of possible controls for gearboxes with epicyclic trains, which the Speciality Equipment and Machinery Corporation (Maryland, USA) decided to use in that same year.

Fleischel's patent led to a strongly disputed lawsuit dealing with industrial property which ended in 1953 when a group of American car manufacturers bought all the shares of the Speciality Equipment and Machinery Corporation.

Viscodrive (1986)

This system, which equips four-wheel steering German cars (VW Golf Synchro and BMW 325 4 × 4), was invented by the English engineer **Harry Ferguson**. When the front wheels are skidding, **Viscodrive** takes over by increasing the power to the back wheels. To ensure satisfactory distribution of the torque, it can be incorporated to a transfer box or a differential.

Bodywork and accessories

Airbag (1981)

This anti-shock air cushion known as the airbag is a **Daimler-Benz** invention. This comes in the form of an air pocket incorporated into the vehicle's steering column. In the event of a frontal collision, the airbag inflates automatically, putting the equivalent of a mattress between the steering wheel and the driver. Mercedes is the first company to equip certain of its models with this system and it has proved very popular in the States.

Eurobag (1988)

Volvo has perfected an inflatable bag designed to protect the driver's face – the Eurobag – after several years' study. Engineers built an electronic head which has 52 sensors that collect 800 pieces of information in the tenth of a second the impact lasts. Volvo has made the head available to other car manufacturers.

Air-conditioning film (1990)

Curtisolar Europe's Glastint was the star of the Eurisko **1990** trade show. It air-conditions the car and reduces noise, while also protecting the windows from vandalism. Developed from a device patented by NASA 15 years ago for the protection of astronauts' visors, it was brought to Europe by **Patrick Curti**, founder of Curtisolar.

Automatic hazard warning lights (1989)

Isaac Baloutch and **Jean-Pierre Louis** patented a new vehicle security invention: the ACS (anti-collision system). This little electronic device automatically switches on the hazard warning lights if the car stops suddenly or hits something.

Bumpers (1905)

In **1905 F. R. Simms** patented the first bumpers to be made from rubber. The Simms Manufacturing Company of Kilburn, London, fitted the bumpers onto a Simms-Welbeck in the summer of 1905. Bumpers had previously been fitted to a Czech vehicle, the Präsident which was built in 1897. Unfortunately, the bumpers fell off after 15km *9 miles*, and were never replaced.

Bump Guard (1990)

The British firm **Avon Tyres** has perfected a new proximity warning device, the Bump Guard, to reduce the risk of an accident for utility (town use) vehicles during low-speed manoeuvres. It is a radar, mounted on the near-side front bumper, which sweeps the road up to 40cm *16in* ahead and to the side. As soon as the sensor detects an obstacle, a light comes on in the cab to warn the driver of hidden danger. This visual warning can be accompanied by a sound alarm, or each system can operate separately. For reverse manoeuvres, Avon Tyres also offers the Avon Backstop braking system, popular among lorry drivers.

Double glazing to stop misting (1989)

The problems of driving in very cold weather and a study of drivers' reactions led **Volvo** to use double glazing in their cars. This overcomes the inconvenience of misting without having to resort to a fan which often makes the car feel cold or draughty. The double glazing

Since 1990 Michelin has been marketing MTM (Michelin Tyre Monitoring), an electronic process for monitoring tyre pressures on the dashboard. For each of the five tyres (spare wheel included), this device shows the fluctuations and differences in pressure, any possible anomalies, etc. First fitted to a luxury BMW coupé, the MTM – which took four years' research – has passed all the most difficult tests, particularly in competition conditions, such as the Paris–Dakar. The first competitor on the horizon is Goodyear, which is preparing its own device for 1992.

also reduces loss of heat from inside the vehicle.

Electronic detector for reversing (1989)

Reversing is still a nightmare for many drivers, especially in the dark, the rain or the snow. It will now be made easy by the electronic detector **Back Sensor** from South Korea. This consists of two detectors which are fitted under the back lights or on the bumper. As you manoeuvre, it warns you about any kind of obstacle, be it another vehicle or a pedestrian.

Emergency battery (1987)

Called the Jump Start, it was invented in **1987** by the American **John Tompkins**. When your battery is flat, Jump Start can be plugged into the cigarette lighter and off you go! Originally invented to overcome the problems of dead batteries on Tompkins' private plane, he quickly realised its potential in the car market.

Fifth door (1961)

The fifth door, or hatchback, which makes it possible to open touring cars from the back, the back shelf folding inwards, first appeared on the Renault 4 in **September 1961**. The Autobianchi Primula followed suit in 1963.

Gas generator (1883)

The first gas generator that could be used to supply internal combustion gas engines was produced by the English engineer **Emerson Dowson** in July 1883. A gas generator turns solid fuel into a gas fuel. Dowson's generator had a 60 percent efficiency. It was used by the Crossley brothers in England and by Deutz in Germany.

Integrated child seat (1990)

A new safety measure for children has been revealed by **Renault** and, after approval, it will be fitted on one of their forthcoming vehicles. It is a seat which, when not in use, is hidden in a retractable housing in the back seat. When it is in place it has the double advantage of enabling the child to look at the scenery as

easily as an adult, and of allowing a conventional adult seat belt to be used, the lower strap being placed completely flat between the child's legs.

Petrol saver (1989)

Patented by the Frenchman **Antoine Piras**, this is an electronic system which automatically switches the engine off when the car stops and switches it on again when the car moves off. It also takes into account variations in the acceleration and deceleration speed. The CA 35's predecessor, which is less effective, was tested on post office cars and enabled them to economise on fuel consumption by 14.5 percent.

Pneumatic tyres (1888)

A Scottish veterinary surgeon working in Belfast, **John Boyd Dunlop** (1840–1921), invented the pneumatic tyre in **1888**. This was one of the most significant leaps forward as far as locomotion by wheels was concerned.

Dunlop had the idea of fitting air-filled tyres to his son's bicycle.

The same idea had already been put forward by a Belgian, Dietz, in 1836, and by a Scottish engineer, Robert W. Thompson, in 1845, but had not been put into practice. Abandoning his old profession, Dunlop patented his invention and founded the first tyre factory, where he utilised Goodyear's vulcanisation process. Through the mediation of a German subsidiary, Dunlop tyres were put on the first mass-produced motorcycles, the Hildebrand & Wolfmüller in 1894. The Dunlop firm immediately received complete support from most manufacturers. On the other hand, it was the French Michelin brothers, André (1853–1931) and Edouard (1859–1940), who in 1895 first used pneumatic tyres on an automobile.

Removable tyre (1891)

Invented in **1891** by the French firm **Michelin**, the removable tyre proved to be revolutionary. A blow out, which formerly meant calling a specialised repairman, could now be fixed by the rider in less than 15 minutes. This invention was an immediate success.

Anti-puncture liquid (1988)

Perfected in the United States by **World Promotions**, it is a liquid mixture of glycol and acrylic fibres in suspension which, as soon as a puncture occurs, concentrates in the affected area and stops the air escaping. The liquid is introduced into the deflated tyres and is evenly spread after a 10km *6 mile* drive (the tyres must be pumped up again, of course!). It is efficient for punctures up to 5mm *⅕in* in diameter.

Tyre that goes grey (1988)

Like humans, this tyre, patented in **1988**, goes grey as it gets older so that one knows exactly when it needs changing. This tyre was invented by the Spaniard **Mariano Romero** and first displayed in Brussels.

Rear-view mirror (1906)

In **1906** a French inventor, **Alfred Faucher**, registered the first patent concerning a 'warning mirror for motorcars'. He had also fitted his car with a 'hand to signal changes of direction', the ancestor of our direction indicators, and with the first rear warning light activated by touching the brake pedal. About ten years later, side mirrors were introduced to complement the central rear-view mirror which was fitted inside the car.

Electronic anti-glare rear-view mirror (1988)

Perfected by **Stewart Automotive Ltd** of Greenock in Scotland, the **Eclipse** rear-view mirror, using microchip technology, automatically tilts within one tenth of a second of being hit by the dazzle of headlights, going back to its original position only after the light conditions are normal again.

Periscope rear-view mirror (1990)

Invented by an Englishman, **Peter Milne**, this new type of interior rear-view mirror does away with the need for external mirrors by using instead a prismatic mirror based on the periscope. A first prism built into the outside of the door reflects the surroundings in an interior mirror, from here a second prism relays it to the driver. Advantages: the car is more streamlined as nothing is protruding from the vehicle, and the risk of mirrors being smashed or vandalised is removed. However, the project is still seeking a manufacturer.

Seat belt (1903)

The seat belt is derived from a patent registered in **1903** by the Frenchman **Gustave Désiré Liebau**, which dealt with 'protective braces for use in motorcars and other vehicles', and from a slightly different model which an American military doctor, Colonel Stapp, tried out on a vehicle travelling at a speed of more than 200km/h *124mph*. First used in aeronautics, the seat belt went

through various stages before being fitted on mass-produced cars by Volvo after the firm conducted tests from 1959 to 1963 that led them to choose the three-point type. The wearing of seat belts in the front seats of a car was made compulsory in Britain in January 1983.

Automatic-fastening belt (1988)

Toyota has fitted an electric system that automatically fastens the seat belt on some of its models for the American market as seat belt regulations are particularly strict in the USA.

Automatic-release seat belt (1989)

Kim Nag-Hyun of the Seóul Polytechnic (South Korea) presented in New York in **March 1989** an electric system which automatically releases the seat belt catch 30 seconds after the car has been stopped by an impact.

Solar ventilator (1990)

To combat the suffocating heat that builds up inside a car when it is parked in the sun, the British firm **Intersolar** has perfected a ventilation panel that uses solar energy to prevent this accumulation of hot air. The device can be easily fitted to the rear window.

The windscreen (1903)

The first windscreens appeared in **1903** and were generally very high, as the cars of the period reached a height of up to 2m *6ft 6in*. Made of ordinary glass, these early windscreens were very dangerous and were considered optional accessories.

Laminated windscreens (1920)

The first windscreens made of laminated glass (invented in 1909 by the French chemist **E. Benedictus** and marketed as of **1920** under

the name Triplex) were reserved for top of the line models for some time. The first car manufacturer to use laminated glass windscreens for a series model was Volvo in 1944 for the PV44.

Resin for windscreens (1972)

In **1972** the American engineer **Gerald Keinath** patented his technique for repairing laminated windscreens with a transparent resin injected with a piston then solidified before being polished by an ultra-violet lamp. Since then this process has been greatly improved, allowing repairs even in the case of significant impact with blistering or radiating cracks.

A COLLAPSIBLE STEERING WHEEL

German cars are renowned for their safety and now, on all 1991 models, Audi have added to that reputation by introducing a new system to reduce the chance of serious injury in front-end accidents – Procon Ten.

This is a mechanical device triggered by the deformation of the front section of the car. When this happens, the engine and gearbox are pushed backwards towards the driver. This movement tightens a stainless steel cable which runs round the gearbox unit and immediately triggers the steering wheel to move forward into the dashboard, thus reducing the danger of the driver smashing his head into it. Simultaneously, the seat belts lock and so reduce the effects of whiplash. The Procon Ten system has won many prizes, including the Golden Safety Award in Germany.

Thanks to the remarkable contraption on the back of Franco Sbarro's latest car, the Robur, it is able to park in the smallest of spaces.

8 TRANSPORT

Windscreen wiper (1916)

The first mechanical windscreen wipers appeared in the United States in 1916. In 1921 the Englishman W. M. Folberth invented windscreen wipers that worked automatically, using compressed air supplied by the engine. The first electric windscreen wipers were manufactured in the United States by Berkshire.

Invisible windscreen wiper (1978)

Rain'x was invented by the American chemical engineer **Howard Ohlhausen** while he was a pilot, and has been used by thousands of motorists in the United States since 1978. Now called Rain Away, it works like an invisible windscreen wiper. It is a transparent hydrophobic substance which repels rain by forming minute droplets which cannot cling to glass. It improves visibility and, above a certain speed, a coat of it applied to the windscreen makes the use of conventional wipers unnecessary.

Sensitive windscreen wiper (1983)

The first windscreen wiper to adjust its speed automatically to the intensity of the rain was developed in 1983 by the Japanese firm **Nissan** and fitted to all their cars.

At the roadside

Belisha beacons (1934)

These orange roadside lights were designed to highlight crossing points so that pedestrians could cross the road more easily and drivers of vehicles would be more cautious when approaching. The roads are now painted with white stripes so that this is known as a zebra crossing. The first Belisha beacon was erected in London in **September 1934** and named after the then Minister of Transport in the National Government, Hore-Belisha.

Black-ice detector (1985)

The British firm **Zero Products** has perfected a very reliable and accurate black-ice detector which may prevent a great number of accidents. After being tested by the Essex police, it is now fitted on Lotus cars. It is a useful accessory with which Zero Products hopes to conquer the European market.

Car registrations (1893)

The first number plates were introduced in Paris in 1893. The British adopted the idea in 1904, the first plate being A1 and going to the 2nd Earl Russell. There is now a thriving trade in personalised number plates; for example, MUS1C was recently offered for sale at almost £100000.

Cat's-eyes (1934)

These reflecting studs in the centre of the road were designed by **Percy Shaw** of Halifax in Yorkshire to help people driving at night. They have a self-cleaning mechanism when pressed down so that they remain bright. They were first used in **April 1934** near Bradford.

Parking meters (1935)

The first 150 parking meters were put into operation on **16 July 1935** in Tulsa (Oklahoma, USA). A journalist called **Carlton Magee** had thought up the parking meter system and shortly afterwards founded the first company that was to build them, the Dual Parking Meter Co.

Space Maker car parks (1976)

In New York, even more than in London or Rome, finding a parking space for your car is practically impossible. This is the reason why the American engineer **Arnold Rosen** thought of adapting the platforms used for planes by the airport maintenance staff. Called Space Maker, his system doubles the capacity of car parks. It has been widely available in the United States since 1976 and has been well received in England and Scandinavia.

Traffic lights (1868)

The first traffic light was set up at the junction of Bridge Street and Palace Yard in London on **10 December 1868**. It was a gas light mounted at the top of a 7m *23ft* steel pole. One side was red and the other green and a lever system made it rotate. Red meant *Stop* and green *Be careful*. That light was quite dangerous: the policeman whose task it was to turn it was badly injured when it exploded on 2 January 1869.

The first electric traffic light was set up under Alfred A. Benesch's insistence at the junction of 105th Street and Euclid Avenue in Cleveland (Ohio, USA) on 5 August 1914. The manufacturer, the Traffic Signal Co of Cleveland, had also fitted it with a bell that rang when the light changed. The first three-colour traffic light was set up in New York in 1918.

Parcoville is a new type of car park, tested in Charleroi, Belgium, where the car is parked automatically.

cycle in 1876 which led to **John Kemp Starley**'s Rover safety bicycle being designed in **1885**. This model brought together the main features of the modern bike: wheels of equal size, geared-up chain drive, direct steering with inclined forks and the diamond shaped frame.

Bicycle with propeller shaft (1989)

A firm from north-east China, **Molun**, has introduced a bicycle that uses a propeller shaft. There are several hundred million cycles on Chinese roads, but they are rather old-fashioned. Molun are aiming to produce a million bicycles with propeller shafts.

Dérailleur gears (1889)

The first two-speed gear changing system fitted on the rear hub appeared in 1889 under the brand name The Cyclist. Tested by Paul de Vivie in 1905, it was improved in 1911 (Panel's patent for the rear *dérailleur*) and in 1925 (Raymond's patent for the front *dérailleur*).

Two-wheelers

Origins

Although no actual example is known to have existed prior to the 18th century, it is likely that the ancient civilisations had already envisaged two-wheeled locomotion. Drawings of two-wheeled vehicles have been discovered in China. The Egyptian obelisk taken from the temple of Luxor in 1836 to ornament the Place de la Concorde in Paris has among its hieroglyphs a representation of a man astride a horizontal bar which is mounted on two wheels. The obelisk dates from the reign of Rameses II (13th century BC).

The bicycle

Celeripede and Velocipede (1790)

The two-wheeled vehicle era started with **Count de Sivrac**'s celeripede in **1790**. This consisted of a two-wheeled wooden frame without a steering mechanism and propelled by no other means than the rider's feet pushing against the ground. The celeripede was renamed velocipede, or dandy-horse, when attempts were made to improve its appearance by making it look like a lion, a horse or even a dragon.

Draisine (1817)

The Draisine was introduced in **1817** in the Luxembourg Gardens in Paris by the German baron **Karl von Drais von Sauerbronn**. It brought two-wheelers back into fashion. The Draisine had a swivelling steering mechanism controlled by a sort of rudder, the ancestor of the handlebars. It was propelled by being 'walked' along the road. After some major improvements, the Draisine became quite popular, especially in England from 1819 where it was called a hobby-horse.
Around 1839 a Scottish blacksmith, **Kirkpatrick Macmillan**, added pedals which drove the rear wheel through a system of cranks.

Velocipede (1861)

In Paris in **1861** the blacksmith **Pierre Michaux** and his son **Ernest** had a brilliant idea. While repairing a dandy-horse, they decided to attach what was subsequently called a pedal-and-gear mechanism to the front-wheel axle. The innovation worked and by 1865 the firm of Michaux & Co. had sold more than 400 vehicles.

Rover safety bicycle (1885)

In 1870 the first ordinary bicycle was built by James Starley in Coventry; it became known as the pennyfarthing because of its huge front wheel.
Harry J. Lawson patented his 'safety' bi-

Vertical pedal bicycle (1978)

This bicycle was patented in **1978** by its two inventors, the Korean **Man Te Seol** and the American **Marione Clark**. The vertical pedal bicycle enables the rider to attain remarkable speeds without getting tired thanks to its 29 gears and the unusual movement of its pedals, which puts much less strain on the legs.

Flexible cycle (1984)

Manufactured in the United States in **1984** by **ACS** (American Cycle Systems), this bicycle has rims which automatically regain their original shape after being distorted, thanks to Zytel, a nylon resin invented in 1954 by **Du Pont de Nemours**.

Alex Garfitt is surely one of the few children to go to school on a monocycle. However, the device is over 100 years old, coming out soon after the pennyfarthing in around 1870.

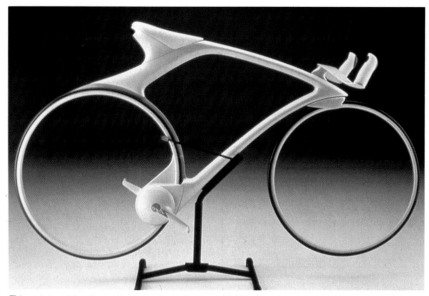

This prototype bicycle was designed by the Japanese M. Mikita and H. Tsuzaki. The wheels are held in place by magnets, while magnetic forces ensure propulsion. It will be a long time before it is for sale.

All-aluminium bicycle (1986)

The **Paris-Peugeot** and **Péchiney** companies have perfected a new featherweight all-aluminium bicycle which first became available in 1987. Originally, a Cegedur-Péchiney patent made it possible to mass-produce equipment previously limited to racing models.

Although it only weighs 8.980kg *19lb 13oz* (1.350kg *2lb 15.6oz* for the frame) this bicycle is very strong. Not many people know that the frame of a bicycle has to undergo considerable stress. When climbing a mountain pass or sprinting, it is under the same sort of stress as the wing connections on an Airbus fuselage.

Selectric (1987)

A French engineer, **François Guerbet**, is the inventor of Selectric, a tiny electric engine that can be adapted to any bicycle. You still have to pedal, but it gives a considerable boost, especially going up hills. This engine is, of course, silent and non-polluting, ideal for town traffic.

Dahon (1989)

The Dahon can be folded or unfolded in less than a minute. Comfortable and strong, its road-holding is good and it can fit into a small case. Its inventors, **Hon Machinery** of Taiwan, hold seven patents to protect its various qualities.

Hubless wheels (1989)

Introduced at the beginning of 1989, the Swiss **Franco Sbarro**'s invention created a sensation. It is a revolutionary wheel which does away with the conventional hub as well as the solid central disc. The rim alone is retained, and that is attached to the outside of the machine and carries the tyre. This gives the impression that the tyre is held on by magic. The effect is striking, and the saving in weight considerable as each wheel weighs only 600g *1lb 5oz*. The wheel's inventor, who had it tested on motorcycles first, is convinced that it will also be suitable for mass-produced cars and racing vehicles, the weight reduction guaranteeing considerable fuel economy. Further experiments are needed, however, to establish whether, from the safety point of view, it might not have unpredictable reactions under certain riding and braking conditions.

Motorcycles

Origins (1818)

On Sunday **5 April 1818** in the Luxembourg Gardens in Paris a Draisine fitted with a steam engine at the back was displayed. The only drawing of the period which has reached us, however, does not show how the power could be transmitted to the wheels. The official name of this astonishing vehicle was the *velocipedraisiavaporiana*.

The Italian Murnigotti was the first, in 1879, to register a patent for a two-wheeled vehicle with a 0.5hp, four-stroke engine. The machine was never built.

Four-stroke motorcycle (1885)

In 1885 the Germans **Wilhelm Maybach** and **Gottlieb Daimler** built a motorcycle with a wooden frame and wooden wheels, powered by a four-stroke internal combustion engine. The engine produced 0.5hp and went at 18km/h *11mph*.

The English, on the other hand, claim that Edward Butler invented the motorcycle a year earlier. But this claim derives only from the patent for a tricycle with a petrol engine, which was not built until three years later.

First mass-produced motorcycle (1894)

In 1894 two Germans, **Heinrich Hildebrand** and **Alois Wolfmüller**, built a motorcycle that was mass-produced with over a thousand units. It was a two-cylinder, 1488cc motorcycle.

De Dion three-wheeler (1895)

The **Marquis de Dion** was the first person to see the potential that the Daimler engine could have on a light economical vehicle. The first tricycle with a four-stroke engine came out in 1895. It had a ¾hp engine with electric ignition. Some 15000 de Dion tricycles were produced up to 1902.

Motorbike (1897)

The motorbike, named the *Motocyclette* by its French inventors **Eugène** and **Michel Werner**, was exhibited for the first time at the Paris Salon in 1897. These two Russian-born journalists had already produced several machines – a phonograph, a cine-projector and a typewriter – when in 1896 they undertook to mount a small engine, designed by H. Labitte, on a bicycle. First, they placed the engine horizontally above the back wheel, then in front of the handlebars with a leather belt linking it to the front wheel to drive the bike. It was an immediate success and thousands of these models were built from 1898 onwards in France and, under licence, in England and Germany.

Military motorcycle (1899)

The military motorcycle was born at the turn of the century, almost at the same time as the civilian one. The first model known dates back to 1899, the year in which the Englishman **F. R. Simms** introduced a de Dion tricycle adapted for use in the Boer War. The tricycle had the front of a quadricycle fitted with a Maxim machine gun.

The motorcycle's true military vocation was discovered in 1914 when the British and the American forces fitted them with sidecars to be used as ambulances or with a machine gun for dispatch riders.

From the road motorcycle modified by the army was born the cross-country motorcycle. The first military motorcycles not derived from civilian ones appeared in 1939: they had a driving wheel on the sidecar and were produced by BMW and Zündapp in Germany; FN and Gillet in Belgium; Gnome and Rhône in France, and Norton in England. The most original one was definitely the French Simca-Sevitane which was completely waterproof and could be turned into an engine to power a landing craft.

Scooter (1902)

The scooter first appeared in France in **1902**, under the name of Autofauteuil (motor-armchair). It was a motorbike equipped with a protective 'apron', small wheels and an open frame to allow the driver to be seated. Invented by **Georges Gauthier**, it was manufactured until 1914.

This type of vehicle took off after 1919 and became very fashionable by 1946 with such models as the Italian Vespa. After a period of being out of favour, the scooter came back into fashion as a result of a Japanese offensive led by Honda and Yamaha from 1982 onwards.

Sidecar (c.1910)

The idea of attaching a sidecar to a bike was discussed as early as 29 April 1894, in the

The prototype Domani was invented by the German Mike Kransers. The engine is situated between the bike and the sidecar and it develops 90hp.

magazine *Le Cycle*. But this addition had to wait until motorcycles became more solid and powerful; sidecars became popular around **1910**. An articulated assembly was perfected in America in 1916. It allowed the motorcycle to lean when going into a curve or around a corner. A motorised sidecar wheel was developed in 1939 and adopted by the best-known makes in all industrial countries.

Snow scooters (1959)

In 1935, after several years' research, a Canadian mechanic, **J. Armand Bombardier** (1907–64), invented a control wheel and a caterpillar track that were both revolutionary. This marked the start of the production of snowmobiles. One of the first models had bodywork similar to a contemporary car and could carry seven passengers.

At the beginning of **1959** Bombardier invented the **Ski-Doo** snowmobile. That model gave birth to a new sport and marked the start of a fantastic expansion of the industry. Today there are about 5 million Ski-Doos on the snow.

Two-stroke engine motorcycle (1900)

The first two-stroke engine fitted on a motorcycle was perfected by the Frenchman **Cormery** who had the invention patented in Paris on **20 August 1900**.

In 1901 another French manufacturer, Léon Cordonnier, registered a patent for his Ixion engine which also marked the beginning of the rotor arm. During the same period, the Englishman Alfred A. Scott was working on the first two-cylinder, two-stroke engine, which obtained its British patent on 11 February 1904 but was not built until 1908, when six were made.

It was not until 1911, when water-cooling appeared, that this vehicle reached its most competitive form. The two-stroke engine was only perfected in the 1930s due to research carried out by the German company DKW. Finally, separate lubrication appeared on

some makes, such as Scott in England in 1914 and DFR in France in 1924.

Four-stroke engine motorcycle

All the improvements carried out since 1895 have been geared to reducing the size and bulk of the motorcycle engine while increasing its power and, as a result, its rate of revolution.

Cooling

The de Dion engine was the first one to be fitted with fins to improve the air-cooling.

As early as 1912 James Booth adopted water cooling on an eight-cylinder, 5500cc engine; that motorcycle weighed 370kg *815lb*.

Valves

The de Dion engine of 1895 was the first to have automatic valves; Peugeot then introduced an engine with side valves in 1903, followed by mechanically operated inlet valves. The push-rod operated overhead valve was introduced as early as 1899 on the French Buchet engine. The distribution system with overhead camshaft really started to develop from 1930, followed by positive controls.

Five-valve cylinder head (1988)

As early as 1977 **Yamaha** started research into a means of making four-stroke engines more efficient than two-stroke ones. This led them to look for a multi-valve cylinder head. After many experiments they arrived at lentiform combustion chambers with five valves (three inlet valves and two exhaust valves). As opposed to the 'roof-shaped' combustion chamber, Yamaha's five-valve chamber does not require a hemispherical piston head to achieve a high rate of compression, and the distance between the spark-plug's electrode and the piston head remains generous. Maximum power is achieved and the torque curve is excellent. The five-valve cylinder head invented by Yamaha is fitted on the 750FZ and the 1000FZR Genesis.

Single-cylinder engine (1897)

The first single-cylinder engine dates back to the invention of the first motorcycle by the **Werner** brothers in **1897** (see above). Its popularity has fluctuated over the years. By using it in 1976 on the XT500, Yamaha created a new type of motorcycle, the Trail.

Six-cylinder engine

The most famous of these engines are quite recent, such as the one which powered the Grand Prix Honda 250. It could develop about 18000rpm and it became world champion in 1966 and 1967. Then came the renowned Honda CBX 1000 and Kawasaki 1300. The only one still in existence is the Benelli 900 Sei (1983). Starting from a Kawasaki 1300, Godier-Genoud has built a turbo-charged model which approaches 170hp. It is currently the most powerful engine around.

Four-cylinder motorcycle (1901)

Holden, an English colonel, built a motorcycle with four opposed cylinders as early as **1901**. Its connecting rods drove the back wheels without the use of a drive belt, like the connecting rods on a locomotive.

Turbocharger (1981)

The first mass-produced motorcycle with a turbocharger was the **Honda CX500 Turbo** in **1981**.

Rotary engine (1908)

In **1908** an Englishman named **Umpleby** built an engine with three combustion chambers and only one piston. This was similar in principle to the Wankel engine (*see* Energy) which only appeared 50 years later. Umpleby's engine was never mass-produced.

In 1974 the Japanese manufacturer Suzuki produced a motorcycle with a Wankel engine, the RE5. At present, the British Army is

With the Pulsar, the tricycle makes a comeback. Developed by the French engineer Philippe Girardi, its size is similar to that of a motorbike and it can accommodate two people sitting in tandem on a saddle. There is half-open bodywork to protect the passengers, and the third wheel increases stability, eliminating any risk of falls and ensuring more efficient braking.

conducting experiments on a rotary engine built by Norton.

Rocket-propelled motorcycle (1983)

The Dutch dragster champion **Henk Vink** built a motorbike propelled by a rocket. Estimated power: 2500hp. It covers 400m *437yd* in just over five seconds from a standing start, crosses the line at more than 400km/h *248mph* and is stopped by parachutes.

Motorcycle with reverse gear (1988)

The Goldwing 1 is the largest and most luxurious machine ever built by Honda. This Rolls-Royce of the two-wheelers comes with a new six-cylinder, 1520cc, 100hp engine. It is the only modern bike with a reverse gear (to make manoeuvring easier).

Transmission (c.1900)

The drive belt, chain and camshaft, which are the three main means of transmission of the engine's power to the back driving wheel, appeared with the first motorcycles, around 1900.

Drive belts

Until 1914 leather, flat or with links, and reinforced rubber were the most common materials used in drive belts. Nowadays only Harley Davidson and Kawasaki still use this technique on some of their models.

Chain (1897)

Adopted almost from the first days of the motorcycle (**1897**), it changed very little until 1972 when the Duplex chain (a double chain) invented by the Englishman **Reynolds** appeared. In 1982 Yamaha's Ténéré was given an O-ring chain, which was waterproof and self-lubricating.

Shaft transmission (1900)

Shaft transmission was invented in **1900** by the Belgian company **Delin**, who first used it on a de Dion engine. However, it was not brought into mass production until 1923, when the first German BMW was put on the market. Not until the 1980s was this type of transmission perfected to become as smooth as the chain.

Variable transmission (1910)

As early as 1910, before gearboxes appeared, variable transmission by pulleys with variable

Philippe Girardi's Pulsar manages to combine safety with attractive lines.

Bike and dragster enthusiast Gilles Moussaoui has succeeded, with the help of the French company Aérospatiale, in attaching a helicopter engine to this bike. Top speed: 328km/h 204mph.

cheek spacing appeared at **Terrot**'s in France and one year later at **Rudge Witworth**'s in England.

This system was not suitable for increasingly powerful machines and was abandoned for motorcycles. An automatic version was fitted on mopeds, the first one being by Motobécane in 1966.

Gearbox (c.1914)

True gearboxes became common on motorbikes just before the First World War. At first the gearbox was controlled manually via a lever and a serrated quadrant fixed on the tank. The pedal control appeared in England in 1923 on the Vélocette but only took precedence after the Second World War.

Electric starter motor (1913)

In 1913 an American firm, **Indian**, introduced

the Hendee Special, with a V-shaped, two-cylinder, 998cc engine. This was the first motorcycle equipped with an electric starter motor, the Dynastart. Too advanced for its time, the Hendee Special was a complete failure, and all Indian models with an electric starter motor were recalled to the factory for removal of this accessory, as unperfected as the fragile batteries supplying its current. The electric starter motor did not make its appearance commercially until the 1960s, on mass-produced Japanese motorcycles.

Front suspension (1903)

The first motorcycle front suspension to be marketed was the very complex **Truffault** fork which was seen in December **1903** at the Paris Salon on a Peugeot motorcycle.

Telescopic fork (1904)

In **1904** a well-known French make, **Terrot**,

Louis de Verdal's beautiful wooden motorcycle took him some 500 hours to build, using different woods (walnut, oak, rosewood, etc.) for each part.

patented what can be considered to be the first telescopic fork. It was used until 1908, the year in which, in England, Scott also introduced a telescopic fork which did not have hydraulic dampers. The pendular fork used by Terrot in France then by Alcyon and Triumph in England appeared in 1909.

Parallelogrammatic fork (1907)

The parallelogrammatic fork was the best-known type of front suspension. Invented in 1907 it was used until after the First World War in various guises.

Telescopic fork with hydraulic damper (1935)

In 1935 the German firm **BMW** conceived the first telescopic fork with hydraulic damper. It was universally adopted when it came out and it is still being used. Only BMW, the firm that invented it, uses a different system, which they introduced in 1955 – the Earles type suspension. That system was very popular until the 1960s, and was fitted on almost all scooters as well as the first Hondas.

Rear suspension (1904)

The concept of rear suspension for velocipedes was invented as far back as 1898. For motorcycles, the first development was the French **Stimula** of 1904, which had rear suspension with a cantilevered rocking arm and a spring under the seat. In 1911 the German firm NSU inaugurated rear suspension with a rocking arm and two near-vertical shock absorbers with helicoidal springs, as used today. The English ASL of 1912 introduced pneumatic suspension, with inflatable front and rear shock absorbers. In addition, the seat contained an inflatable cushion.

All the basic principles of rear suspension

had been invented by the beginning of the century, but the technology was not far enough advanced to apply them. It was only after the Second World War that sliding suspension appeared, then rocker suspension with greater and greater wheel clearance. Finally, in 1979 and 1980, the first variable geometric suspensions were marketed: Honda's Pro Link, Kawasaki's Uni Track, Suzuki's Full Floater, etc. These suspension systems contain a combination spring and shock absorber, activated by an intricate arrangement of articulated levers.

Cast wheels (1972)

Cast wheels appeared as early as 1972 thanks to the Frenchman **Eric Offenstadt**. They were cast in a magnesium alloy and gradually replaced those with spokes. They made possible, among other things, the use of tubeless tyres, which are safer in the event of a puncture.

ABS for motorcycles (1987)

The anti-blocking brake system, perfected by the German firm **Bosch** for cars was fitted for the first time by **BMW** in 1987 onto their top of the range motorbikes. Several years were required to master a technique originally aimed at four-wheeled vehicles. But in both areas, the advent of the ABS system is certainly as important as that of the disc brake was some 20 years ago.

Anti-blocking MC ALB (1988)

This anti-blocking system, which comes into action when the driver slams on the brakes, was developed by **Honda** and is not electronic. Fitted in the hubs, the very compact MC ALB system automatically controls the

degree of braking as well as the tyres' gripping threshold, preventing the rider from executing any sudden manoeuvres which would result in a fall. It comprises high and low pressure pipes linked to the master cylinder and the brake fluid tank. The system is activated automatically by a speed sensor.

Deltabox frame (1988)

A direct derivation from the one used on the 250cc and 500cc winners of the 1986 world championships, this frame consists of rectangular sections made from very high quality alloys. This technique gives optimum resistance to buckling and better road-holding. Strong and light (12.2kg *26lb 14oz*), the Deltabox frame is used on the Yamaha 1000 FZR Genesis.

The railways

Origins

The first British parliamentary decree relating to the creation of a railroad concerned a mining line running between Middleton and Leeds in 1753. The passenger railway was not built until 1830.

Rails (1602)

If we leave out the grooves used by Roman chariots, the first wheel-guiding rails seem to have appeared in 1602 in mines around Newcastle upon Tyne. These rails were made of wood. In 1763 Richard Reynolds made the first cast-iron rails, manufactured as a result of a slump in the iron industry. The first raised metal rails date back to 1789 and were invented by the Englishman William Jessop. Steel rails were invented by Bessemer in 1858. Nowadays all rails are made of steel. On main lines, new rails are delivered already welded in units of up to 800m *875yd*.

Points (1789)

In **1789 William Jessop** also perfected a points system. After the advent of metal tramroads around 1765, forerunners of the points had been invented, but they did not have any moving parts. Jessop's ingenious innovation was to incorporate a moving tongue-rail to this primitive device. His system marked the start of the invention of the points switching system, which remains a collective achievement.

Trevithick's steam engine (1802)

In 1802–03 the Cornish engineer **Richard Trevithick** (1771–1833) built the first steam locomotive at the Coalbrookdale ironworks. Soon afterwards, urged on by Samuel Monfrey, an ironmaster from the Cardiff area, he built a second one.

Tests began on 2 February 1804 which proved conclusive. Trevithick's locomotive, with a six-tonne load, ran on the Pen-y-Darren line (15km *9.3 miles*). A few passenger carriages were added. Empty, its speed was 20km/h *12mph*; loaded, 8km/h *5mph*.

Trevithick invented high-pressure steam machines and also designed several prototype steam cars.

Blenkinsop locomotive (1812)

The first steam locomotive to be mass produced was built by an Englishman named **John Blenkinsop**, beginning in 1812. An engine with an ordinary, non-tubular steam boiler, the Blenkinsop was designed to carry goods and travelled at a very low speed. Its special characteristic was that it ran on a toothed rail.

From 1812 the Blenkinsop ran between Leeds and Middleton.

Stephenson's *Rocket* (1829)

In 1829 the Englishman **George Stephenson** (1781–1848) developed the first high-speed steam locomotive. As early as 1813 he had built a steam locomotive equipped with driving wheels joined by connecting rods. These wheels were smooth and rolled on rails. His *Rocket* won the Rainhill trials in 1829, a contest organised by the contractors for the Liverpool–Manchester railway line. Under the competition's conditions (to pull a 40-tonne train), the *Rocket* attained a speed of 26km/h *16mph*, but with no train to pull it could reach up to 56km/h *35mph*. This exploit marked the birth of the railway.

Passenger carriages (1830)

Although the Stockton and Darlington Railway had, on occasion, carried passengers from its inception in 1825, they had to sit in the coal trucks.

The first passenger carriages as such, which looked like stage coaches, appeared in **September 1830** when the Liverpool to Manchester line was opened. This was the first inter-city service in the world.

Wide tracks (1835)

The 1.435m *4ft 8½in* track width had barely been fixed, when an English engineer, **Isambard Kingdom Brunel**, thought it to be too narrow and developed a 2.13m *7ft* wide track.

In 1835 I. K. Brunel founded the Great Western Railway which was the first to link London to Bristol – on a 2.13m *7ft* wide track, of course.

Much later, Hitler also thought that the existing tracks were too narrow. He therefore planned to build his own wide-track network. In 1942 he gave instructions for the creation of a European super railway, going from Paris to Rostov and Istanbul with offshoots to Brest, Leningrad, Kazan and Baku. The tracks were meant to be 3m *9ft 8in* wide. Electric locomotives weighing 1000 tonnes and developing 30 000hp would have pulled passenger trains at 240km/h *149mph*. . . Unlike Brunel's, Hitler's train never came into being.

Long Boiler locomotive (1841)

The Long Boiler model was perfected by the Englishman **George Stephenson** in 1841. Its main characteristic was longer chimneys. Some of the original models were still in circulation in the 1920s. These machines were the forerunners of the modern steam engine.

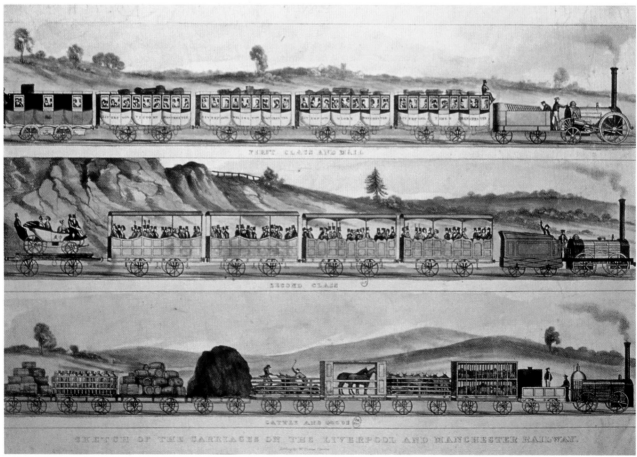

Following the Rainhill trials, Stephenson's Rocket *was chosen as the best engine to pull the first inter-city train between Liverpool and Manchester.*

Crampton locomotive (1846)

In 1846 an Englishman, **Thomas Russell Crampton**, built the first two locomotives embodying a principle he had conceived three years earlier. Crampton's idea was to build a high-speed locomotive modelled on Stephenson's Long Boiler but without the latter's major disadvantage – instability resulting from the overhanging position of the boiler furnace in relation to the wheel axles. Crampton shifted one driving axle to the rear of the firebox, leaving only two axles under the cylindrical body of the boiler. His two locomotives, put into service in Belgium on the line running between Liège and Namur, easily reached a speed of 100km/h *62mph.*

In 1848 Crampton built the *Liverpool*, a locomotive of huge size intended for use on the London–Wolverton line of the London and Northwestern Railway. The engine reached a speed of nearly 127km/h *79mph* but was nevertheless taken out of service because it put too much strain on the rails.

Railway signals (1849)

Originally, train timetables were based on allowing suitable periods of time between departures to avoid the trains catching up with the one in front. Inevitably, there were numerous accidents when the one in front went slower than expected. So, a block-signalling system was adopted by the **New York & Erie Company** in 1849. This meant that no train could enter a block until the one in front had left it. In 1856 an English engineer, Edward Tyer, invented an electric signalling device that was adopted for use in the lower Blaisy tunnel on the Paris–Dijon line.

The automatic block signal was invented by Thomas Hall in the United States in 1867. The signals were then operated by the train. In 1871 Franklin Pope installed on the Boston & Lowell Railroad the first signalling system to be centrally controlled.

In 1878 Edward Tyer invented a system which is still in use in some countries, including Great Britain, to prevent trains on single track lines colliding: the electric staff.

Rack railway (1862)

In 1862 the Swiss **Niklaus Riggenbach** invented the rack railway which was to be used on slopes over 6 percent. He was inspired by John Blenkinsop's system, whereby a cog on the locomotive engaged with a toothed rail.

In 1868 Sylvester Marsch built the Mount Washington line in New Hampshire (USA) ascending slopes that reached gradients of up to 30 percent. In 1870 the first rack railway in Europe was built at Righi, Switzerland. In 1885 a Swiss engineer from Lucerne, Abt, invented a system of triple gears with staggered cogs for the Harz Mountain railway in Germany.

Restaurant car (1863)

The first restaurant car was put into service in the United States between Philadelphia and Baltimore in 1863. In Europe, the first dining car in which food was prepared ran between Leeds and King's Cross, London in 1879; from 1880 a restaurant car service was also available between Berlin and Frankfurt. Such a

The Snow Train of Ontario, Canada, can cope with temperatures of −60°C −76°F.

service had already been tried out in 1867 in Russia.

The first buffet car was created in England in 1899 on the Great Central Railway. It was a forerunner of the snack-bars which have generally replaced the traditional restaurant car.

Sleeping cars (1865)

The first (American) patents for the sleeping car system were registered by **George M. Pullman** in 1864–5 and the maiden voyage of the first de luxe 'Pullman' sleeping car, the Pioneer, dates back to 1865.

In 1867 Pullman founded the Pullman Palace Car Company for the construction and development of luxury sleeping- and restaurant-cars.

Today there are only three Pullman trains left in the world: the Manchester Pullman (London–Manchester), the Merseyside Pullman (London–Liverpool) and the Yorkshire Pullman (London–Leeds), the last two trains having been put back into operation on 13 May 1985. As for couchettes, they appeared in the United States in 1836.

Car-sleepers (1955)

This type of service was created by British Rail which in 1955 put into service the first car-sleeper between London and Perth. In 1956 a car-sleeper link was established between Ostend and Munich as well as between Hamburg and Chiasso.

Air brakes (1869)

Originally, the brakes used on railway carriages consisted of a simple brake shoe that pushed against the wheel. These brakes were manoeuvred by hand. In 1869 an American, **George Westinghouse** (1846–1914), patented automatic air brakes. Compressed air was distributed to each carriage by a central air tank that fed auxiliary air tanks through a triple valve. When the pressure was lowered, a supply of air was released to the

brake cylinder. This system was tried out on a passenger train for the first time in 1872. It contributed to the improvement of rail transport and the same principle has remained in use up to the present day.

Electric locomotive (1879)

After various trials by the American Davenport and the Englishman Davidson in 1839, a small train driven by an electric locomotive – developed by **Werner von Siemens** and **Johann Georg Malske** – circulated within the walls of the Berlin Fair in the summer of 1879. Despite its small dimensions, this locomotive is considered to be the starting-off point for electrically driven vehicles. Preserved by the Siemens Company, this machine still exists.

In 1902 a 200km/h *124mph* speed record was set by an electric locomotive between Zossen and Marienfelde, in Germany.

The first electric railway in the world was that of Giants' Causeway in Ireland, inaugurated in 1884.

Pacific locomotive (1892)

The famous *Pacific* was put into service for the first time in the United States on the Missouri Pacific Railroad in 1892. The *Pacific* developed 2200hp and weighed 93 tonnes.

Atlantic locomotive (1900)

The *Atlantic* locomotive appeared about 1900 on the Philadelphia–Atlantic City line (USA), hence its name. The use of the *Atlantic* spread to Europe in 1901. It then had 1500hp and weighed 64 tonnes.

Diesel locomotive (1912)

The first diesel locomotive was built in 1912 in Winterthur, Switzerland, by the firm **Sulzer**. It weighed 85 tonnes and developed 1200hp; that is weak when compared to the power of steam locomotives of the time.

Magnetic trains

For the past 20 years, a great number of projects dealing with magnetic levitation trains have been studied in large industrial countries. The trains are suspended a few centimetres above a (very special) track and are propelled by linear induction motors.

The challenge is to go faster than the French TGV within an acceptable cost range. It remains to be seen which line will be the first to dare choose a Maglev (*magnetic levitation*) rather than a 'wheels on rails' system.

United States (1967)

The first magnetic levitation vehicle was tried out in the United States in **1967**, at the Pueblo (Colorado) trials centre. In 1973 a linear induction motor engine, developed by Garrett, reached the speed of 402.5km/h *250.1mph*.

Transrapid (1972)

As early as 1971, West Germany produced an 'electroglider' using the magnetic levitation principle. But the first true Maglev vehicle, the **Transrapid**, came out a year later. It has been developed by seven large German companies in association with Lufthansa and the German government, which has pledged subsidies equivalent to £300 million over 15 years.

The 54m *177ft* long train is supported by 64 electromagnets; another 56 help with lateral guidance. Its official maximum speed of 412.6km/h *256.4mph* was recorded on 21 January 1988. The Japanese MLU has only managed to reach 405.3km/h *251.85mph*.

Britain (1983)

Since **1983**, a short line (2km *1¼ miles*) using magnetic levitation has linked Birmingham International station to the airport. But the maximum speed on that line is only 25km/h *15.5mph*.

Birmingham's Maglev train has a long way to go to catch up with the Japanese, but the principle is the same. It floats above a magnetic field carried in the central strip rail.

The Japanese bullet train streaks past Mount Fuji at speeds of up to 210km/h 130mph.

HSST versus MLU in Japan

Magnetic levitation has been used in Japan since 1971 when Japan Air Lines (JAL) produced the HSST, and Japanese National Railways the ML500.

In 1978 the HSST reached a speed of 307km/h *190.8mph* and the ML500 301km/h *187mph*. The latter is said to have reached 407km/h *252.9mph* in 1979 and 517km/h *321.3mph* in 1980. The HSST works on a principle similar to that of the German Transrapid but, according to the specialists, it is more difficult to perfect.

Another type, the MLU 001, literally floats on a field of nobium-titanium superconducting magnets positioned under the floor of the train. In 1987 it reached a speed of 405.3km/h *251.8mph*.

The Maglev (2001)

The Maglev (Magnetic Levitation System) is the Japanese super train of the year 2000, capable of covering the 550km *340 miles* from Tokyo to Osaka in one hour. A special track 40 to 50km *25 to 31 miles* long is being built to test this futuristic train.

High-speed trains

Japanese bullet-trains (1964)

The **Japanese National Railways** inaugurated their first high-speed train line, Tokyo–Osaka (515km *320 miles*) on **1 October 1964**. The maximum speed of these bullet-trains is 210km/h *130mph*, although during one trial, held on 17 October 1985, a speed of 272km/h *169mph* was reached.

At present, this high-speed network (*shinkansen*) numbers three lines: Tokyo–Hakat (1069km *664 miles*), Tokyo–Niigata (297km *184 miles*), Tokyo–Morioka (492km *305 miles*).

Beginning early in 1992 a new generation of *shinkansen* should come into operation. The Super Hikari should reach speeds of around 270km/h *168mph*.

British HST (1973)

To increase the speed of trains on non-electrified main lines, **British Rail** in 1973 created an experimental diesel-electric train comprising two 1680kW locomotives with seven or eight slip coaches in between. It could do 200km/h *125mph* in commercial service and was named the High-Speed Train or HST. In 1979 a mass-produced version was put into operation between London and Bristol. Today there are about a hundred of these trains, known as the 125, in the whole country.

Another high-speed train was researched in 1975–6 by British Rail: the much talked-about APT (Advanced Passenger Train). But too many unsolved technical problems meant the idea had to be abandoned in July 1986.

TGV (1978)

Research geared to creating a high-speed train, the TGV (*Train à Grande Vitesse*), began in France in 1967, the year in which the first gas-turbine train, the TGS, was produced. This TGS gave birth to two great families of trains: the ETG (*Eléments à Turbines à Gaz*) in 1970 and the RTG (*Rames à Turbines à Gaz*) in 1973, a year after the TGV 001, also using a gas turbine, came out. This reached a speed of 318km/h *198mph* in 1972. The first electric TGV was delivered in 1978. One of the trains, No 16, reached 380km/h *236mph* in February 1981, a few months before the new Paris–Lyons line was put into commercial service. In 1985 the TGV's top speed was 270km/h *168mph*. However, in May 1990 a TGV reached 515.3km/h *320.2mph*.

The German ICE (1985)

The German ICE (Intercity Experimental) is the Deutsche Bundesbahn's (DB) high-speed train. Like the TGV, it is designed to travel at high speed on new lines. Two of these are being built at present between Hanover and Würzburg and between Mannheim and Stuttgart.

DB took delivery of the prototype ICE train in April 1985. Comprising two locomotives with three slip coaches in between, the train reached speeds of 317km/h *197mph* in November 1985 and 345km/h *214mph* in 1986.

The ICE is fitted with asynchronous motors, powered by triphase current. The train has continuous power of 2800kW, with a maximum of 4200kW. Under the name of Intercity Express, it will run from 1991 at a cruising speed of 250km/h *155mph*.

Urban transport

Origins

Blaise Pascal (1623–62), the French philosopher, was the inventor of the public transport system. In 1661 he proposed a system of coaches that would 'circulate along predetermined routes in Paris at regular intervals regardless of the number of people, and for the modest price of five sols'.

On 19 January 1662 the King's Counsel authorised the project's financiers, the Marquis de Sourches and the Marquis de Crenan, to begin running coaches in the city of Paris and its suburbs. The first coach went into service on 16 March 1662.

This public transport system attracted a good deal of curiosity, but its success was short-lived, for the coaches, ill-adapted to the tortuous, crowded medieval streets, were far too slow. Lacking patrons, the price rose to six sols, and the company went bankrupt 15 years later.

Taxi (1640)

Nicolas Sauvage, a French coachman, opened the first taxi business in 1640 on the rue Saint-Martin in Paris. He started with a fleet of 20 coaches. In 1703 the police laid down laws for their routes and gave each an easily readable number, thus introducing the first form of vehicle registration.

The real use of the automobile as an individual means of public transport with a meter registering both speed and distance, is attributed to Louis Renault who, in 1904, launched small, specially designed two-cylinder cars.

Tram (1775)

The tram was invented by the Englishman **John Outram** in 1775. This public transport vehicle ran on cast-iron rails and was drawn by two horses. It was not used in the city.

In 1832 John Stephenson built the first urban streetcar between Upper Manhattan and Harlem in New York (USA). It ran for only three years. In 1852 a Frenchman, Emile Loubat, thought of embedding the rails in the road surface. That same year, he used his idea to build the Sixth Avenue line in New York. The cars were horse-drawn and open at both ends.

Electric tram (1888)

The first operational electric tramway line was built in 1888 by the American **Frank J. Sprague**. He obtained a concession for a 27km *17 mile* line to Richmond, Virginia. Ten years later 40000 trams were in use in the United States. Sprague's 'first' had been preceded by a few prototypes: that of Siemens and Halske in Berlin in 1879, and Edison's in Menlo Park in 1880.

Supertram (1991)

This is the name of the urban transport system that the city of Manchester wants to adopt in 1991: a light articulated electric vehicle comprising two streamlined cars with a passenger capacity of 180. Maximum speed: 80km/h *50mph*. A ramp will make the cars accessible to all, including the elderly, the disabled and children in push-chairs.

Bus (1829)

The first omnibus line was inaugurated on **4 July 1829**, in Great Britain, by **George Shillibeer**, a coach builder. The buses had 22 seats and were drawn by three horses, and the conductors wore midshipmen's uniforms. By 1856 the London General Omnibus Company was the largest in the world.

In 1825, 150 years after the first public transport system was abandoned, a former soldier in the French Imperial Army, Colonel Stanislas Baudry, thought of using vehicles derived from the stagecoach (which could hold some 15 passengers, including a conductor) to provide public transportation. Baudry made his vehicles available to Parisian customers of his hot-water bath house, which was in the suburbs. But, after noticing that many people who lived in the suburbs also used his coaches, he expanded the service. His terminus in the city was located at the Place du Commerce, in front of the shop owned by a certain Monsieur Omnes, whose sign included the words Omnes omnibus. Baudry found the word omnibus (which means 'for everybody') appealing, and decided to use it for his transport line.

Motorised bus (1831)

Walter Hancock, an Englishman, provided his country with the first motorised bus in 1831. This bus, powered by a steam engine, could carry ten passengers. The *Infant* was put into service experimentally between Stratford and the City of London that year.

Steam-powered buses were replaced by the petrol-driven bus, first built in 1895 by the German firm Benz. The Benz bus was put into service on 18 March 1895, on a 15km *9 mile*

William Gladstone, four times prime minister of Great Britain, joined those on the first trial trip on London's underground on 24 May 1862, setting off from Edgware Road. Since then travelling conditions may have improved, but there are fewer top hats around.

route in the northern Rhineland. There was room for six to eight passengers and two drivers, who remained outside.

The underground (1863)

The first underground railway was inaugurated in London on **10 January 1863**. It ran between Farringdon and Edgware Road; it was 6.4km *4 miles* long and used steam traction. Since then it has grown considerably, and there is now over 400km *250 miles* in the system taking well over 2 million passengers on average per day.

Otis mini urban train (1985)

The American firm **Otis**, which specialises in lifts, has created a new mini urban train system. It derives both from the lift and the hovercraft: it is pulled by a cable and glides on air cushions. The 'smallest urban train in the world' has been running at Serfaus in Austria since the end of **1985**. Its single track is only 1300m *1422yd* long. The train (there is only one) comprises two 'cabins' which can hold 270 passengers each. There are two other similar systems: one in Tampa, Florida (USA), the other in Sun City (South Africa).

Trolleybus (1882)

The first trolleybuses appeared in Germany in **1882**. They had an electric engine which received current from an overhead cable made up of two wires that provided a constant voltage. However, unlike trams, they were steered by a driver and did not run on rails.

Funicular railway (1879)

In 1835 the Swiss inventor Egben suggested a convenient way of getting to the top of Mont Blanc. First, the ice-cap was cleared, then a huge trench was dug to install the mechanism for the driving wheel and finally the ice was allowed to cover the whole installation. It was not until **1879** that the first funicular railway started operating on the slopes of Mount Vesuvius where the gradient is over 60 percent. It was pulled by two steam engines of 45hp each.

First sub-glacier funicular (1990)

It was built above Les Deux-Alpes in France. The train goes under the Jandri glacier along a 1650m *1 mile* long gallery and comes out at an altitude of 3410m *11 185ft* opposite the Ecrins mountains.

Cable car (1908)

In the 15th century, so the story goes, a squad of soldiers from the Japanese Imperial army who were surrounded at the top of a mountain, managed to escape using a primitive cable car. The first picture of a cable car was drawn by Faustus Wranczi in the 17th century. In the last century, the forerunners of the modern cable car took over from railways in a large number of mines and quarries. The first cable car specifically dedicated to passenger transport was inaugurated on **27 July 1908** in Switzerland; it was nicknamed the 'Wetterhorn lift'.

By air

Balloons

Hot-air balloon (1783)

The first flight by a hot-air balloon took place at Annonay, near Lyons, France, on 4 June 1783. This hot-air balloon was constructed by two brothers, the paper manufacturers **Joseph** (1740–1810) and **Etienne** (1745–99) **de Montgolfier**. The *Montgolfière* was made of pack-cloth covered with paper. The balloon carried a portable stove in which wool and straw were burnt to produce hot air, that is, a gas lighter than air. This first balloon attained an altitude of 1000m *3300ft* and landed after ten minutes. When the news of the flight reached Paris, it caused a sensation.

On **19 September 1783** the Montgolfier brothers repeated their first experiment in front of Louis XVI and his court at Versailles. This time the balloon carried a suspended cage containing the first air passengers: a sheep, a duck, and a cock. This flight was also witnessed by Benjamin Franklin, then United States' ambassador to France.

First human flight (1783)

Jean Pilâtre de Rozier (1756–85) and the **Marquis d'Arlandes** (1746–1809) made the first human flight on **21 November 1783**. Ascending in a basket supported by a hot-air balloon, the first two aeronauts left the Bois de Boulogne, Paris and landed 25 minutes later close to the centre of the city.

Pilâtre de Rozier, the first pilot, was also to become aviation's first victim. He was killed on 15 June 1785, while attempting to cross the English Channel. Soon after departure, the balloon caught fire and crashed 5km *3 miles* from Boulogne.

The modern balloon (1963)

The revival of interest in balloons is due to research done by the US Navy in the early 1950s, and it was in 1963 that touring balloons first appeared. Balloon coverings are now made of very light, synthetic materials; the basket is usually wicker, and the pilot heats the air with the help of a flame from a propane gas burner.

Richard Branson and Per Lindstrand crossed the Atlantic in the *Virgin Atlantic Challenger* on 2–3 July 1987 from Maine, USA to Co. Londonderry, N. Ireland in a hot-air balloon which reached speeds of up to 209km/h *130mph*.

The first festival of American, British and Soviet balloons was held in Leningrad on 27 May 1990, the eve of the city's 288th anniversary.

series of patents for a streamlined dirigible that would not lose its shape but remain rigid. A moveable hangar enabled it to be taken out without risk, no matter what the wind direction was. The first ascent of the LZ1 took place on 2 July 1900.

This airship comprised a 128m *420ft* cylinder with an aluminium frame covered with specially impregnated cotton.

Between 1900 and 1939, 52 000 people had travelled 2 million kilometres *1 250 000 miles* by zeppelin. One accident brought the fashion to an end: the *Hindenburg* burst into flames on arriving at New York on 6 May 1937.

Skyship (1984)

The Skyship 600 fitted with a 12m *39ft* long gondola can carry 12 to 15 passengers. Its manufacturer, **Airship Industries**, claims the airship can fly at a speed of 102km/h *63mph* and has a 55-hour endurance and hence a range of 5500km *3400 miles*. Its polyester envelope is made in France by Zodiac. The craft is powered by two Porsche turbo engines. At present there are about ten skyships in operation worldwide.

Helicopter-balloon (1992)

The Canadian company **Hystar Aerospace** has conceived its future helicopter-balloon in answer to the needs of foresters. At present, practically insoluble transport problems are compelling foresters to cut down whole sections of forest at a time.

The Canadian balloon will be similar in shape to a flying saucer, and topped by a rotor. According to its manufacturer, the helicopter-balloon will be much more reliable than the helistat which was devised by the American engineer Frank Piasecki in 1956, but only flew for the first time in 1984. The helistat has four rotors which are impossible to synchronise.

Aeroplanes

Origins (1809)

People have always dreamed of emulating birds. In the 15th century Leonardo da Vinci observed how birds flew and designed artificial wings and even helicopters. This study was taken up by Borelli in 1680.

Englishman **Sir George Cayley** (1773–1857) is the true father of the aeroplane, pioneering the theory of heavier-than-air flight. In 1809 he perfected a fixed-wing glider with a stabilising tail and in 1853 he built a fixed-wing glider which flew 500m *1640ft*. He was also the first person to think of using propellers to obtain the necessary force to drive the plane.

In 1871 the French engineer Alphonse Pénaud managed to make a model aeroplane propelled by a twisted rubber-band system fly more than 50m *165ft*. This enabled him to set out flight equations for the first time.

In Britain in 1843 William Henson had patented a steam-powered flying machine, but it was his partner John Stringfellow who, in 1848, managed to make a model aeroplane fly a few dozen metres. In 1856 the Frenchman Jean-Marie Le Bris had made the first gliding flight.

Hydrogen balloon (1783)

It was French physicist **Jacques Alexandre Charles** (1746–1823) who invented all the rules governing modern ballooning. The balloon he designed, inflated with hydrogen, went up in the Jardin de Tuileries in Paris on **1 December 1783**, with Charles and Nicolas Robert on board. The American balloonist Wise perfected Charles' balloon by introducing the use of a rip cord. Modern sporting balloons differ from that of Charles only in the use of a non-flammable gas, helium, and in the quality of the covering used.

It was in a mixed hot-air/helium balloon, the *Dutch Viking*, built by the British company Cameron Balloons that, in August 1986, the Dutchman Hen Brink (accompanied by Evelien and Willem Hageman), beat the speed record for crossing the Atlantic by balloon: 51h 14min to cover more than 4000km *2500 miles*.

Airship (1852)

The airship was invented in **1852** by the Frenchman **Henri Giffard**, who perfected a balloon furnished with a means of propulsion. This hydrogen-filled airship was driven by a 3hp steam engine, and it flew for the first time on 24 September 1852, covering a distance of 28km *17 miles* at a speed of 6.9km/h *4.3mph*.

In 1883 the French Tissendier brothers attached an electric motor to a conventional airship. It made two flights, but proved to be unreliable.

The first flight which returned to the take-off point was accomplished on 9 August 1884 by the French Army captains Charles Renard and Arthur Krebs. Their airship, *la France*, was powered by an electric engine.

The Zeppelin (1890)

Count Ferdinand von Zeppelin undertook experiments as early as **1890** and took out a

J.T.C. Moore-Brabazon may deserve credit for being the first British citizen to fly in Britain, but he surely deserves great acclaim for making pigs fly.

First flight (1890)

The glory of getting off the ground for the first time aboard a motorised machine, and making a 'flying leap' goes to the Frenchman **Clément Ader** (1841–1925). On **9 October 1890**, at Armainvilliers, Seine-et-Marne in France, he 'flew' a distance of about 50m *165ft* at 15cm *6in* from the ground on board the *Eole*, a bat-shaped aircraft fitted with a 20hp steam engine. Ader's patent, registered on 19 April 1890, uses the term aeroplane for the first time. His *Avion III*, which still exists, was equipped with two 20hp steam engines. It 'leapt' over a distance of 300m *985ft* at Satory on 14 October 1897 but was damaged. Unable to obtain any financial support, Ader had to give up his research into military uses of flying machines. In the 1880s the German Otto Lilienthal (1848–96) was practising piloting a glider so as to compile information that would enable him to tackle motorised flying.

First sustained flight (1903)

It is undeniable that the first sustained powered flight in the world was accomplished by two Americans: the **Wright** brothers, **Wilbur** (1867–1912) and **Orville** (1871–1948). They flew their first glider on the Kitty Hawk dunes in North Carolina in 1900. They then built a biplane, the *Flyer I*, and on **17 December 1903**, after drawing lots, Orville became the first man to fly aboard a powered machine. During that first trial the aeroplane covered 36.6m *120ft* in 12 seconds. Wilbur

By the time this Coastal Command flying boat arrived at Tower Bridge to help commemorate the Battle of Britain in 1950, the idea was 40 years old. At least the local pets seem to have liked it.

and Orville alternately accomplished two flights of 13 and 15 seconds each. During the fourth flight, Wilbur covered 284m *930ft* in 59 seconds. The *Flyer's* take-off was assisted by a rail along which rolled a carriage carrying the aeroplane.

Seaplane (1910)

The Frenchman **Henri Fabre** (1882–1984) is the father of marine aviation. He built a flat-bottomed seaplane with floats. On **28 March 1910** he took off in it from the Etang de Berre in the South of France. The machine was of the 'canard' type with wings and engine at the back.

In 1905 Gabriel Voisin had already conceived the idea of a glider mounted on parallel floats and towed by a motorboat. Later on, the seaplane was developed in France and in the United States where Derhaut and Curtiss came up with the flying-boat at the same time.

Boeing 247 (1933)

The Boeing 247 – the first airliner – was put into service by United Airlines in the United States in **March** 1933. It carried ten passengers. For the first time, travellers could cross the United States in less than 20 hours. This low-wing, twin-engine aircraft had retractable landing gear, wing de-icers, constant-speed, full-feathering propellers (which permitted the automatic pilot mechanism to be used and also guaranteed maximum engine efficiency under all conditions), and the ability to maintain flight on a single engine.

Douglas DC-3 (1935)

Equipped with the same advanced technology as the Boeing 247 but able to carry more passengers, the Douglas DC-3 was the first transport airplane to fly over the Himalayas, between India and China. American Airways was the first company to put it into service, flying between New York and Chicago, in **1935**. During the Second World War, when it was known as the Dakota, it was frequently used as a military transport aircraft. Over 10 000 of these commercially profitable airliners were built, and they are still in service, notably in Africa and the Third World.

Viscount V-630 (1948)

The Viscount V-630, constructed by the British firm **Vickers-Armstrong**, was a low-wing monoplane powered by four Rolls-Royce turboprop engines. Its cruising speed was 440km/h *273mph*. This airliner made its first flight on **29 July 1948** and was put into service for a period of only two weeks (29 July–14 August 1950) on the London–Paris route. It became the first turboprop to be used for commercial service. However, it was almost immediately dropped in favour of the larger and more powerful Viscount V-700.

Havilland Comet (1949)

The Comet 1, built by the British firm **De Havilland**, made its first flight on **27 July 1949**. Powered by four turbojet engines, each with 2020kg *4453lb* of thrust, this aircraft could cruise at 788km/h *490mph*, at an altitude of 12 000m *39 360ft* carrying 36 passengers. Entering service with BOAC on 2 May 1952, this airliner could fly from London to Johannesburg (10 750km *6680 miles*) in 17h 6min. The Comet was withdrawn from airline service following a series of accidents.

Boeing 707 (1954)

The first trials of the B-367-80 (prototype of the Boeing 707) were made in Seattle, Washington (USA) on **15 July 1954**. The Boeing 707-120 aircraft made its first commercial flight with Pan American Airways on 20 December 1957. This aircraft, whose wings were placed at a 35 degree sweep, was powered by four turbojet engines. It had a wingspan of 39.9m *131ft* and could carry 179 passengers at a cruising speed of 912km/h *567mph*. More than 3000 Boeing 707s were built. Larger and more powerful than any airliner of the period, the Boeing 707 became the standard long-range airliner.

Caravelle (1955)

The revolutionary idea of mounting jet engines at the rear of the fuselage, rather than on the wings, originated with the French Caravelle, which made its first flight on **27 May 1955**. Rear mounting of the jet engines allowed undisturbed airflow over the wings, as in gliders, and brought increased aerodynamic efficiency, better stability, and decreased cabin noise. The Caravelle was also one of the first aeroplanes to have a rear integrated stairway. This efficient, rear-mounted engine system was soon adopted by almost all aircraft manufacturers.

The plane was put into service in 1958 but by 1970 it had been overtaken on the technical front by other airliners and was no longer being manufactured.

Tupolev 144 (1968)

The Soviets supersonic Tupolev 144 has a wing span of 28.8m *94ft 5in*, a length of 64.45m *211ft 4in* and can carry up to 126 passengers. Its maiden flight was on **31 December 1968**.

On 1 November 1977 the Moscow–Alma-Ata line was opened to the public. This run was never satisfactory and an accident in June 1978 brought commercial application of the aircraft to a halt.

Tupolev 155 (1989)

On **18 January 1989** the 20-minute-long test flight of the liquid natural gas-propelled Tupolev 155 proved that it is possible to fly with this type of fuel which is cheaper and less polluting than kerosene.

It is hoped that the 155 will come into operation on some Soviet routes by 1993 when it will carry up to 170 passengers.

Concorde (1969)

On **2 March 1969** the supersonic plane Concorde had its maiden flight. The first commercial flight, for British Airways, linking London to Bahrain took place seven years later, on 21 January 1976. On the same day, an Air France Concorde inaugurated the Paris to Rio de Janeiro link. The Anglo–French plane's birth certificate had been signed on 29 November 1962, by Aérospatiale and British Aircraft Corporation.

This commercial plane – the first supersonic civil aircraft – is the fastest passenger aircraft in the world. It has a 25.56m *83ft 10in* wingspan and is 62.17m *203ft 11in* long. It can carry between 100 and 139 passengers and take off with a total payload of 185 000kg *407 925lb*. Its maximum range is 6200km *3850 miles*. It can 'do' Paris to New York in 3½ hours, flying at an altitude of 18 000m *59 000ft*.

Boeing 747 (1969)

The first flight of a Boeing 747 took place on **9 February 1969**. The aircraft was put into service by Pan American Airways on 21 January 1970. With this aircraft, Boeing launched a new generation of large-capacity planes which became known as jumbo jets. This aircraft has a wingspan of 60m *197ft* and it can cruise (with a full payload) over 7402km *4600 miles* at Mach 0.89.

In January 1990 a 747 was specially fitted out for President Bush's official trips. *Air Force One*, as it is called, has replaced a Boeing 707 as the presidential plane.

Airbus (1973)

The first commercial flight of the Airbus, the first medium-range jumbo jet, took place on **28 October 1973**, in Toulouse, France. The Airbus is a European aircraft as it has been conceived and manufactured by companies from France (**Aérospatiale**), Germany (**MMB**), Spain (**CASA**), Britain (**British Aerospace**) and Belgium (**Belairbus**).

A320 (1988)

The Airbus A320 entered service with Air France and British Airways in **April 1988**. Designed from the outset to be the most economical airliner in its class, while providing considerable improvements in safety and comfort, the A320 is by far the most modern aircraft. It makes the most of new materials (improved metal alloys and composites) as well as the most advanced technology, even surpassing that of Concorde: the A320 is the first civil airliner to use 'fly-by-wire' technology. Fly-by-wire controls driven by computers are used to ease the pilot's workload in routine operations, and safety is enhanced by the built-in protection against dangerous situations.

The A320 is a 150-seat single-aisle twin-jet aircraft with a range of 3500 to 5950km *2175 to 3700 miles* depending on the model. It flew for the first time on 22 February 1987 with Pierre

NEW YORK–TOKYO IN THREE HOURS: THE AIM OF THE HYPERSONICS

The race is on for the AGV, Hotol, NASP-X 30 and Sänger.

Unveiled at the Le Bourget Salon 1987, Aérospatiale's AGV (*Avion à Grande Vitesse* – high speed plane) is powered by four engines with 30 tonnes thrust each (or six engines with 20 tonnes thrust). At an altitude of 30 000m *98 400ft* it will carry 150 passengers at the speed of Mach 5.5 which is more than 5000km/h *3100mph*. And all this while still using conventional runways for take-off and landing.

The British Hotol, created by Rolls-Royce and British Aerospace, will also be able to take off from ordinary airports. It would have a hybrid propulsion with reactors that can 'breathe' the surrounding air during the phase of the flight that goes through the atmosphere.

The Germans, for their part, are also planning an autonomous space aeroplane: Sänger.

The race is definitely on in Europe, but it seems that the various governments already know that they will have to work together. Today, their aim is to ensure they each have a prominent place when it comes to planning and manufacturing the future European hypersonic craft.

The *Orient Express*, as it was baptised by President Reagan, is the National Aerospace Plane (NASP) project, otherwise known as the X-30, which would make it possible to fly from Washington to Tokyo in 2½ hours. It has a passenger capacity of 305 and would fly at Mach 5.

All these space aircraft projects raise numerous technical problems, notably the speed/overheating ratio as the sound barrier is also the heat barrier. But the most serious problem at present is propulsion. Perhaps the ramjet engine, invented by the engineer René Leduc in 1913, will become, because of its extreme simplicity, the ideal candidate to power a hypersonic craft.

Optimists forecast that prototypes will appear in the late 1990s, others say it will only be in the next millennium.

SCHEDULED FOR 2005: THE SUPER CONCORDE

On 5 April 1990 an agreement was signed between British Aerospace and the French company Aérospatiale to study the feasibility of a successor to Concorde, a supersonic jet that would cover a distance of 12,000km *7500 miles* at 2400km/h *1500mph* and carry more than 200 passengers. This advanced supersonic transport (AST) could be in service by the year 2005. One of the most difficult technical problems still to be solved is that of the engine.

Baud, head of flight testing at Airbus, at the controls.

A330 and A340 (1991)

After the A320, the next step in the development of the Airbus family is the A330, a high capacity medium- to long-range widebody twin aircraft (328 seats) with a range of 9300km *5800 miles*, and the A340, a four-engined long range aircraft (13 200 to 14 300km *8200 to 8900 miles*) with 262 to 294 seats, depending on the model. The A330's maiden flight is planned for June 1992, and the A340's in 1991.

Pedal aircraft (1977)

It was the American industrialist **Paul McCready** who renewed popular interest in human propulsion for aircraft. His *Gossamer Condor* was, in 1977, the first aircraft in the world to give a convincing demonstration of human-powered flight.

Crossing the Channel (1979)

On 12 June 1979 McCready's *Gossamer Albatross*, piloted and 'pedalled' by Bryan Allen, managed to cross the Channel. It seemed as if no one could go any further, but the famous MIT (Massachusetts Institute of Technology) decided to take up the challenge. With the help of sponsors such as the Smithsonian Institute, Anheuser-Busch Inc. and United Technology, a team from MIT led by Mark Drela got to work.

Chrysalis and co

A first prototype, the *Chrysalis* biplane, took to the air as early as 1979. On 11 May 1984 the *Monarch*, also a biplane, won the Kremer prize by covering 1500m *1641yd* at an average speed of 32km/h *20mph*. The project's promoters then decided to concentrate their efforts on achieving the mythical feat: crossing the Aegean Sea. The *Light Eagle*, built in 1986 after a great deal of research involving high technology, beat McCready's record on 22 January 1987. Seven years and seven months later, it covered 58.7km *36½ miles* as opposed to 35.9km *22.3 miles*. But that was on a closed circuit.

Daedalus (1988)

Drawing from their experience of the *Light Eagle* the team were able to build *Daedalus*. Its technical specifications are: wingspan 34.14m *112ft*; wing area 30.84m² *332sq ft*; length 8.84m *29ft*; unladen weight 31.75kg *70lb*; speed 24 to 28km/h *15 to 17.4mph*.

On 23 April 1988, piloted by a Greek racing cyclist, Kanellos Kanellopoulos, *Daedalus* took off from Heraklion in northern Crete and, 3h 55min later, he arrived at Santorini, 118km *73.3 miles* away.

Boeing 767 (1978)

This twin-jet, medium-range aircraft was a

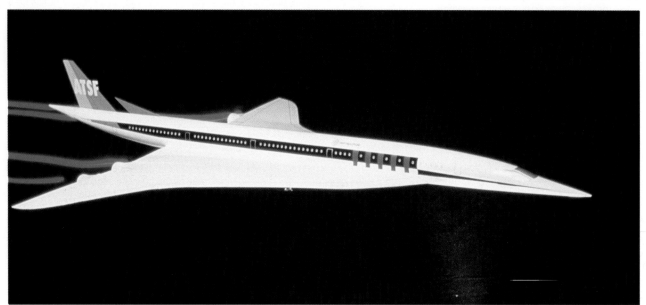

It is hoped that the new Super Concorde will enter service in 2005.

completely new concept. The programme started in **July 1978**. It was the first plane to be launched by **Boeing** since the inception of the 747 in 1969. The first deliveries took place in August 1982.

In April 1988 a Boeing 767 beat the world distance record for a non-stop flight by a twin-jet plane, covering 14 468km *8990 miles* from Halifax (Canada) to Mauritius, a trip lasting 16h 35min.

Glasair (1979)

The Glasair was the first plane in kit form and is still the one that performs best. In the United States more and more people wish to own a plane but cannot afford one. It is for those people that **Thomas S. Hamilton** and **Robert M. Gavinsky** invented, in 1979, the Glasair Taildragger. The Glasair III, which came out in 1986, holds two world records and has a 2250km *1400 mile* range.

Voyager (1986)

In **December 1986** this amazing twin-engine plane, invented by the American **Burt Rutan** and piloted by his brother Dick assisted by Jeana Yeager, Dick's wife, flew non-stop around the world in a little over nine days without refuelling. That's 40 212km *24 987 miles* aboard a propeller plane which consists of little more than fuel tanks: it weighs 900kg *1984lb* unladen and 4210kg *9283lb* when its 17 tanks, which are situated in the wings and the fuselage, are full. *Voyager* is of course built from ultra-light materials which this experiment (or adventure, rather!) served to test once again. It also led on to military applications with the AT3, the prototype of which was tested in 1988.

Joined-wings aircraft (1990)

This new joined-wings design, invented by the American engineer **Julian Wolkovitch**, gives a weight saving of 30 to 40 percent, while retaining the same aerodynamic properties. This weight saving would allow an increase in the number of passengers carried. Its special shape, furthermore, gives the plane better air penetration as well as added protection in the event of an accident. A prototype of the JW-1 is being built by ACA Industries for NASA. The first flight was in **1990**. Wolkovitch is also working on an unmanned joined-wings aircraft.

Canard wings aircraft

The configuration of these planes is the opposite of the usual one as they have large back wings and small fore wings, hence their name: *canard* is the French word for duck. Some early aircraft, such as Fabre's seaplane already had this arrangement. It had been abandoned but was taken up again in the 1980s for amateur aircraft. As they were very successful, **Beechcraft**, a company based in Wichita, Kansas (USA) invented a twin-engine canard plane which could carry 20 passengers. The first prototypes were stolen in 1987. Still in the United States, Burt Rutan, *Voyager's* inventor, also created several canard-style planes.

Solair, *designed by the Munich engineer Günter Rochelt, holds the world record for endurance for a solar plane, completing a 5h 41min flight on 21 August 1983.*

LANDMARKS IN CIVIL AVIATION

Country	Date	Event
France	9 October 1890	First flight in an engine-powered plane, piloted by the Frenchman Clément Ader; a single flying leap of 50m *164ft*.
USA	17 December 1903	Flights by the Wright brothers. Best flight by Wilbur Wright: 284m *932ft* in 59 seconds.
France	13 January 1908	The Frenchman Henri Farman completes the first closed loop in his biplane built by Gabriel Voisin.
France	3 October 1908	George Dickin becomes the first Briton to fly, as a passenger of Wilbur Wright.
UK	16 October 1908	An American, Samuel Cody, was the first to fly in Britain when he covered 423m *1388ft* at Farnborough.
France	25 July 1909	The Frenchman Louis Blériot crosses the Channel (38km *23½ miles*) in 37 mins, landing near Dover Castle.
France	28 March 1910	First flight in a seaplane by the Frenchman Henri Fabre.
USA	February 1914	First regular airline in history between St Petersburg and Tampa, Florida.

UK	14–15 June 1919	First non-stop intercontinental flight: Newfoundland–Ireland by Captain John Alcock and Lieutenant Arthur Brown, in a Vickers Vimy. It took over 16 hours to cover the 3150km *1960 miles.*
France	25 August 1919	The first regular international flight (Paris–London) by the Farman company.
USA	20–21 May 1927	First non-stop, solo trans-Atlantic flight New York–Paris by the American Charles Lindbergh (1902–74) in the Ryan monoplane *Spirit of Saint Louis*: 5809km *3610 miles* in 33h 30min.
Germany	27 August 1939	First flight of a jet-propelled plane, the German Heinkel He-178 piloted by Erich Warsitz.
USA	14 October 1947	The Bell X1 breaks the sound barrier. Pilot Chuck Yeager flew at 1078km/h *670mph* over Edwards Air Force base, California.
UK	2 May 1952	First commercial jet flight: London–Johannesburg (S. Africa), 10750km *6680 miles* in 17h 6min.
UK/France	2 March 1969	First flight by a commercial supersonic aircraft, the Anglo–French Concorde. The first commercial flight took place in 1976.
USA	14–23 December 1986	First non-stop circumnavigation without refuelling by Dick Rutan and Jeana Yeager in *Voyager*.

Hounslow aerodrome, 1919. The beginning of the era of regular flights between London and Paris.

Helicopters

Origins (1480)

The helicopter, in model form, flew for the first time in 1784. The Frenchmen Launoy and Bienvenüe presented their model to the Academy of Science. This very simple machine consisted of two two-bladed propellers arranged at the opposite ends of a spindle so as to contra-rotate, powered by a taut whalebone bow.

In fact, as early as **1480**, Leonardo da Vinci had designed a machine, a sort of airscrew, which had wings rotating around a vertical axis. Borelli in 1680 and Paucton in 1768 studied his theory. In 1862 the Frenchman Ponton d'Amécourt (to whom we owe the word 'helicopter'), and in 1877 the Italian Enrico Forlanini built crafts that were powered by steam engines. These experiments solved many problems and finally paved the way to making piloted machines.

First take-off (1907)

The first take-off by a manned helicopter was accomplished by the Frenchman **Paul Cornu** on **13 November 1907** at Lisieux in France. The machine weighed 260kg *573lb* and was powered by a 24hp Antoinette engine.

Rotor (1908)

The history of the rotor is intimately linked to that of the helicopter. In 1907 a Frenchman, Paul Cornu, had hovered a few feet off the ground for a few seconds. In America in **1908** the Russian-born aeronautical engineer **Igor Sikorsky** (1889–1972) tackled the problem of the blade and rotor mechanism: the rotor ensuring both the lift and propulsion of the aircraft. This problem found many solutions during the evolution of the helicopter. A major invention was the variable cyclic pitch which makes it possible to change the position of the blades as they rotate so as to correct the uneven lift created by the forward motion of the craft.

In 1939 Sikorsky's work led him to fit the VS-300 with a single main rotor. This helicopter, in 1941, beat the world record for range with a one-and-a-half hour flight. (In 1937 a two-rotor system had been fitted on the German helicopter, the Focke-Achgelis FA61.)

New solutions

Since then there have been many different rotors: the first streamlined anti-torque rotor Fenestron perfected by **Aérospatiale** in **1967**; the Starflex, also from Aérospatiale (1973), with a rotor head made of a type of fibreglass and blades made of composites; the tilt-rotors which allow the prototype Bell XV to perform as well as an aeroplane (*see* Helicopter-plane), Sikorsky's contra-rotating rotors, which are still in the experimental stage, etc.

Autogiro (1922)

As early as **1922** the Spaniard **Juan de la Cierva** (1895–1936) had started to work on an autogiro. In 1924 he fitted a four-blade rotor above the cockpit of a Deperdussin monoplane. On 18 September 1928 la Cierva and a passenger, Henri Bouché, crossed the

The first pedal-power helicopter managed to stay airborne for seven seconds in December 1989.

(the first in the world) of a full defrosting system for the rotors of Aérospatiale's Puma. The greatest area of progress at the moment is in the growing use of more economical composites to make the blade and rotor heads.

Helicopter-planes (1988)

The first tilt-rotor aircraft, the V22 Osprey Tilt-Rotor was introduced by the **Bell** company in Dallas, Texas in **January 1988**. The great attraction of this type of aircraft is that they take off like helicopters. Once airborne, the rotors go back to a vertical position and then act as propellers. The first applications were military but a civil version, able to carry about 30 passengers, is being studied.

The Eurofar (1998)

Some European countries – France, Germany, Italy, Great Britain and Spain – joined forces to build a competing machine, the Eurofar. The first full-size prototype is due to appear in 1994. Mass production should start at the beginning of 1995, the first machine to be completed by the end of **1998**.

Miscellaneous

Air hostess (1930)

The first air hostesses were in fact stewards. Before the First World War, the large Zeppelin airships already had staff on board.

In 1919, at the beginning of commercial aviation, it was often the radio operators who served drinks or picnic-style meals. It was not until 1927–8 that the first stewards started to appear on the British Imperial Airways aircraft.

But it was in **May 1930** that Boeing Air Transport, which was to become United Airlines, hired stewardesses for the first time. Ellen Church and seven other young women made up the first team on the San Francisco to Chicago line. In Europe, the first air hostess was Nelly Diener, a Swiss woman hired in 1934 by Swissair. The British, however, lagged far behind. It was not until May 1943 that Rosamund Gilmour became the first air hostess from the UK.

Air speed indicator (1910)

After the pioneer era when pilots only used the controls as their instincts dictated, the factor that preoccupied the early pilots most was speed.

The first speed indicator was built by **Captain Etévé** in 1910. Perfected by the engineer Raoul Badin (1879–1963), it became a little clock called an anemometer, which measures the difference between the dynamic pressure of an aircraft moving through the atmosphere and the static pressure.

Current research, especially for large planes, is moving in the direction of the highly sensitive laser air speed indicator.

Automatic pilot (1914)

The first night flights were made possible thanks to progress made in instrumentation

---

Channel from England to France, aboard the C8II. The autogiro does not allow vertical flight but it was a first step in the tackling of slow flight. Many of these machines were built in England, France, the United States, the USSR and Japan.

First helicopter flight (1924)

Sixteen years after the aeroplane, the first helicopter to fly a distance of one kilometre over a closed circuit was the one flown by the Frenchman **Etienne Oehmichen** on **4 May 1924**. From 1920 to 1925 the Spaniard Marquis Paul Pescara built three helicopters which managed to take off. It was the first time that the complete flight programme of the helicopter, including autorotation, was studied and its principle established. The theory was only put into practice in 1936 when Louis Bréguet and René Dorand invented the Gyroplane Laboratoire which, piloted by Maurice Claisse, went through the complete routine of hovering, flying sideways, long cruising flight and above all the first precision landing using autorotation with the engine off.

First operational helicopters (1940)

The first mass-produced helicopter was the Focke-Achgelis FA 223. The prototype's maiden flight took place in **1940**. The Bell 47 was the first helicopter in the world to receive a civil aviation certificate of airworthiness (8 March 1946). The first operational Soviet helicopter was the MIL Mi-1, built by the Russian company Mikhail Mil and mass produced from 1951.

Jet-powered helicopter (1953)

The only craft of this type to be mass produced was the French SO 1221 Djinn, a two-seater with an unladen weight of 369kg *813lb* which flew for the first time in *1953*.

THE FIRST PEDAL HELICOPTER

Called the Da Vinci, it was built by a group of students from the California Institute of Technology. After a few successful lift-offs in November 1989, it achieved its first take-off (seven seconds) on 10 December in the presence of the National Aeronautic Association (NAA), which recognised the Da Vinci as the first muscle-propelled helicopter. Research had begun in 1981.

Turbojet helicopter (1955)

The first helicopter to be powered by a gas turbine was the SO 1120 Ariel III. The flight took place at Villacoublay on 18 April 1951. But the turbojet's great popularity dates back to **March 1955** when Jean Boulet took off for the first time aboard the Alouette II in France. Invented by **Charles Marchetti** and **René Mouillé** for Aérospatiale, the Alouette II is the first helicopter to be created round a turboshaft engine. It is a five-seater machine whose 'offspring' are still in production.

Recent helicopters

The most prominent recent machines are the middle-size twin-engine ones (3.8 to 4.5 tonnes) created for the business market and oil-rig shuttle services. They are fast, quiet, comfortable and can carry eight to 12 passengers over 500 to 800km *311 to 497 miles* at a speed of between 250 and 280km/h *155 to 175mph*. The Bell 222, and Sikorsky S-76C and the Dauphin 2-N vie for this side of the market. In 1984 a Germano–Japanese competitor appeared, the BK117. Turboshaft engines are now perfectly reliable, quiet and economical. Another step forward was the certification

and in the willingness to replace a human being at the controls of the plane. The first efficient system was produced by the American **Elmer Sperry** and further perfected by his son, Lawrence, on a Curtiss seaplane in 1912.

In **1914 Lawrence Sperry** presented his device at a competition on aeroplane safety which took place in Paris. In order to demonstrate the stability of the plane, he made the flight with both arms in the air, while his passenger held on to the wing of the plane.

The latest automatic-pilot systems have benefited from developments in computer technology.

Ejector seat (1946)

This system was invented with the high speed plane, as jumping from one of these using a conventional parachute would be far too dangerous. Considered possible as early as 1918 by Colonel Holt, preliminary designs were studied more closely in 1939 by the Germans and the Swedes.

The first experiment in which a man was used rather than a dummy was carried out on **26 June 1946** by the Englishman **Bernard Lynch** who jumped out of a Meteor in a seat built by the British company Martin-Baker. He was at an altitude of 2500m *8200ft* and was flying at a speed exceeding 500km/h *310mph*. The first pilot to be saved by his ejector seat was a Swede who had crashed into another plane on 30 June 1946.

The first time a pilot was ejected at supersonic speed was on 26 February 1955 from a F-100 Sabre.

Gyroscope (1852)

In **1852** the French physicist **Léon Foucault** (1819–68) set out to prove the earth's rotation. He hung a 60m *197ft* long pendulum from the centre of the Pantheon's dome thus demonstrating that a pendulum swings on a fixed plane. He then invented a mechanical device including a rotor and called it a *gyroscope*. At the beginning of the 20th century gyroscopes were used as stabilising devices on ships. These heavy and cumbersome systems have nowadays been replaced by automatic pilots.

Gyrocompass (1904)

A true innovation in the domain of navigation was the gyrocompass, invented at the beginning of the 20th century. After Foucault's observations, another Frenchman, G. Trouvé, made a spinning top powered by an electric motor in 1865. After that, the aim was to make gyroscopes for ships. Three names are linked with the development of this aspect: two Germans, Anschütz and Schüler, and an American, E. Sperry. **Anschütz**'s first gyrocompass was patented in 1904; in 1911 Sperry made a gyrocompass suspended by a wire. This type of equipment remained unchanged until the Second World War, from which time radio-navigation began to be developed.

In-flight refuelling (1923)

An American, Wesley May, should be credited for having performed the very first in-flight refuelling. On 12 November 1921 May jumped from the wing of a Lincoln Standard to the wing of a JN-4 with a fuel tank strapped to his back. He then climbed on top of the

Base-jump is a new and especially dangerous sport, whereby one jumps from a cliff of at least 60m 200ft high and waits till the very last possible moment before opening the parachute.

engine and poured the fuel into the upper wing tank.

The first in-flight refuelling using a pipe took place over San Diego, California, on **26 June 1923**. An airplane piloted by US Army **Lieutenant Seifert** refuelled an aeroplane piloted by **Captain Smith** and **Lieutenant Richter**.

From 26 February–2 March 1949, after flying exactly 94h 1min, US Air Force Captain James Gallagher completed the first nonstop, around-the-world flight. His B-50 *Lucky Lady II* was refuelled in the air several times during the flight.

Joystick (1906)

It was the French engineer and airman **Robert Esnault-Pelterie** (1881–1957) who invented the control lever or joystick in **1906**. Unfortunately he did not register a patent and an American firm used his invention in spite of all his efforts to have his rights acknowledged.

Parachute (1802)

The first parachute was patented on **11 October 1802**. It was invented by the Frenchman **André-Jacques Garnerin** (1769–1823) who made a descent in Grosvenor Square, London in September 1802.

A parasol in the hand

Already in ancient times, Chinese acrobats used bamboo and paper parachutes to amuse their audience and, a few centuries later, Leonardo da Vinci (1452–1519) drew a sketch of a parachute.

From a height of 800 metres

In 1783 a French physicist Sebastien Lenormand dropped from a first floor window holding a parasol in each hand. He was the one to give the parachute its name (*para* from parasol, and *chute* which means fall in French). But it was **André-Jacques Garnerin** who made the first true parachute jump on **22 October 1797**. He went up in a balloon above the Parc Monceau in Paris. When he reached an altitude of about 800m *2624ft*, at 5.35pm, he cut the rope which held the balloon and the basket together. The basket went down, hanging from a parachute.

The first drop from an aeroplane was made by the American Captain Albert Berry, who jumped from a biplane above Saint Louis, Missouri on 1 March 1912. The USSR became the first country, in 1935, to use the parachute for military purposes.

Pressurisation (1920)

With the advent of jet transport and the consequent increase in flight altitudes, machines had to be pressurised so that passengers could breathe normally. The first airliner to be pressurised was the Boeing 307 Stratoliner, dating back to before the Second World War, but the first trials took place in **1920**.

Retractable undercarriage (1911)

As is often the case, the idea was conceived in the first years of aeronautics: as early as 1876, the French pioneers Alphonse Pénaud and Paul Gauchot had thought of reducing the aerodynamic resistance produced by the wheels.

The first retractable undercarriage appeared in 1911, on the German monoplane **Wienvziers**, though the undercarriage was a folding one rather than a retractable one. A few years later, the American pilot and engineer Glenn Martin fitted his Martin K-3 Kitten fighter with an undercarriage which could be retracted towards the rear. In 1920, on the American monoplane Dayton-Wright RB racer, the wheels disappeared up into the fuselage. The year 1922 saw the first plane with an undercarriage retracting into the wings: it was the American racer Verville-Sperry R3.

But it was in 1929 that the Frenchman Georges Messier perfected the first retractable undercarriage operated by hydraulic controls.

Rocket belt (1961)

The rocket belt was perfected by America's **Bell Aerosystem Company** and exhibited in **1961**. The device was invented by **Wendell F. Moore**. To date, experimental flights with the belt have not exceeded 200m *656ft* horizontally and 20m *65ft* vertically. The rocket belt consists of two vertical tubes and a fuel tank strapped onto the user's back. Two motorcycle-type handles are used to control it. This belt allows vertical take-offs and stationary flight, and it can rotate 360 degrees.

'Driven' by a 'flying man', the rocket belt made a remarkable sight at the opening ceremonies of the Los Angeles Olympic Games in August 1984.

By sea

Shipping

Steamboats

A boat with a steam boiler (1730)

When use of Newcomen's steam pump had spread into the coal-mining regions of England during the 1730s, a mechanic named Jonathan Hulls used it to equip a tugboat. Placing a crank at the end of the beam of Newcomen's machine, he transformed the back-and-forth movement of the piston into a rotating movement which was transmitted to the paddle wheel of the boat. But the mechanical irregularity of this atmospheric engine and the large quantity of coal that it consumed made Hulls' project impractical and it was forgotten.

Steamboat with a paddle wheel (1783)

Watt's invention of the rotative steam engine, which permitted an increase in the driving power of the engine and used less combustible fuel, led to a breakthrough in the progress of steam-powered navigation. It was in America that steam navigation was to undergo its greatest improvements.

Steamboat with oars (1787)

A curious demonstration, witnessed by George Washington and Benjamin Franklin, took place on the Delaware River during the summer of 1787. Two American builders, **John Fitch** and **James Rumsey**, introduced a boat with oars fixed to a horizontal wooden rod, operating in the same way as ordinary oars but powered not by men but by a steam engine.

The *Clermont*, the first river steamboat (1807)

The *Clermont* was built by the American **Robert Fulton** in New York in **1807**. It was the first successful commercial steamboat. It measured 50m *164ft* long by 5m *16ft* wide, had a capacity of 150 tonnes and its paddle wheels were 5m *16ft* in diameter. Few people, however, believed that this powerful riverboat would succeed, and even though its trial runs had taken place with no major problems, no passengers showed up for its maiden voyage. Only Fulton and his crew made that first run up the Hudson River from New York to Albany. During its night-time voyage, the *Clermont* spread terror: Fulton fired the boiler with pine boughs, which produced a lot of smoke and sparks. This column of flame, along with the noise of the engine and the paddle wheels crashing on the water, terrified the people living along the banks of the river.

The *Savannah*, the first transatlantic steamer (1818)

In **1818 Captain Moses Rogers** of Savannah, Georgia planned to build a steamboat intended for regular service between America and Europe. A corporation launched the operation, acquiring a handsome sailboat and installing a steam engine and paddle wheels. These paddle wheels could be dismounted and folded on deck.

The *Savannah* left port on 26 May 1819, and arrived in Liverpool 25 days later. Its engine had functioned only 18 days of that time, as the captain wanted to take advantage of a favourable wind to economise on coal.

After this successful run, the *Savannah* made its way into the Baltic Sea to Kronstadt and St Petersburg, where it was visited by Tsar Alexander I. But the *Savannah* ended up in obscurity. After returning to the United States, it was reconverted into a passenger sailboat and ended its adventurous career on the Long Island coast. It wound up sinking in the harbour during its last voyage.

An English steamer, *Enterprise*, travelled to India in 1825.

Wind-powered cargo ships (1980)

The last large commercial sailing ship disappeared in 1936. The high price of fuel has now reopened the possibility of using the wind as an auxiliary source of power.

In **1980** the Japanese shipyard **Nippon Kokan** launched the *Skin-Aitoku-Maru*. This is a cargo vessel fitted with two upright wings – each one opening like a book – with a total area of 194.4m² *2098sq ft*. These wing-sails can save up to 50 percent in fuel costs. Five other cargo vessels to be used in the coastal trade have been launched since. Janda (the association for the development of the Japanese Navy) then instigated the building of a sea-going cargo vessel. The *Usuki Pioneer*

Built in 1509–10 the Mary Rose *was one of the first purpose-built warships. It capsized in July 1545 and was only raised in 1982.*

was finished in November 1984. Its two computer-controlled metal sails should give this 16.25m *53.3ft* long cargo ship a saving of about 30 percent in fuel costs. In the United States the 3100-tonne coasting vessel *Mini-Lace*, was fitted in **1980** with a canvas sail which can be made smaller by winding it round the rotating mast. It gives a 20 percent fuel economy.

Wind-driven boat (1870)

In **1870** an old 7m *23ft* lifeboat, renamed the *City of Ragusa*, was equipped by its skipper, **John Buckley**, with a sail and a six-bladed wind engine intended to turn a double-bladed screw propeller in the water. This device's lack of efficiency did not prevent the boat and its crew of two men from crossing the Atlantic.

Turbosail (1982)

The principle of the turbosail was perfected by **Professor Lucien Malavard** and his pupil **Bertrand Charrier** in 1982. A variation on the Magnus effect, it makes it possible, among other things, to avoid rotating the cylinder at high speed.

The turbosail was tried out first on the Cousteau Foundation's *Moulin à Vent I* in 1983 and then on the *Alcyone* (formerly the *Moulin à Vent II*).

The *Alcyone* is driven by the combined action of two diesel engines and two turbosails whose efficiency is four times greater than that of the best sail ever made. This system created a 25–35 percent saving in energy on the maiden voyage of the *Alcyone* in May–June 1985. Computers make it possible to adjust these turbosails according to the wind direction, thus obtaining maximum efficiency.

Hydroplane (1897)

Count Lambert de Versailles presented plans for the first hydroplane as early as 1897. In 1907 the Brazilian airman Alberto Santos-Dumont (1873–1932) reached a speed of 100km/h *62mph* during trials on the Seine. His hydroplane consisted of three aluminium and wood 'cigars' covered with silk.

The hydroplane is a flat-bottomed boat which rises out of the water at high speed. At this point, only the bottom part of its 'steps' remain in contact with the water. Driven by an aerial propeller, the craft can travel along shallow rivers but only over calm water.

Hovercraft (1955)

This type of vessel, also known as a Surface Effect Ship (SES), or Air Cushion Vehicle (ACV) was patented on **12 December 1955** by the Englishman **Sir Christopher Cockerell**.

His hovercraft is a boat that rides on a cushion of air. It does not touch the water but 'hovers' over it.

The 7-tonne prototype, the SR-N1 made its first public appearance at Cowes on 30 May 1959 and caused a sensation. It was highly manoeuvrable and capable of a speed of over 100km/h *62mph*.

On 25 July 1959, the 50th anniversary of Blériot's cross-Channel flight, the first hovercraft crossing was achieved.

The WPC (1990)

Hoverspeed's Wave Piercing Catamaran

Club-Med 1 *is the world's largest liner with sails and was launched in 1990.*

(WPC) is designed to take over from the hovercrafts that cross the Channel between England and France. It is built like a catamaran (the largest in the world: 73m *240ft* long, 27m *89ft* wide, 450 passengers, 80 vehicles). It came into service in **1990**.

Icebreaker (1864)

The *Ermak* was the first English icebreaker. It was built in **1898** by the Armstrong shipyards, following the design of Russia's Admiral Makarov.

However, the first icebreaker was Russian; the *Païlot* left the shipyard in **1864**.

Lenin (1957)

The *Lenin* was the first atomic-powered surface ship. It was an experimental icebreaker developed by the Russians in **1957**. The heart of the *Lenin*, its three nuclear reactors and the associated containment system, weighs 3000 tonnes. In free water the ship can run at 18 knots and can break an ice-cap 2.5m *8.2ft* thick at the constant speed of 2 knots thanks to

its 44000hp engines. It was decommissioned in April 1990.

Atomic-powered ships (1958)

Laid on the stocks on **22 May 1958** in the United States, the *Savannah* was the first commercial atomic-powered ship. Launched in 1959, it was given the name of its famous ancestor, the first steamer ever to cross the Atlantic. It could transport 9500 tonnes of cargo and 60 passengers. Attended by a crew of 100, it could develop 20000hp and reach speeds of 20.5 knots.

Although the *Savannah* was undoubtedly a technical success, she was a commercial failure. The operating company had to take her out of service in 1967.

Magnetic boat (1985)

It was at the Tsukuba exhibition in Japan that, in **1985**, a model of the magnetic boat was first shown to the public. It has no engine (in the strict sense of the term), no sail and no rudder.

The prototype of the world's first magnetic boat was revealed on 11 July 1990 at Mitsubishi's shipyards.

It is propelled by a system of superconducting magnets arranged along the hull. These create a powerful magnetic field in sea water, which is a good electricity conductor. Its Japanese inventor **Yoshiro Saji**, a 60-year-old physicist, has been working on it for about 15 years. The first prototype, the *Yamato 1*, is being built by the Japanese Foundation for Shipbuilding Advancement (Tsukuba) and should be ready around 1991.

Sailing liner (1986)

The *Wind Star* (and its twin sister, the *Wind Song*) is the first sailing liner ever built. Produced by the **Ateliers et Chantiers du Havre** (ACH) at the end of **1986**, the *Wind Star*, commissioned by the American company Windstar Sail Cruises, has a sail area of 2000m² *21 528sq ft*. The masts rise to 58m *190ft* above sea level and the sails are completely computer-controlled. It can carry 180 passengers with a crew of 75. The ship's speed is between 10 and 15 knots. The boats are 134m *440ft* long and have four masts.

Miscellaneous

Anchor (3rd millennium BC)

The first anchors, used by Chinese and Egyptian sailors in the **3rd millennium BC** and later by the Greeks and the Romans, were stones or bags containing sand or pebbles that could simply be thrown overboard. Pliny, Strabo, and other Roman authors attribute the invention of the metal anchor to several different seafaring peoples. The first approach tried was the single-palm grapnel used around 600 BC.

An important improvement was made in the 18th century when better quality, less brittle iron was used, and when the arms were given a new camber. Around 1770 iron-stock anchors completely supplanted wood-stock anchors. (The stock is a bar perpendicular to the shank of an anchor; its purpose is to make

the anchor swing so that one of the flukes grips the bottom.)

In 1821 the Englishman Hawkins engineered the mooring hawse-hole anchor with palms. With this system the stock is no longer necessary, the arms being mounted in such a way that they automatically lean to the same side to grip the bottom. This type of anchor was modified between 1872 and 1887 by the Englishmen C. and A. Martin, S. Baxter and W. Q. Byers.

The CQR anchor, or plough anchor, which the Englishman G. I. Taylor patented in 1933, is of an extremely original design. At the extremity of the shank, a double ploughshare is mounted, and the gripping power this provides is twice as great as that of a standard anchor.

Canal lock (14th century)

The double, or chamber, canal lock is an invention attributed by some to **14th century** Dutch engineers (later to be improved upon by the Italian genius Leonardo da Vinci) and by others to da Vinci himself around 1480. By regulating the conditions of passage, the invention of the chamber lock solved the problem of getting vessels from one reach of water to another and simplified the often dangerous procedure of lowering and lifting boats.

The compass

No one knows when, where or by whom the compass was invented. It was in China, around the year 1000, that the magnetic needle appeared as an aid to navigation. In China, these first instruments pointed to the South. It was only two centuries later that the compass was mentioned for the first time in Europe in the works of an English monk, Alexander Neckam.

Even the origin of the words magnetite, magnetic and magnetism is obscure. They might be connected to an ancient part of Thessaly (Greece) called Magnesia. A legend tells of a shepherd by the name of Magnes whose metal-tipped crook and hobnailed shoes stuck to the ground and enabled him to discover the magic mineral.

As early as the 12th century the magnetic

needle, or steering compass, which in Europe pointed to the North, became essential for sailing in bad weather. In the 14th century, as the steering compass came into general use in the Mediterranean, trade was made easier whatever the weather all the year round.

The compass enabled Christopher Columbus to undertake his westward journey to India which led him to rediscover America, a continent the Vikings had discovered several centuries before and which was probably shown on Soliman the Magnificent's maps that Columbus would have consulted.

Compass card (1876)

It seems that the first compass, or mariner's, card was made by Flavio Giova, an Amalfi craftsman. After centuries of trial and error, the **Thomson** compass was perfected in **1876**: this dry compass had thin cylindrical bars mounted on silk thread and tied to very thin paper – it weighed no more than 20g *¾oz*. The liquid compass, a result of the work of two Englishmen, Dent (1833) and Ritchie (1855) came into general use around 1880. After the First World War, it was strongly challenged by the gyrocompass perfected from the work of the French physicist Léon Foucault and of G. Trouvé.

Lifebelt (1769)

It was a French priest, the **abbé de Lachapelle**, who invented the first lifebelt in **1769**. This device consisted of a canvas waistcoat made of coarse hemp and lined with cork, which allowed the arms to be free. He also suggested that sappers wore his belt when reconnoitring fortresses surrounded by moats. The cork breastplate would also act as protection against the sabre and the gun.

Lighthouses (285 BC)

In **285 BC**, one of the Seven Wonders of the World was built on Pharos (an island in Alexandria harbour, Egypt). This was the lighthouse built according to the instructions of Egypt's King Ptolemy II. This lighthouse is said to have measured over 130m *426ft* in height. A wood fire was kept burning all night at its top. It was destroyed by an earthquake in 1302.

The decisive advance in lighthouse construction was the invention, by the Englishman John Smeaton in 1759, of a cement that could set in water.

As to the light, it was provided by wood fires until the 18th century. In 1780 a Swiss, Argand, designed the flat-wick oil lamp called the Argand burner. In 1901 a new development appeared; this was the petroleum burner, invented by Arthur Kitsen.

The progress made in optics had an impact on lighthouse design. As of 1752 the parabolic reflector designed by the Englishman William Hutchinson increased the power of the light signal.

The most decisive step in the use of lenses was conceived in 1821 by the French engineer Augustin Fresnel. An optical lens was used to focus the light into a beam aimed at the horizon. Escaping light was collected by concentric rings of prisms.

The use of electric lighting (beginning in 1859 in Dungeness, Great Britain) greatly improved the effectiveness of lighthouses.

Mechanical log (1801)

The mechanical log was created by the Englishman **Edward Massey** in 1801. It standardised an already ancient, but imprecise, system. Originally quite rudimentary, the log was simply a wooden block that was thrown into the water towards the bow of the ship and then recovered when it had reached the stern. The apparent speed of the vessel was calculated by taking into account the time the log took to pass from one end of the ship to the other.

Octant (1730)

The first known octant was made by an English mathematician and astronomer, **John Hadley**, in 1730.

Outboard engines (1905)

Two models appeared in 1905: an American engine designed by a Norwegian, **Ole Evinrude**, who called it outboard because it had the characteristic of being screwed vertically to the boat's outer hull; and a German engine built by **Fritz Ziegenspeck**, who named it the Elf-Zett.

Propellers

First propellers (1785)

In 1785 an Englishman, **Joseph Bramah**, patented a 16-blade propeller to drive boats. But the first experiment was made by an American, John Stevens, and an Englishman, Sir Marc Isambard Brunel, who coupled two four-bladed propellers to their one-cylinder steam boiler to sail up the Passaic River in New Jersey (USA).

Screw-propeller (1837)

In 1837 a Swedish engineer **John Ericsson** patented a screw-propeller in America. His propelling system, consisting of two screws, was used on a tugboat, the *Francis Ogden*. In the same period Francis Pettit Smith, a Kent farmer, perfected a similar system and founded a company, the Steam Propulsion Company, which in 1838/9 built a full-sized, sea-going screw ship called the *Archimedes*, which attained 10 knots.

In 1843 Isambard Kingdom Brunel built the first transatlantic steamship powered by a screw-propeller: the *Great Britain*, measuring 98m *321ft* in length. Two years later, the Royal Navy tied two ships back to back: the *Alecto* which was a paddle-steamer and the *Rattler* which had a screw-propeller. With its paddle wheel at full power the *Alecto* was still pulled by the *Rattler*, the screw-propeller had proved its superiority.

Fully cavitating propellers (c.1970)

In the 1970s the US Navy, to obtain a greater speed, perfected fully cavitating propellers which exploit the formation of a depression around the blades of the propeller thus making the most of the pocket of steam created by the whirl of the screw.

The alternative aileron

Scientists from Glasgow University are currently experimenting on an alternative aileron process that could, before long, replace the traditional propeller. This aileron would create a saving of up to 20 percent in fuel.

Studying the drag effects of a propeller can have an important bearing on the design of a boat.

Jean-Pierre Ofroni perfected the SMAL 2, a recreational submarine which has been operational since 1990.

Tide tables (13th century)

The first known tide tables were drawn up in the 13th century by the monks of Saint Albans to give the height of the Thames at London Bridge.

The first printed tables were published in the Nautical Almanac by the Breton Brouscon in 1546. One of the most famous tables is that of Richard and George Holden, published in Liverpool in 1773. For a long time, it was used to determine the tides of that harbour, although these are very irregular. In 1858 the Nautical Almanac, published by the British Admiralty, gave a tide table for all of the harbours in the world. As of 1910 it gave tables for only 26 of them.

Weighted keels (17th century)

In order to prevent sailing ships from capsizing under the lateral force of their sails, it was always necessary to concentrate the weight of the ship as low as possible. When fighting ships had no cargo, they had to be filled with stone ballast that acted as counterweight to the sails.

Towards the end of the 17th century King Charles II had the bottom of one of his yachts covered with lead plates.

In 1796 the Royal Navy had two frigates built, the *Redbridge* and the *Eling*, which had lead ingots fixed to the outside of the hull. In 1844 the American sloop *Maria*, designed by Robert L. Stevens, had lead-lined wooden hull rails. The first sailing ship to be completely lead-ballasted on the outside of the hull was the *Peg Woffington*, owned by the Scot George L. Watson in 1871.

Keel of the *Australia* (1983)

Thanks to an original keel, the America's Cup was won by the yacht *Australia*, in 1983, after 132 years of American domination of the contest.

The designer of the *Australia*, **Ben Lexcen**, envisaged fins under the keel to prevent a loss of lateral pressure. Thanks to this, it was possible to design an even more efficient keel, broader above than below. This keel is beginning to be fitted on cruise ships, allowing them to reduce their draught by 20 to 30 percent with no loss in efficiency.

Weapons

Light weapons

Firing tube (15th century)

With the invention of gunpowder appeared a device which was both an early version of the cannon and the forerunner of the rifle. It consists of a metal tube closed at one end. The gunpowder and shot were loaded into the mouth and the powder was lit by a small opening or priming hole in the side of the tube.

Match-lock (15th century)

Until the middle of the **15th century**, light weapons were fired by holding a lighted fuse to the priming hole or pan of the weapon with the right hand. About this time, the fuse coil was invented which freed the right hand and enabled the user to maintain a firmer hold on the weapon.

Wheel-lock (16th century)

The wheel-lock produced the spark necessary to set off the gunpowder, so that the user no longer had to worry about keeping the fuse alight in order to fire the weapon. **Johann Kiefuss**, a watchmaker from Nuremberg, is generally thought to have invented the wheel-lock in **1517**, but it has also been attributed to Leonardo da Vinci. It was a complicated and costly device which was particularly popular with horsemen as it enabled them to fire one-handed.

Bayonet (16th century)

According to legend, the bayonet was invented, or at least manufactured for the first time, in **1590**, in the French town of Bayonne, after which it was named. It came into common usage towards the end of the 17th century.

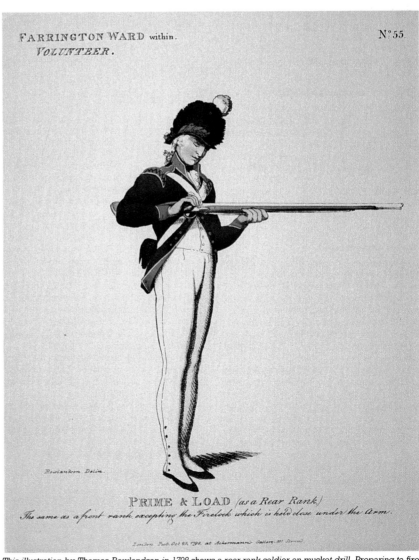

This illustration by Thomas Rowlandson in 1798 shows a rear rank soldier on musket drill. Preparing to fire was a long process.

Cartridge (17th century)

The paper cartridge was an early invention. It was in general use by the Swedish Army c.1630, but it did not become widely used until the 18th century. Originally it contained gunpowder only and did not combine bullets and gunpowder until 1738.

Percussion lock (1807)

In 1807 Alexander John Forsyth, a minister at Belhelvie near Aberdeen in Scotland and a keen hunter, invented the method of firing a percussion cap to ignite the priming. Among other things, it eliminated the misfires caused by wet weather. The well-known toy 'cap pistols' use a small amount of fulminate placed between two paper discs.

Minié bullet (1836)

The Minié bullet, invented by the French Army officers Henri-Gustave Delvigne and Claude-Etienne Minié in 1836, was the first to enable the rifled gun to be used efficiently. Gunsmiths realised that the range of the rifle could be substantially increased but the problem of loading the bullets still had to be solved. The problem was how to obviate tightness, (i.e. retarding friction) caused by rifling. The bullet, with a diameter slightly less than that of the barrel, was automatically propelled by the pressure of the gases. It increased the range of an infantry rifle from 200m *650ft* to more than 1000m *3300ft* and was the most widely used ammunition during the American Civil War.

Integrated priming (19th century)

When rifles could be breech-loaded, inventors had the idea of incorporating the primer into the cartridge. There were many different suggestions, including the pin-fire cartridge invented by the French gunsmith Casimir Lefaucheux in 1836, and rim priming invented by the French gunsmiths Béringer and Nicolas Flobert in 1845. The invention was used intensively during the American Civil War (1861–5) and then spread via Europe to the rest of the world.

Metal cartridge (1861)

There were many drawbacks to cartridges made of paper and other low-resistance materials. Powder often leaked or was affected by poor weather conditions, etc. During the second half of the 19th century, many inventors tackled the problem but the first ammunition with a completely metal case was not tried out in the field until the American Civil War.

In 1865 Gosselin of France presented cases in drawn brass to the Commission of Vincennes, but the level of knowledge of the working of copper was so limited that they did not become widely used. In the same year another Frenchman, Schneider, and two Englishmen, Boxer and Daw, developed ammunition which was made entirely of metal with centre priming. However the case did not consist of a single piece of metal but of a cartridge made of a thin sheet of brass in the form of a coil. No further progress was made until after the Franco–Prussian War (1870–71).

Centre priming (1865)

Centre priming was invented in 1865 by both the English Army officer Boxer and the Frenchman Schneider. It was further improved by the Americans who, from 1867 onwards, manufactured cartridge cases made from a single piece of brass. The development of this type of cartridge led to the invention of repeating rifles.

The invention of nitro powder in 1884 made it possible to reduce the calibre from 11mm to 8mm and subsequently to 7.5mm, 6.5mm and 6mm. These cartridges are still in use today and are effective over a distance of up to 1000m *1095yd*. Several years ago, some very small-calibre cartridges were brought out i.e. 5.56mm which have a high muzzle velocity.

Modern research is directed towards developing caseless ammunition; the first trials were carried out during the Second World War by Germany in 1944. It has already been developed by the German companies Heckler & Koch and Mauser and the former have even presented the prototype of an assault rifle using this type of ammunition at a NATO exhibition. A few problems still have to be resolved before this type of cartridge becomes fully operational.

Flint-lock (17th century)

The flint-lock worked on a similar principle to the wheel-lock: the charge was ignited by a spark produced by a flint moving against the strike-plate. The flint-lock was adopted by the French Army around 1660 and it was later perfected and incorporated into the British Army's Brown Bess.

Revolver (1835)

The idea of repetition by rotation has very early origins. Evidence of it can be seen on a bronze horse pistol dating from around 1680, and attributed to the London gunsmith J. Dafte, which is preserved in the Tower of London. A carbine of a very similar design has also survived and can be seen in the Milwaukee Public Museum in the United States.

In 1814 J. Thomson, a shopkeeper from Islington, north London, patented a flint-lock pistol with a revolving magazine-feed mechanism with nine chambers and a single barrel. In 1818 an American, E. Collier, with the help of Captain Artemus Wheeler and Cornelius Coolidge, followed up with a hunting rifle and a five-shot revolver with a rotating breech. Other inventors followed before a patent was registered on 22 October 1835 by a young man of 21 named Samuel Colt (1814–62), whose name has gone down in history.

The most famous of the many revolvers currently in existence are undoubtedly those manufactured in America, for example the Colt, Ruger and Smith & Wesson.

Although the best-known calibres are the .22, S & W Special 38 and S & W Magnum 35, there are also a few chambered monsters that take high-powered cartridges such as the S & W Magnum 44 and the Casull 44.

Automatic revolver (1895)

The automatic revolver was invented and patented on 16 August 1895 by G. V. Fosberry, a colonel in the British Army. It made use of the recoil action to reset the cocking piece and turn the cylinder one notch. It was brought onto the market in 1901 under the name Webley-Fosberry in the English regulation calibre of .455 and in Colt Automatic 38.

Breech-loading (1841)

The idea had already been in existence for some time when Samuel Pauly, a Swiss gunsmith living in Paris, presented the first true breech-loading rifle to Napoleon I in 1812. The weapon also used closing cartridges made of brass. But the Emperor did not develop it.

The breech bolt rifle was developed in 1835 by the German Johann Nikolaus von Dreyse (1787–1867), a former student of Pauly. The weapon appeared in its final form in 1841 and was adopted by the Prussian Army. In 1866 it enabled them to win an easy victory over Austria at Sadová, and over the Danes in Schleswig-Holstein.

Many old muzzle-loaded weapons were subsequently converted to models with a moveable breech.

Jacketed or armour-plated bullet (1878)

The invention of nitro powder made it possible to obtain considerable muzzle velocities which lead bullets were incapable of. The Swiss Army officer Rubin invented the composite bullet around 1878. It consisted of a lead nucleus encased in a jacket of a more resistant metal such as cupro-nickel, brass or steel, which was sometimes electroplated with copper or other metals. This type of bullet is used exclusively for military purposes and on rifle ranges. A lead-tipped bullet, known as a semi-plated bullet, is used for hunting.

Dum-Dum bullet (1897)

These hollow-tipped bullets, fitted by the English to several models of the .303 military cartridges to improve their stopping power, were developed in 1897. Most of the tests on this type of bullet were carried out at the arsenal at Dum-Dum on the outskirts of Calcutta during British colonial rule. The Dum-Dum bullet, which causes terrible wounds, was banned by The Hague Convention in 1908, but a certain number were, however, used during the Boer War (1899–1902) and in the First World War.

.22 Long Rifle (1847)

In 1847 the Parisian gunsmith Nicolas Flobert had the idea of fitting a shot pellet on to a case. He had just invented the modern version of the cartridge and in particular the .22 or 5.5mm which was exported to the United States where it was greatly improved and extremely successful. This led to the development of the .22 Long Rifle.

Machine guns

Mechanical machine gun (1850)

The mechanical machine gun appeared around 1850. It consisted of either a single barrel with a handle which, when turned, propelled and fired the cartridge, or of several barrels which were loaded and fired in rapid succession. The most popular model, invented by the American Richard J. Gatling (1818–1903), appeared in 1862. The same principle was used for the Vulcan cannon where an electric motor enables 6000 20mm shells to be fired per minute.

Automatic machine gun (1884)

The first continuous-firing automatic machine

gun, operated by the effect of the recoil action, was invented in **1884** by the American **Hiram S. Maxim**. It demonstrated its true value in 1894 when it was adapted for the use of nitro powder. Maxim's basic principle is used today in most types of machine gun.

Researchers introduced different methods of operation, based on his invention. In 1892 the American John Moses Browning invented the first gas-operated machine gun. In 1893 a former officer in the Austro-Hungarian Army, Captain von Odkolek, patented a very similar invention and sold the rights to the French-based company, Hotchkiss. Founded by Benjamin B. Hotchkiss (1828–85), an American living in France, the company had already gained a substantial reputation with its rapid-firing cannons. From the beginning of the century, the company manufactured a number of models culminating in the famous 1914 Model used by the French Army as well as the armies of many other countries.

Automatic rifle or light machine gun (1902)

In **1902 Madsen** of Denmark developed a light machine gun which could be operated and carried by one man. Other models were subsequently produced by other companies. In fact, a distinction was fairly rapidly established between the light machine gun which was easily transported but operated by several men, such as the famous MG 34 and MG 42 which also existed in the form of a heavy machine gun, and the development of the mass weapon operated by one or at the most two men, i.e. the automatic rifle.

The first automatic rifle worthy of the name to be brought into service was the French Army's FM 15, also known as the CSRG after its inventors Chauchat, Suterre and Ribeyrolles, and the company, Gladiator, which had produced the prototypes. Although it was a fairly crude and unreliable weapon, it was produced on a large scale and was even adopted, in the absence of anything better, by the American Army in 1917.

Some of the most famous examples of the automatic rifle are the BAR of John Moses Browning; the ZB 26 developed in Czechoslovakia by the Holek brothers and its English counterpart, the famous Bren Gun; the British Lewis Gun with its circular magazine, and the French, 1924 M29, developed at the Châtellerault factory by a team under the supervision of Colonel Reibel.

Repeaters (1860)

In 1854 Smith and Wesson, the directors of the American company Volcanic, bought the rights for the Hunt & Jennings rifle which, with its tubular magazine, was the first repeating rifle to be produced but which was unusable as it was. They therefore gave B. Tyler Henry the task of making the invention a viable proposition. Unfortunately his research did not produce any results worthy of note, and it was not until **Oliver Winchester** bought the business from the two Americans that the Henry rifle came into being in **1860**.

Automatic pistol (1872)

The first weapon of this type was patented by **Plessner** in **1872**, followed shortly afterwards by Lutze of the United States in 1874. Then came the invention of the French gunsmiths, the Clair brothers: a rather strange, gas-operated weapon which they demonstrated to the army but was not adopted.

The first true automatic was invented by **Hugo Borchardt** in **1893**, and followed by the invention of Theodor Bermann a year later. These German weapons were paralleled in Austria by the first versions of the Mannlicher.

Semi-automatic rifle (c.1890)

The first semi-automatic rifles, which used either the recoil or the action of the combustion gases to operate the repeater mechanism, appeared towards the end of the last century as a result of an invention by a Mexican general, **Mondragon**. His invention was further developed by the French gunsmiths, the **Clair brothers** from St-Etienne, who acquired the patent.

In spite of the fact that a few of these weapons were used on a limited scale during the First World War, e.g. the Meunier rifle or A6, Models 17 and 18 of the RSC rifle and the Mauser automatic aircraft carbine as well as for civilian purposes, e.g. the Winchester 351 SL and the 401 SL aircraft gun, it was not until much later with the Pedersen device and then especially the invention of John Garand of the United States that the weapon was brought into service in 1932.

Silencer (1908)

The silencer was invented in **1908–09** by the American **Hiram Stevens Maxim** (1840–1916). It only worked on shot-by-shot rifles and pistols. H. S. Maxim developed it and subsequently adapted it for car exhausts.

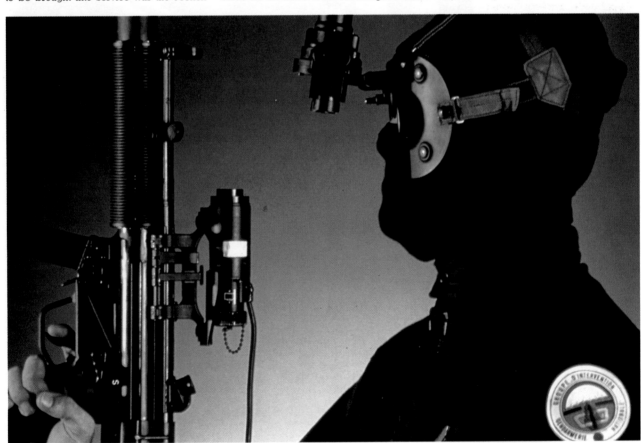

The elite French police corps, the GIGN, are equipped with hi-tech weapons and the TN2-1 visor, which weighs only 450g 16oz and gives great night vision.

Legendary weapons

The Colt

The intelligent and ambitious Samuel Colt, a self-educated man, revolutionised the revolver market by making ingenious improvements to the small repeating handgun. He patented his invention in Paris and London in 1835 and a year later in the United States where he founded the Patent Arms Company in New Jersey.

He began manufacturing the Colt Paterson, but although this was extremely efficient, it was not very successful, and eight years later the company went bankrupt. The inventor then worked relentlessly, and the war between the United States and Mexico in 1846 came at a very opportune moment, enabling Colt to re-launch the company and resume production. In 1847 he brought out the Colt Walker, a six-chamber 44 calibre weapon, and in 1848 the Colt Dragoon, the first American Army regulation revolver. Colt was an astute businessman and, in spite of a distinct lack of enthusiasm on the part of the English arms manufacturers, he set up a factory in London. The British involvement in the Crimean War (1854–6) led to its considerable commercial success which marked the beginning of the Colt empire.

Production in the United States continued to increase. Thousands of revolvers were used by both armies during the American Civil War, and the migration towards the West was responsible for a further increase in orders. By the time Colt died in 1862, the future of the company was assured, and in 1873 it brought out the Colt Peacemaker, followed in 1878 by the Colt Frontier. These revolvers, which sold in vast quantities, were of such high quality that they are still produced today with hardly any modifications.

The Winchester

In 1857 Oliver Winchester, a shirt manufacturer and an extremely

The Colt Frontier came out in 1878 and is still produced today.

shrewd businessman, bought from Hunt and Jennings the patents for the invention of a repeating rifle with a tubular magazine. He founded the New Haven Arms Company and engaged the services of Benjamin Tyler Henry to perfect the weapon. In spite of an extensive publicity campaign organised by Winchester in 1862 to launch Henry's repeating rifle, the American authorities were in no hurry to purchase it. In 1866 Winchester launched a considerably improved model and renamed his company the Winchester Repeating Arms Company. The new weapon, known as the Winchester Yellow Boy, became extremely well known. It had a 44 calibre bore, rim priming Henry cartridge and could be loaded from the right-hand side.

Although Winchester was unable to corner the American military market, which remained

faithful to the Springfield, he sold the weapon in Switzerland and the Ottoman Empire. He went on to launch the 1873 Model, which became known as 'the rifle which won the West' and was used by outlaws and sheriffs alike. Produced until 1919, with sales in excess of 720000, the weapon used the same 44–40 calibre ammunition as the Colt Frontier revolver and became an essential piece of equipment for the frontiersman. The 1886 Model, the most powerful in the Winchester range, was adopted by the Texas Rangers and the light and handy 1894 Model, specially designed for hunters, was so successful that it is still being manufactured today.

The Mauser

In 1871, after the Franco–Prussian War, Kaiser Wilhelm I

decided to equip the German infantry with the Mauser, a strong, single-barrelled rifle. This was the great breakthrough for Peter Paul Mauser, the son of a gunsmith and an extremely clever inventor. He set up his factory in the former Benedictine monastery of Obendorf and devoted himself to perfecting his repeating rifles. In 1888 he found himself having to manufacture the Gewehr 88, a rifle designed not by him but by the German commission for light weapons. Greatly vexed, he made it a point of honour to design a superior weapon himself and a year later came up with the Gewehr 98, which replaced the military commission model and was adopted by the imperial army. It had a magazine which held five 7.92mm cartridges, and was the first breech-loading rifle. The weapon, which had a faultless safety mechanism, proved ex-

Gary Cooper, an American, plays a sergeant in the British Army wielding one of the most famous revolvers – a Lüger, made in Germany.

tremely popular and was soon being used in all areas of combat.

While pursuing this line of research, Mauser also worked on the invention of an automatic pistol. On 20 August 1896 he received the supreme accolade when the Kaiser tried out the Mauser 1896, a 7.63mm calibre pistol with a magazine which held ten cartridges and a 150mm *6in* barrel. Although this very accurate pistol did not win the approval of the German military commission, many German Army officers adopted it. In 1898 the Mauser 1896 began to be exported all over the world. It was used in colonial campaigns and during the Chinese and Russian Revolutions, and Stalin and Churchill both favoured it. Today, the Mauser factories mainly produce hunting rifles.

The Browning

In 1896 John Moses Browning invented the competitor of the Mauser and Lüger, an automatic pistol which used the gases produced by the explosion rather than the energy created by the recoil action. Browning licensed the Belgian National Arms Factory to manufacture his weapon. The compact 1900 Model, which held seven cartridges, was an immediate success and was adopted by the Belgian armed forces. By 1920 nearly 725 000 weapons had been produced.

The enthusiasm of the European military for automatic pistols completely disrupted the weapons market, and the Colt factory in the United States called Browning to the rescue. After extensive tests, the American Army officially adopted the Colt 1911 Model which was also very popular with the general public. Browning produced a simplified version, the 1911 A1, which also proved extremely successful, owing to its reliability and solidity.

Browning died in 1926 when his last model, the GP 35, was still in the design stage. This became one of the most popular weapons in the world for both military and civilian use. The GP 35 is along the same lines as the Colt 1911 mechanically, but Browning had increased the loading capacity from seven to 13 cartridges. It became regulation equipment in many countries. During the Second World War the plans of the pistol were evacuated to Canada. After the war the Belgian National Arms Factory resumed production of the GP 35, which remains standard issue in many countries today.

The Lüger

When Georg Lüger was given the task of improving the Borchardt automatic pistol in 1897, he produced the forerunner of the legendary Parabellum. He modified the handle and simplified the locking system of the articulated bolt mechanism. In 1898 the new weapon was patented. After various tests, the Swiss Army officially adopted the Lüger, which already had the famous shape of the many subsequent models. In 1902 Lüger perfected the 9mm Parabellum cartridge, which was to become the most widely used standard ammunition in the world. In 1904 the German Navy adopted the Lüger P.04 pistol with a 150mm *6in* barrel. American and French forces selected the Lüger for a series of tests.

In 1908 DWM (Deutsche Waffen und Munitions), the manufacturers of the Lüger, cornered a new military market by supplying the Germany Army with the Model P.08, which had a 100mm *4in* barrel. DWM was inundated with orders. The Lüger Parabellum, the first pistol to have a significantly increased firing power, became the world's most widely used military handgun. The production of the P.08, which was interrupted in 1942, was resumed in 1960 by Mauser and Interamco.

Faye Dunaway is seen putting her revolver to somewhat illegal use in Bonnie and Clyde.

Submachine gun (1915)

The first submachine gun was manufactured and brought into service by the Italians in **1915**. It was in fact two combined weapons which used the regulation ammunition for the pistol, i.e. the Glisenti 9mm. The whole thing was named the Villa-Perosa after the factory where it was produced, *Officine di Villa-Perosa*. Its inventor, **Abiel Revelli**, wanted to produce a lightweight machine gun which could be fired on a tripod.

By separating the two weapons and mounting each one on a wooden support in the same way as the carbine, the engineer, Tullio Marengoni, turned it into a *Moschetto automatico* which only fired in bursts. The weapon appeared in 1918 and was immediately followed by an improved version with a double firing level which enabled it to fire shot-by-shot. Both models were produced by the Beretta company. At the same time, in Germany, Theodor Bergmann was developing the MP 18.1 which was the basis for most of the later versions.

Submachine guns are currently being replaced by automatic rifles in many armies. However, they still have considerable advantages for use in close combat, maintaining law and order and special operations.

The most famous examples of the submachine gun are the American Thompson, the German MP 38 and MP 40, the British Sten, the French Mat 49 and the Israeli Uzi.

Mini submachine gun (1932)

The mini submachine gun first appeared in **1932** in the form of the Mauser 96 (1932 Model). It is a very small weapon for special use in certain police and commando units and for the close protection of VIPs. Among the most famous are the American Ingram, the Israeli Mini-Uzi, the Czechoslovakian Skorpion and the Polish WZ 64. Unfortunately, they are known to have been used in a number of terrorist attacks.

Pistol with a firing selector

These pistols make it possible to choose to fire shot-by-shot or in bursts, but, given its dimensions, bursts are often difficult to control. The first versions were the Mauser C 96, known as the Schnellfeuer Pistole, used by certain SS units during the Second World War, and its Spanish copies, the Astra 900 and its derivatives.

In the 1960s the Soviets brought out a similar weapon, the Stetchkin, with the same calibre as the 9mm Makarov, and in 1977 Beretta brought out its R 93, the usefulness of which is not immediately obvious.

Heavy machine gun (1938)

This is the name given to heavy weapons which have to be transported by motor vehicle and operated by an entire team. The most famous version and the first to receive its baptism of fire, in **1938**, was the German four-barrel anti-aircraft gun, known as the 2cm Flakvierling, manufactured by the German company **Mauser**. Nowadays, the firing of these weapons is usually controlled by radar.

Motorised machine gun (1940s)

Towards the end of the **1940s**, the American company **General Electric** revived the Gatling principle, but replaced the need for

In the 1980s the British Army changed its standard service weapon, with noticeable effects for those standing guard at Buckingham Palace. The new model is the one on the left.

'elbow grease' with an electric motor. The McDonnell Douglas Helicopter company has developed another model of motorised machine gun known as the Chain Gun. Both weapons have also been adapted as light machine guns. General Electric's 62mm Minigun was used by troops airlifted by helicopter in Vietnam, and the 7.62mm Chain Gun is used in Kenyan Army helicopters and has been adopted by the British Army as a secondary weapon for their tanks.

Assault rifle (1944)

The first assault rifle to be produced in any quantity was the **1944** German **Sturmgewehr 44**, a name invented by Hitler. It was in fact a lightweight machine gun. In 1947 Mikhail Kalashnikov of the USSR used it as a basis for his famous AK 47.

During the 1950s the Belgians developed the first true assault rifle, the F.A.L., which fired 7.62mm cartridges. The weapon was sold in hundreds of thousands throughout the world.

In 1956 Eugène Stoner of the United States invented the AR-15 which was very similar to the Kalashnikov in terms of its use but very different in terms of design. The Americans appreciated its true value during the Vietnam war, and the AR-15 (the design of which had been bought by Colt) was adopted at the end of the 1960s by the American Army under the name of the M 16. A new version of the rifle, the M 16 A2, was brought into service for the Marines in 1985.

Bullpup (c.1980)

The bullpup rifle was designed as a modern weapon adapted to new forms of combat, but the system dates back to the beginning of the century when the Burton automatic rifle was invented in the United States in 1917. The overall length of this compact rifle is much reduced, although the barrel is of the same length as on a traditional rifle so that its accuracy is in no way affected. The first versions of the rifle were designed in Great Britain in about 1955, but the design was not widely adopted until the end of the 1970s with the AUG manufactured by Steyr-Daimler Puch for the Austrian Army in 1977, the FAMAS designed by GIAT for the French Army in 1979 and the Royal Ordnance's SA 80 for the British Army in 1985.

Stun Gun (1984)

The Stun Gun is a new American invention which has the advantage of immobilising, rather than killing or wounding, by means of a powerful electric charge of between 40000 and 50000V which momentarily dazes and paralyses the victim. It has been tested by the Harris County Constable Department which is responsible for the transportation of dangerous mentally ill patients. The Stun Gun, like its predecessor the Taser, which operated on the same principle but was more unwieldy, is also used by the American police to control prisoners, ward off attacks and so on.

Glock 17 (1986)

Invented by the Austrian **Gaston Glock**, most of the components of this automatic pistol are made of plastic except, of course, the barrel. However, this does not, as was originally thought, enable it to pass undetected through the metal detector control systems used in airports. It is a 9×19 calibre (= 9mm Parabellum) lightweight weapon (650g *1lb 7oz*) which is extremely accurate and reliable.

P.90 (1990)

Designed to compete with light guns such as the Uzi, the P.90 is a 9mm calibre Parabellum made by the **Fabrique Nationale de Herstal** (Belgium). Secret composite materials make it an ultra-light weapon suitable for use by the special services, bodyguards and military personnel requiring a very small gun. The magazine is transparent, which allows the user to keep a constant check on the number of cartridges left.

Available since the beginning of **1990**, the P.90 – equipped with a laser sight – was seen in *Rambo III.*

Artillery

Cannon (14th century)

The first pieces of ordnance, the forerunners of the cannon, appeared with the invention of gunpowder in the **14th century**. They went under various names, bombards, blunderbusses, etc. However, the first document recording the use of the cannon is of Arab origin and dates back to 1304.

Shrapnel shells (1784)

In **1784** an Englishman, **Henry Shrapnel** of the Royal Artillery, invented the exploding shell.

With his invention, Shrapnel wanted to maximise the effect by having hollow iron balls filled with bullets explode on target. Shrapnel was adopted by the British Army in 1803 and came into immediate use against Napoleon, particularly at Waterloo. Shrapnel subsequently became, and remained until very recently, the classic missile of the artillery. During the First World War, it was used against aircraft.

Recoil brake (1897)

Invented in **1897** for the 75mm French field gun, the hydraulic recoil brake marks the birth of modern artillery. Until then, pieces had recoiled by several metres every time they were fired. The 75mm field gun was developed by a team of French artillerymen, General Sainte-Claire Deville, Captain Rimailho and Colonel Deport.

Recoilless gun (c.1910)

This weapon was invented by an American, **Davis**, at the beginning of the 20th century and brought into service for a short time on several English aircraft during the First World War. It had two opposing barrels and a central chamber for the propellant charge. Towards the end of the 1930s, the German companies Krupp and Rheinmetall manufactured several models of the 75mm recoilless gun, one of which was tested by German parachutists in Crete.

Mortar (1917)

The mortar, a very short wide-barrelled piece, appeared about the same time as the pieces of ordnance. The modern version of the mortar was invented by the Englishman, **Stokes**, who developed an 81mm calibre weapon which was brought into service by the British Army in 1917.

In the 1930s a Frenchman, Edgard Brandt, developed an entire series of mortars ranging from 45mm to 155mm. The Stokes-Brandt mortars have been continually improved and form the basis of all modern mortars.

Mountain infantry go through their drill with a 120 mortar.

Armoured vehicles

Armoured vehicles (antiquity)

Horse-drawn chariots were used in ancient times to carry soldiers armed with bows and javelins. They were used by Cyrus, King of Persia, against Croesus, King of Lydia, at the Battle of Thymbreae in 540 BC. The drawings of Leonardo da Vinci also show various projects for armoured chariots, covered with a conical protection of wood.

Armoured car (1902)

In 1902 the French company **Charron, Girardot & Voight** brought out the first armoured car combining all the modern technical possibilities: a motorised vehicle, armour-plating and turret-mounted weapons.

Tank (1908)

In 1908 the Englishman **Roberts** unveiled, near London, an armour-plated, tracked vehicle. In 1912 the Austrian Gunter Burstyn developed a similar vehicle but armed with a gun. However, the military had little faith in his invention.

The trench warfare that took place from 1914 revived the idea of an armoured land vehicle which was studied by the Royal Navy and the French Artillery. In France the idea was promoted by Colonel (later General) Jean Baptiste Estienne. The project for this new vehicle was top secret. It was E. D. Swinton who designed a tank with caterpillar tracks to enable it to crush barbed wire and climb over trenches. The first tank was ready in September 1915, built by William Foster & Co. of Lincoln.

The first battle in which tanks participated took place in France on 15 September 1916 at Flers-Courcelette.

Underwater tank (1944)

In 1944 a team of German engineers took only a few weeks to develop a tracked pocket submarine which was equally capable of travelling on the seabed and on land. This tracked submarine was difficult to detect and carried two torpedoes powerful enough to sink a warship. It was an invention that the Germans did not have time to use.

Special weapons

Hollow charge (1883)

In 1883 the German **Max von Forster** published the results of five years' research carried out on the effects of an explosive charge in the form of a hollow cone.

The principle was developed by Lepidi of France in 1890, Lodati of Italy in 1933, and finally by the Swiss-born Mohaupt brothers. In Germany the method was used from 1940 onwards for the charges used to destroy the Belgian forts in Liège. It was then applied to rifle grenades and later to rockets.

One of the first American tanks goes into action during the First World War.

The JP 233, produced by Hunter Engineering, was used by Allied forces in the Gulf War to knock out runways. A cascade of little bombs cratered the runway and left behind anti-personnel mines.

Anti-tank gun (1918)

The first anti-tank gun to be used effectively at the front was invented by **Fischer**, a lieutenant-colonel from Bavaria, who constructed it while installing a modification of the 37mm revolving gun onto a captured French St-Etienne machine gun carriage. With improved ammunition, it could produce a muzzle velocity of 506m *1660ft* per second and penetrate 16mm *0.63in* of steel at a distance of 450m *1500ft*. Anti-tank guns were gradually replaced by hollow charge projectiles.

Bazooka (1940)

Several inventors claim the credit for the bazooka, or rocket launcher, including the Swiss **Mohaupt** brothers who, at the beginning of the Second World War, sent plans to America for a projectile which subsequently became the T 10 anti-tank grenade and then the active charge of the bazooka. The plans were delivered to New York on **31 December 1940** by Colonel Delalande.

The bazooka consists of a single tube of thin metal which acts as the launcher for a rocket equipped with an explosive head with a hollow charge. It can seriously damage armoured vehicles.

Stalin's Organ (1942)

These batteries of rockets with explosive heads, propelled by solid fuel, were used extensively by the Soviets for bombardments during the Second World War. Their German counterpart was the multi-tube rocket launcher known as the Nebelwerfer. The main disadvantages of this type of weapon were their lack of precision and the fact that they were easily detectable as they gave off large amounts of smoke when fired.

Powder and explosives

Gunpowder (7th century)

During the early years of the Tang Dynasty, the alchemist and pharmacologist **Sun Simao** gave the first description of how to make gunpowder from a mixture of saltpetre, sulphur and charcoal. It is however likely that it had been invented several decades earlier, but that alchemists had closely guarded the secret of their discovery.

Gunpowder has been used in warfare from the 10th century onwards. Manufacturing techniques were subsequently improved many times to keep pace with the development of firearms. The Crusades of the 13th century fought against the Arab countries of central Asia led to the discovery of this explosive by Europeans, and its use then spread into the Mediterranean countries. However, it was not until the 15th century that the European countries produced their first powder guns.

Incendiary compounds

In 674, during the Siege of Constantinople by the Arabs, the Syrian architect **Callinicus** showed the Emperor Constantine the secret of Greek fire, according to an old Chinese tradition. His compound consisted of sulphur, tar, naphtha, oil, fat, resin and charcoal. Firing

CHEMICAL WEAPONS: STILL A THREAT

Chemical warfare was already being practised in the Middle Ages with the use of asphyxiating missiles made from powdered Euphorbia (a poisonous plant) added to vine charcoal. Poisoned bullets and quicklime were also used.

But modern chemical warfare began in 1915 when the Germans released 180 tonnes of chlorine gas upwind of the French positions, with the result that 15000 men were put out of the war. Chlorine was gradually replaced by phosgene and then, on 12 July 1917 at Ypres, the Germans used shells loaded with mustard gas. From June 1918 a quarter of the shells fired by the French also contained mustard gas. Among the German victims was a 29-year-old corporal, Adolf Hitler, but the experience did not deter him, in 1933, from supporting research in the field of nerve gases.

The first of these gases, tabun, was discovered in 1936 by the German company I. G. Farben during research on insecticides. Sarin was discovered in 1939, and soman in 1944 by the German Richard Kuhn, who won the Nobel Prize for Chemistry in 1938, not for this discovery but for his work on vitamins.

These nerve gases are among the most dangerous of their type. They cause the organic muscles to contract which leads to convulsions and prevents breathing. In 1987 some 5000 Kurdish men, women and children in Halabja in northern Iraq died in this way.

Bacteriological weapons, which are being researched as much as chemical weapons, have been used since Roman times and made sporadic appearances up to the 16th century. Today these weapons are included in the arsenals of many world powers. Since 1987 various conferences, committees and comfnissions have undertaken the difficult task of developing projects which aim to impose a total ban on the use of both chemical and bacteriological weapons. However, it will require many years of negotiations to obtain the necessary agreements. These terrible weapons will therefore continue to remain a very real threat until the year 2000.

British soldiers check their chemical protection suits during a training exercise.

GUNPOWDER WHILE SEARCHING FOR IMMORTALITY

It was while searching for the secret of immortality, according to Christopher Cullen, a professor at the School for Oriental and African Studies, London University, that the Chinese are said to have discovered gunpowder. Saltpetre, or potassium nitrate, which Chinese alchemists used in their experiments, has explosive properties, and it was around the year 850 that the scientists realised the danger that came from mixing it with sulphur and carbon.

stone which consisted of gunpowder mixed with saltpetre and sulphur appeared c.1450.

Experiments with phosphorous began in the 19th century. In 1890 thermite was invented. This is a substance with a base of powdered aluminium and metallic oxides which only ignites at high temperatures and is therefore easier to handle. It used to be used for welding tramlines.

In 1910 a French engineer, Sazerac de Forges, invented an incendiary bomb designed to destroy German airships which he tested by throwing it from the first level of the Eiffel Tower. The flame-thrower appeared during the First World War, and the napalm bomb was invented in 1943.

Molotov cocktail (1939)

The Molotov cocktail is used in urban guerrilla warfare and as a close-range anti-tank device. It was invented in 1939 by the Finns during their winter campaign against the Soviets. It would appear, however, that the Molotov cocktail was also used by the Republicans during the Spanish Civil War. This elementary incendiary weapon is quite simply a bottle filled with a petrol-based mixture, a device improvised by those fighting barehanded against armoured vehicles.

The safety fuse or slow match wick (1831)

The safety fuse or slow match wick was invented in 1831 by the Englishman William Bickford (1774–1834). The company, Davey-Bickford, still exists today.

Guncotton (1847)

In 1847 a German chemist, Christian Friedrich Schönbein (1799–1868), who in 1839 isolated ozone by water electrolysis, developed the manufacture of guncotton or nitrocotton. Guncotton consists of nitrocellulose and is an extremely powerful explosive.

Nitroglycerine (1847)

In 1847 the Italian chemist Ascanio Solaro produced nitroglycerine by pouring a half volume of glycerine drop by drop into a mixture of one volume of nitric acid and two volumes of sulphur acid. Nitroglycerine, which was extremely powerful and exploded at the slightest jolt, was responsible for the most terrible accidents. Two Swedes, the Nobel brothers, carried out a study of nitroglycerine. One of them was killed by this dangerous explosive but the other, Albert, courageously continued his experiments.

Dynamite (1866)

During one of his 1866 experiments, Alfred Nobel made a discovery. Nitroglycerine from a broken flask was absorbed by *kieselguhr*, a form of clay used as an insulating substance. Nobel found that the absorbed nitroglycerine retained its explosive qualities but was considerably more stable and much easier to handle. Dynamite was born.

Nuclear weapons

Atomic bomb (1945)

The atomic bomb was the work of a team of American scientists: Arthur H. Compton, Robert Oppenheimer, and the Italian- and Hungarian-born physicists, Enrico Fermi and Leo Szilard, who were both living in the United States. The bomb was exploded, experimentally, for the first time on 16 July 1945 at Alamagardo, 350km *217 miles* to the south of Los Alamos in New Mexico.

A letter written by Albert Einstein (1879–1955) on 2 August 1939 influenced the United States in its decision to build an atomic bomb. President Franklin D. Roosevelt did not find out about the letter until 11 October of that same year, over a month after war had broken out on 1 September.

On 2 December 1942, in their secret laboratory below the terraces of the football ground at the University of Chicago, the research team led by Enrico Fermi succeeded in releasing the first chain reaction in a uranium-graphite atomic pile (*see* Energy).

On 6 August 1945, a uranium 235 bomb was dropped on the Japanese city of Hiroshima killing 80 000 and wounding 50 000. On

This white froth on the surface of the sea is the only visible trace of the underwater nuclear experiments at Mururoa.

The American Strategic Defence Initiative (SDI) or 'Star Wars' programme is going ahead in its entirety, despite the opposition of Congress, and could be implemented from 1996. The Bush administration applied for an additional 22 percent for the 1991 budget. The initiative was given a fillip by several successes in 1989, in particular the performance of the high-power laser MIRACL which shot down a target missile flying at more than twice the speed of sound.

In February 1990 a Delta rocket put two experimental satellites into orbit. The RME (Relay Mirror Experiment) carries a mirror of 50cm *20in* in diameter which is able to reflect back to earth a low strength laser beam sent out from the ground with a precision of 57 millionths of a degree. The second satellite, the LACE (Low-power Atmospheric Compensation Experiment), is there chiefly to measure the efficiency of a system for correcting distortions of the laser beam caused by its passage through the atmosphere.

Another experiment which shows that the SDI is in full swing is the first trial in space of the Brilliant Pebbles system of spatial interceptors. The Brilliant Pebbles project consists of deploying in space, at an altitude of 650km *400 miles*, some 5000 miniature interceptors measuring less than 1m *3ft* in length. Once activated from the ground, they become totally autonomous. Their task is to destroy enemy missiles by colliding with them.

A space probe incorporating certain elements of the Brilliant Pebbles – a semi-autonomous anti-missile satellite constituting one of the key elements of the SDI – was launched during the second half of 1990.

Credit for initiating the SDI programme has been given to President Reagan, who launched the programme in 1983 in the face of much opposition. Perhaps his faith in it is finally beginning to bear fruit.

MICROWAVE ANTI-MISSILE BOMB

The American Department of Energy is studying a new type of nuclear weapon which makes it possible to destroy the electronic equipment aboard missiles in flight. This new bomb, a highly powerful microwave weapon, would produce an electromagnetic pulse (EMP) much greater than that produced by a traditional nuclear bomb, one of the effects of which is to disrupt electronic systems. As missiles are sensitive to electromagnetic pulses, they would thus be rendered harmless. This research is in response to the development of missiles which are difficult to detect in flight.

9 August a plutonium bomb completely destroyed Nagasaki. Japan surrendered and the Second World War was over, but was replaced by the fear of nuclear war.

H bomb (1952)

On **31 October 1952** the United States exploded the first H bomb on the Pacific atoll of Eniwetok. The H bomb was invented by **Edward Teller** as a result of research carried out on the A bomb between 1949 and 1951.

In August of the following year, the USSR exploded a similar bomb, followed by Great Britain in 1957, China in 1967 and France in 1968.

Neutron bomb (1958)

Research on the neutron bomb began in the United States, on the initiative of **Samuel Cohen**, around 1958. The experts prefer to refer to it as the enhanced radiation warhead or the neutron shell.

Neutron rays are particularly deadly, but the device is a 'clean bomb' in the sense that, being less powerful than the H bomb, it destroys all forms of life without affecting the material environment and without causing pollution. Therefore, once the neutrons have dispersed, it is possible to take over enemy installations.

Detection systems

Sonar (1915)

In **1915**, following the sinking of the *Titanic* three years previously, a French professor called **Paul Langevin** developed a system for detecting icebergs and, by extension, submarines, which formed the basis of the Sonar system (the acronym for *Sound Navigation and Ranging*) developed in England in the 1920s. The military derivative, the Asdic (Allied Submarine Detection and Investigation Committee), was installed in 200 Royal Navy destroyers and escort vessels in 1939, and was extremely useful to British and American ships during the final stages of the war. More sophisticated versions are in use today.

Sonar dome (1990)

The first 'sonar dome' of composite material (fibreglass) appeared on **1 March 1990**, a product of the Cherbourg arsenal workshops in France. This submarine nose, designed to protect hyper-sophisticated monitoring equipment, is the first of its kind in Europe, made with an entirely new technology. It is constructed of successive layers of material pre-impregnated with resin, and is vacuum cooked to give it a homogeneity never previously achieved with composites.

Radar (1940)

Radar (the acronym for *Radio Detection and Ranging*) was developed in England in 1940, although a great deal of preliminary research had been carried out by, for example,

Heinrich Rudolph Hertz of Germany in 1886, the Serbian–American inventor Nikola Tesla in 1900, and the German engineer Christian Hülsmeyer who patented a 'detector for objects with a continuous radio wave' in 1904.

In about 1934 Henri Gutton, a research worker in the French wireless company CSF, developed the magnetron which later became the main component of future radar systems. The director of the company, Maurice Ponte, who was married to an Englishwoman, was able to have Gutton's invention sent to England during the war thereby enabling the English to develop their own projects.

At the same time the project of another Frenchman, Pierre David, an electromagnetic system for the detection of aircraft, was tested successfully at Le Bourget. The system, based on an idea conceived in 1928, made it possible to detect an aircraft at a distance of 5000m *3.1 miles*.

Under the pressure of events, research continued during the early stages of the Second World War and resulted in the invention of radar by a British technical research team under the supervision of **Sir Robert Watson-Watt**. Radar proved a determining factor in the anti-aircraft defence system during the Battle of Britain.

By 1991 the UK had developed a new form of radar capable of detecting missiles within a field of 360 degrees. It was the first radar in western Europe able to detect, simultaneously, a threat from both East and West.

Transmission systems

RITA (1985)

In **1985** the French company **Thomson-CSF**, in association with the American company **GTE**, won a contract for more than $4 billion to equip 25 divisions of the American Army with a tactical transmissions system. RITA, an integrated automatic transmissions network, was chosen in preference to the British system Ptarmigan.

Skynet-4B (1988)

This was the first exclusively military satellite and was launched by Ariane-4 in **December 1988**. Skynet-4B, a British communications satellite, is part of the Skynet-4 programme which will become fully operational when it consists of four satellites. Skynet-4B, built by the Space and Communication division of British Aerospace, has a total mass weight of 1433kg *3160lb* during launching and 790kg *1742lb* in its geostationary orbit. It should remain operational for seven years.

Missiles

Ballistic missiles (1942)

The first major steps in the field of missiles took place in Peenemünde in Germany in 1937. Most of the theoretical developments took place between 1939 and 1945, and only technological limitations prevented some of these from being put into practice.

The first trial of the V2, the first operational ballistic missile in history, took place on **13 June 1942**. Its form has been adopted for the modern ground-to-ground missile. It was developed by a research team directed

The Tomahawk cruise missile was one of the great successes of the Gulf War thanks to its pinpoint accuracy.

by **General Walter Dornberger** assisted by **Wernher von Braun** and **Hermann Oberth**.

The main categories of modern missile are the lightweight surface-to-air portable missiles, fired from the shoulder, such as the British Blowpipe, or those which can be transported on light vehicles: the British Rapier and the American Stinger for example; and the intermediate range surface-to-air missiles, for example the Soviet SAM, and the long range land-to-sea, sea-to-sea and air-to-sea missiles, the most famous of which is the French Exocet, employed during the Falklands War in 1982.

Anti-tank missiles belong to a separate category. They are usually 'guided by wire'. The best known are the Franco–German systems, Milan with a range of 2km *1¼ miles* and HOT with a range of 4km *2½ miles*, and the American TOW with a range of 3km *2 miles*.

Intercontinental missiles

The long range intercontinental ballistic missile, ICBM, is the weapon which will maintain the balance of world power. These missiles, with their nuclear warheads, can be launched from underground silos or submarines and are preprogrammed to destroy cities. They have an incredible range, in the order of 9000km *5600 miles*. The most famous are the American Minuteman, which is soon to be replaced by the four-stage MX with a range of 10000km *6200 miles*, and the Soviet SS-19.

Intermediate range missiles

Intermediate range ballistic missiles (IRBM) generally have three nuclear warheads and a range of 5000km *3100 miles*. The best-known are the American Pershing, the Soviet SS-20 and the French S-3.

The submarine-launched ballistic missiles (SLBM) – the Anglo–American Polaris, the Soviet SS-N-20 and the French M-20 – have the same characteristics as the IRBM.

Cruise missiles

Cruise missiles are high-speed, low-altitude pilotless aircraft. They were invented by the Germans in 1944 in the form of the V1, the *Vergeltungswaffe*, or Vengeance Weapon which was powered by a ramjet engine.

In 1982 Boeing delivered the first Air Launch Cruise Missiles (ALCM) to the American Air Force. Twelve of these tiny planes with arrowhead collapsible wings are attached to the underside of the wings of a B52.

Tomahawk BGM-109C (1980s)

The whole cruise programme had a long evolution from 1972, when the idea was first conceived, to its first use in active service in the Gulf War in January 1991. Throughout the **1980s** it had been improved, so that when war broke out it was one of the immediate successes when fired from American warships in the Gulf and the Red Sea.

The Tomahawk is powered by a turbofan jet engine which gives it a range of 1300km *800 miles* at 800km/h *500mph* and cruises along only a few metres or feet above the ground. It is guided by the Tercom system (*terrain contour matching*), which means that it can hug the contours and thus avoid detection by enemy radar. As it approaches its target, still constantly checking its flight path, it switches to a new guidance system DSMAC (Digital Scene Matching Area Correlator) which enables it to check that what it 'sees' matches the information stored in its computers and to adjust accordingly if there are any discrepancies. Then it homes in on its target with pinpoint accuracy so that the 450kg *1000lb* warhead does the maximum damage. It can, of course, be loaded with either conventional or nuclear warheads.

The 'invisible' AGM-129/A (1989)

On **2 March 1989**, the American Air Force tested the new 'invisible' cruise missile, the AGM-129/A, manufactured by **General Dynamics** and **McDonnell Douglas**. It has a greater speed than that of the previous generation of cruise missiles and is virtually undetectable by radar.

Anti-ship missiles

The sinking of the Israeli frigate *Eilat* in 1967 by a small Egyptian patrol boat armed with Styx anti-ship missiles, triggered off and accelerated the programme for the development of such missiles in the western world. The Kormoran was developed jointly by France and West Germany; the MM38, the first version of the Exocet, by France; Otomat by France and Italy; Harpoon by the United States; Penguin by Norway and Gabriel by Israel. They all travel at high subsonic speeds. Any future attempts to counter the anti-missile systems will have to develop missiles with a greater range and with a high penetrating power, i.e. missiles that will reach supersonic speeds (Mach 2). Given the range of speeds and altitudes to be covered the statoreactor is the most satisfactory solution.

Since the autumn of 1988 the American company Northrop has been producing a new missile, Tacit Rainbow, capable of destroying enemy radar systems.

THE PRECISION OF TRIDENT

Trident II is the name of the American Navy's new nuclear missile, whose precision is such that it can hit a submarine from a distance of over 7000km *4350 miles*. American nuclear submarines have been equipped with Trident II since 1990. Each vessel can hold 24 missiles, each capable of carrying 12 independent nuclear warheads – a total of 288 warheads per submarine.

Naval warfare

Submarine (1624)

Origins

The Dutch physicist **Cornelius Drebbel** (1572–1633), inventor of the thermometer and tutor to the children of James I, was responsible for the creation of the first submarine. In fact he applied the theories of the English mathematician William Bourne, who had defined the principle of ballast tanks in 1578. Bourne had also had the idea of a hollow mast to provide ventilation. This was the principle of the schnorkel which was used much later in the German Type XXI submarines

In **1624** Drebbel had an ovoid, wooden submarine built which was propelled by 12 oarsmen in addition to the crew. The trials took place on the Thames between Westminster and Greenwich, much to the amazement of the general public. It would appear that Drebbel had the idea of renewing the air on board chemically, using an alkaline solution, which intrigued the Anglo–Irish physicist Robert Boyle (1627–91). Apparently nobody ever obtained details of this strange mixture.

Bushnell's *Turtle* (1776)

The hull of this single-seater vessel looked like two turtle shells stuck together. This hand-cranked craft was equipped with screw propellers and a sort of brace used to fix a box, containing a large charge of gunpowder and a detonator, to the hull of the ship to be blown up. It was piloted by the American Army sergeant Ezra Lee, who had received instruction from the inventor, **David Bushnell**. In **1776** the *Turtle* attacked the English ship *Eagle* outside New York harbour, but was unsuccessful as the wooden screw of the *Turtle* could not pierce the ship's copper-lined hull. However, a year later it blew up an English schooner and the inventor was rewarded personally by George Washington.

Nautilus (1797)

In **1797** an American mechanic, **Robert Fulton**, designed a propeller-driven submarine which was intended to place explosive charges under the hulls of enemy ships. The *Nautilus*, built in 1798, was tested on the Seine but failed to impress Napoleon. Fulton went to England where his reception was no better. The British Admiralty also turned it down as they believed the submarine would enable weaker nations to sink British warships.

David (1864)

The first feat of arms performed by a submarine carrying a torpedo – actually a simple barrel of gunpowder towed by a long rope – dates back to the American Civil War. During the night of **17 February 1864** a submarine, the *David*, designed by the American naval captain **Horace L. Hunley**, and piloted by a crew of nine men, sank the Union frigate *Housatonic*, which was taking part in the blockade of Charleston. However, the experience was not repeated due to the fact that 34 Confederates were killed in the incident and

because of the measures taken by the Union to protect their ships.

Submersible (1899)

Earlier inventions had been 'submarines' in the true sense of the word. The *Narval*, built in **1899** by **Maxime Laubeuf** (1864–1939), a marine engineer in the French Navy, was a submersible boat which had ballast tanks on the outside of its thick hull in order to withstand pressure more effectively. It was also far superior to its predecessors in certain respects, such as being able to sail on the surface. It was operated underwater by an electric motor and on the surface by an oil-fired steam motor.

In 1875 an Irish-born American engineer, John P. Holland, designed an early submarine which combined most of the basic control systems of the modern submarine, and obtained his first order from the US Navy Department in 1895. The *Holland* was delivered in 1900, followed by five more. These were the first fully operational and efficient submarines in the world, and the Royal Navy commissioned five.

The first truly seaworthy submarine on the open sea was the *Argonaut* designed by another American, Simon Lake, in 1894 and tested in 1898.

The 'classic' submarine

These diesel-electric propelled submarines which are still in use today were developed in 1901. The infamous German U-Boats of the First and Second World Wars and the French *Daphné* are of this type.

The first submersibles were used mainly for shelling on the surface after releasing torpedoes underwater. After the appearance of the German Type XXI, which was able to dive rapidly and was equipped with schnorkels which meant it did not have to resurface to recharge its batteries and replenish its air supply, everything was done below the surface. The Type XXI was the prototype for a whole generation of classic post-war submarines.

Schnorkel (1938)

Originally designed for an American submarine in 1897, the schnorkel ('snort') was

An early German U-Boat is seen leaving Zeebrugge in 1915 aiming to disrupt Allied shipping.

installed on several Dutch submarines in 1939. The German engineer Helmut Walter improved the system and adapted it for German submarines.

The first sea trials were carried out in 1942 by the U-107, under the command of Lieutenant-Commander Hessler, son-in-law of Admiral Dönitz.

The schnorkel consists of a retractable tube of about 8m *26ft* long and 30cm *12in* in diameter which can be raised at right angles to the submarine, thus enabling it to cruise below the surface using its diesel engine. The schnorkel has two pipes, one to take in fresh air, and the other to extract exhaust gases.

Battleship (1850)

A French naval engineer, **Stanislas Henri Laurent Dupuy de Lôme**, developed the first high-speed fighting ship, the *Napoléon*, in **1850**. This was followed by *La Gloire*, an armoured frigate, presented to Napoleon III in 1857. Both were steam-powered and screw-propelled.

In 1859 Dupuy de Lôme was responsible for the construction of two high tonnage ships, the *Magenta* and the *Solferino* which, although similar to earlier warships, were armoured.

In 1854 the American John Ericsson developed the revolving turret which extended the field of fire of a battleship's guns to 360 degrees. His idea was put into practice with the construction of the famous *Monitor* which played a decisive role in the American Civil War, and in particular at the Battle of Hampton Roads.

Dreadnought (1906)

The disappearance of rigging from sailing ships made it possible to install turrets on the midship centre line, so that, as early as **1906**,

the modern form of the battleship was established by the English ship *HMS Dreadnought* which revolutionised naval history. Five armoured rotating turrets housed ten 304mm *12in* breech-loading guns.

Current battleships, such as the *New Jersey*, have been thoroughly modernised and are now equipped with missiles, rapid-firing guns, helicopter platforms, etc.

Torpedo boat (1860)

The first torpedo boats appeared between **1860** and 1865. They were basic small craft equipped with a long moveable pole in the bows. The pole carried an explosive charge which was set off below the surface near the objective after a silent approach under cover of darkness.

The first successful use of the torpedo boat dates back to the Russo–Turkish War of 1877–8.

The counter torpedo boat or destroyer appeared in 1893, the logical answer to the torpedo boat which it eventually replaced.

Sea mine (1861)

Although it had been described in various works at the beginning of the 17th century, the sea mine did not really make an appearance until the American Civil War of **1861–5**. It was widely used during the First World War.

The Second World War saw the development of the magnetic mine which was exploded under the magnetic effect of iron hulls; the acoustic mine, mainly activated by the noise of the propellers; and the low-pressure mine which operated on the basis of the suction effect and the low pressure caused by the movement of the ship.

It was as a result of mine warfare that the

minesweeper was brought into service during the First World War, and the mine detector developed towards the end of the 1960s.

Mobile mine (1980)

Since **1980** the great naval powers, and the United States in particular, have begun to develop a new form of mine: the mobile mine. Nuclear powered submarines, and especially missile launchers, constitute the main objective of this type of mine.

Torpedo mine (1995)

The Swedish Navy is currently researching a new 'intelligent' anti-submarine weapon which could be brought into service during the **1990s**. It is a combination of the mine and the torpedo and will be able to distinguish between allied and enemy submarines. The torpedo mine rests on the seabed from where it uses an acoustic device to record the sounds of passing ships and compare them with programmed sounds in a data bank.

Self-propelled torpedo (1864)

The self-propelled torpedo was invented in **1864** by the captain of a frigate in the Austrian Navy, **Luppis**, and later improved and constructed at Fiume (then an Austrian port) in Yugoslavia in 1867 by the British engineer Robert Whitehead (1823–1905). The torpedo is a tiny independent 'submarine' carrying a heavy explosive charge in its bows and equipped with a self-steering mechanism which enables it to move itself towards the enemy vessel.

At present the torpedo, which is up to 7.3m *24ft* long with a diameter of 53cm *20in*, weighing more than a tonne and loaded with 270kg *595lb* of explosives, can cover a distance of 13km *8 miles* at a speed of 50km/h *31mph*.

The USS Eisenhower *is one of the American Navy's Nimitz class aircraft carriers, the largest in the world, powered by four nuclear-powered steam turbines.*

The French submarine Triomphant *is seen here under construction in a naval shipyard.*

Aircraft carriers (1911)

The first plane to take off from a warship was piloted by an American, Eugene Ely, on 14 November 1910. He took off in a Curtiss biplane, equipped with a 50hp engine, from the American cruiser, *USS Birmingham*.

On **18 January 1911 Eugene Ely** landed the same plane on a specially equipped platform on the quarter-deck of the battleship *Pennsylvania*. He took off again a few minutes later: the aircraft carrier had come into being.

Landing remained a problem for a long time, and the development of the oblique landing runway was a major step forward. During the Second World War, the Americans built 120 aircraft carriers which moved naval combat into the air.

Nimitz (1975)

The five largest aircraft carriers in the world are in the Nimitz class, used by the US Navy, and have an overall length of 330m *1083ft*. Their eight 280 000 shp nuclear reactors propel the 90 000 tonne ships at a speed of more than 30 knots. They have a crew of 6300 men and carry 90 aircraft and helicopters.

Soviet aircraft carriers (1975)

In 1970 the USSR undertook construction of the first aircraft carriers in her history. Since its entry into service in **May 1975**, the *Kiev* has been followed by three other ships of its type. They are called 'aircraft carrier cruisers' by the Russians and are powerfully armed against ships, missiles, aircraft and submarines. The *Kiev* holds a total of 28 aircraft, 16 of which are Forger-type vertical take-off and landing aircraft.

BIK-COM-2 (1983)

Since **1983** the USSR has undertaken the con-struction of a traditional aircraft carrier with an oblique flight deck and steam catapults for the use of unadapted planes. Known in the West under the name BIK-COM-2, the new Soviet carrier could have a displacement of approximately 75 000 tonnes at maximal load, a floating length of 300m *984ft* and a deck width of 73m *239ft*.

Propulsion will be ensured via two nuclear reactors which provide a total power of 200 000hp and allow a speed of 30–32 knots.

Cruiser (c.1920)

The cruiser is not an armoured vessel, but is quick and heavily armed. It took over during the **1920s** from the scouts of the First World War. The cruiser was intended to act as a scout for squadrons and convoys, but its function became gradually extended and generalised to the point where it played an important part, particularly from the beginning of the Second World War.

The biggest and most powerful cruisers currently in service throughout the world are the Kirov class of the Soviet Navy.

Piloted torpedoes (1936)

These slow-speed torpedoes were developed just before the beginning of the Second World War by two Italian naval officers, **Tesei** and **Torschi**. The torpedoes carried a two-man crew at a shallow depth with a charge of TNT which they had to attach to the hulls of ships anchored in enemy harbours. These first frogmen, equipped with aqualungs, attacked the English fleet in Gibraltar in September 1941, and again in the port of Alexandria in December of the same year,

causing serious damage to the battleships *Valiant* and *Queen Elizabeth*.

In 1944 the Germans brought the *Marder* into service. This was a double torpedo in which the upper one contained a single-seater cockpit.

The Japanese developed the *Kaiten*, a sort of miniature submarine used in suicide attacks. It carried an explosive charge and was piloted by volunteers who crashed them into Allied ships.

Nuclear submarine (1955)

The first nuclear submarine was constructed by the **US Navy** at the instigation of **Admiral Hyman G. Rickover**. The *USS Nautilus* was included in the naval budget in 1951, was put on the slipway in 1952 and launched on 21 January 1954. Its first sea mission started on **17 January 1955**, and in May of the same year it beat all records by covering the distance between New London and Puerto Rico, i.e. 1397 nautical miles or 2587km in 84 hours. On 3 August 1958 it became the first submarine to surface at the North Pole in a channel between the ice floes. After ten years it had covered 330 000 nautical miles and used up three 'hearts' with a 6kg *13lb* uranium capacity. To cover the same distance, a standard diesel-electric propelled submarine would have needed 38 million litres of fuel. With a submerged tonnage of 4091 tonnes, *USS Nautilus* carried a crew of 103 at a speed of 20 knots.

The modern nuclear hunter-killer submarines have a submerged speed of the equivalent of about 35 knots. This is due to the carefully designed droplet shape of their hull with its single propeller.

WARSHIPS OF HISTORY

Type	Date	Characteristics
Galley	3rd–2nd millennium BC	The Cretans were already familiar with the galley which, propelled by oars, dominated the Mediterranean for almost three millennia. It had its hour of glory at Salamis on 28 September 480 BC when the 470 Greek vessels of Themistocles defeated the Persian fleet of Xerxes which consisted of more than 1100 ships.
Longship	8th century	Invented by the Vikings, the longship had a characteristic high prow and stern. The prow of the vessel was often decorated with the head of a dragon.
Cog	13th century	Always associated with the period of the Crusades and great discoveries. Not ideally suited to war at sea, it was the predecessor of the vessels which ruled the oceans from the 16th to the 19th century.
Galleon	16th century	The *Great Harry*, built by the English in 1514, and the *Grande Françoise* prefigured modern ocean liners. The perfection of the design of this type of ship was achieved at the end of the 18th century by the skill of the French naval engineer, Jacques-Noël Sané, nicknamed the Vauban of the Navy.
Fire ship	16th century	It made its appearance at the beginning of the 16th century. It was a ship, no longer fit for service, which was filled with inflammable material and launched against enemy ships when the wind was favourable.

Typhoon (1980)

The Soviet submarines of the Typhoon class are the most impressive strategic submarines ever to be brought into service. They have two nuclear reactors which ensure their virtually unlimited autonomy, and appear to be constructed from two thick hulls joined together. Two vessels of this type have been in service since **September 1980**. The superiority of the Soviet submarines, which are, generally speaking, better armed, quieter and capable of cruising at greater depths, is currently a subject which preoccupies certain experts.

Pocket submarine (1987)

Crack naval commando units are currently equipped with 15 or so pocket submarines which enable them to approach enemy ships and coastlines with minimum risk of detection. There is a two-seater and a six-seater version, with a maximum speed of 6 knots.

These submarines, known as SDVs (Swimmer Delivery Vehicles), enable their crews to attach an explosive charge discreetly to the hull of a ship or to take commandos ashore with a minimum of noise. Once its mission has been completed, the SDV heads for the open sea where it is taken aboard a downgraded nuclear missile-launching submarine, specially adapted for the purpose.

Ohio (1990)

The Ohio is the latest nuclear submarine for launching the American SLBM missiles. Ten vessels are planned and construction is already underway. Like the Typhoon, it is 170m *558ft* long and will initially carry 24 Trident-1 missiles with a range of 8000km *5000 miles* and by the end of the 1990s, 24 Trident-2 missiles with a range of 11 000km *6835 miles*.

Aviation

Kite (2nd century BC)

Although it is difficult to say exactly where and how the kite came into being, it is known that it existed in China several centuries BC. Some sources quote its inventor as being **General Han Si** who was the first to use the kite for military purposes in the **2nd century BC**.

In 1903 kite trains were used by the Russian and British navies and armies. In 1906 British Army kites carried observers to a height of 400m *1300ft*. In 1909 the French Army was equipped with kites which, with captured enemy balloons, were used during the First World War to observe the front lines.

Military airship (1902)

A French engineer, **Henri Julliot**, invented the first military airship in 1902. It was a semi-rigid airship nicknamed *le Jaune* because of its colour (yellow), 57m *187ft* long and equipped with a 40hp engine. At the beginning of the First World War, airships were intended to be used for reconnaissance missions, and eventually on bombing missions. At the end of the war, they came into their own when they were used to protect convoys and combat submarines.

During the Second World War, the US Navy successfully used some 170 airships to escort convoys in the Atlantic.

Today, the airship is back, and has been used in various ways for several years: as a tactical platform, for anti-aircraft surveillance, etc.

At the end of 1986 the US Navy launched an appeal for offers to develop a prototype for a large airship to be used for surveillance and advance warning. The new airship, the Sentinel 5000 constructed by Airship Industries in association with Westinghouse, began trials in 1990.

Reconnaissance (1911)

Aircraft were used for military operations for the first time in **1911**. In October of that year, the Italians used Blériot aircraft to carry out reconnaissance missions in Libya. Planes were also used for this purpose during the Balkan Wars of 1912 and 1913. Reconnaissance planes were subsequently transformed into bombers and fighters.

AWACS (1977)

The **Boeing** Airborne Warning and Control System (AWACS), brought out in **1977**, makes it possible to carry out airborne surveillance, control and command simultaneously. It is a system which meets the requirements of tactical forces and aerial defence. A new vertical scanning radar, specially developed for the E-3 system, makes surveillance possible at all altitudes.

Mainstay

The Soviets also have an AWACS system, the Mainstay, as it is referred to by NATO. It is derived from a four-engine heavy transport aircraft, the Ilyushin-76, and will be produced at the rate of five or six aircraft per year. With its four Soloviev turbojets, the Ilyushin takes off over a distance of only 850m *2790ft*, cruises at a speed of between 750 and 800km/h *470 and 500mph* and can cover an overall distance of 6700km *4160 miles*.

Two of the workers on the Zeppelins being built at Short Bros are seen emerging from within the balloon in February 1919.

HIGH ALTITUDE SURVEILLANCE

The D500 is a new single-seater plane with a composite structure, designed to operate at high altitudes (1500 to 18000m *4900 to 59000ft*). It can fly for periods of up to 12 hours without refuelling. First shown to the public on 7 September 1989, the aircraft will be produced by a group of six companies, two American, including the Hughes Aircraft Company, and four German, including MBB. It will be used for surveillance and disarmament verification. The radar (for which the Hughes Company will be responsible) will record images of static and mobile objectives, on the ground and in the air.

Fighter gun (1914)

The first fighter gun, a fixed weapon on the centre line of the plane, was an idea put forward in 1911 and tested in 1912 on a Blériot aircraft equipped with a 37mm revolving gun placed in front of the propeller. In **1914** two Frenchmen, engineer **Raymond Saulnier** and pilot **Roland Garros**, developed a system for firing through the propeller, the blades of which were protected from any impact by steel edges.

In Germany the Dutch manufacturer and pilot Anthony Fokker improved the system of the two Frenchmen and invented a mechanically synchronised firing system whereby the operation of the machine was interrupted by a series of cogs and rods when one of the propeller blades was in front of the gun barrel. The system was first used at the front in July 1915.

Aircraft machine gun (1914)

The first machine gun was used on an aircraft by an American, **Captain De Forest Chandler**. The aircraft was a Wright biplane piloted by **T. de Witt-Milling**, and the gun was a Lewis light machine gun which had to be held at an angle between the knees of the operator. The first planes to use this type of equipment were two Breguet reconnaissance aircraft which took off from the base at Dugny, north of Paris, in **August 1914** equipped with a Hotchkiss 1908 machine gun.

First aircraft guns (1917)

The first guns to be mounted in a plane were the German 20mm Beckers, introduced in **1917** on the Gotha bombers, at the request of the pilots and against the advice of the senior officers. The weapons, which were of modern design, reappeared in Switzerland after the war and gave rise to the group of guns known as the *Oerlikon*.

The newly-formed RAF No. 1 Squadron line up for the camera in 1918. The third plane on the right would appear to have a dog as co-pilot.

BOMBERS				
Type	Date	Constructor	Country	Characteristics
Handley Page 0/100	1916	Handley Page Ltd	UK	Strategic bomber used for night flying.
Breguet XIV	1917	Breguet	France	Archetype of all bombers until 1945. Louis Breguet used Duraluminium in its construction.
DH.4	1917	De Havilland	UK	Single-motor bomber able to carry a bomb load of 203kg *448lb*. Also built in USA.
Tu TB 1	1927	Tupolev	USSR	First monoplane multi-engine bomber. Able to carry a bomb load of 1000kg *2200lb* at 208km/h *129mph*.
Tu TB 3	1932	Tupolev	USSR	First four-engine bomber.
JU 87 Stuka	1938	Junkers Flugzeug-und Motorenwerke AG	Germany	Dive-bomber. Stuka was an abbreviation of *Sturzkampfflugzeug*. It was able to carry a bomb load of 1800kg *3969lb*.
B-29 Superfortress	1942	Boeing	USA	Operational in 1944. A B-29 was used to drop the first atomic bomb on Japan on 6 August 1945.
Arado AR 234 Blitz	1943	Arado Flugzeugwerke GmbH	Germany	The only jet bomber to serve during the Second World War.
A-4 Skyhawk	1956	McDonnell Douglas	USA	Suitable for use on aircraft carriers due to its small dimensions.
B-58 Hustler	1956	Convair	USA	First supersonic bomber.
A-5 Vigilante	1958	North American	USA	Introduced aerodynamic and electric innovations. Fighter and strategic reconnaissance plane. The fastest aircraft in the US Navy.
F-111	1964	General Dynamics	USA	First swing-wing bomber.
Tupolev T-26	1969	State Industry	USSR	Brought into service in 1974. Carries standard, nuclear and thermonuclear bombs. Can operate with supply planes and has a capacity for ten hours' autonomous flying.
B-1B	1986	Rockwell International	USA	Variable geometry supersonic quadrijet. Brought into service in 1986. There have been a lot of problems with this aircraft.
Tupolev Blackjack	1988	State Industry	USSR	Quadrijet with a maximum speed of Mach 2. Missile launcher.
B-2	1989	Northrop	USA	Stealth bomber.

THE HELMET THAT FIRES A CANNON

A helmet which can both receive intelligence and execute commands was unveiled for the first time at Le Bourget in June 1989. It will enable the fighter pilot simply to follow the target with his eyes and then activate the weapons (cannon, air-to-air missiles, etc.) adapted to this system – all in a fraction of a second. Called DASH, it was developed by Elbit, Israel's largest equipment manufacturer.

Bombers (1911)

The first bomb attack from an aircraft was carried out by an Italian lieutenant, **Guilio Gavotti**, on **1 November 1911**, from an Etrich-Taube monoplane on an enemy column during the occupation of Tripolitania (Cyrenaica). The bomb was a spherical Cipelli-type device from which the pin was simply removed and the bomb thrown out of the aircraft.

On 3 August 1914 the effectiveness of aerial bombing was demonstrated when, barely six hours after war had been declared, a German Taube dropped three small bombs on the French town of Lunéville.

Thirty-one years later, virtually to the day,

on 6 August 1945 a huge American bomber, the Boeing B-27 Superfortress *Enola Gay*, dropped the first atomic bomb on the Japanese city of Hiroshima.

Ilya Mourometz (1914)

On **12 February 1914** a biplane rose over Moscow, climbed to an altitude of 200m *650ft* and, with 16 passengers on board, flew for five hours at an average speed of more than 100km/h *60mph*. This biplane was to become the first four-engined bomber in service under the name of *Ilya Mourometz*. It was designed by the engineer **Igor Sikorsky**, who left the Soviet Union after the First World War for the United States, where he became famous as the designer and builder of helicopters. The 73 aircraft built during the conflict carried out more than 400 air raids.

Spitfire (1936)

The forerunner of the Spitfire was the Supermarine S.6B, which won the Schneider Trophy in 1931. The familiar Second World War Spitfire was the result of a private venture, created by a team led by **Reginald Mitchell**. Without this plane, the RAF would have had nothing to match the German fighters. The prototype Spitfire flew in **March 1936**.

MiG aircraft (1940)

The famous Russian MiG aircraft was created in 1938 by the research unit of **A. Mikoyan** and **G. Gurevich**. The first fighter, the MiG-1, was produced in **1940/41**. The MiG-9, the first jet aircraft to be mass produced in the Soviet Union, took to the air on 24 April 1946. The MiG-15 with its arrowhead wings appeared in 1947. The delta wing MiG-21, made in India from 1959, was the first Soviet aircraft to be manufactured in a non-communist country.

MiG-29 Fulcrum (1983)

The single-seater supersonic Soviet fighter, the MiG-29 Fulcrum, was the star of the 1988 Farnborough Air Show. The plane has been in existence since **1983** and its prototype was flying in 1977, but it had always been shrouded in secrecy. A MiG-29 was photographed in July 1986 in Finland. It can fly at speeds greater than Mach 2.2 and has a very short take-off distance of about 400m *1300ft*. There are about 500 MiG-29s currently in service, and the aircraft would appear to be closely based on the American F-18.

Jet fighter (1941)

The first jet aircraft were developed simultaneously by an English pilot and engineer, **Frank Whittle**, and a German engineer, **Ernst Heinkel**. In 1930, at the age of 23, Whittle had registered a patent for a jet engine which he tried to adapt for fighter planes from 1937. The Gloster E28/39 was flown at Cranwell on **15 May 1941**. But Whittle was beaten by the Heinkel company who carried out the first secret flight on 24 August 1939 with a Heinkel He 178 piloted by E. Warsitz. The Heinkel He 280, which was the first aircraft to be designed as a jet fighter, made its maiden flight on **5 April 1941**. Meanwhile, Whittle had vastly improved his engine, which made it possible for Rolls-Royce to manufacture its first turbojet engine.

During the Second World War, the only Allied jet aircraft to become operational was the twin-engined Gloster Meteor. A squadron was used to intercept the V1 flying bombs. The first German jet fighter, the Messerschmitt Me 262, which became operational on 3 October 1944, could fly at a speed of 869 km/h *540mph* at a height of 9000m *30000ft*.

Supersonic plane (1947)

The American **Bell XS-I** (later restyled X-1), piloted by Captain Charles Yeager, was the first aircraft to break the sound barrier on **14 October 1947**, propelled by a rocket engine at a speed of 1078km/h *670mph*. These planes do not take off directly from the ground, but are transported by other aircraft carriers from which they subsequently take off. The rocket engine operates, by definition, without an intake of external air. Its fuel consumption at low altitudes is extremely high. Modern supersonic aircraft achieve much greater speeds, reaching six times the speed of sound.

VTOL (1954)

This type of aircraft shares features with the helicopter and the aeroplane. Its propeller, or propellers, can be used as either a rotor or a standard propeller. In the more recent types of VTOL, such as the Osprey V-22 (see below), the pusher engines which drive the aircraft are able to pivot in such a way that the turbofans function as rotorblades.

The first VTOL craft (Vertical Take-Off and Landing) was the 'Flying Bedstead' constructed in **1954** by **Rolls-Royce**. Two vertically mounted reaction control jets lifted it off the ground.

Convair XFY-1 (1954)

On **2 June 1954** the first vertical take-off and landing of the Convair XFY-1, piloted by J. F. Coleman, took place at Mofett Naval Air Station in California (USA).

This fixed-wing aircraft, equipped with a 5500hp Allison turboprop engine, had the peculiarity of landing on its tail with its nose pointing upwards. It was known as a 'Pogo Stick'.

Hawker Siddeley Harrier (1960)

The Hawker Siddeley Harrier made its maiden flight in **October 1960**. It was designed by the engineer **Sir Sydney Camm** for the British company Hawker Siddeley. It was the first fixed-wing VTOL fighter plane to become fully operational, and has been in service with the RAF since 1969.

Osprey V-22 (1989)

This was the first aircraft with pivoting rotors.

The research into the Osprey concept was begun in early 1982. The prototype of this convertible, built by the **Bell** and **Boeing** companies, flew for the first time on **19 March 1989**. It takes off with its propellers rotating horizontally, like a helicopter, and then travels with them turning vertically, like a plane. On 4 September it flew with its nacelles tilting at an angle of 45°. The aircraft reached a speed of 130 knots at an altitude of 700m *2300ft*. Ten days later, it carried out a complete conversion at 1800m *6000ft*.

The V-22, which is currently reserved for military purposes, could equally well be developed for civilian use. Its manoeuvrability, the fact that it can land in the middle of a city, the number of passengers it can carry, etc, make the VTOL craft, and the Osprey in particular, the plane of the future.

Fastest plane in the world (1964)

On **29 February 1964** Lyndon B. Johnson, President of the United States, revealed the existence of an extraordinary aircraft: the Lockheed A-11. Under the name of SR-71, the craft became a strategic reconnaissance plane designed to replace the Lockheed U-2. It could reach a speed of Mach 3 at an altitude of 21000m *69000ft*. So that it could sustain a continuous speed of Mach 3, the SR-71 was constructed in titanium, which resists temperatures of kinetic heat of the order of 300°C *572°F*.

On 27 July 1976, an SR-1 A beat the world closed loop record over a distance of 1000km *621 miles* at a speed greater than Mach 3. On 28 July it beat the world speed record for straight line flying at a speed of 3529.56km/h *2193.27mph*. The pilots were Captain Eldon Joersz and Major George T. Morgan, Jr. The SR-71 is at present withdrawn from service, but holds many other records.

Inverted-wing aircraft (1984)

The X-29A was officially revealed by **Grumman** at Calverton, USA on **27 August 1984**, in the form of the prototype No. 2. The following

Over a thousand of General Dynamics' F-16s have been sold on the world market. Seen here is the F-16 C, the most powerful model available.

day, tests began on the prototype No. 1. The wing unit of the aircraft is inverted which gives it an advantage in aerodynamic terms and a better lift at low speeds. It can be lighter, smaller and less costly than a conventional aircraft.

The idea of an inverted-wing unit is not a new one since the first operational aircraft of this type was the German experimental quadrijet bomber, the Junkers Ju 287, tested in 1944 and recovered by the Soviets at Dessau.

Variable wing camber (1985)

The F-111-AFTI, Advanced Fighter Technology Integration, developed by **General Dynamics** and produced by the Boeing Military Airplane Corporation, made its maiden flight on **18 October 1985**, at the Edwards Air Force base in the USA.

Its originality lies in its variable wing camber. The wing profile can be adjusted by the pilot who only has to register the altitude, the Mach number, and the manoeuvre he wishes to perform. The automatic pilot system selects the optimum camber.

The biggest aeroplane in the world (1988)

At Le Bourget in June 1985 the Antonov 124 *Ruslan* was unveiled. With a wingspan of 73m *240ft* and 65m *210ft* in length, the Antonov 124 was then the biggest aeroplane in the world and came into service in spring 1986. Since then, however, an even bigger plane has been built: the Antonov 225, which flew for the first time on **21 December 1988**. It reached a speed of 850km/h *530mph* and can carry 150–250 tonnes 4500km *2800 miles* without refuelling. It is 74m *245ft* long and has a wingspan of 87m *285ft*.

C-5B Galaxy (1986)

After **Lockheed Aircraft Co.**'s C-5A Galaxy, which had its maiden flight as long ago as 30 June 1968 (and which, until the arrival of the Antonov, was the biggest plane in the world), the Military Airlift Command launched the C-5B to increase its strategic capability. The first of the 50 C-5Bs contracted for delivery by 1989 was delivered at the end of **1986**.

Sukhoi SU-27 (1986)

The twin-engined SU-27, named 'Flancker' by NATO, is reminiscent in its general shape of the MiG-29, but is heavier and more powerful. In 1986, under the name P-42, it broke several operational speed records in its class previously held by the F-15.

Apparently it came into service in **1986** and more than 100 of them are in use. The USSR, once so secretive, is now eager to present its military achievements to the public, and thus to the Western market. It was in a SU-27 fighter, a plane with great manoeuvrability, that Viktor Pougatchev, head of the test pilots at the Sukhoi construction bureau, perfected his famous acrobatic air attack figure, the Cobra, which was demonstrated at Le Bourget in 1989.

A 5-K 'Kong Yun' (1988)

This is the first prototype of the Chinese fighter plane which made its maiden flight on **17 September 1988** at the Hangzhou airbase near Shanghai. The navigation and attack system was developed by the French company, Thomson-CSF. The assessment of the system was completed in 1989. Chinese pilots have been trained in the use of the equipment in France.

B-2 stealth bomber (1989)

The maiden flight of the B-2, the famous invisible bomber developed by the research division of the US Air Force in conjunction with the American company **Northrop**, took place on **17 July 1989**.

The B-2 is a long-range strategic aircraft which looks like a flying wing; there is no fuselage in the conventional sense of the word, and the cockpit and two engines are incorporated into this 'wing'.

The term invisible obviously does not mean that the plane cannot be seen, but that its overall shape, the materials from which it is built, its paintwork, etc enable it to escape detection by radar as it throws back virtually no electromagnetic waves. The bomber was designed to be completely undetectable: for example, so that there is no release of heat which would enable the B-2 to be picked up by infra-red detectors, the aircraft is not supersonic.

The stealth programme is obviously a costly one. A single B-2 bomber costs $516 million. Including the time spent on research (**John Patierno**, the 'father' of the B-2, has worked on the project for 17 years), and the costs of research and development, it is the most expensive aircraft in the world. The Pentagon has ordered 132 of them and they proved their worth in the Gulf War.

F-117 A (1981)

Another stealth programme, for the development of fighters, exists in the United States, but it is much more discreet. The F-117 A stealth fighter is a twin-engine, single-seater fighter built by **Lockheed**. It made its maiden flight in **June 1981** and was brought into service in 1983.

The Pentagon did not officially admit the existence of the F-117 A stealth fighter until 3 April 1990, but they have been built since 1981.

FIGHTER PLANES

Type	Date	Constructor	Country	Characteristics
Vickers FB.5	1914	Vickers	UK	Nicknamed Gunbus, this two-seater biplane was used by the best British fighter squadrons.
Fokker E.1	1915	Fokker Flugzeugwerke GmbH	Germany	Monoplane, based on the Morane N, installed with the Fokker firing system, i.e. propeller synchronised.
Polikarpov 1-16	1936	State Industry	USSR	Small, robust monoplane fighter with retractable landing gear and closed cockpit.
Messerschmitt Bf 109 (Me 109)	1936	Messerschmitt AG	Germany	Single-seater monoplane. The first of the out-standing fighter planes of WWII. Speed 570km/h *354.2mph*. Archetypal Second World War fighter. Like the Spitfire, it was modified many times during the war.
Supermarine Spitfire	1936	Supermarine Division, Vickers Armstrong Ltd	UK	Great rival of the Messerschmitt. 20 334 aircraft built up to 1947. Speed 570km/h *354.2mph*.
Gloster Meteor	1943	Gloster Aircraft	UK	Used against the V1s. First British jet plane.
Me 262	1944	Messerschmitt AG	Germany	First operational German jet fighter. Speed 869km/h *540mph*.
Me 163 Komet	1944	Messerschmitt AG	Germany	First rocket-powered fighter. Maximum speed 900km/h *560mph*.
Lockheed F-80 Shooting Star	1944	Lockheed	USA	Used during the Korean War, it was the first fighter to win a fight between two jet planes by shooting down a MiG-15.
F-102 Delta Dagger	1948	Convair	USA	The first delta-winged plane. Very advanced in terms of electronics. A modified version, the Delta Dart, exceeded Mach 2 in 1959.
F-86 Sabre	1950	North American	USA	Jet plane with arrowhead wings. 9500 aircraft were built. Extremely fast and manoeuvrable.
MiG-15	1950	Mikoyan and Gurevitch	USSR	Jet plane with arrowhead wings. Rival of the American fighter planes.
Super Sabre F-100	1953	North American	USA	The first fighter to exceed Mach 1 in horizontal flight.
Mirage III	1956	Dassault	France	Remarkable delta-wing fighter, with a French engine, the Altar 101. It exceeded Mach 2.
MiG-25	1965	Mikoyan	USSR	Code name: Foxbat. Still the fastest fighter in the world. It has been detected at a speed of 3395km/h *2109.6mph*, i.e. Mach 3.2.
Grumman F-14 Tomcat	1970	Grumman Aerospace	USA	Its variable sweep wings enable it to fly at speeds of between 200 and 2500km/h *124 and 1550mph*.
F-15 Eagle	1972	McDonnell Douglas	USA	Multi-purpose fighter for use in aerial combat, interception and ground attack. 620 planes built at the beginning of 1981.
F-16	1975	General Dynamics	USA	Remarkable close-range fighter. Light, easy to manoeuvre. Its post-combustion turbofan engine produces a thrust of 11 000kg *24 255lb*.
MiG-29	1977	Mikoyan	USSR	A high-speed, quick take-off supersonic fighter.
F-117 A	1981	Lockheed	USA	A stealth fighter.

F-20 Tigershark	1982	Northrop	USA	Advantages: short take-off, faster climbing speed, ability to turn instantaneously, high load capacity.
Mirage 2000	1984	Dassault-Breguet	France	To replace the Mirage III, V and F1. Used for tactical intervention, back-up and reconnaissance.
Sukhoi SU 27	1986		USSR	A highly manoeuvrable new Soviet jet.
Rafale	1986	Dassault-Breguet	France	The French land and ground forces hope to replace their Crusaders and Etendards with the Rafale in 1996.
ATF	1994	McDonnell Douglas	USA	The Advanced Tactical Fighter is planned to replace the F-15 Eagle.
A-12	1995	McDonnell Douglas and General Dynamics	USA	This fighter plane of the 21st century will share some of the features of the stealth bomber.
EFA	1995–6	British Aerospace	UK, Germany, Italy, Spain	European competitor of the Rafale. It made its first experimental flight in July 1986.

Aircraft of the future

Swedish Griffon (1993)

The maiden flight of the prototype of the Swedish fighter plane, the JAS 39 SAAB Griffon, took place on 9 December 1988. One of the distinguishing features of the Griffon is its small size. It is about half the weight (i.e. 8 tonnes) of the aircraft it is replacing – the JA 37 Viggen – while still being able to carry the same load of weapons.

The Swedes have used carbon-based composites in the plane's construction which account for about 30 percent of the structure. The aircraft will be brought into service in 1993, later than planned after a prototype crashed in February 1989.

Japanese FS-X (1993)

The FS-X is the new Japanese fighter plane. Launched in 1989, the prototype should be operational by 1993, but the first planes in the series will not fly until 1997. The plane, inspired by the F-16 developed by General Dynamics, was constructed by Mitsubishi Heavy Industries using mainly composite materials (carbon fibre reinforced with polyacrylnitrile plastic), which made it possible to reduce the weight by 40 percent. In addition, by using a process which consists of layering 150 sheets of carbon fibre, the Japanese are able to construct the fuselage and the wings in a single piece of composite material.

ATF (1994)

The Advanced Tactical Fighter or ATF will be one of the American planes of the future to be used in aerial combat. It will replace the F-15 Eagle built by McDonnell Douglas but, like its predecessor, it will be a single-seater, twin-engine fighter. In October 1986 two projects were chosen, one by Lockheed and the other by Northrop.

The final choice between the two prototypes was made in 1990 and production should begin in 1994.

The ATF should have a cruising speed of Mach 1.5 and be able to reach a maximum speed of Mach 2.5. It is an interceptor with a long flying range which will use the invisible and undetectable stealth technology. It will also be equipped with a navigation and attack system which will enable it to detect and destroy its adversaries.

P.7 A (1994)

This anti-submarine maritime patroller built by Lockheed (currently still codenamed LRAACA – Long Range Air ASW Capable Aircraft) will replace the P.3 Orion. The two aircraft are similar externally but the P.7 A's avionics are far superior. Its four General Electric 5600V turboprop engines ensure a 25 percent lower fuel consumption than the P.3. The prototype is scheduled to fly at the end of 1991, and mass production to begin in 1992, for delivery in January 1994.

A-12 (1995)

This 21st century fighter plane will replace the A-6 Intruder and could also be used by the US Air Force to replace its land-based bombers. The new aircraft, which is to be designed by McDonnell Douglas and General Dynamics within the framework of the ATA or Advanced Tactical Aircraft, will have some of the characteristics of the stealth bomber. It must be able to take off from an aircraft carrier in order to attack targets on land. The first of these aircraft should be in service by 1995.

Rafale (1996)

Designed by Avions Marcel Dassault-Breguet Aviation, the French-built Rafale made its maiden flight on 4 July 1986. By June 1989 it had completed 423 flights. An M88 jet engine, positioned to the left replacing one of the two General Electric F404s, will make it possible to use demonstrator A as a flying test bed.

The first of the five prototypes of the Rafale D is scheduled to fly in February 1991, and the Marine single-seater prototype at the end of 1991. The Rafale D will possess stealth characteristics, notably its streamlined shape and the use of new materials such as those which absorb radar waves.

The first tactical combat plane should be delivered to the French Air Force at the end of 1996, but the first squadron will not be operational until 1998. The French Air Force has ordered 250 tactical combat planes, while their Navy will employ 86 fighter planes.

EFA (1996)

The European competitor of the Rafale, the prototype of the EFA, the European Fighter Aircraft, developed jointly by the UK, Italy, Germany and Spain, first flew in Germany in 1991. The eighth and final prototype should be flown in 1993, and the plane should be brought into service in 1995–6.

Hornet 2000

This is the American counter proposal for the European 21st century fighter plane.

Fighter helicopters

The first military helicopter (1939)

The Russian-born American manufacturer Igor Sikorsky resumed his research on helicopters just before the Second World War. In the spring of 1939 Sikorsky developed his first prototype, the VS-300. This was improved in January 1941 and became the VS-316 A which, in May 1942, went to Wright Field, Ohio, to undergo military standardisation tests. It was named the XR-4. Orders came from the United States and the United Kingdom where the helicopters were given the name Hoverfly and were brought into service in 1945.

The S 75 ACAP helicopter (1984)

On 16 August 1984 the American Sikorsky S 75 ACAP helicopter made its first public flight which lasted 20 minutes. Constructed from composite materials, the S 75's main interest lies in the fact that it has a lighter structure

HELICOPTERS FOR THE YEAR 2005

The LHX, the American helicopter programme, is designed to replace the AH-1 Cobra, OH-6 Cayuse and OH-58 Kiowa. The US Army has ordered 2096 helicopters, and delivery should take place between 1995 and 2005.

The demonstration phase of the future military helicopter began at the end of April 1990. The first prototype should take to the air in August 1993. The helicopter is planned to come into service in 1996.

The LHX will have a variety of applications: armed reconnaissance, air combat and air/ground attack, combined operations with the Air Force. They will complement the heavy Apaches, which are equipped for anti-tank combat. Two teams are competing for the order: Boeing–Sikorsky and McDonnell Douglas Helicopter–Bell Helicopter Textron. The LHX will fly at a cruising speed of about 315km/h *195mph* and will have a range of 2335km *1450 miles*.

The Apache anti-tank helicopter was given its first serious trial in the Gulf War.

than conventional helicopters, but nevertheless has a better resistance to bullets.

Apache (1984)

The AH 64 A Apache, built by **McDonnell Douglas**, is the most powerful, the heaviest and the most expensive anti-tank helicopter in the western world. It is equipped with 16 laser-guided missiles, 76 rockets and an automatic 30mm gun, and flies at a speed of 360km/h *223mph*. The Apache has been used by the US Army since **1984** and has replaced the AH I Cobra. An improved version of the Apache, particularly in the field of detection, is to be tested at the end of 1993.

NH 90 (1993)

A programme is underway involving **Aérospatiale** of France, **Messerschmitt-Bölkow-Blohm** of Germany, **Agusta** of Italy and **Fokker** of the Netherlands (the UK has withdrawn), to produce the **NH 90**, a medium tonnage aircraft which is intended to replace the Super Puma. There will be an NH 90 military transport helicopter and a naval version for use as an anti-submarine craft. The first flight is scheduled for the beginning of **1993** and deliveries of the helicopter should take place in 1995 and 1996.

The NH 90 will weigh between eight and nine tonnes. It will be able to fly in all weathers, reach a height of 6000m *19 700ft* and have a range of over 700km *435 miles*. A civilian version is planned.

EH 101 (1992)

The British company **Westland** and the Italian company **Agusta** are collaborating in the development of the EH 101, a heavy 30-seater, three-engined helicopter weighing 14 tonnes. The certification should be obtained in 1990 and the Royal Navy should receive its first EH 101 in **1992**.

Sea Dragon (1987)

In **August 1987** the Americans sent the aircraft carrier *Guadalcanal* into the Gulf loaded with Sikorsky MH 53 E mine-sweeper Sea Dragon helicopters, the mine detecting version of the Super Stallion. The Sea Dragon is the largest helicopter in service. It is 27m *88ft* long and its blades have a diameter of 22m *72ft*. The helicopter's efficiency is largely due to its speed, which reaches up to 300km/h *186mph*, and its ability to fly for periods of up to four hours. The mine sweeping can be either mechanical, where the mine has risen to the surface and is destroyed with guns, or is carried out using magnetic and acoustic systems.

A SOVIET APACHE

The Mi-28 is the Soviet fighter helicopter which was unveiled at Le Bourget in June 1989. A two-seater aircraft with the pilot placed behind the weapons operator, it is reminiscent of the American Apache but is superior in some ways. Its missiles and cannon, in particular, are much more powerful.

POWER AND INDUSTRY

Power

Hydraulics

The dam (3000 BC)

The oldest dam on record was built in Egypt about 3000 BC. Initially, dams were used to create reservoirs to supply water to towns and for irrigation, but later they were used to produce energy.

It was the French engineer, François Zola, father of the author, who in 1843–59 constructed the first modern arch dam near Aix-en-Provence, but it was a technique which was not widely adopted. There are two other types of dam: the gravity dam and the cofferdam. The first of these, after being studied mathematically, was constructed on the River Furan at St-Etienne in 1861–6, and the first big dam of the second type was the Panama Dam built in 1912.

One of the most famous dams is the Itaipu Dam in Brazil, constructed in 1982.

Archimedes' screw (3rd century BC)

One of the greatest scientists of antiquity, a Greek from Syracuse, **Archimedes** (287–212 BC), invented the hydraulic screw. This device is made of an inclined cylinder that encases a broad-threaded screw. It is used to raise water, to serve whatever purpose one wishes. The device is introduced into a body of water, then the screw is rapidly turned, so that the water rises from whorl to whorl.

Hydraulic ram (1796)

In **1796** the Frenchmen **Joseph** (1740–1810) and **Etienne** (1745–99) **de Montgolfier** had the idea of utilising the kinetic energy of running water in a pipe to force a portion of the liquid mass to a higher level than its source. The energy was transferred through what they called the ram effect. The principle was to be improved by Amédée Bollée (1844–1917), another builder of hydraulic rams.

A spectacular view of the dam at Cruachan in the West Highlands of Scotland, near Oban.

Francis turbine (1855)

In 1855 *Lowell Hydraulic Experiments* was published by an American of English origin, **James Francis**. In it he describes the invention of a reaction turbine intended for medium to small falls of water. Today it is the most used reaction turbine.

Pelton turbine (1870)

In 1870 the American engineer **Lester Allen Pelton** perfected a turbine which was inspired by the horizontal bucket wheel used in the mountainous regions of California. The turbine is still used for high heads of water which have a low rate of flow, and is the only action turbine in use today.

Kaplan turbine (1912)

In 1912 the Austrian **Viktor Kaplan** (1876–1934) had the idea of developing the propeller type turbine by making it possible to adjust the blade angle, though it was not produced commercially until 1924. The turbine was designed to harness the energy from low heads and wide, slow-flowing rivers, and is used by tidal power stations.

Hydro-electric power (1869)

On 28 September 1869 the French papermaker **Aristide Bergès** (1833–1904) was the first to convert the mechanical energy of a waterfall in the Alps into electrical energy which could operate the machines in his factory. He achieved this by the use of forced conduits.

In 1886–7 he organised an extremely dangerous operation. At a depth of 25m *82ft* below the bottom of Lake Crozet, which stands at an altitude of 1968m *6459ft*, he excavated an overflow gallery, to collect surplus water.

Steam engines

Connecting-rod system (14th–15th century)

One of the most important inventions of the Middle Ages was the connecting-rod system, developed around the end of the 14th and beginning of the 15th century.

The system enabled a continuous circular movement to be converted into a rectilinear up-and-down movement, or vice versa. The absence of such a technique had, until then, seriously limited technical development. The system spread rapidly and its uses were many and varied: saws then pumps and wheels. Two centuries later, it contributed to the development of the steam engine.

Steam engine

Origins (1st century AD)

Steam power dates back to ancient times when the Greek engineer and mathematician **Hero** of Alexandria (1st century AD) described an *aeolipile*, a steam-operated wheel which, at the time, remained a project of purely technical interest without there being any thought of finding other uses for it. Steam power did not really develop until the concept of atmospheric pressure was better understood.

WATER-WHEELS			
Type	Date	Origins	Characteristics
Vertical water-wheel	Between 5th and 3rd century BC	Middle East	An elevating but not a driving wheel. Probably the first water wheel invented.
Undershot water-wheel	1st century BC	Middle East	The first hydraulic engine in history.
Horizontal water-wheel	1st–2nd century AD	Middle East	Paddle-wheel
Overshot water-wheel	4th–5th century AD	Europe (Roman Empire)	Wooden or iron bowls (buckets) replace the blades. The driving wheel used throughout industry in 18th century.
Breast wheel	12th–13th century	Unknown	The blades are on the side of the wheel.
Short bladed undershot paddle-wheel	1827	France	Also called the Poncelet Wheel after its inventor Jean-Victor Poncelet (1788–1867). Forerunner of the turbine.
Angle bladed paddle-wheel	1851	France	Invented and patented by Sagebien, it was a development of the breast wheel. Also used as an elevating wheel.

Atmospheric engine (1661)

The aim of the first steam engines was quite simply to put atmospheric pressure to work. It was the Italian physicist, Evangelista Torricelli who, in 1643, first discovered and demonstrated its existence. A little later, in 1654, the German physicist and mayor of Magdeburg, **Otto von Guericke**, carried out a spectacular experiment which demonstrated the force of this pressure (*see* Science). In 1661 he invented a machine which consisted of a metal cylinder inside which a piston moved up and down. Using his pump he created a partial vacuum inside the cylinder and, quite naturally, the piston plunged downwards within the cylinder, at the same time lifting a weight by means of a system of ropes and pulleys. This was an important date in history since, for the first time, air pressure was seen to be performing a function.

Denis Papin's engine (1679)

It was the French inventor **Denis Papin** who first had the idea of creating a void behind the piston by using the evaporation and condensation properties of water. In 1679 he invented a safety valve for his steam digester, the prototype of the pressure cooker, which gave him the idea of developing a cylindrical machine in which the piston would be steam-operated. In 1679 he was also responsible for the voyage of the first steam ship on the River Fulda in Germany. But he did not have the money necessary to exploit and therefore to reap the benefits of his ideas and inventions. He died in poverty, forgotten, in London in 1714.

Newcomen's engine (1712)

The problem of flooding in mines caused concern to many in the early 18th century and there were several attempts at improving the method of pumping out the water. In 1698 the English engineer Thomas Savery registered a patent for a steam pump which was capable of extracting water from great depths. But the machine, which had no piston or valve, proved dangerous and was abandoned. However, the patent protected the rights for the use of 'power produced by fire for all types of machine'. In order to circumvent the difficulty, **Thomas Newcomen** joined forces with Savery in 1705 and in 1712 constructed the first real steam engine. It was manufactured and sold in large quantities and was the prototype of the machine developed by the

Watt's engine erected for the Birmingham Canal navigations at Smethwick in 1777. It was removed in 1898, having worked for 120 years, to Oaken Hill near Wednesbury.

Scotsman James Watt at the end of the 18th century.

Watt's steam engine (1765)

James Watt (1736–1819) had the brilliant idea of converting the steam engine into an actual steam motor capable of driving the new machinery that was rapidly being developed in the new industries.

In **1765** Watt constructed one of Newcomen's machines, fitted with a condenser which was essential for high efficiency, and then, in 1783, he converted Newcomen's machine into a double-effect machine.

Between 1776 and 1800 Watt joined an important Birmingham manufacturer, Matthew Boulton, and produced about 500 engines, thus making the steam engine the true instrument of the Industrial Revolution.

In 1881 physicists gave the Scotsman's name to the international unit of power: the watt. He was also responsible for the measurement of horse-power as a result of experiments carried out in 1783.

Multiple expansion engine (1803)

In **1803** the Cornish mining engineer **Arthur Woolf** (1776–1837) patented the first multiple expansion engine. This was a machine with two or three cylinders, in which the steam expanded consecutively. Woolf's engine was used for high-pressure machinery.

High-pressure engine (1805)

Around **1805** the Cornishman **Richard Trevithick** (1771–1833) perfected the first high-pressure steam engine. As a mining engineer, Trevithick was well aware of the problems of pumping water from the shafts. He realised that by increasing the pressure on the steam from an engine, he could do away with its condenser, which was cumbersome and heavy.

Trevithick is also the inventor of the first steam locomotive.

Metal ring piston (1816)

In **1816** the Englishman **John Barton** patented a metal ring piston which was subsequently widely adopted for use on cars.

Water-tube boiler (1825)

The first really efficient water-tube boilers were developed from **1825** onwards by the Cornishman **Sir Goldsworthy Gurney** (1793–1875) who wanted to manufacture steam carriages and therefore needed a lightweight boiler. For legal reasons, these inventions were unfortunately never marketed.

During the 1860s Gurney's system reappeared, first in the form of a limited circulation and then a free circulation boiler. The most widely-used examples were developed by the Englishmen Babcock and Wilcox in 1867, and the Frenchmen Belleville and Serpollet in 1886. The boilers of fossil fuel power stations are of the same type.

Electricity

Thermoelectric effect (1823)

In **1823** the German physicist **Thomas Johann Seebeck** (1770–1831) observed that if heat was applied to the junction of two different metals which were joined in a closed circuit, it had the effect of making the needle of a compass deviate. An electric current had therefore been created within the wiring. The Seebeck or thermoelectric effect found a practical application about a century and a half later with semi-conductor techniques.

Magneto (1832)

On the advice of Ampère, the Frenchman **Hippolyte Pixii** (1800–35) built the first magneto-electric (magneto for short) generator in 1832, which was perfected by a machine by Faraday, built in 1830. It was the first induction electric generator and therefore the first machine to convert mechanical energy into electrical energy. It produced an alternating current.

Lead–acid storage battery (1859)

In **1859** a French physicist **Gaston Planté** (1834–89) invented the first electric storage cell: the lead–acid battery.

The German physicist Johann Wilhelm Ritter (1776–1810) had observed in 1803, on a lead plate voltmeter, the principle according to which this kind of secondary cell works.

Lead–acid batteries are still the most common.

Alkaline storage batteries (1914)

Around **1914** the ingenious American inventor **Thomas Edison** (1847–1931) developed the first alkaline storage battery, so called because the electrolyte is not acid but basic: nickel–iron and nickel–cadmium storage cells.

The iron–zinc battery was developed in 1941 by the Frenchman H. André.

The energy storage efficiency of this kind of battery is two to three times superior to that of the lead battery.

Dynamo (1871)

On **17 July 1871** the French Academy of Sciences gave an enthusiastic welcome to the Belgian **Zénobe Gramme** (1826–1901). He had been living in France since 1856 and had invented the dynamo (short for dynamo-electric generator), which was a generator of continuous and completely reversible electric current.

With his invention, which marked the beginning of electrical technology, Gramme combined many of the discoveries and inventions made since the invention of the magneto. Although an early version of the dynamo had been constructed by the Italian Antonio Pacinotti in 1860, it had not advanced beyond the experimental stage. Gramme's dynamo was developed by the German Friedrich von Hefner-Alteneck in 1873.

Alternator (1878)

In **1878** the French company **Gramme**, founded by the Belgian Zénobe Gramme and the Frenchman Hippolyte Fontaine, industrially manufactured the first alternators. A German company founded by Werner von Siemens (1816–92) began producing them at the same time.

An alternator is a device that transforms mechanical energy into electrical energy; it produces an alternating current.

Transformer (1882)

The principle of the transformer, which enables the parameters of electrical current to be modified (i.e. voltage, strength), was demonstrated by the English scientist **Michael Faraday** (1791–1867), who built a transformer in his laboratory.

The modern transformer was invented simultaneously by the French chemist and physicist **Lucien Gaulard**, the American **William Stanley** and the Englishman **John Dixon Gibbs** between **1882** and 1885.

Transmission of electricity (1882)

In 1882 the French engineer **Marcel Deprez** (1842–1918) carried out the first transmission of electricity through high voltage cables. On **25 September 1882** he transmitted a continuous electric current from Miesbach to Munich along a telegraph wire. On 6 February 1883 an amazed crowd, gathered at Porte de la Chapelle in Paris, saw an electric motor start up at the same time as an apparently unconnected dynamo situated next to it. In fact the motor was connected by an electricity line which ran to Le Bourget and back to Paris.

Photo-electric cell (c.1895)

The photo-electric cell was invented by the German physicists **Julius Elster** (1854–1920) and **Hans F. Geitel** (1855–1923) around **1895**. It has the ability to transform a luminous flux into an electric current. Production of the photo-electric cell depends on selenium, a non-metallic crystalline solid, discovered in 1817 by the Swedish chemist Jons Jacob Berzelius.

Magneto-hydrodynamic generator (1959)

In **1959** the **Avro Research Laboratories** in Massachusetts, USA built the first magneto-hydrodynamic generator in a purely experimental form. The generator was capable of directly transforming calorific energy into electrical energy. It was a practical demonstration of theoretical work carried out ten years earlier by the Swedish physicist Hannes Alfvén, Nobel Prize-winner in 1970.

Nickel–iron battery (1983)

The improvement of storage batteries was a constant preoccupation of car manufacturers. One of the lines of research was directed

This Gramme dynamo was constructed in 1877.

CELLS		
Name	**Date**	**Inventor**
Voltaic cell	1800	The first electric cell was invented by the Italian Alessandro Volta.
Thermoelectric cell	1821	Also called thermoelectric couple, invented by the German physicist Thomas Seebeck (1770–1831).
Daniell cell	1836	Named after the British chemist John Frederic Daniell, inventor of the first impolarisable cell.
Bunsen cell	1843	Developing the work of the British physicist William Robert Grove, the German chemist Robert Wilhelm Bunsen (1811–99) invented a more efficient version of the Daniell cell.
Bichromate cell	1870	Developed by the German physicist Henrich Ruhmkorff, it initially bore the name of the original French inventor, Grenet.
Leclanché cell	1877	Developed by the French engineer Georges Leclanché, and improved much later by the French physicist Charles Féry. Still in use today.
Dry cell	1887	Invented by the English physicist Hellesen.
Fuel cell (Bacon cell)	1936	Invented by the American, Bacon, in 1936, it was not produced commercially until 1960 in the USA. A cell fuelled by the hydrogen/oxygen reaction is used in space missiles.

towards new galvanic couples, nickel–iron in particular, which had been considered by the American **Thomas Edison** towards the end of the 19th century.

Since the appearance of the first electric Nissan Micra at the end of **1983**, many prototypes have been produced by Japanese car manufacturers who are convinced of the superiority of this type of battery in terms of durability and power. But they are not as yet being mass-produced. In Europe similar efforts are being made, notably by Mercedes and Peugeot, the latter in collaboration with Saft, a French company specialising in different types of battery, which provided the battery for the prototype of the electric Peugeot 205.

Petroleum

Origins (antiquity)

It seems that hydrocarbons were first used in the Middle East. According to the Bible, Noah used pitch to caulk his ark and Moses' mother used it to coat her son's cradle before she set it afloat upon the Nile.

Pitch was also used by the Egyptians for preserving their mummies and by the Chinese for heating houses, cooking and making bricks as well as for lighting. In Europe, the earliest references to the use of oil are in connection with the greasing of chariot wheels and, in particular, medicine. Oil and bitumen were used in ointments for the treatment of lumbago, blows and swellings.

Catalytic reformation (1949)

Catalytic reformation, which replaced thermal reformation conceived in the 1930s, was invented by **V. Haensel** in 1949 for the Universal Oil Products Company. This operation allowed the composition of petrol to be modified, specifically to increase the octane levels.

Cracking process (1891)

The cracking process is a refining process which enables more fuel to be obtained from a given amount of petroleum, and a certain number of heavy residues from the distillation process to be converted into lightweight products such as petrol and gas oil.

Thermal cracking, invented by the Russian **Vladimir Chukhov** in 1891, was used industrially after the First World War.

In 1913 W. M. Burton, head of manufacturing at Standard Oil of Indiana, patented a cracking process involving high temperatures and high pressure. In 1915 Jesse Dubbs improved the process and Shell became the first licensee.

Catalytic cracking, which creates far superior products to those obtained from thermal cracking, was invented by the Frenchman Eugène Houdry in 1930.

Distillation

The origins of distillation processes, which were often discovered by chance in the very early stages of the history of petroleum, are tied in with its first uses.

In 1556 the German mineralogist Georg Bauer, also known as Georgius Agricola, explained how to distil bulking tar from petroleum in his work *De Re Metallica*. In 1650 the distillation of crude oil brought to boiling point enabled varnish, waxes, grease and lamp oil to be obtained. The first English edition of *De Re Metallica* was published in 1912 by Herbert Clark Hoover, who became President of the United States in 1929.

Oil lamp (1840s)

Outside China, oil was not used as a source of lighting until relatively recently when a colourless liquid was extracted from crude oil which, when lit, burnt with a flame strong enough to provide light without giving off too many unpleasant fumes. This was known as burning oil. In the **1840s** in Scotland **James Young** discovered that an excellent lighting oil could be obtained from the shale rocks of central Scotland.

Petrol (1855)

In **1855** the American chemist **Benjamin Silliman** carried out a series of experiments on distillation based on the studies of the composition of oil made by European chemists. As a result, he obtained a number of products: tar, lubricating oil, naphtha, paint solvents and petrol, which was used as a stain remover and considered of minor importance.

Paraffin (kerosene) (1859)

In 1859 an American, George Henry Bissell, distilled crude oil and marketed part of the distillation under the name kerosene.

Bissell's contractor was Edwin L. Drake, known as Colonel Drake, who will be remembered for carrying out a drilling operation which went down in history. At Titusville on **27 August 1859**, when a depth of 23m *75ft* was reached, the oil shot skywards and started what was to be known as the black gold rush.

Continuous distillation (1873)

As the quantities of crude oil to be treated increased, it became necessary to develop processes that would enable continuous distillation to take place, i.e. in the same place and on the same site. Such processes were developed by the Russian **A. A. Tavrisov** in Baku, Russia in **1873** and by the American Samuel Van Sycle at Titusville, USA, in 1877.

In 1880–81 the Nobel brothers developed a new method of continuous distillation by placing the stills in a cascade.

The distillation column was finally perfected in 1926 by an American company, Power Speciality Company.

Drilling for oil (2nd century BC)

Drilling can be traced back to the Chinese who, from the **2nd century BC**, got petroleum by a drilling process using bamboo tubes and bronze pipes.

Drilling techniques developed with the expansion of industrialised civilisation. One of the first patents in the field was for the rotary drilling method perfected in 1844 by the Englishman Robert Beart, which consisted of a boring bit with toothed rollers rotating around a central rod. The method was improved by the Frenchman Rodolphe Leschot in 1863 and then in 1887 by Chapman's patent which is the basis of the modern rotary method.

Turbo-drilling was introduced by the Soviets in 1922, and electro-drilling in 1949 by the American company Electrodrill Corporation.

In 1980 Elf and the IFP (French Oil Institute) carried out the first horizontal drilling (natural gas) in Lacq and, in 1982, the first offshore horizontal drilling (crude oil) in Rospo. This enabled the Rospo Mare oilfield (French Adriatic) to go into production, the first well in the world to be developed by the technique of horizontal drilling.

The firemen of the oil wells (1915)

On 17 April 1861 the Henry Rouse oil well, to the east of Oil Creek, exploded and caught fire, killing 19 people and injuring ten. It took three days to put the fire out, by covering the well with earth.

It was around **1915** that **K. T. Kinley** had the idea of exploding a charge of dynamite to blow out the fire, a method which was adopted on an increasingly spectacular scale by his son, Myron Kinley, and later by Paul 'Red' Adair.

Methane tanker (1959)

The first methane cargo ship, the *Methane Pioneer*, sailed out of the Gulf of Mexico for England on **31 January 1959**. Constructed for the North Thames Gas Board, it contained 2200 tonnes of liquid methane.

Off-shore drilling for oil (1869)

On **4 May 1869** Thomas F. Rowland filed the first patent for a fixed platform. The first working off-shore oil well was built off the California coast in 1897.

On 21 August 1928 the Italian-born American Louis Giliasso filed a patent for a submersible barge which was constructed in 1933.

The first drilling ship, the *Submarex*, was constructed by the American company Cuss in 1953. The first drilling ship capable of dynamic positioning was the *Cuss 1* by Global Marine which was deployed in 1961.

The first self-elevating mobile platform (conceived in 1869 by Samuel Lewis) was the Delong No. 1, built in 1954. As the Blue Water 1, constructed in 1962, it was the first semi-submersible platform.

Skuld (1988)

Elf Aquitaine's *Skuld* research project culminated in **September 1988** when Frigg Est became operational. This is the world's first underwater hydrocarbon production station. Installed and maintained in the Norwegian North Sea without the use of divers, it is capable of producing 8 billion cubic metres of gas in 110m *360ft* of water. The underwater station, telecontrolled from the installations in the Frigg field 18km *11 miles* away, was designed to operate to depths of up to 600m *2000ft*.

Poseidon (1992)

A project is currently under consideration which deals with the automatic exploitation of oil deposits lying below the sea bed, with a view to reducing as far as possible costly human presence on drilling platforms. The *Poseidon* project, which involves a completely submerged drilling station linked to the mainland, has been developed by the

Oil was first discovered in the North Sea in 1970 and produced a whole new industry in Scotland. Over 20 years on, some 2 million barrels emerge from the British fields every day.

The underwater station developed by the Skuld project has been operational since September 1988.

Institut Français du Pétrole (the French Petroleum Institute), the French company Total and the Norwegian company Statoil. The first Poseidon station should be operational in 1992.

Oil tanker (1886)

The first tanker designed specifically for the purpose was a German ship, the *Glückauf*, launched in 1886. In 1861 barrels of oil extracted at Titusville, Pennsylvania, were transported in a sailing ship, the *Elizabeth Witts*.

Seismography (1914–18)

Seismography is a method of prospecting for oil that is carried out on the surface. It was developed by the German **D. L. Mintrop** during the **First World War**. He used it to locate Allied artillery emplacements. After the war, Mintrop used the method to study underground geological formations, and set up the first seismic exploration company in the United States.

The seismographic method consists of artificially provoking slight disturbances at ground level. The resulting waves traverse underground rock layers and some are reflected back. Waves returning to the surface are analysed to determine the make-up of various rock strata.

Seismography has been greatly advanced by the introduction of data processing. The Geophysical Analysis Group (GAG) and the Massachusetts Institute of Technology (MIT) carried out the first experiments between 1953 and 1957.

Subterranean storage (1916)

It was the German company **Deutsche Erdöl** that, in 1916, patented the first process for storing hydrocarbons in a gaseous form underground.

Well logging (1927)

The first attempt at electrical core sampling, the method by which the nature of the substrata is determined by taking electric measurements, was carried out on **5 September 1927** during a test drilling by a team from the company **Schlumberger Ltd** under the direction of Henri Doll.

Previously, rock samples had been taken by mechanical coring, and the cylindrical shape (core) of the piece of earth or rock taken for the test drilling gave the process its name.

Electrical core drilling was so successful that, as a result, Schlumberger Ltd is today a powerful multinational company.

Engines and ignition devices

Carburettor (1893)

In 1893 the German engineer **Wilhelm Maybach** invented the modern injection carburettor. It is an indispensable part of the engine as

IGNITION SYSTEMS

System	Date	Inventor	Origins	Characteristics
Flame transfer	1836	William Barnett	UK	Enables the pre-compressed fuel mixture to be ignited at regular intervals. Replaced in 1900 by electric ignition.
Ignition tube	1855	Alfred Drake	USA	Although used widely between 1880 and 1905, it lacked precision at moment of ignition. Unusable for vehicles with variable speeds.
Magneto-electric generator	1880	Giesenberg	Germany	Low tension magneto. Developed in France in 1882 by Fernand Forest.
Electric ignition by battery and spark coil	1883 1883	Etienne Lenoir Karl Benz	France Germany	The most widely used system in internal combustion engines.
High voltage magneto	1902	Gottlieb Honold	Germany	The first high voltage magnetos were constructed by Robert Bosch, specialists in the manufacture of electrical equipment for engines. After 1925 the system was replaced by ignition by storage battery and spark coil.
Starter motor	1931	Maurice Gondard	France	The first starter motor for cars by the creator of the Solex carburettor.

it is within the carburettor that the fuel mixture is prepared from air and petrol vapour before being taken in by the cylinder.

The injection carburettor was used for the first time in an engine with two parallel cylinders, known as the Phoenix engine, manufactured by Maybach and Daimler. It was one of the first operational petrol engines intended for use in cars, and was extremely successful.

The carburettor that existed before the development of the injection carburettor was known as the surface carburettor.

Throttle valve (1893)

The carburettor was improved by **Karl Benz** in the same year it was invented (**1893**). Benz installed a throttle valve to regulate the amount of air and gas supplied to the engine. This allowed the speed and power of the engine to be adjusted.

Distributor (1908)

The distributor was the invention of two Americans: **Edward A. Deeds** and **Charles F. Kettering**. While they were both employed by National Cash Register of Dayton, Ohio, E. A. Deeds, trying to perfect the ignition system of a car he was reconstructing, called upon Kettering and his knowledge as an electrical engineer. In **1908** what could be considered the first distributor was perfected. They tested it on Deeds's car and approached Cadillac, who ordered 8000 of them for the 1909 model. Returning by train from the Cadillac factory, Deeds and Kettering thought of the name Delco for the distributor, using the initials of the newly formed company, the Dayton Engineering Laboratories Company.

Induction coil (1841)

The induction coil was invented in **1841** by the French physicists **Antoine Masson** and **Louis**

A modern replica of a German plane of which only 23 examples were built in 1924.

Breguet. It is a device which makes use of the phenomenon of electromagnetic induction to produce a high voltage alternating current. It is fitted to all ignition systems in all internal combustion engines.

Radiator (1897)

The radiator was invented by the German engineer **Wilhelm Maybach** in 1897. After numerous attempts, Maybach perfected a honeycomb radiator. The first examples were built by the German company Daimler Motoren Gesellschaft, where Maybach worked.

Separate combustion chamber (1890)

The first engines to have separate combustion chambers were built in 1890 by the British engineer **Herbert Ackroyd-Stuart**. This system was later refined on certain hot bulb engines.

The combustion chamber plays a very important role in all diesel engines as it ensures that an adequate fuel mixture is achieved.

Antechamber (1909)

The German engineer **Prosper L'Orange**, from the **Benz** company, invented the antechamber in 1909 and completed its development in 1919.

Meanwhile, at the Swedish company Svenska Maskinverken, engineer Harry Laisner worked on a similar project from 1913.

Rotochamber (1919)

In 1919 the English engineer **Harry Ralph Ricardo** constructed his famous T-shaped combustion chamber with a cylinder head, the part of the cylinder where the gas is compressed.

At the time, many manufacturers were trying to use air turbulence to produce an improved fuel mixture. In 1904 a basic model had been developed by Stricland and in 1920 Taylor gave it a hemispherical shape.

Air reserve chamber (1926)

The air reserve chamber, another type of separate combustion chamber, was designed in 1926 by the German engineer **Franz Lang**.

Spark plugs (1885)

In 1885 the Frenchman **Etienne Lenoir** invented an electric spark plug very similar to the one still used today. The igniting of fuel by a spark had already been suggested by the Italian Volta in 1777, and then by Isaac de Rivaz for the internal combustion engine which he described in 1807.

Glass-capped spark plugs (1988)

The new 'Colourtune' spark plug, manufactured by the British company **Gunson Ltd**, has a transparent glass cap which enables better regulation of the ignition as the colour of the spark can be checked. This can be done by replacing just one of the spark plugs with a 'Colourtune' plug. A yellow spark means that the mixture is too rich and that the engine is wasting energy, whereas a blue spark, obtained by regulating the carburettor, indicates a correct mixture.

ENGINES		
Name	Date	Inventor
Piston engine	1673	The Dutch scholar Christiaan Huygens demonstrated the first piston engine before Colbert and the French Academy of Sciences.
Steam engine	1712	In 1712 the Englishman Thomas Newcomen built the first practical steam engine.
Closed circuit, hot air engine	1816	Invented by Robert Stirling of Great Britain and manufactured industrially in 1844. Used today in submarines and spacecraft.
Electric engine	1822	Barlow's wheel, 1822, named after its inventor, can be considered as the first electric engine. In 1838 the German physicist Moritz Hermann von Jacobi equipped a paddle steamer with an electric engine (an AC engine). In 1873 the reversibility of the dynamo (its functioning as a motor) was demonstrated at Vienne by the French engineer Hippolyte Fontaine.
Open circuit, hot air engine	1851	John Ericsson, USA. The engine was used in a liner.
Two-stroke engine without preliminary compression	1860	First internal combustion engine to operate successfully. Invented by the Belgian-born French inventor, Etienne Lenoir.
Atmospheric engine	1867	Invented by the Germans Nikolaus Otto and Eugene Langen. The most widely used internal combustion engine until the invention of the four-stroke engine in 1876.
Brayton engine	1873	Developed by the American Brayton. The first engine to operate successfully with preliminary compression of the fuel mixture.
Four-stroke internal combustion engine	1876	In 1876 the German Nikolaus Otto (1832–91) patented the first gas-operated four-stroke internal combustion engine. The patent constitutes one of the great dates in the history of the motor car.
Double piston engine	1878	Invented by the German Ferdinand Kindermann for the Hannverscher Maschinenbau company, and almost at the same time by Linford of Great Britain in 1879.
Two-stroke internal combustion engine	1879	Invented by the English engineer Dugald Clerck to bypass the patent by Otto (see above). It was less efficient and more polluting but had a much higher fuel rating. It is still used for mopeds and racing bikes.

Water-cooled engine (1823)

In **1823** an Englishman, **Samuel Brown**, invented a water-cooling system. In 1825 Brown founded a company that built several engines of this kind, one of which was fitted on a car and another on a boat.

Sealed circuit water-cooled engine (1960)

In **1960** the French company **Renault** designed a water-cooling system which was totally sealed, therefore waterproof. The usefulness of this system is that it is filled with water and anti-freeze once and for all and never needs replenishing.

Turbo engines

Turbocompressor (1905)

While building a gas turbine, a young Swiss engineer, **A. Büchi**, envisaged replacing the combustion chamber with an internal combustion engine. This would eliminate the inconvenience caused by high pressure and high temperatures.

His research led to supercharged diesel engines. In **1905** he patented the first turbocompressor, and in 1908 Büchi went to work for Sulzer Frères in Switzerland. This company brought out the first turbocharged engine in 1911. It was a four-stroke single cylinder diesel engine with pneumatic fuel injection.

Turbocharged diesel lorries (1953)

The Swedish company **Volvo** was the first to equip lorries with turbocharged diesel engines in **1953**.

Petrol turbo (1967)

One of the most important developments in the history of the motor car in recent years has been the use of the turbocompressor in private cars.

In **1967 SAAB** was the first to use turbocharging on its standard engine, producing greater power from a smaller amount of energy because of the system of supercharging applied to this type of engine.

In 1974 BMW followed suit and subsequently introduced the turbo-diesel in its 5-24 in 1983.

AN ENGINE AS THIN AS A HAIR

This 'micro motor', unveiled in 1988, measures 70 micrometers *0.003in* in diameter and a few micrometers in thickness. Developed by the American Richard S. Muller, Professor of Electrical Engineering and Director of the Berkeley Sensor and Actuator Center (University of Berkeley, California), it was built with the same techniques used in electronics for the manufacture of integrated circuits.

Most of the applications envisaged at the present experimental stage are in the sphere of medicine: the making of instruments for micro-surgery, machines which would be able to move up and down the arteries to scrape off deposits of fat, and so on.

Four-stroke petrol engine	1883	In 1883 the Frenchman Edouard Delamarre-Debouteville and Léon Malandin built the first petrol-fed four-stroke engine. It was experimental and was not produced commercially. On 29 January 1886 the German engineer Karl Benz patented the first truly efficient four-stroke petrol engine.
Synchronous motor	1885	These polyphase motors were a practical application of the discovery of the revolving magnetic field by the Italian physicist Galileo Ferraris. At the same time Nikola Tesla, an American of Croatian origin, perfected the polyphase alternator.
Revolving cylinder engine	1887	Invented by the Frenchman Millet. The most famous was the Gnome engine, built in 1908 by the French engineers Louis and Laurent Seguin. The Gnome and Rhône companies amalgamated and produced a nine-cylinder engine which was the most widely used aeronautical engine of the First World War.
High-power gas engine	1888	Invented by the Frenchmen Léon Malandin and Edouard Delamarre-Debouteville, it developed 100hp. In 1900 the 1000hp barrier was crossed. These motors were mainly designed for industry.
Radial engine	1888	Invented by the Frenchman Fernand Forest, this 12-cylinder, four-bank parallel radial engine (i.e. three cylinders per bank) was widely used in aviation.
Four-cylinder linear engine	1889	Invented by Fernand Forest in France and Wilhelm Maybach in Germany, this engine with its four-stroke cycle is currently the most widely used engine in the European car manufacturing industry.
V engine	1889	Invented by the German engineers Gottlieb Daimler and Wilhelm Maybach. In 1889 the engine was installed in a car designed by Maybach which is today considered as the first modern car.
Engine with pre-combustion chamber	1890	Invented by the English engineer Herbert Ackroyd-Stuart. Forerunner of the surface-ignition engine, also known as the hot bulb engine, which was perfected in 1902 by the Swedish engineer Rundölf.

Opposed cylinder engine	1895	The flat-twin, the first horizontally opposed cylinder engine, developed by the French industrialist Albert de Dion and manufacturer Georges Bouton. In 1896 the German Karl Benz constructed a similar engine. A famous example of this type of engine is the Volkswagen engine of the late 1930s with its four horizontally opposed cylinders.
Diesel engine	1893/97	In 1893 the German engineer Rudolf Diesel (1858–1913) constructed the first prototype of the engine named after him. This four-stroke engine was mass-produced from 1897 onwards. The two-stroke diesel engine, perfected by the German engineer Hugo Güldner, is currently the most powerful internal combustion piston engine. In 1986 eight Japanese car manufacturers set up the Clean Diesel Laboratory, an institute for research into the diesel engine, which aims to develop, within six years, a new diesel engine which causes less pollution.
Rotary engine	1956	Perfected by the German engineer Felix Wankel and constructed by NSU. It is used by the Japanese company Mazda.
Ceramic engine	1995?	One of the formulae for the future. The low thermal conductibility of this material enables considerable savings in energy to be made. Many experiments are being carried out in Japan by Nissan and Isuzu, in France by Peugeot and in Germany by Porsche. In 1985 Nissan began marketing a ceramic turbo-compressor

Turbocompressor for aircraft engines (1917)

In 1917 a French engineer **Auguste Rateau** built the first turbocharged aircraft engine. It produced 50hp and weighed 23kg *51lb* and turned at 30000rpm.

Turboprop (1920)

The turboprop engine, invented in 1920 by the Englishman **A. A. Griffith**, is no more than a gas turbine, the energy from which drives one or several propellers. The main difficulty lies in the high rotation speed of the gas turbine: powerful speed inhibitors are essential so that the propeller can turn at a speed which is compatible with its efficiency. The turboprop was used mainly on planes flying at between 600 and 800km/h *370* and *500 mph*.

Rocket engines

Origins

Used initially in warfare and then for fireworks, the rocket engine was re-introduced into Europe by the English general **Sir William Congreve** around 1800. Until the 20th century its only propellant was gunpowder. The propellant or propergol is the substance which generates the energy required to propel the rocket. Rocket engines propel by reaction the device to which they are attached, by ejecting hot gases produced by a propellant carried on board the missile. The only rocket engine used today is the internal combustion rocket engine which uses chemical fuels and oxidisers: a substance which combines with another substance to produce combustion. Electric and atomic rocket engines are still at the planning stage.

Solid propellant rocket engines

The first rockets were simple cylinders made from cardboard or wood and closed at one end. The principle remains the same, although from 1800 onwards the cylinder was made from metal.

During the First World War, the American Robert Hutchings Goddard (1882–1945)

THE TWO-STROKE ENGINE OF TOMORROW . . .

Since the models brought out by some companies, e.g. DKW, Saab, Wartburg, Suzuki, just after the Second World War, the two-stroke engine has been virtually excluded from the car manufacturing industry and reserved for lightweight machinery such as mopeds, motor saws, outboard motors and lawn mowers.

But in 1973 Ralph Sarich, an engineer of Yugoslavian origin who had settled in Australia, received a prize for his invention of an ingeniously designed thermal engine, with a central piston which described a sort of orbit. With a substantial grant from the Australian government, he went on to set up a company, the Orbital Engine Company, which carried out research into the updating and adaptation of the two-stroke car engine.

The new engine, compared to its four-stroke counterpart, is half the size, a third the weight and less expensive as a result of discarding almost 200 parts of the timing gear.

Agreements have been signed with Ford and General Motors who are carrying out road tests and who will certainly not waste any time in marketing its advantages. In particular, it causes much less pollution than the old two-stroke engines and uses between 20 and 30 percent less petrol.

Sarich's prototype two-stroke engine (see box feature adjacent).

GAS AND STEAM TURBINES

Type	Date	Inventor	Origins	Characteristics
Gas turbine	1791	John Barber	UK	Remained at the project stage.
Steam turbine	1884	Sir Charles Algernon Parsons	UK	Steam, reaction turbine. First turbine built industrially.
Steam action turbine	1889	Carl Gustaf de Laval	Sweden	Low power, single-stage turbine.
Steam turbine with pressure stages	1897–1900	Auguste Rateau	France	Enables slower rotational speeds and higher efficiency.
Internal combustion gas turbine	1903	Armengaud	France	First internal combustion gas turbine to be built. Preceded by patents of Peer (USA, 1890) and Hordenfeldt and Christophe (France, 1894).
Combustion/ gas turbine	1904/5	Stolze	Germany	Same turbine invented in France by Armengaud and Lemale.
Internal combustion gas turbine with preliminary compression	1909/10	Hans Holzwarth	Germany	The first gas turbine to be used in industry.
Closed cycle gas turbine	1940	Prof Ackeret Dr Keller	Switzerland	Developed by the Swiss company Escher-Wyss under the name of the Escher-Wyss aerodynamic turbine.

improved rocket efficiency by 65 percent by increasing the speed of the escaping gases. There were subsequent improvements to efficiency. The solid propellant engines are less complicated than those using liquid propellant but are much less flexible.

Cooling of rocket engines (1933)

In 1933 the Austrian engineer **Eugen Sänger** invented a new cooling system for liquid fuel rocket engines, known as regenerative cooling. It became the most widely adopted system.

Sänger constructed several rocket engines which were used to back up the take-off of the first aeroplanes equipped with turbojet engines, but he soon decided to work on the development of a jet engine which would effect a take-off unaided.

Monopropellant rocket engine (1935)

In 1935 the German scientist **Helmuth Walter**, constructed the first monopropellant rocket engine. This is a liquid fuel rocket engine which uses only one propellant and for this reason is referred to as monopropellant.

In February 1937 a Walter rocket supplying 100kg 220lb of thrust was attached to a German Heinkel Kadett plane as a take-off engine. This was the first rocket-assisted take-off in the history of aviation.

The V2 rocket engine (1942)

Rocket-engine research in Hitler's Germany was carried out under the guidance of

Hermann Oberth. Later it was directed by Oberth's student Wernher von Braun (1912–77). Work was first done at the military base of Kummersdorf, then transferred to the Peenemünde base in 1937.

The infamous V2, which used liquid fuel, made its first flight on **13 June 1942**. Designed by **Wernher von Braun**, it was equipped with a rocket engine built by W. Thiel. (Thiel was killed in 1943 during a bombing raid on the Peenemünde base.)

The engine on the V2s that terrorised London in 1944 and 1945 was the last in a series of rocket engines designed initially to power the V1. The rocket attained a velocity of 760m 2500ft per second. Escape velocity for leaving the earth's gravitational field (for example, in order to put a satellite into orbit) is 11km 7 miles per second, or 15 times faster than the V2.

After the war, the V2 engine served as a model for both the Americans and the Soviets, and von Braun emigrated to the United States to contribute to its rocket programme.

Jet engines

As well as rocket engines, there is another type of engine, the jet engine, which uses air as an oxidiser and which is more correctly referred to as an air-breathing jet engine.

Ramjet engine (1913)

In 1913 the French engineer **Lorin** patented the first ramjet engine, but it was never produced commercially. After the First World War, the project was continued by another

The German manufacturer BMW has launched as a world first a new 12-cylinder hydrogen engine. According to its designer, its performance is comparable to that of a petrol or diesel engine.

French engineer, René Leduc, who constructed the first prototype in 1936. It was not until 1949 that a machine propelled by a ramjet engine made its maiden flight. In spite of some impressive performances the ramjet engine was replaced by the turbojet engine for various technical reasons, such as efficiency, ease of adjustment, etc. But, as a result of recent research by seven engineers from ONERA, the French National Office for Space Study and Research, and Aérospatiale, the ramjet engine has been revived and may well propel the space-craft of the future.

Turbojet engine (1930)

It was the Englishman **Frank Whittle** who first attempted to construct a turbojet engine between 1928 and **1930**.

The turbojet engine is a jet engine: the exhaust gases, produced by reaction, create the thrust of the engine and consequently propel the machine containing the engine.

The first British plane equipped with a turbojet engine was ready to fly on 15 May 1941. The turbojet engine of the Gloster

Nuclear energy

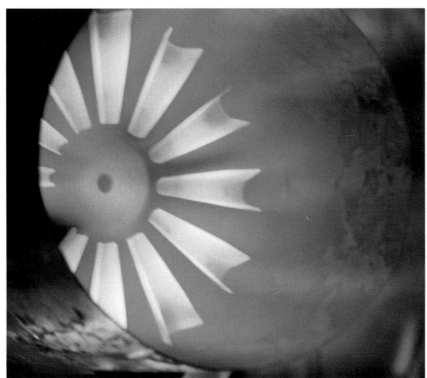

A fighter plane turbojet is tested by the French group ONERA. The idea was first developed by the Englishman Frank Whittle.

Whittle E28 used a turbocompressor and produced a thrust of 375kg *827lb*. In Germany, Hans Pabst von Ohain started similar research in 1936 and a Heinkel fighter plane made its maiden flight in 1939.

Concorde is equipped with Olympus turbojet engines, constructed by the English company Bristol Siddeley.

Turbofan engine (1940)

In 1940 the American company **Metropolitan Vickers** developed a turbofan engine. This engine is intermediate between a turboprop and a turbojet. It has two advantages over these two other engine types: in-flight fuel consumption is 20 percent less, and there is less noise from the exhaust.

The turbofan engine has been widely used. The American firm Pratt & Whitney has built turbojets of this type for the Boeing 707, Boeing 720, Boeing 727, the Caravelle and the Douglas DC-8. General Electric and Rolls-Royce have produced turbofan engines as well.

Turbojet with afterburner (1945)

In 1945 the British company **Rolls-Royce** constructed the first turbojet with an afterburner. Afterburning allows greater thrust to be obtained without substantial increase in engine weight. This increased thrust is particularly useful in take-off.

The biggest drawback of afterburners is the very high fuel consumption. That is why they are only used very briefly, at take-off, and to obtain peak speeds with fighter aircraft.

Pulsejet engine (1940)

In 1940 the principle of the pulsejet was discovered by the German **Paul Schmidt**. He was trying to develop a ramjet that could start up under its own power. The pulsejet was immediately put to use on the German flying bomb, the V1.

Propfan (1985)

After ten years' research carried out under the auspices of **NASA**, the 'propfan' project was disclosed in 1985. It combines a contra-rotating propeller and turbine which produces a very considerable saving on fuel.

The first demonstration flight of the turbojet engine with a jet propeller took place on 20 August 1986 in a Boeing 727. However, despite very satisfactory results, Boeing, the world's leading aircraft constructor, seemed to want to shelve the project. It was McDonnell Douglas who continued the trials with the MD-80, resuming flights on 18 May 1987 in the United States, and taking it to the Farnborough Airshow in England in the autumn of 1988.

Today, more than 160 flights have been carried out with machines equipped with propfan, of which 140 were on the MD-80.

The aim is to produce standard aircraft. Currently being studied are the MD-91 and MD-92. The former will carry 114 passengers, is powered by two General Electric GE36 engines and has a fuel consumption estimated at 40 percent less than that of a conventional aircraft.

GE-90 Reactor (1995)

It will be the largest civil engine in the world. With a thrust of between 75 000 and 95 000lb, it has been designed for the large carrier twinjet planes of the late 1990s, in particular the new Boeing 777. The pioneers of this programme are **General Electric** (USA) and the French **Société Nationale d'Etude et de Construction de Moteurs d'Avion** (SNECMA).

Isotopic separation (1922)

In 1922 the English physicist **William Francis Aston** carried out the first isotopic separation in a laboratory. In order to achieve this, he had used a mass spectrograph which sorted the atoms by using a magnetic field. Isotopic separation involves isolating a particular isotope from a given substance. In fact, a substance never naturally presents itself in isolation, but is always accompanied, usually in very small proportions, by substances with the same atomic number but containing different numbers of neutrons.

Heavy water (1932)

In 1932 the American chemist **Harold Clayton Urey** discovered deuterium and heavy water. He was awarded the Nobel Prize for Chemistry two years later for this discovery.

In 1933, using Urey's method of preparation, the American physicist and chemist Gilbert Newton Lewis successfully prepared a few millilitres of almost pure heavy water by fractional distillation of ordinary water.

The term heavy water, a chemical compound similar to water, is used to describe deuterium (the heavy isotope of hydrogen) oxide. This oxide is contained in all water in virtually constant proportions – that is, one molecule of heavy water to approximately 1000 molecules of water.

Atomic pile (1942)

The first atomic pile was constructed below the football stands at the University of Chicago, under the direction of Italian-born physicist **Enrico Fermi** in December 1942.

The energy produced by atomic fission is given off in the form of heat. This heat is then recovered and transformed, for example, into electrical energy. During fission neutrons are released as well as heat, and these in turn induce more fission. However, in an atomic pile this reaction can be controlled.

Nuclear moderator (1942)

In 1942 **Enrico Fermi**, Italian physicist and Nobel Prize-winner in 1938, used graphite as a moderator in the first atomic pile in Chicago. The probability of fission occurring depends on the energy of the neutron which collides with the fissile nucleus. For the main fissile nuclei, uranium 235 and plutonium 239, the probability increases when the extremely high kinetic energy of the neutron decreases. In order to moderate this energy, substances known as moderators are used. They are composed of lightweight nuclei which, on impact with the neutrons, dissipate their initial energy and slow them down, without capturing them too often.

The only moderators which can be used are: carbon, in the form of industrial graphite; hydrogen in water or certain hydrocarbons; deuterium in heavy water; and pure or oxydised beryllium.

Nuclear power stations (1951)

The first nuclear power station to produce

The cooling towers and the reactor buildings at Calder Hall nuclear power station.

electricity was the **ERR-1** in America, which created 300kW, opened in **1951**. The first civilian nuclear power station was opened in June 1954 at Obninsk in the USSR when a 5000kW (5MW) production reactor was started up. Prior to this, the United States had developed a nuclear-powered engine for military purposes to be used in a submarine and which had an equivalent capacity. But, as it was a prototype and a military project, this first atomic power station did not receive international approval. Britain's first electricity-producing power station was Calder Hall (Unit 1), Cumbria, opened in 1956.

Like all machines, nuclear power stations have a limited life span. It is estimated that, after 20 to 40 years' service, the installations of the reactor are worn out and become dangerous. Already 135 installations throughout the world have been shut down.

Nuclear reactor (1951)

The various types of reactor, and the different materials which could be used, were developed between 1940 and 1945, but the industrial development, which began in 1951 in the United States, required detailed preliminary study.

The largest reactor in the world is the 1450MW Ignalina station in Lithuania, USSR.

There are well over 400 nuclear reactors operating around the world. The USA has the most (108), followed by the USSR (56), France (55) and Britain (40). In all they produce some 17 percent of the world's electricity.

Breeder reactor (1959)

The first breeder reactor was commissioned at **Dounreay** in Scotland in **1959**. A breeder reactor is one which produces more nuclear fuel than it consumes, so that the depletion of the world's stock of fissile uranium (i.e. 7 percent of natural uranium), does not present a threat.

In 1955 France started to consider the development of such a system and, in 1975, the Phénix (Phoenix) breeder reactor (250MW)

The removal of a fuel element at a High Flux Isotope Reactor (HFIR). The fuel element and the reactor are submerged in water. The blue glow is due to Cerenkov radiation, emitted because the charged particles move faster through water than does light. The main product is the isotope californium 252.

Alternative sources of energy

Origins

The history of the human race has been characterised by the search for sources of energy. In the 1970s the oil crisis revived this preoccupation and research was directed towards new sources of energy or new ways of developing old forms of energy. By the end of 1988 an entire programme was proposed within the framework of the European Community to promote renewable sources of energy such as solar, biomass, etc.

Windmill (10th century)

The earliest recorded windmills are those used in Iran during the second half of the 7th century, but the idea did not reach Europe until the 10th century. A windmill at Weedley, near Hull, Humberside, is probably the earliest British example, dating from 1185.

Windmill is the generic term for any mechanism used to harness the kinetic energy of the wind in order to operate a machine, in particular a millstone.

Wind engines (1876)

A modern version of the traditional windmill, the wind engine or aerogenerator, converts the kinetic energy of the wind into mechanical energy and, more precisely in the case of aerogenerators, into electrical energy. Wind engines were first mentioned during the second half of the 19th century. Since then, far from becoming obsolete, the use of wind power energy has continued to develop, particularly in countries which have very windy regions.

In the United States more than 300 000 aerogenerators provide 300 million kW/h every year. This is the country which, in the 1970s, built the most powerful wind engine: it produces more than 2MW.

Rack and pinion windpump (1990)

Although a windpump often seems to be an ideal, environment-friendly, cheap source of power, it has one or two obvious problems: it requires a much stronger gust of wind to get started than it does to keep going; further-

---

came into service at Marcoule on the River Rhône. The reactor was named after the bird which, according to Greek mythology, was able to rise repeatedly from its ashes. The first breeder reactor came into service in the United States in 1963, in the USSR in 1968, and in West Germany in 1977.

Mox (1970)

This is a fuel mixture of uranium and plutonium which was first used in the 1970s. Mox (Mixed Oxide) comes from the reprocessing of natural and enriched uranium-based fuels burnt in nuclear power stations.

Mox provides a solution for the recycling process of nuclear waste. It contains 0.8 percent of the isotope uranium 235 (more than uranium in its natural state), and is all the more interesting because after spending three years in a nuclear reactor, the waste has been converted into a fuel and can be reprocessed and re-used. Experiments have been carried out on this especially in the nuclear power stations of Germany.

Thermonuclear reaction

Thermonuclear fusion

The great hope for the energy of the future is thermonuclear fusion of hydrogen, with a view to reproducing on earth the reactions which take place in space and which result in the fusion of hydrogen atoms.

Research is directed mainly towards the possibility of recuperating energy produced in this way, and building electricity generating stations around the fusion reactors.

The Bethe cycle (1938)

In 1938 the German-born American physicist Hans Albrecht Bethe discovered the nuclear transformation cycle, named after him, which explains the energy of the sun and the stars.

The Lawson criterion (1957)

In 1957 the British physicist John Lawson stated the conditions which must be fulfilled by a plasma of deuterium or tritium before the phenomenon of nuclear fusion can take place, and be maintained, without an external supply of energy.

The Lawson criterion defines the relation that must be reached between the density of the plasma and the length of time of its confinement, the temperature having to reach 100 million K before the reaction can take place.

Today, plasma physicists consider that the

construction of fusion reactors has a good chance of success.

Magnetic confinement (c.1949)

Research on thermonuclear reaction controlled by magnetic confinement began independently in the United States, the USSR and Western Europe towards the end of the 1940s. In the early stages the research was carried out secretly, and some definitive work on plasma physics was done at the Kuratchov Institute in Moscow. For the first time, in 1968, physicists at the Institute brought a plasma to a temperature of 12 million K in a machine called a tokamak.

Tokamaks (1963)

The first tokamak (an abbreviation of the Russian name *Toroidal Kamera Magnetic*, a machine for magnetic confinement which enables plasmas to be studied while in a state of fusion) was invented by the Russian physicist Lev Andreevitch Artsimovitch and first used in 1963.

In the 1970s tokamaks were constructed in many laboratories. In 1978 the Princeton tokamak in the USA reached a temperature of 70 million K, but was still a long way from the Lawson criterion.

In 1983 the Alcato C tokamak at the Massachusetts Institute of Technology (MIT), USA, exceeded the temperature threshold of the Lawson criterion but only by 15 million K. Today, huge tokamaks like the JET (Joint European Torus), installed at Culham in England in 1983, are being built in European laboratories. In October 1988 the JET briefly reached a temperature of 100 million K, ten times hotter than the sun. The aim is to exceed both the threshold of the Lawson criterion and a temperature of 100 million K in order to demonstrate the feasibility of controlled nuclear fusion.

NET (1992)

The programme of the Joint European Torus (JET) is to be continued until 1992 when the Next European Torus (NET) will take over. By the beginning of the next century, NET should have developed a European fusion reactor.

ITER (2015)

The European Community, the United States, Japan and the USSR, which brought its Tokamak-15 into service in 1988, have co-operated in the development of a pilot study for an International Thermonuclear Experimental Reactor (ITER). Their aim is to demonstrate the technological feasibility of thermonuclear reaction which should enable a non-polluting and virtually inexhaustible source of energy to be developed commercially by around 2015–25.

It will be the biggest wind engine park in Europe. Construction began in 1990 near Lelystad in the centre of Holland. The 35 wind engines' combined power totals 10.5MW and they will be able to provide 15 million kW a year and supply 5000 homes with electricity. This will make it possible to save 5 million cubic metres of natural gas a year. Another park containing 60 wind machines is being planned near Rotterdam.

more, when required in remote areas, many are too bulky to be easily and cheaply set up.

Using an old idea from the turn of the century and modern techniques, **IT Power**, under the direction of **Peter Fraenkel**, have developed a small windpump that can start easily and that can be transported without difficulty. They have devised a rack and pinion system to power the piston on the pump, which means that weaker winds will now start it. As the company already had one larger pump on the market, they made this one much smaller, aiming at those who need only to supply water to, say, a farm rather than a whole village.

Hydrogen (1766)

Hydrogen, the most plentiful substance in the universe, could provide the basis of energy in the 21st century.

Discovered in **1766** by the English physicist and chemist **Henry Cavendish**, hydrogen reacts violently when it comes into contact with certain substances, for example chlorine and oxygen. This property makes it a much more energetic fuel than petroleum.

Hydrogen does not exist in a free state on earth and exists in only very small quantities in the atmosphere. However, it is found in many substances, the most common of which is water.

The future of hydrogen as a fuel depends on finding the solutions to certain questions including how to produce large quantities as economically as possible, and transporting and storing it safely.

At present the main problem is that of producing large quantities of hydrogen from water and solar energy.

This new type of energy generator uses wind energy and has both domestic and industrial applications. It was designed by a Toulouse company, ATS Holding, and first shown at the end of 1989. These generators, resembling revolving pyramids, can be of different sizes, depending on the power required. They can work as well with gentle breezes as with gale force winds, unlike current wind engines which do not function with the most gentle breezes, but are risky in high winds.

Biomass

Biomass is the oldest source of energy used by man. With the exception of solar energy, until the 18th century it was our main source of warmth.

The present forms of its development are extremely varied, the most developed being biogas and biofuels.

Ethanol (antiquity)

This is the technical name for ethyl alcohol often known simply as alcohol. The method for obtaining it dates back to antiquity, but its use in industry to produce energy has developed noticeably since 1973.

Ethanol is obtained by fermentation and then refined by distillation. The raw materials are often sugars or starches of vegetable origin.

Methanol (1661)

Methanol or methyl alcohol was discovered in **1661** by the Anglo-Irish philosopher and chemist the **Honourable Robert Boyle** among the distillation products of wood. In 1812 Taylor established a connection with alcohol, but it was the two French chemists Dumas and Péligot who determined its composition in 1835. Like ethanol, methanol is a liquid fuel.

Experiments are currently under way to examine the possibility of using wood alcohol to replace lead in petrol.

Methane (1776)

This gas, discovered in **1776** by the Italian **Count Alessandro Volta** (1745–1827), is produced during the decomposition of organic matter by fermentation. The first use of biomethane dates back to 1857 when a methane plant was built in a leper colony near Bombay in India.

Methane is mainly used in industrial and urban heating. It is currently being tested to decide its suitability as a car fuel.

Geothermal energy (1818)

Geothermal energy is an inexhaustible source of energy produced by the earth's heat. The oldest geothermal installation is in Larderello in Tuscany and dates from 1818. It can be utilised by harnessing underground water which is hot from contact with the rocks.

A distinction is made, depending on the temperature of the water, between low energy geothermics (less than 90°C *194°F*), used for heating homes, greenhouses, fish farms and the drying of crops; medium energy geothermics (between 90°C and 180°C *194°F* and *356°F*), used for refrigeration or to produce electricity by the vaporisation of an organic fluid such as isobutane, which makes it possible to drive turbines linked to generators producing electricity; and, lastly, high energy geothermics (higher than 180°C *356°F*), also used for the production of electricity, but in this case the fluid vaporised is the actual jets of water.

Since 1986 a European research programme has been trying to exploit the heat of the rocks directly in zones where there is no underground water (Soultz geothermic programme on dry rocks).

In terms of high energy geothermics, more than 6000MW are currently being produced throughout the world, particularly in the United States, Mexico, New Zealand, the Philippines and Indonesia. Japan is only just beginning to exploit its vast resources.

Heat pump (1927)

A heat pump is a device that recovers heat from any free source such as air, ground water, etc. It converts mechanical energy into thermal energy. It transfers the heat accumulated through use of a conventional system of radiators and heat pipes. The only energy expended is that needed to run the compressor for transferring the heat. More energy is recovered than is consumed, which makes this a particularly attractive process.

Credit for having thought of the process goes to Lord Kelvin. In 1852 he had already set down the principles of a thermodynamic machine that produced heat as well as cold. Nevertheless it was 75 years before the first heat pump was built by **T. G. N. Haldane** in **1927**. He used it to heat his office in London and his house in Scotland.

Solar energy

Solar furnace (3rd century BC)

The idea of the solar furnace can be traced back to the Greek scholar **Archimedes** (278–212 BC). While defending Syracuse, he armed the soldiers with concave shields which, by concentrating the sun's rays, made the Roman troops under the consul Marcellus believe that they were facing 'soldiers of fire'.

The French chemist Antoine Laurent Lavoisier (1743–95), father of modern chemistry, was the true inventor of the solar furnace. He concentrated the sun's rays in order to achieve the combustion of a diamond in an atmosphere containing oxygen without the use of fuel.

It was not until 1946 that an experimental plant was constructed at Meudon in France where the first large-scale solar furnace enabled a temperature of 3000°C *5430°F* to be reached.

Solar collector (17th century)

Modern solar collectors use the greenhouse effect discovered in the 17th and 18th centuries: the sun's energy passes through glass warming the air, and is trapped there.

It was during the 17th century that greenhouses first appeared in France where the *Jardin du roi* (the King's Garden), now known as the *Jardin des plantes* (the Plant Garden), was created in Paris in 1653. In England they were constructed on a large scale from the end of the 18th century.

During the 1920s a large number of solar collectors were constructed in California and then abandoned in favour of petroleum. The energy crisis of 1973 revived interest in them as a source of energy.

Photovoltaic cell

Origins (1839)

In **1839** the French physicist **Antoine Becquerel** (grandfather of Henri Becquerel who discovered radioactivity) constructed the first photovoltaic cells. However, they were never developed during his lifetime.

In 1990 solar street plans were introduced in Tokyo.

The parabolic reflector at Odeillo-Font-Romeau solar power station in France, where 63 flat orientating mirrors automatically track the motion of the sun and reflect the light onto it. This reflector then concentrates the rays to produce 1000 kilowatts and a temperature of 3800°C 6900°F in the furnace.

A SOLAR MONSTER

The solar-powered electricity plant of Luz International Ltd is situated to the north-east of Los Angeles in the middle of the Mojave desert. It began operating at the beginning of 1990. It is a huge monster as well as a technological wonder. It produces 80MW and is capable of supplying the electricity needs of a population of 115 000. It is environmentally friendly (there are none of the disadvantages associated with electrical power stations, notably acid rain), and will lead to a considerable fall in the emission of carbon dioxide. When the programme is complete, by about 1995, this electricity plant will provide enough electricity to supply the equivalent of a million people!

A HUGE BARRAGE

A project to build a giant hydro-electric barrage, 16km *10 miles* long and driven by the tides, is being studied in the UK. This barrage, costing £5.5 billion (nearly as much as the Channel Tunnel!), would be situated in the estuary of the River Severn, which is subject to tides of exceptional range. It could provide 7 percent of the electricity requirements of the whole country. Building would begin in 1993 and it would be operational by 1999.

Development (1954)

It was the growth of space research during the early 1950s that brought about the manufacture of photoelectric cells. In **1954** American scientists at the Bell Laboratories, **G. L. Pearson**, **C. S. Fuller** and **D. M. Chaplin**, developed a solar battery which consisted of tiny silicon cells whose transformation capacity, although tripled within a few years (6 percent in 1955 and 18 percent in 1978), gave a relatively low rate of efficiency for the high costs of production. However, in the last ten years or so, work carried out on lowering production costs has enabled the system to be used to supplement weak spots in the world's electricity network such as at isolated telecommunication relay stations, in lighting and pumping water in arid and sunny places, etc.

Amorton technology (1987)

The Japanese company **Sanyo** has conceived a photovoltaic cell using the amorphous, i.e. non-crystalline, properties of silicon, and has thereby developed a complete technology, known as Amorton technology, which enables solar energy to be used to an extremely high level of efficiency. The amorphous silicon photocell is currently being developed and could perhaps offer an alternative to nuclear power as a source of electricity in the near future. It is under discussion.

Solar generator (1878)

As early as **1878** a Frenchman, **Augustin Mouchot**, presented a small solar generator at the Paris Exposition. The solar plant furnished enough energy to operate a steam engine. However, this pioneering work was not followed up until similar research was undertaken after 1945. Later, the energy crisis in the 1970s prompted the governments of principal industrial nations actively to encourage the work.

Solar thermal power plant (1960)

The first solar thermal power plant was constructed in Ashkabad, capital of the Soviet Republic of Turkmenistan, in 1960.

The most powerful plant is Solar 1 at Barstow in California (USA) which produces 10MW and began functioning in 1982. In Europe the biggest photovoltaic solar power plant should be opened by late 1991 in Saint-Imier, Switzerland. Covering a total of 4000m² *43 000sq ft*, it will produce approximately 720MW/h.

The oceans as a source of energy

Wave energy (1875)

The idea of using wave energy seems to have been considered scientifically for the first time in **1875** by the Australian **R. S. Deverell**.

In 1889 a very basic form of installation known as Ocean Grove was operating off the coast of New York. In 1980 the Japanese Foundation for Naval Construction started to build a prototype power station, which they called Kaiyo, off the coast of the island of Iriomote.

A power station using wave energy (1985)

In **February 1985** the Norwegians started to build, to the west of the port of Bergen, the first power station in the world to use wave energy to produce electricity. It will produce enough electricity to supply 70 average-sized homes in Norway, i.e. 1.5 million kW/h. The Norwegian government is also investing in another project which consists of using wave energy to force large quantities of water into a funnel so that it can be used by a standard hydraulic power station.

Tidal power station (1966)

In 1955 the French engineer Albert Caquot laid the foundations of a project for a tidal power station in the bay of Granville, and incorporating the bay of Mont-Saint-Michel. The idea was not a new one. A scientific commission had already met in 1919 to discuss the basic operational principles of an electricity power station using tidal energy. In 1943 the technical committee considering the sea as a source of energy recommended that the Mont-Saint-Michel scheme should be abandoned. The project was considered far too ambitious and a decision was taken to begin with a smaller project: the tidal power

A prototype wave power machine on the isle of Islay.

station on the estuary of the River Rance, opened on **26 November 1966**, which has an output of 240MW.

At the moment there are only three tidal power stations in the world: in France, the USSR and Canada where the Bay of Fundy in Nova Scotia has record tides of 20m *66ft*. But

new projects are being considered, in particular the project for the biggest estuary dam in the world producing tidal energy, to be constructed on the River Mersey, near Liverpool. If the project proves viable, by 1995 the dam could be providing 0.5 percent of the electricity used by England and Wales.

Industry

Architecture and construction

Origins

It was in the Neolithic period (between the 9th and 4th millennia BC) that architecture really began. Curiously, this art sprang to life in a part of the world lacking those classic building materials, wood and stone. In the Near East the clayey earth was used to build the first walls, either in the form of puddled clay or unfired bricks, around the 7th millennium BC.

Two series of inventions were to play a decisive role in the development of architecture: iron tools, whose use became

widespread from the 10th century BC; machines such as the pulley (with the block and tackle) and the winch, of which even the most modern machines are only sophisticated examples.

The lever dates back to prehistoric times. The pyramids could not have been constructed without the lever, the mathematical principles of which were described by Archimedes in the 3rd century BC.

Bridge (Neolithic Age)

In the late Stone Age tree trunks and piles of stone were used to construct simple bridges. The idea of building stone arches began with the Sumerians around 3500 BC. The Romans were masters of constructing arches notably thanks to their discovery of natural cement.

In China at the beginning of the 7th century the engineer Li-Chun built the first arched bridge in stone at Zhaoxian, in the province of Hebei.

Suspension bridge (6th century)

The Chinese were building suspension bridges in the **6th century**, although they existed in the form of draw-bridges and foot-bridges made from creepers before that.

If one excepts a chain foot-bridge built over the Tees in 1741, the first metal suspension bridge was constructed on the Merrimac River in Massachusetts in 1809. The first major suspension bridge in Europe was by Thomas Telford over the Menai Straits; it was completed in 1826. Currently the largest bridges are the Verrazano Bridge at the entrance to the port of New York, which spans 1420m

The temple of Amon at Luxor, built by the architect Amenhotep in the 14th century BC.

CHANNEL TUNNEL

The first proposal for a tunnel under the English Channel was made in 1751 by a French engineer, Nicholas Desmaret. Since then, a further 25 possible schemes have been suggested, including one made to Napoleon in 1802 that involved a cobble-stoned passage to be used by horse-drawn carriages. In 1860 there was a proposal to construct a 6m *20ft* high 32km *20 mile* long four-track jetty. In 1882 and 1974 some construction work began but both projects were abandoned for strategic, political and financial reasons.

The Anglo–French Channel Tunnel Treaty was ratified by the British and French governments in 1987 and tunnel boring began in November of that year by Eurotunnel, who contracted the design and construction to the Transmanche Link group.

The Tunnel is planned to open in 1993 carrying passenger, freight and vehicle rail traffic. There will actually be three tunnels: two parallel railway tunnels will run either side of a central service tunnel. The single track railway tunnels – one for each direction of travel – will run underground for 50km *31 miles*, of which 37km *23 miles* will be under the Channel at an average depth of 40m *130ft*.

If all goes to plan, the constructors say 30 million passengers and 15 million tonnes of freight will be carried annually. However, all is not going smoothly on the financial front: Eurotunnel revised its estimated cost of construction from £5.23 billion to over £7 billion two years after work began. At 11.13 am on Saturday 1 December 1990 the two tunnelling teams, one from France, one from Britain, met in the middle.

Graham Fagg and Philippe Cozette exchange flags at the Channel Tunnel breakthrough.

4658ft (1964), and the Humber Bridge (1981) whose central bay of 1542m *5059ft* is the longest in the world.

But numerous projects are either in progress or being planned: a 13.1km *8.1 mile* long bridge (completed in 1988) links the Shikoku and Honshu islands in south-east Japan. The bridge is in fact 11 bridges that 'jump' from islet to islet. A 3300m *10 826ft* long suspension bridge between Sicily and the Italian mainland should be completed by 1995. A 4000m *13 123ft* long bridge is due to be completed between Le Havre and Honfleur in France by 1992.

First metal bridge (1773)

The first metal bridge was built between **1773** and 1779 by the British iron-founder **Abraham Darby**. The Iron Bridge at Coalbrookdale was made of cast-iron and its central arch spanned 30m *98ft*.

The first architect (2800 BC)

The first architect whose name we know is the Egyptian **Imhotep**. It is to him that we owe the world's first large-scale monument constructed entirely in stone: the Step Pyramid at Saqqâra. It was built for the Pharaoh Zoser around **2800 BC**.

Plumbline (3rd millennium BC)

The plumbline and the set square and their judicious combination to find the level were known to the Egyptians at the beginning of the Memphite period or the Old Empire (**2778– 2423 BC**). Both a symbol and a talisman, the mason's hieroglyphic image (a plumbline in a triangle passing through the horizontal line of the base) assured perpetual stability. The Romans were the first to use lead for the weight.

Aqueduct (antiquity)

The aqueduct was born out of necessity in the Middle East and the Mediterranean basin. Cultivated land and entire towns were irrigated by artificial channels that crossed bridges and ran underground. In 703 BC the Assyrian king Sennacherib had a 50km *31 mile* long aqueduct built to supply Nineveh. In Egypt the canals leading from the Nile were often so wide that boats could navigate them.

The arched aqueduct, such as the Pont-du-Gard at Nîmes (AD 23), was developed mainly in Rome and throughout the Roman Empire.

The longest aqueduct today is the Water Project in California, which was built in 1974 and is 1329km *825 miles* long.

Winches, pulleys and cranes

Medieval builders used winches and capstans which were probably very similar to those used by the Romans. The latter introduced many mechanical systems to their building sites such as hydraulic and wind powered cranes and hoists.

The origin of the crane is still quite mysterious, except for a three-pulley crane system which is attributed to Archimedes (287–212 BC).

The pulley, together with the crank and the winch, is first mentioned in *Mechanica*, a work of the Aristotelian school (4th century BC). The invention of the pulley and of the tackle block is attributed to Archytas of Tarentum (430–360 BC) who was an army general, philosopher, mathematician, creator of automata and an innovator in the field of mechanics.

The level (1573)

The water level is described for the first time in the works of a Polish geometrician, **Strumienski**, and would therefore date from **1573**.

The spirit level is the invention of the Frenchman Melchisédech Thévenot (1620–92), an unconventional character, great traveller and keen researcher in the fields of science and technology. It was in his correspondence with the Dutch astronomer Christiaan Huygens between 1661 and 1662 that the first reference to his spirit level can be found. But Thévenot did not publish a description of his instrument until 1681.

Tunnel (1826)

The first railway tunnel was built in England in **1826** on the Liverpool to Manchester railway.

The Mont-Cenis tunnel, the first tunnel through the Alps, was begun in 1857 under the supervision of the Frenchman Germain Sommeiller. During the digging he invented the first pneumatic pick, which allowed the boring of the tunnel to be greatly speeded up.

One of the most famous tunnels in Europe, and one of the most important technical achievements of the 19th century, is the St-Gotthard tunnel which links Germany to Italy via Switzerland. Its construction began in 1872, lasted ten years and was carried out under very difficult conditions.

A new transalpine railway tunnel is under construction: the work, financed by Switzerland, should begin in 1994 and, according to which plan is adopted, will take 14 to 17 years to complete.

The world's longest tunnel (1988)

This railway tunnel, which was officially opened in **March 1988**, links the main Honshu island to Hokaido via the Tsugaru Strait in northern Japan at 240m *787ft* below sea level.

The 53.9km *33 mile* long tunnel was bored through volcanic rock – a technological achievement that has required 25 years to complete, cost an astronomical sum of money and has claimed several lives.

But now, instead of a four-hour crossing which was often made dangerous by storms and typhoons, today's passengers travel at 110km/h *68mph* and complete their journey in just two hours.

Sky-scraper (1885)

The sky-scraper was invented in **1885** in Chicago by the engineer and architect **William Le Baron Jenney**. The upward expansion of the town had begun in the 1850s, principally as a means of escape from the water which transformed the roads into quagmires. But it was perhaps also the fear of fire (Chicago had been devastated by one of the greatest fires in history in 1871) and the necessity to build quickly and high which persuaded architects to replace timbers with a steel backbone which was light, strong and solid. It was thus that William Le Baron Jenney devised the internal structural skeleton which bore the weight of the entire building; the external wall had nothing to support.

The first sky-scraper, the Home Insurance, had only ten floors (two were subsequently added). One of the most famous is the Empire State Building in New York City (architects Shreve, Lamb and Harmon), which was

MACHINE TOOLS

Type	Date	Inventor	Country	Characteristics
Wood-turning	1900 BC	—	Egypt	This is the first machine tool that we know of. The drilling machine is probably contemporary.
Planing machine	1751	N. Focq	France	Invented for planing iron, it was superseded by a tool made by the French locksmith Caillon in 1805.
Planing machine	1835	Joseph Whitworth	UK	Improved the previous models.
Slide lathe	c.1751	J. de Vaucanson	France	Tool used for the manufacture of loom parts.
Reaming machine	1775	John Wilkinson	UK	Polishes and adjusts the diameter of a cylinder while it is being drilled.
Hydraulic press	1796	Joseph Bramah	UK	Provides great pressure which can be applied progressively.
Precision lathe	1797	Henry Maudslay	UK	This type of lathe is one of the oldest and most significant of machine tools.
Circular saw	1799	A. C. Albert	France	The patent for this tool was, however, not granted to this inventor.
Circular saw	1816	A. Brunet and J. J. Cochot	France	Circular saw with tempered steel teeth.
Milling machine	1818	Eli Whitney	USA	Also invented the cotton gin in 1792.
Filing machine	1826	James Nasmyth	UK	Replaced chisel work.
Steam power hammer	1839	James Nasmyth	UK	It was used to forge a drive shaft for the steamship *Great Britain*.
Grinding machine	c.1840	inventor not known	UK	In 1842 the Frenchman Malbec built a grinding tool by using quartz and a rubber compound.
Steam roller	1859	Louis Lemoine	France	A very important invention used in road-building.
Hammer-drill	1861	G. Sommeiller	France	Invented during the construction of the Mont-Cenis tunnel.

The Canary Wharf Tower in London's Docklands is the UK's tallest sky-scraper.

Originally built to last 20 years, the tower was due to be dismantled in 1910 but its scientific role saved it from destruction: the tower held laboratories for the study of astronomy, biology, meteorology and atmospheric pollution, plus radio and television transmitters.

In 1964 it was classified as a historic monument and in its centenary year it attracted over 5½ million visitors.

Steel (antiquity)

Since antiquity certain blacksmiths – notably among the Hittites – have produced tools and weapons from iron mixed with small quantities of carbon. In 18th century England ironfounders, led by **Abraham Darby**, produced small amounts of steel. But it was the discovery of a direct conversion process by **Sir Henry Bessemer** (1813–98) that paved the way towards industrial production of steel.

Stainless steel (c.1912)

Stainless steel was developed between 1903 and **1912** thanks to the simultaneous efforts of Harry Brearly in Britain, F. M. Buckett in America, and Benno Strauss and Edward Maurer in Germany.

Macadam (1815)

Macadam was invented by a Scotsman, **John McAdam** (1756–1836), in **1815**.

At the end of the 18th century the state of European roads was appalling as they had not been renewed since the Middle Ages.

Born in Ayr, Scotland, John McAdam had made his fortune in the United States. On returning to Scotland he started, at his own expense, a series of studies on road surfaces. In 1815 he was appointed Surveyor General of Bristol roads, and was at last able to put his theories into practice. He created a road surface made from crushed stones and sand compacted by road-rollers. Although the name still exists, the McAdam road surfacing

opened on 1 May 1931. For a long time it was the highest in the world at 381m *1250ft*, with 102 floors. Its summit had been planned as an embarkation point for airships.

Tallest sky-scraper

The tallest is the Sears Tower in Chicago which has 110 floors and is 443m *1453ft* high – 475.10m *1558ft* if one includes the antenna. In 1990 Canary Wharf replaced the National Westminster Tower as the tallest building in Britain. It is 244m *800ft* high.

Materials

Iron (2nd millennium BC)

The so-called Iron Age marks the period when iron replaced the use of bronze towards the end of the **2nd millennium BC**. The discovery of iron was, however, made much earlier. A recent translation of a text from the Fayoum region shows that the Egyptians were capable of extracting iron ore some 3500 years BC, but the technique used was rather rudimentary.

The use of iron was developed in Asia Minor (Mesopotamia). It was introduced into Greece towards 1200 BC, where it permitted the growth of architecture: buildings could be made with blocks of stone joined by metal bolts. Iron also allowed beams of great length to be constructed because metal girders spread weight evenly. The Propylaea of the Acropolis in Athens are a magnificent example of this.

But the use of iron in architecture is mainly a 19th century creation. Some important examples of the style include the Coal Exchange in London (1847), the domed Reading Room of the British Museum and the Crystal Palace.

Eiffel Tower (1889)

The Eiffel Tower was built by the engineer **Gustave Eiffel** with the help of Maurice Koelchin, Emile Nouguier and the architect Stephen Sauvestre who was responsible for its decoration. It is a prime example of metal architecture and was inaugurated on **31 March 1889**.

Originally 312.27m *1025ft* high (now 320.75m *1052ft* including transmitters at the top), the tower's steelwork weighed 7340 tonnes, bringing its total weight to 9700 tonnes (inclusive of all installations). Over the years this load was increased to 11440 tonnes but between 1981 and 1983 a load reduction programme bought the total weight down to 10000 tonnes and eventually, with the replacement of the third lift, to 9000 tonnes.

Nineteenth-century sensibilities were somewhat troubled by the smell that emanated during the production of tarmaced pavements. However, the benefits in the long run meant that the idea caught on.

This picture clearly shows the effect of absorbent road surfacing in reducing standing water.

system has been almost completely abandoned. Nowadays, mixtures of cement, cinders or slag are used. Tar is no longer used either, being replaced by asphalt.

Absorbent road surfacing (1983)

The latest innovation in motorway surfaces is an absorbent surfacing which acts like blotting paper when it rains. No more slippery roads, no more danger of aquaplaning, no more fine spray reducing visibility. Hence fewer accidents. This process sometimes uses crushed old tyres mixed with the asphalt. The pioneer in this surfacing is a French company, **Beugnet**, who developed Drainochape, perfected in **1983**. This is already used at accident 'black spots' on a number of French motorways, and by 1995 the whole length of the Autoroute du Nord will be surfaced with it.

Fibreglass (1836)

Contrary to popular belief, fibreglass is already an old invention. In **1836** a Frenchman, **Ignace Dubus-Bonnel**, deposited a patent for the 'weaving of glass, pure or mixed with silk, wool, cotton or linen, and made pliable by steam'. He also included a sample with his patent request, woven on a Jacquard loom. He could thus produce imitation gold or silver brocades by combining silk with a weft of glass fibres which had been coloured with metal particles. Dubus-Bonnel's fabrics won him prizes at the 1839 Paris Exhibition, and the inventor produced the draperies which decorated the hearse used for the reburial of Napoleon's ashes at the Invalides in 1840.

Despite its success on that occasion, the new fibre was subsequently forgotten, probably because of the high costs of production, and would only reappear around 1950.

Currently, most composite materials are made lighter and stronger by the addition of fibreglass. Its uses vary from car bumpers and bonnets, to rocket engine parts, to the masts of surfboards. Some 300 000 objects are today manufactured with fibreglass.

Breeze blocks (1846)

To make it possible to build a wall by simple assembly, with bricks placed rapidly and continuously, the Frenchman **Jean-Aimé Balan** developed a system of hollow blocks made of brick or hydrated sulphate of lime mortar which he patented on **2 February 1846**. This invention opened the way for the breeze blocks which we use today.

Corrugated iron (1853)

From the 18th century painted sheets of metal and tin were used for the roofs of baroque churches. But they rusted easily and lacked rigidity. On **2 September 1853** the Frenchman **Pierre Carpentier** took out a patent for a 'machine to rib galvanised metal sheets'. He had invented corrugated iron and went on to exhibit it at the Paris World Fair in 1855. The galvanisation process, perfected earlier (1837) by Sorel, another Frenchman, provided excellent protection against rust and made it possible to produce very cheaply metal structures and roofs that could resist bad weather.

Carbon fibres (1880)

The first carbon fibre was obtained by calcining a bamboo stalk. This was done by the American **Thomas Edison** who used the fibre as a filament for his glow-lamp in **1880**.

The fibre currently used for the manufacture of composite material was invented in Japan by A. Shindo in 1961 and was later perfected, also in Japan, in 1969. This fibre is obtained by burning very pure polyacrylonitrile fibres in a vacuum. The resulting fibre is 15 times tougher than the best steel, weight for weight. Its principal applications are in sport and aeronautical engineering.

Prefabricated panels (1888)

On **12 December 1888** Frenchman **Georges Espitallier** patented the first prefabricated panels: standard size units made of varnished compressed cardboard and slag-wool. This wool is derived from blast-furnace slag and was developed by the Welshman Edward Parry.

The idea of prefabrication was not however completely new: the Crystal Palace, built in 1851 for the Great Exhibition, was a gigantic prefabricated conservatory which was designed by British engineer and architect Sir Joseph Paxton (1801–65), a pioneer of iron architecture. It took six months to assemble the parts which came from a number of different factories.

Composite materials

Composite materials are made from two or more elements which have complementary properties: often one material withstands traction and the other compression. These compounds have been used for centuries: the first one was probably daub, a mixture of hay and mud. Reinforced concrete was the first modern composite material.

The first very high performance composites were produced in 1964 but have only

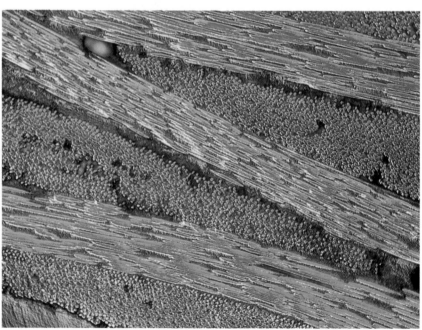

A light micrograph of glass fibres in a polypropylene matrix. Polypropylene is a tough, flexible and synthetic material which becomes soft when heated and hardens on recooling.

had industrial applications since 1970. In 1972 aramide fibre was created by Du Pont. It is lighter and tougher than carbon fibre but may soon be replaced by an even stronger polythene fibre developed by the Dutch manufacturer DSM (1984). Metallurgists have also discovered the benefits of reinforcing metals with carbon fibres.

Besides these spectacular 'super' materials which are used only in small quantities (a few thousand tonnes per year), numerous low cost composite materials are also being developed. The most recent of these are FITs which appeared in 1984. These are thermoplastics reinforced with long fibres. The resulting material is very strong and easy to manipulate.

Carbon-carbon and ceramic-ceramic

There are two main groups of so-called thermostructural materials: carbon-carbons which are composed of carbon material covered by carbon fibres and of which Carbone Industrie, a subsidiary of the company SEP (Société Européenne de Propulsion) is the second largest manufacturer in the world. The second group is made of composite materials based on a ceramic matrix (ceramic-ceramic and ceramic-carbon). These were developed by SEP in 1981 and their licence was sold to the American company Du Pont in 1987.

Unique plants have been built to manufacture these materials which are used in fields that range from space research to medicine. Some types of biocompatible carbon compounds are excellent as bony artificial materials for use in surgery.

Concrete

Mortars (2nd century BC)

Lime has been known to man since antiquity, but lime mortars – used to bind stones together – appeared only around the **2nd century BC** when the Romans began adding volcanic ash to lime to produce a more resistant concrete. It was called pozzolana.

Hydraulic cement (1756)

Medieval builders seem to have lost the Roman recipe for making mortars. Their own were of poor quality until the 12th century, when some improvements were made.

Cement was only re-invented in the middle of the 18th century when, in **1756**, the English engineer **John Smeaton** rediscovered its principle: the presence of clay in limestone. And, 30 years later, the furnace masters Parker and Wyatts perfected a new cement by burning nodules of clayey limestone.

Portland cement (1824)

In 1824 a mason from Leeds, **Joseph Aspdin**, patented Portland cement, so called because it was made by burning a mixture of clay and chalk the colour of Portland stone.

Reinforced concrete (1892)

The non-combustibility of concrete was used by the French engineer **François Hennebique** as a means of fire prevention; this had also been a major factor in the development of iron architecture. He developed a concrete slab

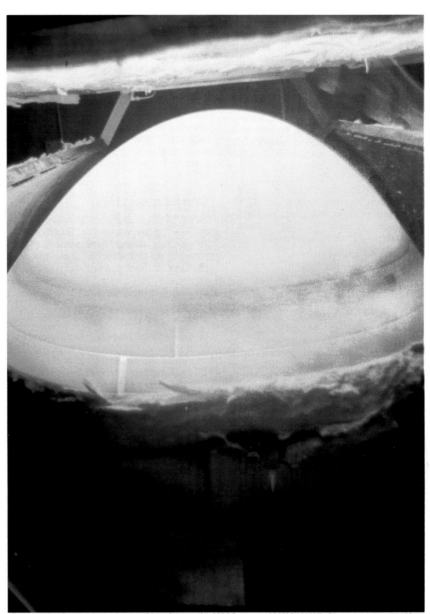

A space shuttle nose cone is tested in a furnace by NASA at over 1000°C 1800°F. The cone is made of a reusable carbon composite constructed out of layers of graphite fibre cloth in a carbon binder with a coating of silicon carbide to ensure that it can withstand the heat on re-entry.

This house was designed by David George and is built entirely from plastic materials, from the joints to the windows, and weighs 23 tonnes. It cost $3 million to build.

and later a monolithic structure similar to timber. These inventions, patented in 1892, led to a widespread use of reinforced concrete and opened new perspectives in architecture.

Cast-iron fibre (1987)

In 1987 the Pont-à-Mousson Research Centre in France launched a new substance designed to reinforce concrete and mortar. It is manufactured from amorphous (i.e. non-crystalline) metallic strips, and is known as Fibraflex. This new fibre is very light, very supple and very strong. A common application today is to reinforce concrete used for the restoration of major constructions such as aqueducts. Research is in hand to extend its use to the manufacture of very thin prefabricated elements.

Glass

The origins of glass

According to the Roman naturalist Pliny the Elder (AD 23–79), glass (or glazing, to be precise) was discovered accidentally by sailors. An Egyptian ship laden with natron (the Egyptians used it – as they did asphalt – to preserve their mummies) ran aground on a Phoenician beach. Unable to find any stones on which to place their cooking pot, the sailors used two blocks of natron. The heat from the fire caused the natron to combine with the sand (silica) on the beach, and thus by happy chance they had discovered glass.

The oldest surviving piece of glass was made during the reign of the Pharaoh Amenophis I between 1557 and 1530 BC. At the time, glass was used for ornamental objects or receptacles, which were sculpted from glass blocks.

Around 300 BC in Alexandria the technique was refined thanks to the invention of moulded glass, by which molten glass was poured into a mould.

Glass-blowing (1st century BC)

The great innovation which was to make glass production available cheaply was glass-blowing, discovered in the 1st century BC. The technique of blown glass (whose composition is very similar to that of modern soda/lime glass) was probably perfected in Syria, but it was the Romans who spread it throughout their empire and beyond.

Venetian glass (10th to 15th centuries)

There were glass-makers in Venice as early as the end of the 10th century, and in 1271 the profession gave itself a statute. The glass-makers were obliged to work on the island of Murano because of the pollution caused by their craft. This isolation helped to protect the secret of the glass-blowers' craft; indeed, the craftsmen were not allowed to leave the country. The invention of Venetian glass is attributed to a glass-maker called Beroverio in 1463.

Crystal glass (1674)

Industrial production of crystal glass was developed by glass-makers in England in the 17th century. George Ravenscroft took out a patent in 1674. Crystal had previously been produced by Venetian craftsmen and by the Bohemians (16th century) whose crystal was brighter than the Venetians'.

Pyrex (1884)

In Germany in 1884 Carl Zeiss invented a glass that contained boracic acid and silica and which was extremely resistant to heat. In 1913 J. T. Littleton of the American company Corning Glass had the idea of using the glass for crockery. C. Sullivan and W. C. Taylor carried out research which led to the development of Pyrex in 1915.

Wired glass (1893)

In 1893 the Frenchman Léon Appert opened the way to the fabrication of wired plate glass. Around 1910 two engineers, completely unknown to each other, simultaneously developed plate glass: Emile Fourcault in Belgium and Irving Colburn in America. In 1952 Alistair Pilkington developed a manufacturing method that was much cheaper than the preceding ones: a layer of molten glass was poured onto a layer of molten tin to produce a perfectly smooth and shiny glass.

Laminated glass (1909)

In 1903 the French chemist Edward Benedictus began research on laminated glass and patented his invention in 1909. The glass was commercialised in 1920 and was first used for car windscreens. Some laminated glass is resistant even to shots from automatic weapons.

Float glass (1958)

This was invented in 1958 by Sir Alistair Pilkington. The production process is still a secret even though patents have been ceded to other manufacturers. The glass has many applications: car windscreens and glass walls, for example. The latter are made from Kappafloat and Planar, 'energetic' glasses which let solar heat in and prevent internal energy from escaping. Extra-thin float glass is being developed for use in optics, photography and aerospace.

It is thanks to float glass that glassmaking, which for a long time was a traditional activity, has become a heavy industry. Float glass is produced in a giant oven capable of producing between 500 and 600 tonnes of glass a day. There are 110 such ovens in the world, 33 of which are in Europe.

Glass without fluoride (1989)

Fluoride facilitates the fusion of glass. Although fluoride fumes in the air are not dangerous for people, they are a threat to coniferous trees. To protect the forest adjacent to its factory in Savoie, Saint-Gobain has developed a manufacturing process in which the use of fluoride is completely eliminated.

Priva-lite (1990)

Launched at the beginning of 1990 by the Belgian company Saint-Roch, Priva-lite glass is a layered glass which is able to become opaque and then transparent again at the press of a button. It is made up of two panes of glass and a film of Taliq Liquid Cristal (an American invention): when the switch is thrown the crystals are activated and they align themselves in such a way that the glass becomes transparent. When at rest, the crystals return to their positions and the glass becomes opaque again.

Liquid crystals enable Priva-lite to become opaque or transparent at the touch of a button.

Clocks and watches

Origins (3rd millennium BC)

The first 'clock', the gnomon, was invented in the **3rd millennium BC** and has been attributed to both the Chinese and the Chaldeans. The gnomon was the precursor of the sundial, invented, according to some sources, by the Greek **Anaximander** of Miletus in the **6th century BC**, and, according to others, by the Chinese and the Egyptians at a much earlier date.

The first artificial clock, the water clock or clepsydra, appeared at about the same time. The Egyptians in 3000 BC used the clepsydra alongside the sundial.

The hourglass

The hourglass, symbol of the passing of time, is also said to have been invented by the Chinese, although the exact date is not known. The first mention of an hourglass is found in a play by Baton, an Athenian comic poet of the 3rd century BC.

Candle clock

In the early centuries AD the Byzantines introduced candle clocks. Candles were marked at regular intervals and, as they burned lower, it was possible to calculate how much time had passed by the number of marks that remained.

Weight-driven and pendulum clocks

Gerbert d'Aurillac (c.938–1003), who became Pope Sylvester II in 999, is said to be the inventor of the weight-driven clock. The Dutch astronomer **Christiaan Huygens** invented the pendulum clock in **1657**. The first portable spring-driven clock was made by the Florentine architect **Brunelleschi** (1377–1446) in **1410**. This was the earliest domestic clock.

Escapement (725)

It seems that the first escapement mechanism was invented by a Chinese **I. Hsing** in **725**. The escapement is one of the most important parts of a timepiece: it controls the transfer of energy from the motor to the hands, and it provides the oscillator with energy which compensates for that lost through friction. The most commonly used kind of escapement nowadays consists of toothed wheels and an anchor, invented by the Frenchman L. Perron in 1798.

Spiral spring (1675)

In 1675 the Dutchman **Christiaan Huygens** (1629–95) invented the balance wheel and spiral spring oscillator. The introduction of the spiral spring into watch design had an effect analogous to that of the pendulum into clocks – another of Huygens' innovations, dating from 1657.

Chronometer (1736)

A watchmaker and astronomer **George Graham** (1673–1751) first used the term chronometer as applied to a small portable

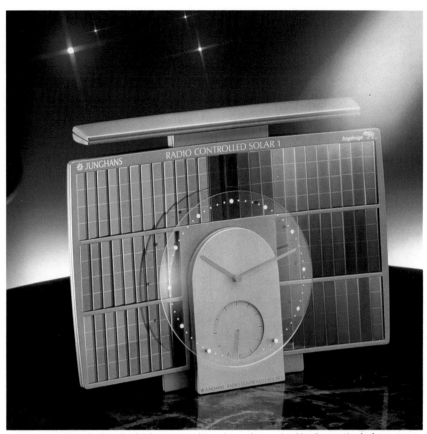

This solar-powered clock is absolutely accurate; it receives pulses emitted by the atomic clock at Braunschweig in Germany.

pendulum. In **1736** John Harrison (1693–1776), another English watchmaker, made the first naval chronometer, in wood, and perfected it in 1761. Accurate time-keeping was necessary on the seas so as to enable sailors to calculate the correct longitude. Harrison's spring-driven chronometer was tested by Captain James Cook on his voyages from 1768.

Winder (1755)

In **1755** the French author **Beaumarchais** invented a watch for Madame de Pompadour that could be wound without a key. She could turn a ring mounted on the face with her fingernail. It was not until 1842 however that the Swiss A. Philippe succeeded in producing a mechanism which allowed the watch to be wound and the hands to be repositioned too. The self-winding watch was invented by a French watch-maker A. L. Perrelet in 1775. The first self-winding wrist watches were patented by H. Cutte and J. Harwood in 1924.

Electric clock (1840)

The electric clock was perfected in **1840** by the Scotsman **Alexander Bain**. At the same time, the English physicist Sir Charles Wheatstone (1802–75) invented electric distribution of time from a so-called mother clock.

Alarm clock (1847)

The first modern alarm clock was invented by the French clock-maker **Antoine Redier** (1817–92) in **1847**. The Braun Voice Control was the first alarm clock to stop ringing at the sound of a voice. It appeared in 1985.

Quartz clock (1920)

Work on the use of quartz as a resonator in clocks began in **1920**, but it was not until 1929 that the American clockmaker **Warren Alvin Marrison** perfected the first clock with a resonator of this type. Quartz watches were commercialised for the first time in 1969 by Seiko. In 1988 there was a major change in the way quartz watches work: the battery was replaced by a tiny dynamo which creates energy to compensate for that consumed. Two companies are behind this development: Seiko, who have been working on the project since 1973, and the French company Jean d'Eve.

Waterproof watch (1926)

In **1926 Hans Wilsdorf** and his Rolex team developed the first completely waterproof watch case. In 1927 Wilsdorf gave an Oyster watch to Mercedes Gleitz, a typist from London, who swam the Channel with it strapped to her wrist.

Atomic clock (1948)

The principle of the atomic clock was laid down by the American chemist **Willard F. Libby** (1908–80), winner of a Nobel Prize for Chemistry in 1960. An atomic clock uses the energy changes within atoms to produce extremely regular waves of electromagnetic radiation.

Talking watch (1987)

The Voice-Master VX-2 replies when its

owner asks the time. But it can also obey 27 different commands once they have been put into the memory: credit card number, telephone number, and so on. Designed by **Citizen** and marketed in Japan in **November 1987**, it has been generally available since 1988.

Aviation chronograph (1990)

An innovation from **Seiko** for pilots: with its four motors, this new chronograph is equipped with navigational aids such as systems for calculating flight time, speed, distance, altitude, climbing speed, etc. It has a double time zone and is accurate to two-tenths of a second.

Metallurgy

Etruscan furnace (7th century BC)

The Etruscans have left us eloquent testimony of their metallurgical techniques. Layers of iron ore and of charcoal were piled over a hollow to a height of about 2m *6ft*. The whole thing was then covered with clayey mud and a flue was made at the top of the dome. Holes were pierced lower down the dome to ensure a good draught. When the smelting was complete, the furnace was demolished and the metal retrieved from the process was then worked by a blacksmith.

Blast furnace (13th century)

The antecedents of blast furnaces date from the **13th century**. In the 14th century waterwheels were used to work bellows. The inventor of the modern blast furnace was **Abraham Darby** (1711–63), an iron-master from Coalbrookdale. Pig-iron (an alloy of iron and at least 2.5 percent carbon) can be obtained directly from iron ore in a modern blast furnace. The second step forward was made by a British engineer born in Germany, Karl Wilhelm von Siemens (1823–83), who in 1857 had the idea of using the heat from the gases inside the furnace to heat the air sent in by the bellows. The open-hearth process was patented in 1858. Since the 1950s iron ore has been crushed into pellets before being placed in the furnace.

METALLURGY: A STRANGE INVENTION

It is highly probable that metallurgy was invented purely by chance. The most likely explanation would appear to be that when prehistoric man discovered fire, which, according to the most recent discoveries made in Africa, he did more than a million years ago, he also discovered traces of the most easily smelted metals in the ashes of his hearth. It was in such a way that extractive or chemical metallurgy was 'invented'. Copper, lead and pewter were among the first metals to be extracted from their ores, nearly 6000 years ago. Bronze, an alloy of copper and pewter, was known to the Egyptians in 3700 BC. The Chinese are thought to have been using iron in at least 2000 BC, after previously using cast iron for a very long period.

In order to produce iron, cast iron must undergo a chemical process to eliminate the carbon which makes it brittle. It was not until 1784 that it became possible to produce large quantities of iron industrially by means of the process known as puddling, invented by the English manufacturer, Henry Cort.

In 1856 the English engineer and inventor Sir Henry Bessemer (1813–98) invented the refractory-lined furnace which enabled good quality steel to be produced.

Another step forward was made in 1878 when electrometallurgy was discovered simultaneously by a Frenchman, Paul-Louis Héroult, and an American chemist, Charles Martin Hall. This in turn enabled aluminium, magnesium, sodium and calcium metallurgy to be developed.

Coke (1735)

The metallurgist **Abraham Darby** was the first to use coke as a fuel in blast furnaces in **1735**. Coke is obtained by heating coal in a confined space at between 900° and 1150°C *1650°F and 2100°F*.

Bessemer converter (1856)

Henry Bessemer (1813–98) perfected a converter in **1856** that allowed him to remove the carbon from pig-iron and to produce steel of a relatively good quality. This discovery, perfected at Bessemer's own cutlery factory in Sheffield, was the basis of the rise of the steel industry.

Thomas converter (1876)

The British inventor **Sydney Gilchrist Thomas** (1850–85) improved the Bessemer process in **1876**, making it possible to refine the phosphoric pig-iron and to eliminate the various other impurities thanks to a basic lining of the converters.

The Bessemer and Thomas processes are virtually obsolete today. They have been replaced by new processes based on the LD (Linz-Donawitz) process developed after the last war by Austrian engineers. It consists of refining the pig-iron with pure oxygen, introduced via a vertical blast pipe.

Electric furnace (1900)

The melting of scrap-iron in an electric furnace was made possible by the invention of the arc furnace by the Frenchman **Paul Héroult** (1863–1914). The first industrial application took place on **9 October 1900**. The process makes it possible to produce quality steel and currently provides 26 percent of the world's steel.

Welding (4th millennium BC)

Heterogeneous welding, which enables two pieces of different types of metal to be joined together, dates back to about 3500 BC. Autogeneous welding is more recent, dating from about 1500 BC. Until the end of the 19th century the only method of welding iron and steel was by forging. In 1877 the American engineer and inventor Elihu Thomson

Refined steel has been produced by the process of continuous casting since the 1960s. This picture shows the cold cages where the castings are cooled.

The hi-tech approach to steel-making can be seen in this control room of a modern works. The days when ingot moulds were necessary are long since gone.

A FIRE-RESISTANT TEXTILE

A small French company, La Société SAB, has developed an extraordinary textile, a world first, which they revealed at the beginning of 1990. The flame-resistant Montségur textile is capable of neutralising up to 90 percent of the residual heat-flow of a fire. During trials this textile was used to arrest the progress of a simulated forest fire, a vertical firescreen 10m *32ft* long and 5m *16ft* high resisted the fire without being damaged. Owing to the semi-transparency of this material, it is possible to watch the progress of the fire through the screen and choose when to intervene. This invention was the brain-child of Jo Rousset, specialist in heuristics, in 1989.

invented resistance welding. In 1807 the Englishman Sir Humphry Davy (1778–1829) invented the electric or carbon arc. In 1885 Bernados invented the carbon arc torch which enabled a filler metal to be used in welding. In 1890 the Russian Nikolai Gavrilovich Slavianov developed the process of arc welding with a consumable electrode and in 1904 Kjeliberg invented the coated electrode. But it was not until 1920 that arc welding became widely used.

Today electron beam welding is being used much more extensively. This was a process developed in 1954 by M. Stohr, an engineer at the Saclay Centre for Nuclear Research. Since 1970 laser welding has also become more common.

Textiles

Origins (prehistoric)

The art of weaving, like that of spinning, goes back to prehistoric times. Although until the end of the 19th century only the wooden hand-loom was known, the idea of mechanising the weaving loom led to a number of further inventions.

In 1606 the Frenchman **C. Dangon** created the *cassin*, a device which made it possible to activate the healds via a series of pulleys. This system allowed the weaving of larger patterns. In 1725 the Frenchman **B. Bouchon** improved on Dangon's invention by substituting for the looped string an endless band of perforated paper by which the simples for any shed could be selected, thus making it possible to set aside a pattern and take it up again. **H. Falcon** perfected the system in 1728, using perforated cards to create the pattern.

Mechanical loom (1785)

The first mechanical loom was invented by the Englishman **Edmund Cartwright** (1743–1823) in 1785. Previously, in 1775, the Frenchman Jacques de Vaucanson (1709–92), a brilliant builder of automatic machines, tried

		SPINNING	
Type	Date	Characteristics	
Spindle	antiquity	Probably the first tool used to spin wool and linen.	
Spinning wheel	16th century	Seems to have originated in the Middle East. It was introduced into Europe towards the beginning of the 16th century.	
Flying shuttle	1733	The Lancashire weaver John Kay developed this spinning machine which was twice as efficient as previous models. Up to then, it had taken two people to weave a wide cloth as the shuttle had to be thrown from one side of the frame to the other. Kay's device returned the shuttle automatically. As a result, the quality of the fabric was improved and a single weaver could work on a broad cloth. This saved on labour costs and doubled productivity	
Spinning jenny	1768	Invented by the Lancashire mechanic Thomas Higgs who named it after one of his daughters, and perfected by James Hargreaves.	
Water-frame	1769	Higgs also invented the water-frame in 1769 which used hydraulic energy. The Preston man Richard Arkwright appropriated this invention and became rich at Higgs' expense. The machine made continuous spinning possible and is the basis for modern mechanical spinning.	
Mule jenny	1779	This was invented by Samuel Crompton to solve the problems associated with spinning cotton. The machine combined features from Arkwright's and Hargreaves' machines: it spun cotton into yarn and then wound the yarn onto spindles.	
Ring throstle	1828	The ring throstle was invented by J. Thorpe and perfected in 1833 by W. Mason. It is still the most commonly used machine for spinning wool, combed cotton and synthetic fibres.	

Microfibre fabrics are too close-knit to allow water through and are therefore waterproof, but air can circulate and so permit perspiration.

to apply a complex automatic action using a perforated cylinder to the weaving loom. Unfortunately, the capacity of this cylinder was too limited. Cartwright's invention, which was improved in 1786, is the basis for present-day looms.

Jacquard loom (1804)

In 1804 in Lyons the Frenchman **Jean-Marie Jacquard** (1752–1834) invented a loom for weaving brocade fabrics and various other machines for weaving and for making fishing nets. Jacquard managed cleverly to combine Falcon and Vaucanson's devices. Jacquard did not take out a patent for this invention, but it made his name. Traditional weavers' looms still use the Jacquard cards to alternate different types of thread and to vary the interlacing of the fibres.

Automatic loom (1822)

In 1822 the Englishman **R. Roberts** invented a fully automatic loom, which was soon adopted throughout Europe. It was later perfected by various technicians and builders, who developed different mechanisms to accommodate more healds. In 1890 the American **J. H. Northrop** designed the automatic loom which, with a few adjustments, is still used today in the textile industry.

Breathing fabric

Thanks to processes patented in Japan synthetic fibres can now be produced that measure less than ten micrometers in diameter: that is to say, approximately three times finer than the fibres used in conventional textiles. The advantages of microfibre fabrics are that their threads are woven together so tightly that they prevent molecules of water from seeping in, but are loose enough to let vapour through. In other words, these fabrics are totally waterproof – which is not the case for most coated or treated fabrics – and they allow perspiration to evaporate.

Biotextiles

The new age in which fibres and fabrics can be made by 'grafting' molecules onto conventional (natural or synthetic) materials has arrived. The results can range from fluoride-activated cottons which are permanently waterproof; fabrics in elastomer-encased fibres which remain crease-free; synthetic textiles which are self-sterilising with antibacterial drugs; fabrics that filter highly selectively.

Furthermore, a number of traditional operations such as drying and fabric preparation can be achieved by the use of these techniques. One of the methods uses particle radiation: electrons penetrate synthetic material and ionise polymeric molecules which separate and give rise to free radicals which are then bound to the desired molecules.

New technology

Optical fibres (1955)

Optical fibres were invented in 1955 by the English professor **Narinder S. Kapany**. They have many applications, notably in the transmission of information (telex, television cables) and in medicine (endoscopes). They are also used in lasers. Their range, their insensibility to parasites and their capacity are vastly superior to those of coaxial cables. They enable the simultaneous transmission of the voice, images (animated or still) and computer signals. Two types of fibre coexist: the multimode fibre (functioning with several electromagnetic modes), which has been on trial since 1986 on the French telephone network, and the monomode fibre, which provides improved quality with a greater output.

Materials that remember (1960s)

Made from special alloys these amazing materials which 'remember' (originally metals but now also plastics) allow the creation of variable shape objects. Thanks to their so-called memory, these materials resume the shape they were first given whenever the

KNITTING MACHINES

Type	Date	Inventor
Stocking frame	1589	William Lee invented the first loom for making stockings. After a number of attempts, he managed to open a mill in Nottingham with the help of his associate, Aston. This showed that his machine could produce materials as fine as silk and ten times faster than by hand.
Rip-stop knitting	1775	This invention is attributed to the British man Crane and allowed the manufacture of ladder-proof knitwear. The first patent covering this type of knitting was not filed until 16 years later by Dawson, another Briton.
Circular loom	1798	Developed by the Frenchman Decroix for the manufacture of seamless stockings. Despite its origins, the loom was first used in England in 1806 where it was introduced by Sir Marc Isambard Brunel (1769–1849).
Power loom	1832	A mill using a rectilinear loom (producing four garments at a time) powered by hydraulic energy was opened in the US by E. Egberts and Timothy Bally in 1832. However, the use of non-human energy had previously been tried in England in 1818. In 1838 a hosiery factory using steam-powered looms was opened by the Briton John Button in Germantown (USA).
Rectilinear shuttle loom	1857	It was successively perfected by the Briton Luke Burton in 1857, by Arthur Paget in 1861 and by William Cotton in 1863 (patent for a loom which produced between two and 12 stockings at a time).
Home knitting machines	1860	They appeared during the 1860s with the machines produced by the Britons John Aiken and Herrick around 1865.

This picture shows the spectacular display created by a spray of optical fibres; they were invented by Narinder S. Kapany in 1955.

temperature at which they were moulded is recreated. This phenomenon had been observed for the first time in 1932 by American researchers, but had remained a scientific curiosity for many years with no obvious industrial application.

In 1960 **William Buehler**, an engineer at the Naval Ordnance Laboratory of White Oak (USA), developed nitinol, a nickel/titanium alloy, capable of changing shape according to the temperature. Since then, these alloys have been developed in the fields of space and aeronautics. In 1969 Raychem developed the first nickel/titanium circuit joints for the Gruman F14 fighter plane. The shape-memory alloys are now enjoying a spectacular breakthrough in many fields: a patent is deposited every two days. The Japanese firm Walcoal has, since 1985, sold a flat bra which, once worn, adapts to the body's shape thanks to an underwire in the memorising alloy, and the heat of the body.

Memory plastics

It would seem that plastic with a memory, an invention being developed by the Japanese group Nippon Zeon, will become the new super-material of the future. It has the same properties as the metal alloys but, thanks to a great molecular mass and to its particular chemical links, it is as elastic as rubber. So, for example, in the future dented car bumpers will reshape themselves when heated to the temperature of manufacture.

Cutting by water jet (1968)

This revolutionary technique invented and patented by the American **Norman Franz** in **1968** has rapidly established itself across the USA. Since the 1970s water jet cutting has been adopted by car manufacturers (at General Motors, a hundred machines cut parts by this method) and was quickly taken up by other industries such as those working with steel, fabrics, chipboard and even minerals. Despite its advantages this process has been slow to establish itself in Europe, although it has been used in Sweden and Germany for a number of years.

The process consists of cutting material with a jet of pure water sometimes mixed with polymers or abrasive substances under a pressure of 2000–4000 bars. Programmed by an optical reader and by a digital console, it allows a variety of substances to be cut with great precision.

Thanks to the possibility of combining several jets, water cutting is neater and more economical than using lasers.

Loegel jet (1984)

Cutting by water jet is also applicable to hard stone such as marble and granite. This technique was perfected in **1984** by a Frenchman from Alsace, **Charles Loegel**, head of the family sandstone quarry in Rotbach, which has been the sole supplier of stone for Strasburg cathedral for many years. In 1986 the Loegel jet was put on the market and is the first system in the world capable of cutting deep into all kinds of rocks.

Biometal (1986)

The United States have pioneered the work on biometals, particularly at the Naval Research Laboratory, since 1979. However, while working on shape-memory alloys in **1986**, **Dai Homma**, vice president of the Toki Corporation of Japan, discovered a true biometal. He found that thin wires (a few tenths of a millimetre in diameter) of a metal with a peculiar crystalline structure contract under direct heat (Joule effect). This type of material could be used to activate robots, thereby making them lighter and greatly simplifying their design.

Solid water (1987)

Aquabloc is a process developed by the Frenchman **Daniel Menant** in 1987. It can take the form of a compressed powder which is sprinkled over an unwanted puddle of water, for example when a bath overflows. In a few minutes, the water turns to solid matter which can then be swept up with a broom. Apart from this purely domestic application, other possible uses include the transportation and storage of solid water to help irrigate underprivileged countries, where it can again be liquified. Daniel Menant has also developed a derivative of his invention for dealing with pollution, as it can help mop up oil slicks.

Anti-noise noise (1988)

An original technology was developed at the acoustics laboratory of the **CNRS** of Marseilles in France by Christian Carmes in **1988**. Based on the principle that a noise has to be heard to be treated, the laboratory has developed a noise-reducing helmet which works by active sound absorption.

Noise passing through the helmet's plastic shell is fed to an electronic device which then treats it and generates a signal which reduces the noise strength. This combination of noise/noise-destructor brings noise levels down by 20 to 40 decibels according to the frequencies.

A similar device has also been developed in the USA by G. B. B. Chaplin who invented this technological paradox. His patents are exploited by Noise Cancellation Technologies. The electronic 'silencer', still at a prototype stage, should find numerous applications in industry for the attenuation (or even the suppression) of engine and machine noise. It should be introduced onto the car market in 1992.

The all-purpose laser

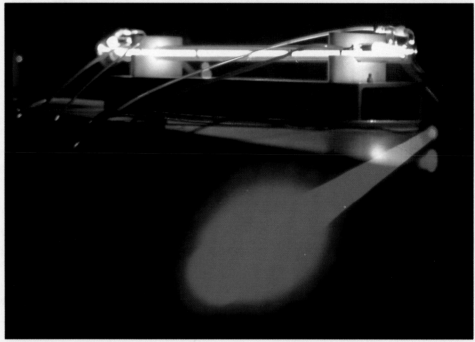

A cutting laser developed by Lectra Systems, the leading French company based in Bordeaux.

In 1917

In 1917 Albert Einstein formulated the principle which was to lead to the invention of the laser. He declared that it was possible to stimulate the emission of electromagnetic radiation by matter by stimulating the electrons of the atoms from which it is composed. This amplification generates a continuous luminous beam, i.e. with a uniform wavelength and particles which are displaced in the same direction.

From maser to laser

In 1954 the Americans J. Gordon, H. J. Zeiger and Charles H. Townes produced the gas maser (Microwave Amplification by Stimulated Emission of Radiation), which gave out an ultra-short wave beam in the radio range.

In 1958 A. L. Schawlow and Charles H. Townes applied the theory to infra-red and optical frequencies. The first light beam amplifier was constructed and tested by Theodore H. Maiman of the Hughes Research Laboratory (California) in 1960.

In the same year, the Soviet physicists N. Bassov and A. Prokhorov produced similar devices. Since then, applied research has won universal recognition for the laser, which now has a current annual market of $3 billion.

The name 'laser'

The name laser (Light Amplification by Stimulated Emission of Radiation) was coined by Richard Gordon Gould, who also invented the gas discharge laser (1957–9), used in particular for compact discs and reading bar codes. It was nearly 30 years (December 1985) before Gould's invention rights for the laser were recognised by the American Supreme Court.

Which type of laser?

Lasers are identified on the basis of whether they use either a material in the solid state (ruby, crystal or chromium with neodymium, yag – yttrium-aluminium-garnet – or silicate dispersed in crystals or glass) which is optically pumped (flash), or a liquid or gaseous medium (helium-neon mixture, argon, carbon dioxide, sulphur dioxide) stimulated by electrical pumping. The diversity of materials can be explained by the need to obtain a beam of variable intensity which has a specific wavelength in relation to the target.

Laser and medicine

The first application of the laser was in 1964, when the ruby laser developed by Maiman was used to treat lesions of the retina. The bistoury-laser (which cuts and cauterises) was invented by D. R. Henriott, E. I. Gordon, D. A. S. Hale and W. Gromnos of Bell Laboratories in the United States, and was in use by 1975.

Since 1976 yag lasers controlled by optical fibres have been used to remove small tumours in the stomach and fatty deposits on the artery walls. Pulsating yag lasers, which give out a high level of power in a very short space of time, were developed in 1979 by Doctor Aaron-Rosa of the Rothschild Foundation and are tending to replace the argon lasers used in optical surgery.

Pulsating devices are also used in conjunction with the endoscope to destroy gallstones and stones in the kidney. After the initial experiments by Doctor Goldman (1968), the sterilising thermic properties of the laser are now used in dental surgery to prevent dental caries, to make incisions into the gum and to seal the enamel.

Other applications

The laser is a universally recognised instrument. There seems to be no limit to its uses. For example:

– *industrial cutting:* first drilling demonstrations by General Electric in 1965

– *detection, range-finding and guidance:* in this field it is the directivity of the laser beam which is used, since lasers in fact describe perfectly straight lines in space and cover large distances owing to their low level of dispersion. This technique has been used in some incredible ways in seismology and astronomy, for example, to measure the distance between the earth and the moon to within 2cm *1in* (Caussol Observatory, 1988).

Seeing by laser

Laser tomography, which makes it possible to see air flows by selectively lighting suspended particles, has moved out of the experimental stage and is being applied in the field of industrial research. In November 1989 it was also announced that a microscope had been developed at the Livermore and Princeton Laboratories (USA) which uses an

X-ray laser and makes it possible to obtain holographic images of the inside of a blood cell.

Cables, CDs and computers

The combination of lasers and optical fibre (as a guidance support) has in particular enabled the transmission capacity of telecommunication networks (new transatlantic cables TAT-8 and 9) to be increased many times over. But it is mainly the results in the field of the high-speed communication (500 Gigahertz) produced by semi-conductor lasers, already in use on the readers of compact discs, which provide the new capacities for the optical light computers currently being developed by IBM and other large manufacturers.

The laser weapon

Several experimental devices, the most famous of which are the American CCLAW, Road Runner and Stingray, have demonstrated their ability to neutralise targets as different as anti-tank missiles, helicopters and armoured vehicles. In 1985 the MIRACL, a 2.2MW deuterium-fluorine laser capable of destroying a target as large as a Titan rocket stage, was developed in the United States by TRW. This was the initial stage in the development of laser anti-missile ballistic missiles which use X-ray or free-electron lasers. These are included in the American SDI programme, which involves Thomson-CSF. At the moment, armies are not using high-powered lasers as weapons, but some, originally designed for range-finding and aiming, would prove to be devastating weapons on the battlefield. The value of the laser weapon lies in its rapid firing capacity and its immediate destructive impact.

The laser and thermonuclear fusion

One current area of research in elemental physics is that of nuclear fusion by laser bombardment of hydrogen isotopes. In order to achieve this, giant lasers have been constructed in the United States (Nova at Livermore), Japan (Gekko) and France (Phébus at Limeil-Valenton). As fusion can only be obtained at temperatures of several million degrees and under pressures of several tens of millions of atmospheres, these devices are designed to produce hyperpowerful impulses over very short periods of time, e.g., for Phébus, 10 terawatts (10 million million watts) in a nanosecond (a billionth of a second).

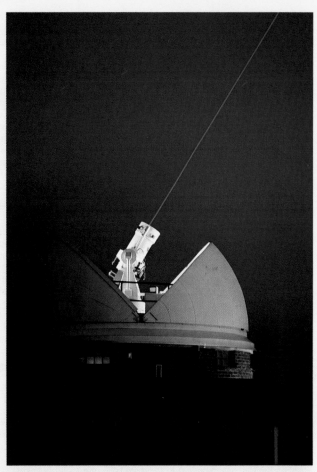

The Satellite Laser Ranging Telescope at Herstmonceux in East Sussex. This telescope can accurately measure the position and distance of a satellite by shining a laser beam at it and recording the reflection.

Earth, Wind and Fire had a spectacular laser show for their concerts. They were one of the most successful bands to emerge from the 1970s disco boom.

Holograms

Holograms (1948)

The hologram (from the Greek *holos*, whole, and *gram*, something written) is a three-dimensional photograph using the interference produced by the superimposition of two laser beams. **Dennis Gabor**, an English physicist of Hungarian origin, discovered the principle of holography in **1948** in the course of his research into electronic microscopy. But it was not until the discovery of the laser that practical applications could be developed.

The Americans E. N. Leith, J. U. Upatnieks and C. W. Stroke from the University of Michigan carried out the first tests in 1963. Since then, holography has developed greatly in the spheres of research, industry and art. The first examples of holography applied to art were achieved by Professor Youri Denisyouk of Moscow, who, towards the end of the 1960s, applied holography to the reproduction of works of art.

Holographic credit card (1984)

In 1984 **Visa** launched an international credit card in the USA which bore a hologram. Besides their aesthetic appeal, holograms reduce the risks of counterfeiting.

Recess holograms (1986)

Thanks to a combination of holography and computing, a team from the Massachusetts Institute of Technology (MIT), directed by **Stephen Benton**, has managed to represent a car in three dimensions. This technique could reduce the design time of a car from five years to 18 months.

Holographic banknote (1988)

On the occasion of the Australian bicentenary the **Commonwealth Reserve Bank** and the **Organisation de Recherche Scientifique et Industrielle** co-operated to launch a new $10 bill by using a new type of hologram which makes it virtually counterfeit-proof. The banknote is made of special plastic sheets and holds a holographic image which changes colour according to the angle of view. The new banknote also has raised marks which makes it easy to identify by touch.

Conoscope (1988)

The result of research begun in 1985 (and made public in **1988**), in collaboration with D. Psaltis, the Conoscope is a holographic camera functioning with natural light. It is the culmination of a simple idea which is also a revolution in three-dimensional imagery. The hologram and the laser have always been indissolubly linked: only this type of coherent artificial beam makes it possible to produce and collect the interference fringes necessary for the creation of a three-dimensional image.

The French scientists **Gabriel Sirat** and **Alain Maruani** from the ENST succeeded in obtaining the same effect by using two beams of natural light dephased by a double refractive crystal. The two beams define a cone in space, hence the name of the device. Since its early applications, the development of the hologram has suffered limitations associated with the use of the laser: taking photos in the dark, the immobility of the subject and the impossibility of digitising the image have contributed to the fact that until now, the animated holographic image has remained a laboratory curiosity. The Conoscope, however, works in broad daylight and produces an image which is accessible to video techniques. And so it is the first-born of the first generation of viable holographic cameras. The three-dimensional film is within its reach.

There are countless other applications: the holographic checking of manufactured articles, the guiding of robots through three-dimensional space and the numbering of objects for computer-aided design, to name but a few examples.

Holographic stamp (1989)

The first holographic stamp was launched in **January 1989** by the Austrian post office. 3 040 000 stamps were issued.

Thierry Vide's holotramic sculptures are inspired by holograms. This sculpture was created for the American company Bendix.

SCIENCE

Mathematics

Number theory

Numeration (3rd millennium BC)

Numbers were first written in the **3rd millennium BC**, as is attested to by the clay tablets discovered in Susa and Uruk (currently Warka in Iraq) and those from Nippur (Babylon, 2200 to 1350 BC). The Babylonian system of numeration is on a base of 60. Our time divisions are a vestige of this. There was no zero; missing units were simply indicated by a space.

The ancient Mayan system was on a base of 20 – the number of fingers and toes. This was a position system and included a final zero which was not an operator.

In the 5th century BC the Greeks used the letters of the alphabet. For units of one thousand, the nine first letters accompanied by an inferior accent to their left were used (α equals 1 and ,α equals 1000). This system, which had no zero, was used for a thousand years. The Hebrews and Arabs adapted this for their own alphabets. Calculations were then made using abacuses. Numbers were represented by pebbles (the word calculation derives from the word *calculus*, meaning pebble).

Modern numeration (5th century)

Around the **5th century AD** decimal position arithmetic appeared in India: it used ten figures from 0 to 9 such as we know today. In 829 the scientist Mohammad Ibn Musa al-Khwârizmî (780–850) published a treatise on algebra in Baghdad in which he adopted this decimal system. A French monk called Gerbert became interested in the Arabic figures during his voyage (980) to Cordoba in Spain, and was able to spread the use of these symbols when he became Pope Sylvester II in April 999. However, it was not until Leonardo Fibonacci, known as Leonard of Pisa, through his *Liber Abaci*, written in 1202, that Arabic numbering began to spread throughout Europe. In 1440, thanks to the invention of

---

FRACTALS

We know that the spatial dimensions of normal geometric objects are always integers. Thus a point has a dimension of zero; a line, or a segment of a line, has a dimension equal to one; a surface element has a dimension equal to two, and so on. Fractals are unusual objects whose dimension, known as the *fractal dimension*, has a non-integer value, for example 4/3 or π. Thus they are objects which are geometrically intermediate between points, lines, surfaces, etc.

Let us take the case of a fractal belonging to a two-dimensional plane, and use a fractal dimension which is bounded between one and two. Such a fractal, which is called a *fractal curve*, occupies (intuitively) 'more space' in the plane than a traditional curve, yet without occupying the entire plane. Fractals in fact have an extremely complex structure with many ramifications and convolutions. Some have regular structures whose features are repeated identically on all scales, and others are completely irregular.

The origin of the notion of fractals dates back to the end of the 19th century. The mathematicians of the time discovered astonishing mathematical objects possessing some of the qualities of fractals. In 1872 Weierstrass built a curve that was continuous but non-differentiable on all its points; and in 1890 Giuseppe Peano obtained a curve which completely filled a square. These results were unexpected and Peano, contemplating his theorem, exclaimed: 'I see it, but I don't believe it!' The first known fractal is probably Georg Cantor's triadic set (1883). It is a fractal with a dimension between zero and one.

It was only in 1919 that Felix Hausdorff invented the fractal dimension. The word 'fractal' itself is recent: it was introduced in 1962 by the Frenchman Benoît Mandelbrot, who suggested that fractals could be useful in the study of natural forms, such as a coastline, for example.

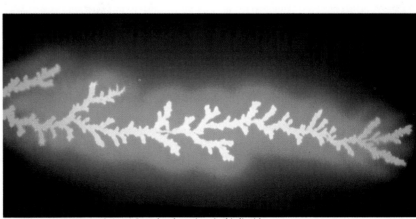

Despite an appearance of chaos, fractal order reigns in this liquid.

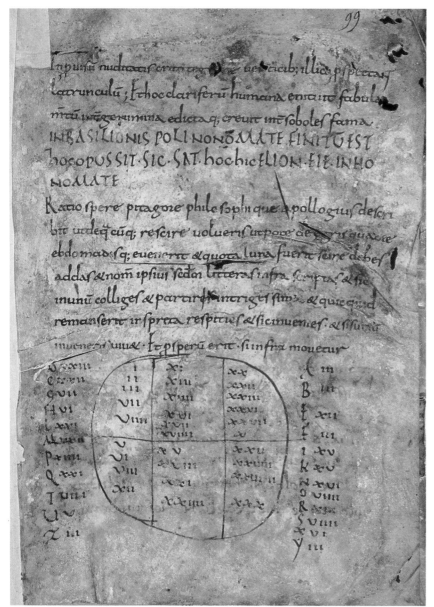

This is part of a manuscript written by the Greek philosopher and mathematician Pythagoras in the 6th century BC.

of base 10 had only been developed for whole numbers. Numbers between whole numbers were expressed as fractions of over the base of 60, which was used for expressing units of time (minutes in the hour) and angles.

The Frenchman **François Viète** declared in **1579** that sixtieths should be replaced by thousandths, hundredths and tenths, and in 1582 the Flemish mathematician and physicist Simon Stevin (1548–1620) suggested using decimal numbers in calculations, but decimals were not widely adopted throughout the 17th century. Stevin also proposed the decimal division of units of measurement. But it was not until the French Revolution that a decimal metric system was established (10 December 1799).

Complex numbers (17th century)

The Italian mathematician **Raphael Bombelli (1526–73)** gave the first definition of complex numbers, which he called 'impossible' or 'imaginary' numbers. He defined these numbers from his study of cubic numbers, and introduced the concept of $\sqrt{-1}$. A complex number is the sum of a real number and an imaginary one e.g. $(a + \sqrt{-1}b)$.

Until 1746 people used these imaginary entities without really knowing how they were structured. In that year, however, the French mathematician Jean Le Rond d'Alembert established their general form $a + b\sqrt{-1}$, assuming the principle of the existence of n roots of an equation of degree n. The Swiss mathematician Leonhard Euler (1707–83) introduced the notation 'i' to designate $\sqrt{-1}$, a notation taken up again by Gauss in 1801.

Transcendental numbers (18th century)

It was in the **18th century** that mathematicians came up with the notion of the transcendental number. We call a number, say $\propto$, transcendental if there does not exist an algebraic equation with rational coefficients with $\propto$ as a root.

In 1844 the French mathematician **Joseph Liouville** gave the first example of a transcendental number. Then in 1873 the Frenchman Charles Hermite showed that 'e' (the base for natural logarithms) was transcendental, and in 1882 the German Ferdinand von Lindemann demonstrated the same for π.

The number π (3rd century BC)

By using polygons of 96 sides, inscribed and excribed to the circle, the Greek scientist **Archimedes** (287–212 BC) demonstrated that the number π is located between

$$3 + \frac{10}{71} \text{ and } 3 + \frac{10}{70}$$

Thus, when Ptolemy (Greek mathematician of the 2nd century AD) adopted the value of 3.1416 for π he noted, to justify it, that it was nearly the mean of the two Archimedean boundaries.

In 1874 an Englishman, William Schanks, calculated the first 707 decimal places of π engraved in the Palace of Discovery in Paris. The first 527 places are exact, but the remainder are wrong. Since then, through the use of the computer, π has been calculated to millions of decimal places.

printing, the shape of these ten figures was definitively fixed.

Zero (4th century BC)

Babylonian numeration was perfected in the **4th century BC** by the appearance of the zero in mathematical texts. The zero was placed either at the beginning of a number or within a number, but never at the end.

The word zero comes from *sunya* which means 'nothing' in Sanskrit; it became *sifr* in Arabic and was Latinised into *zephirum* by Leonardo Fibonacci. It was fixed at zero in 1491 by a Florentine treatise.

Prime numbers (3rd century BC)

In the **3rd century BC** Euclid demonstrated that there are an infinite number of prime numbers. The riddle of Erastosthenes (c.284–c.192 BC) was the first method used to investigate these numbers systematically. Nonetheless, in 1876 a Frenchman, Edouard

Lucas, developed a method to study the primary nature of some large numbers.

The greatest known prime number – $2^{216091} - 1$ (65050 digits) – was discovered by chance in 1985, by a team of technicians in the oil firm Chevron, in Houston, Texas (USA). While they were trying out a super-computer, this new prime number came to the fore: to write it would fill at least ten pages of this book.

Irrational numbers (6th century BC)

Pythagoras (c.580–c.500 BC) demonstrated the impossibility of writing the number $\sqrt{2}$ as a fraction, and hence revealed the existence of irrational numbers. A general form of the theory relating to this exists in Euclid's *Elements*.

Decimal numbers (16th century)

Up until the end of the 16th century the system

Golden number (3rd century BC)

The golden number is the solution, x, of the equation

$$\frac{1}{x} = \frac{x}{1 + x}$$

where x is equal to

$$\frac{1 + \sqrt{5}}{2} \quad (\approx 1.618)$$

and exists in an asymmetrical sharing when the ratio between the largest of the two parts and the smallest is equal to the ratio between the whole and the largest. This number was known before **Euclid**, but it was he who, in the **3rd century BC**, made of it a famous problem by seeking to divide a straight line in mean and extreme ratio or 'golden section'.

The harmony based on this golden number has been studied in numerous arts: in architecture (Phidias, who worked on sculptures in the Parthenon in the 5th century BC, Alberti in the 15th century; Le Corbusier in the 20th century), in music (Pythagorean research on sound intervals), and in painting (Leonardo da Vinci, Raphael).

Geometry

Thales' theorem (7th–6th century BC)

Before Thales, each surveyor or geometer found gadgets with which to measure distances, surfaces, etc. The Greek philosopher and mathematician of the Ionian school **Thales** of Miletus (c.624–c.546 BC) had the very clever idea of measuring heights by using shadow at the time when the 'shadow is equal to the object'. That is when the sun's rays are projected at 45°. In order to measure the height of the Great Pyramid, he refined his method by using the rays at any given hour. He might have left it at that, but he wanted to formulate a theory based on his experiments. The use of the sun's rays caused him to study

---

EULER'S NINE-POINT CIRCLE

The nine-point circle of Leonhard Euler (1707–83) is a circle which can be built very simply from a triangle. It passes through the middle of the sides of the triangle, through the bases of the perpendiculars of the triangle, and through the three points which are equidistant from the apexes of the triangle and the intersection of the perpendiculars.

This circle is famous not only because it is mathematically interesting, but also because it is indicative of Euler's talents. Leonhard Euler was actually blind when he discovered the nine-point circle. He lost his right eye when he was young, and he lost the use of his left eye at the age of 50 through cataracts. Therefore Euler had to visualise the positions of the nine points mentally, without seeing them, before recognising and demonstrating that these points were all situated on the same circle.

---

parallel lines and the ratios between the lengths projected and the initial lengths. He then drew up his theorem, called Thales' theorem: 'parallels are projected from a straight line onto another line of proportional length'. Thales of Miletus thereby introduced the deductive and demonstrative aspect of mathematics to geometry.

Pythagoras' theorem (6th century BC)

Using the work of Thales on parallel lines and projections, and in the same spirit of demonstration, **Pythagoras**, the Greek philosopher and mathematician of the **6th century BC**, became interested in orthogonal projections and demonstrated the theorem which bears his name. This theorem establishes a relationship between the lengths of the sides of a right-angled triangle: that the square on the hypotenuse is equal to the sum of the squares on the other two sides. This relationship had been known since surveyors had begun to practise, but Pythagoras was the first to demonstrate it.

Euclidian assumption (3rd century BC)

The Greek mathematician of Alexandria **Euclid** (**3rd century BC**) worked mainly on a synthesis of his predecessors' work. In his *Elements*, he structured the knowledge of his era by redemonstrating everything from five assumptions which were considered to be true even though they could not be demonstrated. The foremost and best known is: given a point exterior to a straight line, there exists a unique line which is parallel to this straight line. The contrary of this assumption had been imagined by Aristotle. Until the 19th century, mathematicians thought that the demonstration of this assumption was possible. Thus, in the 18th century, numerous mathematicians tried in vain to demonstrate it by absurdity. Two possible negations appeared: at least one point exists by which there is no straight line parallel to a given straight line. The other was: at least one point exists by which at least two distinct parallel lines pass. The fact of having clearly expressed these two contrary thoughts allowed the following century to create two new kinds of geometry.

Trigonometry (3rd–2nd century BC)

During antiquity, trigonometry developed as a technique annexed to astronomy. Thus, the Greek astronomers **Aristarchus** of Samos (c.**300** BC) and **Hipparchus** of Nicea (c.**200** BC), were the precursors of trigonometry. The Alexandrian Ptolemy (AD c.80–c.160) summarised all the knowledge of the era in his treatise, the *Almageste*.

It was the Arabs who, during the 9th and 10th centuries, developed trigonometry as a separate science. Al Khwârizmî (780–850) established the first sine tables, and Habasch al Hasib those of the tangents. The *Perfection of the Almageste* (877–929) by al Bâttâni was a veritable treatise on modern trigonometry and was much more complete than Ptolemy's *Almageste*. The studies were taken up and elaborated upon by the German mathematicians Johan Müller (1436–76) and Georg

Rhaeticus (1514–76). Abraham de Moivre (1667–1754) and Leonhard Euler (1707–83) made a radius and an angle correspond to each complex number, thus allowing trigonometry to be dealt with by means of the exponential form of complex numbers. Trigonometry was thereby integrated into an algebraic theory.

Conic sections (3rd century BC)

Conic sections have been studied in very different ways over the centuries, and are a good example of how geometry has evolved from antiquity to the present.

Apollonius of Perga (c.262–c.180 BC), in his treatise on conic sections, studied various ways of cutting a cone. He then showed how parabolas, hyperbolas and ellipses would be obtained: he also originated these terms.

In the 17th century Descartes translated conic sections into equations and showed that they could be obtained from second degree equations.

Blaise Pascal (1623–62) developed the modern aspect by approaching conic sections from an analytical point of view. In the 20th century, they are part of the general theory of quadratic forms.

Co-ordinates (17th century)

The use of numbers for the univocal location of a point on a surface had been known since the time of Archimedes (3rd century BC). But it was not until the **17th century** that co-ordinates were used in a systematic way in problems of geometry. Legend has it that the French philosopher and mathematician **René Descartes** (1596–1650) had the idea while watching an insect flying by his window. This discovery allowed geometrical problems to be analysed using algebraic techniques; thus, with the French mathematician **Pierre de Fermat** (1601–65), analytic geometry began, where equations and curves were linked.

Vectors (1798)

The Danish geometer **Caspar Wessel**, in **1798**, and the Swiss **Jean-Robert Argand**, in **1806**, wrote two papers on complex numbers. Both of them had the idea of not only representing complex numbers by points A on a plane, but also of identifying them by the vector from the origin 0 to the extremity A on a Cartesian plane. Thus the notion of the $\vec{0A}$ vector was born: the sum of two complex numbers then allowed the sum of two vectors to be worked out. Vectors, quantities specified by both magnitude and direction, are thus geometrical objects, which can undergo the same sort of operations as number sets.

Structure of vectorial space (1844)

The German mathematician **Hermann Grassmann** (1809–77), in his 'theory of linear extension' of **1844**, defined vectorial spaces in more than three dimensions. At the same time the Irish mathematician Sir William Rowan Hamilton (1805–65), with his study of quaternions, elaborated the first vector system. These definitions were very useful to physics at the time when the theory of relativity was developed, in which space-time is considered as a vectorial space in the fourth dimension.

geometrical objects invariable, such as medians and perpendiculars. In studying the structure of these groups, C. F. Klein integrated geometries into one algebraic theory. Thus, in the 20th century, algebra and geometry form part of mathematics.

Algebra

Origins (3rd century)

The word *algebra* comes from the Arabic word *al-jabr*: to reduce. It is generally considered that the work of **Diophantus** of Alexandria (3rd century) was the first step in the history of algebra. It was in his *Thirteen Books of Arithmetic* that mathematicians such as the Frenchmen Pierre de Fermat (1601–65) and François Viète (1540–1603) found the starting point for their own research. François Viète is often considered to be the inventor of modern algebra. He founded the algebraic language in 1591 in his work, *Ars analytica*. The language uses letters not only to indicate unknowns and indeterminates but also to form words or algebraic expressions.

Algebraic symbols (15th–17th century)

The Egyptians used symbols: addition was indicated by two legs walking in the same direction, and subtraction by two legs walking in opposite directions. Conversely, no symbolism is found with the Greeks, where each reasoning process was written out fully.

It was the Germans, the English and the French, in the **15th to 17th centuries**, who introduced symbolic calculation. Our + and − signs, which appear in 1498 in an arithmetic book by the German Jean Widmann D'Eger, were promulgated by the German Michael Stifel in 1544 in his treatise on algebra, *Arithmetica integra*. The root sign $\sqrt{}$ was invented by Cristoff Rudoff in 1526. The sign × is more recent, and Englishman William Oughtred (1637) is credited with using it for the first time. The greater than > and smaller than < signs are due to another Briton Thomas Harriot (1631). Finally, the French philosopher René Descartes created in 1637 the use of figures placed as exponents to designate powers (eg $9 = 3^2$), and the Englishman John Wallis (1656) was responsible for the idea of negative exponents (eg $\frac{1}{9} = 3^{-2}$).

Fermat's last theorem (1637)

The great French mathematician **Pierre de Fermat** (1601–65) asserted in **1637** that he had demonstrated the following theorem: 'There do not exist positive integers x, y, z, n such that $x^n + y^n = z^n$, where n is greater than 2.'

In the 17th century mathematicians were not very interested in demonstrating their theorems. So Fermat never published his proofs, simply stating this last thorem which he believed he had demonstrated. A number of such statements by Fermat were later found to be correct and important, so scientists were accustomed to treat the great mathematician's assertions with considerable respect.

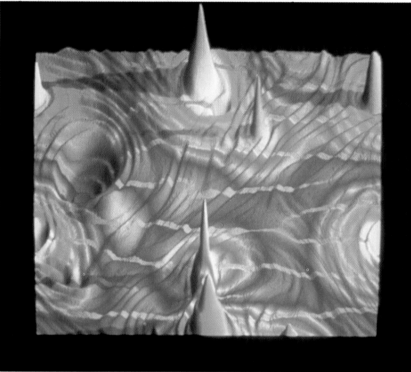

This is a numeric simulation of a turbulence field, based on the mathematical concept of 'wavelets' as developed by J. O. Stromberg of Norway and Yves Meyer of France.

Non-Euclidean geometries (18th century)

In the **18th century** Giovanni Girolamo Saccheri, Johann Heinrich Lambert, Taurinus, Reid and numerous other mathematicians tried to work out the logical consequences of the negatives of Euclid's postulate; but they came up with no complete theories. At the beginning of the 19th century, these theories took shape and developed into two different geometries, both possible and practicable.

Elliptic geometry (19th century)

The German physician and mathematician **Johann Karl Friedrich Gauss** (1777–1855) created a geometry in which a plane was defined as the surface of a sphere with an infinite radius.

The German **Bernhard Riemann** (1826–66), a student of Gauss at Göttingen, continued his work and proposed a revision of classical geometry, allowing elliptical geometry to be considered as a particular case of a more general theory.

Hyperbolic geometry (19th century)

The Hungarian mathematician **Jéanus Bolyai** (1802–60) and the Russian mathematician **Nicolai Ivanovitch Lobatchevski** (1792–1856), created a geometry in which the plane is a hyperbolic surface. Each of its points is shaped like a saddle.

Definition of geometry (1872)

Various works on non-Euclidean geometries at the beginning of the 19th century stirred up passionate debate and violent polemics; they revolutionised the philosophy of knowledge, in fact, more than geometry itself.

Thus it was necessary to bring this work together and create a theory large enough to accommodate these co-existing but different worlds of geometry. The German mathematician **Christian Felix Klein** (1849–1925) in his opening address to the Erlangen congress (the 'Erlangen programme', **1872**), defined geometry as the study of 'groups' or 'collections' of transformations, leaving certain

Fermat's 'Last Theorem' has never been completely proved after 300 years of research and is the mathematical problem for which the greatest number of incorrect proofs have been published. We only know that the theorem is valid for all the values of n between 1 and 30 000, but a complete proof is remarkably elusive. All mathematicians think that the general theorem is true and hope to end up by proving it.

In 1988 a Japanese mathematician, Yoichi Miyaoka, said that he had arrived at a proof, but his colleagues are sceptical.

Algebraic equations

1st and 2nd degree equations (1700 BC)

Some examples of the solution to 1st and 2nd degree equations attached to specific problems were found in the Rhind Papyrus (Egypt), which dates back to 1700 BC. Chinese literature offers examples of solutions to these two systems of equation by two unknown writers, in the work *Nine Chapters on the Art of Calculus* (c.200 BC).

The history of 2nd degree equations goes back to the Babylonian civilisation of the 2nd millennium (1800 BC). The Babylonian arithmeticians knew how to solve all equations of the 2nd degree but did not express them in real number sets. The Greeks in the 3rd century BC made the solution of 2nd degree equations the basis of all their geometry, and in order to make them work for real sets, they replaced the Babylonian calculations with constructions by ruler and compass. The Greek algebraists, however, calculated within the set of positive rational numbers, which left many equations unsolved. It was not until the 16th century and the identification of complex numbers that all 2nd degree equations could be solved.

3rd and 4th degree equations (16th century)

The Italian school of the 16th century brought solutions to the resolution of 3rd and 4th degree equations. The three pioneers were successively **Scipione del Ferro**, **Niccolo Fontana** called Tartaglia (c.1500–57), and **Girolamo Cardano** (1501–76).

Abel and the 5th degree equation (1826)

While he was still a student, the Norwegian mathematician **Niels Henrik Abel** (1802–29) attacked the formidable problem of solving an algebraic equation of the 5th degree. One day he thought he had cracked it, but soon saw that his proof had an error in it. He then decided to prove that it was in fact impossible to solve the general quintic equation. In 1826 he proved his revolutionary result: that it is indeed impossible to solve equations of degree greater than four by means of radicals.

Abel decided to visit the two greatest mathematicians of the time, the German Johann Karl Freidrich Gauss and the Frenchman Augustin Cauchy (1789–1857), and show them his results. But they did not want to acknowledge the genius of the 24-year-old, and could not be bothered to understand his extraordinary paper. Unrecognised and despairing, Abel returned to Norway, where he died of tuberculosis at the age of 27.

In mathematics there are 17 infinite families of regular groups and 26 groups known as sporadic, the largest of which is the Fischer-Greiss monster, named after the mathematicians who predicted its existence.

Theory of probabilities (1656)

The theory of probabilities was born from the study of games of chance. The word hazard, transmitted through Spain, comes from the Arabic *az-zahr* meaning 'the die'. Blaise Pascal and Pierre de Fermat were the first, in their correspondence, to want to 'mathematise' games of chance.

The Dutch scientist **Christiaan Huygens** (1629–95), aware of this correspondence, published in 1656 the first complete account of the calculation of probabilities, *De Ratiociniis in ludo aleae*. Subsequently, Jacques Bernoulli (1654–1705) wrote the work *Ars conjectandi*, a deeper study of the science than that of Huygens. Finally, it was the French mathematician Pierre-Simon de Laplace (1749–1827) who produced work on the application of mathematical analysis to the theory of probabilities which had a philosophical element.

Statistics (1746)

In 1746 a professor from Göttingen, Germany, **Gottfried Achenwall**, created the term statistics. In fact, the gathering of data goes back to antiquity. For example, the Chinese Emperor Yao organised a census of agricultural production in 2238 BC.

The Belgian Adolphe Quetelet, in 1853, was the first to think that statistics might be based on the calculation of probabilities.

The appearance of powerful calculators gave birth to methods of analysis of multidimensional data which are currently enjoying wide popularity.

Matrices (1858)

The study of systems of equations and linear transformations led the English mathematician **Arthur Cayley** (1821–95) to establish tables called matrices, and to define operations on these tables.

Matrix algebra was thus developed, and he published it in a thesis in 1858. His work permitted the further study of the structures of linear transformation groups and prepared

the ideas which were put forth by Christian Felix Klein in his Erlangen programme (1872).

Group structure (19th century)

During the course of the 19th century, many groups were studied at the same time that work was being carried out on various equations. The French mathematician **Augustin Cauchy** studied groups of permutations of roots of algebraic equations. **Evariste Galois** (1811–32) continued this work and developed a theory of groups which unfortunately remains unfinished; he was killed in a duel at the age of 21. His theory, despite some oversights, remained a guide for further research.

During the period 1870 to 1880 the Norwegian mathematician Sophus Lie (1842–99) formulated the theory of continuous groups of transformation or 'Lie groups', notably to study differential equations. These groups were used by Klein in his Erlangen programme. Since then, this group structure has been used in all modern mathematics and physics, in research on atomic structures.

Mathematical logic (1854)

The self-taught Englishman **George Boole** (1815–64) was the creator of symbolic logic. In 1847 he published a short treatise (*Mathematical Analysis of Logic*) in which he maintained that logic must be connected to mathematics and not to philosophy.

In 1854, in his treatise *An Investigation of the Laws of Thought*, Boole set out the results of his thinking. Thus began what is today called Boolean algebra, a system of symbolic logic which codifies non-mathematical logical operations, using the numerical values 0 and 1 only. Logic took its current form with Gottlob Frege in 1879, whose work was made known to the public by the philosopher Bertrand Russell in 1903.

The set of real numbers (19th century)

In the 4th century BC the Greek mathematician and astronomer Eudoxus tried to put into the

Among Sir Isaac Newton's achievements was the formulation of a theory of calculus.

linked and expressed one as a function of the other. He thus used functions and expressed them using the form $\psi(\chi)$. This discovery was made while researching new methods of calculation which developed during the next century under the name of infinitesimal calculation.

Infinitesimal calculus (18th century)

Jean Bernoulli, Professor of Mathematics in Basle, Switzerland, explained and made known the calculation methods of Leibnitz and introduced them to France around 1691. He was also the professor of **Leonhard Euler** (1707–83), who ordered and developed the work of his predecessors. Euler provided the first general theory of variation calculus, clarified the notion of the function, and reassembled all these results in his *Institutiones calculi differentialis* (1755) and *Institutiones calculi integralis* (1768–70).

Independently of the work of Leibnitz and of Euler, the English physicist and mathematician **Sir Isaac Newton** (1642–1727) formulated a theory of calculus which deals with exactly the same problems. Therefore, at practically the same time, infinitesimal calculus made its appearance in various scientific communities. In the 19th century integral calculus made considerable progress thanks to the work of the German Georg Friedrich Bernhard Riemann (1826–66).

Topology (19th–20th centuries)

Topology is that part of mathematics which studies the ideas, *a priori* intuitive, of continuity and limit. Until the beginning of the 19th century, mathematicians had used these ideas without defining them correctly. The German mathematician **David Hilbert** (1862–1943) sought to make them axiomatic and introduced 'neighbourhoods'. The Frenchman Maurice Fréchet and the Hungarian Frederick Riesz, at the beginning of the 20th century, defined respectively the notions of 'metric theory' and of 'topology'. Finally, around 1940, the definition of 'filters' by the French mathematician Henri Cartan rounded off the history of the idea of limit. **Jules Henri Poincaré** (1854–1912) is considered to be the inventor of algebraic and differential topology.

Non-standard analysis (1960s)

Non-standard analysis was invented in the **1960s** by the American mathematician **A. Robinson**. It is a new branch of mathematics which makes it possible to define rigorously and to use in a practical manner numbers which are intuitively qualified as infinitely large or infinitely small. Robinson effectively showed that it is possible to construct logically a new analysis, called non-standard, in which the sets of numbers of standard analysis (the usual analysis) are complemented by infinitely greater or smaller numbers which are greater or smaller than all the standard numbers.

This new analysis ensures greater rigour in many calculations and makes an important contribution to the study of complex geometric objects such as fractals and of chaotic physical phenomena.

form of a set numbers not limited to the rational, which he sensed were insufficient. He was not successful, neither were any number of later mathematicians of antiquity, who were reluctant to deal with irrational numbers.

It was not until the **19th century** that the Danish-born German mathematician **Georg Cantor** (1845–1918) studied irrational quantities and the notion of 'continuity', taking account of the 'continuum' aspect of the law of real numbers, formed by an infinity of distinct points, each representing a number. This gave rise to many paradoxes which challenged intuitive ideas. Cantor, aware of the break with traditional good sense, had to struggle for several years to convince his contemporaries of this arithmetic of the infinite. When he died on 6 January 1918, his work had become universally accepted.

Theory of groups (19th and 20th centuries)

Since the work of the German philosopher and mathematician Gottfried Wilhelm von Leibnitz (1646–1716) it appeared indispensable to create notations and symbols to systematise logic. In his algebra, **George Boole** made the union and the intersection of groups correspond to addition and multiplication, on the one hand, and the 'or' and 'and' on the other. Thus, parallel to logical symbols, symbols and a theory of groups appeared.

The Italian mathematician and logician **Giuseppe Peano** (1858–1932) introduced in 1895 the symbol ϵ which signifies 'belonging to', $\cup$ for the combination of two sets and $\cap$ for their intersection. The German Schröder in 1877 introduced $\subset$ for inclusion.

With the work of Cantor on real groups, paradoxes appeared which led Peano to define the cardinal number of a group. The French mathematician Emile Borel (1871–1956) introduced the notion of innumerable groupings which opened up 20th century research to topology and the theory of measurement.

Analysis

Logarithm (1614)

Archimedes (3rd century BC), in his *Study of the Grains of Sand*, calculated the number of grains of sand necessary to fill the universe, and was close to becoming the inventor of logarithms. The Frenchman Nicolas Chuquet (1445–1500) invented arithmetical and geometrical progressions, as well as negative exponents, but it was the Scotsman **John Napier** (1550–1617) who invented logarithms in 1614 while doing research on a new method of numerical calculation. His system allows the replacement of multiplications by additions, and divisions by subtractions, using the smallest numbers. However, he did not find his results satisfactory and so developed, together with his friend, the Englishman Henry Briggs (1561–1631), the decimal or common logarithm. He was then able to calculate each of the first 31 000 prime numbers to 14 decimal places.

Functions (17th century)

Gottfried Wilhelm von Leibnitz had the idea of treating problems by analogy; in effect, he was interested in the similarities between various problems. In particular, he noted in his correspondence with the Swiss mathematician Jean Bernoulli (1667–1748) that some variables, such as time and distance, might be

Physics

Standards

Weights and measures

The first units of measure were most often derived from the human body: the thumb (inch), the forearm (cubit), the distance between the tip of the king's nose and the tip of his middle finger in medieval England (yard). Or they had some relation to physical activity, such as the league, which equalled an hour's walking. The Celts used the capacity of two cupped hands united as a measure, while the ancient Egyptians derived their measure for liquids from the mouthful or draught.

For centuries units of measure spread throughout Europe in haphazard fashion. However, developments in the areas of science and technology created a need for a single, coherent system.

In France, weights and measures became standardised with the institution of the decimal metric system. In the English-speaking countries, the Système International d'Unités was not adopted until the second half of the 20th century: Britain's official conversion to the metric system was only completed in 1980.

Metric system (1795)

The principle of mandatory units for weights and measures was established in France during the Revolution. A decree issued on **7 April 1795** instituted the metric system, established the names of the units and, for the first time, legally defined the metre as a fraction of the distance between the North Pole and the Equator, measured on the meridian from Barcelona to Dunkirk.

Begun in June 1792, the measurement of the meridian arc by the Frenchmen **J.-B. Delambre** and **Pierre Méchain** was not completed until the end of **1798**. For this geodesic operation, the two astronomers used the repeating circle, recently invented by **Charles de Borda**, which made it possible to measure angles to the nearest second (each degree is divided into 60 minutes and each minute into 60 seconds). The choice of the name 'metre' is attributed to Borda; it is also the name that had previously been chosen by the Italian **Tito Livio Burattini** in a treatise published in **1675**, in which he suggested using the length of a pendulum marking the seconds as a universal unit of length, and this he called the catholic metre. The unit of weight became the kilogramme.

On 22 June 1799 the first standard metre rule and the kilogramme weight were placed in the French National Archive in Paris. That same year the metric system became compulsory in France, but its use spread very slowly. It was not considered fully established until 1840.

The Système International d'Unités (SI) (1960)

This system of units defined, in **1960**, the seven base units from which all other units derive. They are:
– length (the metre)
– mass (the kilogramme)
– time (the second)
– electric current (the ampere)
– thermodynamic temperature (the Kelvin, which equals the degree Celsius, but the Kelvin scale begins at absolute zero and not 0°C; 0°C = 273.16K)
– amount of substance (the mole)
– luminous intensity (the candela).

The SI metre is no longer defined as the distance between two marks on a platinum-iridium bar, kept at the International Bureau of Weights and Measures at Sevrès in France, but as the light-metre (as from 1986), which is to say the 299792458th part of the distance travelled by light in a vacuum in one second.

Planck's constant (1898)

The German physicist **Max Planck** (1858–1947), after discovering the quantum of interaction h (*see* Quantum theory), noted in **1898** that h could be used to establish an absolute scale of units.

These units have no proportional relation to the ordinary physical world. If you wanted to test this scale physically, with the aid of a particle accelerator constructed by present day techniques, you would need an accelerator the size of our galaxy, that is about 100 000 light-years in diameter.

It is thought that the Planck constant is the limit on this side of which quantum effects appear in the gravitational field. It is not understood at present, however, how these effects could intervene.

Foundations of physics

Cosmological model (antiquity)

In the **5th century BC** the Pythagoreans (i.e. the disciples of the renowned Greek scholar and philosopher Pythagoras), together with

Ptolemy's cosmological system (Earth at the centre of the universe) was unchallenged until Copernicus.

the Greek Eudoxus of Cnidus, imagined a system of concentric spheres, whose rotational axes, variously inclined, passed through a common centre: the earth. This cosmological system was systematised by the last astronomer of antiquity, Ptolemy (AD c.80–c.160) of Alexandria.

The Copernican system (16th century)

The Pole **Nicolaus Copernicus** (1473–1543), doctor of law, canon and passionate astronomer, seems to have developed in the early **16th century** the cosmogony for which he would become famous: that the earth itself rotates and, like the other planets, it rotates around the sun.

Copernicus understood the Church, and he must have anticipated the general outcry from the theologians when his theory ruined their certainty that the earth, and thus man, the 'image of God', was the centre of the universe. So Copernicus did not hasten to publish his book, *De revolutionibus orbium cœlestium libri VI*, and put it into the hands of his friend Georg Rhaethicus. The work appeared a few days before Copernicus died, on 24 May 1543.

A little-known but very interesting fact to remember: 18 centuries before Copernicus, the Greek Aristarchus of Samos (c.310–c.230 BC) had been the first to conceive of a heliocentric universe. Unlike his contemporaries, he thought that the earth and the other planets went round the sun, and not vice versa. Moreover, he had noted the rotation of the earth itself.

Laws of dynamics (17th century)

In his *Discourses and Demonstrations Concerning Two New Sciences*, published in **1638**, **Galileo** stated the principle of inertia according to which a body not subject to the action of external forces has a rectilinear and uniform movement. And in the *Principia (Philosophiae naturalis principia mathematica)*, published in **1687**, **Sir Isaac Newton** (1642–1727) stated the fundamental principle of dynamics, according to which a body, subject to an external force, gathers acceleration in proportion to that force.

Albert Einstein, the greatest scientist of the 20th century, at Oxford in May 1932.

The French astronomer Jean Picard (1620–82) from the Observatoire de Paris – who was the first to measure the earth's diameter precisely – had a young Dane, Olaüs Römer as his assistant. The latter carried out observations of the four large satellites of Jupiter discovered by Galileo some 70 years earlier. He measured the intervals of time between the successive eclipses of the satellites by Jupiter and noted that these were regularly shorter or longer depending on whether Jupiter and the earth were closer together or further apart in their respective orbits around the sun.

Römer understood that this phenomenon was due to delays in the light from Jupiter reaching earth. He then calculated that, to explain all these observations, light travelled at a speed of 300 000km/sec *186 400 miles per second*. At last, after 2000 years of controversy, it was established that light did not travel instantly, but has a finite and measurable speed.

Absolute space (1687)

Isaac Newton (1642–1727) believed in the existence of 'absolute space', in which objects at rest or in motion at a constant speed are not subject to any force of inertia. To illustrate this idea, he carried out the following experiment: having attached a bucket of water to a rope previously coiled upon itself and having waited until the water was at rest in the bucket, he allowed the rope to uncoil itself and thus rotate the bucket. He observed that the surface of the water, which in turn was affected by the rotation of the bucket, took on a concave form.

Newton's interpretation was that the water initially at rest is at rest in absolute space and is therefore not subject to any forces of inertia: its surface is flat. But then, the water in rotation is in rotation in relation to absolute space and is therefore subject to forces of inertia which curve its surface.

Mach's hypothesis (1889)

These ideas were prevalent until in **1889** the physicist and philosopher **Ernest Mach** – who introduced the famous Mach number for measuring supersonic speed – noted that it was not Newton's absolute space but rather all the matter in the universe, and in particular all the stars, far away but numerous, that determine the forces of inertia. Thus the water in Newton's bucket is subject to forces of inertia as it is in rotation in relation to the distribution of distant stars.

This hypothesis, known as Mach's principle, is most certainly correct: Newton's absolute space does not exist.

Quantum theory (1900)

At the end of the last century, no law had been discovered to account for the phenomenon of heat and light radiation by a solid, white-hot body. In **1900** the German physicist **Max Planck** guessed that radiation did not occur in a continuous fashion but in small discrete units, separate quantities or quanta. This discovery, which enabled scientists to explain heat radiation, turned physics upside down, especially in the sphere of classical mechanics which became inoperable in the area of infinitely small quantities.

Thanks to this theory, **Albert Einstein** explained in **1905** the photo-electric effect by showing that light, which comprises both waves and particles, moves by quanta, tiny packets of light, which were later called photons.

The Danish physicist **Niels Bohr** built on this

quantum theory a model of an atom, describing in 1911 the movement of electrons inside the atom. This model enabled him to achieve remarkable results in the fields of the spectroscopy of gaseous matter and of X-ray physics.

Wave mechanics (1924)

The Frenchman **Louis de Broglie** produced the wave theory of matter in **1924**, which also derived from quantum theory. It was perfected by E. Schrödinger.

Statistical determinism (1927)

In **1927** the German **Werner Heisenberg** stated that the absolute principle of determinism in classical mechanics (the same causes produce the same effects) was no longer true of wave mechanics. He introduced the idea of statistical determinism, which allowed the calculation of probabilities only.

Today, quantum mechanics has become the basic tool of modern physics, but it has not yet yielded up all its secrets.

Fundamental forces

The elementary particles of matter may act among themselves in various ways, because of forces or what we call 'interactions'. Four fundamental forces are known at present, of which two were known to antiquity – gravitational and electromagnetic forces – and two of which are the fruit of 20th century research: weak and strong interactions.

The process of interaction, according to modern theories, is like the superimposition of elementary interactions occurring when a particle is exchanged, characterised by the force called an 'intermediary boson'. The particles interact a bit like rugby players, passing the ball from one to another. In the case of electromagnetic force, the particle that is exchanged (the boson) is the famous light-particle invented by **Einstein** in 1905, the photon.

In 1986 the physicist Ephraïm Fischbach and his colleagues at the University of Washington suggested the possibility of a fifth force, but its existence has not been confirmed since.

Electromagnetic force (1820–64)

It is this force which links atoms and molecules to form ordinary solid bodies. Thus, if your elbow doesn't sink into the wood of your desk while you are writing, it is because the electrons in the atoms of your desk and of your elbow push against each other by means of electromagnetic interaction.

The relationship between electricity and

magnetism was discovered in **1820** by the Danish scientist **Christian Oersted** in an experiment during which he noticed that a magnetic needle was deflected by an electric current. The French physicist André Marie Ampère later generalised these observations, but it was the Scotsman **James Clerk Maxwell** who, in **1864**, formulated the general laws of electromagnetism and showed that light was nothing but an electromagnetic wave.

Since the 1930s a number of physicists such as the Englishman P. A. M. Dirac and the Americans Richard Feynman and Julian Schwinger have developed the modern theory of electromagnetic interaction between electrons (with the exchange of photons).

Force of gravity (1687/1915)

Responsible for the movements of great masses on a large scale (the rotation of the earth around the sun, the movement of the galaxies, the expansion of the universe, etc.), the force of gravity, whose laws were first stated by **Sir Isaac Newton** in **1687**, is the weakest of known forces. Today it has a very special status because it has been interpreted since **Einstein (1915)** as a manifestation of the curvature of space-time. With regard to gravitational force, the boson which plays a role analogous to the photon is called the *graviton*.

Weak force (1934/1974)

It has been known since **Enrico Fermi's** work in **1934** that this force is manifested during certain radioactive processes, such as the spontaneous disintegration of the neutron. In 1974 the physicists **Sheldon Glashow** (US), **Abdus Salam** (Pakistan) and **Steven Weinberg** (US) decided that the existence of three exchange particles, the intermediary bosons W^+, W^- and Z^0, played a role analogous to that of the photon and the graviton for weak force. (For this work they won the Nobel Prize for Physics in 1979.) These three particles were observed at the European Centre for Nuclear Research (CERN) in Geneva by the physicists Carlo Rubbia (Italy) and Simon van der Meer (Holland), who won the Nobel Prize for Physics in 1984. Their discovery was certainly one of the most important in particle physics in the second half of the 20th century.

Strong force (1935/1965)

Strong interaction, discovered by the Japanese **Hideki Yukawa** in **1935**, is principally responsible for the cohesion of atomic nuclei: it is this which maintains the links at the centre of the atom between the protons and neutrons which constitute the nucleus. More precisely, the protons and neutrons are made up of quarks and the strong force is what binds the quarks to each other. A difficult theory known as quantum chromodynamics has been elaborated by various physicists since **Nambu (1965)**, and suggests that quarks interact among themselves by the exchange of eight bosons which are called gluons, massless particles which transmit the forces that bind quarks together.

Theory of superstrings (1984)

The concept of superstrings in its present form, was invented by the Englishman **Michael Green** and the American **John Schwarz**. The theory had its origins in work done by the Japanese Yoichiro Nambu in the late 1950s, while Frenchmen Joel Scherk and André Neveu were among those who made important contributions to its development. Ordinarily in physics, one thinks of elementary particles as points, without dimensions. The new idea is to replace the concept of the particle, an object with zero dimension, with the concept of a string, which has one dimension. Then one could think of interpreting particles and their associated waves as excited states of a vibrating string, and thus arrive at a classification of particles and a unification of the four fundamental forces (see above).

For example, it has been shown that the lowest state of vibration of a string may be identified with the graviton, the hypothetical particle of the gravitational field. A notable characteristic of superstrings is that they necessarily evolve in a space-time having more dimensions than the four usually allowed to space-time.

Since **August 1984**, when Green and Schwarz proved a very important result for the theory of superstrings, dozens of physicists have been working on the subject, and thousands of articles have been published. Known as the Theory of Everything, it can answer important questions like: How did the universe begin? What is matter? What is the origin of time? Developments are still being made in the field of superstrings.

Hydrodynamics

Archimedes' principle

Archimedes (c.287–212 BC) was the first to formulate the principle of floating bodies which bears his name: all bodies weighed when immersed in fluid (liquid or gas) show a

The visualisation of aerodynamic flows through hydraulic analogy.

loss of weight equal to the weight of fluid they displace.

After having discovered this principle, as we know, Archimedes cried Eureka! ('I've found it!'). Less well-known are the circumstances of this discovery: the ruler of Syracuse, Hiero II, a naturally suspicious man, had given some pure gold to a jeweller so that he could melt it down and make a royal crown. Archimedes was put in control of this work. He then had the idea of immersing in a receptacle filled to the brim with water first the crown, then gold and silver equal in weight to that of the crown. After each experiment, so the story goes, he weighed the water that had overflowed. He finally showed that the figure of the first weighing had fallen between the figures of the next two: it weighed less than pure gold and more than silver. Thus it was proved that the crown had been made of a mixture of gold and silver.

Hydrostatic paradox (1586)

The Flemish physicist and mathematician **Simon Stevin** (1548–1620), known as Simon of Bruges, was inspector of dykes for the States of Holland and, in that capacity, directly interested in the internal forces of liquids, was the first to make a truly scientific study of these forces.

In **1586** Stevin's three books on mechanics were published. These contained his famous hydrostatic paradox: the pressure of a liquid at the bottom of a receptacle depends solely on the depth of the liquid and not on the shape of the receptacle. Conversely, the weight of the liquid depends on the shape of the receptacle.

Fundamental principle (17th century)

Taking the fundamental relationship as a starting point, **Blaise Pascal** (1623–62) also deduced his fundamental principle: pressure applied to any one point of an incompressible fluid at rest is transmitted without loss to all other parts of the fluid.

Characteristic numbers

Reynolds number

The English physicist and engineer **Osborne Reynolds** (1842–1912) carried out research in the field of hydrodynamics, studying the flow of viscous fluids. Reynolds number is a dimensionless coefficient expressing the relationship between the inert forces and the viscous forces.

Froude number

The English physicist and engineer **William Froude** (1810–79) was the first to study by experimental means the resistance of a fluid to motion. To carry out his experiments, he devised the first model tank.

Mach number

The Austrian physicist and philosopher **Ernst Mach** (1838–1916) was the first person to recognise the role of velocity in aerodynamic flows. The Mach number (M) is the ratio of the inertial forces to the square root of the forces of pressure. If M is greater than 1, then the object is supersonic (or greater than the speed of sound in air which is 240 metres per second *760.6mph*). If M is less than 1, the object is subsonic.

Gravitation

The centre of gravity (3rd century BC)

The greatest scientist of antiquity, the Greek **Archimedes** (born in Syracuse in 287 BC), first determined the centres of gravity of homogeneous solids defined geometrically, such as the cylinder, the sphere and the cone. Archimedes developed this idea in his *Book of Balances*. In this book he also displayed his rigorous law of levers.

Falling bodies

The Italian physicist and astronomer **Galileo** (1564–1642) demonstrated by experiment that falling bodies accelerate at a rate which is independent of their nature and composition. According to legend, he threw a wooden ball and a lead ball from the top of the tower of Pisa, and noted that they reached the ground at the same time (disregarding a slight resistance in the air). In 1686 **Isaac Newton** came to the same conclusions as the result of experiments with oscillating pendulums. And in 1888 the Hungarian baron and physicist **Lorand Eötvös** (1848–1919) showed, with the aid of torsion pendulums that the 'universality' of falling bodies was correct to within a billionth or more.

None of these experiments was satisfactorily explained until 1915, when **Einstein** discovered the general theory of relativity.

Kepler's laws (17th century)

The German astronomer **Johannes Kepler** (1571–1630) undertook a systematic study of the movement of the planets, in particular that of the planet Mars.

He stated three laws which bear his name. They had the great merit that calculations on the basis of these laws proved to coincide with observations. The first two laws were published in *Astronomia Nova* in **1609**, and the third in *Harmonices Mundi* in **1619**.

The laws of universal attraction (1685)

One evening in 1665 **Isaac Newton** was musing in his garden. The moon was full. An apple fell at his feet, and Newton wondered why the moon, too, did not fall to earth. This question led the man of science to state in his *Philosophiae naturalis principia mathematica* (**1685**) the laws of universal attraction. However, the discovery of the laws which govern the universe cannot be reduced to this one anecdote, related by Voltaire, and anyway not verified.

Before Newton, the German astronomer Johannes Kepler, starting out from the notebook of the Danish astronomer Tycho Brahe, had established between 1601 and 1618 the three laws which bear his name and which enable us to calculate a planet's orbit around the sun and its rotation period. At the same time, Galileo issued many observations on the trajectory of projectiles and, for the first time, in 1609 had looked at the sky through an astronomical lens. Before these men, Copernicus and then Giordano Bruno, condemned to death and burnt at the stake by the Inquisition in 1600, had fallen foul of official theory which made the earth the centre of the universe.

It thus fell to Newton to unify the astronomical knowledge of his time in the famous law of universal attraction.

Principle of relativity (17th century)

Contrary to general belief, the principle of relativity is not a notion invented by Einstein. **Galileo** (17th century) already thought that natural phenomena were insensible to the state of motion of the laboratory in which they took place, as long as the speed of this motion was uniform.

Albert Einstein, guided by the experiments of the Americans Michelson and Morley (1887), issued a hypothesis in 1905 concerning the constancy of the speed of light: 'The velocity of light is independent of the motion of the observer who measures it.'

Allied to the principle of relativity, this hypothesis in Einstein's hands had revolutionary consequences. For example, Einstein showed that two observers moving relative to one another would assign different times to the occurrence of an event. This surprising effect, together with a number of others, formed Einstein's theory of relativity in 1905. All other theories in physics are today based on this theory and, especially, on the general theory of relativity (1915) which concerns the gravitational field.

WHAT IS SPACE-TIME?

Space-time is the geometric framework in which the events of nature take place. It has four dimensions: the three usual dimensions of space – length, width, and depth – plus an additional dimension, that of time. An event in space-time is therefore the datum of the place where and the moment when the event occurred. Why are space and time, which appear to be of very different natures at first glance, linked in a single entity, space-time? It is because space-time makes it possible to interpret the theories of relativity most fruitfully. In 1907, two years after the publication of Einstein's Specific Relativity theory, Hermann Minkowski – who had taught Einstein at the Zurich Polytechnicum – demonstrated that in his former pupil's theory there was a mathematical quantity that could be interpreted as the distance between events taking place in space and time. In Minkowski's hands Specific Relativity became a geometric theory of space and time, with straight lines, planes, rotations and distances, as in traditional geometry.

Later it was realised that Minkowski's space-time was flat, like the space in Euclid's two-dimensional geometry. And in 1915 Einstein showed that gravitational fields curve space-time in such a way that the true space-time of the universe has a curved geometry.

These ultra-sensitive gyroscopes will test in space certain effects anticipated by the theory of relativity.

The general theory of relativity (1915)

In 1915 the German-born physicist **Albert Einstein** (1879–1955) put the finishing touch to an extraordinary theory that was very complex for its time. This theory showed how the gravitational law of Newton could be made compatible with the laws of relativity.

The theory of relativity interpreted the field of gravity not as the usual field of forces, but as a manifestation of the space-time curve. For example, the sun curves space-time around itself, and thus the earth is obliged to circle the sun along a curved line, which is roughly elliptical.

Today, the general theory of relativity is largely accepted. It has been so thoroughly verified by experiments and observation that physicists think that even the most mysterious objects evolving from this theory, such as black holes, must really exist in nature.

Gravitational waves (2000?)

In the general theory of relativity, the gravitational interaction between two bodies such as the earth and the sun moves in waves, at a speed equal to the speed of light. These are thus called gravitational waves. There are a number of experiments being made throughout the world in order to observe these waves. They are emitted by objects far off in the universe, such as exploding or colliding stars. No further observation can be made yet, because gravitational waves are of an extremely weak intensity. Astrophysicists, however, in observing the object called the binary pulsar PSR 1913+16 have proved that gravitational waves really exist. The proof of their existence constitutes the most important contemporary test of the theory of relativity.

Matter

Gases (17th century)

The Flemish doctor and chemist **Jean Baptiste van Helmont** (1577–1644) was the first to recognise the existence of different gases, such as carbon dioxide and oxygen, which were identified as such much later. Until the 17th century the knowledge of these states of matter was purely empirical.

The Greeks designated the immense dark space which existed before things began as 'chaos'. Van Helmont invented the word 'gas' from the sound of their word.

Air (17th century)

In antiquity air was – with earth, water and fire – one of the four natural elements. **John Mayow** (1640–79), an English chemist and pupil of Boyle, was the first to show that air was a mixture of gases.

Oxygen and nitrogen (18th century)

It was in **1777**, in a paper that was not published until 1782, that **Antoine-Laurent de Lavoisier** (1743–94), the founder of modern chemistry – in the wake of the English chemist Joseph Priestley and the Swede Carl Wilhelm Scheele – named life-giving air 'oxygen' (*oxygène*, literally: that which produces an acid), and non-vital air 'nitrogen' (*azote*, literally: that which does not maintain life). In **1772** the Scottish physician and botanist Daniel Rutherford (1749–1819) had distinguished between 'noxious air' (nitrogen) and carbon dioxide in his doctoral thesis, *De aere mephitico*.

Rare gases

First precise analysis (1783)

In **1783** the English chemist **Henry Cavendish** (1731–1810) made the first relatively precise analysis of air. He found 20.8 percent oxygen, 78.2 percent nitrogen and indicated the presence of a 'bubble' which represented about one percent of the volume of gas analysed. This bubble appeared to be endowed with a remarkable inertia.

Argon (1894)

In 1894 two English scientists, **Sir William Ramsay** (1852–1916) and **Lord John William Rayleigh** (1842–1919) detected the presence of an inert gas in the air through spectroscopic analysis. They called it argon, which means 'lazy' in Greek.

Helium (1895)

In 1895 Ramsay and the Swedish chemist **Per Theodor Cleve** (1840–1905) identified the presence of helium in cleveite, an ore. Helium in the atmosphere had been reported by the French astronomer Jules Janssen (1840–1907) at the time of the eclipse of the sun on 18 August 1868.

Neon, krypton, xenon (1898)

In 1898 Ramsay and the English chemist **Morris William Travers** (1872–1966) isolated other rare gases in the air: neon, krypton and xenon.

Radon (1900)

In **1900** the German **Ernst Dorn** discovered the last inert gas, radon, in the radioactive disintegration products of radium. Radon is a dangerous gas. In the United States it was discovered in 1986 that it could contaminate houses in certain regions. At present, 12 percent of American houses contain enough radon to make their inhabitants run the same risk of lung cancer as if they had smoked half a pack of cigarettes every day of their lives.

Water (1781)

The Swiss doctor Paracelsus (1493–1541) was the first person to draw attention to the existence of hydrogen.

In 1781 the English chemist **Henry Cavendish** (1731–1810) had the idea of burning oxygen and hydrogen together. He measured the quantities of the two gases and observed that they were converted into a quantity of water whose weight was the same as the sum of the weights of the two gases.

Lavoisier repeated and completed Cavendish's experiments. He had the idea of vaporising the water and separating the vapour into its two constituents, which he then combined to form water again. This series of experiments led him to state his famous law of the conservation of matter in a chemical reaction which states that the sum total of matter in the universe cannot be changed.

Changes of state

Atmospheric pressure (1643)

The Italian physicist and mathematician, pupil of Galileo, **Evangelista Torricelli** (1608–47) was the first to measure air pressure, in 1643. To prove the existence of atmospheric pressure, he used mercury, which is 13 times denser than water, so that he could work on more easily measurable heights. He filled a crucible and a glass tube with mercury, and inverted the open end of the tube over the crucible. The mercury level went down in the tube and stabilised at 76cm *30in* from the open surface of the crucible. Torricelli deduced from this that air exercised pressure on this surface, balanced by the hydrostatic pressure exercised by the 76cm *30in* of mercury in the tube. Torricelli's tube was the first barometer. The term barometer was invented by the Frenchman Edme Marlotte.

Vacuum (1654)

The German engineer **Otto von Guericke** (1602–86), a native of Magdeburg, developed the first vacuum pump. In 1654 von Guericke demonstrated it to the nobility of the Holy Empire.

He joined together two hollow bronze hemispheres, each 50cm *20in* in diameter. Creating a vacuum in the sphere, he harnessed two horses to each hemisphere. The horses pulled: nothing happened. He had two more horses added: still nothing. It took eight horses harnessed to each hemisphere to pull them apart.

A man of science, von Guericke was also a showman. During his experiments, he demonstrated that when burning candles were snuffed out in a vacuum, animals quickly expired, and bells no longer rang. These 'miracles' made his fellow countrymen take him for a magician.

Expansion of gases (1661)

In 1661 the Irish self-educated scientist **Robert Boyle** (1627–91) demonstrated that the variation in the volume of a gas is inversely proportional to the variation in its pressure. He was interested in the experiments of van Helmont and Pascal and directed his research towards the compressibility of gases. Using a simple graduated J tube and mercury, Boyle proved that the volume of the air imprisoned in the tube can be reduced by half by doubling the pressure exerted by the mercury.

Charles' Law (1798)

In 1798 Jacques Charles (1746–1823), a French physicist and ballooning enthusiast (he was the first person to think of filling balloons with hydrogen) pronounced the following law: if a gas is held at a constant pressure, its volume is directly proportional to its absolute temperature.

Gay-Lussac's Law (1804)

In 1804 the French physicist and chemist **Joseph Louis Gay-Lussac** (1778–1850) discovered that the volume of gas at a given temperature t is related to the volume at 0°C/*32°F* (if the pressure is constant) in the same way as the relationship discovered by Jacques Charles.

Ideal gas (19th century)

The French physicist **Emile Clapeyron** (1799–1864) was the first to use the notion of ideal or perfect gas. Ideal gas is a purely theoretical perfect fluid, which represents the limit of a real gas state in which the temperature tends towards absolute zero, and where the pressure becomes very high.

Liquifaction of gases

Origins (1818)

In 1818 the Englishman **Michael Faraday** (1791–1867) discovered a means of liquifying gas (i.e. transforming it from the gaseous state to the liquid state) by increasing the pressure when cooling the gas. The son of a blacksmith, Faraday started out as an errand boy in a bookshop and later became a bookbinder. An avid reader, he taught himself physics. To perfect his scientific knowledge, he enrolled in an evening course taught by Sir Humphry Davy and became his assistant at the Royal Institution.

In 1818 Faraday oriented his research in a direction that was entirely new for the day: studying the effects of pressure and cold on gases. Faraday successfully liquified hydrogen sulphide and sulphuric anhydride but did not succeed with oxygen, hydrogen or nitrogen.

Liquid oxygen (1877)

In 1877 the Frenchman **Louis-Paul Cailletet** (1832–1913), an ironmaster in Burgundy, invented a pump which enabled him to obtain and maintain pressures of hundreds of atmospheres.

He managed to liquify oxygen by causing the sudden expansion of gas in a capillary tube in which he decreased the pressure from 300 to 1 atmosphere which dropped the temperature to −118.9°C −*182°F*.

A few days after the success of this experiment, **Raoul-Pierre Pictet** (1846–1929), Professor of Physics at the University of Geneva, published the results of similar research.

The Irish chemist Thomas Andrews (1813–85) also liquified gases independently, and discovered the 'critical temperature'

which Cailletet and Pictet used in their further work on liquifaction.

Liquid air (1895)

In 1895 the inventor and industrialist **Karl von Linde** (1842–1934) succeeded in liquifying air by compression and expansion with intermediary cooling. He was thus able to separate the gases and prepare almost pure liquid oxygen.

In 1902 the French scientist Georges Claude (1870–1960) invented another process for liquifying air, by expanding the gas and applying an outside force. From the liquid air, he isolated oxygen, nitrogen and argon in liquid form by fractional distillation. He thus put in train the first industrial process for liquifying gases.

Liquid hydrogen (1899)

In 1899 the Englishman **Sir James Dewar** (1842–1923) used Linde's air liquifaction process to obtain boiling liquid hydrogen.

Liquid helium (1908)

In 1908 the Dutch physicist **Heike Kamerlingh Onnes** (1853–1926) liquified helium in his cryogenic laboratory in Leyden. Helium was the last gas to be liquified. Research did not end there, however. In 1971, in liquifying helium 3 (an isotope of helium 4, the gas's normal form) at less than 2.7mK, it was discovered that this also had the property of superfluidity (already discovered in helium 4); it has almost no viscosity.

Note that Onnes also discovered supraconductivity, now called superconductivity, in 1911: that is, the property of certain metals or alloys, at temperatures close to absolute zero, to lose their resistance to electrical currents.

Thermodynamics

Origins

In 1849 the Glasgow engineer **Sir William Thomson** (the future Lord Kelvin, 1824–1907) invented the term thermodynamics to describe the study of relations between thermal and mechanical phenomena, but the discipline as such may be said to have been founded by the Frenchman Sadi Carnot (1796–1832). Thermodynamics is the mathematical formulation of the parameters defining a system in the exchange of energy. These parameters are temperature, pressure and volume.

Carnot principle (1824)

After studying the steam engine invented in 1703 by the Englishman Thomas Newcomen (1663–1729), **Sadi Carnot** (1796–1832) stated in his only published work, *Reflections on the Motive Power of Fire* (1824), that mechanical energy could be produced by simple transfer of heat.

Work–heat equivalence (1842)

The German physicist and doctor **Julius Robert von Mayer** (1814–78), following Carnot, was interested in gases and the motor

By studying Newcomen's engine, Carnot developed the principle that bears his name.

power of heat. In **1842** he published the results of his research in *Annalen der Chemie und Pharmaciae*. He stated intuitively the theory that was later to be called the principle of work–heat equivalence.

This principle was confirmed by the numerous and exact measurements made by the Englishman **James Prescott Joule** (1818–89), working at the same time (between 1840 and 1845), turning his famous current meter in an isolated enclosure, filled with a liquid whose temperature he measured as it rose. Thus he was able to evaluate the quantity of heat set free by clearly defined mechanical work.

Temperature (1848)

In 1848 **Sir William Thomson** (Lord Kelvin) stated the zero principle of dynamics. This principle enabled him to define thermodynamic temperature and to establish an objective method of measuring it.

When two systems are each in thermal equilibrium with a third, they are in thermal equilibrium with each other. This equilibrium is expressed by their equal temperatures. If you give a conventional value to the temperature of a system in a given physical state, the other temperatures can be determined by what are called thermodynamic measures.

In 1961 the General Conference on Weights and Measures chose as the standard unit of thermodynamic temperature the Kelvin (K), defined as the degree on the thermodynamic scale of absolute temperatures at which the triple point of water is 273.16K (the

equivalent of 0°C). At this temperature, ice, water and steam can co-exist in equilibrium.

According to this convention the freezing and boiling points of water at one atmosphere are respectively 273.15K and 373.15K. The temperature interval measured by one Kelvin is equal to that which measures 1°C.

Principles of thermodynamics (1852/1906)

In 1852 **Sir William Thomson** stated the first two laws of thermodynamics based on the work of Carnot, von Mayer and Joule. The third principle was formulated in **1906** by the German physicist **Walter Hermann Nernst** (1864–1941).

Electricity and magnetism

Electrostatics

Origins

The Greeks had already observed the phenomenon of electricity, as Thales of Miletus (c.624–c.546 BC) relates in his writing, around 600 BC, describing the electrostatic power of a fossil resin found on the Baltic seashore: amber, which the Greeks called *elektron*.

Other phenomena had been recorded, such as the flash or electrotherapical response of a torpedo fish under a drop of water, but no links had been established between them.

First electrical machine (1672)

The first electrical generator was invented by the German physicist **Otto von Guericke** in the second half of the 17th century. It consisted of a revolving ball of sulphur to which friction was applied by a person's hands. Thanks to this machine, Guericke discovered in **1672** that the static electricity could cause the surface of the sulphur ball to glow, that is, he understood electroluminescence.

In 1708 the English doctor William Wall made the connection between electroluminescence and lightning.

Conductors (18th century)

Between **1727** and **1729** the English physicist **Stephen Gray** (1670–1736) discovered conductivity and carried out the first experiment of transporting electricity over a distance, using silk threads attached to a glass tube, which was rubbed, and an ivory ball.

In **1740** the French inventor **Jean Desaguliers** proposed that solids through which electricity freely circulates, such as iron and copper, should be called conductors, and those through which it does not circulate, such as glass or amber, should be called insulators.

Leyden jar (1745)

At this period electrical friction machines were perfected and became more powerful. The possibility was even discovered of accumulating strong electrical charges on a conductor isolated by glass or air. In **1745** the German **Ewald Jürgen von Kleist** made the first condenser, a few months before the invention of the famous Leyden jar, built by the Dutchman **Petrus van Musschenbroek**. The jar became a curiosity and attraction in the courts of Europe, the great and the wealthy across the continent coming to see how electric charges were produced. It is a glass jar coated inside and outside with tinfoil or other conducting material.

Lightning-conductor (1752)

The ground was prepared for **Benjamin Franklin**'s (1706–90) famous experiment of **1752**, when he flew a kite with a metal tip in a thunderstorm. The tip was joined to a piece of insulating silk holding the wet string, and thereby to an iron key which, dangling free in the air near the technician, filled the role of the condenser. Thanks to this contrivance, a dangerous one, Franklin could charge up a Leyden jar and prove that thunderclouds contained electricity.

Franklin made a fortune by inventing and selling lightning-conductors, and also became the most important politician in the United States. He is considered to be the first scientist of the New World.

Coulomb Laws (1785)

Between 1784 and 1789 the French engineer and physicist **Charles de Coulomb** invented his famous torsion balance, which enabled

Volta displays his newly-invented battery to Napoleon. Using a stack of discs of copper, zinc and cardboard moistened with salt solution, he demonstrated that he could produce a flow of electricity.

him to establish the fundamental laws of electrostatics (**1785**).

Volta's battery (1799)

In 1791 the Italian physiologist Luigi Galvani (1737–98) noted by chance that the muscles of a dissected frog contracted when they were touched at the same time by two different metals. He thought that the muscles contained a fluid which he called animal electricity.

Another Italian, **Alessandro Volta** (1745–1827) repeated Galvani's experiment and his work led him to invent in **1799** the first chemical battery, made up of alternating layers of silver, blotting paper impregnated with sulphuric acid, and zinc. The chemical generation of electricity was born. This invention led to Volta's being made a count by Napoleon Bonaparte in 1801.

In 1831 the English physicist Michael Faraday managed to produce an electric current by induction, rotating a metal disc across magnetic lines of force. The first generators worked by steam engines soon made their appearance. These large and not very powerful machines provided an alternating current.

Superconductivity (1911)

First discovered in mercury in **1911** by the Dutch scientist **Heike Kamerlingh Onnes**, who succeeded in liquifying helium at 4.2° Kelvin, that is −268.96°C −425.128°F, superconductivity is the property of certain metals or alloys, at very low temperatures, to lose their resistance to electricity. For a long time it was thought that this temperature would be in the range 0°–20°K.

After Kamerlingh Onnes's discovery, research stayed at the level of laboratory curiosity for a long time, until suddenly progress was made in a totally unexpected way, because of materials known for their insulating power and not as conductors: ceramics. The first work with these was carried out in the laboratory for crystallography and material sciences in the University of Caen in France.

But it was in 1986 that superconductivity really took off with the results obtained in IBM's Zurich laboratories on ceramic superconductors by two scientists, K. A. Müller (Swiss) and J. G. Bednorz (West German) which earned them the Nobel Prize for Physics in 1987. Their superconductivity record at −238°C −396.4°F launched an era of other records, which in their turn open up astonishing perspectives on tomorrow's technology: trains running by magnetic levitation, the stockpiling of enormous amounts of energy, new kinds of computer, etc.

Some scientists think that discoveries about superconductors could be as important in the future as was the invention of the transistor or the laser in the past. But, at the moment, there is a halt in further developments.

Electrodynamics

Ohm's Law (1827)

In **1827** the German physicist **Georg Simon Ohm** (1789–1854) used a hydraulic analogy to formulate a precise definition of the quantity of electricity, the electromotive force, and the intensity of a current, thereby formulating the law that bears his name. Ohm likened electric current to a liquid flow and the electric potential created by an electromotive force to a difference in level.

Joule effect (1841)

When a current passes through a homogeneous conductor, the conductor heats up. After 1882 this effect carried the name of the English physicist **James Prescott Joule** (1818–89), who formulated the law in **1841**.

The heat engendered by the passage of the current turns the filaments of incandescent lamps red. Elements are still used to produce heat in cookers, electric radiators, etc. The principle of the fuse is also based on this effect: a metal wire with a low fusion temperature is inserted into an electric circuit; if the intensity increases to an abnormal degree, the wire melts and the circuit is broken.

Electric discharge in gases

An electric discharge corresponds to the passage of charges, that is to the current in an environment which is a low conductor or insulator.

This superconducting cable is composed of 1600 filaments yet it is only 1.25mm 0.05in in diameter.

THE POLES AND EARTH'S MAGNETISM

We know that the magnetic needle of a compass always points towards the North Pole. This phenomenon is due to the existence of a magnetic field around the earth. In 1600 the Englishman William Gilbert was the first to realise that the earth is in fact a giant magnet whose magnetic poles are situated not far from the earth's geographic poles, meaning the points through which the earth's rotational axis passes. The lines of the earth's magnetic field run from south to north and form a gigantic structure around the earth.

What is the origin of this magnetic field? Inside the earth there is a zone called the outer core, situated at a depth of between 3000 and 5000km *1850* and *3100 miles*, in which molten iron circulates as the earth revolves. This liquid iron is a conductor of electric currents, and it is these electric currents which create the magnetic field through what is known as the 'dynamo effect'.

The earth's magnetic field would appear to originate inside the earth (as the German physicist and mathematician C. F. Gauss suspected in 1830), and its direct cause is the rotation of the earth. However, although we have strong reasons to believe in the accuracy of this theory, we do not have any formal proof.

The external regions of the earth's magnetic field, which form what is known as the magnetosphere, are subject to the action of the solar wind. This compresses the lines of the field and stretches them away from the sun to form a huge magnetic tail, rather like the tails of comets, which stretch more than 10 million kilometres *6 200 000 miles* from earth. The outer magnetic field is shaped like a gigantic cylinder centred around the earth–sun axis – a discovery made by means of probes and artificial satellites.

Paschen's Law

Two physicists, one German, **Friedrich Paschen** (1865–1947), and the other Irish, **Sir John Townsend** (1868–1957), showed that the breakdown potential of a gas between parallel plate electrodes is a function of the product of the gas pressure and the electrode separation. This potential is minimal for a determined value of the product in question. Paschen discovered this law empirically, and Townsend expressed it scientifically.

Neon tube (1909)

In 1909 the French scientist **Georges Claude** (1870–1960) invented the neon tube. This is a tube containing neon at low pressure, in which the gas becomes luminous when a certain voltage is applied to the electrodes. The neon light is one of the best-known applications of glow discharge.

Electromagnetism

Origins (1819)

In 1819 the Danish scientist **Christian Oersted** (1777–1851) proved that the passing of an electric current creates a magnetic field in the space surrounding the conductor. This phenomenon is induction: the current induces a magnetic field.

In 1820 the French scientist François Arago (1786–1853) made the first electromagnet. In 1820 also, the French mathematician André-Marie Ampère (1775–1836) developed his theory of the magnetic reactions of live electricity. He studied the reciprocal reactions of currents and magnets.

Induction (1831)

In 1831, while studying the results obtained by Oersted and Ampère, the Englishman **Michael Faraday** (1791–1867) discovered the principle of electromagnetic induction. Faraday's discovery had enormous technological ramifications. Among other things, it served as the basis for electricity-producing machines known as generators: the magneto, which produces a magnetic field by a permanent magnet; the dynamo, for producing direct current; and the alternator, for alternating current.

Foucault current

The self-educated French physicist **Jean Bernard Léon Foucault** (1819–68) was the first to demonstrate the existence of electric currents inducted by an alternating magnetic field in a massive conductor. Named in honour of their discoverer, these currents create a magnetic induction whose flow opposes that of the alternating magnetic field that produces them. The mechanical force resulting from the passage of these currents is therefore always a resisting force.

Foucault currents, also known as eddy currents, have many applications, including induction-heating and electromagnetic braking systems.

Electromagnetic waves (1864)

James Clerk Maxwell (1831–79), a pupil of Michael Faraday, was one of the most illustrious physicists of the 19th century, and in 1864 was the first to suppose the existence of electromagnetic waves. Although Maxwell was not able to prove his theory experimentally, he hypothesised that light has an electromagnetic nature.

Electronics

Cathode rays (19th century)

Around 1850 the German **Heinrich Geissler** (1815–79), who had been a glass blower before becoming a manufacturer of laboratory equipment, constructed glass containers equipped with electrodes, in which he created a vacuum. He thus obtained very attractive lighting effects that varied with the shape of the container and the type of gas used. This phenomenon was further observed by two more Germans, Julius Plücker (1801–68) in 1854, and Johann Hittorf (1824–1914) in 1869.

In 1879 the Englishman **William Crookes** (1832–1912) carried out experiments proving once and for all that rays were emitted by the cathode of such glass tubes.

In 1895 the Frenchman **Jean Perrin** (1870–1942) demonstrated that cathode rays are charged with negative electricity and that they are deflected by electric or magnetic fields.

In 1897 the Englishman **Sir Joseph Thomson** (1846–1940) calculated the ratio between the charge and the mass of the particles emitted. It then became apparent that these particles were electrons. The existence of electrons was first hypothesised in 1874 by the Irishman George Stoney (1826–1911), who named them in 1891.

Cathode-ray oscilloscope (1897)

In 1897 the German physicist **Karl Ferdinand Braun** (1850–1918) perfected the cathode-ray oscilloscope. The trajectory of cathode rays is rectilinear, but, in an electric field, they are deflected in proportion to the voltage applied. The cathode-ray oscilloscope can display the transient or repeated wave forms on a fluorescent surface.

The cathode-ray tube is the device that creates an image on television screens. In this case, a signal is induced in the television's aerial by a signal given by the transmitter of the broadcasting network.

Semi-conductors (1929)

A semi-conductor is a solid with an electrical conductivity somewhere between that of an insulator and that of a metal. An insulator when at low temperatures, a semi-conductor becomes a conductor when subject to increased heat or light. The odd phenomenon of electrical conductivity had already been noted by Michael Faraday (1839, in his experiments with silver sulphide) and by Karl Ferdinand Braun (1874, on galenite), without having been explained.

The first coherent theory of conductivity in solids (covering the properties of insulators, conductors and semi-conductors) was produced by **Felix Bloch** (born in 1905), a Swiss physicist who became an American citizen in 1939. In 1929 he suggested a theory of bands. Between 1925 and 1935, Bloch and scientists from various countries perfected the theory of semi-conductors.

The understanding of the semi-conductor mechanism was the basis for the invention of the transistor, which was to revolutionise electronics.

Electronic gate (1986)

The **Bell laboratories** at AT&T and Cornell University in the USA established in **1986** the speed record for semi-conductors: they created an electronic gate prototype, capable of interrupting an electric signal in 5.8 millionths of a second (i.e. 5.8 pico-seconds). During this time a light ray could only travel 1.6mm *0.063in*. Some parts of the circuit measure just a third of a micron.

Atomic and nuclear physics

Atom (5th century BC)

The Greek philosophers of the **5th century BC** were the first to suggest that all matter was made up of invisible particles: atoms.

Atomic theories

The first modern atomic theory was created by the English physicist **John Dalton** (1766–1844), who in 1801 adopted the Classical hypothesis of the indivisibility of matter, and gave it a scientific basis. In 1810 the Frenchman **Joseph Louis Gay-Lussac**, experimenting with chemical actions in gases, established that gases combine in simple proportions by volume, and that the volumes of the products are related to the original volumes, thus refuting Dalton's theory.

The phenomenon was explained by the Italian **Amedeo di Quaregna e Ceretto**, Count Avogadro (1776–1856), who distinguished clearly between the atom and the molecule.

In 1897 the indivisible nature of the atom was taken up again by the Englishman Sir Joseph John Thomson and the Frenchman Jean Baptiste Perrin, who won the Nobel Prize for Physics in 1906 and 1926 respectively.

Rutherford's atom (1911)

The explosion of a radioactive atom discharges alpha particles with great energy. When a beam of alpha rays passes through a thin metal plate, some particles are widely deflected. To explain this phenomenon, revealed by the experiments of the German Hans Geiger (1882–1945) and his team, the New Zealander **Ernest Rutherford** (1871–1937; later Lord Rutherford, winner of the Nobel Prize for Chemistry in 1908) in **1911** went back to Jean Perrin's hypothesis of the nuclear structure of atoms. That is that all the mass and all the positive charges are concentrated in a small central nucleus, which creates an intense field of attraction in which electrons revolve around the nucleus in the same way that the earth revolves round the sun.

Rutherford calculated that these positive particles are about 1836 times the mass of the electrons: he called them protons. The neutral atom helium has a nucleus made up of two protons, around which revolve two electrons.

Bohr's atom (1913)

The Danish physicist **Niels Bohr** (1885–1962, Nobel Prize for Physics in 1922), inspired by the quantum theory proposed in 1900 by Max Planck (1858–1947), suggested in **1913** a theory explaining the radiation emitted by atoms, when under electric discharge, for example.

Arnold Sommerfeld (1868–1951), a German mathematician and physicist, began in 1915 to apply relativist mechanics and quantum theory to the atom to explain the fine structure of spectral lines from hydrogen. He explained that the circular orbits suggested by Bohr were in fact elliptical orbits.

The atom in wave mechanics (1925–6)

The Bohr–Sommerfeld model, in which the electrons were precisely located on an orbit, precluded the development of atomic mechanics that could take account of all the phenomena involving atoms.

Two physicists developed a satisfactory theory from **1925–6**. The Austrian **Erwin Schrödinger** (Nobel Prize for Physics, 1933) applied to the atom the Frenchman Louis de Broglie's idea: an electron, or any other particle, has a wave associated with it.

The German **Werner Heisenberg** (Nobel Prize for Physics, 1932) formulated his uncertainty principle which said that it was impossible simultaneously to determine the position and the momentum of a particle with absolute certainty, enabling the combination of Schrödinger's formalist mathematics with a physical interpretation which satisfied the wave–particle duality.

The periodic table of elements (1869)

A fundamental stage in the development of chemistry, and of modern science in general, the table was the work of the Russian **Dimitri Mendeleev** (1834–1907) in **1869**. It enabled scientists to establish relationships between various chemical elements that had been considered as independent entities, and to understand why certain elements had the same properties.

The interesting thing about this classification is that it shows the periodic variations of chemical and physical properties in the chemical elements when they are classed in ascending order of their atomic mass.

The 110th element (1987)

The 110th element, according to Mendeleev's periodic table, was synthesised for the first time in **August 1987** by researchers in the **Doubna Nuclear Research Institute** near Moscow. This new element was obtained from a U-400 cyclotron, at the end of two years' work by **Professor Yuri Aganessian**. Experiments are under way to obtain a 111th element.

Avogadro's number (1811)

In 1811 the Italian **Amedeo di Quaregna e Ceretto (Count Avogadro)** (1776–1856),

Professor of Physics at the University of Turin, established a law that was named after him. Avogadro assumed that in analogous conditions of temperature and pressure, equal volumes of gas contain the same number of molecules.

Avogadro's hypothesis did not gain immediate recognition. It was not until some 50 years later that an Italian chemist, **Stanislao Cannizzaro** (1828–1910), demonstrated the necessity for adopting Avogadro's concept as the basis for a coherent atomic theory. Cannizzaro honoured Avogadro by giving his name to an atomic constant. He defined the Avogadro number as the number of gaseous molecules contained in a gram-molecule of any substance, that is, the quantity of that substance occupying a volume of 22.4 litres *9.48cu.ft* in typical conditions of temperature and pressure.

Natural radioactivity (1896)

In nature, some heavy nuclei emit natural radioactivity. The Frenchman **Henri Becquerel** (1852–1908) discovered this phenomenon in Paris in **1896** while performing experiments on uranium. In fact, it was the discovery of X-rays that led to the discovery of radioactivity.

One cloudy day in Paris, Becquerel set up an experiment designed to verify whether a sample of pitchblende (a black mineral composed of uranium and potassium) exposed to sunlight emitted X-rays. Unable to complete his work because of the weather conditions, Becquerel put his equipment away. He resumed the experiment another day when the weather had improved, placing the samples of pitchblende on a photographic plate that had not been removed from its wrapping. When later developing the plate, he was surprised to see an image appear whose contours followed the outline of the ore sample perfectly. What could possibly be the origin of the 'energy' in the mineral that was capable of leaving an impression on a photographic plate?

Radium and polonium (1898)

Becquerel took the matter up with his friends **Pierre Curie** (1859–1906) and his wife, **Marie** (1867–1934). Examining the pitchblende

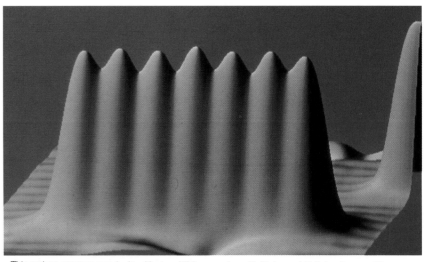

This curious structure was 'written' by two IBM researchers, D. Eigler and E. Schweitzer, and it demonstrates that each atom can be moved and very precisely repositioned.

more closely, Pierre and Marie Curie discovered that the radiation had been caused by at least one substance that was much more radioactive than uranium. Finally, after two years of unrelenting and meticulous work, the Curies revealed the existence of not one but two elements that emitted this strange radiation: radium and polonium. The second one was named in honour of Marie Curie, née Sklodowska, who was Polish by birth. For these discoveries Henri Becquerel shared the 1903 Nobel Prize for Physics with Pierre and Marie Curie.

Radioactive disintegration (1902)

Sir Frederick Soddy, English physicist and chemist (1877–1956, winner of the Nobel Prize for Chemistry in 1921), explained the phenomenon of radioactive decay of atomic nuclei, thus paving the way for research in nuclear energy.

Geiger counter (1913)

The Geiger counter was invented in 1913 by the New Zealand physicist Ernest Rutherford and his German assistant, Hans Geiger. This enabled them to locate and count alpha particles, a constituent of the rays emitted by radioactive decay.

Artificial radioactivity (1934)

In 1934, in Paris, Irène (1897–1956) and Frédéric (1900–1958) Joliot-Curie (the daughter and son-in-law of Pierre and Marie Curie) obtained radioactive phosphorus by bombarding aluminium with alpha particles (the nuclei of helium).

In their natural state, certain elements such as radium, neptunium and actinium are radioactive. Nuclear reactions, on the other hand, bring into play the disintegration of atomic nuclei, thus obtaining radioactive nuclei unknown in nature: these elements are said to have an artificial radioactivity.

This discovery earned the Joliot-Curies the Nobel Prize for Chemistry in 1935, and has enabled the fabrication of isotopes used in medicine, biology, metallurgy, etc.

Transuranian elements (1940)

The discovery of artificial radioactivity in 1934 led physicists of the time to think that there might be bodies with atomic numbers greater than Z92, the number of uranium in the periodic table. These are called transuranian bodies. The first one was discovered in June 1940 at the University of California at Berkeley by E. M. McMillan and P. H. Abelson. They called it neptunium, and it has an atomic mass of Z93. At the end of 1940 G. T. Seaborg, J. W. Kennedy and A. C. Wahl discovered plutonium, of mass Z94.

The latest element was discovered at Doubna in 1987. Its atomic mass is Z110. Theoreticians such as Sven Gosta Nilsson and the Swedish school think that Z114 could exist.

X-rays (1895)

In September 1895 in Würzburg the German physicist Wilhelm Conrad Röntgen (1845–1923) discovered X-rays. Röntgen called the rays 'X' because their nature was then unknown. It was not defined until 1912, by another German physicist, Max von Laue (1879–1960), who managed to diffract them through a lattice of crystal.

X-rays are electromagnetic waves, which pass through material that is normally opaque to light. These rays have a very short wavelength.

The discovery of X-rays immediately created a considerable stir. Röntgen, a national hero before the century was out, was awarded the Nobel Prize for Physics in 1901.

Nuclear magnetic resonance (1946)

Now a means of medical investigation, NMR is a physical phenomenon which was discovered in 1946 by the Swiss-born American physicists Felix Bloch and Edward Mills Purcell, who jointly obtained the Nobel Prize for Physics in 1952.

NMR or nuclear induction is a method of

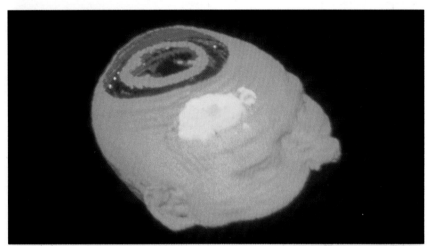

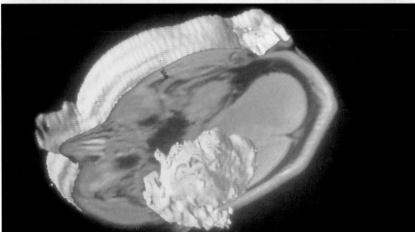

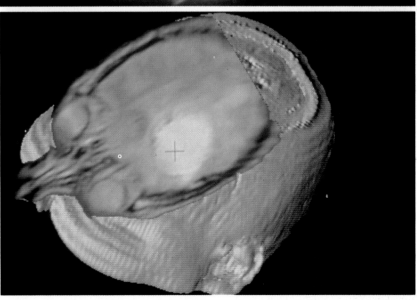

These three views of the same skull show a tumour from three different angles, thanks to nuclear magnetic resonance. Because of this, the surgeon can decide where best to make the incision to operate.

measuring the magnetic field of atomic nuclei, using a particular property of the proton whose behaviour is closely linked to its environment.

It is especially useful in analysis, as it allows the precise detection of specific atoms in a number of areas: in botany, in geology, in food technology, etc.

Carbon 14 (1947)

In **1947 William Frank Libby**, an American chemist specialising in the radioactivity of living organisms and recipient of the 1960 Nobel Prize for Chemistry, explained the formation of carbon 14 in the atmosphere. Carbon 14 is an isotope of common carbon, carbon 12. It has two more neutrons than carbon 12.

Carbon dating

The dating of ancient objects by means of carbon 14 is based on the extent of the residual activity of isotope 14 in carbon.

A number of other radioactive isotopes, contained in samples from this or that event, allow the occurrence to be dated along the same principles (measuring the residual activity of a radioactive isotope whose period is known). Argon–potassium dating is much used. Such a process, used on the charcoal of the Lascaux caves in France, enabled scientists to date the habitation of the caves to 13 000 years BC.

One of the most famous recent examples of carbon dating has been its use on the Holy Shroud of Turin, considered by many Christians to be Christ's shroud. Three institutions – the British Museum, the University of Arizona and the Federal Institute of Technology in Zurich – took part in this work, the results of which were made known at the end of 1988: in fact, the shroud dates back to the Middle Ages.

Particles

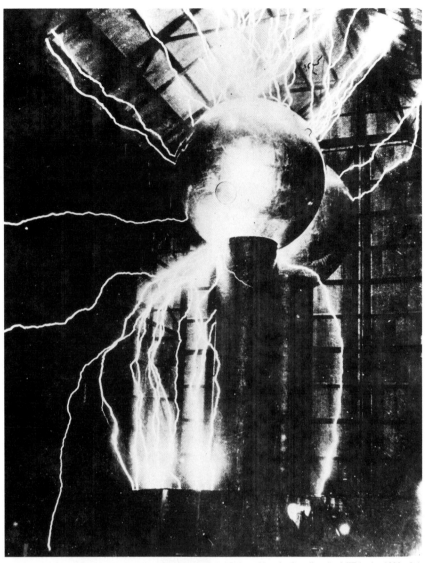

This is one of the first Van de Graaff generators, built by Robert Van de Graaff at the MIT in the 1930s. It is a high voltage electrostatic generator and one of the first sub-atomic particle accelerators. It can produce such high electrical potentials that man-made lightning is created.

Elementary particles

An elementary particle is one which is 'indivisible', which has neither dimension nor internal structure. Of course some particles may appear to be elementary at one time in scientific history, and then later be revealed as complex. This was the case, for example, with the proton and the neutron.

At present elementary particles are organised in two categories: the leptons and the quarks, with which antiparticles are also associated. The existence of the latter was suggested by the English physicist **P. A. M. Dirac** in **1929**. Even by observing them closely by the most powerful particle accelerators, no one has been able to detect the slightest internal structure in leptons, quarks and their antiparticles.

Leptons

The electron (1875)

This was the first lepton to be discovered. Its existence was deduced from electromagnetic experiments made by **Sir Joseph John Thomson** from **1875**. Its negative electric charge was precisely determined by the American R. A. Millikan in 1916. The positron, which is the antiparticle associated with the electron, was discovered in cosmic rays in 1932 by the American C. D. Anderson.

The neutrino (1933)

The existence of this lepton was postulated by the Austrian-born Swiss physicist **Wolfgang Pauli** in **1933**, to explain certain phenomena in beta radioactivity and it was named neutrino (tiny neutron) by the Italian Enrico Fermi. It is an extremely light particle, which can travel through dense matter like the earth without difficulty because it hardly interacts with matter. It was directly identified towards the end of the 1950s by the Americans Reines and George Arthur Cowan.

It is now known that there are in fact three types of neutrino, associated respectively with the electron, the muon and the tau.

The muon (1937)

Discovered in **1937** by **C. D. Anderson** in collaboration with **Neddemeyer**, the mass of the muon is 206.77 times that of the electron. It was created in an accelerator in 1939.

The tau (1976)

This came to the fore during an experiment on collisions between electrons and positrons, run by **Professor Martin L. Perl** and his team at Stanford (USA) in **1976**. Its mass is 3600 times that of the electron.

Quarks (1964)

In **1964** the physicists **Murray Gell-Mann** and **George Zweig** independently postulated the existence of quarks (although Zweig called them 'aces') as the fundamental constituents of protons and neutrons. There are now thought to be six quarks, known by their English names: Up, Down, Strange, Charm, Bottom, and Top. A team at the European Centre for Nuclear Research (CERN) found experimental evidence of Top's existence in 1984, and estimated its mass at 30–50 billion electron volts.

The physicist Greenberg proved that quarks must have a new kind of charge, which he called colour, which takes the form of three different shades, conventionally blue, red and green.

Composite particles

These are not elementary particles but are made up of elementary particles linked together. There are lots of composite particles in nature; the proton, the neutron and the pion are the most important examples.

The proton (1886)

The discovery of the proton goes back to an experiment conducted by the German physicist **E. Goldstein** in 1886. It is the main constituent of the atomic nucleus, with a positive charge, and is made up of three quarks.

WHAT DO PARTICLE ACCELERATORS DO?

Knowledge of the innermost structure of matter is in fact the main concern of scientists, whatever their specific field. On this depends our understanding, and perhaps our control, of the universe.

In order to penetrate the organisation of matter, we must break it down to its most elementary particles. This is what researchers are doing when they use particle accelerators. By bombarding their targets with electrons, neutrons, positrons or antiprotons at a great speed, or by causing head-on collisions between these particles, scientists are able to penetrate even further into this field of knowledge.

The neutron (1932)

This is the second constituent of the atomic nucleus, which was discovered by the Englishman **James Chadwick** in 1932, following on from the work done by W. Bothe in Germany and the Joliot-Curies in France. Its name comes from the fact that it is electrically neutral. It is made up of two Down quarks and one Up.

The pion (1935)

In 1935 the Japanese physicist **Hideki Yukawa** postulated the existence of a new particle to explain the transmission of nuclear force: the π-meson or pion. He predicted that it would have about 200 times the mass of an electron. The pion was actually discovered in 1947. It is made up of a quark and an antiquark (the antiparticle associated with the quark).

Bosons

These are particles associated with classic waves. They appear also as the particles exchanged during the process of fundamental interactions. Their name derives from the fact that they obey Bose–Einstein statistics.

The photon (1923)

'Invented' by Albert Einstein in 1905 to explain the photoelectric effect, the photon is a light particle. It 'carries' the electromagnetic force between charged particles. The American physicist **A. H. Compton** found evidence of its existence in 1923.

The graviton (21st century)

This is a particle in the gravitational field. At

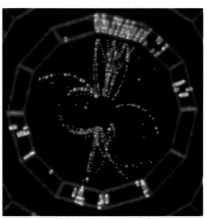

The disintegration of Z° in quark and anti-quark appear in the form of two sprays of particles.

present it only exists as an abstract concept. It is thought that gravitational waves may be formed from a large number of gravitons.

Weak interaction bosons (1983)

There are three of these, called W⁻, W⁺ and Z⁰, which were found to exist by a team of 200 research workers led by the Italian **Carlo Rubbia** and the Dutchman **Simon van der Meer** at CERN in Geneva in 1983.

Gluons (1982)

There are eight gluons responsible for strong nuclear interactions. They have never been seen, but an experiment conducted in 1982 by a group of American research workers from Brookhaven and the City College in New York seems to prove their existence.

Professor Chan Joshi has been working in California on the creation of a plasma particle accelerator.

Chemistry

Inorganic chemistry

Acids

Nitric acid (1838)

The preparation of nitric acid by the catalytic oxidation of ammonia gas was discovered in **1838** by the French chemist **Frédéric Kuhlmann**; the catalyst used in the reaction was platinum.

Using this method, the German chemist Wilhelm (1853–1932) made nitric acid on a small scale. But when another German chemist, Carl Bosch (1874–1940) replaced platinum with a catalyst based on iron, manganese and bismuth, the production of nitric acid on an industrial scale could be considered. The resulting production of nitrates replaced·the natural nitrates which had been imported from Chile.

Sulphuric acid (18th century)

The first sulphuric acid plants were created in England in the **18th century**. They used the leaden condensing chamber developed in 1746 by the Scottish chemical engineer John Roebuck (1718–94). For the first time a link was formed between the laboratory and industry.

In 1774 steam replaced water in the process, which changed from discontinuous to continuous.

Aluminium (1886)

In 1822 the French mineralogist Pierre Berthier (1782–1861) discovered near the village of Les Baux, in Provence, the first deposits of an ore which he named bauxite. It was in fact hydrous alumina (aluminium oxide).

In 1825 the Danish scientist Hans Christian Oersted obtained aluminium in a powdered form, and in 1827 it was created in the form of an ingot by the German scientist Friedrich Wöhler (1800–82).

In **1886** the French metallurgist **Paul-Louis Héroult** (1863–1914) and the American **Charles Martin Hall** (1863–1914) discovered independently, but almost simultaneously, the process of electrolysis, still in use, which was to give rise to the aluminium industry.

Since then, because of technological progress, aluminium has never ceased to grow in importance.

Ammonia (1908)

By applying the laws of chemical equilibrium, the German chemist **Fritz Haber** succeeded in **1908** in synthesising ammonia using the elements which make up this substance: nitrogen and hydrogen.

The industrial development of the procedure in 1909 by BASF was the work of another German chemist, Carl Bosch. By converting atmospheric nitrogen into ammonia, this process ensured a ready supply of fertilisers.

Cadmium (1817)

This silver-white metal, with its slight tinge of blue, was produced for the first time in the laboratory in **1817** by the German chemist **Frederic Strohmeyer** using its oxide present in a sample of zinc carbonate. In 1818 Strohmeyer proposed the name cadmium for this newly discovered metal because it was mainly recovered from the zinc *cadmia fornacum*, flowers formed on the walls of ovens used to distil zinc.

Industrial production of cadmium began in 1827 in Upper Silesia. The main uses of cadmium and its compounds are electroplating alloys and car radiators. In addition, cadmium rods are used to control the flux of neutrons in nuclear reactors.

Ceramics (7th millennium BC)

Terracotta pottery, invented simultaneously in Turkey, Syria and Kurdistan in the **7th millennium BC**, was the first technique to transform matter of mineral origin by the use of fire. With pottery, man had invented the first artificial material.

In general, antique pottery had one major drawback: it was not watertight. Thus, through the centuries, men attempted to perfect a watertight clay as well as the exterior varnishing.

Alexandre Brongniart, in the mid-19th century, created the precursor of modern pottery, before the appearance of industrial ceramics around the 1950s, with neoceramics based on the principle of calcination, and oxide ceramics. Because they hardly expand, the latter are very resistant to heat and are thus used in the aerospace industry.

Transparent ceramics (1988)

A transparent ceramic used in the new scanner-detectors has been commercially produced since **1988** by the American firm **General Electrics**. These new detectors are made up of 900 sensitive elements (from photodiodes to silicon) placed side by side and covered with a block of transparent ceramic. This material (HiLight Ceramic) acts as a scintillator when hit by X-rays.

Superconductive ceramics (1988)

The American company **Du Pont** has applied for a patent for a superconductive ceramic, which is more stable and easier to manage than the non-resistant materials currently in use for carrying electricity.

Expandable ceramics (1990)

Another innovation in the field of ceramics is the development of superplastic ceramics. The Japanese scientist **Fumihiro Wakai** and the research teams of Mitsubishi and the University of Osaka have produced ceramics which can undergo deformation (elongation) through heating.

Chlorine (1774)

In **1774** the Swedish chemist and pharmacist **Carl Wilhelm Scheele** (1742–86) discovered chlorine, by causing hydrochloric acid to

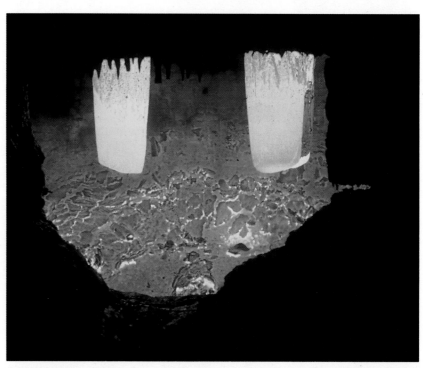

Two large graphite electrodes glow over the molten metal in a furnace after a firing. The electrodes are made by the BOC Group for applications in electric arc furnaces that are typically employed for the production of metal alloys.

react with manganese dioxide. From salt-petre Scheele also discovered tartric, oxalic and lactic acids and glycerine.

In 1810 the English chemist **Sir Humphry Davy** (1778–1829) recognised chlorine as a new element. A constituent of all living organisms, it does not exist in a free state in nature. It is found only in the form of chlorides (hydrochloric acid salts).

Cobalt (1735)

This metal was isolated for the first time in 1735 by the Swedish chemist **Georg Brandt** from copper minerals found in the Harz region. The word cobalt is derived from the Middle High German word *Kobalt*, which means goblin, because the vapours given off during the fusion of copper minerals, which contain cobalt, are toxic.

In 1910 it was discovered that this metal improved high-speed steel, and metallurgists became interested in it. Cobalt is used in alloys that are resistant to high temperatures, in magnetic materials and in hardwearing alloys that resist corrosion.

Germanium (1885)

While analysing argyrodite ore, the German chemist **Clemens Winkler** discovered in 1885 a new metal, which he named germanium, after its country of origin. Germanium is easy to purify and is used as a solid semi-conductor in transistors and rectifiers.

Germanium dioxide is used in the composition of glass with a high refractive index. It is also a good catalyst in the polymerisation of polyester.

Porcelain (6th century)

The first porcelain that can be definitely dated was manufactured in China in the 6th century. In 1698 a German industrialist, Baron Schnorr, discovered the first European deposits of kaolin in Saxony. At the same time, the Germans von Schirnahaus (1651–1708) and Johan Friedrich Böttger (1682–1719) perfected the process for making porcelain.

In 1752 the discovery of kaolin deposits in Saint-Yrieix-la-Perche in central France led to the rapid development of porcelain factories in Limoges.

Semi-crystals (1984)

A geometric rule requires that the elementary figure of a crystal possesses symmetrical axes of the order of two, three, four or six only. Symmetry of the order of five is impossible in practice, for the simple reason that a pentagon does not have its edges touching in space.

In 1984, however, four research workers announced the discovery of a structure in matter symmetrical to the order of five. The discovery was made jointly by **Dan Schechtmann** and **Ilon Blech** of the institute of technology, Technion, in Haifa; by **Denis Gratias** of the centre for metallurgical chemistry at CRNS in France, and by **John Cahn** of the National Bureau of Standards in Washington. They chose to call this new stable state of matter semi-crystal, not entirely a crystal and not entirely amorphous.

In 1985 mathematical models created by computer showed that this impossible structure was feasible in a six-dimensional space, and in July 1986 a team at the Péchiney research centre in France managed to create a cupro-manganese alloy made up of single crystals observable by the naked eye.

This discovery enables scientists to envisage the fabrication of new alloys whose resistance and lightness could completely alter the industrial scene. Makers of aeroplanes are watching these new developments with particular attention.

Excellent conductors of heat and very stable up to temperatures of 400°C semi-crystals are ideal to coat hot-plates on cookers and frying pans. The technique was patented in 1988 by Jean-Marie Dubois, a chemist and director of research at the French CNRS. Pans thus coated will be able to cook an omelette in 5–10 seconds and meat in 35–40 seconds.

Silicon (1823)

This is the most common element on the surface of the globe (28 percent) after oxygen, with which it is associated in the form of silica (flint) or silicates (clay). It was isolated in its pure state for the first time in 1823 by the Swedish chemist **Jöns Jakob Berzelius** (1779–1848), one of the creators of modern chemistry. It has important uses in metallurgy, where it increases the resistance of steel to corrosion. It is also used in the making of light alloys, such as alpax (aluminium–silicon), which have many uses: pistols, casings, bicycle wheels, electrical appliances, etc.

It is increasingly used to make semiconductors in the electronics industry, and in the plastics industry.

It is used in the plastics industry and, of course, in electronics for the manufacture of silicon chips. In the United States, the name Silicon Valley was given to the Santa Clara region in California, where most of the factories using silicon as a raw material in the manufacture of semiconductors are concentrated.

Tungsten (1781)

Discovered in 1781 by the Swedish chemist **Carl Wilhelm Scheele**, tungsten is a hard, malleable element. Its name means heavy stone in Swedish. Tungsten is the most fire resistant element known to date, with a melting point of 3410°C 6170°F.

Tungsten is used in the manufacture of lamp filaments, and in the composition of silver, copper, zinc, pewter, argyrodite and germanite based minerals. The main sources are found in China, Korea, the United States and the USSR.

Organic chemistry

Organic chemistry is a branch of chemistry which deals with carbon and its compounds. The carbon on earth is of organic origin. Plants produce it through photosynthesis. Coal and oil (hydrocarbons) are a result of the fossilisation of living organisms.

Bakelite (1907)

In 1907 **Leo Hendrik Baekeland** (1863–1944), a Belgian chemist living in the United States, invented the first duroplastic resin, bakelite. It was designed as a rubber substitute, as rubber was prone to drying out and cracking. Bakelite could be shaped and set under extreme heat and pressure and would then remain hard and heat-resistant. It was ideal for such objects as pan handles.

Formaldehyde (1868)

Discovered in 1868 by **August Wilhelm von Hofmann** (1818–92), it is used in the textile industry, in papermaking, tannery, dyeing, photography and joinery (wood glues). It is also a base of synthetic resins and insulating foam which is injected into partitions.

Moreover, formaldehyde is used, because of its antiseptic properties, as a disinfectant in solution, known as formol. Formol is easily polymerised into metaldehyde, in which form it is used as blocks for lighting barbecues.

Inspection of tapped rubber trees in a Malayan plantation. The latex from within the tree flows gradually down the bole of the tree and into a bowl. Tapping is done early in the day.

DREAMING THE STRUCTURE OF BENZENE

Benzene is a hydrocarbon with the formula C_6H_6, and the question of its structure was one of the oldest mysteries of organic chemistry. The German chemist August Kakule (1829–96) had long been searching for an answer to this question when one night he dreamed of a snake biting its own tail. In the morning he understood that to explain all the chemical properties of benzene the molecule had to bite its own tail just like the snake: it had to have a cyclical structure in which the six atoms of carbon are arranged in a circle, their six linkages forming a hexagon.

RUBBER AND PLASTIC

Invention	Date	Characteristics
Rubber	1736	Natural rubber was discovered by the French naturalist Charles Marie de La Condamine, on an assignment in Peru.
Nitrocellulose	1833	Obtained by two French chemists T. J. Pelouze and H. Braconnot. First industrial use as cotton-powder by the German C. F. Schoenbein, 1847.
Vulcanisation	1839	This technique, which stabilises the properties of rubber and makes it usable, was invented by the American Charles Goodyear.
Artificial rubber	1860	The isolation of isoprene by the Englishman Charles G. Williams. First successful use: G. Bourchardat (France), 1880, and Tilden, 1884.
Cellulose acetate	1869	Obtained by J. Schutzenberger. Patents for industrial production: Charles Cross and Edward J. Bevan, 1884.
Celluloid	1870	Invented by the American Hyatt brothers for making billiard balls, a mouldable mixture of camphor and nitrated cellulose.
Rayon	1891	In 1891 Charles Cross obtained the patent for fabricating cellulose xanthate, the basis of cellulose. In 1921 Edward Bevan obtained a patent for obtaining rayon from acetate.
Cellophane	1908	Invented in 1908 (trademark registered in 1912) by J. E. Branderburger, who regenerated cellulose xanthate in order to make not fibres but a transparent film: cellophane.
Bakelite	1909	The first synthetic plastic material, patented by a Belgian named Hendrik Baekeland, living in the USA. This phenoplastic remains interesting because it will not melt after its first heating and setting, and is a good insulator.
PVC	1913	In 1913 the German Professor Klatte patented the polymerisation of a gas, vinyl chloride. It was put into industrial production in 1931 by I. G. Farben. PVC is used in many things: soles of shoes, fibres, bottles. Its near relation is vinyl polyacetate (used in microchips).
Polymers	1922	The structure of polymers, made up of very long chains of thousands, even hundreds of thousands, of atoms, these chains spreading out or forming links with each other, was discovered in 1922 by the German chemist Hermann Staudinger (Nobel Prize for Chemistry, 1953). In 1980 the Norwegian John Ugelstad, of the University of Trondheim, invented a process for making polymers from particles of the same size, which is particularly interesting for medical science.
Plexiglass	1924	In 1924 Barker and Skinner made an organic glass, the polymethacrylate of methyl, commercialised in 1934 by Rohm under the name Plexiglass (from 'plastic flexible glass'). The organic glass in spectacles comes from the same family.
Polystyrene	1933	Perfected by Wuff (Germany). Good-looking, it is used for pens and toys. A family of styrene polymers ensued, among them the stretch polystyrene invented by BASF in 1951.
Polyamides (nylon, kevlar)	1935	In 1935 W. H. Carothers perfected at Du Pont (USA) the first polymide fibres. He patented polymide 6-6 or nylon in 1937. In 1965 Stephanie Kwolek, at Du Pont, created kevlar, a descendant of bakelite and nylon. One of the latest Du Pont polymides is kapton. Although polymides are best known as fibres, they also make excellent technical plastics. The latest to be created, Dinyl and Pebax, are French.
Polyurethanes	1937	Invented by Otto Bayer. Many different forms and uses.
Teflon	1938	Known as Teflon, the tetrafluorethylene polymer was discovered by Roy J. Plunkett, an engineer at Du Pont (USA) in 1938 (patented in 1939). The idea of spreading it over a metal was invented by Marc Gregoire in 1954 (used for saucepans, etc.).
Polyesters	1938	First synthesised in 1901 (Smith). First used in 1927. First heat-resistant polyesters (Ellis, 1938). Reinforced by glass fibres (US Rubber, 1942). There is an enormous variety of polyesters. PET belongs to the family of linear thermoplastic polyesters, and was obtained by the Englishmen Dickson and Whinfield in 1940, and commercialised in 1946 under the name of Dacron.

Polyethylenes	1939	The first grams of low density polyethylene (PED) were obtained by Fawcett and Gibson for ICI (UK) in 1935. Industrial production began in 1939. Used notably in radar construction which enabled the British victory over the Luftwaffe in 1940. Excellent insulator. High density polyethylene (PEHD) obtained by Karl Ziegler of Germany (Nobel Prize for Chemistry, 1963) in 1953. In 1985 DSM (Holland) and Allied (USA) produced a polyethylene fibre 30 times stronger than the best steel of the same weight.
Polypropylene	1954	The polymerisation of propylene perfected by Giulio Natta (Italy) in 1954.
Peba	1981	A new family of synthetic materials created by Gérard Delens (ATOCHEM), intermediary between rubber and plastics.
Biodegradable plastic	1989	First plastic made from natural materials.

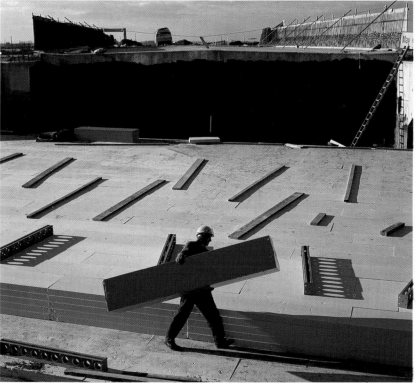

Construction workers are here seen laying part of a trunk road using large polystyrene blocks instead of the normal infill. The technique was developed in Scandinavia and has recently been adopted in the UK. It is cheap, quick and much safer to use. The blocks are covered by a thick layer of plastic.

This photograph of cellophane was taken in polarised light. The basis of this plastic is wood pulp and it was first made in 1908.

Lead tetraethyl (1923)

Lead tetraethyl, put onto the market in América in **1923** by the **Ethyl Corporation**, is an anti-knock agent which, when added to petrol, increases the octane level and thus its efficiency. It also prevents deterioration of the engine. However, in 1965, the American scientist Clark C. Patterson denounced its harmful effects. Inhaled or accidentally ingested (from polluted plants for example) lead tetraethyl enters the blood stream and affects the central nervous system.

Liquid crystals (1929)

The French physicist **Friedel** in **1929** discovered products which could be presented in a stable state and were intermediary between solids and liquids. One family of these products is now well-known: that of liquid crystals. Unlike solid crystals, their molecules can change direction under certain circumstances, in particular, when submitted to a very weak electric current, their transparence is altered. It is this property which is used in watch display panels; any figure can be formed from just seven segments.

In 1971 the Swiss company Hoffmann-La Roche perfected the first panel of liquid crystals.

From 1973 liquid crystals made their appearance in many objects of everyday use: watch-dials, calculator screens, electronic games, portable computers, etc.

Nicotine (1828)

In 1562 the Frenchman **Jean Nicot** extracted a juice from tobacco (brought from America by Christopher Columbus) that accelerated the healing of wounds.

However, it was not until **1828** that **R. Posselt** and **R. Reimann** isolated nicotine in its pure state. Ingested, it is a violent poison which has been used for criminal ends, and its toxicity is utilised in plant medicine to destroy parasites.

Synthetic diamonds (1955)

Ever since it has been known that the diamond is nothing more than ordinary carbon in a practically pure state and in a form of very regular crystals, attempts have been made to produce the gem artificially.

In 1894 the French chemist Henri Moissan thought that he had manufactured diamonds by heating carbon to a very high temperature under great pressure. However, it wasn't until **1955** that the American company **General**

Electric produced true synthetic diamonds by heating carbon to 2600°C *4700°F* at a pressure exceeding 100000 atmospheres.

These tiny diamonds (hardly longer than a millimetre) are often black and are used in industry. But it is possible, by increasing the temperature at which they are formed, to create transparent diamonds for use in jewellery. Due to the cost of production and the time it takes, these artificial diamonds are more expensive than natural ones, and not as beautiful.

Synthetic jade (1984)

On 30 November 1984 the American company General Electric announced an important first: the creation in a laboratory of a sample of synthetic jade. This was the result of the work of two chemists: Robert C. DeVries and James F. Fleischer.

Urea (1828)

This organic substance exists naturally in the blood (0.20 to 0.50g to the litre) and in urine (2.5g to the litre), where it was discovered. Its synthesis in 1828 by the German chemist Friedrich Wöhler marked a turning point in demonstrating for the first time that an organic substance can be obtained independently of any living organism.

Analytical chemistry

Mass spectrography (19th century)

The discovery of the electron in 1897 by Sir Joseph John Thomson proved that the atom was not single and indivisible but made up of several particles. Researchers very soon delved into the innermost structure of matter and came up with evidence for the existence, at the heart of the same natural substance, of two or more atoms chemically similar but of different atomic mass. They called these isotopes, and the process used was called mass spectography. The differences between such atoms came from the number of neutrons contained in their atomic nuclei, which varied from one isotope to another. Thus uranium ore has three isotopes: uranium 238 (92 protons, 146 neutrons), uranium 235 (92 protons, 143 neutrons) and uranium 234 (92 protons, 142 neutrons). It is the same for most natural bodies, except for a few such as aluminium.

For his work on the nature of isotopes the Englishman Frederick Soddy (1877–1956) gained the Nobel Prize for Chemistry in 1921.

Mass spectrograph (c.1919)

By separating isotopes from a body, it became possible to make a very precise analysis of them. The mass spectrograph was created by the Englishman Francis Aston, an assistant of J. J. Thomson. It enabled Thomson to analyse in 1919 the neon atom, and to show that it is made up of two isotopes: neon 20 and neon 22. Aston then continued with the

analysis of many bodies, and received the Nobel Prize for Chemistry in 1922.

The mass spectrograph, which uses the difference in deflection of isotopes in a magnetic field, remains a powerful analytical tool. In effect, it allows the composition of all bodies to be precisely determined. For example, in the search for traces of explosive in the case of a murder attempt, it is possible to use this technique to find the exact nature of the explosive used, as certain isotopes are explosive and others are not.

Biology and genetics

The cell (1665)

The English scientist Robert Hooke (1635–1703) was the first to use the word cell (from *cellula*, little room) to describe the miniature empty structures which he observed in 1665, with the aid of a rudimentary microscope, when he cut into a piece of cork. Cork being a dead tissue, Hooke in fact was only looking at the outer walls of cells. At the same period, Antony van Leeuwenhoek in Holland was using a somewhat better microscope to observe some isolated cells, such as those in drops of blood, sperm and bacteria.

It was not until 1824 that the Frenchman René Dutrochet established that living tissue was made up of juxtaposed cells. Then in 1833, the Scot Robert Brown (1773–1858) described the cell nucleus. Today we describe a cell as being made up of a cytoplasm and a nucleus enclosed by a membrane.

Chromosomes (1888)

Chromosomes are short rods, usually curved (measuring 0.005mm *0.000194in* in humans), that are found in the cell nucleus. The German anatomist G. Waldeyer named them in 1888. The essential constituent of chromosomes is DNA.

Clones (1981)

Clones are genetically identical organisms derived originally from a single individual. The best-known clones are cuttings: a section of a plant which is artificially or naturally removed and which is able to take root and provide a completely new plant.

The Swiss Professor Illmensée and his team tried the same kind of experiment, but this time on animals. By stimulation of the cells from a mouse ovary, he obtained in 1981 three perfectly functional baby mice, who had been born without a father. These young mice are an identical copy of their mother, as they have exactly the same genetic make-up.

Darwinism (1859)

In his book entitled *On the Origin of Species by Natural Selection*, published in 1859, the English naturalist and biologist Charles Darwin (1809–82) studied the problem of evolution of the species. According to him, the species are not unchangeable, the result of

distinct creations, but are progressively transformed by selection of the individuals who are best adapted to their environment (survival of the fittest).

Gametes (5th century BC)

The first person to suspect the existence of male and female reproductive cells was the Greek doctor Hippocrates (c.460–c.377 BC): in effect, he accepted that the formation of the human embryo involved male and female seeds.

These two seeds are the spermatazoon and the ovum. The former is the characteristic cell of the sperm produced by the testicles. A man produces about 200 million of these per day. The ovum is produced by the ovary. At birth, a girl has about 400000 ova whose number then diminishes; by puberty there are only 10000, of which only 400 achieve maturity.

The gene (1910)

The key person in the saga of the gene is a southern gentleman born in Lexington, Virginia (USA) in 1866: Thomas Hunt Morgan. In 1910, while he was working on the fruit-fly *Drosophila melanogaster*, an insect which usually has red eyes, he observed a mutant male with white eyes. Morgan crossed it with a normal red-eyed female, and noted that all the first-generation descendants had red eyes. However, among their descendants, he found flies with white eyes again. The characteristic white eye had been transmitted, according to Mendelian laws, by a fragment of chromosome to which Morgan gave the name *gene*. Today it is reckoned that a person's genetic inheritance consists of around 500000 genes divided among 46 chromosomes. The essential constituent of genes is DNA.

Synthesis of the first artificial gene (1973)

This was achieved in 1973 by the Indian researcher Har Gabind Khorama, at MIT in Cambridge (USA). It involved a double helix of DNA, corresponding to the precursor of ribo-nucleic acid, the gene for tyrosine transfer-RNA. The gene is made up of 199 nucleotides.

Genetic code (1943)

The first experimental arguments in favour of the transmission of hereditary characteristics through DNA information go back to 1943 with the work of the Italian-born American microbiologist Salvador Luria.

We have since learnt that each hereditary characteristic is coded in the form of a message in a tiny fragment of DNA, or the gene, and that the translation of this message produces a specific protein which materialises the hereditary characteristic. The synthesis of the protein requires the intervention of RNA, on which the gene's message is recopied. This message must then be translated in order to produce the protein.

Genetic engineering (1974)

It was in 1974 that the term genetic engineering made its appearance in the scientific world. The association of the word 'engineering' with 'genetics' – or the science of genes – came about because of the new possibility open to researchers breaking up DNA, separating out the genes and recombining them in another DNA molecule.

Genetic engineering is thus the collection of techniques that enable scientists to break into DNA, isolate genes, identify their structure, modify them if necessary and finally, to introduce them into an organism which might be different from the one from which they were originally taken.

Genetic engineering quickly established itself as a basic technique in all areas of biology. But alongside these fundamental activities, it has also made possible the manufacture of rare substances, or those difficult to extract. Medicine and industry have found new methods of production by using organisms – most often genetically modified bacteria – to work on such projects as the synthesis of insulin, a new vaccination against hepatitis-B, or alcohol from biomass for use as a fuel. A new technique, genetic engineering is far from having exhausted all its opportunities.

Genetic fingerprinting (1985)

Professor Alec J. Jeffreys, head of the genetic laboratory at the University of Leicester, has developed a revolutionary and virtually infallible procedure for detecting criminals by analysing their blood, or their sperm in cases of rape: genetic fingerprinting.

The procedure stems from the principle that DNA, which is found in cell nuclei, varies from person to person. These variations, or genetic imprints, can be photographed. The photo, which looks like the bar-codes on packets in supermarkets, allows each person to be genetically identified.

This new technique, which continues the work undertaken by the American Professor Southern, the Southern Blot process, will soon replace simple fingerprinting and is used for research into paternity.

Heredity (1865)

In **1865** the Moravian-born botanist **Gregor Johann Mendel** (1822–84) demonstrated that hereditary characteristics are transmitted via distinct elements, which are today called genes. Two sets of experiments allowed him to reach this conclusion. The first set consisted of crossing peas of stable lines that differed among themselves in a couple of characteristics; for example, peas with smooth or wrinkled seeds were crossed with those with green or yellow cotyledons. The crossing of such plants produced first-generation plants in which dominant characteristics were revealed; for example, the hybrids obtained by the crossing of smooth yellow peas with wrinkled green peas were smooth and yellow. But when the hybrids were crossed, the parental green and wrinkled characteristics appeared in a quarter of the second-generation hybrids.

From these observations, Mendel deduced that hereditary factors determining traits went in pairs, and that the recessive characteristic was only expressed in the plant when both parents had that characteristic. Such experiments allowed Mendel to determine that in peas the smooth and yellow characteristics are dominant, while the green and wrinkled characteristics are recessive. He also drew

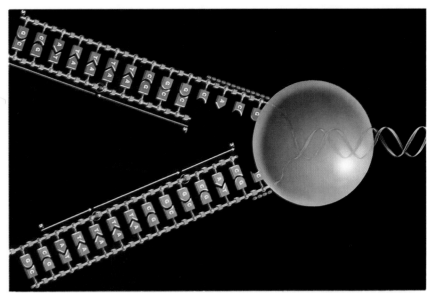

A mechanism for the replication of DNA. The DNA double helix consists of two strands of nucleotides and each strand is joined through hydrogen bonding between the bases adenine (A), thymine (T), guanine (G) and cytosine (C). A always pairs with T, and C with G. The resulting sequence along the molecule determines genetic information.

A researcher studies a DNA sequence. Because each sequence is unique to that person, it is a fool-proof method of identifying someone.

Biotechnology: The meeting point between life and industry

The term 'biotechnology' was used for the first time towards the end of 1979 in a report by Professors F. Gros, F. Jacob and R. Royer on the 'biological revolution', to describe technologies which used the properties of living organisms for practical and industrial purposes. Biotechnology is now a fast developing area and provides a link between several disciplines: genetic engineering, enzymology, microbiology, biology, molecular biology, immunology, biochemistry and animal and vegetable biology. The total value of the world market in this field is estimated at £11 billion for 1990, and is likely to reach £40 billion by the year 2000. The main areas of its applications are agronomy, the pharmaceutical and medical sectors, energy and the environment.

Medicine

Early research in the field of biotechnology lead to the development in 1975 of monoclonal antibodies by the German, Georg Koehler, and the Argentinian, César Milstein. In 1984 they were jointly awarded the Nobel Prize for Medicine for their discovery, which enabled early diagnosis of hereditary illnesses such as mucoviscidosis.

There were other important inventions in the field of medicine which were the direct result of biotechnology. These included the TPA tissue activator (1984), the growth hormone (1979), insulin (1982) and interferon (1984). An anti-rabies vaccine developed in vitro on cultures of VERO cells from a line of cells from the African vervet monkey – Vervet Origin – was adapted for industrial production as a result of biotechnology; a vaccine against hepatitis B was developed by genetic engineering at the Chiron Laboratories, USA, in 1982; a preliminary anti-rabies vaccine was developed by genetic engineering (Pasteur/Mérieux), as well as bio-materials such as haemostatic sponges based on collagen extracted from the hide of calves.

Genetics

Biotechnology made it possible to discover ribozymes (RNA with catalytic properties), for which Sidney Altman and Thomas R. Cech received the Nobel Prize for Chemistry in 1989; and also to develop the PCR (Polymerase Chain Reaction), a reaction for the amplification of tiny, distinct fragments of DNA), a technique which, combined with automation and computer technology, will play an extremely important role in the development of the human genome.

Animal transgenosis

Genetic engineering has made it possible to select the most productive strains of plants and animals and to develop transgenic organisms. The first of these were the 'giant' mice into which the Americans R. Brinster and R. Palmiter transplanted the growth hormone in 1982. The experiment used a method developed in 1980 by M. R. Capecchi (USA) for injecting a gene into eggs which had just been fertilised, a method which is used effectively in fish farming, but which has proved less efficient with pigs and rabbits and even less so with ruminants.

OncoMice

The first animal to be patented as a result of genetic modifications was the OncoMouse, produced by the American scientists Philip Leder and Timothy Stewart and patented in 1984. It carries human oncogenes and is used in cancer research (the Greek word *onkos* means 'tumour'). Other mice 'manufactured' in this way are the SCID (Severe Combined Immune Deficiency) mice used in immunology research . . .

Plant transgenosis

The first plant of this type was produced as a result of research carried out at the University of Ghent in Belgium in 1984. It was a kanamycin (antibiotic) resistant tobacco plant. In 1987 the company developed tobacco, potato and tomato plants capable of selecting a particular type of herbicide or resisting attack by certain parasites. In the case of tobacco a toxin was produced which enabled it to combat the *Manduca sexta*, a caterpillar particularly harmful to tobacco. The first large-scale experiments were undertaken in the United States in 1988, and have already proved that it will be possible for American farmers to grow tobacco without the use of insecticides. Other research on tobacco includes the development of plants resistant to triazines by Ciba-Geigy and Monsanto (USA) in 1986.

Beauty products

Pharmacists and cosmeticists are both involved in this area of production which, by placing cultures from vegetable cells in bioreactors, obtains large quantities of substances with colouring, aromatic and medicinal properties. This method is replacing the extraction of such substances from plants. The first of these products to be marketed was shikonine, used in 'Biolipstick' by Kanebo and developed by Mitsui Petrochemical Industries (Japan) in 1984.

Environment

Biotechnology is also used in the treatment of sewage and waste products, thanks to the development of a bacterial stock with cleaning properties. Since 1986 sulphur has been eliminated from coal in the Netherlands, West Germany and Turkey by the use of the *sulfobulus* bacteria, and in Japan the *thiobacillus* is used in the purification of acidic water and the removal of the heavy metals which accumulate in inland seas.

One of the areas for the future development of biotechnology is the production of energy by the action of bacteria on agricultural, industrial and urban waste. For example, in 1975 the first rubbish dump to produce methane gas using bacterial action was opened in Palos Verdes, California.

Foods of the future

These are also in the hands of the biotechnologists. There have been many new food additives created such as: aspartam, glycerol (a preservative developed by B. Zyrbriggen and produced since 1986 by using mutated yeast cultures), vitamin C (an antioxidant invented by T. Sonoyama and produced in Japan since 1982 using mutated bacterial cultures) and anethole (a flavouring agent obtained in 1980 from fennel plants cloned in vitro by Pernod Ricard). Other foods of the future include seaweed (the edible seaweeds, *nori* and *wakame*, are being intensively cultivated in Japan).

The lettuces on the right have been enhanced by biotechnology.

up laws that bear his name and which, by revealing the segregation of characteristics, prove that hereditary factors behave independently: they join together and separate across generations and hybridisations, according to the statistical norms of chance.

HLA system (1958)

In 1958 the Frenchman **Jean Dausset** first described the HLA system (for Human Leucocyte Antigen) in white globules. The HLA system is a series of proteins present at the surface of all the cells of an individual. These proteins are analogous to fingerprints. They vary from one individual to another and in some way may be thought of as a person's identity card. Today it is known that tolerance to grafts depends on the resemblance of the HLA systems of the donor and the recipient.

Immune system (1877)

Last century Louis Pasteur came up with the idea that living beings possessed within themselves the means of fighting against sickness. When in 1877 the Russian scientist **Ilya Metchnikoff**, who had discovered that certain cells in living organisms were capable of 'eating' and 'digesting' microbes, passed through Paris, Pasteur asked whether he would join his team. So many stages were involved in the progressive discovery of the immune system, such as 'tissue immunity' described in 1922 by Levaditi and Nicolau, that it was not until the 1950s that a clear idea was formed of the defence system belonging to each organism.

In vitro culture (1907)

In vitro cultivation is a method by which a living organism, animal or vegetable, or a part of this organism (cells, tissues, organs), is sustained outside its natural environment.

The culture in vitro of animal cells and tissues was invented in 1907 by the American **R. G. Harrison**, and perfected in 1910 by the Frenchman Alexis Carrel. This method, with regard to vegetable cells and tissues, was invented between 1931 and 1938 by the Frenchmen Roger Gautheret and Pierre Nobécourt, also by the American Philip White.

In vitro cultures are used in research to obtain medical products (serums, vaccines, antibiotics), to produce plants that are protected against viruses, and to propagate plants from buds or cuttings.

One of the most spectacular recent successes of in vitro culture is the saving of the date palm, which has been afflicted since the beginning of the century with a terrible blight. Bayoud disease is a fungus which attacks the roots and eventually kills the tree. In Morocco, which is particularly affected, the disease destroys between 150 000 and 200 000 trees a year, bringing devastation and the progressive destruction of the palm groves. This has a knock-on effect on the micro-climate and thus on the crops and on animal rearing, leading eventually to the exodus of the population.

In vitro plant propagation (1952)

In 1952 the French researchers **G. Morel** and **J. Martin** of INRA (National Institute of

Male rapeseed plants – sterile on the left and fertile on the right. This crop has become increasingly commonly grown over the last decade or so.

Agronomical Research) obtained from a few cells, placed in an artificial environment, a genuine dwarf plant, that could be transplanted to serve as the basis for producing perfect plants.

The success of Morel and Martin's method enabled diseased plants to be regenerated and to proliferate rapidly in their improved form. It is used now to produce roses, orchids, potatoes, fruit trees, etc.

In vitro synthesis of proteins (1954)

The American biochemist **Du Vigneaud** achieved the first synthesis of two proteins in 1954. This concerned hormones usually secreted by the post-pituitary gland: oxytocin and vasopressin, each of which is made up of nine amino acids. In 1969 the first synthesis of a large molecule was achieved in the USA by Bruce Merrifield and Gutte, of the Rockefeller Institute (later University, New York).

They brought about the attachment of a string of 124 amino acids to each other, anchored to some polystyrene. For this technique, which took over three weeks, they used electronic equipment which enabled 369 chemical reactions to take place automatically, in 11 931 stages.

The Merrifield method is now used to produce numerous syntheses. Moreover, the grafting of two cellular fragments, each belonging to different species, can produce proteins. All these 'miraculous' operations are grouped under the name of genetic engineering.

In 1984 Bruce Merrifield won the Nobel Prize for Chemistry for synthesising chains of amino acids or polypeptides.

Lamarckism (1809)

In 1809 the French botanist **J. B. P. A. de Monet de Lamarck** (1744–1829) published his *Zoological Philosophy* in which he set out his theory of evolution: transformism.

According to Lamarck, the species are transformed with time, under the influence of their surroundings, and through the intermediary of their habits and needs. This theory of mutability had its hour of glory, then fell out of favour. However, there has been a revival of interest since the studies carried out by biologists at Harvard Medical School (USA) on mutant *Escherichia coli* bacteria.

Microbiology (1857)

In 1857 the Frenchman **Louis Pasteur** (1822–95) discovered yeast (microscopic fungi) and explained the fermentation process. Pasteur extended his research to bacteria: this was the beginning of microbiology.

Bacteriology (1870)

From 1870 **Louis Pasteur** cultivated and identified *staphylococcus*, *streptomyces* and *streptococcus*. He was thus the inventor of bacteriology.

Pasteur proved that, if the environment was favourable, all cultivated germs could multiply. Since then, many culture environments have been experimented with, thus allowing the isolation of many germs, which these days are known and identified. Each germ carries the name of the person who discovered it.

Virology (1898)

Between 1880 and 1885, while working on rabies, Pasteur realised that he had come up against the problem of an illness, then incurable, whose agent he could not cultivate. In fact this was not a bacteria, but a virus. Eventually he was able to develop the vaccine.

In 1898 the Dutchman **Martinus Willem Beijerinck** (1851–1931) discovered micro-organisms even smaller than bacteria: they passed through the finest porcelain filters. Beijerinck also discovered the virus which caused tobacco mosaic disease. This was the birth of virology. In 1935 the American biochemist Wendell Meredith Stanley (1904–71) succeeded for the first time in crystallising a virus.

In 1959, thanks to electronic microscopy, X-ray diffractions and biochemical methods, the Frenchman André Lwoff established a definition of the virus based on the presence of nucleic acids, which made for progress in virology.

Synthesis of a virus (1968)

In 1968 two American researchers, **Arthur Kornberg** and **Robert L. Sinsheimer**, succeeded in completely synthesising a virus, using only two enzymes – a polymerase DNA and a lipase DNA – extracted and purified from colonies of colon bacilli.

Mutations (1901)

The first observations of mutations were made by the Dutch botanist **Hugo de Vries** in 1901. In cultivating and studying plants of different species, he observed some that did not correspond to what would be expected from their original seed. These individual plants were different from their progenitors and their differences were inherited by their offspring. Hugo de Vries gave the name mutations to these hereditary variations. Later, it was proved that the modifications sprang from alterations in the genes. Mutations are observed among animals as well as vegetables. Today experimental mutations can be obtained by using radiation and chemical products.

Nucleic acids (1953)

Deoxyribo-nucleic acid (DNA)

In 1944 the American bacteriologist **O. T. Avery** of the Rockefeller Institute in New York demonstrated that the transmission of hereditary characteristics from one bacterium to another takes place due to the intermediary DNA molecules. Due to this discovery, it was recognised that genes, whose primordial role in the phenomenon of hereditary transmission was known, are made up of DNA.

In 1953, using diffraction via X-rays, the electron microscope and chromatography, the American **James Watson** and the Englishman **Francis Crick** described the exact structure of the DNA molecule in the British magazine *Nature*. Their work earned them the Nobel Prize for Physiology and Medicine in 1962. The DNA molecule exists in the form of a double-strand helix made up of a series of units called the nucleotides.

Ribo-nucleic acid (RNA)

RNA is also composed of a set of nucleotides, each comprising a sugar (ribose), and four bases, adenine, cytosine, guanine and uracil.

James D. Watson and Francis Crick pose in front of a DNA model. Their discoveries in the 1950s earned them a Nobel Prize in 1962.

RNA plays an important part in the synthesis of proteins.

Oncology (1981)

Cancer genes or oncogenes were discovered in 1981 by three separate American research teams: that of **Professor Robert Weinberg** at the Centre for Cancer Research, part of the famous Massachusetts Institute of Technology; that of **Dr Geoffrey Cooper** at the Sydney Farber Cancer Institute in Boston; and that of **Professor Michael Wigler** of Cold Spring Laboratory on Long Island.

Cancer genes are not in themselves generators of cancer. They only become so when they are affected either by carcinogenic substances, ionising radiation or by viruses. Recently various cancer genes have been isolated, for cancer of the colon, the bladder, the kidneys and for a form of leukaemia.

Protein (1953)

A protein can be represented as a chain of amino acids, of which there are 20 different kinds. The English biochemist **Frederick Sanger** was the first to work out the sequence of amino acids in various protein molecules, in 1953. He determined the sequence for insulin.

Proteins form the main structural components of most animal cells: they constitute connective tissues, skin, hair, ligaments and tendons. Proteins also take part in metabolic processes, when they are called enzymes. Some hormones are also proteins; insulin is an example. Today, insulin can be produced by synthesis.

Astronomy

Origins

With mathematics, astronomy is definitely one of the two oldest sciences and the observation of stars probably dates back to prehistory. Born from the needs of daily life as well as from the fears and beliefs of primitive people when faced with unexplained phenomena, it had pride of place as far as the Sumerians and Babylonians were concerned (4th and 5th millennia), and was often confused with astrology, the mystical interpretation of astronomical events to which it owes much. In order to observe the stars, the first astronomers used an index bar which was a simple rectilinear rod, as well as a compass, that is to say, a double articulated index bar. They also had the astrolabe – an instrument which allowed one to measure the position of the stars above the horizon – said to have been invented by Hipparchus, the Greek astronomer who lived in the 2nd century BC.

Lenses and telescopes

Galileo and the astronomical lens (1609)

It was in **1609** that the Italian scientist **Galileo Galilei** (1564–1642) first used a magnifying lens to observe the sky. This was his improved version of a lens originally invented in Holland.

Within a short period of time, Galileo made an extraordinary number of discoveries. He found the following:
– the marks on the sun which demonstrated a fact which at the time seemed incredible: that the star of the day was an 'imperfect' entity;
– the four large moons of the planet Jupiter: Io, Europa, Ganymede and Callisto, now called the Galilean satellites;
– the phases of the planet Venus, proving that Venus, like the moon, can be lit by the sun from the side. This observation gave substantial support to the theory that the earth revolved around the sun;
– the rings of Saturn, which Galileo could not

A representation of the cosmos from the Middle Ages: a scientist breaks through the celestial vault to discover how the stars move.

correctly interpret and which seemed to him to be rather like curious growths resembling ears;
– the myriad of stars that make up the Milky Way;
– the moon's mountains and craters.

In 1633 Galileo was forced by the Roman Catholic Church to renounce the theory of elliptical planetary rotation and was placed under permanent house arrest at his home in Florence where he spent the last nine years of his life.

Telescope (1672)

The first telescope was built in **1672** by **Isaac Newton**, the famous British physicist, mathematician and astronomer (1642–1727), who set out in the *Principia* in 1687 the famous laws of universal gravitation. The instrument was

perfected in the 17th and 18th centuries, in particular by the British astronomer William Herschel and the German astronomer Johannes Hevelius. It was in 1842 that another Englishman, William Parsons, built the first giant telescopes in the garden of his house.

Giant telescopes

Mount Palomar (1948)

The huge telescope on Mount Palomar in California is equipped with a lens that has a 5m *16ft 5in* aperture. It was brought into service on **3 June 1948**.

The telescope was initiated by George Hellery Hale, an astronomer and inventor of the spectroheliograph, and built with the aid of a $6 million donation from the Rockefeller Foundation.

Hale's giant telescope has become difficult

The New Technology Telescope (NTT) of the European Southern Observatory (ESO), based on a revolutionary new concept, was set in operation on 6 February 1990. Installed on the 800km² *310sq mile* site of the observatory, on Mount La Silla in Chile, it has been operational since March 1989. It has three features which make it a totally new instrument: its adaptive optics (Zeiss), its mechanics, and its remote control. The images produced at the end of 1989 were of unparalleled clarity and make it currently the most advanced instrument in the world. The NTT is the 14th telescope that ESO have installed at La Silla. A small organisation founded in 1962, ESO currently includes eight countries: Germany, France, Italy, Belgium, Denmark, the Netherlands, Sweden and Switzerland. Its scientists and the instruments they have designed make it one of the top observatories in the world.

A long-exposure photograph of the Keck telescope, which will be the largest in the world when it becomes operational around the end of 1991. Each of the 36 mirrors is 1.8m 5ft 11in wide and 7.5cm 3in thick. A computer-controlled tracking system will adjust the alignment of each segment 100 times every second, so that the light from each will combine to form a single image.

to use because of the increasing level of pollution coming from the neighbouring city of Los Angeles.

Zelentchouk (1974)

The Zelentchouk observatory telescope, located at an altitude of 2050m *6728ft* in the Caucasus Mountains, USSR, is today the largest in the world. The telescope, with its 6m *19ft 8in* aperture was designed by Doctor Icannissiani. It went into operation in **1974** after extreme difficulties in manufacturing its enormous 42-tonne lens. This was made by the Lomo centre in Leningrad and is 1½ million times more powerful than the human eye.

Infra-red telescope (1977)

The largest infra-red telescope in the world, equipped with a lens with a 3.8m *12ft 6in* aperture, was installed in **1977** by British scientists at an altitude of 4200m *13780ft* on the top of Mount Mauna Kea, an extinct volcano on the island of Hawaii.

Multiple-lens telescope

The world's first multiple-lens telescope was installed at the Mount Hopkins Observatory, Arizona by the Smithsonian Astrophysical Observatory (SAO) and the University of Arizona. It comprised six lenses with a 1.85m

6ft 1in aperture and is the equivalent of a single-lens telescope with a 4.5m *14ft 9in* aperture.

This new kind of optical telescope was devised by astronomers in order to reduce the size as well as the cost of the instruments without sacrificing performance.

Keck Observatory (1991)

A sum of $70 million was offered by the **Keck Foundation** at the California Institute of Technology for the construction of the largest optical telescope in the world. Work began on 12 September 1985 on the summit of Mauna Kea, a dead volcano on one of the Hawaiian islands.

The mirror of this enormous telescope, which will allow one to observe objects of magnitude 26, in other words, 200 million times smaller than objects discernible by the naked eye, is to be built using 36 identical hexagonal parts, juxtaposed in order to form a single mirror measuring 10m *32ft 10in* in diameter.

It is expected that the telescope will be ready for use in **1991**.

VLT (1997)

The **European Southern Observatory** (ESO) decided in 1987 to build what will be the

largest telescope in the world, the VLT or Very Large Telescope. It will take ten years to build, but the first part is expected to be ready for use in 1994/5.

The VLT will comprise four astronomic lenses with 8m *26ft 3in* diameter mirrors. A 16m *52ft 6in* chamber will extend it further.

It will allow scientists to observe stars inside interstellar clouds, and even to look into the centre of galaxies, and will make it possible to locate potential black holes. The telescope will probably be located in Chile.

The location of the telescope will probably be in Chile, where the NTT has just been set up. The VLT will benefit from the techniques of adaptive optics used on the NTT. These techniques permit a considerable improvement in the quality of the image by eliminating the effects of atmospheric turbulence.

Radio astronomy

First radio telescope (1932)

The very first radio telescope was developed in **1932**, quite accidentally, by an American radioelectrical engineer of Czechoslovak origin, **Karl Jansky**.

A 'continuous whistle'

Employed by Bell Telephone to trace the origins of parasitic signals causing obstructions to radiotelephonic traffic on the North Atlantic, Jansky built a receiver which he had invented himself in Holmdel, New Jersey, USA. With this apparatus he captured the first unfamiliar noises coming from outer space: 'a continuous whistle' coming from the constellation of Sagittarius, at the centre of our galaxy, 250 000 000 billion kilometres *155 350 000 billion miles* away.

Although this news caused a sensation, Jansky abandoned radio astronomy in 1938 on account of the indifference which greeted his discovery. However, his name is remembered in the unit of measurement of the radioelectric flux of the stars.

Reber radio telescope (1937)

The first proper radio telescope was built in **1937** by an American engineer of Dutch origin, **Grote Reber**. A keen radio buff, he used his savings to build an instrument in his garden in Wheaton near Chicago (USA). It comprised a parabolic antenna with a diameter of about 3m *9ft 10in*, and was azimuthal like all modern radio telescopes. After two years of patience and unsuccessful experimentation, Reber finally received a signal with a wavelength of 1.87m *6ft 2in*.

With this success behind him, Reber tried in 1941 to draw the radioelectric map of our galaxy. This document, published in 1944, marked the beginnings of radio astronomy as a new scientific discipline, officially recognised by astronomers who were eager to use it.

The largest radio telescope in the world (1986)

In **July** and **August 1986** American astronomers from NASA's **Jet Propulsion Laboratory** developed the largest radio telescope ever built, by electronically linking aerials on earth and on board a satellite. The parabolic aerials

GIANT RADIO TELESCOPES

Type	Date	Origin	Characteristics
Jodrell Bank	1957	UK	The first large radio telescope to be put into operation. Designed by the British physicist Sir Bernard Lovell.
Nançay	1958	France	Installed in Sologne, the Nançay radio telescope is a semi-mobile instrument with an adjustable reflector.
Eifelsberg	1962	W. Germany	The largest radio telescope with a mobile antenna. Equipped with a parabolic antenna measuring 100m *328ft* in diameter.
Ratan 600	1974	USSR	The largest Soviet radio telescope.
Arecibo	1974	USA	Set up on the island of Puerto Rico, this is a fixed-antenna instrument the reflector of which comprises 38 778 sheets of aluminium. Inaugurated in 1963, it was put into operation in 1974; under the SETI (Search for Extraterrestrial Intelligence) programme, a 169-second message was sent at a frequency of 2380MHz towards the M13 global star cluster (100 000 stars) in the Hercules constellation. Distance: 25 000 light years. Possible reply: in 500 centuries' time!

measuring 70m *230ft* in diameter, located in Japan and Australia, were in contact with one measuring 5m *16ft 5in* in diameter belonging to the TDRS communication satellite in a geostationary orbit 35 900km *22 300 miles* above the earth. The telescope thus created measured 18 000km *11 185 miles* in radius, that is to say, the largest ever developed. It has made it possible to observe three quasars which astronomers believe to be between 15 and 20 billion years old.

Radio-astronomic observatories (c.1950)

The first radio-astronomic observatories were created in Cambridge and in Sydney, Australia, after the Second World War, thanks to the progress made in the areas of radar and electronics during that conflict.

The International Union of Telecommunications (IUT) contributed valuable aid to radio astronomers by deciding, in 1959, to reserve a frequency band of approximately 1420MHz exclusively for the study of signals emitted by cosmic hydrogen over 21cm *8.3in* in wavelength.

One such transmission, which had been announced by the young Dutch astronomer **H. C. van de Hulst** in 1944, was indeed detected in 1951 by the American physicists H. I. Ewen and E. M. Purcell, with the help of a spectroscope.

Since 1990 British radio-astronomers have had at their disposal a radio telescope equivalent to a 200m *656ft* long antenna thanks to the installation of a 32m *105ft* aerial near Cambridge on 8 December 1989. This antenna, weighing nearly 100 tonnes, will complete the network of seven radio-astronomic observatories built on the same principle as Jodrell Bank.

Radio interferometer (1960)

The synthesised aperture interferometer was developed in **1960** by the British radio astronomer **Sir Martin Ryle**, who in 1974 received the Nobel Prize for Physics with his colleague Anthony Hewish. Synthesised aperture interferometry is a method which, using two or more antennae, allows one to gather simultaneously with a single receiver several signals from the same source and to make a true chart of the area observed with a resolution similar to that which would have been obtained by using a very large instrument.

The first large radio interferometer was developed by Sir Martin Ryle in 1964 at Cambridge, by using three telescopes 1.6km *1 mile* apart.

VLA (1977)

The largest radio interferometer is the Very Large Array (VLA), built near to Socorro in the New Mexican desert in America.

The VLA comprises 27 metal parabolas measuring 25m *82ft* in diameter, distributed along three bases 25km *15½ miles* long arranged in a Y shape. The whole unit forms the equivalent of a giant dome measuring 27km *16¾ miles* in diameter.

Radar astronomy (1946)

Radar astronomy is a particular technique in which radio telescopes are no longer used simply as passive receivers but like radars, that is, in an active manner, first as transmitters, then as receivers.

Since **1946**, radar echoes with rather weak transmission power have been obtained from the moon, as well as from other bodies, in order to measure their distances and their movements. This same technique was recently used with the Arecibo radio telescope to establish the first topographical map of the surface of the planet Venus.

Airborne telescopes

First observations (1927)

The first astronomical observations carried out by aeroplane date back to **29 June 1927**, when a twin-engine British Imperial Airways plane was used to photograph a total eclipse of the sun from above the London fog. This observation technique has since been used successfully with Concorde.

Kuiper Observatory (1975)

Since 1965 **NASA** has been equipped with observatory jet aircraft, the Learjet and the Convair 990, which have enabled scientists to discover, in particular, the infra-red emission from the centre of our galaxy. Since **1975** NASA has also used a giant four-engined C 141 Starlifter, specially equipped for astronomy and for research into infra-red radiation. This plane, named the Kuiper Observatory after the famous American astrophysician of Dutch origin, Gerard P. Kuiper (1905–73), may be used on more than 200 nights a year. It is capable of flying for three hours with nine

Thanks to the VLA, astronomers will be able to receive the signals emitted by Voyager 2, *even at a distance of 4.5 billion km 2.8 billion miles.*

tonnes of observation equipment, at an altitude of more than 14 000m *46 000ft*. The Kuiper Observatory, equipped with a telescope with a 91cm *35.8in* aperture, has already made several important discoveries such as, for example, the discovery of the rings of Uranus in 1977.

Space astronomy

Space radio astronomy (1968)

The first radio astronomy satellites were those of the Radio Astronomy Explorer (RAE 1 and 2) from **NASA**, launched in **July 1968** and June 1973 respectively.

The first radio telescope in space was put into orbit by the USSR in July 1979 on the orbital station of *Salyut 6*. This radio telescope, KRT 10, weighing 200kg *441lb*, had an antenna with a diameter of 10m *33ft*, carried by a cargo vessel called *Progress*, and sent into orbit for the purpose of observing centimetre and decimetre waves. The Soviets carried out their interferometry observations of various radio sources in this way in conjunction with an observation station in the Crimea.

Astronomic satellites (1946)

The first observations by means of astronomic satellites were carried out in **1946** by Americans who used V2s salvaged in Germany. However, this technique did not allow for long observations. The first astronomic satellites were launched by the United States (notably *Explorer 1* in 1958, under the direction of Joseph Van Allen, enabling the radiation rings circling the earth to be discovered: the Van Allen rings) and by the USSR (the Cosmos satellites, beginning in 1962, which are not exclusively for the purposes of astronomy).

Uhuru (1970)

Launched from Kenya on **12 December 1970**, *Uhuru* was the first satellite to be dedicated to X-ray astronomy.

After *Uhuru*, other X-ray satellites were launched. In 1978 the *Einstein* satellite was launched in commemoration of the centenary of the birth of the great physicist in 1979. The European satellite *Exosat*, launched in 1983 by an American Delta rocket, completed its mission in 1986.

The next X-ray mission, that of NASA's AXAF satellite (Advanced X-Ray Astrophysics Facility), is planned for the 1990s and is expected to last ten years.

COS-B (1975)

Launched in **August 1975**, the COS-B satellite, developed by the **European Space Agency** (ESA), was wholly dedicated to gamma astronomy or high energy astronomy. The mission finished at the end of April 1982.

The COS-B's mission will be continued during the 1990s by NASA's GRO satellite (Gamma Ray Observatory).

IUE (1978)

The International Ultra-violet Explorer was launched on **26 January 1978** as a joint venture between NASA, the European Space Agency and the Engineering Research Council.

Its mission was to observe the stars and the

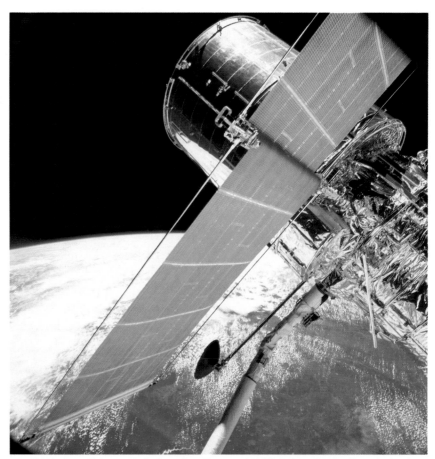

The Hubble Space Telescope is deployed from Discovery *in 1990. At this point it is still attached to the shuttle via the remote manipulator arm (bottom) and is seen unfurling the first of its two solar panels (foreground). At the left is one of the two dish antennae which relay data and commands to and from the telescope. Sadly, it is yet to work properly.*

Hipparcos *is working better than expected and so it should be able to map around 120 000 stars over the next three years.*

sun within the wavelengths of the ultra-violet spectrum. Among the data received by this satellite are some of prime importance with regard to the origin of life on earth.

It was the only ultra-violet explorer in operation and remained so until work was completed on the Hubble Space Telescope.

IRAS (1983)

Launched on **26 January 1983** by a Thor-Delta rocket, the IRAS (Infra-Red Astronomy Satellite) stopped functioning on 22 November of the same year. Built with the cooperation of the United States (NASA), the United Kingdom and Holland, its purpose was to transmit data on bodies in the universe too cold to emit light visible to the human eye.

In the ten months it was in operation, IRAS drew up a cartographical map of the whole sky and found some 200000 sources of infrared rays.

The continuation of its mission will be guaranteed from 1992 by the European Space Agency's (ESA's) satellite observatory.

Astro-C (1987)

On **5 February 1987** the Japanese Institute of Space and Astronomy Sciences (ISAS) launched the Astro-C satellite, the purpose of which was to observe neutron stars and perhaps black holes. The satellite, equipped with X-ray and gamma equipment, is presently in orbit at an altitude of about 530km *330 miles*.

Space telescope (1990)

Planned for several years, the Hubble Space Telescope (NASA's space telescope in collaboration with the ESA) was put into orbit 512km *318 miles* above earth on **25 April 1990** by the space shuttle *Discovery*. Its mission was to transmit to earth pictures free from atmospheric impurities, that is to say, exceedingly clear images. Two cameras, two spectrometers and a photometer allowed the telescope to function within the visible, infrared and ultra-violet spectrum. Hundreds of experiments were planned for the 15 years it was expected to be in operation.

Its usefulness has been temporarily reduced, however, as one of the mirrors is defective and produces only blurred images that are no clearer than those supplied by conventional telescopes. A mission is planned to rectify the problem.

Hipparcos (1989)

The European Space Agency's scientific satellite, *Hipparcos*, called the 'surveyor of the stars' by astronomers, was launched by the European rocket *Ariane 4* on the night of **8–9 August 1989**.

When it was unable to fire its apogee motor, which should have sent it into geostationary orbit at an altitude of 36000km *22370 miles*, its mission was revised, and since then *Hipparcos* has worked on a modified orbit. This satellite is due to measure the positions of more than 100000 stars and to draw up a map of the sky with a precision never seen before.

Lomonossov (1996)

According to the plans announced by the USSR, this will be the twin brother of *Hipparcos*. The launch of this space observatory is expected in **1995** or **1996**.

Astrophysics

Cepheid stars (1784)

The cepheid stars take their name from the first among them: Delta Cephei, discovered in **1784** by the British astronomer **John Goodricke**. These relatively rare stars (today only 700 of them are known) have a variable luminosity or magnitude.

They are of great importance since they enable scientists to calculate distances within the universe. In fact, there is a linear relationship between the rhythm of the variation of their brightness and their average luminosity. This relationship was proven by the American astronomer Henrietta Leavitt in 1912.

The Pole Star is a cepheid star whose period of variation is approximately four days.

White dwarfs (1779)

Some stars, whose mass does not exceed that of the sun by more than one and a half times, cave in at the end of their lives giving rise to celestial bodies called white dwarfs.

It is not possible to give a date on which a white dwarf was first discovered, but that of the planetary nebula, the Lyre, was sighted by **Antoine Dargulier** in **1779**. The existence of Sirius's companion, Sirius B, was calculated in 1834 by the German Friedrich Bessel, and observed in 1862 by the American optician and astronomer Alvan Graham Clark. Neither of these men understood the exact nature of the subject of their observations.

Eridani B (1910)

It was in **1910**, with the discovery of Eridani B, that scientists became curious about this object with its peculiar temperature and density.

In 1917 it was established that Sirius B and Van Maanen star had the same characteristics as Eridani B.

A short time afterwards, the quantum theory was to provide answers to questions posed by astronomers: it is a quantum principle, called the Pauli principle which enables the white dwarf stars to be stabilised.

Neutron stars and pulsars (1967)

Although their existence was heralded in 1932 using the quantum theory, it was not confirmed until more than 30 years later.

They were discovered in **1967** by the British astronomer **Jocelyn Bell** when she was working with Anthony Hewish at the Radio Astronomy Observatory at Cambridge University.

In 1964 she had detected in the sky a very regular radio source which emitted a signal

every 1.33730113 seconds. The Cambridge team came to the conclusion that it was a neutron star, the remains of a large star which, after exploding, left a residue the density of which is measured in millions of tonnes per cm³ with an approximate diameter of 15km *9¼ miles*.

The pulsars (or pulsating stars) discovered by Jocelyn Bell are neutron stars which, in emitting radio signals, are reference points in the universe.

There are now more than 300 known pulsars, the frequency of their emissions varies between more than 620 times per second to once every 4.3 seconds.

Black holes (1967)

The existence of black holes comes within Einstein's theory of general relativity, but was predicted by the French astronomer and mathematician Pierre de Laplace in 1796.

Black holes are the collapsed remains of giant stars the extreme gravity of which would prevent even electromagnetic waves from escaping, including light waves. Their mass would bore a hole in space from which nothing could escape. Such objects could only be detected by the effect produced on objects in the area surrounding them.

Astrophysicists are therefore carrying out research on systems where stars seem to orbit around invisible bodies the mass of which must be superior to that of a neutron star. At present there are three systems which could be considered as serious candidates: Cygnus X-1, LMC X-1 and LMC X-3. However, they all lend themselves to different interpretations and cannot at present be considered as undeniable proof of the existence of black holes.

THE BREATH OF THE SOLAR WIND

The solar wind was discovered by Biermann in 1951. He noticed that part of the tail of comets was pushed by a wind of particles (electrons and protons) coming from the sun and moving at speeds of some hundreds of kilometres per second. The presence of this solar wind was explained as follows: the attraction of the sun is too weak to retain completely the outer region of the sun known as the solar corona, which therefore tends to escape naturally into space and to inundate the solar system with particles.

In the future the solar wind could be used to drive space vessels equipped with enormous solar sails, in the same way that a normal wind drives sailing boats.

A space race to the moon using a 'solar sail' is to be held in 1992 to commemorate the fifth centenary of the discovery of America by Christopher Columbus.

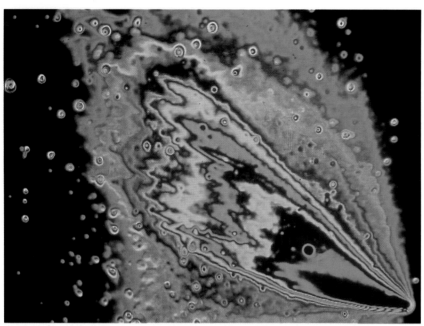

The comet West 75 N as it was observed on 5 March 1976. Subsequently its core fragmented into meteoroids.

The name 'black hole' was first coined by **Professor John Wheeler** at a meeting in New York City on **29 December 1967**.

Quasars

During the 1950s and 1960s radio astronomers drew up a chart of celestial radio sources. At Cambridge University a catalogue of them, entitled *3C*, was drawn up which is considered to be the most important on the subject. By observing, in 1961, one of the radio objects discovered by Cambridge, the astronomer Matthews managed to locate it very precisely. Using a telescope, he discovered a star which was shown to be rather special. In 1963 Hazard, Mackey and Shimming made a second similar discovery.

Quasars have extremely high luminosity and so can be seen at great distances, despite their relatively small size. There are over 3000 quasars known to man and their luminosity can exceed that of the sun by many billions of times.

Distant galaxies

After examination of the results of the objects observed, which were named quasars (quasi-stellar radio sources) in reference to their stellar form, they were identified as being very remote and very bright galaxies.

More than 20 years after their discovery, it is not known which source of energy feeds the quasars to make them so bright and so active. At present about 3000 quasars have been recognised and recorded by astronomers, one of which, discovered in 1987 by Stephen Warren, is the most distant object ever observed.

The distance separating us from the quasars is such that it cannot be measured either in light years or in parsecs (1 pc = 3.26 light years), because there is no point of reference on which to base a measurement. To express their remoteness one uses the quantity of red in the light we receive from them. However, estimates are in terms of billions of light years.

Gravitational mirages (1979)

One day in **1979** the British astronomers **Carswell**, **Walsh** and **Weymann** were extremely surprised to find that two quasars close to each other in the sky were each emitting an absolutely identical light.

It was not long before this phenomenon was explained. It is known that light is not generally propagated in a straight line but that it is sent off course by the field of gravitation of heavy bodies. The astronomers were seeing two images of one and the same quasar, the light of which had reached earth following two different trajectories passing on either side of an enormous galaxy situated between the quasar and us, and acting as a light deflector.

This quasar is now called the double quasar and the phenomenon of the multiplication of images is called gravitational mirage. Many other examples have been discovered since 1979.

Einstein's rings (1987)

A different type of gravitational mirage was discovered in **1987** by an observation team in **Toulouse**. This team made the observation that the arc of light in the star cluster of galaxies Abell 370 come from further afield than does the star cluster itself. It is very likely, therefore, that this is what is called an Einstein ring, that is to say, a deformed image which looks like the ring of a distant quasar as a result of a gravitational mirage due to Abell 370. An image such as this, in the shape of a ring, very occasionally appears in cases where the quasar, the star cluster and earth are perfectly aligned along the same line of sight.

The most distant galaxy (1988)

The 0902+34 galaxy is the most remote galaxy ever observed. It was discovered in **1988** by **Simon Lilly** of the University of Hawaii using a Canada–France–Hawaii telescope. Only a few quasars are found further away than this galaxy.

The 0902+34 is observed as it was at a time when the universe was only 15 percent of its present age. The galaxy is, of course, young, and its light seems to indicate that intense star formations occur there.

The existence of such a distant galaxy demonstrates that the universe itself cannot be much less than 15 billion years old.

Hidden mass in the universe (1913)

Since the time of the pioneering work by the American astronomer **Fritz Zwicky** in **1913**, it has been very widely believed that 90 percent of the total matter in the universe is invisible. In fact, all the indications would lead one to believe that, surrounding the galaxies, and in particular our galaxy, there is a giant

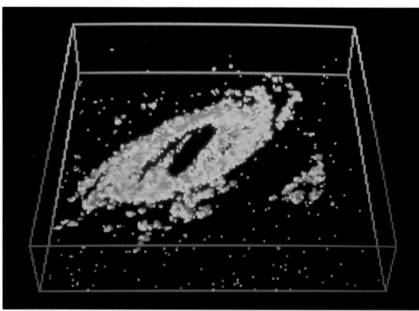

This is a three-dimensional representation of a galaxy completed from data gathered by the VLA (see page 115).

spherical halo composed of invisible matter. What is the composition of this matter? Black holes? Neutrinos? Numerous theories have been put forward over the last few years, none of which is entirely satisfactory.

The enigma of solar neutrinos

Since the work of the German-born American **Hans Bethe** in 1938, it is believed that the nuclear reactions occurring inside the sun, which also serve to supply the latter with light and energy, are well understood.

All the calculations demonstrate that the sun must emit, on account of its nuclear reactions, a certain quantity of very light particles which are called neutrinos. The detection of neutrinos coming from the sun has been undertaken by several laboratories throughout the world, in particular the Davies Laboratory in America.

All the experiments show that the sun, mysteriously, emits only a third of the calculated number of neutrinos. Could this be because neutrinos exist in three different forms and that not all these forms are recognised? Astrophysicists are puzzled and some of them have their doubts as to our understanding of the inside of the sun.

Rockets

Rocket (13th century)

The first rockets were, it seems, built in China and India in the distant past. According to Chinese legend, a mandarin once attempted to fly hanging from two paper kites driven by a large number of rockets. What is certain is that some rockets were in operation as early as the **13th century**: Tartars used them in 1241 at the Battle of Legnica (Lower Silesia, now in Poland).

The only rocket engine used today is the internal combustion rocket engine which uses chemical fuels. Other types of rocket engines, nuclear and electrical, are still only at the planning stage.

First liquid-fuelled rocket (1895)

The exact date of the first liquid-fuelled rocket is not known. Certain people date the invention back to 1895, when a Peruvian engineer, **Pedro P. Poulet**, built and patented an engine with a 10cm *4in* diameter into which was injected a mixture of nitrogen peroxide and petroleum, lit by a candle. Americans readily attribute the first rocket to their compatriot Robert H. Goddard.

The first European to launch a liquid-fuelled rocket was the German Johannes Winkler, whose small rocket HW I (fuelled by liquid oxygen and methane) was launched on 21 February 1931 in Germany at Breslau (now Wroclaw in Poland).

Space rocket (1957)

Although the origins of space rockets goes back over 40 years, in particular to the German V2, it was only on **4 October 1957** that a rocket escaped from the earth's gravitational pull and sent the famous *Sputnik 1* into orbit. Since 1957 more than 2500 rockets have been launched.

Sputnik 1 was launched from Baikonur near the Aral Sea, USSR and was put into orbit at a speed of over 28500km/h *17700mph*. It weighed only 83.6kg *184.3lb*.

Ariane (1979)

Launched for the first time in **December 1979**, the Ariane rocket was invented and perfected for a very precise task: to place satellites in geostationary orbit. For this task, which requires a satellite to be positioned at an altitude of 36000km *22370 miles* above the equator, the rocket is assisted by the location of its launching site, Kourou in French Guiana, which is only five degrees from the equator.

Although it has a launching capacity of 1750kg *3860lb* for the geostationary orbit (GTO), *Ariane 1* was abandoned in February 1986, at the time that *Spot* was launched, in favour of models 2 and 3 which were capable of launching 2600kg *5733lb* GTO.

It is worth noting that Ariane is the European space rocket, built with the participation of ten western European countries: Belgium, Denmark, France, Germany, Great Britain, Italy, Netherlands, Spain, Sweden, Switzerland. Members of the European Space Agency (ESA), decided in 1973 to build Ariane, and construction was carried out by about 60 companies from the ten participating countries.

Ariane 4 (1988)

Ariane 4 came into operation in **1988**, the first launcher in the world to provide different options. According to the wishes of the customer and the mass and form of the satellites to be launched, there could in theory be about 40 different versions of the rocket. In practical terms, however, Arianespace will market six different versions, the differences between which will be based on the form and volume of the cap containing the satellites, and on the extra engines which will run on either solid or liquid fuel. Depending on the version, the rocket has a capacity of between 1900 and 4200kg *4190lb* and *9260lb* GTO.

Ariane 5 (1995)

During the last few years of this century *Ariane 5*, with its entirely new conception, will be able to devote itself to several missions. Capable of placing 6800kg *15000lb* in geostationary orbit, or 21 tonnes in a lower orbit of 500km *310 miles*, the rocket will also be able to launch the spacecraft *Hermès*. It is expected to undertake its first mission is **1995**.

Space shuttle (1981)

The NASA space shuttle is the first rocket in the history of astronautics that can be recovered and used again. It is a real aerospace vehicle that weighs more than 2000 tonnes and lifts off like a rocket: vertically. The main part, the orbiter, is a kind of delta-winged aircraft that weighs 100 tonnes and is placed into orbit around the earth at low altitude (160 to 1100km *100 to 683 miles*). The orbiter re-enters the atmosphere as a glider, and lands on the runway horizontally, like a plane. The shuttle can carry a 39-tonne payload and a crew of between four and seven people, two of whom are the pilots.

Thanks to its jointed arm, the shuttle can

The first voyage of Ariane 5 *is planned for 1995.*

A southern dawn as seen from the shuttle Atlantis. *Unfortunately, a hydrogen leak was subsequently discovered and considerably set back the 1991 programme.*

place all sorts of satellites into orbit. This revolutionary rocket prefigures the space-ships of the future, which, like all other means of transport, will be reusable.

Initiated by President Richard Nixon in 1972, the shuttle (as well as its prototype *Enterprise* which was used for test landings) was constructed principally by Rockwell International.

The first shuttle, *Columbia*, had its maiden flight on **12 April 1981**, with **John Young** and **Robert Crippen** at the controls. *Columbia* lifted off from Cape Canaveral, Florida, and landed 54 hours later at Edwards Air Force Base in California.

The second shuttle, *Challenger*, had its first flight in April 1983 but was destroyed in a tragic accident on 28 January 1986. The third shuttle, *Discovery*, had its first flight in August 1984, and the fourth, *Atlantis*, in 1985.

Walking in space

Some highly successful missions have been accomplished by space shuttles and a par-ticularly spectacular one was that by *Chal-lenger* between 4 and 9 April 1983. During this, two astronauts, Story Musgrave and Do-nald Peterson, tied to the space ship, 'walked'

THE MYSTERIOUS ROCKET PROTON

Long kept secret, the Soviet factory which produces Proton civil rockets opened its doors to foreign visitors for the first time on 16 October 1989. The booster rocket D, or Proton, was designed at the beginning of the 1960s by Vladimir Chelomei. It can send into low orbit loads weighing up to 22 tonnes and can send satellites of 2.5 tonnes into geostationary orbit. It is also capable of sending automatic probes to Mars and Venus. Out of the first 180 launches (up till the end of 1989) Proton had only nine failures.

in space. On a *Challenger* trip in February 1984 Bruce McCandless was seen riding a 'scooter' in space.

After a 32-month hold-up in the pro-gramme, flights started again on 28 Septem-ber 1988 when *Discovery* was launched. *Atlantis* followed it on 2 December. In January 1990 *Columbia* managed the spectacular feat of recovering the space lab LDEF (Long Duration Exposure Facility) which had been in orbit since 1984. Unfortunately, the dis-covery of problems can have serious con-sequences and the programme was again delayed in July 1990.

Hermès, the European space shuttle (1998)

The beginning of the preparatory programme for the European space shuttle *Hermès* was originally announced in December 1986. In charge of the shuttle will be the French com-pany Aérospatiale, with Dassault responsible for the aeronautics. The final design for *Hermès* will be completed in 1991. The first automatic space flight, launched by *Ariane 5*, is planned for **1998**. The first manned flight is planned for April 1999.

Ejector seats for *Hermès*

A number of modifications were introduced into the design of *Hermès* before the defini-tive version. For example, it was decided no longer to have an ejectable cabin, which would hamper the spacecraft by adding an extra three tonnes to its weight. This ex-tremely complex feature had been de-veloped after the *Challenger* disaster in January 1986. Instead, the three crew mem-bers of the *Hermès* have ejector seats similar to those designed for *Bourane*.

Hotol

A project running in competition with *Hermès* is the British rocket-propelled plane *Hotol*, designed by **Alan Bond** of the Atomic Energy Authority (AEA).

Hotol would be able to take off from ordi-nary airports and will be equipped with a hybrid propulsion system, 'breathing' the

surrounding air in the atmospheric phase of the flight. However, at present the project seems to be facing numerous problems.

Sänger (2004)

Parallel to the European project *Hermès*, Germany plans to have its own space pro-gramme which could be implemented around 1995.

The main project in this programme is the space shuttle *Sänger*, named after the Ger-man physicist, Eugen Sänger (1905–64), one of the pioneers of the development of liquid-fuelled rockets. Like *Hotol*, the German space shuttle would not need a rocket launcher. Preliminary studies will begin, but the de-cision whether or not to build *Sänger* will not take place before the year **2004**.

Soviet shuttle (1988)

The Soviet space shuttle, *Bourane* or 'snow storm', was first launched on **15 November 1988**. Propelled by a giant rocket called Ener-gia, *Bourane* (which weighs 105 tonnes at take-off) lifted off unmanned, in automatic mode. Forty-seven minutes later, the shuttle was circling in orbit. After going twice round the earth at an altitude of 250km *155 miles*, *Bourane* switched on its retrorockets and re-turned to a runway 12km *7½ miles* from its launch site.

If the landing of the Soviet shuttle can be compared to that of its US cousins *Discovery*, *Atlantis* and *Columbia* (all land without an engine, gliding down), the lift-off is very dif-ferent. Unlike the US shuttles, at the moment of lift-off, *Bourane* is in a totally passive state: the four engines on the first stage of Energia (800 tonnes of thrust each) ignite at the same time as the rockets on the second stage (200 tonnes of thrust each). The first burn kerosene and oxygen, the second, liquid hydrogen and oxygen.

After 10 min 30 sec of propulsion *Bourane* separates from the rest of the rocket at an altitude of 110km *68 miles*. Finally, at 160km *100 miles* altitude, *Bourane's* principal engine comes into action and propels the shuttle to its circular orbit, at an altitude of 250km *155 miles*, which it reaches 47 minutes after lift-off.

Capable of carrying a crew of two to four cosmonauts as well as six passengers (scien-tists and mission experts), *Bourane*, just like the American shuttles, has an enormous cargo hold. It can lift off carrying a 30-tonne load and is able to bring back 20 tonnes to earth (maxi-mum landing weight: 82 tonnes).

Bourane's second flight will probably not take place, again without a crew, until 1992.

Pegasus (1990)

On **5 April 1990** NASA launched a commercial rocket, *Pegasus*, to send two small satellites into orbit (one experimental satellite for the US Navy and PEGSAT), from a specially con-verted B-52 bomber. *Pegasus* is the fruit of the efforts of an American company formed jointly by the **Orbital Science Corporation** and **Hercules Aerospace**. It is innovative in that it is the first launcher rocket to use an aeroplane for the lift-off phase (hence saving fuel), and also because it is the only machine currently performing as a light launcher, as opposed to the very powerful launchers which are costly for small loads.

Satellites

Transit 1 (1960)

This satellite, launched by the United States in 1960, was the first to provide navigation aid to vehicles on earth. Using special equipment, a vehicle on earth can ascertain its position through triangulation.

Vostok 1 (1961)

The first manned spacecraft, *Vostok 1*, was also the first artificial satellite with a man on board. On **12 April 1961** the young cosmonaut Yuri A. Gagarin circumnavigated the earth at an altitude of 327km *203 miles* in 108 minutes. The first woman in space (on the sixth and last flight of a *Vostok*) was Valentina Tereschkova in 1963.

Landsat (1972)

In **1972 NASA** launched *Landsat 1* under the name of ERTS-1 (Earth Resource Technology Satellite). Observation satellites like *Landsat 1* are used for a variety of purposes: cartography; in the search for minerals or water; to follow the movement of swarms of locusts, etc.

Microsatellites (1990)

They are known as Lightsats, Piggy bags, Secondary passengers, although others have preferred to call them auxiliary loads. One thing is certain: microsatellites have a future ahead of them since a study carried out by the company Arianespace predicted that a dozen satellites would be launched in **1990**, 20 in existence by 1993 and about 40 by 1996.

These microsatellites would however have to adhere to certain rules. They must be electrically 'transparent' – there must be no interference with the launcher – not require any significant modifications, they must not go above a certain volume (250kg *550lb* in total per Ariane launcher) and they must not have any impact on the insurance conditions of the main satellite and launcher.

Orbital stations

Salyut (1971)

The USSR was the first country to launch a manned orbital station. Since **April 1971** the Soviets have put into orbit seven Salyut orbital stations. The last to date, *Salyut 7*, was launched on 19 April 1982. It was manned by seven Soviet cosmonauts, one of whom was the second woman cosmonaut ever.

Although clearly smaller than the American orbital station Skylab, this station is capable of carrying a crew of four cosmonauts for one week. However, long flights lasting several months are generally manned by a two-person crew.

Mir orbital station (1986)

The Mir orbital station (*Mir* means peace in Russian), which has been going round the earth at an altitude of between 300 and 400km *186* and *249 miles* since **29 February 1986**, entered the record books for the longest human stay in space: 366 days passed on board the station by the pair Moussa Manarov and Vladimir Titov. Having left earth on 21 December 1987, the two men returned a year and one day later.

It is worth noting that during this last mission, the Soviet station (15m *49ft* in length, 4.2m *13ft 9in* in diameter with a useable space of 100m³ *3531cu ft*) for the very first time held six cosmonauts at one time, three of whom remained several months on board the Mir before returning to earth.

What is the purpose of the station?

The station – which is locked alongside the astrophysical module Kvant – has many uses: first, to analyse changes undergone by the human body during a long period in a weightless state (reduction in muscles, weakening of bones, etc). The main purpose of this is to prepare for long interplanetary trips such as to Mars in around 2020; second, to carry out observations of earth, as well as of the planets and stars which surround us; finally, to carry out experiments in an atmosphere which is weightless such as the creation of alloys and new crystals, preparation of ultra-pure medicines, experiments on the growth of plants and so on.

In order to enhance still further the performance of the orbital station, the Soviets sent a second scientific module, Kvant 2, in 1989; while in June 1990 Kristall was launched to make semi-conductors in a weightless environment.

Experimental space station (1984)

Christened LDEF (Long Duration Exposure Facility), this experimental space station was released in **1984**. It was the size of a coach, weighing 12 tonnes and was to have been returned to earth ten months later. However, it had to stay in space much longer on account of delays which had built up in NASA's programme. It was therefore recovered by the space shuttle *Columbia* on 12 January 1990 after spending more than five years in space, exposed to meteorites, cosmic rays and corrosion.

LDEF is the first satellite of its size to be brought back to earth without being burnt by the dense layers of the atmosphere. The host of information gathered will have a direct impact on the choice of materials to be used for the construction of the station Freedom, which has to last for 30 years.

Freedom (1999)

The LDEF is the forerunner of the permanent space station Freedom which should be fully operational by about **1999**.

This orbital station will not be solely American, since Europe (the ESA) will be represented by *Columbus*, the European part of the future station, which is to comprise the following: a permanently habitable module laboratory linked to the station; an autonomous module, which will fly in conjunction with it but at different altitudes; a platform in polar orbit containing meteorological and observational instruments; the programme (and the name) *Columbus* covers a series of three modules, including a linked laboratory which will be launched by the American shuttle, while the independent module will be launched by *Ariane 5*.

The American orbital space station was launched in 1984 by President Ronald Reagan and it is an international civil programme. The first part of the programme comprises a 'girder' carrying at its centre of gravity an accommodation module which is permanently occupied and three laboratory modules (the US module, *Columbus* and JEM, the Japanese Experimental Module).

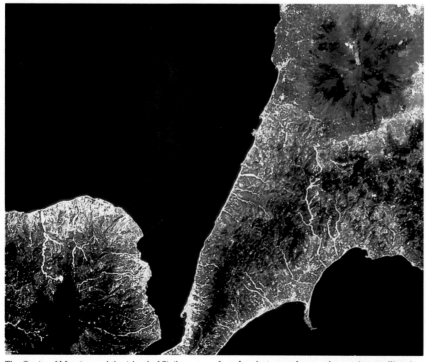

The Straits of Messina and the island of Sicily as seen from Landsat, one of many observation satellites in orbit around the planet.

Space laboratory

Skylab (1973)

On **14 May 1973** the United States launched Skylab, the biggest orbital station ever built. Eleven days later, a team of three astronauts transported by an Apollo craft took up their positions aboard it. The 75-tonne Skylab was built by **McDonnell Douglas** and **Martin Marietta** with elements recovered from the Apollo programme. Built into the *Saturn 5* stage of a *Saturn 5* rocket, Skylab had a living space of 350m³ *12 400cu ft* of unprecedented comfort for a manned spacecraft (kitchen, beds, shower, etc). Sent into circular orbit around the earth at an altitude of about 500km *310 miles*, Skylab contained a vast amount of scientific equipment, including an astronomical observatory.

The station was occupied by three successive teams of three astronauts. Skylab made it possible to take more than 175 000 photos of the sun and more than 46 000 of the earth. Skylab's mission was completed at the end of 1973. After the station had been momentarily placed in a higher orbit by the last crew, it was not possible to bring it back to earth. During an attempt to do so in 1979, the orbital laboratory burst into flames as it re-entered the atmosphere and crashed into a sparsely populated part of Australia.

Spacelab (1983)

Europe has also built a habitable orbital laboratory. Spacelab, built by the German firm **ERNO** and industrialists from ten European countries (Belgium, Denmark, France, Germany, Great Britain, Italy, the Netherlands, Spain, Sweden and Switzerland), is comprised of a pressurised module where up to four astronauts can work, and pallets carrying instruments directly exposed to the space vacuum. The whole laboratory weighs a maximum of 11.3 tonnes, of which 5.5 to 9.1 tonnes comprises scientific and technical instruments.

Spacelab's first flight was in **November 1983**. The shuttle *Columbia*, which launched the laboratory, had a crew of six men, including the first non-American astronaut, 42-year-old Urf Merbold (Germany), an expert in crystallography. The project cost $1 billion. Spacelab is now run by NASA.

Space vehicles

LEM lunar module

The Lunar Exploration Module (LEM), nicknamed 'space spider' on account of its shape, was developed by the American company **Grumman** to make safer those phases which are without a doubt the most critical in space travel, that is to say, landing and take-off. This 15-tonne 'space lift', built in aluminium and covered with gold leaf, allowed a crew of two astronauts to land on the moon within 12 minutes and to take off within seven. They could then rejoin the Apollo cabin which was revolving round the moon at an altitude of about 100km *62 miles*, with the third astronaut involved in the mission on board.

The LEM performed without breaking down throughout all the Apollo flights. On 11 April 1970 it even saved the crew on the Apollo 13 mission after the explosion in mid-flight of an oxygen tank in the cabin.

First walk on the moon (1969)

It was during the Apollo 11 mission that on **20 July 1969** two Americans, **Neil Armstrong** and **Edwin 'Buzz' Aldrin**, made an old dream come true: they walked on the moon. They stayed there for 21h 36min.

Abandoned after the last Apollo flight in 1972, the moon could very well become an astronauts' paradise during the next few decades. In the Soviet and American files are dozens of projects; there may even be a joint US–Soviet mission.

Manned Manoeuvring Unit (MMU) (1984)

In **February 1984** a *Challenger* mission enabled the astronaut **Bruce McCandless**, aged 46, to use the MMU or Manned Manoeuvring Unit for the first time. This $10 million project allows the astronaut complete independence. McCandless was away from the space shuttle for 90 minutes while the latter was more than 270km *168 miles* above Hawaii.

It was the first time that a man had 'wandered' in space in this way without being tied to anything. The freedom it gave was extraordinary but it was not without its dangers. If there was a breakdown or defect in the equipment, the astronaut would have been completely on his own in space.

Life in space

Space design

Anxious to improve the comfort of the orbital station Skylab, NASA called upon the most famous talent in industrial design, **Raymond Loewy**, a Frenchman who has been established in the United States since 1919.

Raymond Loewy was involved with the interior design of the Skylab living quarters – the arrangement of rooms, choice of colours, etc. He also insisted on there being a porthole through which the crew could observe the earth: this was one of the reasons why the mission was so successful.

Some of his ideas were also used in the design of the habitable section of the shuttle. All of Raymond Loewy's preliminary sketches, 3500 of which were drawn up for NASA, were sold at auction by Sotheby's in London in July 1981 when the designer was celebrating his 88th birthday.

Space suits

All American astronauts and Soviet cosmonauts (with the exception of the Soyuz crews, one of which paid for the oversight with their lives) now wear waterproof suits during space flights, at least on board the transport vessels.

First space suits (1934)

The space suits worn by the first American

The French space suit EVA is specially designed for training astronauts in water tests.

THE FIRST FARE-PAYING PASSENGER IN SPACE

While it may still be some years before there are any hotels in space, in December 1990 history was made when 48-year-old Toyohiro Akiyama became the first man whose presence in space was due to the money paid to send him there – a small matter of $39 million.

In fact the money was paid by the Tokyo Broadcasting System (TBS), the largest private television network in Japan. Akiyama was chosen from a total of 163 applicants to go to space and had to undergo 14 months of training before he was ready, which meant that he even had to give up smoking – something that he often complained about during his broadcasts from space.

He took off from Baikonur in Central Asia in a Soyuz TM-11 on an eight-day mission, during which his major experiment involved setting free some Japanese tree frogs to see whether, being weightless, they would think themselves to be in water or on dry land. The results were inconclusive, much to the disappointment of the eight-year-old girl who had suggested the experiment in the first place.

Perhaps the people who were most satisfied by this space mission were the TBS, who had sold advertising space on the side of the space ship and at the launching site, and had also seen their ratings leap in Japan. For them it had been $39 million well spent.

astronauts were derived from those developed earlier for pilots of jet planes. At the request of the American aviator Wiley Post, the tyre manufacturer **B. F. Goodrich** produced the first pressurised space suit that could be worn in the cockpit of an aeroplane in **1934**. The space suits worn during the American space flights Mercury, Gemini and Apollo were developed respectively by the American firms B. F. Goodrich, David Clark and ILC. They were supple suits made from plastic material, with sealed seams at the joints.

AX-5 and ZPS Mk-3 (1996/7)

These are two new types of space suits intended to be used during journeys outside the space station in **1996/7**. Tested since February 1988 by **NASA**, they should allow trips of eight hours; so, with three trips a week this would be a total of between 1000 and 2000 hours of use per year without the need for them to be sent back to earth for maintenance. The ZPS Mk-3 weighs only 68kg *150lb*, as against 83kg *183lb* for the AX-5. The outdoor space suit weighs 45kg *99lb*.

They are like independent cubicles

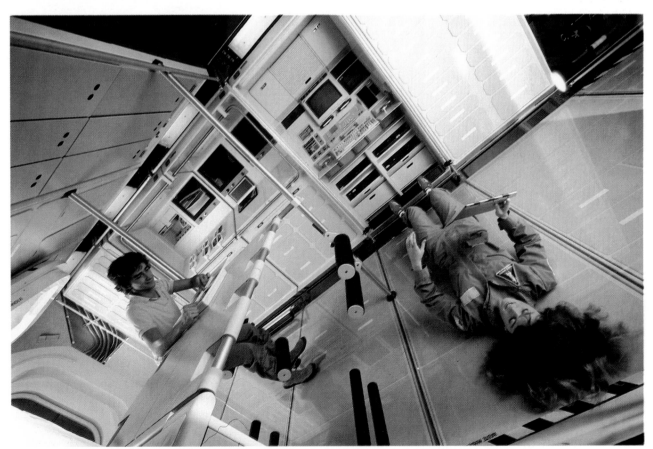

A view of the habitation module onboard a life-size mock-up of the permanently manned space station being planned by NASA. The station will initially consist of four modules linked together. Once operational the station will allow continuous work in a number of areas, such as life sciences. This mock-up will be home to eight volunteers to see how habitable it is.

equipped with all modern conveniences and the astronaut, wearing underwear which automatically regulates temperature, puts on the suit using an opening at the back, and then closes himself in before screwing on the transparent helmet.

Space shower (1990s)

Nothing could be better for the astronauts' morale than to be able to wash in comfort (almost). This is why **NASA** has developed a special shower intended to be used in weightless conditions and which will be fitted on board the orbital station. It is expected to be put into operation in the **1990s**.

93 percent recycled water

After having tried for three years and spent $400000, the Johnson Space Centre presented this unusual piece of sanitary equipment: a cell measuring 1.85m *6ft 1in* in height by 1m *3ft 3in* in diameter, made of plexiglass preventing any liquid from escaping.

A shower head sprays and then sucks up the water, 93 percent of which will be recycled, since it is very important to avoid over-consumption of water. Tests have shown that on average it uses 4 litres *7 pints* a minute, compared with a shower used on earth which generally uses up 20 litres *35 pints* a minute! Taking water into space is expensive for NASA: several thousand dollars a litre. Thanks to recycling, each astronaut will be able to have a shower every two days; at present astronauts on space shuttles are allowed only to wash themselves with a sponge!

The NASA engineer **Rafael Garcia**, who designed the equipment, must find a solution to the problem posed by micro-organisms which sometimes develop in a shower. He will then attempt to develop a space machine for washing dirty clothes.

Exploration of the cosmos

Space probes

Origins (1920s)

The idea of sending space probes to the planets goes back to the beginning of space exploration around **1920**.

The German **Hermann J. Oberth** described in two published works (appearing in 1923 and 1929) the broad principle of interplanetary space flight. During this time, another German called **Walter Hohmann** became the first person to calculate the conditions of such space flights (flight time, mass of propellants, etc) as well as the best orbits for reaching the planets. Some of these orbits are still used today and are known by the name Hohmann orbits as a tribute to their inventor.

Luna 9: towards the moon (1966)

It was on **3 February 1966** with the Soviet space probe *Luna 9* that an artificial satellite landed on the moon for the first time.

The United States also achieved this feat on

The planet Neptune is famous in the history of science as it was discovered by calculation before it was first seen. In 1846 Le Verrier in France and Adams in England predicted its position and its mass from the effects on its neighbouring planet, Uranus. Neptune was discovered very close to the predicted position. A century and a half later very little was still known about this planet: even in the best telescopes Neptune appears as a simple blue ball. But it has been established that Neptune has at least two moons, a large one, Triton, and a small one, Nereïd, and also rings, or rather arcs of rings (discovered in 1984 from earth by a French team led by A. Brahic). On 25 August 1989 the American probe *Voyager 2* at last flew over the planet after a journey of 4.5 billion km *2.8 billion miles* which lasted 12 years.

As always in planetary exploration, the human imagination is surpassed by the beauty and diversity of nature. Neptune is a magnificent gas-covered planet coloured a deep blue, like the oceans on earth. The blue colour is due not to the oceans covering its surface but to an atmosphere of methane. Triton, Neptune's large moon, is a cold body, with extensive polar caps. The surface, easily visible through an atmosphere of nitrogen and methane, appears to be streaked with many flaws. Planetologists thought they could detect geysers spewing gaseous nitrogen into the atmosphere. This phenomenon would be unique in the solar system. Many other observations and discoveries were made by *Voyager 2*, in particular it found six new satellites of Neptune, which will be analysed by scientists in the years to come. Meanwhile, the probe will continue its journey until leaving the solar system around the year 2015.

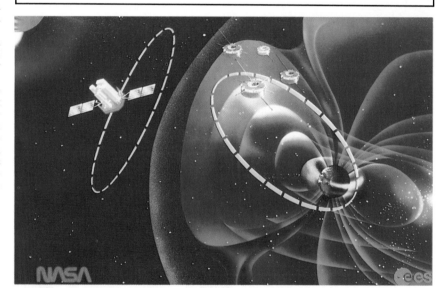

Many probes have been sent out into space to enable us to know more about the solar system, and eventually beyond, but Ulysses is aiming for the sun.

2 June 1966 with the landing of the automatic probe *Surveyor 1*, which transmitted 11 150 photographs of the surroundings (Sea of Tempests). This was followed in 1967 by the probe *Surveyor 5* which carried out the first analyses of lunar soil.

Then, in September 1970, the USSR sent the *Luna 16* probe which carried out the first core-sampling of lunar soil.

Towards other planets (1970)

The USSR also launched the probe *Venera 7* which landed on the planet Venus for the first time on **15 December 1970** and then *Venera 9* and *10* which landed on Venus on 22 and 25 October 1975, transmitting the first images from Venus's surface.

The United States sent the probe *Mariner 10*, which, in March 1974, passed less than 1000km *620 miles* from Mercury, the nearest planet to the sun.

The United States also successfully carried out their first flights over Jupiter and Saturn,

the largest planets in the solar system. First, it was *Pioneer 10* and *11* which flew above the two planets in December 1973 and December 1974 respectively. Subsequently, it was the probes *Voyager 1* and *2* which flew over Jupiter and Saturn, this time getting even closer, as well as over their numerous satellites, before continuing on their flights towards Uranus and Neptune.

Magellan, Ulysses and *Galileo* (1989)

The first of the probes, *Magellan*, was launched towards Venus during the Atlantis mission in **May 1989**. *Galileo* set off towards Jupiter on 18 October 1989, while *Ulysses*, the European probe, headed off towards the sun in the early 1990s.

Cobe (1990)

A probe for distant exploration, Cobe (Cosmic Background Explorer) was launched in the United States in 1990 by a Delta rocket. The purpose of this probe is to research Big Bang, the giant explosion which, according to

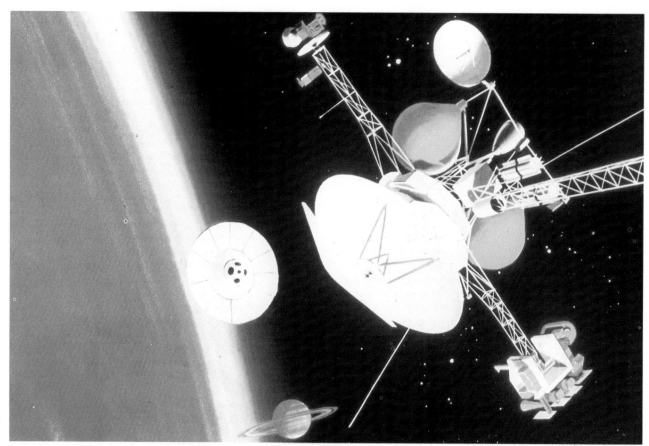

The Cassini *space probe should reach Saturn in October 2002.*

certain scientists, triggered off the expansion of the universe 15 billion years ago.

Soho (1993)

In **1993** or 1995, under the ESA 'Soho' programme, five probes will be launched to examine more closely the relationship between the earth and the sun.

Cassini space probe (1996)

In **November 1988** the European Space Agency (ESA) took up the American–European *Cassini* project (named after the astronomer Jean Dominique Cassini, first director of the Paris Observatory founded in 1672 by Louis XIV). The project discovered a division in the rings of the planet Saturn.

Planned since 1982 by the Frenchman **Daniel Gautier** and the German **Wing Ipp**, the space probe *Cassini* should be launched on 9 April 1996 by an American rocket Titan 4/Centaur G. It will reach Saturn in October 2002, after a journey of 1450 million kilometres *900 million miles*.

For four years *Cassini* will revolve round the system formed by Saturn and its large satellite Titan. The European *Huygens* probe (named after the Dutch astronomer Christiaan Huygens who discovered Titan) will then be detached from *Cassini* and released into Titan's dense nitrogen atmosphere. After being slowed down by an aerodynamic shield, it should reach the unknown surface of Titan and carry out numerous measurements.

The density of the probe has been calculated so that the probe will float if Titan's surface is formed by an ocean composed of ethane, methane and liquid nitrogen.

Bizarre inventions of the past

Burglar-proof bicycle (1900)

Bicycle theft is an ever-growing problem; more and more complex systems and locks are developed to try to prevent bikes from mysteriously vanishing. Perhaps **Adolph A. Neubauer** had the most effective solution in 1900. Any thief cycling away on a bike equipped with his device would soon find a spike coming up out of the seat and get a very painful punishment.

A selective cat-flap

The prolific inventor **Arthur Paul Pedrick**, who used to work in the British Patents Office, came up with an ingenious solution to the problem faced by many cat owners: their cat was not the only one to use the cat-flap and so strange felines would wander in and deposit gifts of dead birds or eat the food intended for the owner's cat. Pedrick designed a cat-flap that was colour sensitive. It could be programmed to register the colour of the cat in residence and would open only when a cat of that colour approached the door. All others would find their way barred.

Safety coffin (1896)

It is only comparatively recently that it has become possible to be completely sure that someone is dead and not just in a deep trance or coma. There were many horrifying tales of people who had been buried alive. Several inventors came up with ideas for means by which someone in a coffin could alert others to their predicament and so avoid a grizzly end.

The Russian **Count Karnicé-Karnicki** was one of the most prolific of these inventors. His most sophisticated device was patented in 1896. A glass ball was placed on the chest of the deceased, from it went a tube of 9cm *3.5in* diameter which went up through the lid of the coffin and out into the air above, reaching some 1.3m *4ft* above ground. The smallest

A 1930s invention from Geneva. This mica mask protects women's delicate skin from bad weather, but as a fashion accessory it leaves something to be desired.

The Patent Travelling Squirt, 1841. This lithograph is based on the idea of Charles Golightly for a new form of air travel. Sadly, the Squirt was too undignified for many potential fliers – not to mention the problems of landing!

movement in the coffin caused the ball to move, which sent a signal up the tube to an iron box on top. The box would then open, a lamp would be lit, a bell would ring and a flag would be raised, thus giving ample notice that someone was alive six feet under. The tube could then be used as a means of communication until the coffin was raised.

A spinning bowler hat (1896)

On **10 March 1896 James C. Boyle** patented an unusual hat. Concealed inside a seemingly normal bowler was a series of finger-like projections which rested on the head. When its wearer nodded his head, a weight tipped, setting off a clockwork motor that automatically tilted the hat forward, spun it round and replaced it – to the astonishment of passers-by.

A hat protector (1914)

Frank P. Snow's 1914 hat protector guaranteed that any hat thief would never again commit the same crime. For, hidden inside the hat rim, was a vicious spike that gave a nasty shock to the unaccustomed wearer – or to the forgetful owner who failed to de-activate it!

Chicken spectacles (1903)

In **1903 Andrew Jackson** of Tennessee was granted a patent for spectacles for chickens. This was not due to an outbreak of short-sighted hens bumping into barn doors. In fact

A new type of plane designed by W. O. Ayers of New Haven, Connecticut (USA) in 1885. It was to be run by compressed air condensed in the two drums in front of and behind the driver.

THE FLYING SAUCER NOW DEPARTING FROM EUSTON

In 1973 the engineering division of British Rail applied for a patent for a flying saucer powered by nuclear fusion and capable of transporting 22 passengers on earth or in outer space, despite the fact that they did not have the technology to construct such a machine. However, by 1976, they had abandoned their attempts at building flying saucers and allowed their patent to lapse. Instead they concentrated on the much more knotty problem of getting the trains to run on time.

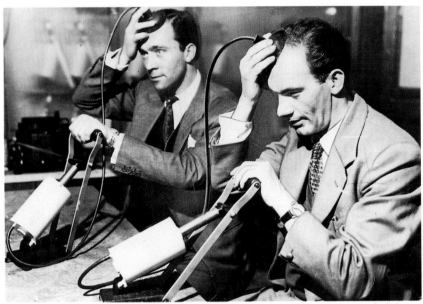

In 1955 Tony Voitechovsky, chairman of the London club Curls, designed this apparatus to make hair grow again. It stimulated the circulation around the bald patch.

they were eye protectors designed for fowls to prevent other chickens from pecking at their eyes.

Phonomotor (1878)

The great American inventor **Thomas Edison** placed over 1200 patents during his life, including such important inventions as the gramophone and the light bulb. But they were not all as successful as these. For example, in **1878** he took out a patent for a 'Vocal Engine' or 'Phonomotor' – a voice-powered motor for driving sewing machines and other appliances. The inspiration for this exciting device came when a lady friend told him that she found pedalling her sewing machine tiring. Now all the operator had to do was to talk non-stop – perhaps by reading aloud, or maybe out of habit – which the phonomotor converted into power and operated the equipment. Sadly, Edison's friend found that constant talking made her even more tired than pedalling, and the invention got no further. Maybe this invention will make a comeback in these days of ever increasing fuel costs.

A rifle to fire round corners (1916)

Wars often inspire inventors to devise weapons to bring a speedy end to the conflict. **Jones Wister** of Philadelphia believed that he could bring an end to the stalemate of the First World War with a weapon to revolutionise trench warfare – a rifle that could shoot round corners. It consisted of a curved extension which fitted to the end of the barrel of a

These individual bomb shelters, perfected by British engineers, were installed in Buckingham Palace in 1939. It is not recorded whether or not they were used, but the living conditions do not look to be particularly palatial.

LUNETTES POUR CHIENS — A

7792. Lunettes coques peau, monture nickel pur, nez peau, verres blancs plans, attache à élastique.

Prix ..... 3. »

7796. Lunettes coques jersey, à ressort se prolongeant derrière la tête, monture nickel pur, garniture peau doublée, verres blancs plans, attache à élastique .. 8. »

NOTA. — *Les lunettes pour chiens existent en 4 tailles, basées sur l'écartement des yeux, pris de centre d centre : 83, 103, 121 et 145*m*/*m*. (Bien indiquer la taille désirée).

The French truly take care of their pets. Advertised here are two models of spectacles for the fashion-conscious hound in turn-of-the-century Paris.

conventional rifle, with a periscope replacing the sights. Although there is no evidence that Wister's invention was ever used, a similar attachment, known as the *Krummlauf* appeared during the Second World War and was actually used by German troops.

Bizarre inventions of today

Aquatic bicycle (1990)

If the pedalo can be considered as being among the more agreeable sporting activities, the aquatic bicycle invented by the Italian **Giorgio Botti Caffoni** and unveiled at the Geneva Salon in 1990, is a totally novel idea. This bicycle, equipped with a propeller powered by the pedals, allows the body to be immersed up to the hips, therefore requiring greater physical effort, in complete safety.

Jumping Balloon (1989)

How is it possible to jump 100m *328ft* in a single giant stride? The Frenchman **Alain Erval** invented the Jumping Balloon in 1989 which makes it possible to jump as high as 30m *98ft*. The novelty for those who like a thrill is that the helium-filled balloon does not have a basket – there is only a simple harness attached to the body, which alone creates the necessary momentum.

Luminous collar for dogs and cats (1989)

Insomniac dogs and cats are often the unfortunate victims of drivers who are not necessarily reckless but just do not see them until it is too late. A Frenchman, **M. Charvet**, has invented a collar, called *Luciole* (firefly), which was shown at the Salon Expo 1989. The collar is equipped with a system of reflecting flashing lights which vary in brightness according to the surrounding luminosity. Ideal for a black dog in the dark!

Page-turner for musicians (1990)

Not all musicians are lucky enough to have someone to turn the pages of their scores while they play. The system invented by the Swiss **Sebastian Jaggi**, launched at the Geneva Salon in 1990, will put an end to the musician's nightmare of watching the capricious score close under his helpless gaze.

Seat belt for dogs (1989)

Animals are also victims of road accidents. To ensure their safety, **Hervé Piolat** has invented a seat belt for dogs, which has been on the market since 1989. It clips round the dog's chest and is attached to the rear seat belt. The danger is further reduced as the dog is unable to jump up at the driver.

Carisa Traut called this novel hat a 'Bee-bee'. To buy it in the shops would be quite a sting.

Modern life has brought new dangers for pets and in some cases the only way to protect them is the seat belt for cats and dogs.

The Best store is in the earthquake zone of California, so you can imagine how terrified onlookers are when they see it coming apart.

Vernon Guy of Nevada has spent his leisure time making chain saw motor-powered roller skates.

The Venetian Livio di Marchi constructed this car, based on the 1930 Jaguar, entirely out of wood. The Italians, known for their love of cars, often suffer in Venice. Could this be the solution?

Madcap inventor Philip Garner has come up with yet another bizarre invention. This time it is a catapult to help high-jump athletes – but will it get past the Olympic Committee?

Andy the goose was born without feet, so he was given some shoes to enable him to walk and swim.

A new discipline for very fit sports enthusiasts – the cross-country monocycle, developed by Pierre Rochat in an inspired moment.

This bicycle for lovers, designed by the American Robert Barrett, is not such hard work.

At 3.26 p.m. on 4 August 1974 in the Los Angeles Stadium in Ashley a whippet leaped to catch a frisbee – and a sport was born. The first championships were held in 1977, but the sport still awaits TV coverage.

Shock absorbers for crutches (1987)

Having to walk with crutches is restrictive enough, but there is an additional physical effort involved, as the body suffers the shocks caused every time the crutches touch the ground. For greater comfort, the Frenchman **Philippe Puyo** has invented shock absorbers for crutches, which have been available since **1987**. The end of each crutch has a spring which absorbs the shock and helps the crutch adhere more firmly to the ground, ensuring greater safety.

Skiing dogs (1989)

Winter sports do not usually crop up as a dog's idea of fun. In **1989** the Frenchman **Laurent Boyer** had the bright idea of inventing a pair of little skis, attached by a metal bar which adjusts according to the animal's size and equipped with little shoes. Black run here we come!

Ultrasound gun (1988)

Unfortunately, dishonourable intentions can sometimes bring forth inventions. For example, there is the well-known case of the Englishman who apparently invented an ultrasound gun. Ultrasound affects animals especially and, in some cases, can cause them to panic. Used on horses, they can disrupt or stimulate their behaviour on the race track. At the time it was alleged that such a gun was used to rig the famous King George VI and Queen Elizabeth Diamond Stakes handicap at Ascot in **1988**. The favourite Ile de Chypre was several lengths ahead of the other horses when, to everyone's astonishment, a few yards from the finishing post, the horse reared and flung jockey Greville Starkey to the ground. The 'explanation' given was that the gun was concealed in a pair of binoculars and fired. However, there has been much controversy as to whether the 'gun' was ever actually used, or whether it could have been fired in the way mentioned.

Underwater pedalo (1989)

Instead of touring the coastline in a pedalo, why not use one to admire the underwater landscape? The Englishman **Henry A. Perry** has invented something making it possible to do just that: an underwater pedalo for two people. One person pedals while the other steers it and controls the air supply. Unlike the traditional pedalo, it is more of a sport than a leisure activity; the first underwater pedalo race was held in Florida in **1989**.

Walking on water (1990)

Anything can inspire the imagination, even miracles! The Italian **Paolo Pegoraro** displayed an invention at the **1990** Geneva Salon which actually makes it possible to walk on water. With two floats the size of a pair of skis, the Wavewalker is an original means of walking safely on reasonably calm surfaces.

The Tantrum brick allows the viewer to let off steam without causing any damage.

Tom McClean, among other records, holds the one for crossing the Atlantic in the smallest yacht.

Philip Garner's aid for waiters rushed off their feet. He has also invented a motorised pepper mill.

UNUSUAL, BIZARRE, USEFUL . . . WILLIAM JOHNSON'S INVENTIONS

If you are furious at the rubbish shown on television, then William Johnson's latest invention is for you. It is the Tantrum brick and has been available since 1990: you pick it up, throw it violently at the TV set and hey presto, it switches itself off. No damage to the screen, of course, because the brick is made of foam. A micro-transmitter inside it transmits the message to the 'receiver' (in this case, the TV set) which picks up the signal and stops.

William Johnson is also the inventor of an electronic shoe for runners, marketed by Adidas in 1984 under the name of Micropacer. The shoe contains a small computer which makes it possible to keep a constant check on performance during training.

And then there is the personal hydrofoil, baptised the Flying Frog, invented in 1987 but not yet on the market; the ring-watch; the Anti-Snoring device – which, as its name suggests, is a small object placed in the ear to prevent snoring (available since 1990); a natural process for stopping the massacre of elephants by substituting an Amazonian nut for their ivory tusks.

This motorbike without wheels won the 11th Honda ideas competition for employees of the company and could be the shape of things to come.

Examination techniques

Microscope (16th century)

It would seem that the microscope was invented towards the end of the **16th century** by the Dutch optician **Hans Jansen**, with the help of his son Zacharias. Described by Galileo in 1609, this microscope was quite basic and had minimal powers of magnification.

Another Dutchman, Antonie van Leeuwenhoek (1632–1723) was the first to observe spermatozoa, muscular striation and certain oral bacteria, although magnification was still less than 200 times actual size. The first modern microscopes were constructed after 1880.

Electron microscope (1926)

In **1926** the German **Hans Busch** laid the theoretical foundations for the electron microscope. In 1928 two of his fellow countrymen, Max Knoll and Ernst Ruska, from the Technische Hochschule in Berlin, carried out experiments based on his research which led to the development of the first operational electron microscope in 1933. It was perfected by Ernst Ruska who, with Heinrich Rohrer and Gerd Binning, was awarded the Nobel Prize for Physics in 1986 for the invention of the tunnel effect microscope.

Three-dimensional electron microscope (1985)

Living cells could not be observed using the electron microscope as the beam of electrons directed at the target had to circulate in a high vacuum. In **1985** scientists from the **Massachusetts Institute of Technology** (MIT), directed by Alan Nelson, invented a new process which consisted of placing the sample in a cavity which retained enough air to produce about 1/10th atmospheric pressure and so made it possible to keep the cells alive.

The second advantage of the process was that a three-dimensional image could be projected onto a television screen, by means of a technique based on medical X-ray scanners, which is why the procedure is known as scanning.

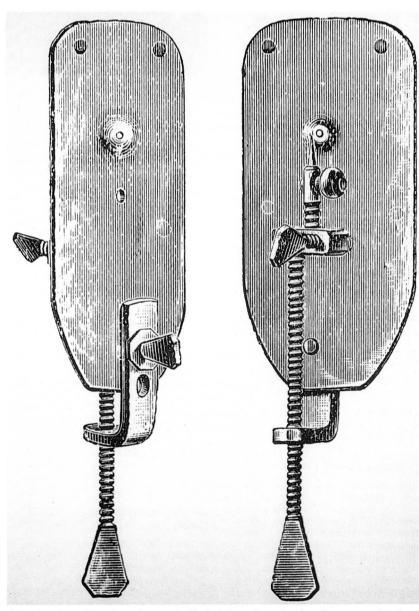

A drawing of one of Antonie van Leeuwenhoek's single-lens microscopes, based on an example in the University of Utrecht, showing back and front views. The lens is held in a pair of metal plates, with a specimen pin attached to a device for adjusting its height.

Tunnel effect microscope (1980)

In 1980 **Gerd Binning** of West Germany and **Heinrich Rohrer** of Switzerland, both working in the IBM research laboratory in Zurich, developed the tunnel effect microscope for which they received the Nobel Prize for Physics in 1986. Based on a principle of quantum mechanics, anticipated at the end of the 1920s, it makes it possible for the surface of a sample to be viewed atom by atom, with a magnification of 100 million times.

Thermometer (1626)

The first clinical thermometer was a water thermometer invented in **1626** by the Italian physician **Santorio**, otherwise known as Sanctorius. The model of the modern clinical thermometer – a graduated glass tube containing mercury – was developed by the English physician Sir Thomas Allbutt, in 1867.

There are now various types of medical thermometer available, including the disposable oral thermometer invented by an American physician, Louis Weinstein.

Percussion (1761)

Percussion was invented in **1761** by the Austrian physician **L. Auenbrügger**. This clinical mode of exploration allows the condition of certain organs to be deduced by the noise obtained when they are tapped with the fingers. The system was improved by Baron Jean Corvisart (1755–1821), Napoleon's personal physician, and then by the Austrian Skoda, who improved it considerably.

Auscultation (19th century)

With the exception of the medical observations of Hippocrates (460–377 BC), the first true auscultation was performed by the French doctor **René Théophile Hyacinthe Laënnec** (1781–1826) using a makeshift stethoscope made from a sheet of paper rolled into a cylinder. He devised this method because of his embarrassment at having to place his ear on the naked chests of his female patients – the previous method of listening to the heart.

The stethoscope in the true sense of the word, from the Greek *stethos* meaning breast, was invented in 1815 when Laënnec replaced the sheet of paper with a wooden cylinder. The device was further modified and improved by Joseph Skoda of Austria and Cammam of the United States, to become the binaural stethoscope as we know it. The electron stethoscope was invented in 1980 by the Americans Groom and Boone.

Measuring blood pressure (1819)

Taking the pulse has long been one of the main methods of making a diagnosis. In **1819** the French doctor and physicist **Jean-Louis Poiseuille** (1799–1869) invented the manometer, a mercury gauge for measuring blood pressure. It was succeeded by the sphygmomanometer, from the Greek *sphygmos* meaning pulse, which was a pulsometer developed by an Austrian physician, Siegfried Carl von Basch, in 1881, and by the French physician Pierre Potain in 1889. This was followed by the broad armband invented in 1896 by the Italian Scipione Riva-Rocci which exerted a more consistent and

Tunnel effect microscopy enables us to see here a picture of atoms of gold on a graphite surface. This microscope was invented by Binning and Rohrer.

reliable pressure. In 1905 the Russian physician N. S. Korotkov perfected the method by developing a device which examined the arteries by means of auscultation rather than palpation.

Electrocardiograph (1887)

The first human electrocardiogram was recorded in **1887** by **Augustus Désiré Waller** (1856–1922), a physiologist from London University, born in Paris.

In 1901 Willem Einthoven, Professor of Physiology at the University of Leiden in Holland, and former colleague of the French physicist and 1908 Nobel Prize-winner Gabriel Lippmann, developed the loop galvanometer. This made him the true inventor of the electrocardiograph (ECG), a piece of equipment that weighed 300kg *661lb* and required five people to operate it.

Carrying out an electrocardiogram is very straightforward, though interpreting the results is not. It is now possible for a pregnant woman to place an ultrasound probe on her abdomen to monitor the baby's heart. The result can then be sent by the woman by telephone to her doctor who can then assess the health of the baby, thus saving everyone a great deal of time and effort.

Electro-encephalogram (EEG) (1929)

In **1929** the spontaneous electrical activity of the brain was recorded for the first time by **Hans Berger**, Professor of Neuropsychiatry at the German University of Jena. But his recording was met with scepticism because of the weakness of the signal. It was not until the English physiologist and 1932 Nobel Prize-winner Edgar Douglas Adrian circulated the results in 1934 and defended Berger that the

latter received the support of scientific and medical circles.

In 1984 an Englishman, Professor Stores, carried out an experimental continuous recording of an electro-encephalogram for a period of 24 hours.

Radio-immunology (1970s)

Radio-immunology, invented by the American physicians **Solomon Berson** and **Rosalyn Yalow**, for which the latter won the Nobel Prize for Medicine in 1977, is a combination of two techniques. The first, which is biological, uses the specificity of the immune reaction in order to identify a given organic substance, while the second is physical and marks these substances by introducing radioactive atoms into their molecules.

Test for hepatitis-B (1984)

This test was developed in **1984** by a working party consisting of Diagnostic Pasteur and the French National Blood Transfusion Centre. It was marketed by Diagnostic Pasteur under the name Monolisa, 'mono' for monoclonal antibody and 'lisa' for the ELISA technique (i.e. enzyme *l*inked *i*mmuno *s*orbent *a*ssay). It makes it possible for hepatitis-B to be traced quickly.

Tracing hepatitis-C (1989)

A hepatitis virus which is neither A nor B, and which should therefore logically be referred to as hepatitis-C, has just been identified in the blood by the research team of **Doctor Qui-Lim-Choo** of the Chiron Corporation, a Californian biotechnology company. The hepatitis-C virus is the most common cause of the illnesses which tend to follow blood transfusions such as hepatitis, cirrhosis and cancer of the liver. This is an important discovery which could enable a vaccine to be developed. In **November 1989** the virus was successfully traced for the first time.

Due to the rapid advances in virology, two further hepatitis viruses have been identified: D and E. Hepatitis-D is found only in B-infected people, while hepatitis-E is known as Epidemic Non A-Non B.

The algometer (1988)

Developed by the companies **3M** and **Racia** and based on the work of **Doctor Claude Willer** of the Hôpital Saint-Antoine in Paris, the algometer, an instrument for measuring sensitivity to pain, measures the threshold above which a stimulus is experienced as pain. It has been tested on hundreds of patients and has been shown to be an objective and accurate method of measurement. It will be used to test the efficiency of certain medicines, to prescribe the required dosage of analgesics as well as to measure the level of analgesia during the administration of an anaesthetic.

LipoScan (1989)

Americans can now carry out on-the-spot cholesterol checks by using the LipoScan (TM)-TC, developed by **Home Diagnostics Inc.** and marketed in **1989**.

A few years ago the same laboratories brought out a similar test, the DiaScan (TM)-S, which allowed diabetics to check the daily level of glucose in their blood.

Rapid diagnosis of tuberculosis (1989)

Since **November 1989** a technique for the rapid diagnosis of tuberculosis and other infections caused by mycobacteria has made it possible to detect the bacterium in three days as opposed to the previous minimum of six weeks. This process was developed jointly by the **Institut Pasteur** in Paris and Unit 82 of **INSERM**, the French national institute of health and medical research. The genetic material (DNA) of the bacteria is enlarged in vitro and specific molecular probes make it possible to identify the type of mycobacteria in question.

Detection of Down's syndrome (1990)

Building on the work done by an American, **Professor Bogart** from San Diego, the French geneticist **Professor André Boué** has developed a blood test which makes it possible to detect two-thirds of cases before birth. The HT21 test (developed by the Clonatec laboratory) is a blood marker which measures the levels of a particular hormone (HCG), the pregnancy hormone, in the blood. A very high level indicates, in two cases out of three, that the foetus is trisomic (i.e. having three chromosome No 21s rather than two – any foetus with trisomy 21 will have Down's syndrome), although this initial diagnosis needs to be confirmed by a study of the chromosomes. The HT21 test must be carried out between the 15th and 17th week of pregnancy: as the levels of HCG are too low to be detectable any earlier. The test became available at the end of **1990**.

Medical photography

Endoscope (1826)

This is a technique which enables organs to be examined internally, to detect and even treat certain forms of damage. The first instrument was developed by a French doctor, **Pierre Salomon Ségalas** who, in **1826**, performed the first endoscopy of the bladder using a speculum lit by candles. In 1853 another French urologist, Antonin Desormeaux, performed the first rectal endoscopy. The first laryngoscopy was performed in 1829 using an instrument invented by the English physician Benjamin Babington. The first gastroscopy was performed in 1842; the first electric cystoscopy in 1878 by the German surgeon and urologist Max Nitze; the first tracheobroncho-scopy in 1897 and the first arthroscopy in 1951 by Watanabe.

In the 1960s the range of investigations performed by endoscopy was greatly increased and extended due to the development of glass fibre instruments which are both extremely supple and excellent conductors of light.

Radiology (1895)

On **8 November 1895** the German physicist **Wilhelm Conrad Röntgen** discovered X-rays while working in his laboratory. On 22 December he X-rayed his wife's hand and was able to see the carpus, the phalanges, etc. In 1901 Röntgen received the Nobel Prize for Physics for his discovery.

In 1912 another German physicist, Max von

A photograph of a foetus in the fifth month of its development, taken by an endoscopic camera. At this stage the foetus can already perform simple reflex actions, such as sucking its thumb. While the eyes remain closed, the ear is developed and so the foetus can respond to noise. The technique of endoscopy has been hugely advanced by the progress in the field of glass fibres.

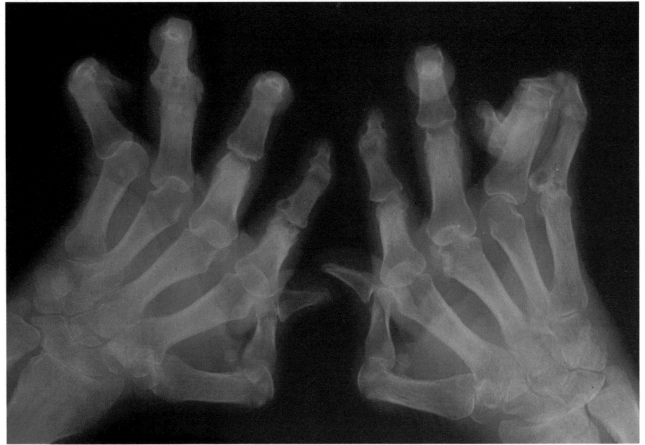

The first X-ray of a hand, that of Röntgen's wife, took place on 2 December 1895. This picture shows a pair of hands deformed by polyarthritis – a common problem, especially among the old.

Laue, demonstrated that X-rays resemble visible light in that they are electromagnetic waves, but with a very short wavelength which enables them to pass through opaque matter.

Radiography was initially used for examining the skeleton, but was extended to the other organs by the use of injections of contrasting substances.

Tomography, a process by which a thin layer of an organ is X-rayed to a specific depth, was discovered by the Frenchman André Bocage in 1915. The first tomographies were carried out in 1928.

The first X-ray of the skull was carried out by Walker in 1896; the first encephalogram or X-ray photograph of the brain by the American surgeon Walter Dandy in 1918; the first arteriogram by the Portuguese physician Antonio de Egas Moniz and urologist Reynaldo Dos Santos in 1927; and the first X-ray of the pulmonary blood vessels and the cardiac chambers by Ameuille in 1938. Today, traditional radiology accounts for no more than half of medical photography.

Ultrasound (1952)

The principle of the echogram is the application of sonar to the human body. An ultrasonic source transmits a signal which is reflected by the obstacles in its path. Ultrasound was first used in the field of medicine in 1952 by the American physician **Robert Lee Wild**, and then by his fellow American, Leskell, who was the first to observe the heart using ultrasound. In 1958 the English physician Ian

Donald carried out the first echogram of the uterus. The method was not widely used until after 1970, but today it can be used to examine any organ. It is used mainly in the fields of gynaecology and cardiology.

Thermal analysis (1950s)

Thermal analysis is another painless and harmless method of examination developed during the 1950s by English and American scientists. It is a method of photographing the tissues using infra-red rays that brings out the differences in temperature due to changes in vascularisation. It is used particularly as a means of checking for cysts and inflammation in the breasts but is replaced by mammography when it is a question of detecting malignant tumours. In 1980 the microwave thermal analysis process was developed by a French research team led by Professor Y. Leroy of Lille University of Science and Technology.

Scintiscanning (1961)

This technique of medical photography was used for the first time in 1961. It is based on the principle of introducing a radioactive substance such as phosphorus, iodine or thallium into the body which then attaches itself to the organ to be examined. Nearly all organs can be scanned in this way, although the technique is currently used mainly for the thyroid gland and the bones. The method has great potential for the future. The use of computers since 1975 has enabled the resultant images to be improved.

Scanner (1972)

The scanner is the result of the combination of the X-ray and the computer. Perfected in 1972 by **Sir Godfrey Newbold Hounsfield**, a British engineer working for EMI, the scanner or tomodensitometer makes it possible to take photographs of cross-sections of tissue in which the detail is 100 times larger than those produced by the traditional X-ray method.

Photography by magnetic resonance (1972)

The appearance of this technique in 1972 revolutionised the field of medical photography. It produced clearer and more detailed pictures than the scanner, with the added advantage that it did not use X-rays. The phenomenon of nuclear magnetic resonance (NMR) was discovered in 1948 by the American physicists Felix Bloch and Edward Mills Purcell. In 1972 it was introduced into the medical world by **P. C. Lauterbur**, Professor of Chemistry at the State University of New York at Stony Brook, and the biophysicist **Raymond Damadian**. The technique uses high frequency electromagnetic radiation which produces changes of energy within the cells which in turn enable the nature of the tissues being studied to be identified. The first pictures of the human body achieved in this way were obtained by Damadian in 1977. At present the technique is used mainly in the field of neurology, but it has other very promising possibilities.

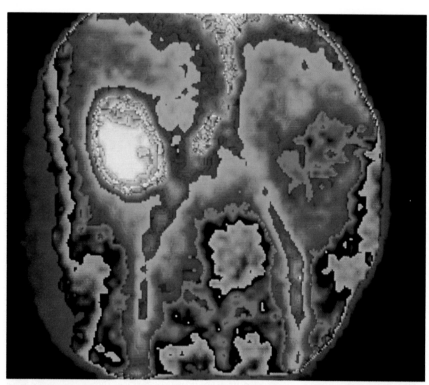

This scintiscan shows the left kidney (on the right), which is not working, and a new kidney, which has been transplanted (on the left) and is directly connected to the bladder.

Magnetic resonance angiography (1989)

This new system of creating magnetic resonance images makes it possible to measure the blood flow without injecting anything into the veins or arteries. It was first demonstrated in **1989** by scientists from the **General Electric** (USA) research and development laboratories. It works by creating a magnetic field. As the cells pass through the field they generate a current and this current is then described pictorially on a television screen.

Vaccination

Variolation (11th century)

For quite some time, the only response possible to smallpox epidemics was to flee the area. Nonetheless, variolation, which was the first known of all immunisation methods, was discovered in the Far East many centuries ago.

The principle behind variolation is that smallpox, like some other diseases, once contracted and cured, will not occur again in that person.

Preventive variolation by the application of dried crusts of smallpox lesions to nasal mucous membranes was used regularly in the Far East almost 800 years before Jenner's discovery. It was not known in Europe until 1717. At this time Lady Mary Wortley Montagu, the wife of the British ambassador to Constantinople, revealed that she had had her three-year-old son variolated.

The eradication of smallpox

For ten years, there has not been a single case of smallpox throughout the world. In producing the figures which enabled it to claim such a victory, the World Health Organisation (WHO) in Geneva considers that this is one of the most important medical facts of the 20th century. In 1967 it was estimated that two million people would die from the disease which affected 10–15 million people annually. The campaign to eradicate smallpox, which took place between 1967 and 1979, cost about $300 million.

Microbes (1762)

The first microbes were discovered by an Austrian doctor, **M. A. Plenciz** (1705–86), who published his 'Medico-Physical Studies' in **1762**.

Most of the microbes that we know were discovered by the end of the 19th century.

Vaccination (1796)

On **14 May 1796** Edward Jenner (1749–1823), having done considerable work on cowpox (a disease of the cow udder whose French name is *vaccine*), took a sample of the material from a pustule on the hand of a dairymaid, contaminated by the cows, and put it into the arm of a young boy named James Phipps. Ten days later, a pustule appeared on the boy and healed quite normally.

In a second experimental phase, Jenner inoculated the boy with smallpox; there was no harmful effect. The experiment was a

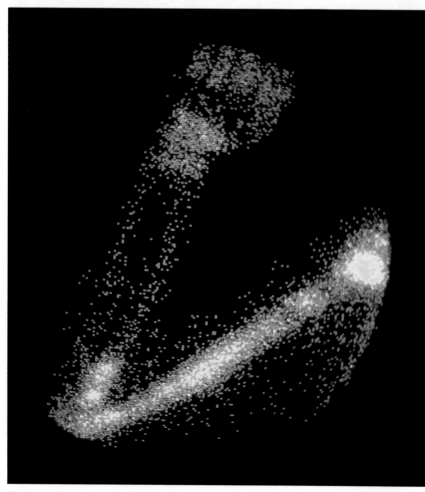

This false colour gamma scan shows secondary bone cancer in the left arm. The areas of increased uptake of radioactivity, known as hot spots, are shown by the pale blue regions. The diagnosis would be confirmed by X-ray.

The Cow-Pock — or — the Wonderful Effects of the New Inoculation! — Vide the Publications of ÿ Anti-Vaccine Society.

This caricature by Gillray in 1802 shows the early scepticism about the benefits of vaccination. The inoculator is Pearson and the page is Woodville – these two physicians were much more prominent at the time than Jenner.

complete success, and in 1798 Jenner published his results. In 1799 he perfected his idea and his technique and called it vaccination after the disease initially treated.

The method spread widely in Europe, the East and the United States. Some 60 years later, Pasteur would make a discovery of still

THE BATTLE AGAINST HEPATITIS-B

A new vaccine against hepatitis-B, obtained by genetic engineering at the laboratories of the American company Smith Kline and French, is now on the market. It is heat-fast, which means that travellers can carry it with them. In 1989 SKF donated a million doses to the World Health Organisation as a contribution to its eradication campaign. It is estimated that there are 200–300 million chronic carriers of the hepatitis-B virus throughout the world. In parts of Africa and Asia up to 15 percent of the population are carriers, while in the UK the incidence is only 0.1 percent. Carriers of the hepatitis-B virus are up to 300 times more likely to develop liver cancer.

greater general interest in the area of disease prevention. However, although the biological principle was different, Pasteur kept the term vaccination, as a posthumous tribute to Jenner.

Later developments

Assisted by his students, E. Roux and C. Chamberland, **Louis Pasteur** (1822–95) first isolated a number of bacteria which cause disease in man.

Pasteur made his first attempt at vaccination to fight the viral disease of rabies. On 6 July 1885 Pasteur injected Joseph Meister, who had been bitten by a rabid dog, with dried spinal marrow taken from rabbits he had inoculated with the virus. The result was conclusive.

In 1922 a French veterinary surgeon, **Gaston Ramon** (1886–1963), managed to isolate a diphtheria toxin and weakened it in formaldehyde. He thus paved the way to vaccines that cause no ill effects to the recipient.

Microbiology (19th century)

The German **Robert Koch** (1843–1910) shares with **Louis Pasteur** the title of founder of the science of microbiology. Koch became famous in 1882 when he discovered the tuberculosis bacillus. In 1883 he detected the cholera vibrion in less than a month during an epidemic that raged in Alexandria, Egypt.

Other parasites (1880)

Besides bacteria and viruses, a number of other disease-causing micro-organisms exist.

In 1880 the Frenchman **A. Laveran** identified the haematozoan, the protozoan responsible for malaria.

In 1881 the Englishman **R. Ross** and the Cuban **C. Finlay** discovered the role of the filariae (parasitic worms found in hot climates) in the transmission of malaria and yellow fever. In 1883 the Englishman **P. Manson** completed his studies by investigating the role of mosquitoes in the transmission of these filariae.

In 1895 the Australian **D. Bruce** investigated the role of tsetse flies in the transmission of sleeping sickness.

Serums (1890)

Serums, obtained by taking samples of blood serum from a diseased or vaccinated patient (serum which thus contains the desired antibodies), allow either preventative or curative action to be taken against numerous diseases and also against bites and stings from venomous animals, by providing the contaminated individual with protective antibodies.

The principal preventative serums were discovered before 1900:
Anti-diphtheria: discovered in 1890 by the German **E. von Behring**, the Japanese **S.**

William Haast of Miami, Florida, has spent his entire life researching serums for snake bites. To immunise himself, he has been bitten on 148 occasions and then had a blood transfusion to help others.

Kitasato, the Frenchmen **E. Roux**, **L. Martin** and **A. Chaillou**.
Anti-tetanus: discovered in **1890** by the **Behring**, **Kitasato**, **Roux** and **Vaillard**.
Anti-plague: discovered in **1894** by the Swiss **A. Yersin**.
Anti-anthrax: discovered in **1895** by the Italian **A. Sclavo** and the Frenchman **E. Marchoux**.
Anti-cholera: discovered in **1896** by the Frenchman **E. Roux**, the Russian **I. Metchnikoff**, and the Italian **A. Salimbeni**.

The virus (1892)

The first virus to be characterised was detected in **1892** by the Russian microbiologist **Dmitry Ivanovsky**. It is the cause of tobacco mosaic, a disease which attacks a variety of plants.

Initially, the existence of viruses was only suspected, as they are not visible under the optical microscope (they can be several hundred times smaller than a red blood cell), but from 1933 onwards, with the development of the electron microscope, the list of identified viruses kept increasing. Today, certain viruses are identified even before the illnesses which they could cause have chance to appear. In 1956 Werner christened them orphan viruses, i.e. viruses that are looking for an illness.

Culture of hepatitis-B virus (1986)

The hepatitis-B virus, which is responsible for the most serious forms of jaundice, has been cultivated in the laboratory since **1986**. The success is due to a Franco–American team led by **Professor Max Essex** of Harvard University (USA). Tests and vaccines had already been developed, but the above research has now made it possible to test anti-viral medication, which is a major step forward in the fight against this extremely infectious disease.

The heart and lungs

Blood circulation (13th century)

It is generally thought that the British physicist William Harvey discovered the circulation of blood in 1628. In fact a 13th century Arab physician, **Ibn al-Nafis al-Quarashi**, had already mentioned the existence of a pulmonary circulation in a work dedicated to the Persian philosopher and scientist Ibn Sina or Avicenna. This work passed unnoticed until it was referred to in 1552 by the Spanish theologian and physician Miguel Serveto in his theological and medical work, *Restitutio Christianismi*, for which he was burnt at the stake.

From 1550 onwards, several physiologists of the Paduan School, including Matteo Colombo, Carpi and Hieronymus Fabricius of Aquapendente, studied the problem. William Harvey based his work on that of his predecessors and had the inspired idea of considering the heart as a pump which was operated by muscular pressure. Proof of the existence of capillary vessels linking the arterial and venous systems was supplied in 1661 by the Italian anatomist Marcello Malpighi.

Blood transfusion (1667)

There seems to be some question as to who should be given credit for the development and use of blood transfusion techniques. Early work in the field of blood transfusion was carried out in England by R. Lower, in France by J. Denis, in Germany by Mayor, and in Italy by F. Folli. Nevertheless, it is practically certain that Lower was the promoter of experimental transfusion in animals, and that Denis was the first to use it for humans. In **1667 Denis** injected one litre of arterial blood taken from a lamb into a young man who had previously been bled. By virtue of its principle and because of the severe dangers inherent in its use, the method was immediately condemned and forbidden.

In 1821 the study of transfusion in animals was again taken up. The method was defined in 1875, but interhuman transfusion was developed only as of 1900, when the work of the Austrian K. Landsteiner demonstrated the existence of four large blood groups. In 1910 the Czech serologist Jansky designated these groups by the letters A, B, AB and O.

In 1940 Landsteiner crowned his achievements by identifying, with Wiener and Levine, the Rhesus factor. It is named after the kind of monkey in which it was first identified. The discovery provided an explanation for the haemolytic reaction in newborn babies.

Blood storage (1917)

At the beginning of this century the problem of blood storage and transportation was the subject of research by Artus, Pages and Peckelharing. In 1914 Hustin made use of the anti-coagulant properties of sodium citrate.

In early **1917 Hédon**, a doctor from Montpellier in southern France, demonstrated that the transfusion of blood with added sodium citrate was possible. On 13 and 15 May of the same year, **Jeanbrau** successfully performed the first three transfusions of stored blood.

Plasmapheresis (1957)

Plasmapheresis is a method which consists of taking blood from a donor and separating the plasma from the corpuscles immediately so as to be able to return the latter to the donor. It was invented in **1957** by **Professors Stokes** and **Smolens**, of the University of Pennsylvania.

TPA: the enzyme that prevents heart attacks (1984)

TPA (Tissue Plasminogen Activator) is an enzyme that has a thrombolytic effect, i.e. it dissolves blood clots which can damage the heart. It was produced in **1984** by the American company **Genentech**, based on the research of Doctor Collen of Louvain in Belgium. Its commercial production was undertaken in 1986 by Carl Thomas GmbH, a West German pharmaceutical company.

An international study in 1988 showed that if a patient was given TPA with aspirin within six hours of a heart attack taking place, the damage done would be limited. It is still expensive, costing £850 a shot.

A hormone for the red corpuscles (1988)

For the first time a hormone which plays an essential part in the physiology of the blood – erythropoietin – is going to be produced commercially as a result of the genetic engineering carried out by the **Ortho-Cilag Laboratory**. It is a medication which marks a major step forward in the treatment of patients suffering from renal insufficiency who are treated by dialysis and who are often unable

Aron Huq soon after his laser heart operation, a technique developed by the British surgeon S. Quereshi whereby the patient is not opened up.

to produce enough of this hormone. The result is anaemia which requires continual blood transfusions.

Artificial heart (1957)

The artificial heart was invented by **Willem Kolff** who began his research in **1957** at the Cleveland Clinic in the United States. In 1970 he joined scientists from other countries at the University of Utah, to develop models for the artificial heart.

In 1976 one of his colleagues, Doctor Robert Jarvik, invented the Jarvik 7, an artificial pneumatic heart which operated on compressed air and was connected, at the time, to a compressor which weighed 150kg *330lb*.

It is implanted in a patient in a situation where there is no alternative form of treatment. On 2 December 1982 the Jarvik 7 was implanted for the first time by Doctor William De Vries into a voluntary patient, Mr Barney Clarke.

Since then some 90 Jarviks (the Jarvik 8 came out in 1986) have been implanted throughout the world. However, the benefits of the process were widely disputed, even as an interim measure for those awaiting a heart transplant, and at the end of 1989 it was banned in the USA.

Other artificial hearts

In addition to the Jarvik, other artificial hearts include the Pen State, developed by Doctor William Pierce, and the Buecherl System, developed by Professor Emil S. Buecherl of Berlin. In **July 1990** the American firm **Novacor** announced the development of a heart assistance device which has the same function as an artificial heart. This is a miniature apparatus, which can be implanted directly into the patient's body. The first implantation into a human being is expected to happen in 1992.

The heart pump (1989)

The Hemopump, developed by **Doctor Richard K. Wampler**, is a miniature turbine which is designed to take over temporarily from the cardiac muscle in a situation where the latter is receiving an insufficient supply of blood. This temporary heart, 6cm *2.3in* long and 6cm *2.3in* in diameter, is inserted percutaneously and directed along the femoral artery to the left ventricle, which is responsible for pushing the blood into the aorta. Once in place, the pump, which is operated by an electric motor outside the body, rotates at a rate of 28 000 rpm to ensure a supply of blood. The Hemopump is extremely valuable in that it provides support at such critical moments as restarting the heart after a heart attack and recuperation before an operation. Its use is limited in that it can only be left in place for a maximum of six days.

The pacemaker (1958)

The cardiac pacemaker was invented in **1958** by **Doctor Ake Senning** of Sweden. The first implants took place in the early 1960s. The pacemaker is capable of stimulating other organs as well as the heart.

In October 1986 a baby was born in Manchester suffering from a congenital malformation of the heart. It was given a cardiac pacemaker when it was only three days old. This

---

CARDIOMYOPLASTY: A REVOLUTIONARY TECHNIQUE

On 24 January 1985 two Frenchmen, Professor Alain Carpentier and his assistant, Doctor Carlos Chachques, a scientist at INSERM in Paris, used, for the first time, a revolutionary technique which they had devised as an alternative to a heart transplant: cardiomyoplasty. This technique consists of replacing part of the defective cardiac muscle with another muscle which returns the contraction of the heart to as near normal as possible. For this to happen, the more rapid rhythm of the contractions of the booster muscle (in the case of this first operation it was a back muscle) has to be converted to the heart's unique rhythm of slow contractions. Only when the muscle has been re-educated can the operation take place. It is very lengthy and even more difficult than a transplant, but offers hope to all those patients who are unsuited to heart transplants or cannot find suitable donors.

A false colour X-ray of a heart pacemaker in place inside a patient's chest. The first effective pacemakers were developed in the 1960s.

A MAJOR BREAKTHROUGH: ARTIFICIAL BLOOD

In February 1979 a Japanese doctor, Ryochi Naito, injected himself for the first time with 200ml ⅓pt of artificial blood, fluosol DA, which is a totally synthetic derivative of petroleum and milky white in colour, capable of supplying essential haemoglobin to the organism, making artificial blood a viable possibility.

In 1966 two Americans from the University of Cincinnati, Professors Glark and Gollan, had demonstrated that a mouse submerged in liquid perfluocarbons could survive because there was enough oxygen in the liquid to prevent it from dying of suffocation. But these fluocarbons did not mix with the blood.

In 1967 an American professor, Henry A. Slaviter from the University of Pennsylvania, succeeded in emulsifying the perfluocarbons by adding albumin, a natural protein found in blood. But, in spite of this step forward, the emulsion ran the risk of agglomerating and blocking some of the capillary vessels.

Ryochi Naito was the first to experiment successfully. In April 1979, during an operation at the Fukushima Centre, an emergency injection of fluosol DA was given to a man with such a rare blood group that a transfusion would have been impossible.

After 25 years' intensive experimentation, a major breakthrough now sees two types of artificial blood on the way. There is white blood, based on fluosol DA, which originates in Japan and is manufactured by the Green Cross. In the USA the Alliance Pharmaceutical Corporation and the Baxter Laboratories are hot on their heels. In December 1989 authorisation was granted there for the use of white blood in certain types of cardio-vascular surgery. Red blood, meanwhile, which will be produced by the fragmentation and recovery of natural red corpuscles from expired blood donations, is still at the experimental stage, for the technique has not yet been mastered.

Another direction for the research is emerging: manufacturing haemoglobin, the oxygen-carrying part of blood, through genetic engineering. A Frenchman, Doctor Poyart of the Kremlin-Bicêtre Hospital in Paris, is working on this in conjunction with the CNTS, the French national blood transfusion centre. This market is attracting a number of firms, notably the American company Baxter and Ajinomoto of Japan.

Some elements of plasma, blood with the cells removed, are currently produced by biotechnology. Factor-8 coagulant (manufactured by Genentech USA) is produced by similar means and is of especial use to those suffering from the most common types of haemophilia. Albumin allows drugs to be carried in the blood and prevents them, and any endogenous substances, from being degraded, as well as preventing fluid loss from the blood to the tissues, a process known as oedema.

---

was the first operation to be carried out in Europe on such a young child.

The programmed pacemaker (1986)

In 1986 a German company, Biotronik, developed a programmed cardiac pacemaker based on blood temperature, which is a good indicator of the level of activity of the patient. For example, as the patient climbs the stairs, the blood temperature rises and the device increases the heart rate accordingly.

The pacemaker pill (1986)

In 1986 an American company, Arzco Medicals Electronics, brought out the first pacemaker 'pill': an electrode contained in a gelatine capsule.

The nuclear pacemaker (1988)

In November 1988 a 47-year-old man made history by being the first person ever to receive a double pulse nuclear cardiac pacemaker. The Pulsar N-1, which operates by using a tiny pastille of plutonium coated with titanium, was implanted under the skin next to the chest. It should last for between 20 and 40 years, whereas single pulse nuclear pacemakers, which act only on a single cardiac function, last for 16 years. Today, between 3000 and 4000 people are fitted with a single pulse pacemaker.

Angioplasty (1964)

In 1954 an American doctor, Charles Daughter, had the idea of inserting a tiny balloon

inside an artery and inflating it at the point at which the artery had become constricted. The idea was put into practice for the first time in Zurich, by the Swiss doctor Andreas Grüntzig in 1964, since when the technique has been greatly developed.

The personal defibrillator (1970)

Certain irregularities in the muscular contractions of the heart cause what is known as a ventricular fibrillation, i.e. uncontrolled contractions of the cardiac muscle. The defibrillator, developed in 1970 in the United States by Professor Michel Mirowski, is implanted directly onto the heart, making it possible to identify any irregularity in the contractions and for immediate action to be taken. In this way the risks entailed in an emergency admission to hospital can be eliminated and the patient's chances of survival increased.

The device was not marketed until the beginning of the 1980s and has not yet caught on in the UK.

Iron lung (1927)

Philip Drinken, an American professor at Harvard University, designed the iron lung in 1927. It was tested on a young girl at Boston Hospital on 12 October 1928.

The first model was made from bizarre objects: two vacuum cleaners alternately produced a positive and a negative pressure on the patient's thorax.

Surgery

Origins (Neolithic times)

The first recorded surgical operation, an amputation, dates back to Neolithic times, between 5000 and 2500 BC. But the skeleton of a Neanderthal man, about 45000 years old, found in the Zagros Mountains in Iraq, seems also to have undergone an amputation. Its missing right arm was due neither to chance nor to an accident.

The sorcerers, doctors and surgeons of the time were also the first to perform trepanation (the removal of part of the skull) on living patients, some of whom appear to have survived this terrifying operation. In fact, some of the trepanned skulls show evidence of healing.

Treatment for fractures (3000 BC)

The Egyptians invented the earliest form of support for fractures. Around 3000 BC Athotis recommended strips of cloth soaked in mud.

Plaster (1798)

In 1798 William Eton, a member of the British Consulate in Persia, noticed that plaster was used there to support fractures. In 1850 a Dutch military doctor from the Royal Hospital, Antonius Mathijsen, developed a method whereby strips of linen sprinkled with dry plaster were prepared in advance and soaked when required.

Glass fibre and resin plaster (1982)

In 1982 the American company 3M developed the Scotchcast, a glass fibre strip impregnated with a polyurethane-based resin. This plaster-resin, which is extremely resistant, is waterproof and is only a third of the weight of a traditional plaster cast.

Dressings and bandages (7th century BC)

The first evidence is recorded on slate tablets discovered during the digs in Assur and Nineveh in Assyria and written by one of the best-known medical practitioners of the 7th century BC, Arad-Manai. In 1825 the French surgeon Antoine Labarraque introduced the chemical disinfection of wounds. In 1840 the English physicians Sir Astley Cooper, Robert Liston, Syme and Macartnay introduced a new form of dressing, a piece of cotton cloth which had been moistened and covered with sticking plaster. In 1864 another English surgeon, Joseph Lister, used dressings moistened with diluted carbolic acid which acted as an antiseptic.

Soluble dressings (1947)

The soluble dressing was invented simultaneously in 1947 by Jenkins in the United States and Robert Monod in France. It consists of a small gelatin sponge that can absorb 20 to 50 times its weight in blood, before gradually dissolving in the body.

Anaesthesia

We know from very early documents that certain methods were used to suppress pain during medical operations. The Assyrians, for

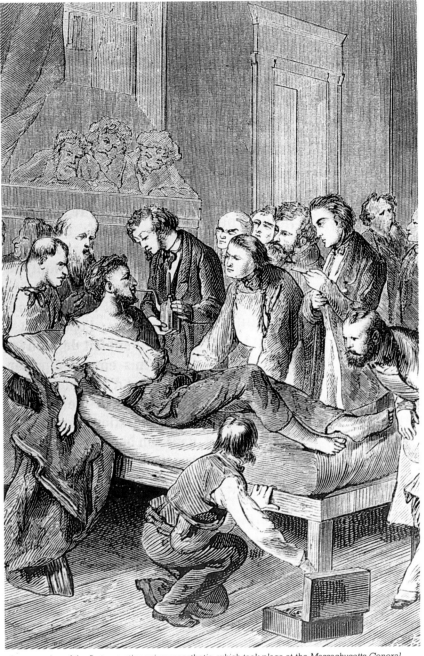

An engraving of the first operation using anaesthetic, which took place at the Massachusetts General Hospital on 14 October 1846. It was performed by Dr John Collins Warren, while the sulphuric acid ether was administered by Dr William T. G. Morton. The operation, to remove a neck tumour, was a success and the idea soon caught on.

and Robert Liston, a Scottish surgeon, introduced it to Europe.

Chloroform became popular after ether. Doctor Simpson, a professor of obstetrics in Edinburgh, used the gas, which had been available since 1831, in a pure form in ~~1834~~. After Queen Victoria had been given chloroform during the delivery of her seventh child, anaesthesia was adopted in all hospitals.

Local anaesthetic (1884)

Local anaesthetic was developed in **1884** using cocaine, by the Austrian ophthalmic surgeon **Karl Köller**. The effect of cocaine was subsequently improved by the addition of adrenalin in 1902, and then it was replaced in 1904 by lignocaine.

However, the earliest written record of local anaesthetic dates back to Pliny the Elder who, in his *Natural History*, gives the recipe for an anaesthetic poultice made from crushed mandrake leaves mixed with polenta.

Epidural anaesthetic (1885)

The epidural anaesthetic was described for the first time in **1885** by an American neurologist, **J. Leonard Corning**. This regional anaesthetic is carried out by injecting an analgesic into the epidural space, i.e. the space surrounding the spinal cord, between the eleventh dorsal and the fourth lumbar vertebrae. This deadens the pelvic organs (the uterus, kidneys, prostate, etc). It was rediscovered in France in 1901 at the Hôpital Tenon by the French surgeon Fernand Cathelin and physician Jean Athanase Sicard, and then neglected until 1970 when it began to be widely used, particularly in obstetrics.

Cryoanaesthesia (1978)

According to 17th century medical texts, doctors in Finland used a technique whereby, in order to reduce fractures and to replace joints, limbs were bathed in iced water. The process made the operation virtually painless. More recently, in **1978**, the **Spembly Llord Method** has enabled an English manufacturer to market ST-2000 Neurostat equipment which extends the range of this technique. These specially shaped cryosounds are able to reach deep-seated nerves and relieve very different types of pain such as backache, post-operative pain or pain resulting from a trapped nerve.

Autopsy (3rd century BC)

The study of anatomy began to develop as a result of the autopsy. Ancient religions prohibited the mutilation of the body. It was not until the **3rd century BC**, and during the reigns of Ptolemy I Soter and Ptolemy II Philadelphus, that the first examinations of a corpse were carried out in Alexandria by the famous Greek anatomists and physicians Herophilus and Erasistratus. For a long time after this the practice was prohibited.

Papal authorisation

It was not until the medical renaissance of the 13th and 14th centuries in Bologna and Padua, and then only with papal authorisation, that the Italian physician Mondino dei Liucci (c.1270–c.1362) was able to publish accounts of the dissections he had performed, in his *Anatomia*.

example, cut off the circulation to the brain by pressing on the carotid arteries while performing a circumcision.

During the 1st century AD, Pliny the Elder referred to a method of making painless incisions and injections by the use of the mandrake. But before the discovery of anaesthetics, the main obstacle to the surgeon's work was the pain suffered by the patient.

Anaesthetic gases (1799)

In **1799** the English chemist **Sir Humphry Davy** (1778–1829) described the analgesic and laughter-provoking effect of nitrous oxide (laughing gas). To demonstrate these effects, he inhaled the gas to ease the pain brought on by an abscess on his tooth.

Some dentists, notably the American Horace Wells in 1844, used this chemical compound when extracting teeth. Wells said 'A new era is beginning in dental surgery. It hurts no more than a pin prick.' Wells died in 1848 from a wound to the femoral artery and, as a final recourse, inhaled the gas while dying.

General anaesthesia (1842)

General anaesthesia with ether was first used by the American **C. W. Long** in 1842. Americans William Morton and John Collins Warren operated on a neck tumour at Massachusetts General Hospital on 14 October 1846 after placing the patient under general anaesthesia with ether. After their success, the use of ether spread throughout the United States,

A lecture on pathology at the University of Leyden in 1610. The engraving shows how the fashionable would go along to view, while dogs were allowed in without hindrance. However, the man selling a human skin at the front right was a figment of the artist's imagination.

Plastic surgery (3rd century BC)

The great progress made in the field of anatomy during the **3rd century BC** in Alexandria encouraged surgeons to attempt the first operations in facial plastic surgery. **Amynthas** of Alexandria performed the first operation on a nose.

Plastic surgery as we know it appeared around the same time on both sides of the Atlantic. In **1891 Roe** of the United States, and in 1898 Joseph of Germany, invented rhinoplastic surgery, i.e. the alteration of the shape of the nose by surgery for purely aesthetic reasons. In 1907 the French surgeon Hippolyte Morestin described his method for the resection of enlarged breasts. In Vienna, in 1928 and 1930 respectively, H. Biesenberger and E. Schwarzmann made important contributions to mammary plastic surgery.

The facelift (1925)

In **1925** a surgeon, **Suzanne Noël**, performed facelift operations under local anaesthetic in the patient's home. Techniques and results in this field are improving all the time, thanks to the great demand for a younger look, especially in the United States where it has become a billion-dollar business, though it is Rio de Janeiro which has the greatest density of plastic surgeons in the world. In the UK very few facelift operations are carried out each year.

Liposuction (1977)

In **1977** a French surgeon **Yves-Gérard Illouz** perfected a technique for fat suction known as liposuction, which makes it possible to reduce the bulk of the stomach, the thighs, the hip and even the face without scarring. After a simple incision of 1cm *0.4in*, the fat is extracted using a foam-tipped canula connected to an aspirator. The method has been very successful in the United States where, in 1987, 90 000 women turned to liposuction. In the UK the total number of these operations can be counted in hundreds per year.

Transplants

Origins (17th century)

In the **17th century** the Boiani, a family of surgeons from southern Italy who practised empirical medicine, developed a way of rebuilding the face based on the method of layering vines carried on in their region. They were the first surgeons to transplant skin tissue by a method still in use today, the skin graft.

But grafting was not developed further until 1958, with the discoveries relating to the HLA system made by the French haematologist and immunologist Professor Jean-Baptiste Dausset, Nobel Prize-winner for Physiology and Medicine in 1980.

Cyclosporin-A (1972)

The second important stage occurred in **1972** when **Doctor J.-F. Borel** of the **Sandoz Laboratories** in Basle, Switzerland, discovered the immunosuppressive properties of cyclosporin-A. This is a substance found in a mushroom which grows on the Hardangervidda, a high plateau in southern Norway. The first tests on humans took place in 1978 and cyclosporin-A came into general use for bone marrow and organ transplants in 1983. A similar substance, known as FK506, has recently been extracted from a type of mushroom growing on Mount Tsukuba in Japan.

Major successes

Hair: N. Orentreich, New York, 1959; the technique invented by Doctor Yamada of Japan in 1985 according to which artificial hairs are implanted individually; the technique of implanting into a cushion of air, invented in 1986 by Doctor Gilbert Ozun of the Hôpital Foch in Paris.

Heart: The first heart transplant was performed on a chimpanzee by J. D. Hary of Chicago in 1964. The first human heart transplant was performed by Doctor Christiaan

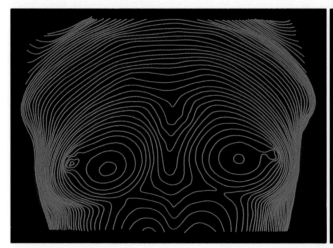
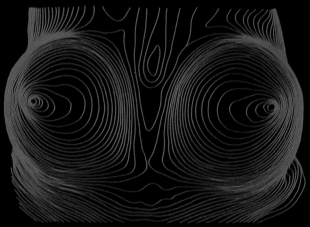

The picture on the left shows a contour map of a young woman's breasts prior to the surgical implantation of silicon for cosmetic reasons. The picture on the right shows the same woman after the implantations. Such cosmetic surgery seems to be most popular in the United States, but it was in Europe that the early developments were made in this field.

A CURE FOR BALDNESS?

In October 1990 Terence Kealey, a researcher at Cambridge University, published the results of some work he had been doing in the *Journal of Cell Science*. In it he announced that he and his PhD student Michael Philpott had managed to make hair follicles grow after they had been removed from the scalp.

He had made the discovery almost by chance. Kealey had been studying sweat glands as part of his research into cystic fibrosis, because children with the disease have a distinctive salty sweat. While looking at the sweat glands he was also isolating the hair follicles, and so he decided to study them too.

It is yet to be seen whether Kealey's discovery will have any long-term significance, but at the moment there are high hopes that within a few years he could have produced a drug which could restore hair – and bring happiness to all those who wish they were not bald.

Barnard in Cape Town, South Africa in 1967. The first successful heart transplant was performed by Professors Cabrol and Giraudon on Emmanuel Vitria on 27 November 1968. Vitria died in 1987, 18 years after the transplant. The first infant heart transplant was performed in London in 1984 by Professor Magdi Yacoub, who also carried out a heart and lung transplant on a baby in 1986.

Cornea: Elschwig, Prague in 1914.

Arm: Ronald A. Malt and J. McKhann, in Boston, USA, in 1962.

Liver: T. Sarzl (1983, USA): the first liver transplant; in 1988 a double transplant of half a liver was performed on two women suffering from acute hepatic insufficiency by Professor H. Bismuth of the Hôpital Paul Brousse in Paris.

Bone marrow: Thomas, USA, 1957.

Bone: R. L. and Jean Judet, Paris, 1950.

Skin: Jacques-Louis Reverdin, Geneva, 1969.

Kidney: Performed by R. Lawler of Chicago in 1950, the patient survived for five years. The first completely successful transplant was carried out by the American physician John Putnam Merrill of Boston in 1954.

Testicle: In 1977 S. Silver of Sacramento, USA, transplanted a testicle from one twin to another. In 1984 Wang Linglong of Hubei, China performed transplants between brothers and parents.

Aortic valve: The French surgeons, J. P Binet and A. Carpentier of the Hôpital Marie-Lannelongue had the first success in 1965. The same surgeons inserted a synthetic valve in 1970.

Brain: Two groups, led by Hitchcock and Lindvall, independently showed that embryonic brain tissue could be introduced into specific areas of the brain of patients suffering from Parkinson's disease and cause an improvement.

THE LATEST TRANSPLANTS

In March 1989 for the first time a simultaneous heart and pancreas transplant was performed in the United States on a patient suffering from severe diabetes complicated by a weak heart.

In September 1989, a year after a Canadian team of neurologists led by Doctor Alan Hudson carried out the first ever nerve transplant on a young boy whose thigh had been slashed by the propeller of a yacht, it was announced that the operation had been successful.

First in utero transplant (1989)

A world first took place at the Hôtel-Dieu hospital in Lyons in **1989**, when **Professors Touraine** and **Raudran** and their teams carried out an in utero transplant. It was performed on a 28-week-old foetus suffering from 'bare lymphocyte syndrome', a rare disease characterised by a very serious immunity deficiency which requires the baby to be placed in an isolation tent from birth so as to avoid any possibility of infection, because even a simple cold could be fatal as there are so few antibodies to combat it. While there the baby gradually builds up its immunities and after several months is able to venture out into the world.

Skin culture (1950)

In **1950 Professor Howard Green** of the Massachusetts Institute of Technology (MIT) discovered that the fibroblasts of human skin multiplied extremely well when a sort of 'fertiliser' made from cancerous 3T3 cells was added. The cells were irradiated to prevent them from reproducing while at the same time allowing them to produce the required nutrient, with the result that cell culture was achieved.

As a result of this discovery, the research team led by Howard Green developed a technique which enabled 60cm^2 *9.3sq in* of skin to be obtained in 20 days from 1mm^2 of skin taken from a newborn baby.

Synthetic skin (1986)

In **1986** two American scientists, **Professor John Burke**, a surgeon at the Massachusetts General Hospital, and **Professor Ioanis Yannas**, of the Polymer Laboratory at the MIT, saved several hopeless cases by performing synthetic skin grafts. Their work was based on the patent held by two Americans, Howard Green and Eugene Bell, who created a second artificial layer of skin from beef collagen, which is well received by the human body, and from silicone plastic. This 'skin' is then sterilised and frozen in alcohol. The technique enables epidermis to be recreated.

Appendectomy (1735)

The English military surgeon **Claudius Amyan** performed the first successful appendectomy in 1735.

On 27 April 1887 in Philadelphia George Thomas Morton (the son of William Morton, one of the pioneers of anaesthesia) operated on a young man who was suffering from acute appendicitis thereby saving his life.

Sutures (1820)

The French surgeon **Pierre-François Percy** (1754–1825) invented wire sutures in 1820. Catgut sutures appeared in 1920. It is interesting that the famous Hispano–Moorish surgeon Abulcasis was already using catgut in the 10th century as he liked its suppleness, its strength and the fact that it is resorbent.

Terylene sutures were invented in 1950, and in 1964 the American company 3M invented the Steristrip, a type of dressing which knits the wound together but avoids stitch marks.

Asepsis (1844)

Asepsis, or medical and surgical hygiene, was invented by a Hungarian physicist, **Ignaz Phillip Semmelweis**, in 1844. Asepsis by boiling and by dry heat autoclave was first achieved by the French surgeons Octave Terrillon and Louis-Félix Terrier in 1883. In 1889 the American surgeon William Stewart Halsted introduced the use of rubber gloves.

Dr Solomon Snyder and his team in Baltimore, USA, managed to grow and reproduce in vitro human neurones taken from a child of two. This has important implications for medicine.

Antisepsis (1867)

The English surgeon **Joseph Lister** (1827–1912) concentrated his efforts on antiseptics. Prior to all operations, he sprayed carbolic acid in the room, and disinfected the instruments and the area of the patient's skin where the incision was to be made. He published the results of his work in *The Lancet* in 1867.

One of the first antiseptics was honey, which the Egyptians used on wounds.

Neurosurgery (1918)

Modern neurosurgery was first introduced in the United States in 1918 by **Harvey Williams Cushing**. It was introduced in France in 1936 by Thierry de Martel and Clovis Vincent who invented the technique of carrying out brain surgery while the patient remained seated. In the same year, the Portuguese physician Antonio de Egas Moniz invented arteriography.

Some important dates

In 1937 Fiambert first performed a lobotomy, which has now been virtually abandoned.

In 1950 Talairach of France invented the stereotaxy. One of the first applications of this process was in surgery for Parkinson's disease, performed by the French surgeon Fenelon.

In 1960 another French surgeon, Guiot, operated on a tumour of the pituitary gland through the nose.

In 1962 a radiologist, Djindjian, and the neurosurgeon Hudart performed the first arteriography of the spinal chord, which enabled operations to be carried out on angiomas of the marrow.

Since 1970 Serbedinko of the USSR has been avoiding operations by inserting a probe into the artery. At the end of a probe is a tiny balloon which the surgeon releases at the point chosen to block or embolise the artery.

Cerebral radiotherapy (1982)

The multi-beam convergent irradiation unit is a unique piece of equipment. It makes it possible to treat brain lesions which were hitherto inaccessible. The first version was invented in 1982 by the Argentinian neurosurgeon **Oswald Betti**.

Cryosurgery (c.1960)

Cryosurgery is a method by which pathological tissue is destroyed by the use of extreme cold, i.e. below −40°C *−40°F*. It has the advantages of being painless and causing no risk of haemorrhage. In about 1960 the American neurosurgeon **Irving S. Cooper** (sponsored by Union Carbide), developed a cryosound using liquid nitrogen which reached a temperature of −180°C *−292°F*. Other instruments were used for cataract surgery and the treatment of tumours of the larynx, and haemorrhoids. In 1964 M. J. Gonder and W. A. Soanes used cryosurgery to treat adenomas of the prostate gland. In 1975 a German surgeon, A. J. Keller, invented cryocautery.

Cryogenic probes (1986)

In 1986 **Patrick Lepivert**, a French doctor from Nice, in collaboration with the Centre for Nuclear Research in Grenoble, developed tiny cryogenic probes which could be used in the treatment of varicose veins. These probes, which are adapted to the size of the veins, make it possible to operate without using an anaesthetic, and to avoid postoperative complications and scars. The development of these micro-probes should enable them to be used in the same way as laser beams, and at a much lower cost, to destroy inoperable tumours in the colon and digestive tract.

Shock waves against kidney stones (1982)

In 1982 three German professors in Munich, **Christian Chaussy**, **Egbert Schmied** and **Walter Brendel**, working with the Dornier company (manufacturers of fighter planes), developed a device that can disintegrate kidney stones by shock waves. The stones are broken down into tiny grains of about 1.5mm *0.0585in* which can then be removed during urination.

Treatment of gall stones by laser (1986)

In 1986 a German doctor, **Ludwig Demling** from the University Hospital of Nuremberg in West Germany, obtained extremely interesting results by the internal use of a laser. An endoscope is inserted into the gall-bladder where it is directed at the stone or stones and the surgeon fires a shot with the laser which destroys them without damaging the surrounding tissue.

Pencil-laser (1987)

This is a surgical laser which, according to its inventors, **Professor Jean Lemaire** and his research team at the French University of Science and Technology in Lille, is as easy to use as a pencil. This CO₂ type laser, known as the Optro 20, was presented in 1987 as the first in Europe to combine the most recent developments in the fields of optics and electronics.

Transparent X-ray table (1989)

Orthopaedic surgery, which is used for example when treating road accident victims, often uses X-ray treatment before, during and after operations. An invention has been available since 1989 which eliminates the visual obstacle of the operating table. It is a table made of composite materials that are completely transparent to X-rays. Developed jointly by two French surgeons **Gindrey** and **Letourneur**, the table, known as the T 3000 and manufactured by Tasserit, has two positive advantages. By completely eliminating the image of the metal parts of the table, the intensity of the rays can be reduced by 50 percent. Also, the operation time is shorter so the patient does not require such a strong anaesthetic.

Gynaecology

Contraception

The vaginal tampon was already being used in Egypt in the time of the Pharaohs. Other Mediterranean peoples such as the Syrians used small sponges soaked in liquids such as spiced vinegar water which were supposed to have spermicidal properties. In 1984 there was a return to these origins when a sponge impregnated with spermicide came on to the market.

Modern spermicides, brought out in the 1970s in pessary or cream form, are 97 percent reliable. One of the most reliable of these products is Nonoxynol-9 which is also noted for its protection against AIDS.

Sheath (16th century)

The invention of the sheath is attributed to the Italian **Gabriele Fallopia** (1523–62), Professor of Anatomy at the University of Padua from 1551 to 1562. The sheath was made of cloth and was intended primarily as a means of combating venereal disease; its contraceptive value was secondary. Only when penicillin reduced the fear of syphilis this century

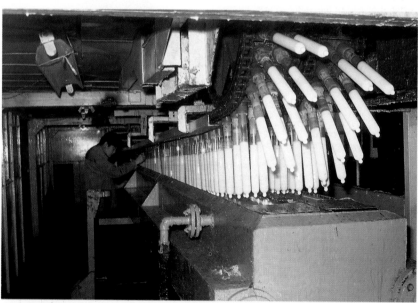

A condom factory in China. Despite massive efforts by the government to control the population growth in China, it is still rising by about a million every month.

did the condom become used primarily for contraceptive purposes. Condom, a physician residing at the court of Charles II, was the inventor of the modern contraceptive which was named after him. Nowadays the contraceptive is widely available and its importance as a protection against infection, and particularly against the spread of AIDS, has grown. The rubber sheath was first used in the 1870s.

Diaphragm (1881)

In 1881 in Holland the first birth control clinic was opened under the direction of Doctors Rutgers and Aletta Jacobs. They advised women to use the diaphragm developed by the German **Mensiga**.

Coil (1928)

The first effective intra-uterine device was the silver ring designed by the German **Ernst Grafenberg** in 1928. Measuring 1.5mm *0.0585in* in diameter, it was made of silver thread rolled into a spiral.

The pill (1954)

The pill was invented in 1954 by the American **Gregory Pincus** of the Worcester Foundation for Experimental Biology, Massachusetts, and **John Rock**. These doctors worked for five years to develop a definitive contraceptive that would be 'without danger, sure, simple, practical, suitable for all women, and ethically acceptable for the couple'. The initial clinical tests were performed in 1954, and the first large-scale experimentation took place in 1956 in San Juan, Puerto Rico with 1308 female volunteers.

The first pill to be marketed was Enovid 10 in 1960, manufactured by G. D. Searle Inc. of Illinois, USA. It became available in the UK in January 1961.

Feeding bottle (antiquity)

Feeding bottles have been used since antiquity. At first they were in the form of jugs with two openings, one to fill the container, and the other, in the shape of a beak, to feed the baby.

Until the end of the 18th century, the teat was made from a small piece of rolled linen, one end of which soaked in the container while the other was sucked by the child. Teats were also made of sponge, softened leather or dried cow udders.

When rubber was discovered in the second half of the 19th century, teats made from this new, hygienic material became popular.

Caesarean section (7th century BC)

The Caesarean is an operation that was first mentioned in a law set out by **Numa Pompilius** (715–672 BC), the legendary second king of Rome. According to his law, no woman who had died during her pregnancy could be buried until her infant had been removed via an abdominal incision. The name of the first of the Roman emperors, Caesar, is derived from the Latin word for cut *caedere*, because one of his forebears had given birth by Caesarean section.

The first modern Caesarean seems to have been performed in 1610 by the German surgeon Trautmann.

Obstetric forceps (17th century)

Obstetric forceps were invented in the 17th century by the English surgeon **Peter Chamberlen**. Until then, a kind of hook, known as a head-hook, had been used. The French surgeon and obstetrician André Levret improved the technique of the instrument, particularly the curve of the blades, in the 18th century. In 1838 there were 144 different types of forceps. After further improvements, the forceps of the French obstetrician Stéphane Tarnier were generally adopted.

Incubators (1880)

The incubator was invented by **Budin** of France in 1880. These first wooden incubators were heated by saucepans of hot water placed beneath them. In 1894 **Lion**, a French doctor from Nice, invented the first incubator for premature babies.

Sanitary towels (1921)

The American company **Kimberley-Clark** of Wisconsin marketed the first commercial sanitary towels under the name of Kotex in 1921.

Ernest Mahler, a German chemist working in the United States, had invented a cotton substitute made from wood pulp to compensate for the lack of dressings in hospitals. Nurses acquired the habit of using these cellulose-padded dressings as hygienic menstrual towels.

When the Kimberley-Clark company, which was already manufacturing cotton-wool bandages, learnt of this, they began marketing them.

Tampons (1937)

In the 1930s the American **Earl Hass** thought of a way to modify the surgical tampon. He wanted to eliminate the inconvenience and the embarrassment caused by use of the sanitary towel. In 1937 he applied for a patent and founded the Tampax Company. After some improvements, the use of the tampon spread throughout the world after the Second World War.

Anti-pregnancy vaccination (1990s)

The World Health Organisation (WHO) in Geneva is currently sponsoring the first tests on a contraceptive vaccine for which 30 women have volunteered. The testing began in February 1986, at the Flinders Medical Centre in Adelaide, Australia. The vaccine has been developed over the past ten years by Ohio State University, USA, in collaboration with WHO and various pharmaceutical laboratories, and could be on the market by the middle of the 1990s.

The babies of science

Test-tube babies (1978)

The first test-tube baby was 13 years old on 25 July 1991: Louise Brown was born on 25 July 1978 at Oldham Hospital. Louise's scientific 'fathers' were **Doctors Patrick Steptoe** and **Robert Edwards**. They were the first to perform this scientific exploit. An ovum taken from the mother was fertilised in a test tube by spermatozoa from the father and the resulting embryo was re-implanted in the mother's womb. Today, thousands of test-tube babies have been born throughout the world.

Frozen embryos (1984)

On 11 April 1984 Zoe, the first 'frozen' baby, was born in Melbourne, Australia. This was made possible by **Doctors Linda Mohr** and

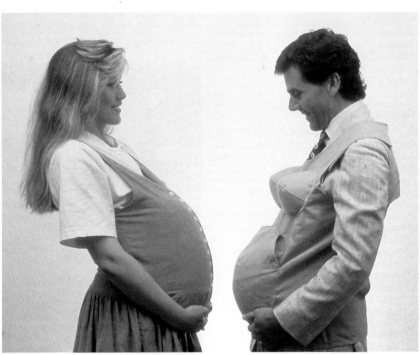

American mother Linda Ware and psychotherapist Dan Neuhart developed this false stomach to help men to understand the discomfort suffered by a pregnant woman.

Alan Frounson, biologists at the Queen Victoria Hospital. Zoe was born from an embryo formed in a test tube and preserved for two months in liquid nitrogen at a temperature of −196°C −321°F.

In April 1987 it was announced that the first English test-tube twins would be born . . . 18 months apart. Amy and Elisabeth were conceived on the same day, but one embryo was re-implanted straight away and the other 18 months later.

A mother without ovaries (1988)

In **December 1988** Europe witnessed a scientific miracle. A 37-year-old woman without ovaries gave birth to a daughter. A little over a year before, the woman had had to have her ovaries removed, and she and her husband decided on a test-tube fertilisation. The two resulting embryos were re-implanted in the mother's womb after the removal of her ovaries. One of them embedded itself and, with the help of hormone treatment, the pregnancy was successful.

Therapeutics

Acupuncture (2000 BC)

The **Chinese** have been practising acupuncture, one of the branches of their traditional medicine, since about **2000 BC**. The theory is that the cause of a disease can be explained by a disruption in the flow of energy, which can be remedied by action taken on one or more of the points situated along the meridians: pathways along which energy is transmitted around the body by oscillation and

In vitro fertilisation brings theological dilemmas for Muslims over the interpretation of the Koran. These are the first Saudi test-tube babies.

Moxibustion – the burning of a cone of compacted dried herbs on a particular acupuncture point to stimulate energy. This technique can be used in conjunction with acupuncture to treat disease. According to the Chinese, illness is associated with an imbalance of vital energy (ch'i) flowing through the body in 12 pathways or meridians each corresponding to one of the vital organs.

Great diseases, great doctors: an unending struggle

Since the beginning of time, people have been terrified of contagious diseases. Today, it is AIDS, previously it was the plague, cholera, syphilis, smallpox and tuberculosis. Tropical countries still suffer an alarming number of scourges, such as bilharzia, sleeping sickness, malaria and leishmaniasis, for which no complete cure has yet been found and which are often fatal. No sooner does a cure emerge than another strain of the disease appears which is even more virulent and obstinate. The history of man is inseparable from the history of medicine: it is the history of a relentless struggle.

Plague

The word 'plague' was the name given to any epidemic disease which claimed large numbers of victims. The first recognised plague epidemic occurred in AD 542.

25 million dead

The second pandemic occurred between 1346 and 1353. It started in India, spreading to the Middle East and then Italy. In five years it killed 25 million people throughout Europe: a quarter of the population. In Britain the population fell from about 3 700 000 in 1350 to 2 000 000 in 1377. The disease gradually died out, although it persisted within Europe, reappearing in certain centres: Venice in 1487, Milan at the beginning of the 16th century where it claimed the lives of 190 000 of the 250 000 inhabitants, London in 1665, Marseilles in 1720.

Doctors were powerless to stop it, although they continued to carry out their duty at the risk of their own lives.

Hong Kong, 1894

During the third pandemic in 1894, the plague bacillus of the rat, as well as the human bacillus, was identified in Hong Kong by the Swiss-born French bacteriologist Alexandre Yersin, who had been sent by the Institut Pasteur to study, *in situ*, the disease which had just broken out in China. In 1898 P. L. Simond identified the role played by the flea in the transmission of the disease. In 1897 Waldemar Haffkinse developed the first anti-plague vaccine.

50 years of pandemic

During the third pandemic which lasted for 50 years and killed 12 million people in India between 1898 and 1948, there were only 91 cases recorded in Europe. It was followed by minor epidemics in Algeria in 1930 and 1944. Today, the plague is still endemic in several regions throughout the world. The early use of antibiotics as soon as the disease is diagnosed has affected the outcome of the disease which is no longer necessarily fatal. Despite this, 134 died of the plague in 1988.

Leprosy

Leprosy is a legendary disease. It is one of the oldest diseases in the world. The name comes from the Greek *lepsi* meaning scales, and *lepein* meaning to scrape or chafe.

The earliest descriptions of the disease were imprecise and passed on by word of mouth. It appears to have existed endemically in India and along the banks of the Nile well before the birth of Christ. In Egypt, the examination of the skeleton of a Coptic mummy of the 5th century AD constitutes the earliest osteological proof of the existence of leprosy. It appeared much later in Europe. It is thought that it reached Greece from the East, following the campaigns of Darius, King of Persia. Subsequently, the legions of Alexander the Great and Julius Caesar helped to spread the disease.

Lazar houses

In the parable, Lazarus, covered in sores, lay at the gate of the rich man. This is the origin of the term lazar house. With the return of the Crusaders, there was a new outbreak of leprosy. During the 13th century there were as many as 20 000 lazar houses in Europe. However, the first to be recorded was at Saint-Claude in the Jura Mountains around AD 460.

The disease was spread northwards by the barbarian invasions to places such as Iceland and Norway. It was in fact a Norwegian doctor, Armauer Gerhard Hansen, who discovered the leprosy bacillus in 1873, while working among lepers in his country. This was a major step forward.

Today

Leprosy is still rife in regions such as Central and Southern America, the West Indies, Africa and Asia. It persists in Europe in the Balkans and Portugal. In all, at least 10 million people have the disease worldwide, of whom only 4 million can be treated. However, research by the New Zealander Professor Jim Watson could lead to a vaccine within ten years.

Cholera

Cholera, which has always been endemic in India, particularly in Bengal, for a long time spread no further than South East Asia. Suddenly, with the development of navigation and trade which took place during the 19th century, it spread throughout the world in a matter of 20 or so years. 1817 saw the first of six pandemics which affected the whole of the Eastern World. It reached Europe in 1823 and by 1837 had claimed more than a million victims.

The comma bacillus

During the fourth pandemic in 1883, which was particularly virulent in the Mediterranean and Egypt, the German doctor Robert Koch, also famous for his work on tuberculosis, went to Alexandria to study the disease. He was responsible for discovering the cholera vibrio or comma bacillus.

Today

The disease is still active in India and South East Asia, although there is a very effective vaccine which is compulsory for trav-

A plague doctor in protective clothing in 1656. The beak purified the air, while the wand enabled the doctor to avoid touching the patient.

ellers visiting tropical countries. However, there is no guarantee that there will not be a new outbreak of the disease in countries with a more temperate climate.

Syphilis

The exact origin of the disease is not known, and there are many theories as to how it first appeared. An engraving by Albert Dürer, dated 1484, suggests that syphilis was in existence at the time. Syphilis is also supposed to have been identified on skeletons from central Russia dating back to 2000 BC.

The New World and war

There was an epidemic of syphilis throughout Europe after the sailors with Christopher Columbus returned from the New World in 1493. Wars, with their accompanying migrations of men (and prostitutes), were dangerous propagators of this disease.

The unhappy shepherd

In 1530, when the disease broke out again in Venice, a city with 11 654 known prostitutes, the Italian doctor, Frascator, named the disease syphilis after the unhappy hero of his poem *Syphilis sive Morbus Gallicus* (Syphilis, or the Disease of France). The shepherd, Syphilis, has offended Apollo who afflicts him with a terrible disease which has the most awful symptoms. The skin falls away from his limbs, leaving his bones exposed, his teeth fall out and his breath becomes fetid. But he is saved by the miracle remedy, lignum vitae, which was recommended at the time. Treatments using lignum vitae and

This 16th century illustration shows Franciscan monks treating lepers.

mercury were in fact carried out until 1907! It is difficult to say how many victims were claimed by syphilis during the course of the centuries. But it is possible that, in the absence of any really effective cure, tens of millions of people died from the disease.

A major step forward

From the 19th century onwards, iodine and iodide were prescribed. After 1910, an arsenic-based preparation was used which had been developed by the German doctor Paul Ehrlich (1854–1915). This changed the outcome of the illness.

In 1905 a major step had been made with the discovery of the agent responsible for the disease, *treponema pallidum*, by the German microbiologist Fritz R. Schaudinn (1871–1906), and the

syphilis specialist Erich Hoffman.

The real cure for syphilis only came with the discovery of penicillin. This does not mean, however, that the disease has disappeared. Far from it! There are about 65 million people throughout the world who currently have syphilis; but at least it can now be treated effectively, particularly if it is diagnosed in its early stages.

Malaria

Malaria has been in existence since ancient times, and it is likely that Alexander the Great suffered from it during his campaign in Mesopotamia during the 6th century BC.

The disease is endemic in all hot regions throughout the world, and particularly in swampy areas.

A voluntary scientist

The pathogenic agent *Plasmodium* was discovered by the French doctor Alphonse Laveran in 1881. In 1907 this remarkable man, who for 25 years carried out voluntary research at the Institut Pasteur, was awarded the Nobel Prize, half of which was devoted to his research in tropical pathology.

Resistant to quinine

After the discovery of quinine in 1820 by the French chemists Joseph Pelletier and Joseph Bienaimé Caventou, it became possible to treat patients suffering from the disease and to protect those who were not affected.

Today the anopheles mosquito has become resistant to insecticides, and *Plasmodium* has become immune to quinine.

A possible vaccine

Malaria is the most widespread and the most serious of the transmitted diseases. It threatens half the world's population and is one of the main fatal illnesses. About 100 million people contract the disease each year, of which some 2 million die. In the UK there were 2000 cases of imported malaria in 1984 and three deaths. The Institut Pasteur and several other laboratories worldwide are trying to develop a vaccine, a task which is made more difficult by the many transformations undergone by the pathogenic agent during the contamination process. However, it appears that the Colombian doctor Manuel Elkin Patarroyo is about to make a major breakthrough.

During the great cholera epidemic of 1832, smoking was thought to be a good preventive measure.

vibration. This action usually consists of the insertion of needles, but also of the application of heat (moxas) or massage. Today, even electric currents and laser beams are used.

Antibiotics (1889)

In the course of his work, Louis Pasteur noted the vital competition that makes some bacteria fight against each other. This fact was repeatedly confirmed and was attributed to the action of an *antibiote* by the French scientist **Vuillemin** in **1889**. Penicillin was the first antibiotic discovered, and it remains the most important because of its curative effects and its almost complete absence of toxicity.

Penicillin (1928)

It was by chance that the Scottish bacteriologist **Alexander Fleming** (1881–1955), working at St Mary's Hospital in London, discovered penicillin. While working on staphylococci in **1928**, he discovered that they were destroyed by the mould which had contaminated them.

A team of researchers at Sir William Dunn School of Pathology at Oxford, Howard Florey, Ernst Chain and N. G. Heatley, continued Fleming's work and concentrated extracts of *Penicillium notatum* in order to obtain purified penicillin, which is more active. Mass production of penicillin began in 1943.

It is interesting to note that during the 9th and 10th centuries, Arab doctors of the Baghdad School were already using the curative properties of a mould that appeared in farinaceous foods. Vegetable dust blown into a patient's nose and mouth was used as a cure for ailments such as catarrh.

Anti-cholesterol machine (1986)

This process was invented in **1986** by a German biochemist, **Wilhelm Stoffel**. It is based on haemodialysis, a system of filtering the blood, and is used for people whose kidneys do not function. It enables the particles of so-called bad cholesterol (Low Density Lipoprotein, LDL) to be eliminated, while the good cholesterol (High Density Lipoprotein, HDL) is completely restored to the patient after the filtering process. Such a technique can be applied to patients who suffer from inherited diseases resulting in an excess of cholesterol since birth and, regardless of diet, will give them a quality of life which would have been impossible until now.

Statins (1990s)

One of the major causes of heart disease is a high level of cholesterol in the blood. Previously it has been necessary to go on a low-fat diet to reduce the cholesterol level. But, for those who like dairy and animal products, this can be a very difficult thing to do. Now, thanks to a new type of drug called statins, it should soon be possible to eat what one wants without suffering for doing so, and without relying on a machine.

Doctor Rory Collins of Oxford University is directing a study with 30 000 volunteers to test the effectiveness of the product, which is thought to reduce cholesterol levels by almost a half. If the results are good, statins could be on the market soon. There are many, however, who believe that it is more important to rely on diet for a solution.

THE STRUGGLE AGAINST ALZHEIMER'S DISEASE

Alzheimer's disease is thought to be one of the biggest killers in the Western world, after such well-known causes as heart disease, cancer and strokes. In the UK perhaps as many as 20 percent of the over 80s suffer from this illness which progressively acts upon people's memories and personalities by destroying the acetylcholine in the brain, one of the important transmitters of the memory.

The new drug, Cognex or THA, acts to maintain the efficiency of the acetylcholine and so prevent any further deterioration in the brain's capacity to complete simple tasks. The drug has been tested since 1988 and has brought good results, and so the English company Parke-Davis are hoping to bring it onto the market soon. They believe that as many as 500 000 could benefit from taking the drug.

Penicillin as seen through polarisation. The first paper on the subject was published in August 1940 and opened the way to one of the great medical developments of the century.

Antihistamine (1937)

An antihistamine is a drug that combats the effects of histamine, an amine released by the body during allergic reactions, and is used especially to fight allergies, a type of condition that was discovered in 1906 by the Austrian C. von Picquet. The first active antihistamine was discovered in **1937** by **Bouet** and **Staub**. The first synthesised antihistamine was created by the Frenchman Halpern in 1942.

Antipyretic agent (5th–4th century BC)

The first antipyretic agent (a remedy that lowers the temperature and relieves fever) was discovered by **Hippocrates** and was based on camomile.

Anti-sugar medication (1985)

The **Servier Laboratories** have developed a medication which enables weight to be lost naturally by reducing the need for sugar. This anti-sugar medication has already been successfully tested in the United States by Professor Wurtman of the Massachusetts Institute of Technology (MIT), and has been available, subject to medical advice, since **1985**.

A MARKER GENE

In January 1990 the first experiment in transferring human genes was carried out in the United States by Professor Steven Rosenberg and his team. Professor Rosenberg has already gained international renown for his discoveries relating to interleukins. Gene transfer, however, is not an actual therapy, replacing a damaged gene by inserting a normal gene in its place, but is an experiment in genetic marking combining immunotherapy and genetic therapy.

Rosenberg wanted to follow the itinerary through the organism of a very special type of lymphocyte (TIL), whose effects against tumours are encouraging. To trace them, he coupled them with a marker gene. The results of this experiment should provide information on the mechanisms at work, on the effectiveness and the dangers, and will thus probably shed new light on genetic therapy itself. Some countries have banned all genetic manipulation in humans because of the technical and ethical risks.

Aspirin (1853)

Aspirin or acetylsalicylic acid was synthesised by the Frenchman **Charles Frederick von Gerhardt** at the University of Montpellier in 1853, but he was not particularly interested in its practical use.

In 1893 Felix Hoffman, a young German chemist working at Bayer in Dusseldorf, rediscovered aspirin to treat his rheumatic father. Bayer began to market the drug in 1899 under the name Aspirin, formed from acetyl + *spir*aeic + *in* which was a popular ending for the names of medicines at the time. It became available in the UK in October 1905. In the Treaty of Versailles in 1919 Germany surrendered the brand name to the Allies as part of her war reparations.

Recent studies have shown what had been suspected for a long time: that taken in moderation, aspirin is good for the heart.

The worldwide consumption of aspirins: 100 billion tablets per year. Its main rival, Paracetamol, first appeared in 1878.

Chewing gum for smokers (1986)

Nicoret was conceived by the Swedish company **Pharmacia Les Therapeutics AB** as an aid to fight the desire for tobacco. It is a product based on nicotine which is released as the gum is chewed and absorbed directly via the mucus in the mouth.

Chemotherapy (1964)

Chemotherapy is the treatment of illnesses, particularly cancer, by chemical substances or drugs. In **1964** an American professor, **G. Rosen**, used chemotherapy for the first time, and before trying any other form of treatment, on two types of cancer. His work was based on experiments carried out on rats by Professor Brooke.

The German surgeon working in Boston, Emil Frey, referred to the new technique as initial or neo-adjuvant chemotherapy.

Chiropractic (1897)

In **1897** a hypnotist, **Daniel David Palmer**, having discovered that he could cure patients by putting pressure on their backs and manipulating their spines, founded the first school of chiropractic, in Iowa.

The profession has been recognised since 1977 in the USA, where there are now 23 000 trained chiropractors. In the UK there are 450 practitioners registered with the British Chiropractic Association, all of whom have undergone a four-year training course before qualifying.

Electrotherapy (1786)

In **1786** in Bologna, the anatomist **Luigi Galvani** established that, on contact with two different metals, the muscles of a frog twitched convulsively. He realised that this contraction was due to an electric current passing through the frog. After the successful treatment in **1795** by a Frenchman, **J. Hallé**, of a patient with facial paralysis, the laws of nerve stimulation were the subject of a great deal of research, notably by Magendie, Faraday and Du Bois-Reymond. This work led to the development of electrodiagnostics and electrotherapy.

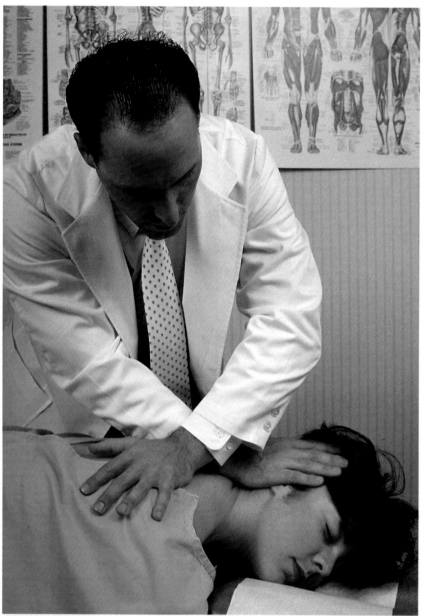

Chiropractic is based on the theory that nearly all disorders can be traced to an incorrect alignment of bones. Here, the chiropractor attempts a remedy by removing nerve interference through manual adjustment of the spinal column; by releasing the pressure in the spine the effect is referred on to the organ to which the nerve is connected.

From 1960 electrostimulation found a major application with the perfecting of the cardiac pacemaker.

Homeopathy (1796)

The German **C. S. Hahnemann** (1755–1843) created homeopathy in **1796**. In 1790 he had been struck by descriptions of the properties of the cinchona, a South American tree with medicinal bark, and by the incoherence of the explanations given for them, and decided to test its action on himself. He took large doses of cinchona over several days and indeed suffered the symptoms of an intermittent febrile state, identical to the fevers that cinchona cured.

Hahnemann then extended his experiments to deadly nightshade, Digitalis, and mercury and verified the law of similitude: any substance capable of inducing certain symptoms in a healthy person is also able to make the analogous symptoms disappear in a sick person.

Hahnemann based his theory on extensive experimentation with healthy subjects, and this led him to pronounce the second fundamental principle of homeopathy: the remedy acts not by virtue of its quantity, but in proportion to its dilution.

Many people have turned to homeopathy when conventional medicine has failed them. For example, Queen Elizabeth II takes very small quantities of arsenic to relieve her chronic sinusitis.

Immunotherapy

Immunotherapy is a recent science. It is a method of treatment based on the reactions of the natural defences of the organism against illness.

The following dates are important in the fight against AIDS.

1983: The team of Professor Luc Montagnier of the Institut Pasteur in Paris isolated LAV. In the same year, a research team from the National Cancer Institute, led by Robert Gallo, discovered the retrovirus HTLV 3 which is identical to LAV.

1986: A second AIDS virus was isolated by the team of Professor Montagnier in collaboration with Portuguese doctors. This virus, HIV 2, is particularly virulent in Africa.

At the same time, the Franco–American team of Doctor Max Essex of the Dana Farber Institute of Boston and Doctor Francis Barin of Tours described another virus, HTLV 4. But it seems likely that HIV 2 and HTLV 4 are one and the same virus.

1987: The Institut Pasteur published the sequel to the virus HIV 2 and brought out a second diagnostic test, Elavia. The first test, ELISA, was developed by the same team in 1985.

1988: Research was carried out in the United States by scientists of the Frederick Center, Maryland and a team from the Center for Disease Control in Atlanta on a second generation of (rapid) detection tests which will make it possible to detect the virus as soon as it enters the organism.

1989: No decisive progress was made in this year.

1990: The Sixth Conference on AIDS, which took place in San Francisco from 20 to 24 June produced no important revelations – just a few leads, a few hopes, including the notion of cofactors acting as stimulators of the virus, put forward by Professor Montagnier. Research to find a vaccine continues, with 30 trials under way. Meanwhile the drug AZT, developed by Doctor S. Broder of Bethseda, Maryland, which has been so disparaged, is still the only anti-viral drug able to check the progress of the disease, despite its toxicity. However, by the end of the year, medical opinion was almost completely united against the drug.

Interferon (1957)

Interferon was first discovered in **1957** by a British virologist, **Alick Isaacs** and **J. Lindenmann** of Switzerland. It is one of the substances (a protein) produced by an organism to combat viruses. In 1969 these substances, active in the immune system which is connected to the lymphatic system, were called lymphokines. Earlier, in 1966, the Americans J. David and V. Blum had identified in a culture of T-lymphocytes (a type of white corpuscle), a factor which inhibited the migration of macrophages (another type of white corpuscle). This was the first in a series of discoveries which were extremely promising for the future of therapeutics.

Interferon was subsequently subdivided into categories and was not really developed further until it became possible to produce it by genetic engineering towards the end of the 1970s. Interferon 2A was marketed in 1987, after being tested for two years on tricholeucocyte leukaemia and Kaposi's sarcoma.

Interleukins (1979)

Other very well known substances which act as a defence are the interleukins, so called in 1979 because they act between lymphocytes (or lympholeukocytes), either causing the production of more lymphocytes or provoking the latter to produce other substances.

Interleukins 2 and 3 (1985 and 1986)

The most recently discovered of the interleukins, which are also subdivided into categories, is interleukin 3. It was discovered in **1986** by **Doctors Steven Clark** and **Yu Chang Yang** of the Genetic Institute in Cambridge, USA. The anti-cancer effect of interleukin 2 was demonstrated in **1985** by the American **Doctor Steven Rosenberg**. Although they provide an excellent defence against viruses, interleukins can have a toxic effect if they are administered in large quantities. For example, interleukin 2 has the side effect of giving people 'flu-like fever, but this can be easily controlled and is also a much less serious problem than the side effects of chemotherapy. The *British Medical Journal* concluded in 1990 that people should not be put off the drug.

TNF (1975)

TNF, or Tumor Necrosis Factor, was discovered in **1975** by **Carswell** and his colleagues at the Sloan Kettering Memorial Institute in New York. It is a protein produced by certain white corpuscles which selects and attacks tumorous cells. The production, study and classification of all these proteins has led to a review of knowledge in the field of immunology. These substances have potentially far-reaching effects and implications, not only in the fields of cancer research and virology, but also in the areas of parasitic, inflammatory, infectious and allergic diseases, and in vaccinations and transplants.

Insulin (1921)

Discovered by the Romanian **Paulesco** in **1921**, insulin was isolated a few months later by the 1923 Nobel Prize-winners, the Canadian physiologists John James Macleod and Sir Frederick Grant Banting, of the University of Toronto, and the American physiologist Charles Herbert Best.

Synthetic insulin was obtained in 1964 by Panatotis and Kastoyannis of the University of Pittsburgh, USA.

In 1978 the Eli Lilly Laboratories successfully synthesised the human insulin gene, which was a major step in the production of insulin by genetic engineering.

In 1982 the first human insulin obtained by genetic engineering appeared on the market.

Novolet (1990)

This is the name of the new insulin syringe which is the smallest and lightest in the world. Developed by the Danish medical group **Novo Nordisk**, it is disposable and made from biodegradable plastic. It holds enough insulin to meet a diabetic's needs for three to seven days. The patient injects the necessary dose simply by pressure. When the syringe is empty, it is discarded.

The British have developed an insulin pen which gives a set dose and is easy to use. It won a design award.

Intravenous injection (16th century)

Elshots was the first to inject medicinal products into human veins in the middle of the **16th century**. However, we know that 'intravenous infusions' had already been tested on animals.

In 1655 Schmidt treated syphilis by intravenous injection.

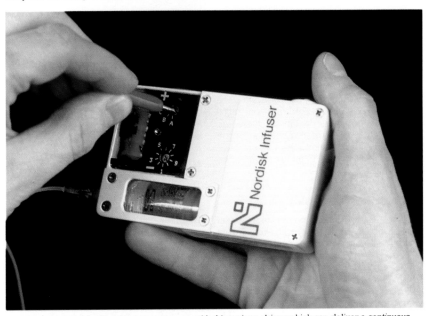

Nordisk, makers of the Novolet, have come up with this syringe-driver which can deliver a continuous dosage of insulin subcutaneously to diabetics. The device is carried in a holster belted around the waist. It is essentially a battery-powered syringe which slowly delivers a small dose of insulin over a 24-hour period, thus maintaining stable levels of blood/insulin.

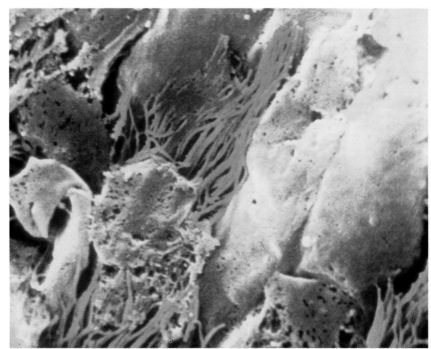

Mucoviscidosis is characterised by the development of mucus in the lungs, as seen here. The gene of this fatal disease was discovered in 1989.

A CURE FOR MIGRAINE?

A new drug from Glaxo's laboratories, Sumatriptan, currently being tested in several countries, promises to be a revolutionary treatment for migraine which will put a stop to eight out of ten attacks within minutes. It is currently waiting for approval before being put on the market. Migraine still remains a mysterious ailment despite the amount of research that has gone into it. Given that the attacks can last up to three days and be very painful, and that normal painkillers are ineffective against it, the new drug represents a huge breakthrough and brings hope to migraine sufferers. It should be available by the end of 1991 and can be taken either orally or subcutaneously.

A DISCOVERY OF FUNDAMENTAL IMPORTANCE

August 1989 saw the discovery of the gene which causes mucoviscidosis, a form of cystic fibrosis which affects the intestine, pancreas and liver as well as the lungs and is one of the most serious and most common hereditary diseases, by an American and Canadian team led by Doctor Lap Chee Tsui, of the Hospital for Sick Children, Toronto, and Doctor Francis Collins, of the University of Michigan. This defective gene was identified and located in a particular region (made up of a million bases) of the long arm of Chromosome 7. The discovery is the result of several years' research and was made possible by the use of new techniques in molecular biology, and the use of restriction enzymes which cut chromosomes in very specific positions and permit DNA to be divided into different sites depending on which enzyme is used. This localisation paves the way for further research: for example, into ante-natal diagnosis, and the development of drugs to correct anomalies in the metabolism of certain glands, such as the pancreas and bronchial mucous membrane, caused by this gene.

A similar process is under way for pre-natal diagnosis of many diseases. A huge and expensive project being carried out around the world aims to identify and map all the genes. These diagnostic tests, as with those for Down's syndrome mentioned earlier, are usually offered only to those parents where abortion is a viable proposition. Previously doctors could test for cystic fibrosis only when the baby was born by looking to see if it had a high sweat sodium concentration.

Osteopathy (1892)

Osteopathy entered the history of medicine in **1892**, when a Missouri doctor, **Andrew Taylor Still**, founded the American School of Osteopathy. Osteopathy consists of using manual manipulation of the osteomuscular system, especially the spine, for therapeutic purposes. Today there are around 19 000 osteopaths in the United States, while in the UK over 1500 are registered.

Painkillers

Bracelet for the treatment of neuralgia (18th century)

During the **18th century**, bracelets and necklaces for the treatment of neuralgia were extremely popular. An Austrian physician, **Franz Anton Mesmer** (1734–1815), who lived in Paris, made a considerable amount of money by selling 'magnets which would draw out the pain'. The doctrine of mesmerism, based on 'animal magnetism', was named after him.

Energy-pak (1983)

Invented by **Doctor Kokoshinegg** and **Professor Bischko** from Vienna in **1983**, the Energy-pak is a soft pack which is applied to the painful area. It relieves muscular or inflammatory pain through an alternating magnetic field.

Cryogel (1985)

This is a soft cushion containing a cooling agent which is activated when refrigerated and stays cool for up to an hour. Developed by **3M Santé**, it is recommended for ailments such as haematoma, bruises, insect bites and strained muscles.

Patch (1981)

The first of these transdermal medicaments was developed by the **Ciba-Geigy** laboratories in Switzerland in conjunction with the American **Alza Corp**. Known as Scopoderm TTS (Transdermal Therapeutic System), and launched in the USA in **1981**, it consists of a sticker containing a drug to combat seasickness and, as its name suggests, it is absorbed directly through the skin. Two other patches

Jetnet (1988)

The handling of cutting instruments and hypodermics used in even minor operations is a source of contamination which, particularly in the case of AIDS, represents a very real danger for medical staff. A new system has been developed by **3M** which ensures the complete isolation of used instruments and eliminates the need for direct contact. Presented in **1988**, Jetnet consists of a hermetically sealed plastic receptacle with a cover in which there is a clamp-operated mechanism. Scalpel blades, needles and other instruments can be separated, kept in sealed receptacles and then incinerated without ever being touched by the person using them. The cover can be sterilised and re-used. The level of prevention achieved in this way is considered to be complete.

Monoclonal antibodies (1975)

The first research on monoclonal antibodies was published in **May 1975** by two immunologists, **Georges Köhler** of Germany and **César Milstein** of Argentina, both working in Cambridge, England. In 1984 they were awarded the Nobel Prize for their research which consisted of combining, in a test tube, lymphocytes from mice, which produce antibodies, with myeloma (cancer) cells. In this way they obtained hybrid cells or hybridomas that were able to survive indefinitely, continuously producing a single antibody specific to the illness against which the animal had been immunised. In therapeutics, monoclonal antibodies are able to direct a chemical substance against a given target located by the antibody which acts as a vector.

followed, one to treat angina and the other to relieve symptoms of the menopause by hormone replacement.

A new application will soon be on the market, Nicotell TTS, again made by Ciba-Geigy, which uses transdermal technology to combat tobacco addiction, by supplying small quantities of nicotine to those trying to give up smoking. Among the advantages of the patch system are the absence of effects on the mucosa – cells lining the gut, and the regular and constant release of the drug into the system.

Psychoanalysis (1885)

Psychoanalysis is at once a method of understanding psychological and psychopathological phenomena, and of treating mental illness. It was developed around 1885 by the Austrian doctor Sigmund Freud (1856–1939) in Vienna. Freud did not invent the idea of the psychic unconscious, but he undertook a systematic exploration of it.

At first received with considerable scepticism by the medical community due to its novel propositions regarding sexuality, psychoanalysis has acquired a more and more important place in medicine and in psychology.

Quinine (1820)

In the 17th century the Indians of Peru entrusted the secret of the 'sacred bark', or cinchona bark, to the Jesuit missionaries who were both numerous and powerful in the country at the time. In 1820 the French pharmacists Joseph Pelletier and Joseph Bienaimé Caventou isolated the alkaloid contained in the cinchona bark: quinine. It was partially synthesised in 1931 by Rabe, but it was not until 1944 that total synthesis was achieved by Doerning.

Radiotherapy (1934)

Radiotherapy, the use of rays for therapeutic purposes, was developed after the discovery of X-rays in 1895, and of radioactivity. It became an area of specialisation independent of radiodiagnosis in 1934 when the French chemist Irène Joliot-Curie (1897–1956) and her husband Jean-Frédéric Joliot (1900–58) discovered artificial radioactivity. The first apparatus capable of transmitting radiation which could reach relatively deep-seated tumours was fed by a current of 250000 volts. This method was gradually abandoned and replaced in 1956 by the cobalt bomb.

Sleeping pill (1st century BC)

The first sleeping pill was invented during early Roman times by the medical writer Celsus, who gave patients suffering from insomnia a pill made from the mandrake and henbane. Today it is known that both these plants are narcotics.

Syringe (1657)

The principle of the syringe was established by the Italian Gattinara in the 15th century, but it was not until the 17th century that practical trials were carried out by the Englishman C. Wren and the Irish scientist Robert Boyle in 1657.

The Englishman Fergusson was the first to use glass, whose transparency allowed the injection to be monitored. However, it was the Frenchman Luer who produced the first all-glass syringe in 1869 and risks of infection fell as a result of its use.

Finally it is to the Irishman Rynd in 1845 and the Scot Wood in 1853 that we owe the method of subcutaneous injection.

Safety hypodermic (1987)

In 1987 the French doctor Jean-Louis Brunet of the Hôpital de la Croix-Rousse in Lyons, patented a safety device which can be attached to hypodermic needles or vacutainers for taking blood samples. It eliminates any risk of contamination from the blood in illnesses such as AIDS and hepatitis.

The system enables the used needle to be automatically re-capped as soon as it is withdrawn from the vein or muscle.

A similar type of invention in the same area is the disposable hypodermic which is impossible to re-use. It was invented by four Danish medical assistants working with drug-users in Aarhus on the east coast of Denmark.

The time pill (1986)

Benzodiazepines, or tranquillisers, were discovered by the American doctors Fred W. Turck and Susan Losee Olsen, and scientists of the Northwestern University of Evanston, Illinois. Better known as Valium and Librium etc, they are used in the treatment of insomnia and enable biological rhythms to be reset when they have been disturbed by a time change, for example. According to the time they are administered, the pills can either bring forward or put back our biological clock which, among other things, synchronises our sleeping/waking rhythm. One of the first people to have identified this biological cycle of approximately 25 hours, known as the circadian rhythm, was the spelaeologist Michel Siffre, during one of his underground expeditions in 1972.

Vitamins (1910)

Although the influence of vitamins on the body was only demonstrated in 1910, their effect had long been suspected, particularly in connection with deficiency diseases such as scurvy and beriberi. The English navigator Captain James Cook had been one of the first to mention them in a letter dated 7 March 1777 and addressed to the Royal Society of London.

In 1910 the Polish chemist Casimir Funk isolated vitamin B1 in unpolished rice and gave the name vitamine to this 'amine' which was so essential to life.

In 1936 the American chemist Robert R. Williams synthesised vitamin B1, and in 1959 a German physicist, Dieter Muting, invented an anti-mosquito pill based on vitamin B1. Vitamin C was isolated in 1928 by Saint Györgyi from the juice of the capsicum, and synthesised in 1933 by the Swiss chemist, Tadeus Reichstein.

Eyes and ears

Spectacles (1280)

Very early on in history, various attempts were made to remedy sight defects. However, the magnifying glass was not invented until the 11th century.

In 1280 the Florentine physicist Salvino degli Armati (1245–1317) developed two eye glasses which, at a certain degree of thickness and with a certain curve, magnified objects. He can therefore be said to have invented spectacles. He told his secret to his friend Alessandro della Spina, a Dominican friar from the Monastery of Saint Catherine of Pisa, who subsequently revealed it. At this point the spectacles had convex lenses for long-sighted people.

Concave lenses for short-sighted people appeared at the end of the 15th century.

The first spectacles consisted of two lenses made of beryl, a sort of crystal, set in a circle of wood or horn. They were later joined by a stud.

Bifocals (1780)

The American Benjamin Franklin invented bifocals for long-sighted people in 1780; in those days, bifocals were simply two lenses bound together by a metal frame. Bifocals made from one piece of glass were developed by Bentron and Emerson for the Carl Zeiss company in 1910. In 1908 J. L. Borsch had invented a process that allowed the two lenses to be soldered together.

Varilux Pilote (1985)

The Varilux Pilote spectacles were invented in 1983 by Essilor Svenska, sponsored by the Swedish airline SAS, and have been on the market since 1985. They make it possible to see at close range not only by lowering the eyes, but also by raising them. This makes them extremely suitable for the professional activities of those who, like airline pilots, need to be able to see at close range above as well as below eye-level.

Contact lenses

Origins

The first person to think of contact lenses was Leonardo da Vinci. In his Codex on the Eye,

In this pair of spectacles the grid improves the man's vision by framing his gaze – techniques have come a long way since the first spectacles in the Middle Ages.

Anti-rain glasses (1989)

Anyone who wears glasses and plays a sport knows only too well that, when it is raining or snowing, before long it becomes virtually impossible to see anything.

The unmarkable, anti-rain lenses invented by the Japanese researchers for **Nikon**, are a real innovation. Water slides over the surface of the glass without clinging or leaving marks. They have been on the market in England since **1989**, but are still expensive.

The cataract operation (1748)

The first description of a cataract operation by 'lowering the cornea' was given by the surgeon Anthyllus in the 2nd century AD.

In **1748** the French opthalmologist **Jacques Daviel** performed the first cataract operation by extraction of the crystalline lens. At the time, the reputation of Daviel was equalled only by that of the British surgeon William Cheselden who had restored the sight of a patient who had been blind since birth.

Operation by ultra-sound (1976)

In **1976** the American **Charles Kelman** invented an instrument which made it possible to remove the cataract through a tiny incision after fragmenting it with ultra-sound. The operation was performed under local anaesthetic.

In 1986 Doctor Kelman also invented a completely harmless, flexible ocular implant, which can be inserted into the eye by making an incision in the cornea of 3mm ⅛in.

Operation by laser (1979)

In **1979** Professor **Danièle Aron-Rosa** developed an operation technique using a super-quick-acting Yag laser which made it possible to operate without making an incision in the patient's eye.

Microlase (1987)

This is a new type of laser for treating eye diseases, including glaucoma and complications arising from diabetes. It uses laser diodes similar to those developed for the compact disc player. As it produces neither sound signal nor light beam, patients are unaware of anything and can keep their eyes open during the operation. Invented in **1987**

he described an optical method for correcting refraction defects by immersing the eye in a water-filled tube that was sealed with a lens.

In 1686 the Frenchman René Descartes performed the experiment and it was performed again at the end of the 18th century by two Englishmen, Thomas Young and John Herschel. Herschel's experiment involved applying a layer of gelatin to the eye, held in place by a lens. This was to correct his astigmatism.

1887: glass contact lenses made their appearance due to the efforts of August Müller in Germany, Doctor A. E. Fick and Sulzer in Switzerland, and Kalt in France.

1936: the German company I. G. Farben made the first Plexiglas contact lenses. This same material is used today for hard lenses.

1945: an American, Tuohy, invented the corneal lens which covers only the cornea.

1964: the Czech Wichterle developed flexible hydrophilic lenses.

Holographic lenses (1987)

These lenses are for people who are both short- and long-sighted. They are called Diffrax, use a technique based on holography, and their entire surface corrects the vision. Even in half light they adapt to the vision of the wearer. They were invented by the English company **Pilkington**, which is well-known for its range of inventions in the field of glassware, and came onto the market at the beginning of 1987.

Disposable lenses (1989)

The first disposable contact lenses, developed by the American laboratories **Vistakon**, have been brought onto the market. They are designed to be worn continuously for a week at a time and then discarded and replaced by a new pair. They are suitable for mildly short-sighted people.

Light-sensitive sunglasses (1938)

Doctor Edwin Land, the founder of the Polaroid company, invented polarising sunglasses which eliminate reflections in **1938**. As early as 1939 a chemist at Corning Glass, Doctor R. H. Dalton, had begun to develop glasses sensitive to variations in light. His invention, patented by Corning in 1964, was put on the market in 1967 as Photogray.

THE OCULAR ENDOSCOPE

Until recently, 20 percent of the eye socket could not be examined, for it is hidden by the iris. In order to be able to see this part of the eye, two French doctors, Claude and Joseph Léon, have developed the surgical ocular endoscope. This is the smallest endoscope there is, and is linked to a Bivision module, making it possible to incorporate the endoscopic image into the field of observation of an operating microscope. This means that during the operation the surgeon can examine the images provided by the endoscope without taking his eyes from the microscope, and act accordingly. It was unveiled in 1990.

RADAR FOR THE BLIND

Professor Giampiero Soardo of the University of Turin has developed the world's first electronic guidance system for the blind. It will enable them to find their way on their own, aided by radar instructions emitted by transmitters along the street. This system was demonstrated in Florence in spring 1990, and was installed over an experimental area in the city's historic centre. The process could in future be extended to bus stops, where a bus's destination would be indicated by infra-red signals, and also to telephone booths. The blind person will carry a receiver which activates nearby transmitters and costs under £100.

by two British scientists, **Doctor Anthony Raven** and **Professor John Marshall**, it has been available since 1989.

The corneal graft (1949)

This form of treatment for certain types of myopia and severe hypermetropia is known as refractive lamellar keratoplasty and rectifies the curve of the cornea. The idea was first conceived in **1949** by the opthalmic surgeon **Professor Barraquer** of Bogota, Colombia.

Since 1983 keratoplasty has been performed at the Rothschild Foundation in the departments run by the American surgeons **Doctor Ganem** and **Professor P. Couderc**.

Artificial crystalline lens (1952)

Invented in **1952** by the English doctor **Harold Ridley**, this polymethylmethacrylate (PMMA) or Plexiglas lens is placed behind the iris.

Multifocal crystalline lens (1989)

A new ocular implant has revolutionised cataract surgery by making it possible for the eye to accommodate without the patient having to wear spectacles.

Previously the artificial crystalline lens which replaces the opaque natural lens has restored the patient's vision without being able to accommodate. The lens is usually adjusted for long vision so that the patient has had to wear spectacles for close work.

The multifocal intra-ocular implant developed by the American company **3M** diffracts the light in such a way that there are two focal points, one for long and one for short vision. This device, and other similar ones, is currently being studied in many centres throughout Europe and by the Food and Drugs Administration (FDA) in the United States.

Crystalline bifocals (1989)

Macular degeneration (the macula is a yellow spot on the retina where vision is especially good) associated with age is one of the primary causes of blindness in those over 60.

It is a slow deterioration of the central region of the retina, and there is no effective treatment for it. Sufferers gradually become unable to read or write and are unable to see anything clearly. Magnifying glasses and other enlarging systems can be helpful but

are often impractical for elderly people. Hence the idea of using a system based on Galileo's telescope, in which the eyepiece is made up of a bifocal implant, concave at the centre, and the object-glass is in the form of a pair of glasses with very convex lenses.

This implant was devised by **Professors Ben-Sira** and **Lipshitz** of the University of Jerusalem, in collaboration with the Israeli company **Hanita**, which has been manufacturing it since **1989**. More than 500 implants have already been carried out worldwide.

Incision of the cornea (1955)

This method of treatment, radial keratotomy, consists of making radial incisions on the inner surface of the cornea in order to correct myopia. It is intended to replace the use of spectacles and contact lenses. It was developed in **1955** by **T. Sato** of Japan only to be abandoned

and then resumed in 1979 by the Soviet practitioner Sviatoslav Fiodorov who, with 50 surgeons, created a sort of production line in his hospital in Moscow which carried out 22 000 operations in one year. This system enables the most able specialists to concentrate on the important part of the operation, while the initial and final stages are supervised and dealt with by other practitioners.

Electric hearing-aid (1901)

The American **Miller Reese Hutchinson** was 26 years old when he invented the first electro-acoustic apparatus designed to amplify sounds for the deaf. One of the first users of the invention was Queen Alexandra, consort to King Edward VII, who wore her Acousticon during the coronation ceremony. She presented a medal to the young inventor as a mark of her gratitude.

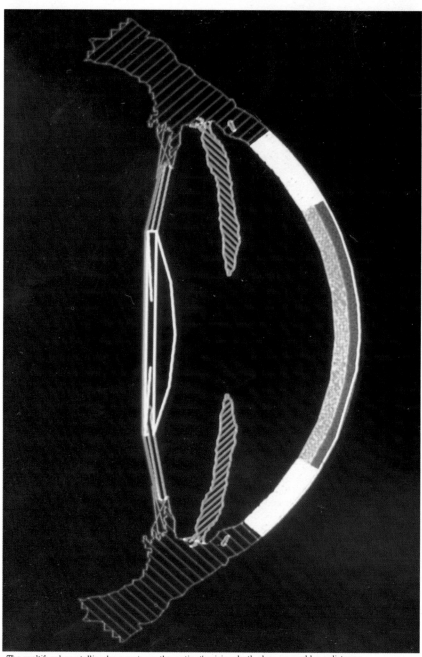

The multifocal crystalline lens restores the patient's vision, both close up and long distance.

Implants for the severely deaf (1961)

In 1961 Georg von Békésy, a Hungarian physicist and physiologist living in the United States, was awarded the Nobel Prize for Physiology and Medicine for his discoveries concerning the stimulation mechanism of the inner ear or cochlea.

In 1973 the company 3M developed a cochlear implant which made it possible for severely deaf people to hear and interpret most sounds.

Scientists throughout the world have pursued similar lines of research with considerable success. In 1977 the Bertin implant was developed by the French doctors Pialoux, Claude Chouard and MacLeod, and in 1981 an Australian, Professor Graeme Clark, produced the 'bionic ear'. In 1988 the most recent model of the device was implanted in a five-year-old girl who had been completely deaf since birth. It was the first time that such an implant had been performed on a child of that age.

Dental surgery

Dentures (16th century)

The earliest complete denture on record was found in a grave in Switzerland that dates from the early 16th century. The dentures appear to have been made from the femur of an ox which was cut and then carved. The upper and lower sections were joined by a metal wire.

Dentures were more widely used when it became possible to place the false teeth on a base which could then rest on the jawbone and adapt to its shape. In 1864 the American company Goodyear brought out a vulcanised rubber which made it possible to produce this type of base.

False teeth (1788)

Until the 19th century, false teeth were made from the bones of familiar or exotic animals; hippopotamus bones were the most widely used as they were the strongest. But these teeth became worn, turning brown and giving off a nauseating smell and had to be changed every 18 months to two years. So, different materials were sought.

As early as 1770 the French apothecary A. Duchâteau had tried to produce a complete denture made from a mineral paste.

In 1788 Dubois de Chemant, a Parisian dentist, produced hardwearing dentures by taking a wax impression from which he made a plaster model.

In 1817 the first porcelain teeth appeared in the United States, and in 1825 S. W. Stockton of Philadelphia commercialised what had previously been a rather unsophisticated process.

Crowns and bridges (3rd century BC)

A piece of a dental plate made in gold was found in Tanagra in Greece. The plate, which consisted of four elements, had been made to replace the two lateral incisors. It appears that the tomb in which it was found could date back to the 3rd century BC. The two central incisors had bands round them and acted as a support for the extension of the false teeth which they held in place. This is the earliest existing evidence of a bridge.

In his *Traité des Dents* (Treatise on Teeth) the French dentist Pierre Fauchard (1678–1761) discusses different ways of achieving fixed dental plates, the bridges promoted by W. H. Dwinelle almost a century later in 1856.

Crowns made from porcelain or industrial resin, known as jacket crowns, appeared around 1895.

Solid ceramic (1979)

This new type of ceramic developed by Doctor Sozio of the United States makes it possible to construct artificial teeth that are superior to the original. The material is so solid that it does not require any reinforced metallic support.

Dental implants (1965)

Dental implant as a method of treatment for people who have had all or some of their teeth removed has existed for the last 30 years. Pegs are inserted into the jaw which act as a support for false teeth. But it is a method which, over the years, has produced many failures. In 1965 positive progress was made as a result of a method of implantation developed by a Swedish professor, Per Ingvar Branemark, a biologist at the University of Gothenburg. The method, which has a success rate of 81 percent for the upper jaw and 91 percent for the lower jaw, is the only one recognised by the American Dental Association.

Fillings (9th century)

The method of filling dental cavities resulting from dental caries is attributed to the famous 9th century Muslim physician Abu Zakariya Yuhanna Ibn Masawaih (776–855), also known as Mesuë Major, who used gold for his fillings.

WHEN WILL THERE BE AN ANTI-CARIES VACCINE?

A French scientist, Doctor Jean-Paul Klein of the Strasbourg INSERM, has been working for 15 years on an anti-caries vaccine, the aim of which is to prevent the bacteria from reproducing and 'colonising' the surface of the teeth. This vaccine, which will be taken orally and will coat the teeth, will make it possible to reduce by half the need for dental treatment throughout the world and to resolve the problems created by sugar consumption. It may be available within a few years but is still very expensive and needs further research.

In the 15th century, important progress was made by the use of gold leaf which made it possible to fill the cavities completely, a technique developed by the Italian surgeon Giovanni Arcolani. In 1853 Makins replaced gold foil with porous gold. This was replaced by soft or non-cohesive gold, and then by cohesive or adhesive gold used by Arthur in 1855.

Amalgams (1819)

In 1819 Charles Bell recommended a mixture of mercury and silver to fill cavities. In 1850 Regnart suggested adding mercury to an alloy to lower the melting point.

Fillings with molten metal appeared in 1884, when they were used for inlays by Aguilhon de Sarran, and in 1886, when Litch used them for onlays.

Compounds (1963)

In 1963 Bowen of the United States discovered a formula for a synthetic resin, for rebuilding and restoring teeth.

Since then, many improvements have been made in the fields of resistance to erosion and adhesive quality. Nowadays, adhesives are

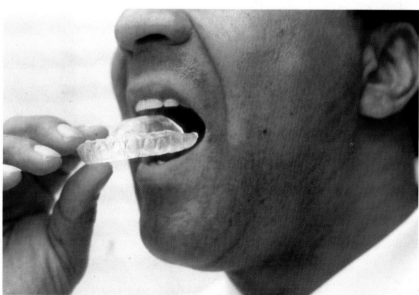

This dental plate, tested on six volunteers, is in fact a cure for snoring. Invented by Professor Morris Clark of the University of Colorado, it pushes the jaw forward to improve air circulation.

A world first: using mother-of-pearl in human bone tissue. Bioracine, an artificial tooth root which has been on the market since 1989, is the invention of twin brothers, both dental surgeons, from Guadaloupe, Serge and Georges Camprasse. This first mother-of-pearl implant is a non-biodegradable transplant which does not stimulate rejection and is bioactive, etc. It comes not only in the form of a tooth root but could also be used as a transplant for any of the bones in the fingers and toes, kneecap, facial bones, the chain of tiny bones in the inner ear, and so on. Its field of application is vast.

being used which prevent the recurrence of dental caries.

The use of ultra-violet rays, blue light and halogen lamps gives a better polymerisation of the product. This also gives the dentist more time to concentrate on the delicate operation of putting the composite in place.

Toothpaste (1st century AD)

The earliest formula for toothpaste was given at the end of the **1st century AD** by a Roman doctor, **Scribonius Largus**. It consisted of a mixture of vinegar, honey, salt and ground glass!

Pliny the Elder recommended urine as a mouthwash, and this use of urine, particularly as a treatment for dental caries, persisted until the 19th century. The explanation given was that urine, which was warm and acidic, neutralised the decaying action of the cold, damp secretions from the pituitary gland which flowed from the brain into the mouth.

Extraction of teeth

In China the instruments preferred for pulling teeth were the fingers. For five or six hours a day, tooth-pullers practised pulling out nails hammered into thick planks.

The invention of the first pair of dental pliers is traditionally attributed to the famous doctor and anatomist **Erasistrates** of Alexandria during the 2nd century BC.

Celsus, the great Roman medical theoretician of the 1st century AD, suggested placing a piece of flock soaked in the sap of tithymalis, a variety of euphorbia, in the painful cavity, a method which broke the tooth into pieces.

In the early 16th century, an instrument appeared which made it possible to extract teeth without the risk of crushing them or fracturing the crown. The invention was known as the pelican and was attributed to the Italian surgeon, Giovanni Arcolani. The first so-called anatomic forceps were designed by the London-based French surgeon, J.-M. Everard (1800–82) in collaboration with Sir John Tomes (1815–59).

Dental transplants (11th century)

The Muslim physician and surgeon **Abulcasis** of Cordoba (Abul Kasim or Abu al-Qasim Khalaf ibn Abbas as-Zahrawi) advised that teeth that were knocked out accidentally should be reimplanted. He had them held in place for several weeks with ligatures which enabled them to re-root.

Towards the end of the 13th century Nicolas Falucci developed the transplantation technique whereby teeth were taken from a donor, living or dead. During the 18th century, transplantations became very popular.

Oral anaesthetic (14th century)

The first evidence of an oral anaesthetic is provided by a surgeon from Padua, grandfather of the famous Italian religious and political reformer, **Girolamo Savonarola**. He made his patients chew tiny cloth sachets filled with henbane, poppy seeds and mandrake. The sap from these plants produced an insensitivity of the mucous membrane which made it possible to make a painless incision.

The mouthwash (15th century)

In the **15th century** the Italian surgeon from the Salerno School **Giovanni Plateario** was the first to recommend a mouthwash to accelerate post-operative healing. This was a major step forward at a time when the risk of oral sepsis, or infection, was extremely high.

Dental equipment

In his treatise on medicine and surgery Abulcasis, the Muslim physician from Cordoba (see above), describes an impressive dental arsenal consisting of pliers, elevators and ligatures which has long been the prerogative of the dental surgeon.

Happily, the process of dental extraction has greatly improved since 1773.

The dentist's chair (16th century)

In the early 16th century Giovanni Plateario abandoned the standard operating position whereby the patient's head was held tightly between the surgeon's knees. He adopted a low chair with a shorter back rest which gave the dentist easier access to the patient's mouth.

The following dates represent the main stages in the development of the dentist's chair: *1810:* chair with a folding stool for the dentist; *1848:* the headrest; *1855:* the jack-operated chair invented by Ball; *1871:* the swivel chair invented by Harris; *1872:* the iron chair operated by a pneumatic jack and which could be tipped backwards, invented by Alexander Morrison; *1877:* the chair operated by hydraulic pump, invented by the Johnston brothers; *1950:* the electrically operated chair.

The drill (1st century AD)

The first surgical drill dates back to the 1st century AD. The Roman surgeon **Archigenes** developed an instrument which was set in motion by a rope and which drove a drill by rotation.

The mechanical drill (1864)

In 1864 **Harrington** of England had the idea of activating a drill using a clock mechanism in which the spring could be wound up and then released.

In 1868 an American, Green, introduced a drill driven by pedal-operated bellows.

On 7 February 1871 the American J. B. Morrisson introduced a model which could achieve a speed of between 600 and 800rpm. In 1874 Green constructed a system which was activated by an electric wheel and

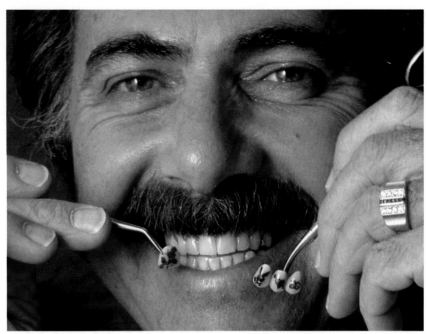

A visit to the dentist brings terror to many; having a tattoo is a painful experience – so perhaps these tooth tattoos are for the very brave only.

reached a rotational speed of between 1200 and 4000rpm.

Since 1958, air-driven turbine-operated drills can reach a rotational speed of between 300 000 and 400 000rpm.

Dental scanner (1987)

The dental scanner or T-Scan was invented by two Americans, an information technologist called **Rob Golden** and a dentist called **William Maness**, who consider their invention the most important since the discovery of X-rays. The scanner is a small device shaped like a jawbone. As the patient 'bites' the scanner, an image is simultaneously projected onto a screen which gives the dentist an immediate view of the teeth and enables him to see what treatment may be necessary. It provides a quick method of examination which means treatment can be carried out without delay.

Agriculture

Agricultural machines

Ploughing and sowing

Origins (4th–3rd millennia BC)

The history of the invention of agricultural machines truly begins with the industrial age. However, the 18th and 19th century inventors were heirs to a tradition that was many thousands of years old.

The earliest evidence we have of agricultural activity – which doubtless began long before – appears in pictograms representing the swing plough, an implement with a symmetrical ploughshare that ploughed a shallow furrow (**4th millennium BC** in Mesopotamia, **3rd millennium BC** in Egypt and, in Europe, the rock engravings of the Valley of Wonders, 3500 BC). The plough proper, a tool with an asymmetrical ploughshare that makes deep ploughing possible, is more recent (1st century AD).

Industrial plough (1730)

In **1730** the Dutchman **Joseph Foljambe** developed the Rotherham plough (so-called after the important manufacturing town in South Yorkshire), which marked the beginnings of industrial manufacture.

The first plough made entirely of cast iron was made by the Englishman Robert Ransome in 1785. By 1789 he had further developed the ploughshare so that it was self-sharpening and it had interchangeable parts. In France in 1825 Fondeur, a blacksmith from the Aisne region, invented the first metal swivel plough with a joined front axle.

In 1837 the American John Deere patented the first steel plough, with an all-in-one ploughshare and mouldboard, and F.S.

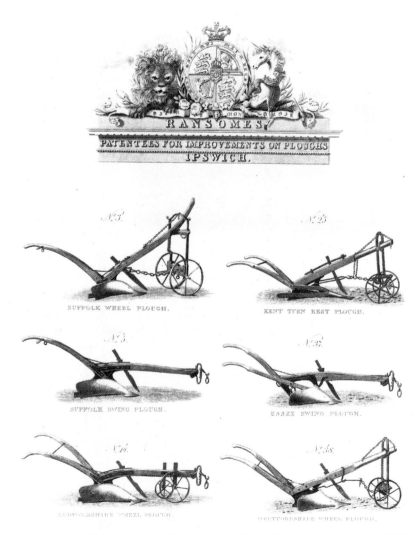

Robert Ransome went into the plough-making business in 1785 with the first-ever plough made entirely of cast iron. These are engravings of some of the company's models around 1830.

Davenport patented the two-wheeled Sulky in 1864, which was supplanted by the three-wheeled Sulky, known as the Flying Dutchman, in 1884. The disc plough first appeared in the United States in 1847 and the version built by John Shearer and Sons in 1877 was particularly successful in Australia.

Tractor-drawn plough (19th century)

In the second half of the 19th century steam engines sometimes replaced animals to draw the plough, machines such as those built by the Englishmen John Heathcoat in 1832 and John Fowler in 1852; the steam cultivator by Halkett in 1860; steam tractors from the American firm Case, from 1829, and the steam locotractor built by the Frenchman Albaret in 1856.

It was not until the 20th century that the tractor-mounted plough first appeared.

Seeders and dibbles (prehistory)

If we regard the digging stick as the ancestor of this family of tools, then it is fair to say that seeders and dibbles go back into prehistory.

In 1660 the Italian Taddeo Calvani invented a seeder consisting of a box which was mounted on two wheels.

In the industrial age there were a number of inventions in the field of seeders: the Englishman **Jethro Tull**'s seed drill in **1700**, which was the first to sow seeds in regular rows (thus making weeding much easier). Other improvements were the ploughshare seeder of another Englishman, James Smyth in 1800, the Frenchman François Dombasle's cylinder seeder in 1805, etc.

Harrow (c.800)

The harrow, in the form of thorny branches or bushes, was already known to the Egyptians, and the Romans used logs stuck with wooden spikes.

However, the harrow that we know today – a rectangular or triangular implement which is pulled along by animal or machine – dates from around **800**.

In the 19th century the harrow entered the industrial age. In England in 1840 James Smith invented the flexible harrow with metal chains; in 1854 the American H. Johnson patented the disc harrow; in 1869 another American, Davis L. Garver, developed the vibrating harrow and in 1872 the Frenchman Emile Puzenat invented the zigzag harrow.

Of all agricultural machines the harrow is perhaps the one whose form has changed the least, since today's tractor-drawn harrows have triangular or rectangular frames, like those of the Middle Ages.

Clod-crusher (1841)

The use of the roller to break up clods of earth dates back to the end of the 16th century, but the type used today is the crosskil, named after its inventor, the Englishman **William Crosskil**, who patented it in **1841** and used a serrated roller.

Memotronic (1990)

Massey-Ferguson, the world's leading agri-

Type	Date	Country	Characteristics
		TRACTORS	
Burger Tractor	1889	USA	First kerosene tractor.
Froelich Tractor	1892	USA	First petrol tractor.
Hart & Pan Tractor	1902	USA	Coining of the word tractor by this company to replace gasoline traction engine.
Crawler Tractor	1904	USA	Invented by Benjamin Holt to increase the bearing surface of steam machines. It ran on petrol after 1906.
Gougis Tractor	1906	France	First tractor able to drive a binder attachment.
Ford Tractor	1907	USA	First Ford tractor. Axle and steering from the Ford motor car. Includes a binder.
Wallis Club	1913	USA	First of the lighter, faster and more powerful tractors (Bull tractors).
Ford Tractor	1917	USA	First tractor with a cast-iron chassis. Petrol or paraffin engine. Four steel wheels.
Farmhall Tractor	1924	USA	Multi-purpose tractor (ploughing, harrowing, etc.). Produced by International Harvester. A revolution in the concept of the tractor.
Tractor with tyres	1928	USA	First tractor with rubber tyres improvised in the lemon plantations of Florida. Subsequently manufactured by F. B. Goodrich Co. (1931) and Firestone Tire and Rubber Co. (1932).
Tool Carrier Tractor	1939	Ireland	Invented by H. Ferguson (1939) preceded by the Tourand system (France, 1907) and International Harvester (USA, 1918).

cultural tractor manufacturer, launched their award-winning Memotronic system in 1990. It links the Datatronic onboard computer to a PC in the farm office. A software package enables the farmer to select information to be transferred before work commences. When the work is completed, further data is added and the information is stored on cassette and analysed by the farmer. Farming has become a truly hi-tech industry now.

Haymaking, reaping and harvesting

Reaper (1822)

The American **Jeremiah Bailey** was the true inventor of the mechanical reaper. Patented in **1822**, his rotary reaper used a cutting disc which turned horizontally a few centimetres from the ground.

The cutting arm, which is specifically for haymaking, was invented by the American William Manning in 1831, but it was not manufactured industrially until 1850.

Tedder (1820)

In **1820** Englishman **Robert Salmon** designed a machine which lifted cut grass and turned it over so that it could be completely dried by the action of the sun and wind. In one day the machine could do the work of 15 women, and even more if the horse kept up a good pace.

However, this implement was too brutal and spread the hay around, and these disadvantages prevented its development. Twenty years later, fork tedders were invented. These were used up until the 1930s, when there were replaced by machines that combine raking, tedding and draining.

Harvester (1st century AD)

The harvester already existed at the beginning of the Christian era. It was widely used in Gaul and throughout the Roman world, and Pliny the Elder (AD 23–79) gives a very precise description of it. Thanks to fragments of stone carvings found during excavations in Belgium, at Montauban-Buzenol, it has been possible to build a picture of this ancient harvester, and a replica has been made. Strangely, the harvester disappeared into oblivion after this and only reappeared in mechanised form in the industrial age.

After 1800 many different types of harvester were produced, among them notably the combine harvester, invented by the American Lane in 1818 and put into operation in 1838 as a result of improvements by Moore and Hascall; Cyrus McCormick's tractor-drawn reaper in 1831; the self-binders from the Americans John F. Appleby (1858) and Walter Wood (1871), and the self-propelling combine harvester, whose prototype was put forward in 1888 by the American Best and which did not come into full operation until 1944, when it was launched by the American firm Massey-Harris.

The world leader in the field is now the American company New Holland, with 27.8 percent of the market.

Axial threshing (1975)

The American companies **International Harvester** and **New Holland** began to research into an axial threshing combine harvester in 1962, but the first prototype was not built until **1975**. With its central rotor and system of separation, this machine represents the greatest development since motorisation.

Pollen aspirator (1988)

Among other things, pollen is used in medical research on allergies, the development of hybrid seeds for reafforestation and the genetic improvement of some plants, such as larch. In order to increase and speed up pollen collection, **Patrick Baldet** and the Seeds and Forest Plants division of CEMAGREF in France developed a self-propelling machine which encloses the tree in a sort of 'cage'. Collection is carried out by vacuum suction within this cage. It took three years to develop this pollen harvest machine, which was first used in **1988**.

Agronomy

Hydroponics (1860)

The growing of plants without soil, or hydroponics, has become a part of daily life. Tomatoes, cucumbers, lettuces, lemons, oranges and avocados, coming from Holland or Israel, are all now grown without the medium of soil, which has been replaced by renewable nutrient solutions.

This is up-to-the-minute technology, but the invention is an old one. Indeed, it was in **1860**

A combine harvester is seen here loading wheat into a trailer towed by a tractor. The first combine harvester was invented as early as 1818.

Corn can be grown in greenhouses by the method of hydroponics, whereby the plant grows in water with diluted nutrients and minerals.

that two German scientists, **Ferdinand Gustav Sachs** and **Knopp**, succeeded in growing plants on a simple mineral solution.

In 1914 a Frenchman called Mazé, drew attention to the role that rare elements, which are present as impurities in ordinary water, could have in hydroponics. However, it was not until 1940 that molybdenum, a fertilising element, completed the list of elements thought to be indispensable to the constitution of nutrient solutions.

From then on, the use of hydroponic cultures in the field of agriculture could seriously be envisaged. Relatively large-scale production made it possible to feed American troops in the Pacific islands during the Second World War.

The growing of plants without soil, using both hydroponics and aeroponics (when the water and mineral salts are sprayed directly on to the roots), has been extensively developed over the last ten years and will make it possible in the near future to plant real gardens, orchards or cottage gardens to feed the space towns of the future.

The first tomatoes officially labelled 'hydroponic' were marketed in Canada in 1988.

Insecticides (1st century AD)

As far back as 2000 years ago, the Chinese were using powdered Oriental Chrysanthemum (Pyrethrum) to kill fleas. In the Middle Ages and during the Renaissance, entomologists prescribed arsenic against insect infestations, following the example of the Borgias, who used it to rid themselves of their enemies. In 1681 the first arsenic compounds for treating plants were recorded.

Many tropical plants were used against insects, such as Tumbo from Brazil and Ecuador, Nikoe from Surinam, etc. Their roots contain a powder called rotenone, which affects the nervous system of insects. Its properties were discovered in 1920. Rotenone was replaced by DDT, which was first synthesised in 1873 by Othmar Zeidler and perfected by the Swiss biochemist Paul Müller, who won the Nobel Prize for Medicine in 1948 for his discovery. It was Müller who gave it its name (short for dichlorodiphenyltrichloroethane) and patented it in 1940. DDT is a highly polluting product and is now partially or entirely banned in many countries.

In the 1940s BHC, a compound of chlorine, was developed in Britain. It was particularly useful in controlling locusts, mosquitos and tsetse fly, rather than as a crop spray because it tended to taint the food.

Fastac (1979)

In 1979, taking their inspiration from chemical structures similar to those of the pyrethrum, the American company **Shell** developed a new synthesised insecticide: Fastac. Fastac is a high performance insecticide, harmless to some insects, notably bees, which gather nectar from treated plants.

A NEW HERBICIDE

Scientists had noticed that some types of sorghum, a crop which is widely grown in the Tropics, were able to defend themselves against fungal diseases. They discovered that these plants, when attacked by a fungus, secreted a poison strong enough to kill it (indeed, it also damages the leaf around where the poison is used, but this affects only a small area and is therefore much less harmful than the fungus would have been).

Ralph Nicholson and Beth Snyder from Purdue University in the United States managed to synthesise a substance which would trigger off the production of the poison. So, when it is sprayed onto weeds of the same group as sorghum, they secrete the poison, but, unlike the sorghum plants, they do so everywhere, thus poisoning themselves in defence against an imagined attack. This new herbicide would be very beneficial to farmers as it would not affect other plants, nor would it damage the environment as is the case with so many other chemical products.

The Eloria Noyesi caterpillar is only 2.5cm lin long, but it feeds exclusively on the leaves of the coca plant. Perhaps it will soon be enlisted in the fight against drugs.

Fertilisers (1817)

Substances have long been used to increase yields and encourage growth, the earliest being animal manure. Guano from seabirds was one such, and was particularly popular in the 19th century. It was only by that time that there was any understanding of the chemical requirements of soil, and the importance of such substances as nitrogen in promoting growth.

One of the first compounds that was added to the soil was superphosphate, originally a mixture of bones and sulphuric acid, devised by the Irishman **James Murray** in 1817. Nitrates became so widely used by the end of the 19th century that there was a danger of running out of supplies unless a method was discovered which enabled the manufacture of artifical nitrates; this was the Haber process to make ammonia. Yields were dramatically increased by the addition of nitrates to the soil, but there is concern about the effect they have on the water supply.

Fungicides (c.1850)

About 1850 farmers began to use sulphur, first as a powder and then in the form of a paste, because its fungicidal properties had been recognised. The Bordeaux mixture of copper sulphate and lime became widely used later in the century.

Fungicides are used to fight diseases caused by microscopic fungi. However some fungi can have beneficial effects. In 1985 scientists from INRA, the French national centre for agronomic research, isolated a fungus microbe which makes it possible to accelerate the process of degradation of lignite (wood): an invention which will be of great service to the economic development of biomass.

Biological pest control (1873)

The first example of biological pest control dates back to 1873, when **C. V. Riley** sent from North America an acarid, the *Rhizoglyphus*

phylloxerae, to **Jules Planchon**, his French correspondent. The acarid was to destroy the microscopic aphid which caused phylloxera of the vine.

The principle of biological pest control is to use the rivalry between two animal species to exterminate parasite species which damage plants. In 1888 **A. Koebek** introduced the Australian ladybird beetle *Rodolia cardinalis* into the citrus orchards of California. This species feeds on *Icerya purchasi*, which ravages citrus crops. The ladybird was a great success, destroying the pest and so this method was subsequently used throughout the world.

Sprayer (1884)

Although the idea of a sprayer was introduced as early as 1781 by the Abbé Rosier in his educational book *Cours d'agriculture*, the first prototype developed by the Frenchman **Victor Vermorel** did not appear until 1884.

Vermorel based his invention on the spray diffuser developed by the American entomologist Riley who had demonstrated to wine growers in the Hérault region that it was possible to treat mildew by spraying the vines with copper sulphate. Vermorel perfected Riley's device by adding a pump to the spray nozzle. In 1887 he introduced a very convenient portable spray, worn on the back. Mechanical sprays appeared in 1889.

Spray planes (1924)

The first planes to be purpose-built for spraying operations were designed by **Huff-Daland Co.** of Ogdensburg, New York State and accomplished this mission in the Mississippi delta in **1924**.

In 1921 ex-First World War planes (Curtis JN6Hs) were used in agriculture for the first time, to spray arsenate powder on catalpa forests to destroy the hawk-moth larvae which were attacking the trees.

The first liquid larvicides were sprayed in 1930 in New Jersey and California to exterminate mosquito larvae.

Insecticides are all too often pollutants, but insects damage crops. To solve the problem without harming the environment, these enormous insect aspirators have been developed in the United States.

project took four years of research and development by INRA scientists.

Self-destructing virus (1987)

Scientists from the Institute of Virology in Oxford have developed a new weapon against insects: a self-destructing killer virus. Through genetic engineering, this virus has been stripped of its natural defences. Once it is swallowed by the insect, the micro-organism dies all by itself. The first experiments took place in Scotland on a caterpillar that attacks pine trees. This procedure would be less dangerous than the usual chemical pesticides which kill indiscriminately. Another method of fighting viruses is to 'vaccinate' plants. The first 'vaccinated' plant is a form of tobacco, which came into being as a result of the work of the CNRS and the IBMP in Strasbourg.

Animal husbandry

Artificial insemination (1780)

While the first and perhaps mythical instance of artificial insemination applied to horses in 1322 is attributed to the Arabs, the true forerunner was the Italian **Lazzaro Spallanzani** (1729–99), who carried out the first recognised experiment of insemination on a bitch in **1780**.

Despite the success of this experiment, it was not until the 20th century that new research was carried out, notably in Russia with the work of Ivanov in 1907, and Milanov in 1933.

Artificial insemination was mainly developed after the Second World War and became a common practice, particularly for cattle, when it became easier to keep semen in storage.

Barbed wire (1874)

In **1874 Joseph Gliden** from Illinois (USA) built the first machine capable of producing barbed wire in large quantities. This cheap mode of fencing quickly spread throughout vast regions of western America. However, disputes soon broke out between farmers who were installing fences and big stock breeders who were accustomed to herding their cattle cross country as they pleased.

RESURRECTION FOR THE ELM?

The elm gradually disappeared in Britain and elsewhere in Europe as a result of a devastating disease against which no effective chemical protection has so far been found. But to prevent a tree that has been such a valuable part of our European heritage over the centuries from disappearing for ever, scientists from many countries have been busy. Professor Smaley (University of Wisconsin) isolated the first natural hybrid, which grows in Japan. Three disease-resistant varieties have been tested in the United States then sent to scientists at INRA, the French national institute for agronomic research. After three years of research and tests, only one of the three hybrids now appears to be disease-resistant. It has been marketed since 1989, under the name of Resista, by a limited number of tree nurseries under the scientific and technical supervision of an official body.

Herbicides (1932)

One of any farmer's greatest problems is that of weeds: how can one prevent the growth of weeds while allowing the crop to grow? Hope came when the Dutchman F. W. Went discovered in 1926 some substances which could control growth. From here it was only a short step to develop a chemical which would attack only weeds. Indeed, in **1932** dinitro-ortho-cresol (DNOL) was patented in France, which was crudely but effectively able to discriminate between different sorts of plants.

After further improvements in the effectiveness of herbicides, ICI developed in the 1950s a new group of chemicals, the best-known of which is paraquat. Paraquat will kill weeds on the surface but is not effective at any depth of soil. This meant that instead of ploughing and harrowing, the farmer could now spray the land and then sow the crop soon after, thus saving a great deal of labour.

Parasite farming (1984)

Since **1984** the first industrial farming of a useful insect (*Encarsia formosa*) has been in progress. This insect is intended to control the populations of another insect which attacks greenhouse tomatoes and cucumbers. The

---

PERFUME FOR COWS

According to Professors Keith Cummins and Lawrence Myers at the University of Auburn, Alabama, spraying cows with aniseed essence has a calming effect, thus creating favourable conditions for maximising the milk yield. The smell of aniseed (in the stressful context of present cattle-rearing conditions) masks the cows' individual smells and consequently reduces the aggressive tendencies which lower their milk yield.

A beekeeper in full protective clothing removes a brood frame from a bee hive. These frames slot into the brood chamber where the queen bee, tended by worker bees, lays her eggs. At the right of the picture is a metal frame called a queen excluder – the holes in the frame are too small for the queen to crawl through and so prevent her from laying eggs in the wrong part of the hive.

Beekeeping (3rd millennium BC)

The Greeks attributed the invention of beekeeping to Aristaeus, the son of Apollo, and the Egyptians had a myth to explain the origins of bees and honey, according to which the latter was the tears of the god Ra. The first Egyptian beekeepers started under the Old Kingdom (between 2780 and 2280 BC). They made great use of honey, since they did not know about sugar.

Cream separator (1878)

The cream separator, based on a system using centrifugal force, was patented in 1878 by the Swede **Carl Gustaf de Laval**. Before Laval's separator, milk was left to stand and separation occurred as a result of the different weights of buttermilk and cream.

The centrifuge principle was afterwards put to use in many industrial fields and in biological laboratories.

Distance alarm (1987)

Denis Carrier, a Canadian inventor from Notre-Dame-du-Nord, Quebec, developed this distance alarm (patented in the United States in 1987), which is intended to be used by farmers who have an animal that is about to give birth.

Embryo transplantation (1975)

The first genetic experiments on embryo transplantation in cattle were tried out in 1975 in the laboratories of British doctors **Rawson** and **Polch**.

Milk refrigeration (1850)

The first system for refrigerating milk was invented in 1850 by the American **Lawrence**. His invention represented a great step forward. Until this point, the temperature of milk as it came from the udder (38.5°C *101.3°F*, the cow's body temperature) was extremely favourable to the proliferation of bacteria. Fast refrigeration was thus one of the fundamental stages in the preservation of milk for distribution, and permitted the development of the dairy industry.

Milking machines (1862)

The invention of the milking machine dates from the 19th century. The first model was made by the American **L.O. Colvin** in 1862. After this, in 1889, the Scotsman William Murchland developed a constant suction machine.

In 1895 another Scotsman, Doctor Alexander Shields, had the idea of using the principle of the pulser, which gave rise to intermittent suction. This was less painful for the cow than Murchland's machine, which caused inflammation. The process was perfected by Hulbert and Park in 1902 and by Gillies in 1903.

New breeds (1868)

Over recent years research on animal biology has made it possible to create new breeds, such as the Renitelo, a new breed of very robust bovines which was created in 1962 by the Madagascans from three strains of zebu.

The smallest horse in the world (40–60cm *16-24in* at the withers), the Falabella, was the successful outcome of work by a vet of Irish origin, **Patrick Falabella**. Falabella moved to Argentina in the last century and began his research in 1868. It was continued by his descendants, who also experimented unsuccessfully on increasing the size of horses. But the family have never revealed their secret of how it was done.

In 1984 an Israeli scientist, Dan Rattner, invented the gobex, a cross between goat and ibex.

A chimera (half goat, half sheep) is just one of the new animals that it has become possible to create thanks to the latest developments in genetic engineering.

In 1986 there was a zoological event of double importance at the Nantes Veterinary School: the natural birth of the first female chabin. It is quite exceptional for a male chabin, a cross between a sheep and a goat, not to be sterile. This baby chabin is the offspring of a female chabin and a ram.

At the end of 1987 a lamb was born to a mother who was entirely 'manufactured' (a chimera, half goat, half sheep) from a few cells from a goat embryo which were inserted into a sheep embryo. This genetic engineering was carried out by a team of reproduction physiologists at the University of California, headed by Gary Anderson.

Refrigerated abattoirs (1873)

In the latter half of the 19th century, confronted with the problem of supplying meat to the towns of eastern America, the American **Daniel Holden** and his brother were the first to envisage, in **1873**, the preservation of meat in refrigerated abattoirs. Before that, meat was salted or smoked at the slaughterhouses where the animals were actually reared, an operation which could only be carried out in winter, or possibly in the summer (as in Chicago in 1853) thanks to a large supply of natural ice.

Fishfarming

Origins (antiquity)

It was the Romans who first had the idea of farming marine animals, fish or crustaceans, in enclosed waters (fishponds). The Chinese also used artificial spawning grounds.

Artificial fertilising of fish eggs (1420)

The invention of the artificial fertilisation of fish eggs in **1420** is attributed to **Dom Pinchon**, a monk at the Abbaye de Réome near Montbard on the French Côte d'Or. Anxious to provide the Christians with sufficient food

for the many days of abstinence, the monk thought up a system for fertilising eggs which would provide enough fish to make it possible to observe the fast days. This fertilisation process was described in 1763 by the German naturalist Jacobi, who reinvented Dom Pinchon's box, calling it a hatching box.

In **1701** the Swedish naturalist **C. F. Lund** invented a spawning box, one of the first of its kind.

Aquaculture (1933)

In **1933** the Japanese **Professor Fujinaga** first solved the problem of getting shrimps (*Penaeus japonicus*) to reproduce in captivity.

Between 1890 and 1910 billions of cod and lobster larvae had been released into the ocean by American biologists to multiply, in

the hope of improving productivity: in vain. Professor Fujinaga's experiments at last opened the way to modern aquaculture, whose production (in fresh and salt water) is today more than 25 million tonnes per annum.

Algae farming (1972)

In **1972** the American **Howard A. Wilcox** put forward the idea of using algae to produce methane as an energy source. His calculations showed that if a 'field' 856km *532 miles* long of algae of the species *Macrocystis pyrifera* could be cultivated in the ocean, the entire annual gas consumption of the United States could be produced. The idea is to harvest the algae, which the action of the sun's rays causes to grow very fast, and then to use a bacterium to digest it, with a resulting emission of methane.

Mussel beds (1235)

After being shipwrecked on the French coast in **1235**, an Irishman, **Patrick Walton**, settled there. Between tall wooden stakes planted in the sea he stretched nets to catch birds. He soon noticed that these stakes became covered in mussels, which seemed to grow remarkably well there. He had the idea of planting many more stakes, close together and linked by racks. He called these strange barriers 'bout choat', which became *bouchot*, the French term for these mussel beds.

Oyster farming (2nd century BC)

The first oyster farmer recorded by history was a Roman named **Sergius Orata**. He built an oyster bed on his property, in Lake Lucrin, near Naples, at the beginning of the **2nd century BC**.

Orata built fishponds that connected with the sea but protected the oyster brood from waves. The young oysters were provided with posts to which they could cling and grow in proper conditions of temperature and light. Sergius Orata's know-how was such that he made a fortune selling his oysters. His contemporaries said of him, 'He could grow

Floating cages in a sea farm run by the French marine research group IFREMER. The idea of fishfarming is very old.

oysters on a roof.' Lake Lucrin disappeared in 1583 after an earthquake and a volcanic eruption.

Currently, Japan is the number one producer of oysters in the world.

Cultured pearls (c.1899)

At the end of the last century (the patent came into the public domain in 1921), **Kokichi Mikimoto** from Japan invented a procedure which made it possible, with pearl oysters, to obtain cultured pearls. Natural pearls are those formed without any deliberate outside action.

Natural pearls were more sought after (and thus more expensive) than diamonds until the invention of cultured pearls. They were mainly gathered in the tropical seas by divers who went to a depth of 40m *131ft* without breathing apparatus and helped by weights held between the feet – a dangerous operation.

In the hands of sometimes unscrupulous dealers, the intensive exploitation of pearl oysters was slowly but surely exhausting the natural beds in Ceylon, Japan, the Red Sea, Polynesia and the Persian Gulf when the invention of cultured pearls opened up new horizons.

Pearls have since been cultivated in specialised 'sea farms' and have become a product almost like any other. It takes three years for a pearl to form around a core of nacre which is implanted in the pearl oyster. One oyster can take two to three grafts during its life, but no more. In 1985 about 68 000 pearls were produced in this way by Japanese pearl farms, which, since 1968, have faced competition from the pearl farms of French Polynesia, whose pearls are highly prized. A connoisseur may pay up to $10 000 for a single cultured pearl, if it is of the right lustre and perfectly formed.

Domestic animals

Cat (2100 BC)

Nearly all of the proof we have on the domestication of the cat comes from ancient Egypt. The first record of the domestic cat's existence dates from approximately **2100 BC**. Any previous traces are probably those of a wild species. It was the Romans who introduced the cat to Europe.

It was only about a hundred years ago that cats began to be selected for reproduction. Towards the middle of the 19th century, breeding and exhibiting began in Britain.

Among the more curious of the 'invented' breeds are the Scottish Fold (a cat with pendulous ears, bred by **William Ross** in Scotland in **1961**); the Manx, the tailless cat from the Isle of Man whose origins are not known; from Germany the Rex, with short, curly hair (**1946**); and the Bobtail, with its pompom tail, which was brought to the United States from Japan in the early **1950s**.

Dog (Neolithic period)

The dog has accompanied man ever since the latter began a more settled existence; that is, around **5000 BC**.

Breeds of dog such as the mastiff and the

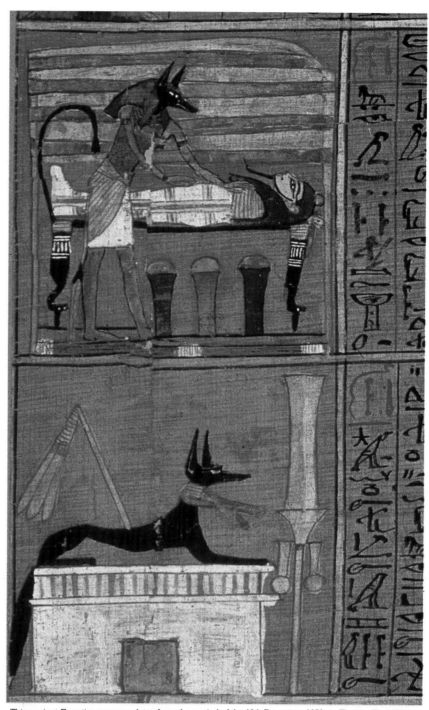

This ancient Egyptian papyrus dates from the period of the 19th Dynasty, c.1250 BC. The top illustration shows a man with a mask of the head of Anubis, the Egyptian god (half dog, half jackal) who conducted the dead to their judgement, while below sits Anubis himself. In Egypt dogs were venerated – cases of severe cruelty to dogs could even bring a sentence of death.

greyhound are ancient, featuring in Assyrian sculpture and Egyptian art of the Old Empire (between 2780 and 2280 BC).

The German shepherd (alsatian) first appeared around 2000 BC and is the descendant of the Persian shepherd. However, the standards for this breed were not established until the end of the 19th century by Max von Stephaniz.

Other breeds are more recent: the boxer appeared at the end of the 19th century, while the characteristics of the cocker spaniel were only established in 1893. The Pekinese was originally the exclusive property of the Imperial family of China and the Empress Tseu-Hi (1835–1908) set out the breeding regulations.

Tinned food for dogs and cats (1865)

When did 'Whiskas', 'Chum' and other tinned foods for cats and dogs first come on the market? The first industrialised food for domestic animals was a cake for dogs, manufactured in the United States around **1865** by **James Spratt**. In 1907 the Bennett Biscuit Company began to manufacture dog biscuits in the shape of bones.

Gardening

Tools

Frames and glass cloches (antiquity)

It is thought that the Romans were already familiar with the use of glass shelters and artificial heat to counter the difficulties of producing certain vegetables during the winter months. But it was not until 1600, when Olivier de Serres, the first French agronomist, wrote his *Théatre d'agriculture et mesnage des champs*, that glass cloches were recommended for growing melons. The glass coldframe is probably a 16th-century Dutch invention.

Garden hose (1850)

Imitating rain so as to provide plants with water is a procedure that was described in 800 by a Benedictine monk. At that time water was poured from a jug and allowed to run between the fingers onto the ground.

Around **1850** the first gutta-percha hoses began to replace watering cans and the watering cart drawn by a donkey.

Automatic watering kit (1968)

A real transformation of garden watering techniques grew out of an invention by two Germans, Kress and Kestner, from the **Gardena** company. Using moulded plastic components they developed a system of automatic connections which could be simply clicked together without any tools (or leaks) to assemble all the equipment necessary for watering (hoses, nozzles, taps, etc.). In 20 years 200 million Gardena kits were sold.

Hedge-trimmer (1880)

In **1880** an Englishman, **R. Hornsby**, invented a machine for cutting hedges, made entirely of metal. Drawn by two horses, it was supported on two large wheels and had a seat in the front for the driver and one in the back for the man operating the cutting arm made from two big vertical blades.

Lawn mower (1831)

The invention of the lawn mower in **1831** was due to two Englishmen: **Edwin Budding** for the design and **Ferrabee** for the manufacture. The horses' hooves were covered by rubber boots so that they would not damage the lawn while pulling the cylindrical blades of the machine.

At the beginning of the second half of the 19th century, the steam mower was produced, followed by the motor-driven lawn mower. Black and Decker produced the first successful lightweight model in 1969.

Flymo (1963)

A mower based on the hovercraft principle was produced by **Flymo** in Britain in **1963**. This mower with a vertical blade has a fan which creates an air cushion under its plastic skirt. The machine is therefore very light to

An advert for the Ransomes, Sims and Head lawn mower that was produced in Ipswich. The idea did not take off until the 1870s, when lawn tennis became popular.

use, even on slopes, and is practical for negotiating obstacles.

A German, Heinz Zipfel, updated the air cushion system, creating the Fremo GMS in 1977. This machine mows however long the grass is, collects the cut grass, is not damaged by damp (and can therefore mow in all weathers), and makes it possible to mow even quite steep slopes, etc. The system has been patented in five countries, including France, Germany and the United States.

Plantophon (1987)

Presented at the Brussels Trade Fair in **1987**, this 'telephone' for plants was invented by a Belgian, **M. Heusquin**. It is shaped like a probe and penetrates into the heart of the plant. When the plant is thirsty, a little red light flashes, accompanied by an audible signal which repeats every five seconds. Once the plant has drunk its fill, the device gives a little bleep and a green light comes on when the desired level of water has been reached.

Secateurs (1815)

Forced into exile by the French Revolution, the **Marquis Bertrand de Moleville**, a former minister of Louis XVI, kept himself busy by

Lawn mower racing has become a popular sport.

Trees and flowers

Bonsai (3rd century BC)

The Chinese started cultivating 'pun-sai' trees in the Qin dynasty (**3rd century BC**). These were almost certainly trees naturally dwarfed by bad weather or soil, which were then replanted in decorated pots by connoisseurs to recreate miniature landscapes.

Bonsai culture became an art during the Tang dynasty (between the 7th and 10th centuries AD). Long the preserve of the nobility, it gradually reached all strata of the population after the beginning of the 17th century.

It was not until the 12th century that bonsai trees began to arouse the interest and then the passion of the Japanese, who then developed the techniques which make miniaturisation possible.

Dahlia (1789)

The first dahlia was sent from Mexico to Madrid in **1789**. It was given its name by the Spanish botanist **Cavanilles** in honour of the Swedish botanist Andreas Dahl, himself a student of Carolus Linnaeus, the Swedish founder of the modern classification of plants.

Orchid (1898)

In **1898** the Frenchman **Noël Bernard** discovered that orchid seeds, in order to germinate and guarantee the first stage of development of the embryo, need to be in contact with a microscopic fungus that lives in symbiosis in the plant's roots. Bernard invented a way to allow the seed to germinate independent of the plant.

In 1922 an American, Doctor Lewis Knudson, developed an environment which allowed germination without the presence of the fungus.

Tulip (1554)

Augier de Busbecq, Austrian ambassador at the court of Soliman the Magnificent, was also an amateur botanist. In **1554** he discovered a

---

FIRST LAWN MOWER CHAMPIONSHIP

The first European lawn mower championship took place in October 1989 on the Saint-Pardoux racetrack near the French town of Limoges. This unique machine sport, created 16 years ago in the UK by Jim Garin, a former rally driver, is a real speed race (without mowing). Some of these high-powered vehicles, equipped with car engines, can reach speeds of up to 90km/h *55mph*.

---

developing a tool which has become almost a symbol for gardeners: the secateurs.

Spade (prehistory)

The first appearance of this digging instrument probably dates back to **prehistoric times**, when humanity moved from the gathering to the agricultural stage.

The low Latin word *becca* or *besca* tells us that the spade was already used by the Romans, who were great horticulturalists and builders of gardens.

Tree replanter (1985)

It is very difficult to transplant an adult tree without damaging it or ruining its chances of settling in its new location. The Hydra-Brute Tree Replanter, an American invention from **Lakeshore Industrial** brought out in **1985**, is very easy to handle and currently has the best performance of any implement of its kind. It does everything – digging up the tree, transporting and replanting it – and it can be operated by one person.

Water grabber (1984)

The water grabber, invented by the nurseryman **Léon Beck** and marketed in **1984**, looks like a grain of salt or a fragment of a grain of rice; but when it is immersed in water it will absorb up to 700 times its volume in a few hours. Using this invention, flowers and plants can water themselves, with a real independent reservoir at their disposal.

The water grabber has had worldwide success and has been marketed in the United States since 1986.

Wheelbarrow (12th century)

The origins of the wheelbarrow are obscure. In Europe one of the oldest representations of a wheelbarrow, used on cathedral building sites, dates from the **12th century**. But the wheelbarrow must already have been in use in Asia, and more specifically in China. Moreover the latter has an astonishing variety of vehicles on the wheelbarrow theme, the common feature of all of them being that, like all other wheelbarrows, they have a single wheel.

Celebrations at the christening of the new tulip Europa. *Despite the Dutch reputation in this field, it was an Austrian who brought the flower to Europe in the 16th century.*

170 AGRICULTURE

flower in Persia and sent seeds and bulbs to Vienna.

A French botanist sent the first tulips to a trial garden in Leyden, Holland, some years later at the reign of the Dutch tulip began.

However, it was not until the 1730s that tulip mania began and fortunes were gained and lost because of the flower as it spread to gardens throughout Europe and then to the rest of the world.

Black tulip (1986)

After its long existence as a legend, the black tulip is now a reality. In 1979 the Dutch horticulturalist **Geert Hageman** put pollen from the 'Wienerwald' variety on the stamen of a 'Queen of the Night', creating the first black tulip. It was not until **1986** that the bulb he thus obtained and raised produced its first flower. The demands of reproduction meant that only three bulbs existed in 1987 and a dozen in 1988. Fields of black tulips are still some way off.

Fruit and vegetables

Apricot (c.330 BC)

The apricot tree came from China with the caravans of the silk route, before becoming established in the Middle East, then gradually spreading to the rest of Europe. History tells us that it was brought to the Graeco-Roman world by Alexander the Great around 330 BC.

It is thought the name comes from the Arabic· al-birqūq, itself derived from the Latin praecoquum, meaning 'early ripener', since the tree is one of the first to flower in spring.

Asparagus (antiquity)

Asparagus seems to have first appeared on the Baltic shore (or in the Mediterranean Basin, according to some). It was greatly appreciated by the ancient Egyptians, then by the Greeks. The Romans began to grow it seriously; however, it remained a luxury for rich gourmets.

It made its way on to our tables during the Renaissance, but did not become widely available until 1875.

Carrot (16th century)

The wild carrot came from Afghanistan long before the time of Christ. The Greeks and Romans did not set much store by it and it was used only for limited medicinal purposes before the **16th century**, when the **Italians** brought it to our attention. Although it was tasty, the carrot of the time had almost nothing in common with the vegetable of today. It was a thin white or yellow root and fairly tough. It took centuries of selection and hybridisation to give it the orange colour it has had since the early 19th century.

Chicory (1850)

In the underground passages of the Brussels Botanical Gardens, where he was Head Gardener, **M. Bréziers** had the idea of forcing a few roots of the chicory used in coffee and then eating the young shoots. The original strain has been extensively hybridised and selected so that today we can enjoy this gently bitter salad vegetable all through the winter.

Clementine (1900)

It was **Father Clement Rodier**, a monk with a passionate interest in agronomy living near Oran in Algeria, who invented the clementine in 1900. He created it by fertilising mandarin orange flowers with pollen from a bitter orange tree.

Granny Smith and Golden Delicious (19th century)

It was Miss **Granny Smith** who, in Australia in **1868**, first grew this green apple flecked with white, with juicy, tart-tasting flesh. As for the famous Golden Delicious, it was born in West Virginia at the end of the **19th century** in the orchards of **Anderson H. Mullins**. By 1914 this apple was already widely known and planted in various parts of the United States.

Grapefruit (1809)

Count Odette Phillippe, a surgeon in Napoleon's army captured at the battle of Trafalgar, was imprisoned by the British in the Bahamas. It was there that he discovered the *Citrus paradisi* or grapefruit, which grew there in abundance. When he was freed two years later, he set himself up as a doctor in Charleston, South Carolina, before moving to Florida, where, in **1809**, he established a citrus fruit plantation using seeds and plants from the Bahamas. Sixty years later, the grapefruit was a major source of revenue for Texas, Arizona and California.

It was not until 1914 that the fruit crossed the Atlantic and arrived in Palestine, where large orchards were planted.

Green grapefruit (1985)

This new fruit obtained in **1985** by Israeli scientists from **Jaffa** is the result of hybridisation between the white grapefruit and the shaddock. It has a sweet taste and was named 'Sweetie' by its inventors. Its skin is a fine spring green with a tinge of yellow.

A MINI-PUMPKIN

This new pumpkin, the size of a melon, is a Belgian invention which has been available since the end of 1989. It was created by Jean-Pierre Jadinon, a director of Promagri, at the request of a canning company – and its employees, exhausted from handling normal pumpkins which can sometimes be over 1m *3ft* in diameter and weigh over 35kg *77lb*. Research and successive selection from more than 150 *cucurbitaceae* seeds from California and New Zealand led to this mini graded vegetable, to be sold henceforth under the name 'Merveille de Tourinnes' (Tourinnes Wonder), after the village to the south-east of Brussels where a famous pumpkin fair is held every August.

Haricot bean (1529)

The haricot bean was imported from America in **1529** by **Piero Valeriano** for Pope Clement VII. It was called *phaseolus*, then *fayol*, finally acquiring the name haricot when it replaced broad beans in the traditional mutton stew or 'haricot of mutton'.

Kiwi fruit (1959)

Chinese gooseberry and Yang Tao are just two of the names given to *Actinidia chinensis*, a plant discovered on the banks of the Yang-Tse River in 1845 and brought to the West at the end of the last century.

In 1906 this prolific creeper arrived in New Zealand where it aroused the interests of the local farmers who were the first in the world to plant orchards and export this new fruit.

The New Zealanders wanted to mark the originality of their product and in 1959 chose to give this fruit the name of the symbolic bird of their country: kiwi.

An autochrome of a Paris market on 21 June 1914 highlights the French love of good, fresh produce, a reputation that lingers to this day.

Lemon (1000 BC)

Some say the lemon tree first appeared in the foothills of the Himalayas, others say it was in the Malayan archipelago. Whatever the case, it was cultivated by the Chinese some 3000 years ago.

The Romans were the first Westerners to introduce it into their gardens. They called the fruit the 'apple of the Mede', in reference to a people who lived in what is now Iran. The fruit was mainly used for medicinal purposes, as an antidote to poisons and venom and as an insect repellent.

It was not until the Crusades that the lemon tree became properly established in the Mediterranean countries, even though the Arabs had already done much to spread it during their conquests.

The lemon was one of the few gifts from the Old to the New World, thanks to Spanish and Portuguese navigators.

One of the lemon's greatest glories was that it made possible the prevention of the terrible scurvy which had been decimating ships' crews at sea. In the mid-18th century **James Lindt**, a Royal Navy surgeon, discovered the remarkable anti-scurvy properties of this fruit.

It was not until 1932, a century and a half later, that the lemon's anti-scurvy properties could be attributed to its high vitamin C content.

Orange (15th century)

For a long time it was believed that oranges were the famous 'golden fruit' of the garden of the Hesperides, the three nymphs of the setting sun, which was later located as being at the foot of the Atlas Mountains. But this was just a legend, since neither the Greeks nor the Romans knew about oranges.

The bitter Seville orange was no doubt brought to the Mediterranean basin by Arab navigators and was rediscovered by the Crusaders in Palestine. But the sweet orange that we enjoy today is a mutation of a fruit which originated in India or China and did not appear in Europe until the beginning of the **15th century**.

Pineapple (1493)

It seems that Christopher Columbus and his companions were the first Europeans ever to taste a pineapple when they landed in Guadeloupe. The Indians of the Caribbean

---

LEEK

Already famous for its world record-breaking plants (18 world records including a 3.5m *11ft 6in* geranium and a chrysanthemum bearing 2400 flowers), the universal liquid fertiliser Algoflash, developed by the French chemist François Santini and the Algochimie laboratories, caused a stir among British vegetable growers in 1989. This 100 percent soluble fertiliser, which supplies nutritional substances directly to the roots when the plant needs them, enabled Gordon Clarke to grow a leek 40cm *16in* in circumference and 1.5m *4ft 11in* in length. A leek of which the Welsh can be justly proud.

---

had long been growing this fruit, which they called Nana, which means 'flavour'. Its exceptional qualities soon made it the Nana Nana, or flavour of flavours, from which its Latin name *Ananas comosus* is derived. However, the English were more struck by its appearance than its taste and called it the pineapple.

In Europe the first attempts to grow pineapples under glass took place in Italy at the beginning of the 17th century, and then in the greenhouses of the Botanical Gardens of Leyden in Holland.

Over the last 20 years, and as a result of fast transportation, the pineapple has become an ordinary product.

Pomato (1978)

This is a hybrid plant, artificially formed in 1978 by the German **Professor Georg Melchers** by combining protoplasts from a potato and a tomato. The fusion of protoplasts from different plant species is a technique destined to have a great future in agriculture.

Potato (1554)

The potato was first introduced into Europe in **1554** by the Spanish conquistador **Pizarro**, who brought it from South America where it had long been cultivated by the Indians of the Andes Mountains in Chile and Peru. A few years later it was introduced to the British Isles by Sir Walter Raleigh (who also brought tobacco back from the New World). Over the next century or so it spread across Europe,

becoming especially important in Ireland and Germany. The French regarded the potato as unfit for human consumption.

Strawberry (1714)

It is to **François Frézier**, an officer of the French Navy and author of a *Treatise on Fireworks*, that we owe the pleasure of eating today's fat juicy strawberries. Frézier had been sent to the South American coast in **1714** to study the fortifications of Chile and Peru. The five plants of *Fragaria chiloensis* (Chilean strawberry) that he brought back to Brittany in France did not bear fruit, but they pollinated other species which had been brought from Virginia, to give the first of our modern strawberries.

Tomato (1596)

Of South American origin, the tomato was brought to Europe in 1596. At first cultivated as a curiosity, it was considered to be a violent poison.

This vegetable-fruit had to wait more than two centuries before its alimentary qualities were recognised. The President of the United States, Thomas Jefferson, cultivated the tomato in his garden but didn't eat the fruit.

It is only in the last hundred years or so that the tomato has become commonplace in Britain.

Watercress (c.1550)

This fast-growing salad vegetable has always grown in ditches and on the banks of streams in countries with a damp climate. But it was not until the middle of the **16th century** that a German, **Nicholas Messinger**, developed the first watercress beds at Erfurt. For several centuries these remained a German speciality.

Williams' pear (1770)

It was in the garden of **Mr Stair**, a schoolmaster at Aldermaston in Berkshire, that the Williams' pear, one of the finest varieties, first appeared in **1770**. Was it the result of deliberate hybridisation or of a mutation in his orchard? Nobody knows, and the inventor of this tasty fruit did not even leave it his name. It was a neighbouring nurseryman, Mr Williams, who bred, marketed and gave his name to the new fruit.

Pollution and 'green' inventions

Rivers and oceans

An automatic warning station (1988)

Two years after the disaster which seriously polluted the Rhine, an automatic warning station, the first link in a chain which is to be set up along the entire length of the river, was opened on **18 November 1988** at Huningue in the Haut-Rhin, France. The station is equipped with a total organic carbon detector, a dissolved hydrocarbon detector, a heavy metal detector, a fluorometer for detecting dye molecules, and a pesticide detector.

The equipment, each element of which is controlled by an independent microprocessor, is completed by a selection–rejection mechanism (the memory bank of the river) and a co-ordinator equipped with a printer as well as a visual display unit. The station also has a tele-data transmission system linked to stations controlling hydraulic structures such as sluices, locks and dams which have to be adjusted in order to limit the effects of pollution.

A clean-up operation on the Thames (1889)

In 1889 the first sewage treatment plant was built on the Thames. The river's 336km *209 miles* were so polluted by the middle of the 19th century, that only eels could survive in it. As a result of the construction of the first plant, which was followed by others, the river became repopulated with many other species of fish. But, in 1945, the population of London had reached 8 million and the Thames was again becoming a dead river. Once more, extensive measures were taken to control pollution and give the river a new lease of life.

Inipol (1989)

Inipol EAP 22 is an oil-absorbing formula developed by **Elf-Aquitaine**'s research teams which speeds up the natural process by which hydrocarbons are broken down in the sea. The originality of this product lies in its positive discrimination in favour of those species of micro-organisms living naturally in the sea which are able to break down hydrocarbons without disrupting the environment. Inipol EAP 22 was chosen by the Environment Protection Agency (USA) and Exxon for use in the summer of 1989 on the polluted coasts of Alaska, with excellent results.

Pleurodeiratest (1989)

The pleurodeira, a primitive salamander, is able to detect micropollution in water that could cause cancer.

FIRST 'GREEN' VAPORETTO

Threatened by pollution and high tides, Venice is going to be equipped with its first environment-friendly vaporetto, the launch used for public transport.

Made from aluminium, and fitted with a non-pollutant electric engine, this new boat is not quite as fast as the traditional vaporetto, but this relative slowness reduces water displacement to a minimum and consequently reduces the shock to the piles and the foundations of the buildings. The innovative design of the keel is also aimed at reducing water displacement. The designers and manufacturers of this new invention are the Italian companies Ansaldo (shipbuilding), Alutekna (aluminium) and Magneti Marelli (electrical appliances).

Engineers practise using Inipol to control a film of oil.

Industrial effluent is discharged from a chemical plant at Hartlepool, Cleveland into the North Sea.

This archaic amphibian, 30cm *12in* in length, is a native of Morocco and the Iberian peninsula. Its aptitude for detecting pollutants contained in water was discovered at the beginning of the 1980s by two scientists, **André Jaylet** and **Robert Siboulet**. However, it is only now that the health authorities in France and other countries including the Netherlands are showing an interest. The pleurodeira is currently being bred by the million in aquariums in Toulouse, France.

A sponge to control oil slicks (1975–87)

At first it looks like an ordinary white powder, but it completely absorbs petroleum on contact, becoming plasticised and forming a sort of solid, rubbery pancake so when the powder is sprinkled on water it can be easily removed once it has been transformed into an oily sponge.

The product, which has the added advantage that it does not harm animal or plant life, has been used in Japan since 1983 to control oil slicks and pollution in the ports. The Japanese are used to seeing these giant sponges saturated with petroleum hydrocarbons being removed by the cleaning squads. But, contrary to popular belief, polynorbornene, which is marketed in Japan under the brand names Fixol and TFN-2, is in fact a French invention.

In **1975 Claude Stein** and **André Marbach**, researchers for the French industrial group **CdF Chimie**, developed the product which was originally intended to be used in the manufacture of a special type of shock absorbent rubber. It proved to be highly absorbent of petroleum products and so it was decided to use it in the fight against pollution. But, for various economic and legal reasons, this use

of polynorbornene was abandoned in Europe, although it proved itself at the time of the *Amoco-Cadiz* disaster in 1978.

However, there are outlets for the sponge in Japan and the United States, where the pollution laws are different, although things are beginning to change in Europe. One of the main areas in which it will be used is in the fight against pyralin pollution, a product used as an electric insulator in transformers, which is non-biodegradable and filters into the ground, polluting cultivated land as it moves along the underground water table.

Protection of the environment

First anti-pollution edict (1382)

In **1382 King Charles VI** of France published an edict that outlawed the emission of foul smelling gases in Paris.

In England in the 18th century, a decree forbad the lighting of fires when parliamentary sessions were taking place at Westminster.

Nearer our own time, in 1967, the Council of Europe first defined atmospheric pollution.

Modern legislation (1864)

The first legislation on atmospheric pollution during the industrial age came into force in the United States on 1 January 1864. Known as the **Alkali Act**, it was a response to complaints from people living in the vicinity of factories using the Leblanc method to produce alkaline carbonate, a substance which had been used since 1823 and which released large quantities of hydrochloric acid into the atmosphere.

Nature conservation (1864)

The modern concept of nature conservation was invented in 1864 by the American diplomat **George Perkins Marsh** (1801–82). In a short work entitled *Man and Nature*, he explained how it was possible to preserve nature from the effects of the human race by using popular organisations to protect it on a national level.

The fight against smog (1952)

On 8 September 1952 London was in the grip of the worst smog on record. Cars drove into each other, aircraft were unable to find runways and pedestrians fell into the Thames. Some 4000 people died of respiratory disorders in the weeks that followed. As a result, the British government decided to introduce measures which formed the legislation known as the **Clean Air Act**.

Within 30 years or so, the number of hours of sunshine in London have more than doubled, and over 150 different species of bird have returned to the capital compared with about 60 at the time of the smog.

BIOPOL: NATURE'S PLASTIC

On 25 April 1990 ICI announced the first commercial application of Biopol. It was the culmination of 15 years of research to find a plastic material that did not depend on fossil fuels for its manufacture and would be fully biodegradable.

Biopol is the trade name for the homopolymer polyhydroxybutyrate (PHB) which was first discovered in 1926 by Lemoigne at the Pasteur Institute in Paris. Some attempts at commercialisation in the 1950s and 1960s failed and ICI came onto the scene in the 1970s following the first oil crisis.

ICI use micro-organisms of the genus *Alcaligenes*, which are widely found in nature and convert sugar or starch quickly and safely by a process of fermentation, to produce a plastic in the form of a white powder. The composition of this powder can be adapted to provide a hard or flexible material – whatever is required – by altering the balance of the raw materials. It is then made into a form that can be used for a wide variety of purposes (the first commercial application was as a shampoo bottle).

Not only can Biopol be produced in a natural way, it is also fully biodegradable. So, once buried in the soil, it will totally degrade to carbon dioxide and water over a period of weeks. In 1991 some 200–300 tonnes have been produced, a figure which is expected to reach the thousands by the mid 1990s.

First ecological movement (1968)

The first ecological movement was founded in 1968 by **Cliff Humphrey**, an American student from the University of Berkeley in California.

Acorns for treating industrial effluent (1989)

KAERI, the South Korean institute for hi-tech energy research, has obtained a patent in the United States (with others to follow soon in France, Japan and Germany) for a new process for the treatment of industrial effluent. It consists of an acid, obtained from acorns, which is capable of separating off the heavy metals contained in the effluent, including uranium. It was two scientists from the institute, Chang-In-Sun and Yun Myong-Hwan, who discovered the de-polluting properties of acornic acid. The new process has proved effective for effluent containing nickel, cadmium, mercury and lead. Approximately 1kg *2.2lb* of acorns should be sufficient to treat 3.5 tonnes of effluent.

Anti-nitrate process (1990)

Etienne Tillié is a French civil engineer working in the petrology and mineralogy laboratory at Nice University and specialising in the analysis of industrial waste. Tillié has developed a technique capable of eliminating nearly all the nitrates and phosphates contained in polluted water, whether it is industrial effluent or sewage. The process, which according to its inventor is 'efficient and economical', could be used in existing sewage purification plants.

Smog remains an especially serious problem in many Eastern bloc countries.

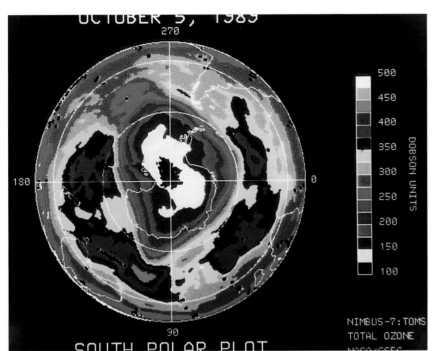

This satellite map shows the severe depletion, or 'hole', in the ozone layer over Antarctica. This is most likely caused by pollution of the atmosphere by chlorofluorocarbons (CFCs) used in aerosols and refrigerants. The most severe depletion so far recorded was in 1987, and each year it is at its peak in October. The pink and purple areas show where the problem is worst.

STILL ON THE AGENDA:
PROTECTING THE OZONE LAYER

The Montreal Protocol, signed in 1987 and designed to protect the ozone layer through the gradual elimination of CFCs (chlorofluorocarbons) and other gases (such as halon, used in extinguishers), was reinforced at the meeting of the 55 signatory countries which took place in June 1990 in London. The setting up of a fund to protect the ozone layer is also under discussion. Running costs for the first three years would amount to $240–60 million.

A layer of ozone, produced by the action of the sun's short ultra-violet rays (0.12 to 0.20μ) on oxygen, surrounds the earth at an altitude of 25km *15½ miles*. Because of its absorbent properties, ozone is able to stop ultra-violet rays with a wavelength of less than 0.20μ from entering the earth's atmosphere. Without this protective layer it would be impossible to survive because of the powerful thermic effect of the part of the solar spectrum below 0.20μ.

There is a considerable amount of evidence which proves that this protective layer is being destroyed. Between 1979 and 1984 it was reduced by 20 percent above the South Pole and continues to be depleted.

The precise causes of this depletion of the ozone layer are not known, but it is certain that chlorofluorocarbons, or CFCs, the gases used in aerosols, refrigerator cooling systems and the manufacture of certain plastics, are a very strong contributory factor. These gases are non-biodegradable and on reaching the upper atmosphere they are destroyed by the ultra-violet rays, giving off chlorine which in turn reacts with the ozone to produce a chloric compound and oxygen.

Until 1987 the annual production of CFCs was 1.1 million tonnes. At the end of the year, leading manufacturers throughout the world met in Montreal to decide on a research programme with a view to discovering a gas which would not harm the ozone layer but which had the same industrial properties as CFCs.

Ozone (O_3), a gaseous element formed from three oxygen atoms, was discovered in 1781 by the Dutch physicist Martinus van Marum, who noticed its smell in air through which electric sparks had passed. In 1840 the German chemist Christian Friedrich Schönbein gave it the name ozone, from the Greek *ozein*, meaning having a smell, and its formula was established by Soret.

Anti-pollution filter (1989)

The modern motorist suffers irritation to the eyes and the mucous membranes from dust and exhaust fumes. To combat the problem, the Swiss company **Incen** launched the Icleen filter in **1989**. Placed in the car's ventilation system, this filter absorbs the toxic particles.

Biodegradable washing powder (1964)

Because standard detergents did not break down naturally, in 1956 a professional organisation in Britain asked manufacturers to develop biodegradable washing powders. In **1964** West Germany was the first country to

---

make the use of washing powders containing biodegradable products compulsory.

An environment-friendly chainsaw (1989)

This piece of equipment has been on the market since **1989**. It was developed by the German company **Stihl**, the second largest chainsaw manufacturer in the world, and is fitted with a catalyst which reduces the amount of exhaust fumes. This is the first time that such a device has been developed for a two-stroke engine.

Environment-friendly refrigerators (1989)

The first refrigerators have been produced which contain half the usual amount of freon gas in their foam insulators. Freon belongs to the chlorofluorocarbon (CFC) family held responsible for the deterioration of the stratospheric ozone layer.

The initiative in the decision to reduce the production and use of CFCs was taken by the Swedish group, **Electrolux**, the current world leaders in the production of household electrical appliances.

ERTS-1 (1972)

The satellite ERTS-1 (Earth Resource Technology Satellite), launched on **23 July 1972** by **NASA**, can be considered the first ecological satellite. Renamed *Landsat 1*, and weighing 930kg *2050lb*, this observer of the earth was set at an altitude of 930km *577 miles* on a circular orbit. It passed over the same point every 18 days and its cameras and infra-red sensors were able to trace the changes and development of different types of pollution: tree diseases, swarms of insects, etc.

ERTS-1 was followed by the launch of a second ERTS in 1973, then by numerous other American, Soviet and French satellites: *Meteor, Priroda* and *Spot*.

HFA 22

Atochem, the only French company producing CFCs, has developed a CFC substitute for aerosols, HFA 22, which is non-flammable and has a very low level of toxicity. Its adverse effect on the ozone layer is 95 percent less than that of CFC-11 and 12 and its contribution to the greenhouse effect is minimal. About a third of the CFCs produced are used in the aerosol industry, except in the United States where aerosols containing CFCs were banned ten years ago. Switzerland followed suit in 1991. The largest Japanese manufacturer of glass, the Asahi Glass Company, has developed two substitutes for freon gas, used in aerosols and the refrigerator industry: HCFC-225ca and HCFC-225. The Japanese have undertaken to reduce their production of freon by 50 percent before 1998.

Incineration by electron torch (1990)

An experimental plant for the high temperature incineration (4000°C *7200°F*) of solid chemical waste using an electron torch, has been constructed at Pont-de-Chaix in France. It is the first of its kind in Europe. The French electricity company **EDF** has collaborated in the construction of the plant which could solve the tricky problem of the destruction of chemical waste. The first tests took place in **May 1990**.

The electron torch, which operates on the basis of a fluid composed of electrically neutral gas molecules, positive ions and negative electrons, was so named in 1928 by the American chemist, Irving Langmuir, winner of the Nobel Prize for Physics in 1932. Looking towards the future, it is hoped that it will one day be possible to use electron torches (at temperatures of several million degrees) to destroy nuclear waste.

The 'Refuse Pyramid' (2005)

This strange construction consisting entirely of rubbish will actually exceed the height of the Pyramid of Cheops (146.6m *480ft*). It is to be built on the Fresh Kills rubbish tip on Staten Island, south of Manhattan in New York, where since 1948 some 100 million tonnes of waste have been dumped. The New York authorities have decided to build a monument from their refuse, a rather special mountain which, at a height of 156m *511ft* by the year **2005**, the estimated date of its completion, will be one of the highest on the east coast of America.

One way of saving scarce resources is to use alternative forms of fuel. This plant in Bridgeport, Connecticut, USA, receives 2500 tonnes of rubbish every day which is dumped into this pit. Cranes transfer the waste to the feed hoppers of three high-temperature furnaces (1400°C 2500°F). Steam raised drives a turbine coupled to a generator which produces 67MW electricity.

The Puente Hills rubbish dump outside Los Angeles is probably the most modern tip in the world. Every day 13000 tonnes of rubbish are compressed, and the gas given off by decomposition is collected and recycled to provide energy.

THE DUSTBINS OF EUROPE: WASTE RECYCLING FOR INDUSTRY

In March 1990 an association of 22 international industrial companies was set up for the recuperation and recycling of used packaging (mainly tin, aluminium, plastics and glass). The association is headed by Jean Gandois, managing director of the French group Péchiney, the world's biggest producer of aluminium cans. This recycling project involves the door-to-door collection of waste material, and the association has run two experimental projects: one in Dunkirk, in France, and another in Sheffield. Among the founder members of the Association Européenne pour la Récupération et le Recyclage (European association for waste recovery and recycling) are Coca-Cola, Cadbury Schweppes, Heineken, Nestlé, l'Oréal, Pepsi-Cola and Péchiney.

A CFC RECLAIMER

The frozen food company Iceland won the top prize in the British Innovation Awards in 1990 with a device that reclaims CFCs from old refrigerators. It is in two parts – a small cylinder to collect the refrigerant at the store and a larger unit to which it is transferred afterwards. It is cheap to produce, safe and easy to use and was developed using existing technology.

Derbyshire County Council's mobile CFC-extracting machine, which is used remove CFCs from discarded refrigerators.

Because of interference with the main supply rivers to the Aral Sea in the Soviet republic of Kazakhstan, the Aral Sea is drying up at an alarming rate.

Engines and fuel

Anti-pollution engine (1988)

This engine with its low pollution 'weak mixture' was developed by the Japanese company **Toyota** and presented at the Geneva Motor Show in **March 1988**. It conforms to the most demanding anti-pollution standards and does not need a catalytic exhaust.

Meanwhile the Dutch company DAF has developed a series of very clean engines for utility vehicles, which they unveiled in **1990**. According to DAF, these will be the most environment-friendly engines ever to come on the market.

Avocet (1989)

While it would be environmentally beneficial to use methanol as a fuel for motor vehicles instead of diesel, it is difficult to do so because of the cost of conversion and because there are ignition difficulties. This is where Avocet comes in.

Avocet is an additive which improves ignition, reduces corrosion and also diminishes pollution. Vehicles run on alcohol with this additive have produced startling results: soot emissions are reduced by about 80 percent, while nitrogen oxide emissions fall by between 50 and 70 percent.

ICI, who launched Avocet in **1989** after seven years' development, have been conducting trials in America, Canada, New Zealand, France and Sweden, with excellent results. It is easy to convert engines to use Avocet and it will be especially useful in reducing the pollution caused by heavy goods vehicles, one of the worst polluters.

Catalytic exhaust (1909)

The need for lead-free petrol has revived interest in an invention that was first patented on **17 April 1909** by **Michel Frenkel** of France: the 'method of deodorising exhaust fumes'. The catalytic exhaust was developed by General Motors in 1974 and has become compulsory in the United States.

In October 1987 Switzerland also made the catalytic exhaust compulsory in an attempt to combat the harmful effects of pollution, in particular the destruction of her forests which have been reduced by 40 percent.

At the end of 1988 the American company Ford produced a new platinum-free catalytic exhaust which complies with the required standards but is much less expensive, and which has been fitted on some models of their cars since 1989. The catalytic exhaust converts the polluting exhaust fumes into harmless substances by means of a series of chemical reactions. In the final stages of these reactions, a precious metal, usually platinum, is used.

Saving the lakes (1989)

Several processes to combat the effects of acid rain are currently being developed or researched. Following ten years of research at the limnology (the science of lakes) laboratories of the **University of Lund**, in Sweden, the Swedes have been dropping briquets of sodium carbonate (washing soda) to the bottom of their lakes to neutralise the acidity. Excellent results have been obtained on Lake Lilla Galtsjön, where the ecosystem has been restored. Two other Swedish lakes were treated in **1989**. The Canadians and the Americans are going to adapt this process for use in their great lakes.

Also in Canada, to combat the acid rain destroying the forests, Doctor L. Hakka of Union Carbide of Canada Ltd's technical centre has developed the Cansolv process, which uses a solvent to remove the sulphur oxide from the fumes of thermal electric power stations, reducing pollution.

Surveillance of the ozone layer (1989)

On **22 March 1989** a research programme was implemented at the University of Wuppertal in West Germany to develop a system for monitoring changes in the ozone layer by satellite. The system, known as CRISTA (a telescope for observing the atmosphere and a cryogenic spectroradiometer), will be on board the German satellite Astrospas, which is due to be launched in 1993.

UBT insulation (1990)

The German group **Bosch-Siemens Hausgeräte** has found a substitute for CFC in the manufacture of polyurethane foam necessary for the insulation of refrigerators and freezers. The first appliances, available since summer **1990**, contain a new insulator called UBT, and a patent is pending.

Environment-friendly diesel (1989)

The German manufacturers **Volkswagen** have developed a new diesel engine for their Golf which is less harmful to the environment. It is a 60hp engine fitted with a turbo-compressor which, by improving fuel combustion, reduces the harmful effect of the

A device for measuring the levels of carbon monoxide (CO) and hydrocarbons emitted from the exhaust of an ordinary car.

exhaust fumes. It is also designed to take an oxidising catalyst.

Diesel engines are currently under scrutiny in Germany where they are suspected of dispersing carcinogenic soot particles into the atmosphere.

Environment-friendly fuel (1980)

Thanks to the diesel multifuel direct injection engine, it is possible to run a car on renewable energy (unrefined vegetable oils) instead of only on a fossil fuel (petrol), supplies of which are becoming exhausted. This engine, which was patented in **1980**, and tested in France in 1984 and in the United States in 1985, was produced by the German company **Elsbett**. After being tried on 200 prototypes throughout the world, it is being fully developed, especially for agricultural engines. In Austria large-scale trials are under way in the province of Styria to produce rapeseed oil as a substitute for gas oil for tractors. In Malaysia, palm tree oil is used. The pollution caused by an engine of this kind is minimal.

Unleaded petrol (1975)

The petrol obtained by refining crude oil is lead free. Chemists decided to add alkyl leads in the 1920s in order to increase the performance of the internal combustion engine. The American company, General Motors, was responsible for the widespread introduction of the process.

However, the exhaust fumes have proved to have an extremely high level of pollution and, in view of the damage they have caused, particularly in the destruction of forests, it was decided to produce lead-free petrol. It has

been on sale in America since **1975** and in Japan since 1977. However, the first unleaded petrol was not available in the UK until January 1986.

Meteorology

Origins

One of the first readings of meteorological observations on record dates back to the Yin Dynasty, c.1300 BC. However, the scientific study of meteorology began in about 340 BC with the publication of Aristotle's *Meteorologica*, which constitutes the first treatise on the atmosphere. In 278 BC Aratus did recommend the use of frogs as a means of forecasting the weather!

From 1855 the French astronomer Urbain Le Verrier (1811–77) was responsible for setting up a network of meteorological data between the various European observatories.

Rain gauge (4th century BC)

This very ancient apparatus was used in India in the **4th century BC**. It was then found around 1440 in Korea.

In the West, the use of the rain gauge became common after 1639, thanks to the work of the Italian Benedetto Castelli.

Thermometer (1593)

The first thermometer was invented in **1593**

by the Italian **Galileo** (1564–1642). It was a gas thermometer which introduced changes in temperature but could not measure them. A few years later, in 1612, the Italian Santorio developed the water thermometer.

The first alcohol thermometers appeared in 1641, in Italy. One of the earliest was made in about 1645 by the Italian enameller Mariani to the specifications of Grand Duke Ferdinand II (1610–70) of Tuscany.

Fahrenheit thermometer (1715)

The German physicist **Daniel Gabriel Fahrenheit** (1686–1736) invented his thermometer in **1715**. He replaced the alcohol with mercury, which has a very low freezing point (−38.8°C *−37.8°F*) and a very high boiling point (357°C *675°F*), and developed a scale of degrees which is named after him. These highly reliable thermometers were soon adopted in England, where he lived, and where the Fahrenheit scale is still used, as it is in the United States and Australia.

Celsius thermometer (1741)

In **1741** the Swedish physicist **Anders Celsius** (1701–44) built a mercury thermometer on which he fixed the freezing point of water at 0 and the boiling point at 100. He divided the space between into a hundred degrees.

The World Conference of Weights and Measures adopted the expression 'degrees Celsius' (represented by the symbol °C) in October 1948. Today, under the name Kelvin (the Kelvin scale takes as its starting point not the freezing point of water but of absolute zero: −273.16°C *−459.69°F*), it is one of the six base units of the international system.

Barometer (1643)

The mercury barometer was the invention of the Italian physicist and geometer **Evangelista Torricelli** (1608–47), a student of Galileo.

Using this apparatus, Torricelli succeeded in demonstrating that air had its own, variable, weight, and that the weight variations (atmospheric pressure) could be measured by studying changes in the height of the mercury column in the tube.

Ship's barometer (18th century)

The first ship's mercury barometers made their appearance during the **18th century** although they were not immediately popular with sailors who preferred the old empirical methods of predicting the weather.

In 1858 an English admiral called Fitzroy had the idea of providing all fishing ports with a barometer.

Anemometer or wind gauge (1644)

The air-speed meter with blades was invented in **1644** by the English mathematician and astronomer **Robert Hooke** (1635–1703). The principle of this system for measuring wind speed was established in 1450 by the Italian Leone Battista Alberti. The pressure anemometer was invented in 1775 by the Irish physicist James Lind, and the windmill type anemometer still used today was perfected in 1846 by another Irishman, the astronomer Thomas R. Robinson.

Admiral Beaufort (1774–1857) devised the scale of wind force which bears his name. By observing the state of the sea it is possible to estimate the strength of the wind. The system can also be used on land too.

Hygrometer (1664)

This apparatus, which makes it possible to measure the amount of moisture in the air, was invented in 1664 by Francesco Folli. It was superseded in 1781 by the hair hygrometer perfected by the Swiss physicist Horace Bénédict de Saussure: here the hair increases in length as the moisture content becomes higher. Later came the condensation hygrometer.

Meteorological map (1686)

The first known meteorological map was drawn in 1686 by the famous British astronomer Edmund Halley (1656–1742) on his return from a voyage to the southern hemisphere. It was he who provided the first explanation of prevailing winds, monsoons and trade winds.

Beaufort scale (1806)

This scale, graded from 0 to 12, which is used to record wind force, was proposed in 1806 by the English admiral Sir Francis Beaufort (1774–1857). Used by all Royal Navy ships from 1834, it makes it possible to standardise the information recorded in ships' log books. The Beaufort scale was adopted by all navies in 1854 and then by international meteorology from 1874. It is still of crucial importance for all navigators.

Weather balloons (1898)

The first weather balloon, designed to explore the atmosphere at high altitude automatically, were sent up in 1898. This was when Léon Teisserenc de Bort (1855–1913), the French meteorologist, launched his first balloons from Trappes and discovered the stratosphere.

Weather radar (1949)

In 1924 the Englishmen E.V. Appleton and M.A.F. Barnett demonstrated the existence of the ionosphere (the area of the atmosphere in which the air is highly ionised), using the reflection of continuous waves.

However, the first programme using radar for weather study was carried out in 1949 in the United States for the Thunderstorm Project, under the direction of M.H. Byers and R.R. Braham.

Weather radar allows scientists to track weather balloons equipped with reflectors, helps the detection of large storm clouds and rain, and enables the internal structure of some cloud masses to be examined.

Sodar (1968/9)

The sodar (sound detection and ranging) is a radar that, using sound waves that are emitted vertically and broadcast back by turbulence caused by changes in temperature, allows the three components of wind to be measured. The principle behind this device was described in 1968/9 by the Americans L.G. McAllister and G.G. Little.

Doppler sodar (1979)

In 1979 the French company Bertin patented the Doppler sodar as a result of research carried out by J.-M. Fage. Sodar was developed in order to improve the safety of air traffic by providing a continuous measurement of wind by means of teledetection. The thermal structure of the atmosphere at high altitudes – its head – is also measured. Wind sheer and the movement of atmospheric pollution can be monitored.

The Doppler effect was described by Christian Doppler, an Austrian mathematician and physicist who lived from 1803 to 1853. The effect concerns changes in wavelength that occur when the source of a vibration moves closer or further away.

Lidar (1976)

Lidar is a colidar (coherent light detection and ranging). The transmitter is a laser and the receiver a telescope supported by a photocell detector. American electrical engineers Louis D. Smullin and G. Fiocco were the first to use the Lidar for meteorological purposes in 1976, in order to detect aerosols at a distance of up to 140km *87 miles*.

The French company Crouzet is working in collaboration with the American company Spectron to develop the Lidar so that it can be incorporated into the control panel of an aeroplane and make it possible for air crews to detect wind sheers.

Anti-hail cannon and radar (1989)

In late 1989 the Franco–Quebec company Carballan International installed the first anti-hail cannon in north America. This cannon will bombard hail clouds with positive ions, causing the destabilisation of the molecules of ice through electrolysis. The hail will be transformed and fall as drizzle or light snow. This cannon is combined with a meteorological radar system perfected by the American firm Sperry. This radar system locates the hail cloud and automatically activates the cannon.

Weather satellite (1960)

The first weather satellite was launched by the United States on 1 April 1960. The *Tiros 1* satellite was built by RCA.

On 24 August 1964 *Nimbus 1* was launched; this satellite produced the first good quality night photographs.

The first geostationary satellite was launched over the Pacific Ocean on 6 December 1966.

Meteosat (1977)

On 23 November 1977 Meteosat, the first European geostationary satellite, was launched in the United States. Initially designed to have

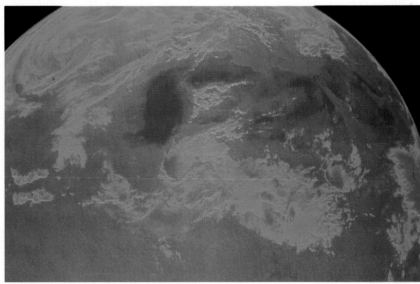

An artificial colour image of thermal flows, ranging from pale blue (cold) to violet (hot).

a lifespan of three years, *Meteosat-1* in fact kept working for eight years, providing meteorologists with the maps and satellite pictures seen daily on our television screens. It has not been in use since the end of 1985 and is at present drifting in orbit, having been replaced by *Meteosat-2* which was brought into service in June 1981.

The radiometer of *Meteosat-2* has scanned the earth's surface more than 110000 times, which is twice as often as any other device of this type installed on board a geostationary satellite.

In 1989 *Meteosat-4* (MOP-1) was launched. It was built by SNIAS, the French aerospace company, under the auspices of the European Space Agency (ESA), after problems with *Meteosat-3*. In 1990 *Meteosat-5* was launched.

Geophysics

Origins (6th century BC)

In the **6th century** BC the Greek scholars **Thales** and **Anaximander** of Miletus were the first to collate the various pieces of information about the properties of the earth. They can justly be considered the founders of geophysics.

In the 4th century BC the Greek geographer Pytheas, born at Massilia (modern Marseilles), put forward the idea that the earth was round. He was a skilled astronomer and mathematician and undertook long voyages to prove his theory. He reached the ancient Kingdom of Thule (probably Iceland or the Faroe Islands) and explored the Germanic coastline of the North Sea. He was also the first to explain the effect of the moon upon the tides.

The brilliant Greek philosopher, Aristotle (384–322 BC), set down the geophysical knowledge of his time in two of his works, *On the Heavens* and *Meteorologica*, which continued to be influential works in the field until the 17th century.

The Greek mathematician, astronomer, geographer and philosopher Eratosthenes (284–192 BC) continued the teachings of Aristotle and was the first to produce a fairly exact calculation of the circumference of the earth.

A subsequently incorrect interpretation of the measurements of Eratosthenes was to have surprising consequences. In the 2nd century AD the Greek astronomer and geographer Claudius Ptolemaeus of Alexandria (Ptolemy) made an erroneous calculation of the circumference of the earth based on the work of one of Eratosthenes' successors, Posidonios of Rhodes (135–50 BC). His calculation, preserved by the Arabs and rediscovered in Europe during the 14th century, provided the cartographic information used by Christopher Columbus when he discovered America by chance. He believed, on the basis of these calculations, that it would be quicker to reach the Far East by heading off in a westerly direction.

Geographical map (575 BC)

There is a strong possibility that it was **Anaximander** of Miletus who compiled the first map of the world in **575** BC.

The Greek astronomer, mathematician

KELVIN VERSUS DARWIN: HOW OLD IS THE EARTH?

The great British physicist William Thompson, Lord Kelvin (1824–1907) is known for his extensive research on electricity and thermodynamics. He invented the absolute temperature scale, or Kelvin scale. However, he stirred up considerable debate when he calculated the age of the earth. Starting with the supposition that it began life as a molten body, which then cooled slowly until it reached its present temperature, Kelvin came to the conclusion the earth must be between 20 and 200 million years old.

At the same time, Charles Darwin (1802–82) presented his theory of evolution. For this theory to hold true, however, and for the species to have had the time to evolve that the theory required, the earth had to be billions of years old.

Darwin was very shaken by Kelvin's conclusions, especially as the latter was very confident that he was correct. Unfortunately the author of *The Origin of Species* died without knowing that he was right, for the earth is in fact 4.7 billion years old, and there had indeed been ample time for life to evolve as he described it, from the very first cells right through to man.

The knowledge we now have about the earth's age is the result not of calculation but of a variety of geological and astrophysical measurements; and we know that it is the natural radioactivity of rocks that has kept our planet at its present temperature for so long.

It was thanks to the misleading maps of Ptolemy that Christopher Columbus found America by mistake. Here he is seen leaving his caravel to take the tender to the shore.

and geographer Ptolemy of Alexandria (AD 90–168), compiled 26 maps which were used until the 16th century.

In the Middle Ages, the only valid maps were the *portulans* and maps compiled on the basis of information supplied by sailors, used for navigation between ports and giving detailed descriptions of coastlines. The earliest of these to be preserved is the Pisan map compiled in Genoa in 1285.

During the Renaissance, sailors developed the science of measurement. In 1569 the Flemish cartographer Gerhard Kremer, known as Mercator (1512–94), produced maps of the whole of the known world on 18 sheets, taking into account the relief, or sphericity, of the earth.

The first maps of European countries appeared around 1530, though the earliest printed map of Britain, based on Ptolemy's outline, was printed in Italy in 1477.

The first map of North America was produced in Boston in 1677 by John Foster.

Volcanoes and earthquakes

Origins (5th century BC)

Empedocles, the Sicilian-born Greek philosopher and naturalist, was responsible for the earliest studies in vulcanology in the **5th century BC**. His observations, which were carried out on site (Mount Etna in Sicily is still the most important active volcano in Europe), led to the realisation that there was molten igneous matter at the centre of the earth.

The origins of the continents

The German meteorologist **Alfred Wegener** had the inspired idea in **1912** that the continents are moving. This came as a result of the realisation that South America fitted into the Gulf of Guinea. Therefore, it appeared that the Atlantic Ocean had been created by the separation of Europe and America. Alfred Wegener's theory of continental drift was not acknowledged by the scientific circles of his time. It was not until the beginning of the 1960s that his idea was considered seriously.

During a Franco–American scientific expedition in the summer of 1974, the rift in the seabed which separated the two continents was observed for the first time.

Wegener's theory is now accepted by most scientists under the name of plate tectonics. They believe that the continents are in fact moving in relation to each other on ten or so plates. Sometimes the plates slide one above the other or collide, as happens in Japan where the collision of three plates off the coast of Tokyo creates incredible tension which produces volcanic eruptions and earthquakes.

Seismograph (132 BC)

The earliest known seismograph was invented in China in **132 BC** by **Zhang Heng**, a royal astronomer in the Han dynasty. The device, which he called a seismoscope, unlike modern seismographs did not record all the features of an earthquake but simply registered the direction of the main tremor.

Zhang Heng's system was improved but

then forgotten about, and it was not until the 18th century that seismometers were invented anew in the West, as a result of the work of the French mechanic (and priest) **Jean de Hautefeuille** and the Italian **Salsano**.

The recording seismograph was perfected at the end of the 19th century and, on 27 April 1894, Charles Howard Darwin's system using a bifilary pendulum enabled him to observe, from Birmingham, the tremors of an earthquake which was just then devastating Greece.

Evaluation of intensity (1857)

In **1857** the British seismologist and engineer **Robert Mallet** was the first to try to evaluate the intensity of earthquakes.

In 1880 Rossi of Italy and Forel of Switzerland developed a scale, graded from one to ten, to evaluate the extent of the damage caused by earthquakes in inhabited areas. In 1902 the scale was extended to 12 degrees by the Italian vulcanologist, Mercalli.

In 1931 Wadati of Japan suggested a scale which was applied to both inhabited and uninhabited regions.

The Richter scale (1935)

The Richter scale, developed in **1935** by the American **Charles Richter** in collaboration with the German-born American geophysicist **Beno Gutenberg**, is based on the conversion of the intensity of seismic waves recorded by seismographs into logarithmic calculations. The scale made it possible for earthquakes to be classified on the basis of energy rather than superficial effects.

The scene of devastation after an earthquake hit the town of Fukui, Japan, in June 1948. Many of the buildings that survived the quake were burned down in the fire which followed.

Forecasting earthquakes (1971)

Since 1971 an American team from the **Lamont Doherty Geological Observatory** has been working with seismologists from the California Institute of Technology, CalTech, to develop methods which will make it possible to forecast earthquakes by establishing the characteristic conditions which precede an earthquake. They were able to predict some small earthquakes in Alaska and, most recently, that at Loma Prieta in California on 17 October 1989. Specialists from CalTech use lasers to observe the two edges of the famous San Andreas Fault in California, an area which is very prone to earthquakes.

In 1988 a researcher from the University of California, Leon Knopoff, and two members of the Russian Academy of Science, Vladimir Keilis-Borok and I.M. Rotwain, announced that they had developed a new method of forecasting involving a complicated mathematical formula based on the seismic activity preceding 14 tremors which occurred in the United States between 1938 and 1984 and which registered more than 6.4 on the Richter scale. The formula was subsequently applied to 20 earthquakes that had occurred in other parts of the world since 1963 with the result that it was possible to 'forecast' 16 of them.

The VAN method (1983)

The VAN method of forecasting earthquakes was developed in **January 1983** by three engineers from the Institute of Physics of the University of Athens, **P. Varostos**, **K. Alexopoulos** and **K. Nomicos**. Although still in the experimental stage, it has produced some interesting results and can be considered as an important step towards an improved method of forecasting earthquakes.

Forecasting volcanic eruptions

As a result of research made public in **1987**, **Professor Bruce Crowe** and his team from the Los Alamos Centre for Volcanic Research in New Mexico consider that it will one day be possible to forecast volcanic eruptions by the analysis of gases and particles given off by the volcano. Basic variations in the amount of gold, platinum and iridium contained in the gases and particles could indicate an imminent eruption. The sudden appearance of precious metals in minute quantities before certain eruptions is a phenomenon which has intrigued vulcanologists for a long time.

A computer for volcanoes (1985)

Professor Kosuke Kamo from the University of Kyoto in Japan developed a computer-linked recording system capable of forecasting volcanic eruptions. The system, which is placed near the crater, can detect very slight changes in volcanic activity. It was this system which, by recording an increase of one millimetre on a crater, made it possible to forecast the eruption of a volcano on the Sakurajima Island on **3 December 1985**.

ERS-1 (1991)

ERS-1 (European Remote Satellite), the first European satellite specifically designed to chart global environmental developments, was launched in 1991. This ESA project, which involves many companies including Matra, Fokker and SAAB, is under the management of the German company Dornier. ERS-1's communications equipment is made up of four main elements: synthetic aperture radar (SAR), a wind diffusion meter, a radar altimeter and an infra-red radiometer. This equipment will enable ERS-1 to maintain a constant surveillance of the oceans, to localise pack-ice and follow the development of icebergs, to draw up a complete map of shallow water sand banks and to detect shoals of fish. It will also enable scientists to learn more about the oceans, as well as bringing further advances in climatology and weather forecasting. Its first customer is NASA. ERS-1 will be sent by an *Ariane-4* rocket into quasi-polar orbit at an altitude of 785km *488 miles*. Its successor, ERS-2, is planned for 1994.

Oceanography

First oceanic exploration (1872)

On **21 December 1872** the British schooner *Challenger*, the first oceanography ship in history, set sail. The *Challenger* was not to return until 1874, having set up 362 stations in all the seas of the globe. This schooner, weighing 2306 tonnes, had been chartered by the members of the Royal Society to study everything to do with the sea, following a purely chance discovery: in 1860 the transatlantic telegraph cable, laid two years previously, had been brought up from a depth of

A lava flow on Réunion, an island situated between Madagascar and Mauritius. There are over 1300 active volcanoes in the world today.

1800m *5900ft* to be repaired. The scientists and technicians on board were greatly surprised to find it covered with strange forms of plant and animal life, never seen before. It was during the course of *Challenger's* 1872–4 voyage that polymetallic nodules were first discovered.

Underwater exploration

Diving equipment

The diving bell (4th century BC)

The diving bell, which already existed in ancient times, was described in detail by Aristotle (384–322 BC). There is no trace of it during the Middle Ages, but it reappears in Italy and Spain during the 16th century. In 1538, to the amazement of several thousand onlookers, including Charles V, two Greeks went to the bottom of the River Tagus in Toledo, Spain, and resurfaced without getting wet and without their lamp being blown out.

In 1552 Venetian fishermen carried out similar experiments in the Adriatic in the presence of the doge and senators. About the same time, the Venetians also invented a 'diver's hood' known as the bagpipes.

Halley's bell (1721)

In 1721 the British scientist and astronomer Edmund Halley developed the first diving bell really worthy of the name. It was perfected in 1786 by the English civil engineer, John Smeaton (1724–92).

The diving barrel (1721)

The progression from the diving bell to the early versions of the diving suit happened almost imperceptibly, so that it is impossible to give a precise indication of the origins of the first equipment which allowed the diver freedom of movement. However, it is generally thought that in 1721 John Lethbridge designed a piece of equipment shaped like a barrel with two holes for the arms and a glass peephole so that the diver could see underwater. The equipment was not particularly practical as the diver was forced to lie on his stomach and to return repeatedly to the surface in order to breathe.

A basic diving suit (1796)

The first diving suit in the true sense of the word was invented in 1796 by the German Klingert from Breslau (now Wroclaw in Poland). It consisted of a domed cylinder made of thick tinplate which completely covered the head and torso of the diver, leaving his arms free. A short-sleeved bodice and a pair of leather trunks protected his limbs from the water pressure, and the whole thing was completely watertight. Two glass-covered holes at eye-level enabled the diver to see. A tube, one end of which was above the surface, was fitted to a hole level with the diver's nose, while a second tube, placed next to it, was intended to evacuate exhaled air. Two lead weights were attached to the diver's waist to provide ballast.

Diving suit with air pump (1829)

The first really effective diving equipment was invented in 1829 by the Englishman Augustus Siebe, who was commissioned to supply the French Navy until 1857.

Diving suit with automatic air regulator (1865)

This piece of equipment, which played an essential part in the development of the diving suit, was the result of collaboration between a mining engineer, Benoît Rouquayrol, and a ship's lieutenant, Auguste Denayrousse, in 1865. The air regulator fulfilled the function of an artificial lung in the sense that the diver's lungs actually regulated the intake of air by acting directly on a distribution valve. This forerunner of the air 'bottle' was developed in 1936 by the French naval officer and inventor, Yves Le Prieur. Rouquayrol and Denayrousse were also responsible for inventing what can be considered the forerunner of the diving mask and breathing tube in about 1870. The mask was further developed by another naval officer, de Corlieu, who also invented flippers.

The aqualung (1867)

This version of the diving suit was presented at the Paris Universal Exhibition in 1867 by the New York Underwater Company. It consisted of a metal helmet and waterproof suit, but the diver also carried a tank of air on his back. The air was compressed at 17 atmospheres, and was enough to last one man for three hours at a depth of 20m *65ft*.

Air bottle (1936)

In 1936 the French inventor Yves Le Prieur developed equipment which consisted of a bottle filled with air compressed at 150kg/cm² *2134lb per sq in* and a pressure-reducing valve linked to the bottle which distributed air at a suitable pressure to a waterproof mask covering the face.

An early salvage operation from around 1750 using Halley's bell.

Cousteau aqualung (1943)

The final stage was reached in **1943** with the aqualung developed by the French underwater explorer and engineer **Jacques-Yves Cousteau**, in collaboration with E. Gagnan. The aqualung had a pressure-reducing valve invented by Gagnan during the war to enable cars to run on gas, and was the first modern version of the aqualung as we know it.

Bathyscaphe (1948)

This diving apparatus was invented and tried out in **1948** by the Swiss physicist **Auguste Piccard** (1884–1962). The first bathyscaphe descended, without a passenger, off the coast of Dakar, to a depth of 138m *453ft*. The American model *Trieste*, built by Professor Piccard in 1953, holds the diving record. On 23 January 1960 it reached a depth of 10 916m *35 815ft* in the deepest part of any ocean in the world, in the Marianas Trench near Guam in the Pacific.

The *Nautilus* (1985)

The *Nautilus*, weighing only 18 tonnes and able to carry three men, was developed in **1985** by **IFREMER**, the French institute for oceanic research. It consists of a titanium sphere, 2m *6½ft* in diameter and 15cm *6in* thick, and is equipped with remote handling equipment in the form of two carbon fibre arms.

It proved particularly efficient during the exploration of the wreck of the *Titanic* during the summer of 1987. During an 18-month mission in the Atlantic and the Pacific, from Martinique to Japan via Hawaii and New Caledonia, the *Nautilus* made 198 dives, taking about 150 000 pictures of the ocean floor.

Shinkai 6500 (1989)

The Shinkai 6500 is the new Japanese oceanographic research submarine which is capable of descending to 6500 metres *21 320ft*, a depth which no other submarine has reached. Constructed by **Mitsubishi Heavy Industries Ltd**, the Shinkai 6500 carries three people and can explore 98 percent of the seabed, compared with 97 percent for the *Nautilus*.

Robot diver (1986)

Jason Jnr was the name given to the robot used in America in **1986** by the **Woods Hole Oceanographic Institute** in the exploration of the seabed and in particular of the wreck of the *Titanic*. Attached by a cable to the submarine *Alvin* at a depth of 3800m *12 464ft*, *Jason Jnr* was lowered to the wreck which lay at a depth of 4000m *13 120ft*.

The Jason project has been fully operational since 1988. It consists of two interconnected remote-controlled vehicles, equipped with cameras and a control arm. The two robots, controlled from a ship on the surface, can reach a depth of 6000m *19 680ft*.

Submarine helicopter (1986)

The first submarine helicopter, known as *Deep Rover*, was constructed in **1986** by the Californian firm **Deep Ocean Engineering Company**. *Deep Rover* is a completely independent unit which can take a diver to a depth of 1000m *3280ft* for a period of up to eight hours. Its main advantage is that the occupant breathes air at normal atmospheric pressure which eliminates the need for decompression stages. From behind the panoramic window

of his cabin, the pilot controls the movement of two remote controlled arms which can perform such tasks as welding, bolting, sawing, etc. It is designed to carry out inspection and repair work on pipelines and oil rigs.

Scubaphone (1986)

In **1986** a longstanding dream came true for **Thomas Murdoch**, **Steen Saloman** and **Bent Larsen**, the founders of Orcatron Manufacturing in Vancouver, Canada. They developed the Scubaphone, a radio system which makes it possible for divers to communicate clearly with each other underwater at a distance of up to 1200m *3936ft*, or with the surface at a depth of up to 80m *262ft*. The system is incorporated into a special helmet containing batteries, with a microphone fitted into the mask. Microelectronic circuits eliminate distortion caused by variations in temperature and pressure and filter any radio interference. The signal is converted into an acoustic wave and then reconverted on reception.

Mir-1 and Mir-2 (1987)

The Soviets began testing their first two research submarines in the Atlantic at the end of **1987**. Mir-1 and Mir-2, capable of operating at a depth of more than 6000m *19 680ft*, were constructed by the Finnish shipyards, Rauma-Repola under the scientific and technical supervision of the Russian Academy of Sciences. They have several advantages over foreign submarines of the same type. They have a greater travelling speed and operating range, a large energy reserve, the ability to change depth without discharging ballast, two manipulator arms and underwater

DeepStar 4000, a manned research submersible, can reach depths of 1200m 4000ft. Here, it is on the seabed near Cozumel, off the coast of Mexico.

drilling equipment. Both the Mir-1 and Mir-2 carry a crew of three people and have reached a depth of 6170m *20237ft* and 6120m *20073ft* respectively.

Aquarius (1987)

At the end of **1987** a technically highly advanced underwater station known as Aquarius was brought into service for an unspecified period. It is located on the floor of the Caribbean, off the coast of St Croix in the Virgin Islands. The station consists of three compartments and can hold up to six people. It is 13m *42½ft* long by 4m *13ft* wide and is 5m *16ft* high. It replaces the Hydrolab station which provided a base for 200 missions between 1966 and 1985. The missions, carried out under the auspices of the American Administration for Oceans and the Atmosphere, were concerned with ichthyology (the study of fish), oceanography and underwater engineering.

A WORLD FIRST:
THE ACCLIMATISATION OF A CORAL REEF

The Oceanographic Museum of Monaco has succeeded in acclimatising a living coral reef from the Red Sea for the first time in the world. The methods used are unique in that the coral, the molluscs and the fish live in a closed system without it being necessary to feed them or to treat the water. The aquarium is thus an independent ecosystem.

Professor Jean Jaubert of the biology and marine ecology laboratory at the University of Nice, in France, has perfected the *microcéan* process, based on the combined action of various organisms and micro-organisms introduced into a layer of sand at the bottom of the aquarium. The first experiments have given conclusive results. The coral has grown and reproduced and the fish even lay their eggs on it.

For Professor Jaubert, the world's coral reefs – which cover 200 million km² *77 million sq miles* – represent an exceptional biological heritage, and their importance is comparable to that of the Amazonian forests, for they regulate the carbon dioxide content of the atmosphere and are instrumental in the temperature control of the planet. The most famous area of coral, the Great Barrier Reef of Australia, is currently threatened by pollution from the land. It is thought that phosphates used by farmers are being washed out to sea and killing the coral.

The picture on the left shows a healthy coral reef, while that on the right is of damaged coral. This is an increasing problem in some parts of the Great Barrier Reef off the coast of Australia where chemicals used by farmers find their way into streams and eventually to the coast, thus causing destruction to one of the world's natural wonders.

Language and literature

Writing

The invention of writing seemed so extraordinary that more than one civilisation claimed it came from their gods. Today, some experts date back the origins of writing to the signs painted or engraved by our distant ancestor *Homo sapiens* some 40 000 years ago.

Cuneiform (4th millennium BC)

Originally semi-pictographic, cuneiform is the most ancient writing system documented. It was developed by the Sumerians in the **4th** and **3rd** millennia BC. The term cuneiform refers to the extremely angular aspect of the signs. A young teacher from Göttingen in Germany, **Georg Friedrich Grotenfend** (1775–1853) was the first person, in 1802, to present a translation of cuneiform. Soon afterwards **Henry Creswicke Rawlinson** (1810–95), a British major working for the East India Company, also solved the enigma.

Hieroglyphics (3rd millennium BC)

The appearance of hieroglyphics, the most ancient and characteristic form of Egyptian writing, coincided with the unification of Egypt: around 3000 BC. Their use was maintained until the 3rd century AD.

Hieroglyphics are picture symbols; hieratic writing is a cursive form of hieroglyphics that was used by the priests until the 5th century AD. Demotic writing also came from the same source and gave seven of its letters to the Coptic alphabet, which was used in Egypt after its conquest by the Arabs in 641.

In 1822 the French Egyptologist **J. F. Champollion** (1790–1832) deciphered the hieroglyphic and demotic characters inscribed on the Rosetta stone, a basalt slab dating from the reign of Ptolemy V (196 BC).

Ideograms (3rd millennium BC)

Chinese writing is said to have been invented by the country's emperors in the **3rd millennium BC**. The most ancient documents discovered date from between the 14th and 12th century BC. Korea, Japan and Vietnam later adopted aspects of the language. Chinese is the only ancient language still in use, and it often forms the only link between the billion Chinese who speak many different dialects.

The alphabet (2nd millennium BC)

These abstract signs representing language and thought date back to the second half of the **2nd millennium BC**. Discoveries made in Râs Shamrah in the Middle East, confirm the theory that it was the **Phoenicians** who invented the alphabet during this period.

Comprising 22 signs, the Phoenician alphabet is the root of all Western alphabets.

Greek alphabet (c.1000 BC)

The Greeks borrowed their alphabet from the Phoenicians and adapted it to their language around 1000 BC. However, the fundamental innovation of the Greek alphabet was the introduction and rigorous notation of vowels. It is the first two letters in the Greek alphabet, *alpha* and *beta*, that are the root of the word alphabet.

Latin alphabet (c.600 BC)

The earliest evidence of Latin writing we have dates back to the **7th** and **6th centuries** BC. The Latin alphabet derived originally from the Greek and was passed on by the Etruscans. The Roman Empire was to impose this alphabet on the whole of the Western world. A century before Christ, the Latin alphabet comprised 21 letters to which y and z were added from the Ionian alphabet. In the Middle Ages j, u, and w were introduced, to give us the alphabet we use today.

Arabic alphabet (512)

The first proven inscription in Arabic dates back to AD 512.

This language, which had Semitic origins and is the sister of Hebrew, is also related to Phoenician writing. The alphabet comprises 28 letters, all consonants, three of which serve as long vowels as well as diphthongs.

Cyrillic alphabet (862)

It was a theologian and missionary of Greek origin, **Saint Cyril** (c. AD 827–69), nicknamed the philosopher, who in 862 invented the Cyrillic alphabet for the purpose of translating the Bible for Slavic peoples to whom he wished to preach the Gospel.

This Glagolitic alphabet (from *glagolu*, meaning word in old Church Slavic) was modified towards the beginning of the 10th century through the introduction of 24 Greek letters. The present Russian alphabet derives from it.

The religious schism which occurred at the beginning of the 9th century gradually split

Writing aids and materials

Papyrus (c.3000 BC)

The **Egyptians** are usually credited with the invention of papyrus around **3000 BC**. The stem of a reed cultivated in the Nile Valley constituted the raw material.

Parchment (2nd century BC)

It was, no doubt, the commercial and cultural rivalry between the Pharaoh Ptolemy and the King of Pergamum in Asia Minor, which, between **197** and **156 BC**, brought about the invention of parchment. The Pharaoh, taking umbrage at the growing reputation of Pergamum as a cultural centre, must have stopped providing it with papyrus, thus obliging the scribes of Pergamum to invent a new material. Parchment is made from the skin of sheep, goat or calf (vellum).

Paper (2nd century BC)

The earliest example of paper was discovered in 1965 in a tomb excavated by archaeologists in the Xian region of China. Analysis has shown that this paper had been made from hemp fibres mixed with a small quantity of linen during the Han dynasty in the **2nd century BC**. However, it was not until the reign of Emperor Hedi (AD 88–106) that paper suitable for writing purposes began to be used. The inventor of this was Cai Lun, one of the Emperor's eunuchs who developed an inexpensive method using bark from trees, linen scraps, old rags and disused fishing nets.

The techniques rapidly improved and paper reached neighbouring countries first (Vietnam, Korea and Japan), and then Arab countries in the 8th century. It was the Arabs who introduced paper to Europe when they brought it to Spain.

The Silos missal, from near Burgos in Spain,

A page from The Sutra of the Ten Kings of the World, *the Shi Wáng Jing Tú, discovered by Mark Stein at Dun Huang in China.*

the Slavic world into two alphabetic areas: Russians, Ukrainians, Bulgars and Serbs adopted the Cyrillic alphabet along with Greek Orthodoxy; the Poles, Czechs, Slovaks, Slovenes and Croatians adopted the Latin alphabet and Roman Catholicism.

Sign language (1620)

The first sign language alphabet was compiled in **1620** by **J. P. Bonnet**. He was a private tutor at the Spanish Court where, at that time, there were many deaf people.

Braille (1829)

In **1829 Louis Braille** (1809–52), a professor at the French Institute for the Blind, published a writing system based on raised dots. Braille had been accidentally blinded at the age of three by his father's tools.

Raised letters for the blind had been proposed by another Frenchman, Valentin Hany, some years earlier, but Braille's system of six dots was easier to read with the fingertips.

This is a modern papyrus, but the art of making it was discovered long ago by the Egyptians.

is the oldest manuscript on European paper. It dates back to the beginning of the 11th century.

Very long paper (1799)

On **18 January 1799** Nicholas Robert, employed in Paris at the bookshop and printers François Didot, obtained a patent 'for the manufacture of an extraordinary paper, measuring between 12 and 15m *39ft* and *49ft* long, without the need for any workman and by purely mechanical means'. This invention was improved by an Englishman, Bryan Donkin, in 1803. It enabled the paper mill to free itself from the traditional method of manufacturing paper – sheet by sheet in a tank.

Digital paper (1989)

Digital paper, sometimes called optical paper, is intended for use in data processing. Unlike traditional paper, it is composed of four layers of materials placed one on top of the other, including polyester which is fine yet strong.

The first sheet of digital paper was manufactured in **1989** by the British company **Image Data**, a subsidiary of ICI.

Pencil (16th century)

In **1564** the discovery of graphite in Cumbria led to the invention of lead pencils. In the 18th century the Cumbrian graphite mines had become a royal monopoly, the exploitation of which was subject to many rules since graphite was also used in cannon foundries. Each workman was searched upon leaving the works and theft was a capital offence punishable by hanging.

The interruption of relations between Britain and France in 1792 led the French engineer Jacques Nicolas Conté to invent graphite and clay pencils covered in cedar wood. Demand crossed international borders and his pencils were soon to reach all parts of the world.

Propelling pencil (1915)

The first automatic propelling pencil, called the Ever-Sharp Pencil, was invented in **1915** by the Japanese **Rokuji Hayakawa**, founder in 1912 of a company to which the propelling pencil gave its name. The Sharp Corporation has since broadened its activities, particularly in electronics.

Rubber (18th century)

Made from a rubber base that erases pen or pencil marks, the rubber is believed to have been invented in the mid-**18th century** by a Portuguese physicist named **Magalhaens**, or Magellan (1722–90), who perfected numerous instruments for use in physics and astronomy. A rubber was mentioned for the first time in 1770 by the British chemist J. Priestley. Today, plastic and synthetic rubber are commonly used to manufacture erasers.

Ink (2500 BC)

It was the Chinese who invented ink in **2500 BC**. It was made with smoke, glue and aromatic substances.

Evidence has been found in Egyptian hypogea of papyrus covered in black or red ink applied with a reed and even a quill pen.

Paper-making in Nepal: the fibres are left to dry in the sun.

The fibres are then moistened and reduced to paper pulp – the work of children.

TYPEWRITERS			
Inventor	Date	Country	Characteristics
William Petty	1660	UK	Manual system with two pens. This is the forerunner of the typewriter.
Henry Hill	1714	UK	Queen Anne granted a patent for this machine which was never built.
Pelegrino Turri	1808	Italy	Earliest example of typewriting, although the machine has not survived.

Xavier Progin	1833	France	First modern circular machine with bars bearing the characters.
Alexander Bain	1841	UK	The familiar inked ribbon was devised.
Malling Hansen	1870	Denmark	First typewriter marketed.
Christopher Latham Sholes	c.1870	USA	The 'literary piano', prototype of a machine sold to Remington which was marketed as from 1874 under the name Remington Model 1.
George C. Blickensderfer	1889	USA	First portable typewriter in a case: the Blick.
Dr T. Cahill	1901	USA	First electric machine. The company went bankrupt after having built 40 examples at a cost of $3925!
R. G. Thomson	1933	USA	Developed the Electromatic, launched by IBM in 1933.
IBM	1965	USA	Launched the first electronic typewriter with a memory (magnetic tape), the 72BM.
Rank Xerox	1972	USA	The first electronic typewriter with a live memory and with a daisy wheel invented by Dr Andrew Gabor.
Matsushita	1984	Japan	First typewriter without keys. The Panaword keyboard is a sensitive sheet. The user writes his message by hand, on a screen.
Dr Andrew Gabor	1989	USA	At the Xerox research centre at Palo Alto (PARC) he developed an entirely silent machine, using a revolutionary method of printing. Xerox Piano came on the market in 1990.

Clean ink (1985)

In **1985** the American **Rodger L. Gamblin** patented an ink which does not run and which does not soil readers' fingers. Its main use has been in printing newspapers.

Fountain pen (1884)

Nobody knows exactly how far back the revolutionary idea of adding an ink reservoir to a quill pen goes. In her *Memoirs*, Catherine the Great of Russia noted that she used an 'endless quill' in 1748. Was she referring to one of the first pens?

Between 1880 and 1900, fountain pen inventions proliferated; more than 400 patents were registered.

The inventor of the first proper fountain pen was the American **Lewis E. Waterman**, an insurance broker, who had had enough of almost losing contracts due to malfunctioning pens. He threw himself into the task of solving the problem of ink flow and, on **12 February 1884**, obtained the first patent for what was to become the Waterman Regular.

The ink cartridge was invented by M. Perrand, director of Jif-Waterman, in 1927 and patented in 1935.

Ballpoint pen (1938)

The ballpoint pen was invented in **1938** by **Laszlo Biro** (1899–1985), a Hungarian journalist. During a visit to the print shop of the magazine for which he wrote, Biro was impressed by the advantages of quick-drying ink. He proceeded to make a prototype of a pen based on the same principle.

To escape the Nazi threat, he settled in Argentina in 1940 and there developed his invention. He patented it on 10 June 1943, and his pens were sold in Buenos Aires from 1945. They were also adopted by the RAF in 1944 to resolve the problems pilots faced, flying at high altitudes.

Bic (1953)

In **1953** a French baron, **Bich**, developed an industrial process for manufacturing ballpoint pens that dramatically lowered the cost of production. The Bic was born, and each year we buy three billion of them.

Erasable ballpoint pen (1979)

It was the American firm **Gillette** which, in **1979**, launched the first erasable ballpoint pen, the Eraser Mate. One result of this product was that banks in the United States cautioned their depositors against using the pen to write cheques.

Felt-tipped pen (1963)

The Japanese firm **Pentel** were the first to develop a felt pen with an acrylic tip. It was invented and marketed in **1963**.

Pentel also invented the first felt-tipped ballpoint pen in 1973, the Ball Pentel; and in 1981 they launched the first ceramic nib: the Ceramicron.

Anti-fraud felt-tip pen (1985)

The French company **Reynolds** has, since **1985**, sold a felt-tip (and ballpoint) anti-fraud pen which contains unerasable security ink. This pen was designed by Reynolds at the request of the banks to make the falsification of cheques more difficult.

Shorthand (antiquity)

The invention of shorthand goes back to ancient times. The Greek Xenophon (c.430–355 BC) could record his conversations with Socrates thanks to his semiology (writing by symbols). In Rome Marcus Tullius Tiro developed one of the first systems for abridged writing in order to take down Cicero's speeches.

Use of shorthand disappeared subsequently only to re-emerge in the 17th century. The initiative came from England, where in 1602 J. Willis wrote a treatise on shorthand.

Various methods have since been introduced. Of these, the most famous are those by Isaac Pitman (1837) and John Robert Gregg (1888).

Punctuation (2nd century BC)

The invention of punctuation is due to **Aristophanes** of Byzantium (257–180 BC). The Greek grammarian directed the famous Library in Alexandria and developed a system comprising three signs corresponding to our full stop, semi-colon and colon. It wasn't until the 16th century, however, with the invention of printing, that its usage was really respected. However, the rules of punctuation remained highly unreliable until the middle of the 19th century.

Printing

Origins (868)

Printing was already a widespread practice in China under the Tang dynasty (618–907):

A four-colour web offset machine for printing magazines. At this stage the magazine has been printed and the web is cut into two prior to going to be folded.

books on magic, scholastic manuals and so on were produced. The discovery in the Dunhuang caves of a copy of the *Diamond Sutra* printed in **868** gives us the name of the printer, **Wang Zhe**.

Chinese printing prospered under the Sung dynasty (960–1279), and in the year 1000 an important Buddhist Sutra was published. In 1041 the Chinese Bi Sheng made mobile characters out of fired clay. The casting of metal characters was developed mostly in Korea around 1392.

Printing (c.1447)

Around **1447** the German printer **Johanne Gensfleisch** called **Gutenberg** (c.1398–1468) developed, along with his associates, the technique of moveable characters. In addition, he perfected the material necessary for the quality and conservation of characters: an alloy of lead, antimony and tin.

Around 1455 in Mainz, Gutenberg printed the *Biblia sacra latina*, known as the 42-line-per-page Bible. It was the first Latin edition of the Bible printed in moveable characters. Gutenberg's business partner, Johann Fust, took him to court for repayment of a loan advanced earlier, gained possession of the moveable type characters, and took all the Bible's profits. However, Gutenberg was able to start up a new printing business by 1465. In 1477 William Caxton (c.1422–91) set up the first printing press in England.

Improvement of the printing press

Around 1800 Lord Stanhope got rid of wood completely in presses and used metal in-

stead. He multiplied newspaper productivity tenfold, reaching 3000 sheets per day.

The first printing press run by a steam machine was developed by the German F. Koenig in 1812. Later, Koenig, in association with A. Bauer, constructed the first cylinder press, which was followed by many others. In London, a single machine was able to print overnight the 4000 copies of the London edition of *The Times*.

Rotary press (1845)

The first rotary press was patented by the American **Richard Hoe** in **1845** in the United States. It was first put into operation the following year.

Xylography

This is one of the oldest and simplest methods of printing an illustration using a block of wood. Combined with typography, it led to the production of beautiful illustrated books at the end of the Middle Ages (14th to 15th centuries).

Intaglio (1450)

This process uses engraved or etched surfaces to hold the ink. The first method was copper-plate engraving, developed in **1450**.

Engraving with burin on a copper plate was followed, at the beginning of the 16th century, by the use of aqua fortis (the old name for nitric acid). Aqua fortis produces depressed lines in the plate at points where the protective varnish has been scraped away.

Lithography (1796)

In **1796** the German typographer **Alois Senefelder** (1771–1834) invented lithography, a method of printing by transfer. He realised that a drawing done with a soft-lead pencil on limestone (the word lithography comes from the Greek *lithos* meaning stone) is water-resistant. However, the unmarked stone absorbs water. If a coat of greasy ink is spread over the surface of the stone, it will not stick to the wet spots, only to the greased areas. The stone has therefore only to be placed in a press and it reproduces the initial drawings.

Senefelder rapidly improved his method. Instead of water, he used a solution of gum-arabic and nitric acid, which is completely impervious to printer's ink.

Photogravure (1822)

We owe the invention of photogravure to **Nicéphore Niepce** around **1822**, who went on to invent photography. In fact, his invention first gave rise to a printing form (engraved copper plate) capable of producing existing images by means of a press. Replacing man-driven tools by light, photogravure contributed to the growth of typography and gave rise to heliogravure and offset printing.

Heliogravure (1875)

The heliogravure printing process was invented by the Austrian **Karl Klietsch** in **1875**.

An industrial intaglio process, heliogravure became widely used in the printing of magazines and catalogues.

Offset (1904)

Invented by the American lithographer **W. Rubel** in 1904, offset came out of the lithographic process he perfected. The word offset covers the same transfer technique (direct apposition) as lithography. Offset is not done on stone but on a sheet of zinc.

Publishing

Book publishing

Genuine publishing houses already existed in ancient Greek and Roman times. Athens and Rome boasted printed works of which several hundred copies were published.

It was, of course, only with the invention of the industrial print shop that publishing really took off, and the bookshop came soon after. The latter was born in London with the bookstore of Wynkyn de Worde, successor to Caxton, and publisher of the first book to be produced in English in England in 1495.

But it was not until the late 16th century that bookshops began to specialise in selling books from one field or another, and it was only then that publishers charged them with the task of distributing their products.

Book (2nd millennium BC)

Although the book first appeared in China in the **2nd millennium BC**, it was only between the 2nd and 4th centuries that it appeared in the West in the form we know. During this period, it went from being the volume (a scroll of papyrus or parchment), which was not very manageable, to the more portable codex (a volume of manuscripts where sheets are inserted and folded together).

Cookery book (AD 62)

The cookery book dates back to the famous treatise *De re coquinaria* published by the Roman gastronome **Apicius** in AD 62. It describes the feasts of the Emperor Claudius I (10 BC–AD 54) and his successive wives, Messalina and Agrippina.

Paperback (1935)

Penguin produced the first mass-market books in **1935** with the introduction of the paperback. Priced at just 6d (2½p) they were within the price range of large numbers of people who might not before have considered buying books.

Library (1700 BC)

The first libraries appeared in Chaldea in **1700 BC**, their 'books' were baked clay tablets. In 540 BC Pisistratus endowed Athens with the first public library. The British Library has over 16 million volumes in all.

Dictionary (600 BC)

The oldest dictionary to have been found dates back to **600 BC**. It comes from Mesopotamia and is written in Akkadian, the language of the Assyrians and the Babylonians. In China, the Hou Chin dictionary did not appear until 150 BC.

In 1480 the English printer **William Caxton** published the first bilingual English–French dictionary for tourists. It had 36 pages.

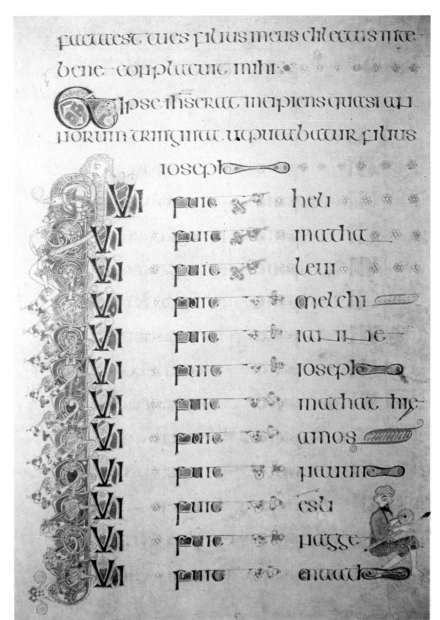

An extract from The Book of Kells, *which has been held in the library of Trinity College, Dublin, since the mid 17th century. This extract shows the genealogy of Christ.*

In 290 BC King Ptolemy founded a library in Alexandria which was to become one of the most important intellectual centres of the classical period. Egypt has decided to revive this tradition by building an ultra-modern library devoted to antiquity and the origins of Christianity and Islam. Designed by a Norwegian firm, it should be completed by 1995.

TYPESETTING MACHINES

Type	Date	Inventor	Country	Characteristics
Machine with moveable characters	1041	Bi Sheng	China	First moveable characters made of clay.
Machine with metal characters	1403		Korea	Some 30 years later, the introduction of a phonetic alphabet in Korea was to make the characters easier to manipulate.
First European machine	c.1447	Gutenberg	Germany	He invented a mould for the casting of metal characters representing the letters of the alphabet. Printed by moveable type.
Linotype	1886	Ottmar Mergenthaler	USA	A machine which made printing letters by casting characters line by line. This machine was built to an order placed by the editor of the *New York Herald Tribune*.
Monotype	1887	Tolbert Lanston	USA	Cast and typeset individual characters from hot metal. It enabled the typesetting of 9000 characters per hour.
Photocomposition	1953	Louis Moyroud and René Higonnet	USA	The first phototypesetters were put into operation; invented by two Frenchmen living in the USA.

The first polyglot dictionary, based on Latin and Italian, then extended to German, English and French, was the famous *Dictionary of the Latin Language* (1509). It was the work of the Italian scholar, Ambrogio Calepino.

In 1755 the English lexicographer Doctor Johnson (1709–84) produced *A Dictionary of the English Language*.

Encyclopaedia (4th century BC)

The oldest known encyclopaedia was written by **Speusippus** in Athens around **370 BC**. The most famous one in the English-speaking world is the *Encyclopaedia Britannica*, first published in Edinburgh in 1768. It now contains over 32 000 pages and 44 million words. Even this massive work is dwarfed by the Spanish *La Enciclopedia Universal Ilustrada Europeo-Americana*.

Newspaper (1605)

The first gazette to come out regularly appeared in Antwerp in **1605** under the title *Nieuwe Tijdinghen*. Its creator was the printer **Abraham Verhoeven**.

It was widely imitated in Europe and, from 1609, two weekly gazettes appeared in Germany, one of which, *die Relation aller fürnemmen und gedenkwürdigen Historien*, published in Strasbourg, mentions in its 37th edition the invention of Galileo's telescope.

The first newspaper in English was the *Corrant of Italy, Germany, etc* printed in Amsterdam by George Veseler in 1620.

The first daily newspaper was brought out by the German Thimotheus Ritzch from Leipzig. It appeared for the first time in 1650 under the title *Einkommende Zeitungen*. Subsequently called the *Liepzig Journal* (*Leipziger Zeitung*), it continued to appear until 1918!

The earliest newspaper published in Britain was the *Worcester Post Man*, later known as *Berrow's Worcester Journal*, which first appeared in 1690.

Audiovisual

Radio

Theoretical bases

Electromagnetic waves (1865)

It was the British physicist **James Clark Maxwell** (1831–79) who demonstrated the existence of electromagnetic waves. This discovery was at the root of the invention of radiotelegraphy, some 25 years later.

Maxwell demonstrated that light was the result of electromagnetic vibrations of a certain wavelength. His theory, put forward in **1865**, allowed scientists to predict the propagation, reflection and diffraction of light. Moreover, it showed how electromagnetic waves other than light waves could be propagated.

Hertzian waves (1888)

In **1888**, at the age of 31, the German **Heinrich Rudolf Hertz** (1857–94), Professor of Physics at the Polytechnic of Karlsruhe, detected, created and used electromagnetic waves. After becoming familiar with Maxwell's theories, Heinrich Hertz manufactured a rudimentary transmitter called the resonator. With the help of this resonator Hertz verified all of Maxwell's theories. For the first time, waves, subsequently called Hertzian waves, were produced and then detected at a distance.

This invention was in turn to enable Guglielmo Marconi to invent the wireless.

Stereophony (1881)

The first transmission in stereo was arranged by **Clément Ader**, the pioneer of aviation, at the time of the first exhibition on electricity, held in Paris in **1881**. For the event, Ader had invented a telephonic 'stereoscopic' system which, each evening, enabled an enthusiastic public to follow performances at the Opera, some 3km *2 miles* away.

However, stereophonic sound, such as we know it today, emerged in the 1930s when numerous systems were developed. After several experiments carried out during the decades which followed, the definitive method was adopted in 1964.

The Edison effect (1883)

In **1883 Thomas Alva Edison** (1847–1931) invented the first incandescent light bulb.

This bulb reveals the Edison effect: a metal heated until red-hot emits an electron cloud. Radio tubes were able to make use of this effect in order to transmit sounds.

Coherer (1888)

The Frenchman **Edouard Branly** (1844–1940), doctor of sciences and of medicine and Professor of Physics at the Catholic Institute in Paris, detected radio waves in **1888**. After two years of research and improvements, he presented his radio detector to the Academy of Sciences on 24 November 1890. This device converted radio waves into usable electric current. Edouard Branly established that the radio waves could be detected tens of metres away and even through walls. Wireless telegraphy was about to be born.

The Englishman Sir Oliver Lodge (1851–1940) perfected and named the apparatus the coherer and it is under this name that it has been passed down.

Syntony of circuits (1894)

In **1894** the Englishman **Sir Oliver Joseph Lodge**, a professor at the University of Birmingham, introduced a new idea: tuning.

It seems obvious today that the receiver should be tuned to the wavelength of the transmitter from which one wishes to tap a signal. By applying the work of Lord Kelvin, Lodge, a forerunner in this field, established the system of tuning which for many years has been called syntony. Another pioneer of syntony in the United States was the Croatian Nicola Tesla (1856–1943).

Aerial (1895)

In 1895 the Russian **Aleksandr Stepanovick Popov** invented the aerial.

As assistant professor at the School of Torpedos in Kronstadt, he had used the methods of Branly and Lodge for the purposes of detecting distant storms. He noticed that sensitivity was increased when he used a long vertical wire for the reception of waves produced by lightning. A lightning conductor was therefore the first aerial.

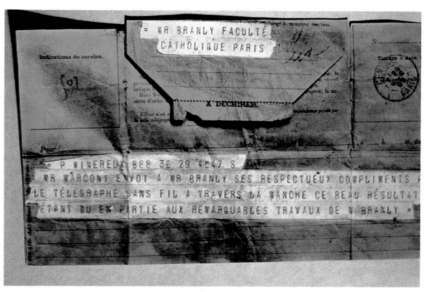

This is the first cross-Channel telegram, sent by Marconi to Branly on 28 March 1899. In it he thanks Branly for his work, without which the telegram would have been impossible.

It is to Aleksandr Popov that we owe the first radio electric link in Morse transmitted over a distance of 250m *820ft*. The first words transmitted were 'Heinrich Hertz' on 24 March 1896.

Although Popov was the inventor of the aerial, in 1891 Branly had shown that by equipping his apparatus with long metal rods their range would be improved.

Wireless telegraphy (1895)

It was the Italian **Guglielmo Marconi** (1874–1937) who was able to bring together previous research and who invented wireless telegraphy and the radio.

At the age of 21, in **1895**, he succeeded in making the first wireless link over a distance of 2400m *1½ miles*.

On 28 March 1899 he carried out the first telegraphic transmission between Dover and Wimereux, south of Calais – a distance of 50km *31 miles* – as well as, on 12 December 1901, with the co-operation of the Englishman Sir John Fleming (1849–1945), the first radio-telegraphic link across the Atlantic between Cornwall and Newfoundland, 3400km *2113 miles* apart.

Diode (1904)

Marconi's collaborator **Sir John Ambrose Fleming** (1849–1945) created the diode in 1904. He placed a plate in front of a heated wire (the filament) in a vacuum tube. The diode was the first radio tube, but it did not much advance the wireless sets of the time.

Triode (1906)

Lee De Forest (1873–1961), an American, invented the first triode in **1906** and named it the Audion.

With the Audion, the radio was equipped with an extremely sensitive apparatus. Due to the auxiliary electrode, it became possible to gauge transmission power with precision and thus to transmit voice vibrations, music and other sounds in all their subtle nuances.

Lee De Forest's invention is the basis of not

only radio but also television, radar and the first computers.

Crystal set (1910)

In **1910**, the work of two American researchers, **Dunwoody** and **Pickard**, on crystals led to the invention of the crystal set, which was the first radio. Galena is a lead sulphur crystal that, combined with some simple elements, permitted thousands of amateurs to build their own wireless sets and to receive the first radio broadcasting transmissions.

Variable frequency receiver (1917)

This was invented in **1917** by the American **Edwin H. Armstrong**. At the time, it was very difficult to achieve proper receiver adjustment as receivers were equipped with a great many buttons, and tuning in to a different frequency involved complicated manipulations. The superheterodyne, or variable frequency, receiver allowed the listener to search for stations with a single button. It considerably simplified receiver adjustments and also facilitated their industrial manufacture.

Presently, 99 percent of radio and television receivers, radar connections via satellite, etc. employ the principle of the superheterodyne.

First portable radio (1922)

It was in **1922** that **J. McWilliams Stone** of Chicago (USA) invented the Operadio, the first portable radio receiver. It cost $180 and weighed nearly 10kg *22lb*.

Car radio (1922)

The invention of the car radio can be attributed to the American **George Frost**, who, in 1922, at the age of 18, installed a radio in a Model T Ford. The first industrially produced car radio was the Philco Transitone, manufactured by the Philadelphia Storage Battery Company in 1927.

Radio control (1974)

In **1974** the German company **Blaupunkt** experimented with the ARI radio control system (the car radio tunes in automatically to the station transmitting information on road traffic). Since then, ARI has been adopted in several European countries such as Switzerland, Spain and Germany.

Frequency modulation (FM) (1933)

The American **Edwin H. Armstrong** began studying the principle of frequency modulation in 1925. This consists in modifying the frequency (or wavelength) of a transmission to adapt it to the rhythm of sound variations.

He studied the principal transmission and reception circuits in 1933 (his first patent was taken out on **24 January 1933**) and he demonstrated that noise can be decreased by increasing the frequency band (contrary to what takes place in amplitude modulation). In 1938 General Electric installed the first transmitter of this type in Schenectady, New York, and this was followed by the Yankee Network. FM was also adopted in 1939 for police patrol radios in the United States.

Transistor (1948)

In **1948** three Bell Laboratories scientists, **John Bardeen**, **Walter Brattain** and **William Shockley**, published the results of the work that would win them the Nobel Prize for Physics in 1956. They had invented the transistor, which replaced the vacuum tube and revolutionised the field of electronics.

It took some years before the first transistor radio appeared. In August 1955 the Sony TR-55 was launched, soon to be followed by many more transistors, as the new radios were called.

Television and video

Nipkow scanning disc (1884)

It was a German student, **Paul Nipkow**, who came up with the idea of cutting up images into lines. His 'electric telescope', patented in **1884**, was a pierced disc which turned in front of the object to be analysed and detailed all its points, line by line. This method, called the Nipkow disc, was the basis of television. It made mechanical television possible until 1935.

Cathode-ray tube (1897)

It was in **1897** that the German physicist **Karl Ferdinand Braun** (1850–1919) invented the cathode-ray tube. It was a kind of vacuum tube in which a fluorescent screen is bombarded by a stream of high-energy electrons. This cathodic oscillator won him the Nobel Prize for Physics in 1909.

Mechanical television (1923)

The Scottish engineer **John Logie Baird** (1888–

A portable Braun radio is contained in this leather handbag – the ultimate fashion accessory for the music fan of 1958.

1946) was one of the pioneers of television. In **1923** he applied for a patent for the use of the Nipkow disc within a mechanical television system. The first experiment was successfully carried out three years later, in 1926. The image obtained comprised only eight lines. He later invented the 240-line mechanically scanned system of television.

Mechanical television used a Nipkow disc (or one of its derivatives) for capturing images. For reception another disc was used which was synchronous with the first, linked to a neon bulb.

In 1928 he developed a television system in colour, although it was still mechanical. In 1930 he established an experimental mechanical television network with the help of the BBC.

From 1930 onwards John Logie Baird marketed his Televisor, the first mass market transmitter. However, his efforts proved unsuccessful.

Television camera (1923)

The iconoscope was the first television camera and the result of the work of the Russian-born American **Vladimir Kosma Zworykin** (1889–1982). Zworykin conceived of an electronic analysis procedure that led to the creation of the iconoscope: a camera tube that converts an optical image into electrical pulses. For this he gained the title 'father of television'.

After having applied for a patent for the procedure in **December 1923**, Zworykin performed an initial demonstration of his invention in the RCA (Radio Corporation of America) electronic research laboratories in 1930. The iconoscope was developed as of 1933. It was used for experimental broadcasts carried out by RCA and NBC from the top of the Empire State Building in New York in 1936.

Zworykin was also the inventor of a receiver tube called the cinescope, which appeared in 1929.

Electronic television (1926)

Virtually unknown in Europe, the Japanese **Kenjiro Takayanagi** almost certainly invented electronic television before Zworykin. In **1926** Takayanagi succeeded in transmitting and picking up the image of a Japanese character. The image comprised 40 lines and 14 frames per second. Only the camera used was mechanical.

A high-definition television (HDTV) camera in use at a tennis tournament. An HDTV image resembles that of a cinema screen, both in terms of format and resolution. The images comprise 1125 horizontal lines (compared to the 625 more commonly in use throughout Europe). The picture is wider, with a width to height ratio of 5:3, whereas in current systems it is 4:3.

This early television receiver, produced by GEC, was said to be suitable for viewing by a party of up to 15 – but that was in the days when one would invite friends and family round to watch TV.

The beginning of television (1932)

It was in London in **1932** that the **BBC** undertook to transmit the first regular television programmes. These were based upon the mechanical method of John Logie Baird, perfected in 1932.

The first real television station was built in Berlin, Germany, in 1935, in anticipation of the Olympic Games. In 1936 in the United States, the Federal Communication Commission opted for a system of 441 lines. In the same year, NBC carried out experiments with the help of an iconoscope from the Empire State Building in New York.

The first live journalistic reporting was undertaken in Britain by the BBC in 1937 at the coronation of King George VI.

Rotating television set (1989)

In **1989** the Danish firm **Bang & Olufsen** developed the Beovision MX 5000, a television set with a programmable motorised base. It can pivot up to 120°, depending from where you want to watch it.

Ghost screen

Hold a certain type of viewfinder to your eyes and you will see, floating in space, the virtual image of a 30cm *12in* screen located about 50cm *20in* from the television viewer. **Allen Becker** patented this Private Eye, which was developed by Reflection Technology, a firm closely linked to MIT. The company has not divulged much information about this amazing invention, but it seems to be one of the civilian by-products of MIT research into holographic viewfinders for combat aircraft. Doubtless more will be revealed soon.

Video recorders

First video recording (1951)

The first company to carry out a demonstration of black and white video recording was **Mincom**, a branch of the M/Scotch company in the United States in **1951**.

In 1954 the RCA corporation built the first video recorder to be recognised as such. The following year, the BBC unveiled the VERA (Vision Electronic Recording Apparatus), a real monster which consumed 17km *10½ miles* of tape per hour!

Ampex solution (1953)

It was the Californian corporation **Ampex** who, in **1953**, resolved the problem of tape consumption by adopting a system which made it possible to maintain an acceptable speed. This method is still in use today on professional or mass media video recorders.

The team of Ampex researchers was led by **Charles P. Ginsberg** and **Charles E. Anderson**. They were joined by a 19-year-old student called **Ray Dolby**, who was soon to become a household name.

On 2 March 1955 Charles E. Anderson carried out a very convincing demonstration of a method for recording sound by modulating the frequency. After further improvements, this video recorder was finally launched on the market in April 1956 under the name Ampex VR 1000.

First retransmission of a recorded television programme (1956)

This took place on **30 November 1956**, on an Ampex VR 1000. That day the CBS studio at Television City in Hollywood recorded the *Douglas Edwards and the News* programme broadcast from New York, in order to retransmit it three hours later.

Ray Dolby helped to invent the video recorder while aged only 19.

VIDEODISCS		
Type	**Date**	**Inventor**
Phonovision	1927	Scotsman John Logie Baird carried out his first experiment using video signals on a disc to store images. His system was called phonovision.
Phonovid	1965	First attempt at a commercial venture on the part of the US firm Westinghouse (Phonovid method). Only 200 still images per disc can be recorded.
Teldec	1970	AEG-Telefunken (W. Germany) and Decca (UK) came together to create the first commercial videodisc called the Teldec. Marketed 1974/5 and was a failure.
Laservision	1972	Improvement of laser-read videodisc by Philips (Laservision) marketed in 1980 in the USA and in 1982 in Europe.
Selectavision	1974	The American company RCA opted for a capacitance reading system called Selectavision. Launched in March 1980 with a large advertising campaign, it proved to be a failure and in 1984 RCA were forced to abandon Selectavision.
VHD	1978	The Japanese company JVC developed a third videodisc system, the VHD (Very High Density), halfway between RCA's Selectavision and Philips' Laservision. It was first marketed in 1983.
AHD	1983	JVC developed the AHD (Audio High Density) system. Originally intended for audio-digital recording, the AHD procedure is completely compatible with the VHD on account of its decoder.
Laservision	1984	The Laservision system received strong support from two quarters: Sony and Hitachi. During this time Pioneer developed a compatible reader of compact dics and Laservision and made the first Laservision videodisc with digital sound (similar to an audio compact disc). In Europe it seems the Laservision system is strictly for professional users.
VHD	1986	Improvement of the standard VHD by JVC. One version offered three-dimensional images. Introduction of Dolby surround method, used in the cinema.
CDV	1987	Announcement of CDV (Compact Disc Video), developed by Sony and Philips. It offered a remarkably clear picture and digital hi-fi sound.
Laserdisc	1990	A major advance on Laserdisc, a new application of CDV. The big American studios proposed films from their catalogue for this medium.

Magnetic video tape (1956)

The first video tape marketed was developed in **1956** by two researchers from the American firm 3M, **Mel Sater** and **Joe Mazzitello**. Working day and night the two men succeeded in unveiling their invention the very day that Ampex Corporation placed the first video recorder on the market. This first Scotch 179 reel was 5cm *2in* wide, nearly 800m *875yd* long, and weighed 10kg *22lb 8oz*.

First colour video recorder (1958)

The first colour video recorder was also built by **Ampex**. It was launched in **1958**, two years after the first video recorder, under the name VR 1000 B. It was followed in 1963 by a transistor version, the VR 110.

Meanwhile the Japanese had been steadily working on video recorder technology:

in 1958 Toshiba announced the first single-head video recorder;

in 1959 JVC developed the first two-head video recorder, the KVI;

in 1962 Shiba Electric (now Hitachi), in co-operation with Asahi Broadcasting, presented a professional transistorised video recorder;

in 1964 Sony marketed the first video recorder for the general public.

Video cassette recorders (1970)

In addition to professional video recorders,

manufacturers also designed models intended for the mass market. It was for this purpose that video cassette recorders were developed (as opposed to tapes).

Towards the end of the 1960s **Matsushita**, **JVC** and **Sony** together developed the standard U-Matic. The first models were launched on the market in **1970**. Subsequently the standard U-Matic gained in prestige to the point where, today, it is considered to be the standard professional recorder.

Mass market video formats

There are three main formats of mass market video recorders and they are all incompatible with each other. They are as follows:

Betamax (1975)

Invented by the Japanese company **Sony**, the Betamax was launched in **1975**. Today Betamax has been almost completely abandoned despite its technical superiority to VHS.

VHS (1975)

The VHS format (Video Home System) was launched by **JVC** in **October 1975** and marketed from 1976. The VHS now holds a dominant position in the world market, with more than 80 percent of sales.

A variation of the VHS model, the VHS-C was launched by JVC in 1982. It was then intended for the portable video and uses smaller video cassettes which can be re-read on a traditional VHS recorder thanks to an adaptor.

In July 1985 JVC launched the VHS HQ (High Quality). In March 1987 JVC brought out a Super VHS in Japan increasing the number of horizontal lines on the image from 240 to 400.

The most modern VCRs, such as the Sony SLV-777, have Nicam stereo, jog and shuttle dials (which improve picture-search and freeze-frame control), inputs for camcorders and a built-in edit function which splits the TV screen into two pictures.

The 8mm (1982)

On **20 January 1982** Sony, Hitachi, JVC, Matsushita and Philips signed an agreement for the joint establishment of standards for a new format called 8mm (because of the width of the tape), designed for camcorders.

Digital video recorder (1985)

In **May 1985**, at the Symposium of Montreux, **Sony** introduced the first video recorder with a digital recording facility. This model was solely for professional use.

Since then digital video recorders have become commonplace. The effects which can be produced are very varied. For instance, it is possible to superimpose a reduced secondary image on to a corner of the screen. It is also possible to choose the speed of the tape with faster and slower options, etc.

Window video recorders (1987)

In **1987** some ten firms, including Hitachi, NEC, Toshiba, JVC, Zenith and RCA, introduced VHS recorders with a microprocessor that can produce the following special effects: it can stop at a particular image; allows simultaneous viewing of recorded film and television (one of the two images selected

appears on a corner of the screen); lets the viewer watch one channel and have eight other programmes in little windows on the screen.

Video Walkman (1988)

Like its audio predecessor, this is also a **Sony** invention. Marketed in Japan since **August 1988**, it is both a television receiver and an 8mm format video recorder; and it weighs just 1.1kg *2½lb*. The latest version, the GV-300, has hi-fi stereo sound.

Video recorder with screen (1989)

Philips have launched the first video recorder that has integrated liquid crystal display (LCD). This allows you to play a cassette at the same time as watching a television channel or vice-versa, to display settings, to check how a recording is progressing, and so on. Meanwhile, Panasonic have brought out the Maclord AV Gear, a portable video recorder with LCD, which is designed for S-VHS-C cassettes.

VHS/VHS-C recorder (1990)

To play VHS-C cassettes on a home video recorder, you used to have to use an adaptor. Now **Panasonic** and **JVC** have developed a recorder that is entirely compatible with both formats, and makes it possible to play either equally well with the same loading mechanism.

Panasonic went even further in 1991 with the NV-W1 which can play, record or copy in any format: PAL (the European TV format with 625 lines of resolution), NTSC (the American System with 525 lines) and the French Secam. It is, however, extremely expensive.

Video cameras and camcorders

Betamovie (1982)

This was the first camcorder: a video camera and recorder combined. Launched at the Japan Electronic Show in Tokyo in **October**

1982 by **Sony**, it uses normal Betamax cassettes allowing up to 3h 35min recording time.

8mm camcorders (1983)

The first prototype 8mm camcorders were brought out in the autumn of **1983** by **Sanyo** and **Philips**. However, the first one to go on the market was the Kodavision, launched in 1984 by Kodak, but produced by Matsushita.

In January 1985, Sony launched Video 8, which could record 90 minutes of images at normal speed and 180 at slow speed. In the same year Sony launched the Handycam, a very simple camcorder that only records, but which is very compact and light (1.3kg *2lb 14oz*). In 1991 Sony launched the MPK-TR which will work up to 40m *130ft* under water. Even the microphone is still effective at that depth.

Video-Movie (1984)

In Japan in **1984 JVC** launched the Video-Movie, a VHS-C format camcorder, and in January 1986, in response to Sony's Handycam, they launched the GR-C7. This was 1.3kg *2lb 14oz*, with CCD transducer, automatic focus and recording and playback facilities. Then in September 1986 JVC announced the GR-C9, ultra-light (990g *2lb 3oz* with battery), with automatic focus and CCD transducer. Like the Handycam, it cannot play back recordings.

Folding camcorder (1990)

From **Hitachi** comes the VMC-1-S, the world's slimmest camcorder (69mm *2.7in* thick). Very compact, it folds in on itself for storage, and records on to VHS-C utilising the latest innovations – automatic focus, titling, automatic exposure program and so on.

Concept C (1990)

In Japan in spring **1990**, in the search for the ever smaller product, **JVC** launched a modular camcorder, the Concept C. In S-VHS-C format, it comprises a recording component, a camera-syntoniser component, an LCD screen and an electrical supply unit, which are all detachable.

JVC's Concept C – all elements of the camcorder are removable, so one can carry only the camera.

Telecommunications

Post

Postal service (6th century BC)

Cyrus the Great (558–528 BC), the founder of the Persian Empire, is said to have been the first to introduce a postal service. Cyrus had conquered a vast area and found, therefore, that messengers bearing missives and information were inadequate. This is the reason why the King organised a postal service with staging posts at regular intervals which would look after the horses after a reasonable day's journey.

The Romans copied this method of organisation and created, during the reign of Augustus (27 BC–AD 14), the *Cursus publicus*. Military routes were marked with *mutationes* which were staging posts providing rested horses and *mansiones* which were inns reserved for official travellers.

Monks' postal system

In the Middle Ages, Europe had many monasteries and abbeys. In order to communicate with each other, a roll of parchment, called a *rotula*, was used on which the first abbey would write its message. As the *rotula* went round, abbeys would add to it. The parchments could become very long: the Saint Vital Rotula announcing the death of its abbot measures 9.5m *31ft* in length and 0.25m *10in* in width.

Directories (1785)

The first city directory was for the city and suburbs of Philadelphia, between 1st Street to the north and Maiden Street to the south, 10th Street to the west and Delaware Street to the east. Published by **John Macpherson** on **1 October 1785**, it included 6250 names and addresses.

Envelope (1820)

A Brighton resident called **Brewer** stated in **1820** that he had invented the envelope. However, several envelopes dating back to 1615 are preserved in Geneva, Switzerland. At that time a letter would be folded and covered with silk thread with a wax stamp fixing the two ends together. Later the letter was wrapped in a folded white sheet on which the receiver's address would be written.

Stamps (1834)

The Scot **James Chalmers** printed the first stamp in Dundee in **1834**, but it was not until 1840 that stamps were used, following the British postal reform carried out by **Sir Rowland Hill** (1795–1879), who introduced penny postage.

The first adhesive stamp, which went into use in Great Britain on **6 May 1840**, was the Penny Black which bore the profile of Queen Victoria on a dark background.

Perforated stamps (1854)

The first apparatus for separating stamps was invented in 1847 by the Englishman **Henry Archer**. It could only make slits, but its inventor perfected it one year later and the machine could then perforate a series of small holes. The first perforated stamp was the Penny Red, issued in **February 1854**.

Postcard (1861)

The postcard was invented in Philadelphia, USA in 1861 by **John P. Charlton**, who obtained a copyright for it and then sold his rights to a stationer named Harry L. Lipman. The latter published the cards with a picture and the words 'Lipman postcard, patent pending'.

The pre-stamped postcard was conceived by the Austrian Emmanuel Herrman, of the Neustadt Military Academy in Vienna. The first of these were made available on 1 October 1869.

Telegraphy

Chappe's telegraph (1793)

After a preliminary demonstration in March 1791, a French engineer, **Claude Chappe**, sent his first telegraphic message a distance of about 15km *9 miles* between Saint-Martin-du-Tertre and Paris on **12 July 1793**.

Chappe's telegraph was a relay of semaphore signals from stations positioned about 12km *7½ miles* apart at fairly high points so that someone with field-glasses could see the signals being made.

Electric telegraph (1833)

In 1827 the German Steinheil discovered that a single earthed electric wire could be used as a transmission line. In **1833** the English physicist and chemist **Michael Faraday**

Left: the Pony Express passes some workmen putting up the telegraph poles that were to make the riders' job obsolete. Right: one of the first operational telegraph machines.

END OF THE SOS

This was the most famous of all telegraphed messages: three dots, followed by three dashes, then three dots again. First used in 1906 at the Berlin radio-telegraphic conference, it will disappear in 1999, to be replaced by GMDSS, an alarm system that uses beacons – doubtless more efficient, but far less romantic. The first SOS in the history of navigation was sent out by the *Titanic* on 14 April 1912; let's hope that the last will not be for such a tragic occasion.

(1791–1867) demonstrated that an electric current could be induced by moving a conductor within the field of influence of a magnet. If variants are used in accordance with a code common both to the sender and receiver, those two people will be able to send messages to each other.

It is on the basis of these principles that the Russian diplomat Pavel Schilling created an experimental telegraph in St Petersburg. His early death interrupted the experiment. The Englishman Sir William Cooke (1806–79), an Indian Army officer, and the great physicist Sir Charles Wheatstone (1802–75), continued Schilling's work and patented the first electric signal in June 1837.

With the help of a telegraphic message, the police were able to arrest a murderer, John Tawell, travelling on the 7.42 train from Paddington on 1 January 1845. This arrest increased the popularity of the telegraph in Britain.

Morse telegraph (1837)

On **28 September 1837** the American **Samuel F. B. Morse** (1791–1872) applied for a patent for electric telegraphy. However, his most original contribution was, without doubt, the invention of Morse code whereby letters are translated by a succession of dots and dashes.

On 30 December 1842, after a great deal of effort, he managed to obtain a grant of $30 000 to build an experimental line from Washington DC to Baltimore, which was opened on 24 May 1844. After a number of setbacks Samuel Morse, who saw his invention being contested, had his rights confirmed by a judgement of the Supreme Court. The telegraph subsequently experienced enormous growth and Morse became rich and famous.

Although its only purpose is to act as a support in the event of the radio system failing, the Morse code, 150 years after it was invented, is still taught to Navy radio controllers.

Underwater telegraphic cable

First cable under the Channel (1851)

In **1851** the first important telegraph cable was laid between Dover and Calais by the British steam ship *Blazer*. The British technician **Jacob Brett** was the main promoter of the operation which was made possible thanks to progress in many techniques. For example, the German engineer Werner von Siemens had developed a machine that could apply

gutta-percha onto cables, thereby ensuring that they were insulated.

First transatlantic cable (1866)

On **27 July 1866** the first transatlantic telegraph cable was completed. The American **Cyrus Field** (1819–92) had been the instigator of this operation which cost him almost his entire fortune. The first four attempts (one in 1857, two in 1858 and one in 1865) had ended in failure.

Telephone

Telephone (1876)

Candidates for the title of the inventor of the telephone are legion, with each country claiming its own. Before 1876 numerous researchers described some form of telephone system. 7 mar ?

On **14 January 1876** two men, **Alexander Graham Bell** (1847–1922) and **Elisha Gray** (1835–1901) filed applications for patents at the Patents Office in New York. The first did so at noon, the second at 2pm. It is on this two hours' difference that the judges made a decision in Bell's favour after a long court case between the inventors.

Born in Edinburgh, Bell was aware of the problems surrounding deafness from a young age. His mother was deaf and his father was a specialist in the education of deaf children. The family emigrated to the United States and it was there that Bell became fascinated with telegraphy and later invented the telephone.

Bell invents the telephone by accident

In 1875 Bell was working with his assistant Watson towards improving the telegraph. All of a sudden, on 2 June, Watson made a mistake. A bad contact by a clamping screw which was too tight changed what should have been an intermittent transmission into a continuous current. Bell, who was at the other end of the wire, distinctly heard the sound of the contactor dropping. Bell spent the next winter making calculations and filed an application for a patent. However, it was not until 6 March 1876 that he succeeded in transmitting intelligible words to his colleague: 'Come here, Watson, I want you.'

The telephone had been born. The world was to learn about his invention when Bell demonstrated it at the United States Centenary Exhibition held in Philadelphia in June 1876.

There are now approaching half a billion phones worldwide.

Telephone exchange (1878)·

Manual exchange

In **1878** the first manual telephone exchange opened in New Haven, Connecticut (USA). It served 21 subscribers, one of whom was the writer Mark Twain.

Automatic exchange (1891)

In **1891** an American undertaker from Kansas City, **Almon B. Strowger**, applied for a patent for the first automatic telephone exchange. Strowger had discovered that his competitor's wife, an operator at the local manual telephone exchange, was the first to learn of deaths in the city. Doubtless, she was direct-

ing the calls sent to Strowger's enterprise to her husband. It is thus easy to understand Strowger's interest in an automatic telephone system.

Pay phones (1889)

William Gray from Hartford, Connecticut (USA) was granted the patent number 408709 on **13 August 1889** for a piece of apparatus that enabled telephones to be used with coins. The first telephone equipped in this way was installed in the bank at Hartford. In 1891 William Gray, Amos Whitney and Francis Pratt formed a company which installed pay phones in large stores.

Radiotelephone (1900)

The ancestor of the radiotelephone is Chichester Bell and Charles Sumner Tainter's graphophone. The first demonstration took place on 15 February 1885. Radiotelephony is a means of communication by radio waves rather than along telephone wires.

The first proper radiotelephone was produced by **Reginald A. Fessenden**, who demonstrated the device in **December 1900** at Cob Point, Maryland, USA.

The first transatlantic transmission was made by AT&T in 1915 between Virginia (USA) and the Eiffel Tower in Paris.

Portable radiotelephone (1979)

This apparatus, known as the cellular telephone, is causing a revolution in the field of communications.

It was in Sweden under the instigation of the **Ericsson Company** that it first appeared in **1979**. The area to be covered is divided into a certain number of small cells, each one served by a receiver. The unit is controlled by a data processing system. In 1986 some 200 000 Swedes, Danes and Finns already used a mobile telephone. Four years later the number had more than doubled, while Britain already had 500 000 mobile phone users.

Telex (1916)

The first teleprinter, which made it possible to send written messages through telephone lines, was invented in **1916** by **Markrum Co.** of Chicago. The system became operational in 1928 and was extended at a national level by the Bell Laboratories in 1931 under the name telex from *tele*printer *ex*change. Today it is being overhauled by the fax machine.

Phototelegraphy (1924)

The first ancestor of the fax machine was Englishman A. Bain's electrical picture transmitter, 1843. In 1906 a German, Arthur Korn, transmitted a portrait of the crown prince by telephotography over a distance of 1800km *1120 miles*, and in 1907 the French scientist Edouard Belin (1876–1963) developed an apparatus that worked along similar lines, which he called the belinograph.

In **1924** the **Bell Laboratories** carried out a preliminary demonstration of phototelegraphy. This was a transmission by telephone of photographs from the Chicago and Cleveland Conventions to New York when candidates for the Presidential Election were appointed. This method had been perfected by the

The Desk-Fax, produced by Western Union in 1953, enabled people to send telegrams and cablegrams automatically from their desk at the push of a button.

The Swatch Twin Phone, invented by the same company that produce the famous watch, enables two people to talk to a third from the same place. It has been available in Switzerland since 1989.

engineers Ives and Gray from the Bell Laboratories.

Fax

The name is an abbreviation of facsimile. It is a direct descendant of all the earlier systems that were widely used in Japanese industry, mainly because of the difficulty of transmitting ideograms. Starting from virtually none in 1973, the global number of fax machines is growing exponentially and by the end of 1989 there were already well over 10 million in use worldwide, with Japan still leading the way. The fax has become a must for businesses.

Visiophone (1929)

It was around 1929 that American engineers experimented with visiophone, a device that enables two speakers to see each other on a screen while on the telephone. During the 1970s Bell Laboratories marketed the Picturephone in the United States but the exorbitant price led to its failure. Subsequently numerous prototypes have emerged throughout the world, in particular in Japan (the Scopephone by NTT, for example).

Hertz relays (1942)

Telephone transmission by ultra-short waves used in Hertz relays was perfected in the United States in the AT&T laboratories by **Harold T. Friis** around **1942**. They were a direct result of the war effort made by the Bell Laboratories.

Communications terminal (1976)

This little radiocommunications apparatus is not really a telephone proper, since it only works in one direction, that is, receiving messages. Eurosignal – from the German company **Bosch** – was the first, invented in **1976**. It makes it possible to receive messages at a distance, by using the telephone. In 1989 there were 10 million subscribers worldwide.

A European communications network is due to come into operation at the beginning of 1992.

Vocal control telephone (1983)

The first telephone unit to be controlled vocally was invented in **June 1983** by the American **Garth A. Clowes** and then marketed in 1984 under the name TTC 6012. This is a device which responds to the sound of the voice, either directly or through a memory capable of storing 80 numbers. The device is able to recognise the voice of three different people.

Recent developments on this principle are: a mobile telephone controlled by the human voice, developed by a Danish firm, Dancall, in co-operation with British Telecom in 1987.

Pocket telephone (1989)

Soon public telephones will be obsolete: all one will need is a cordless telephone not much larger than a packet of cigarettes. Many companies are competing to get ahead in this market which, by 1995, is estimated to be worth billions of pounds.

Pointel (1978)

Developed by **Pactel** (UK) in 1978, and called CT2 (Cordless Telephone 2), it is as small as a cigarette packet and weighs 125g *5oz*. It can be used to telephone anywhere, provided you are within 200m of a relay. The disadvantage is that it does not take incoming calls; this is because it is not yet possible to locate the mobile.

DECT (1993)

The Digital European Cordless Telephone is currently under development, notably in Sweden by **Ericsson**, one of the world leaders in radiotelephony. It is bidirectional – which means it can handle outgoing and incoming calls – as well as digital, and will be far more advanced and universal than Pointel. Ericsson brought the CT3 on the market in Sweden at the end of 1990. It will be available worldwide by **1993**.

Communication cables and satellites

Cable television (1927)

The first cable television transmission was carried out in the United States by the **Bell Telephone Company** in **1927**. The experiment took place between Washington and New York. A Nipkow scanning disc was used for the transmission and another for the reception.

This cable technique was then taken up again for the purposes of reaching those areas without access to traditional Hertzian transmission.

In 1949 a small town in Oregon, USA, suffered from bad reception of programmes transmitted from Seattle on account of the mountains which surround it. It was decided that a large aerial would be installed on high ground. From there a cable network transmitted programmes, without any risk of parasitic oscillation.

Rapid growth of cable television (1960s)

It was not until the **1960s** that cable television experienced real growth in the United States and Canada. Today 22 million Americans are subscribers to different cable systems (paid by subscription), 2.5 million of which are Disney Channel subscribers.

The development of optical fibres in place of traditional coaxial cable (invented by the Americans Affel and Espensched in 1929) makes it possible to go from passive viewing of programmes to active audience participation – users are able to choose their programmes and to participate directly in the contents of the programmes themselves (quick surveys, questionnaires, games, etc.).

First transatlantic telephone cable (1956)

On **26 September 1956** the first cable telephonic transatlantic link was made. The cable made it possible to transmit 588 conversations – more than all radiotelephone traffic in the previous ten days. In order to carry out this operation successfully, the American company AT&T, the British GPO and the Canadian company Canadian Overseas Telecommunications worked together.

Olympus was sent into orbit in 1989 to demonstrate the new developments in telecommunications.

First fibre optic transatlantic cable (1988)

The first fibre optic transatlantic cable, the TAT-8, has linked the United States with the UK and France since **1988**. The cable is 6620km *4114 miles* long and carries television, telephone and data processing signals. The partners in this venture are DGT (France), American Telegraph and Telephone (AT&T), and British Telecom International. It can handle 37 500 simultaneous conversations.

Telecommunications satellite (1960)

In 1945 the science-fiction writer Arthur C. Clarke published the first theoretical analysis of an artificial satellite system, in the radio buffs' magazine *Wireless World*.

On **12 August 1960 NASA** launched its first American telecommunications satellite called *Echo 1*. It was simply a 30m *98ft* diameter balloon, the metallic surface of which reflected radio signals without either magnifying or diverting them. Unfortunately, *Echo 1* did not withstand meteorites for very long.

Telstar (1962)

On **10 July 1962 NASA** launched the first truly efficient civil telecommunications satellite on behalf of the American company AT&T: Telstar.

Satellite television (1962)

There are two types of satellites used in television: direct television satellites (DBS) and telecommunications satellites (still called 'point-to-point' satellites), which are now very widespread. The first of these was Telstar which was launched in **1962**. However, the line between these two types of satellite is becoming blurred.

Teletext (1963)

Teletext, or broadcast videography, is a system for transmitting data sent as television signals to television receivers. The system is based on the demonstration that was made in **1963** by three French engineers, which showed the possibility of transmitting information using the vertical intervals between the video lines.

Ceefax

Developed by the **BBC** and **British Telecom**, the Ceefax standard took over from Antiope and became dominant at the European level. Furthermore, Grundig is testing a system of programming video recorders using Ceefax broadcasts; in this system, a message tells the recorder when a programme is beginning, thus enabling it to record from the start (it is well known that they are not always on time!) to the finish.

ECS satellite (1983)

Under the auspices of the **Eutelsat** organisation, the first ECS satellite (European Communications Satellite) was sent into orbit by the Ariane rocket in **1983**. It was called ECS 1 and its main purpose was to re-transmit various television programmes (Sky Channel, Music Box, etc.) to European networks. The fourth satellite of this series, ECS 4, was launched in June 1986.

INFORMATION TECHNOLOGY

The first machines

The abacus (3000 BC)

The abacus, ancestor of the calculator and of the computer, is of Babylonian origin and dates from around 3000 BC. The word abacus is derived from the Semitic term for dust. In its old form the abacus was in fact a slab of wood covered in fine sand on which figures were written with a stylus. The abacus later took the form of a bead frame. Nowadays, the bead frame is still used in India, China *(suan pan)*, Japan *(soroban)*, and the Soviet Union *(tschoty)*. An abacus performs four mathematical operations: addition, subtraction, multiplication and division.

Arithmetical machine (1624)

The German **Wilhelm Schickard**, a professor at the University of Heidelberg, built, in **1624**, the first arithmetical machine capable of performing the four basic operations. He called it a calculator clock.

Pascaline (1642)

In **1642 Blaise Pascal** (1623–62) made the first calculating machine, which was the true ancestor of our modern pocket calculator. Pascal was a highly gifted young man, for he invented this machine at the age of 19, while working on conic sections, to help his father collect taxes in the central region of France. Counting whole numbers, cogwheels in a mechanical gear system performed additions or subtractions which could involve up to eight columns of figures at a time. This machine, which Pascal named the Pascaline in 1645, worked in the same way as a car milometer.

Stepped reckoner (1671)

In **1671 Gottfried Wilhelm von Leibnitz** (1646–1716), the German philosopher and mathematician, invented a mechanical calculator which was similar to the Pascaline, but more refined. Pascal's machine could only count. Leibnitz's could multiply, divide and calculate square roots. However, both of

Jacquard's loom was the first machine to use numerical control.

these calculators were based on the same mechanical technique, 'single step' calculation. They repeated the same operation, such as, for example, a series of additions. Many modern computer programs also work in this way.

Numerical control (1805)

Without realising the importance of his invention, the Frenchman **Joseph-Marie Jacquard** (1752–1834) used numerical control in the operation of a mechanical loom.

The automatic sequence-controlled computer built at Manchester University was hailed as 'a marvel of our time' in 1949.

The Jacquard loom was, in **1805**, the first machine to use a punched hole in a card to represent a number and thus control the pattern of its weave.

Analytical engine (1835)

In **1835** the Englishman **Charles Babbage** (1792–1871), who was Professor of Mathematics at Cambridge University, presented the concept of an 'analytical engine'. This machine, which was completely new, was in fact the world's first digital computer.

The analytical engine combined arithmetical operations with decisions based on its own calculations. It used a system of 50 cogwheels, and data was entered by means of punched cards.

The first ever programs were written for this machine by Ada, Countess Lovelace. Unfortunately 19th century technology was not sufficiently advanced to put most of Lovelace and Babbage's brilliant discoveries into practice. Thus only a rudimentary version of the analytical engine was built.

Electric totaliser (1886)

Hermann Hollerith (1860–1929), an American statistician, found fame by combining Babbage and Jacquard's system of punched cards with electromagnetic inventions. He thus made a major contribution to the development of computer technology. In **1886**, when he was working on the American population census, he tried placing punched cards over little bowls of mercury. He then dropped metal pins through the holes into the mercury, to complete an electrical circuit. This system of electromechanical detection enabled Hollerith's totaliser to classify data and enter it into a ledger. His systems were put to good use during the 1890 census.

Hollerith went on to develop punching and sorting machines, which were precursors of today's computer peripherals. In 1911 he helped to set up the Computing Tabulating

Recording Company, which became the International Business Machines Corporation (IBM) in 1957.

First attempt to build a computer: the Z1 (1931)

Early in the 1930s the German engineer **Konrad Zuse** made computers that operated in binary mode. The Z1 was followed by the mechanical Z2, then by the Z3, a relay computer which could perform a multiplication in three to four seconds.

Zuse was hindered by the slowness of his machines and in 1940 he suggested to the German government that electromechanical relays should be replaced by electronic tubes. But Hitler, certain that the war would be won, reduced investment in this area. Zuse worked on and by 1944 was developing the Z4, but all his machines were destroyed in the bombardment of Berlin.

Binary computer (1939)

The first binary computer was made in **1939** by the American mathematician **George R. Stibitz** at the Bell Laboratories and was called the Model 1 Relay Computer or Complex Number Calculator.

It consisted of a logical mechanism in which the data output consisted of the sum of the data entered. Stibitz used telephone relays in his computer, which functioned in the binary 'all or nothing' mode (in other words they only used the digits 1 and 0), with the aim of developing a universal computer. He assembled the computer in one weekend, using a few discarded relays, two lightbulbs and fragments of a tobacco jar.

The first computers

The ABC tube computer (1939)

The idea was already there: a German, Schreyer (a friend of Zuse's) had obtained his

doctorate by demonstrating the importance of vacuum tubes in digital calculation; but it was mathematician and physicist **John Vincent Atanasoff** who was the first to apply it. Assisted by one of his students, Clifford Berry, this professor at Iowa State College built a binary machine designed to solve the complex equations used in physics. It became known as the ABC (Atanasoff Berry Computer) and had no rivals until 1942. However, since neither Atanasoff nor Iowa State College registered a patent, the invention of the tube computer was long attributed to John W. Mauchly and J. Presper Eckert, although these two did in fact draw heavily on the ABC to build the ENIAC (Electronic Numerical Integrator and Calculator).

Colossus (1943)

Right from the start of the Second World War, British number theorists tried to find a way of decoding German messages. They put **Doctor Alan Mathison Turing** at the head of a team charged with solving this problem.

Before the war Alan Turing had clarified the notion of calculability and adapted the notion of algorithms to calculate certain functions. He had thus postulated the Turing machine, which was theoretically capable of calculating any calculable function. In **1943** at Bletchley Park, the first electromechanical computer, Colossus, went into operation. It was formulated by **Professor Max H. A. Newman** and built by **T. H. Flowers**. This computer contained more than 2000 electronic tubes and could process 5000 characters a second.

It was a specialised machine, which did its job very well: right until the end of the war, the British government was kept informed about German plans thanks to the decoding powers of Colossus.

Harvard Mark 1 (1944)

The first fully automatic calculator in the world was Harvard Mark 1, at that time called the IBM Automatic Sequence Controlled Calcula-

quences of operations, and the use of registers – an idea that was picked up by every other manufacturer.

A register is a device used by the computer to store information for high-speed access. The bits of data stored in the register could represent a binary number, an alphabetic character, or a computer instruction.

Universal electronic computer (1946)

After signing a contract in 1943 with the Ballistic Research Laboratory, **John W. Mauchly** and **J. Presper Eckert**, two American scientists from the University of Pennsylvania, set to work. In **1946** they presented ENIAC (the acronym for Electronic Numerical Integrator and Calculator), the first universal electronic computer. It weighed 30 tonnes, occupied a surface area of 160m² *1720sq ft* and contained 18000 electronic tubes. By means of electronics, it brought speed to the world of computers. It was used to calculate ballistic trajectories.

Stored program computer (1948)

John von Neumann joined the team at the Institute of Advanced Study in Princeton, New Jersey, and it was here that the idea of a machine with a stored program was conceived. In 1946 Neumann, with Arthur W. Burks and H. H. Goldstine, published 'Preliminary Discussion of the Logical Design of an Electronic Computing Instrument'. This was a crucial document in the history of computer science: the program became a sequence of numbers stored in the computer's memory. EDVAC (Electronic Discrete Variable Automatic Computer) was capable of operating on and therefore changing the stored instructions and was thus able to alter its own program.

The first machine to incorporate von Neumann's principles was built at Manchester University in **1948**. In 1950 the first computer intended for business use came onto the market: the Universal Automatic Computer (UNIVAC I).

Concepts

Algorithm (18th century BC)

In the **18th century BC**, Babylonian mathematicians of the time of Hammurabi formulated algorithms in order to solve certain numerical problems. An algorithm is a series of elementary actions designed to solve a problem.

The idea of mechanising algorithms goes back to the year 1000, particularly to the work of the Frenchman Gerbert d'Aurilliac (c.938–1003), who became Pope Sylvester II.

A computer program is the translation of an algorithm into a well-defined language.

Mechanised calculation (1617)

In **1617** the Scotsman **John Napier** (1550–1617) found a way of expressing division by a series of subtractions and multiplication by a series of additions. He thus became the inventor of logarithms.

Napier's technique, which made it possible

tor. The machine was presented by **Howard Aiken** of Harvard University, and its development had been encouraged and financed by T. J. Watson, then president of IBM. It weighed five tonnes and contained 800km *500 miles* of tape.

This calculator improved on Babbage's dream and included two innovations: a clock intended to synchronise the diverse se-

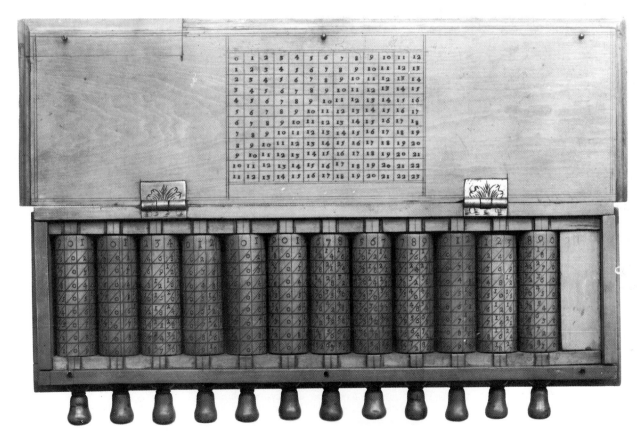

John Napier's calculating machine helped him to devise the idea of logarithms.

COMPUTERS MODELLED ON THE BRAIN?

Neurocomputer science – the science of computers whose architecture is modelled on that of the brain – began in the 1940s, and the first machine actually to be built was Frank Rosenblatt's Perceptron (USA) in 1949. Although other machines were built, scientists in the mid-1960s chose to move in the direction of artificial intelligence, which seemed more promising. However, the limitations of the latter and of expert systems on the one hand, and the work of John Hopfield (1980, USA) and the discovery of learning algorithms on the other, have led a number of scientists to return to the earlier research.

The importance of neuronal computers lies in the fact that they are able to work on imprecise data, for example, recognition of badly-written manuscript figures, and are also capable of learning. Their 'neurons' (simple components) are all interconnected and work in parallel, whereas traditional computers function sequentially, that is, one item of information follows another.

Many universities and companies in the United States, Japan and France have projects under way. The first applications of these are in the field of the recognition of shapes and signals.

to perform any calculation simply by repeating the same operation several times, opened the way to calculation using mechanical means.

Computer program (1835)

While Charles Babbage was designing his analytic engine, **Ada, Countess Lovelace** (1815–52) was writing programs for it.

In fact it has recently been revealed that without the help of the Countess (who was the daughter of the famous poet Lord Byron), Babbage's machine would certainly not have been built.

The Countess Lovelace was thus the first programmer. Her work foreshadowed such techniques as subroutines and automatic programming.

Coding (19th century)

The invention of coding can be attributed to the American **Hermann Hollerith**. The coding of punched cards is often called the Hollerith code, in memory of this scientific forerunner. Later notable contributions were made by the Frenchman Emile Baudot, who invented the telegraphic code which was patented in 1874. However, coding goes back to the first mechanisms to use punched cards: Jacquard's looms and Babbage's machine.

Binary logic (1859)

George Boole (1815–64), an English logician and mathematician, developed symbolic logic and, specifically, binary logic operators such as AND, OR, etc. Boole's rigorous system makes it possible to mechanise logic,

operating with 0 and 1 only: 0 meaning off and 1 meaning on. This is how electronic logic circuits work in computers today.

Cybernetics (1940)

Cybernetics, as a science, was invented by **Norbert Wiener in 1940**, but the word was not coined until 1948 by Wiener and A. Rosenblueth. It comes from the Greek word *kubernêtés* meaning a steersman or pilot.

Cybernetics is the study of automatic-communication and control mechanisms in machines as well as in humans.

Bit (1946)

The term 'bit' was created by **John Tukey** in 1946, while he was working on the ENIAC.

It is a contraction of the two words 'binary digit'. A bit is a binary unit of information. It refers to either of the two elements, 0 and 1, by means of which information is coded in a computer.

The computer scientist's bit is in fact the same as the thing that telegraphists had for years been calling a 'moment', using five-moment codes (Baudot code) and eight-moment codes (bytes).

Real time working (1946)

A system is said to work in real time when it provides an immediate result. A highly accurate computer, the BINAC (Binary Automatic Computer), was developed in **1946** by the Americans **J. P. Eckert** and **J. W. Mauchly**. It consisted of two computers which simultaneously carried out the same calculations, whose results were then compared. The BINAC was the first computer to work in real time. Its accuracy was phenomenal for its day: in 1949 one of the two processors which made up BINAC worked faultlessly for 44 hours nonstop.

Byte (1961)

A byte is a group of eight bits, or eight binary elements. The byte appeared as a basic unit of information on the Stretch, a high-powered, transistorised computer built by **IBM** in **1961**. Today the byte is universally used to represent a character (a letter or figure).

Computer capacity is usually given in kilobytes (one kb equals 1024 bytes), megabytes (one Mb equals 1024kb), gigabytes (one Gb equals 1024Mb) or terabytes (one Tb equals 1024Gb). Note that $1024 = 2^{10}$.

Time-sharing system (1961)

A team headed by **F. Corbato** at the Massachusetts Institute of Technology (MIT) designed, in **1961**, the Compatible Time Sharing System (CTSS) for the exploitation of IBMs 700 and 7090. The first time-sharing system to be marketed was on the PDP1 in 1962.

Work stations (1980)

Work stations are in fact simply computers, misleadingly named by the American firm **Apollo** which invented them. Current models are very powerful, more so than minicomputers. A work station is a machine in the form of a microcomputer, designed to

carry out a precise function – calculation or drawing (which requires a powerful processing capacity) – and linked to a central system and shared peripherals (file storage, flatbed plotters).

Supercomputers

Cray 1 (1976)

The first commercial supercomputer (or supercalculator), the Cray 1, was created under the supervision of **Seymour Cray** in 1976. It contained 200 000 integrated circuits, was freon-cooled and could perform 150 million operations per second.

Bestseller: the Cray X-MP (1982)

In **1982 Steve Chen**, a Taiwanese immigrant to the United States where he did his engineering studies, designed the world's first computer featuring parallel architecture, the Cray X-MP.

The Crays were overtaken by Control Data's Cyber 205, which performs 700 million operations a second.

Seymour Cray regained the advantage with the Cray 2, revealed in 1986. It has a two gigabyte central memory and performs 1.6 billion operations a second. Its architecture is very compact to facilitate the movement of information, and to stop it overheating it is submerged in a fluorocarbon fluid.

Cray Y-MP (1988)

At the beginning of **1988 Cray**, who still dominate the market with 60 percent of supercomputers in service (since Control Data left the field open to Cray Research by abandoning the ETA 10 and the supercomputer market), presented the Cray Y-MP. It is capable of performing 2 billion operations per second and costs $20 million. It is used by NASA, for instance, but should also be of interest to the biotechnological, aerodynamic and chemical industries, since it enables the generation of complex three-dimensional simulations.

Connection machine (1987)

This fascinating supercomputer is the product of six years of research led by **David Hills** (36). Backed by a team of people who left MIT (which has continued to support them), he set up the Thinking Machines Corp. The Connection Machine works using parallel architecture, unlike the Crays, and it contains up to 64 000 processors. In themselves none of these is particularly powerful, but they are all connected to each other. This provides incredible powers of calculation: more than 2 billion operations per second for the most powerful version, which is installed at the Los Alamos military base (USA).

Optical computer (1990)

A hand-held computer, weighing a few grammes and containing billions of pieces of data, is now theoretically possible thanks to an invention by **Alan Huang**. This engineer at

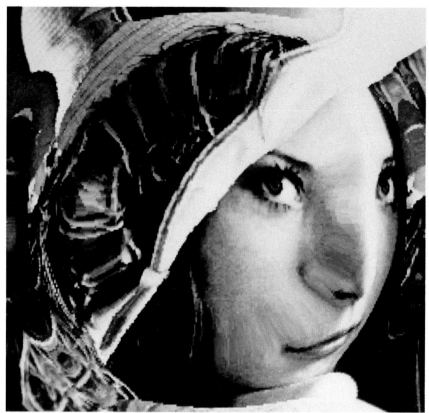

The Connection Machine here reproduces the effect of a drop of water falling into a basin.

AT&T, the American telecommunications giant, uses photons – light particles – to carry data, a technique that makes it possible to achieve calculation speeds a thousand times greater than that of usual electronic transport, without wasting energy.

It is not yet known whether this process – a prototype of which was presented in **1990** – poses insurmountable technical problems. An answer is expected in the 21st century.

Supercomputers with superconductors (1989)

Superconductors allow the passage of electrons without resistance or heating, which are two of the fundamental problems for computer designers. On **13 December 1989**, two Japanese scientists announced that they had succeeded in using elements in superconductive materials to make microprocessors and memories; the latter must be kept at a temperature of $-269°C$ $-452°F$.

These components are based on the Josephson effect: according to the British physicist Brian Josephson, a current can pass between two superconductors if they are placed sufficiently close together.

Microcomputers

Electronic pocket calculator (1972)

The first electronic pocket calculator was developed by the Americans **J. S. Kilby**, **J. D. Merryman** and **J. H. van Tassel** of **Texas Instruments**. The patent was applied for in **1972** and granted in 1978. The calculator is preserved at the Smithsonian Institute in Washington.

In 1973 Hewlett-Packard brought out pocket calculators that were programmed to suit the needs of a particular domain (for example, finance or economics). In 1976 the same American company marketed the first programmable calculators, which were true pocket computers.

Micral (1971)

The first microcomputer in the world was French. At the end of **1971 François Gernelle**, an engineer with R2E, designed it to respond to the French agricultural research institute's need for automatic regulation. R2E's boss, André Truong Trong Thi, a Frenchman of Vietnamese origins, was won over by the invention and decided to manufacture computers built around a single microprocessor. This very first microcomputer was called Micral. When R2E was bought by Bull, all that remained of Micral was the brand name.

Altair 8800 (1974)

Many companies have argued over who launched the first American microcomputer. But the one which really set things in motion was the Altair, produced by the company MITS, which was set up by **H. Edward Roberts**. In **December 1974** the magazine *Popular Electronics* published a bombshell of

Discovered in 1986, the new superconducting ceramic materials are the subject of a great deal of worldwide research. Here a small cylindrical magnet floats freely above a nitrogen-cooled superconducting ceramic. The vapour is caused by liquid nitrogen, which bathes the ceramic and maintains it within the superconducting temperature range.

an article: readers were invited to buy through the post a kit with which they could build themselves a real computer, based on Intel's 8080 microprocessor. It cost $397 and was extremely basic compared to today's microcomputers. In place of a keyboard it had 25 switches which had to be moved in a cumbersome sequence in order to start the machine, and it had a 256 byte random access memory (2000 times less than many of today's PCs). Nonetheless, 200 orders were received on the first day.

IBM 5100 (1975)

Six years before their famous PC, **IBM** had already built a microcomputer, the 5100. However, its distribution remained confidential.

Apple II (1977)

The Apple II, brought out for the first time in the United States in **May 1977**, was the first commercial product of the legendary company founded by **Steve Jobs** and **Stephen Wozniak**. It was an improvement on the first Apple of which about 100 had been manufactured the previous year and which was simply a kit sold directly to members of the Homebrew Club, the first computing club in the United States. The big advantage of the Apple was its user-friendliness.

IBM PC (1981)

It was on **12 August 1981** that the number one company in world computer science announced its entry into the microcomputing market with the IBM PC. The arrival of this microcomputer, designed by a team of young computer scientists headed by **Philip Estridge**, created a real standard throughout the world.

Apple Macintosh (1984)

At the beginning of **1984 Apple** presented the Macintosh, the most original microcomputer and the one most likely to revolutionise the way in which non-specialist users interact with their machines. The Apple team which developed the Macintosh, personally led by **Steve Jobs**, took up ideas that had been used in the same company's Lisa in 1983: a mouse, a high definition screen and graphic symbols representing programs and data.

These techniques had been outlined several years earlier at Rank Xerox's PARC Laboratory. They saved the user from having to be concerned with the internal workings of the computer.

Macintosh II and Macintosh SE (1987)

When on **2 March 1987** Apple launched two microcomputers which could accept software designed for both Macintosh and for the IBM PC, they brought together two worlds which had hitherto been thought incompatible.

Amstrad PC 1512 (1986)

Amstrad created a real stir in **September 1986** when they announced their PC 1512: this microcomputer, which was compatible with the IBM PC but twice as fast and easier to use, cost a third the price. In Europe this machine

Computer Critters had the ingenious idea of disguising computers as soft toys, and they will soon be marketed internationally. At the moment, however, there are sales of $3 million a year in the US.

opened up IBM standard to home users for the first time.

Alan Sugar, Amstrad's Managing Director, is happy to admit that he understands nothing of computer science. All the same he is a formidable negotiator. He begins by setting the price for his future products – always much lower than those of his competitors – then he argues every step of the way with his suppliers in order to hold to those prices.

In this way in 1984 Amstrad, a British producer of hi-fi systems, launched a cheap high performance home computer, the Amstrad 464, and the company joined the club of microcomputer producers.

The IBM Personal System/2 (1987)

On **2 April 1987 IBM** changed the rules of the microcomputing game by launching a new range of microcomputers called Personal System/2, or PS/2, with a different design from that of the previous PC and PC-AT.

The models in the PS/2 series are faster, more compact and easier to use, their screens are easier to read, they have greater RAM and mass memory and are designed to run several programs at once. Nevertheless, they are quite expensive and have not conquered a market dominated by PC compatibles.

NeXT (1989)

After leaving Apple, **Steve Jobs** came up with a new computer aimed at academics and researchers. This machine looks like a black cube and is produced by his new company, **NeXT**. It uses a Motorola 68030 microprocessor and four coprocessors and has the first erasable optical disk as its mass memory, with a capacity of 256 Mb (millions of bytes or characters). Jobs joined forces with powerful allies (notably IBM and Canon) before announcing in 1990 that they were bringing the first machines on to the market. These are now aimed at all businesses.

Atari's Portfolio (1989)

Since the launch of the first portables in Europe in 1984 the market has not stopped growing. **Atari** currently hold the record for the smallest IBM compatible computer with the Portfolio: 450g *1lb*, 20 × 11 × 3cm *8 × 4.4 × 1.2in.*

DOUG ENGELBART, INVENTOR OF THE 'RAPPORT' BETWEEN MAN AND MACHINE

If today's microcomputers are a thousand times easier to use than their predecessors, it is all thanks to people like Doug Engelbart. From the end of the 1950s onwards, this scientist from the Stanford Research Institute had visionary ideas that are still revolutionising the world of computer science. His most famous invention is definitely the mouse, but he was also behind most concepts related to interactivity: the screen with several windows, the Hypercard software's hypertext, integrated help systems, idea processing programs and composite text/image files were all conceived of at a time when the punched card was the only means of communication between people and computers.

Software

Operating systems

Origins (1954)

An operating system is software (or a program) which is used not by the person using the computer, but by the computer itself. It comes between the machine's electronic circuits and the application software (for example, word processing, accountancy) with which the user is in contact.

It acts like the conductor of an orchestra, co-ordinating the functioning of the computer's different elements. In microcomputing it is also a tool for standardisation, since it enables any software to function (with some modifications) on several different computers, provided they use the same operating system. Each one is designed for a particular type of microprocessor. The first operating system dates back to large computers: **Gene Amdahl** designed it in **1954** on an IBM 704.

Unix (1970)

The Unix operating system grew out of research done at Bell Laboratories and at the University of California at Berkeley. It was originally designed for minicomputers by **Ken Thompson** and **Dennis Ritchie**. Today there are versions of it for almost every sort of machine, from portables to supercomputers. The name Unix itself dates from **1970**, and the first version was marketed in 1975.

The main advantage of this rather complex operating system on a microcomputer is that it is multi-task and multi-user, which explains its growing share of the market.

CP/M (1976)

In **1976 Gary Kildall** invented the first operating system for microcomputers. He was working on assembling systems from components of different origins and found it a tedious chore having to rewrite all his programs every time he tried to read different floppy disks on the same central unit. The adaptor software that he wrote at the time was the core for the CP/M operating system. For some reason, Gary Kildall chose to give his company the grandiose name of Intergalactic Digital Research! The fact remains that CP/M rose to the rank of standard operating system for eight-bit professional microcomputers equipped with a Zilog Z 80 microprocessor.

However, when IBM approached Intergalactic Digital Research, to design the operating system for its PC (personal computer), the firm rejected the secrecy clause, thus unwittingly choosing the path that would lead it into decline. The market was taken over by Microsoft, who designed MS-DOS.

MS-DOS (1981)

In **1981** IBM asked **Microsoft** (a small company which has since expanded greatly) to provide them with an operating system for their future microcomputer, the PC. Bill Gates, who was Microsoft's young owner at the time, then bought Seattle Computer Products' Tim Patterson's 16-bit operating system SCP-DOS. Having adapted it, he christened it MS-DOS and delivered it to IBM (who call it PC-DOS). MS-DOS has since been considerably improved and is today the most widely used for professional microcomputers, since it is used by all IBM compatibles.

It was conceived and jointly launched by the two companies, under the direction of Bill Gates, to work with the PS/2.

OS/2 (1987)

In **April 1987 Microsoft** and **IBM** launched a new operating system which makes it possible for the first time to get the full use from microcomputers which use the Intel 80286 processor. However, it has not been well received.

Interface software

Integrating (or interface) software consists of utility programs situated between operating systems and applications software. They make for easier movement from one application to the next, with each taking place in a different window displayed on the screen. They are also intended to facilitate the adaptation of applications software from one type of computer to another.

Visi-On (1982)

The American company **Visicorp** was the first to come up with the idea of integrated software. Visi-On, which was first launched in **November 1982**, consisted of an integrating module on to which the required applications modules, such as word processing, spreadsheet, graphics, or file management applications, could be grafted. Visi-On could only use applications specifically designed for it and ultimately failed.

Windows (1985)

This was launched in **November 1985** by **Microsoft**. It required more than 50 man-years of work. In April 1987 it was adopted as the standard integrator by IBM.

Windows 3-0 (1990)

Launched with great ceremony by **Bill Gates** himself on **22 May 1990**, this is truly a threat to Macintosh. For this new integrating software makes it possible to use IBM-PCs and compatibles (an OS/2 version is to follow) with as much ease as an Apple; the different programs or options appear in windows on the screen, which can be called up using the keyboard. It is multitask and can even be used with some application softwares that were not specifically designed for it. The story of Bill Gates, Microsoft's founder (*see* MS/DOS) is the archetypal success story in information technology. Co-author of the first Basic, he combines genius for programming with a talent for management. Behind his youthful appearance hides one of the few minds that can influence the microcomputer's future. At the age of 35, he is already a dollar multi-millionaire.

Postscript (1985)

It was the American company **Adobe Systems** that developed the page description language Postscript, which was first used in

Bill Gates, the man who set up Microsoft.

microcomputing in Apple's Laserwrite printer, launched in **January 1985**.

It functions as an interface between the software and the laser printer, allowing the user to print directly onto the page. Its adoption by Apple, and then in March 1987 by IBM, ensured it would be standard equipment.

Languages

All software of whatever type is written using a programming language, which has its own vocabulary (its instructions list) and syntax. The most basic language (from which all others are ultimately derived) is machine language, a series of binary or hexadecimal numbers which are directly comprehensible to the computer but hard for the programmer to manipulate.

Assembler (1950)

Assemblers are types of languages close to machine language, but at a higher level, therefore easier to use. They are specific to a particular computer or microprocessor. Signs of the first assembler can be found in **1950** in the EDSAC, one of the ancestors of the large computers of today, which was developed in Cambridge by **M. V. Wilkes'** team. The first commercial assembler was the SAP (Symbolic Assembly Program), which was developed by the United Aircraft Corporation and installed on an IBM 704.

Artificial intelligence programming languages (1956)

Logical reasoning and formal calculus have led to entirely new programming methods. Today more than a hundred languages are used in the field of artificial intelligence (AI).

The first AI programming language IPL (Information Processing Language) was invented in 1956 by American scientists **A. Newell**, **D. Shaw** and **F. Simon**. It was developed specifically to write the LT (Logic Theorist) program, capable of resolving mathematical logic problems.

Lisp (1958)

Although old by computer standards, Lisp is the most commonly used language in artificial intelligence. As early as 1958, **J. McCarthy** had developed the particular concept of list processing that forms the basis of this language whose name is a contraction of 'list' and 'processing'. Since Lisp needs a lot of memory it generally requires fairly large computers to run properly, but microcomputer-based versions have been written.

Cobol (1959)

Cobol (*C*ommon *B*usiness *O*rientated *L*anguage), the prime language for business management applications, was launched in 1959 under the aegis of the Conference on Data Systems Languages in the United States. It belongs to the world of large computers, but although it now seems very dated it is still widely used.

Basic (1965)

Invented in 1965 at Dartmouth College (USA) by **Thomas E. Kurtz** and **John G. Kemeny**, Basic was originally designed to help students to learn programming. Basic stands for '*B*eginners *A*ll-purpose *S*ymbolic *I*nstruction *C*ode'. It was developed at a time when microcomputers did not exist and was adapted for use on them in 1974 by Bill Gates and Paul Allen, the founders of Microsoft. Today Basic is the standard language of all home and office microcomputing and its reputation as a beginner's language with little power is becoming increasingly unjustified.

Pascal (1969)

Named after the French mathematician, Pascal was developed in 1969 in the United States by **Niklaus Wirth**. The idea governing its design was to give programming students their own language, which was well structured and would instil good writing habits. It is more powerful than Basic and is often used in microcomputing, in universities and to write wide-circulation professional software.

C (1972)

This language is rapidly gaining popularity in the development of wide distribution software applications. C was created in 1972 at the Bell Laboratories in the USA by **Dennis Ritchie** – one of the inventors of the Unix operating systems – specifically to help the development of Unix. C has the innovative feature of mixing high level code (which is easy to manipulate) with low level code (which is efficient). It is based on BCPL, a language developed at the Massachusetts

Institute of Technology and at Cambridge University.

Prolog (1973)

One of the main languages adapted to artificial intelligence is French. Prolog was designed in 1973 by **Alain Colmerauer** and his team at the University of Luminy-Marseilles, France. Its basic principle, which draws on mathematical logic, was revolutionary: instead of telling the computer how to solve a given problem – as happens with traditional languages, which are called procedural – the programmer simply sets out the data for the problem. Prolog then gets on with finding the solution. Although Prolog can function on supercomputers, it has recently come into use on microcomputers.

Ada (1979)

Ada was developed in 1979 after five years of effort by a team from CIL-Honeywell-Bull, headed by the Frenchman **Jean Ichbiach**, in response to a invitation to tender by the American Defence Department in 1974.

This language takes its name from Ada, Countess Lovelace, who may be regarded as the earliest programmer.

Ada has become a world standard. It is in general use for military and space applications, air control, etc.

Alsys, the company set up by Jean Ichbiach in 1980, is involved in microcomputers too, and in 1987 produced Ada compilers for them.

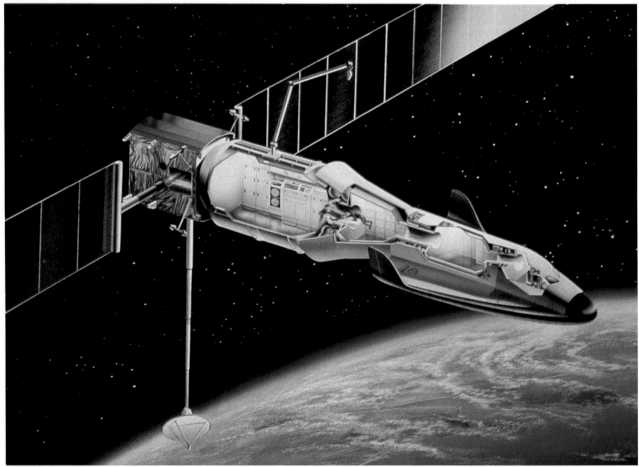

Hermes will use the computer language Ada to undertake some of its important tasks in space.

Applications software

The term applications software refers to programs which deliver a specific service directly to the user, such as word processing, printing payslips, or playing games.

Visicalc (1979)

Visicalc was invented by two Americans, **Dan Bricklin** and **Bob Frankston**, and launched in **1979** on Apple computers. It was the world's first spreadsheet and an excellent example of how lively the minds of microcomputing inventors are. Certainly, before Visicalc, no programmer working on large computers had thought of such a program, which combines a table of figures with a table of formulae which determine the relations between the figures. As a result, it is possible to construct very complex models (for example, the provisional budget of a company), and to see in an instant what would happen if one of the hypotheses were changed: the spreadsheet automatically recalculates all the figures. Today the spreadsheet programs are among the most widely used software on microcomputers, and there are hundreds of them. Similar tools have been developed for large computers.

Wordstar (1979)

The first major word processing software for microcomputers was launched in **1979** by the American company **Micropro**. It is still on the market today and has given rise to a whole host of programs of the same type.

The version 5.5, available since the end of 1989, is better than the original: it has a dictionary of 100000 words, mathematical functions, graphics, etc.

dBase II (1980)

Launched in **1980** by the American firm **Ashton-Tate**, dBase II is the archetypal database management software for microcomputers. It makes it possible to classify, sort and select information according to numerous criteria. It was developed in October 1979 by **C. Wayne Ratcliffe**, who had marketed it under the name Vulcan before selling it to Ashton-Tate. New versions will soon be launched.

1-2-3 (1982)

This software with its strange name has given rise to a whole new generation of integrated software. It was designed by one man, **Jonathan Sachs**, and launched in **October 1982** by the American company Lotus. Its particular feature is that it combines three functions in one microcomputer program. It is above all a very high-power spreadsheet, but is also combined with a small file management facility and most importantly with a graphics module which makes it possible to visualise in curve form any group of figures presented in the spreadsheet. 1-2-3 is still one of the most widely used software products on PC compatibles.

Mac Paint (1984)

Written by **Bill Atkinson** in **1984**, Mac Paint led to thousands of beginners becoming interested in computers. This graphics software, specially designed for the Apple Macintosh, works on an instinctive basis: the user draws by moving the mouse on the desk after selecting one of the symbols 'pencil', 'paintbrush', 'spray' and even 'rubber' which are displayed on the screen and give lines of different appearance and thickness. The user simply selects a paint pot to colour in a shape, the lasso to grasp part of the drawing and move it elsewhere, and so on. Since its creation, Mac Paint has had countless imitators.

Mac Write (1984)

Mac Write was presented in **1984** at the same time as the Mac Paint software, and was designed for use on the Macintosh. It was the first word processing software intended to be used without training. **Randy Wigginton**, **Ed Ruder** and **Don Breuner** from Encore Systems designed it for Apple.

Page Maker (1985)

On **15 July 1985** the American company **Aldus** perfected revolutionary software designed for the Apple Macintosh and called Page Maker. It was the first software to enable a single individual to write, lay out, paginate and print a newspaper or book, including illustrations, using only a microcomputer and a laser printer.

Since then the product has been much improved and, with the 3.0 of 1989, has become PC compatible.

Artificial intelligence

AI is a scientific discipline consisting of writing computer programs that attempt to model human intelligence. AI formalises human knowledge and reasoning, whereas data processing merely manipulates information.

According to this definition, AI could date back to 450 BC when the Greek philosopher Socrates envisaged reducing all reasoning to a simple calculation in the form of something like geometry.

Fundamental papers relating to AI were published as early as 1953 in America. However, the term was used officially for the first time at the International Joint Conference on Artificial Intelligence held at Washington (USA) in 1969.

Today, the most popular application of AI is in building expert systems.

Expert systems

An expert system (ES) is a software program characterised by its ability to reason by logical inference starting from a problem set by the user. The system uses a base of knowledge and a set of rules called production rules, drawn up by a human expert.

In the early 1960s some researchers were already putting forward the idea that the laws of reason, combined with the power of a computer, could produce systems that go beyond the capacity of human experts. However, there are severe theoretical reservations.

The first operational ES appeared in the early 1970s. There are very many of them today, in different domains.

Oldest expert system (1961)

In **1961 J. R. Slagle** produced a thesis at the Massachusetts Institute of Technology (MIT) on a heuristic program for solving problems related to symbolic mathematics. This was the beginning of SAINT (*Symbolic Automatic Integrator*), which culminated in MACSYMA, presented in 1971 by two MIT researchers, W. A. Martin and R. J. Fateman. Today an improved version of MACSYMA surpasses most human experts in performing symbolic differential and integral calculus. Today there are thousands of expert systems in such varied fields as medicine, chemistry, mining prospection, teaching, etc.

Components

Electronic tube (1906)

It was not until **1906** that an American inventor, **Lee De Forest** (1873–1961) developed the necessary element for the practical application of Boole's binary system. The electronic tube controlled the movement of electrons across a vacuum inside a hermetically sealed glass bulb. Also known as an 'electronic valve', the main feature of this component was a direct current of electrons that produced the two conditions indispensable to binary logic: stop and go. On this basis, circuits could be produced according to binary logic, thus marking the dawn of the age of electronic computers.

Transistor (1947)

The transistor was invented at the end of **1947** by three physicists at the Bell Laboratories,

USA: **William B. Shockley**, **John Bardeen** and **Walter H. Brattain**. The transistor is a true semiconductor triode. It is the electronic component which characterised the second generation of computers. It is a solid-state component, and rapidly became widespread. It was originally made with germanium but after 1960 transistors used silicon, which is more stable.

Transistors can detect, amplify and correct currents; they can also break them. They can produce very high frequency electromagnetic waves and open or close circuits in the space of a millionth of a second. They have allowed advances to be made in information technology, communications, aeronautics and have also made electronic watches and pacemakers possible.

Quantum effect transistor (1989)

Presented as the transistor of the year 2000, a quantum effect transistor has been developed by the research centre of **Texas Instruments** in Dallas (USA). It works on the basis of the wave behaviour of electrons and on the tunnel effect, which in particular requires a control of nano-electronics (electronics on the scale of a billionth of a metre).

A hundred times smaller than today's transistors, it reaches execution speeds a thousand times faster.

This new transistor, which has been studied since 1982, was developed for the US Army.

Integrated circuit (1959)

On 12 September 1958 **Jack St Clair Kilby**, a young American engineer from the University of Illinois who had recently been taken on at Texas Instruments, showed the results of his work to some of his colleagues. He had assembled a few transistors and capacitors on a single support. This discovery was to revolutionise the electronics world. A patent for this first integrated circuit was applied for in **1959** and granted in 1964.

An integrated circuit is an electronic mechanism in which different components (transistors, resistances, capacitors, etc.) are diffused or implanted, then connected up within a thin layer of semi-conductor, such as silicon, enabling the formation of complex electronic circuits which carry out complete functions.

Microprocessor (1971)

In **1971 Marcian E. Hoff**, then working for Intel, developed the first microprocessor which he baptised the 4004. Hoff brought together the elementary functions of a computer on a single electronic component (an integrated circuit). It contained the equivalent of 230 transistors and was a 4-bit processor.

Intel was set up in 1968 by Robert Noyce (1927–90), together with a few friends who were working at Fairchild. They were known as the Fairchildren, founders of Silicon Valley. Noyce had already been involved in the invention of the integrated circuit with Kilby.

Z 80 (1976)

In **1976 Zilog** launched one of the microprocessors that did most for the microcomputing boom, the Z 80. The operating system CP/M and leading software (Word-

star, dBase II) were written for this 8-bit processor.

6502 (1976)

In **1976 Chuck Peddle**, one of microcomputing's great pioneers, developed the 6502, an 8-bit microprocessor marketed by the American company MOS Technologies. It was chosen by Stephen Wozniak and Steve Jobs to equip their first Apple II, and has had a fairytale career: it is still a core element in the latest versions of the Apple II, and an extraordinary software library has been designed around it.

8086 (1978)

In **June 1978 Intel** launched the first 16-bit

A circular silicon wafer, comprising numerous individual integrated circuits, is photographed inside a processing oven during one of the stages of manufacture. Kilby's invention has transformed the world of computers.

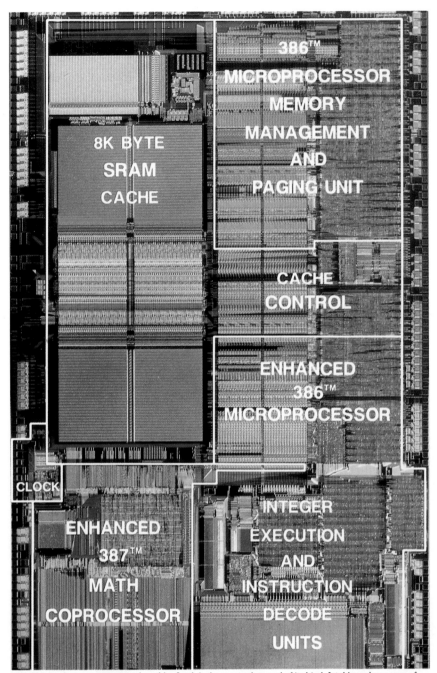

This 32-bit microprocessor, produced by Intel, is the most advanced of its kind. Intel have been one of the most successful companies in this field.

was calculation. With the growing stress on user-friendliness, the manipulation of graphics has come to take up an increasing proportion of microcomputer power. This is why in **1986 Texas Instruments** and **Intel** each separately launched graphics processors designed to ease the burden of the main processor. Texas' 34010 is particularly used in extension cards for IBM PC compatibles and Intel's 82786 is its direct competitor.

Integration

Because the integration of electronic components grew out of many different technologies, its beginnings are hard to trace. The problem was to produce increasingly complex and small integrated circuits. In the case of a computer, the time taken by a signal to go from one circuit to the next limits its performance. Increasing the micro-electronic density inside a package is then of prime importance.

In the early 1970s electronic engineers began talking about large scale integration (LSI). This meant a single 'chip' could hold around 500 components. Some five years later very large scale integration (VLSI) appeared, with up to 10000 active elements. Now one talks in terms of millions.

Microframe (1989)

A good example of integration: 10 million transistors in 25cm² *4sq in*: the SCAMP (*Single Chip A Mainframe Processor*) from **Unisys** contains as many circuits as a minicomputer. The machine built with this processor, the Microframe, measures 17 × 58 × 43cm *7 × 23 × 17in* and weighs 23kg *50lb*. It was designed as a microcomputer and in fact is very like one, while having the power of a mini.

Transputer (1983)

According to some specialists, this is the most important invention in computer science since the microprocessor. It was designed by **Ian Barron** for **Inmos** (UK) around a very high integration microprocessor featuring a new microscopic architecture which enabled it to carry out parallel processing of information.

microprocessor to have commercial success, the 8086. It was developed by a team headed by **Bill Pohlman**. It has considerable strategic importance, since one of its versions, the 8088, an 8–16-bit processor, was chosen by IBM to equip their first microcomputer, the PC. Since then, IBM has bought part of Intel's capital, and all their microcomputers use Intel microprocessors.

80386 (1985)

In **1985 Intel** launched their 32-bit microprocessor, the 80386, which offers microcomputers performance at the level of yesterday's minicomputers (it is capable of carrying out 3–4 million instructions a second), while being compatible with the software designed for its predecessors (8086 and 80286). In particular, it can run several programs designed

for an 8086 simultaneously, each working as though it had a real 8086 entirely at its disposal. The first microcomputers using the 80386 appeared at the end of 1986.

68000 (1979)

In the United States in **1979 Motorola** launched the 68000, the first of a series of microprocessors competing with those of Intel. This 16–32-bit processor is known above all for having been chosen by Apple for their Macintosh and, secondarily, by Atari for their ST series of personal microcomputers. It gave rise to several other versions, notably the 68020 used by the Macintosh II.

Graphics processors (1986)

At first the main function of microprocessors

Classical computers, by contrast, work 'serially', one bit at a time.

The first transputer, Inmos's T 414, was highly regarded but did not sell well. But the performance of the T 800, which went into mass production in November 1987, is impressive. Its architecture gives it 12 times more power than Intel's 80386 microprocessor. Its originality lies in the way that it enables design of multiprocessor systems whose architecture can be modified by software, depending on the problems to be solved.

The European program to build a supercomputer is based on the transputer.

Internal memory (1947)

The internal memory of a computer is the mechanism which enables it provisionally to store information just before, during and after it is processed. In **1947**, at Manchester University, the Englishman **F. C. Williams** experimented with electrostatic tubes used as a memory. In 1949, at Cambridge University, EDSAC, one of the computer's first ancestors, used delay lines. These were tubes filled with water or mercury, blocked off at both ends with crystals which transformed electronic signals into sonic vibrations. Because sound travels more slowly than electricity, it was possible to store some information in them. Legend has it that Alan Turing advised putting

gin in the delay lines. Then, in 1949, Jay Forrester used ferrite cores for the memory of the Whirlwind. Cores continued to be used until 1964, when they gave way to semi-conductors.

Random access memory (1970)

The first component of dynamic *R*andom *A*ccess *M*emory, or RAM, was produced in **1970** by **Inter**. This circuit, developed by **Bob Abbott** under the direction of **Les Vadasz**, was called 1103 by the American company and had only a 1 K-bit capacity (1024 bits or units of information). Random access memory, which can be both written to and read, forms the usable working memory of computers.

Current DRAMs

Texas Instruments holds most of the patents relating to DRAM, which is a type of semiconductor memory that saves information as long as it is plugged in, and which currently dominates the market.

In February 1987 IBM announced that they had developed the commercial manufacture of a 4-bit component, and many other manufacturers followed them. Then on 13 February 1990 IBM announced that they had begun experimental construction of 16-bit memories. Other manufacturers are working on the development of such memories, but have not

yet reached the production stage.

A 64-bit DRAM (1995)

In 1990 the German group **Siemens** together with **IBM** announced that they were joining forces to develop a 64-bit superchip. These new microprocessors should be produced and marketed by the mid 1990s; the development budget is estimated at $580 million.

SRAM: 4-bit (1990)

The Japanese currently seem to be leading the field of SRAM, or Static Random Access Memory. Unlike a DRAM, an SRAM does not need constant reactivating to save the information in its millions of cells.

Sony, Hitachi and Toshiba have all independently announced the development of a new generation of 4-bit SRAMs; current SRAMs are 1-bit.

Mass memory

The first mass memory, in other words a medium enabling the permanent storage of data, was invented long before computer science by the Frenchman **Joseph-Marie Jacquard** in **1805**. This was the punched card, and it was designed for his loom. Hermann Hollerith used it again in 1890 on his machine designed

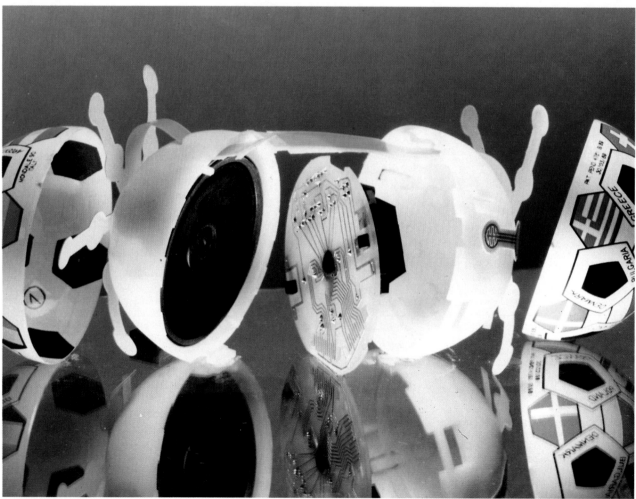

Texas Instruments and Malbo developed the musical football for the 1990 World Cup – press the flag of your country and it plays the anthem.

for the American census. Then came magnetic tape, tested for the first time on an EDVAC in 1949, and removable disks, which were first marketed by IBM in 1962.

Floppy disks (1950)

Floppy disks, universally used on microcomputers, were invented in 1950 at the Imperial University in Tokyo by **Doctor Yoshiro Nakamats**, an inventor who boasts of having 2360 patents for objects as diverse as golf clubs and loudspeakers. He granted the sales licence for the disk to IBM.

Hard disk card (1985)

In 1985 the American company **Plus Development Corporation** revolutionised mass memory technology by launching an extension card designed for IBM PCs equipped with an extra-flat hard disk of 10 Mb. Before this, hard disks (large capacity fixed magnetic media) were awkward and fragile. The Hardcard, as it is called, is only 2.5cm *1in* thick. Many other producers have followed this lead.

CD-ROM (1985)

The CD-ROM, invented by **Philips** and promoted throughout the world in collaboration with **Sony**, is simply a laser-read compact disc, similar to those used in hi-fi systems, but adapted to computing uses. It has the advantage of containing a thousand times more data than a diskette. Its disadvantage is that the data on it can be read, but new data cannot be written on to it.

The CD-ROM began to take off in 1988. It found professional outlets: Renault decided to put all the technical documentation for its network (12000 graphics plates and 80000 pages of text) on to CD-ROM; training courses for Airbus pilots are now on CD-ROM, etc. But its main markets are professional and in teaching.

Interactive compact disc or CD-I (1989)

Put forward by **Philips** and **Sony** at the first CD-ROM conference in Seattle organised by Microsoft in March 1986, the CD-I arrived on the professional market in 1989 and should reach a wider public in 1992.

Derived from CD-ROM technology, it stores interactive programs, combining high quality sound, animated images and texts. The disc is read by a reader resembling a hi-fi laser deck connected to a television screen and stereo system, and which is in reality a powerful computer.

Write once optical disk (1988)

Write once optical disks, called WORM (*Write Once Read Many* times), have been the object of much research. They have been marketed by **IBM** since 1988.

A 16 M-bit EPROM (1990)

In **February 1990** the Japanese giant NEC announced the development of the first erasable and programmable 16 M-bit memory (EPROM). NEC has succeeded in putting 18 million transistors and other components on a 7.1 × 17.1mm *0.28 × 0.67in* silicon chip.

Computer peripherals

The terminal (1940)

The first experiment that involved a terminal connected to a remote computer was conducted in 1940 by **Bell Laboratories**. The computer was in New York and the terminal at Dartmouth College, New Hampshire.

Light pen (1963)

Light pens are accessories with which users can draw on their screens, as they would do with a real pen. A light pen enables them to move part of a drawing, to 'take' a colour from a 'palette' and use it to 'paint' the surface they touch with the tip, and to command different functions. The first light pen was presented in 1963 at the Massachusetts Institute of Technology (MIT) by **I. E. Sutherland**, who was associated with the conversational graphics system Sketchpad. Today this accessory is chiefly used on computer-aided design (CAD) consoles.

The mouse (1965)

The mouse is a small device that slides in all directions on a desk and which makes it possible to interact naturally with the computer. Its use was popularised by Apple with the Lisa and the Macintosh models in 1983. However, it was the little-known American inventor **Douglas Engelbart** who conceived and designed it. His brilliant idea was to have the computer operator place his or her hand on a small box or mouse. A sphere on the underside of the mouse is used to measure movements which are then transmitted to the computer via a lead – the tail of the mouse. These movements are translated to the cursor on the screen: if the mouse is pushed to the right the cursor goes to the right; if the mouse is pushed away from the user the cursor moves up, and so on. This revolutionary input device, originally found only on Apple computers, was adopted by IBM in 1987.

Mouse-keyboard (1990)

A Californian computer scientist, **Kirk MacKenzie**, has invented a mouse equipped with a keyboard. The Power Mouse adapts to programs designed for use with a mouse, to which it brings keyboard facilities, or vice versa. It went on the market in spring 1990 in the United States.

Dataglove (1988)

After three years of research, two engineers from a small Californian company, VPL Research, **Thomas Zimmerman** and **L. Harvill** have developed the Dataglove. The glove consists of fibre optic strands sandwiched between the layers of fabric along each finger. A remarkable piece of equipment, this glove allows the user to 'dive' into a display unit and enables him or her to manipulate in three dimensions the objects represented on the screen.

Tactile screen (1985)

In 1985 **Zenith** (USA) presented the first tactile screen system, based on surface acoustic wave technology: all the user has to do to give a command is touch a section of the screen.

Ergonomic keyboard (1990)

The fight against QWERTY (the traditional layout of keyboards) continues: American **Willy Diernisse** has patented a new type of keyboard, which makes it possible to increase typing speed a great deal. According to the inventor, after 65 hours of training the typist of the future will be able to type 100 words a minute; with today's keyboards, the average is 70 wpm after 100 hours' training.

Optical keyboard (1990)

There are no electrical or electronic contacts in this keyboard, patented by **Alain Souloumiac** in 1986 and put on the market in April 1990. Instead, it uses light to identify movement of the keys, which are themselves connected to optical fibres. This keyboard can safely be used in surroundings where

The PowerMouse, developed by Kit MacKenzie, adapts to programs for the mouse or the keyboard.

there is a danger of explosion, and is un-affected by either electromagnetic impulses or static electricity. Water cannot harm it – not even a cup of coffee can! Last but not least, it is undetectable by pirates or the simply curious.

Recognising handwriting (1990)

It is not always easy to use a computer if you have to take notes standing up, as is the case for people in many jobs: sales, the police or maintenance personnel, for example. Grid-pad has been designed for them. It is a portable computer shaped like a pad of paper, which can be written on and it can read – as yet capital letters only. Gridpad is PC compatible.

The inventor was **Jeff Hawkins**. In his early 30s, he has been around in Silicon Valley for ten years, and in 1983 went into Grid, a small firm specialising in portables. However, in 1986 he decided to return to studying and specialised in neurobiology at Berkeley. It was his research there that finally led to the invention of the Gridpad. He is now working on artificial intelligence projects.

Eye control (1986)

In **1986** the American company **Analytics Inc.** developed a prototype computer which obeys sounds and the eye. It uses an infra-red beam to record eye movements. The user stares at a point on the screen, then gives a command to a micro and the machine carries it out immediately. This system could facilitate the control of robots or the selection of compo-nents on an assembly line.

Speech recognition (1950)

The first machine to recognise ten numbers pronounced by a human voice as a series of sonic signals was built at the Bell Laboratories in the United States by **K. H. Davies**. That was in **1950**. Since then progress has been slow.

Speech synthesis (1933)

The first electric speech machine, the Voder (Voice Demonstrator), was built in **1933** by the American **H. W. Dudley**. It was followed in 1939 by the Vocoder (Voice Coder). Speech synthesis is based on the theory of visible speech, formulated in 1948 by the Americans **R. K. Potter**, **G. A. Kopp** and **H. C. Green**, who showed how phonemes (vocal sounds) cor-respond to graphic traces.

Speech synthesis, which poses far fewer theoretical problems than speech recogni-tion, is used in many domains, such as industry, cars and games.

Printer (1953)

The printer enables data provided by the computer to be printed on paper. The first fast printer worthy of the name was developed in **1953** by **Remington Rand** (USA). It printed 600 lines of 120 characters a minute.

The most widely used technologies fall into two types: impact printers (using dot matrix or daisy wheels) and non-impact printers (thermal or laser transfer).

Dot matrix printer (1957)

Dot matrix printing is an invention which has had the greatest success: the majority of

Gridpad is the first portable computer that is capable of recognising handwriting. Its development cost many millions of pounds.

Palm Top is an electronic notebook that can recognise Japanese lettering. Developed by Sony, it is only available in Japan.

printers use this principle. The print head has a vertical row of needles which are propelled forward electromagnetically as the head runs over each line. The first dot matrix printers were marketed by **IBM** in **1957**.

Thermal printer (1966)

Invented in **1966** by **Texas Instruments**, thermal printing was first used for microcomputers. The print head is made of resistant needles which are heated when an electric current is passed through them. This technique requires special paper and gave way to 'thermal transfer', where the needle does not directly heat the paper but an inked ribbon. IBM retained this technology on its recent typewriter-printers.

Daisy wheel printer (1978)

The American company **Diablo**, since bought by Rank Xerox, invented this procedure which was inspired by techniques used on typewriters.

Laser printer (1975)

The first laser printer was introduced by **IBM** in **1975**. It was an extremely expensive and bulky machine, designed for high-speed printing. In 1978 the IBM 3800 was followed by the ND2 from Siemens and the 9700 from Xerox, but it was not until 1984 – with Hewlett-Packard's Laserjet – that the laser printer began to expand into the world of microcomputers. It works on a similar principle to that of offset printing: a laser beam 'paints' the letters on to a roller and the sheets of paper are printed by rotation. In 1988 colour laser printers came on to the market.

Applications

Computer graphics (1950)

The art of computer graphics can be traced back to the graphics made for wallpaper by Burnett in California from 1937 onwards. These graphics were based on Lissajous figures. But it was **Ben F. Laposky** who, in **1950**, really founded the art of computer graphics.

Computer graphics are pure products of computer technology and two or three years ago still represented something of a feat (both technically and financially!). Today, still graphics are two a penny and can be produced on microcomputers. As for animated graphics – which are frequently used in television advertisements for example – these can be so perfect and 'real', that they are sometimes quite disturbing.

The work of the companies Robert Abel Associates, Digital Equipment Corporation (USA) and Sogitec (France) has now become famous in this field.

Automatic translation (1950)

In 1946 **W. Weaver** and **A. D. Booth** thought of using a computer to help with translation. But the techniques had not been perfected, and it was not until **1950** that Weaver and Booth could try out their idea.

In 1970 Doctor P. Thomas developed a universal translation system, SYSTRAN. It was first put to spectacular use during the meeting of Apollo and Soyuz in 1975. It was adopted by the European Community in 1981.

There are some systems that can translate in particular fields or with a limited vocabulary. But none of these systems can work without human intervention or error for any text of some difficulty.

Music (1956)

Composers were the first to use computers for artistic creation. The first of these were the Americans **M. Hiller** and **M. Isaacson** in their work on the *Illiac Suite* in **1956**. Also important are the works of M. Phillipot and I. Xenakis, C. Risset and M. Matthews from the Bell Laboratories (USA), and lastly those of the Vincennes Group.

At the end of the 1970s, computers became widely used in all fields of music (from pop music shows to teaching).

Cinema (1964)

The film industry was quick to grasp the possibilities of computer graphics. One interesting example is the pioneering work of **Peter Foldes** in his film *The Hunger*, but Steven Lisberger was the first to use all the computer's possibilities in the shooting of *Tron* in 1982.

Image animation (1951)

Computerised image animation was first experimented on at the **Massachusetts Institute of Technology** (MIT) in **1951**. But it was not until the early 1960s that the potential of the technique was fully understood. Today it is used in the fields of medicine, architecture (with models in three dimensions), space exploration and chemistry.

Flight simulators (1970)

Around **1970 General Electric** supplied NASA with the first flight simulation programs. The power of today's machines provides amazing possibilities and all pilots are now trained on simulators. The advantages of this are obvious: pilots can try out difficult manoeuvres without risk of losing their lives or destroying a plane.

The world of simulation (1988)

Simulation is now present in almost every domain: such phenomena as nuclear power plant accidents, a pollution cloud over the Alps, molecules that do not exist, Formula 1 cars that are faster than real ones and chariot races can all be simulated. From hi-tech industry to electronic games, computer graphics recreate reality. Things have reached the point where Californian scientists have made an astounding wager: the aim of the Biosphere 2 program is to simulate all the ecosystems of the planet.

Digital control (1956)

The digital control of machine-tools first appeared in **1956**, the year that the *Automatically Programmed Tools* (APT) language was created for the US Air Force.

Computer-aided design (CAD) (1960)

Computer-aided design began in the **1960s** in the context of the major American military aeronautics programmes.

The term refers to a set of techniques which can be used to create data that describe an object to be designed, to manipulate that data in a conversational mode and to arrive at a finished form of the design.

After its adoption by the military, CAD penetrated civil aeronautics and the motor and computing industries. It enables an object (for

Istar can create 3-D images of sites by processing numeric data gathered from observation satellites. This has enabled technicians to produce this view of the venue for the Winter Olympics.

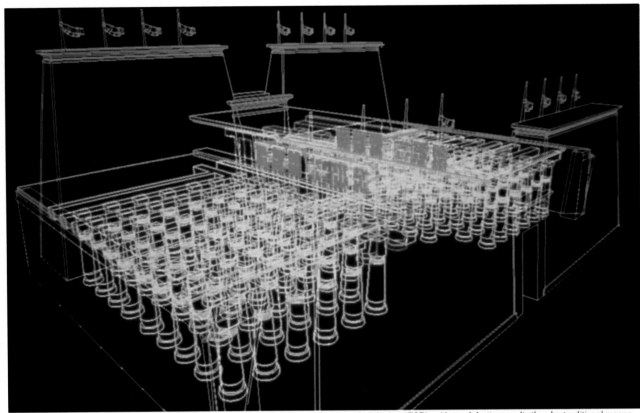

Scientists have begun to reconstruct the Temple of Amon in Egypt by using computer-aided design (CAD), with much better results than by traditional means.

example, a car) to be drawn in three dimensions and to be examined in a great number of theoretical circumstances, even before the building has begun. Today CAD plays an essential role in almost all fields of industry.

Robots

Automata

The first automata are to be found in antiquity at the time of Hero of Alexandria (1st century AD). The Arabs kept the tradition going. In 809 Sultan Harun ar-Rashid gave an animated clock to Charlemagne.

But it was not until the work of Jacques de Vaucanson (1709–82) that a machine was built that perfectly imitated natural animation. In Paris in 1738 Vaucanson exhibited a duck which astounded everyone: it flapped its wings, swam, smoothed its feathers with its beak, drank and pecked; furthermore, after a certain time it evacuated the food it had taken in, in the form of a soft substance.

The torch was then taken up by two Swiss: Pierre and Henry-Louis Droz. In 1773 they constructed a drawing machine. Their creation was so perfect that they were put on trial for witchcraft. Fortunately for them, there was growing public interest in scientific methods and the verdict was in their favour.

Androids

In our imagination, robots are destined to replace people in certain tasks and should therefore look like them. But industrial robots, whose numbers are ever-increasing, look just like machines, whereas androids look like us.

There are many notable androids in operation: *Lincoln* at Disneyland, Bernard Szajner's *Einstein*, Pascal Pinteau's *Leonardo da Vinci*, and so on.

The word 'robot' (1920)

The word 'robot' was coined in 1920 by Czech dramatist **Karel Capek** for his play *R.U.R. (Rossum's Universal Robots)*. The term comes from the Slavonic root *rab*, meaning 'slave', which became the Czech word *robota* or forced labourer.

First industrial robot (1962)

The first robot designed for industrial use appeared in 1962 with the creation of Unimates, mass produced by **Unimation Inc.** of Dambury, Connecticut (USA). Today, tens

of thousands of robots are at work in factories throughout the world, with thousands of intelligent robots performing the most varied tasks.

Robots in medicine

Robot patient (1980)

The first of these was the Japanese company **Koken**'s robot patient in 1980, which was designed to help teaching in universities. The following year Michael Gordon, a professor of cardiology in Miami, created *Harvey*, a robot which could simulate 26 illnesses. Replicas of *Harvey* are widely available.

Robot nurse (1983)

Melkong (Medical Electric King Kong) was

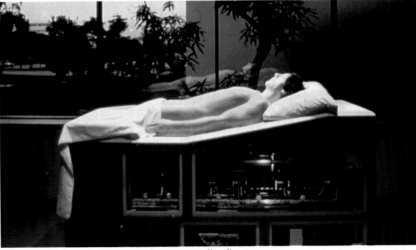

This is Harvey, *the robot that can simulate many cardiac diseases.*

created by **Professor Hiroyasu Funakubo** of Japan. It can hold a patient in its arms, wash him, put him to bed, and tuck in the sheets!

Police robots (1983)

Denning Mobile Robotics (Massachusetts, USA) has been working on security robots since **1983**. The Denning robots are also capable of guarding factories and banks from robbers.

Walking robots (1983)

One of the major areas of research in robotics is that of giving robots the means of moving, in particular so that they can work in hostile environments where people cannot go.

There are many prototypes:
- *bipeds:* Certainly the most remarkable is the WHL-II, conceived by **Ichiro Kato** and built by Hitachi.
- *quadrupeds:* The Japanese Titan III can move over uneven ground and also climb stairs.
- *multi-legged:* The most developed of these are undoubtedly Odex 1, 2, 3, from the American company **Odetics**, which can overcome obstacles while carrying a load of 500kg *1102lb.*

Domestic robots (1986)

Hero 2000 was born in **1986**. Its big brother, Hero 1, was designed in 1982 by the American company **Heathkit**. The aim of both was educational: they were designed to initiate young people into robotics, but they can also teach languages. They can also carry out a number of useful tasks, such as carrying packages. Many, less ambitious, personal robots can be programmed to perform a certain number of tasks, but fundamentally these are just modern automata.

A robot for nuclear power plants (1988)

Using its two jointed caterpillar tracks, Centaur II, developed by the **French Commission for Atomic Energy** jointly with the **Cyberg** company, can move around in all sectors of nuclear installations in the case of incidents giving rise to dangerous radiation levels. It is autonomous and waterproof and can perform a certain number of simple operations.

Robot barman (1990)

The Robotender, from **Honeybee Robotics**, New York, can pick up glasses, pour drinks and prepare a hundred cocktails, mixing anything from kir to Manhattans perfectly. But it puts the glass down on the bar and does not serve the customer directly.

Robot shearer (1991)

In Australia there are 165 million sheep to shear. Hence the need to invent a mechanised shearing procedure. After ten years of research the Australian company **Merino Wool Harvesting** has developed prototype robot shearers, capable of shearing a sheep in 100 seconds instead of the three minutes taken by a human. These robots are due to come on to the market in **1991**.

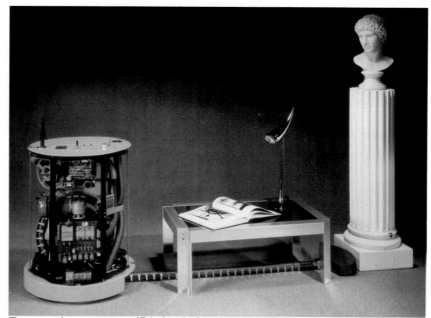

There are only ten prototypes of Tekodex, *the first robot vacuum cleaner, which was designed by Bernard and André Jonas.*

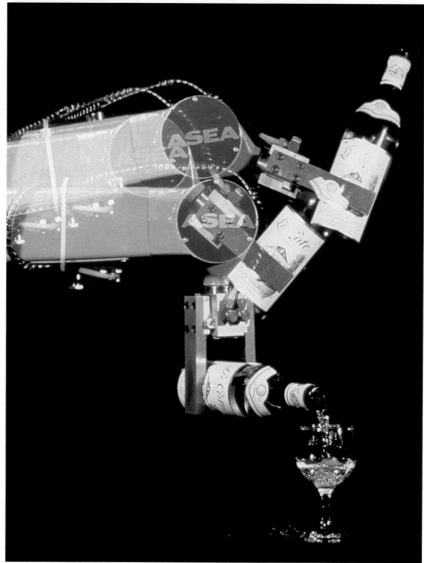

This robot barman can prepare perfectly up to a hundred cocktails.

A 17th-century illustration of a French kitchen.

In the kitchen

Artificial flavouring (1874)

In 1874 two Germans **Doctor Wilhelm Haarman** and **Professor Ferdinand Tiemann**, synthesised vanillan, the principal component in vanilla husk. Two years later Karl Reimer conceived a chemical compound which fully reproduced the flavour of vanilla. This was the beginning of artificial flavouring.

Beer (4th millennium BC)

Man has been drinking beer for thousands of years: in India (c.3200 BC), in China (c.3000 BC) and above all in the Middle East where the Sumerians reserved 40 percent of their cereal crop for brewing. In Egypt beer was considered to be the national drink. It was, however, very different from the beverage we know today. Less liquid than our beer, it resembled a kind of drinkable 'bread' but had nonetheless a high alcohol content (13 to 15 degrees proof) and was generally made from barley. In the Middle Ages monks introduced hops into the recipe and from the 12th century professional brewers appeared.

The Germans are the world's greatest beer drinkers, consuming over 250 pints per head each year. The British, by comparison, drink only 195 pints. Budweiser is the world's bestselling brand.

Alcohol-free beer (19th century)

Alcohol-free beer was created in France at the end of the 19th century (between 1873 and 1900).

Breakfast cereals (1898)

Corn flakes were popularised in 1898 by the American **Will Keith Kellogg**. Before that, Henry D. Perky of Denver, Colorado (USA), was the first, in 1893, to have the idea of making ready prepared breakfast cereals. Having met a man who nursed his stomach pains by eating boiled wheat soaked in milk every morning, Perky came up with a product made from wheat, which he called Shredded Wheat.

Will Keith Kellogg was employed by his elder brother, a doctor at the Battle Creek Sanitarium in Michigan. Working at night in the hospital kitchen, Will boiled wheat in an effort to help the doctor search for a digestible substitute for bread. One day in 1894, after a batch of boiled wheat accidentally was left to stand, the brothers tried again. Unknowingly, they had tempered the wheat by letting it stand. The compressed wheat was flaked off rollers with blades devised by Will. Thus was the modern-day breakfast cereal born. Granose Flakes were launched in 1894, which became Corn Flakes in 1898.

Camembert (1790)

It is not known whether **Marie Harel** got the recipe from her mother, Marie-Catherine Fontaine, or from a non-juror priest from the Brie district whom she sheltered at the start of the Revolution. What we do know is that her cheese was very successful at the Camembert markets in Orne, France. Her daughter and son-in-law, who were excellent business people, took over from her, establishing the cheese's reputation and giving it its name.

Carbonated mineral water (1741)

Fizzy mineral water was invented in Whitehaven, Cumbria, by **William Brownrigg** in 1741. He had the idea of adding carbonic acid (which produces bubbles) to ordinary spring water and then bottling it. The bubbles would appear when the bottle was opened.

Carton (1951)

It was **Ruben Rausing**, a Swedish industrialist specialising in packs for dry foodstuffs (flour, sugar, etc.), who revolutionised the packaging of liquids and drinks in 1951. Combining the most highly developed paper, aluminium and plastic technologies, he created the tetrahedral carton, a totally new form of packaging in form, manufacture and cost price.

In 1961 Ruben Rausing and his Tetra Pak company made their decisive expansion with the first aseptically filled cartons of UHT-treated long-life milk. Following dairy products, a whole range of goods including fruit juices, soups, cream and wine, were to be packaged in 'brick' form.

This has brought about a real revolution in our daily life, with Tetra Pak now present in 98 countries. If one placed end to end all the packing sold by Tetra Pak in 1988, it would reach 14 times further than the distance between the earth and moon.

Champagne (around 1695)

Until the end of the 17th century the wine of Champagne was kept in barrels. It then became clear that it was easier to keep the wine in bottles, and it was decided to preserve the young wine systematically in bottles, even before fermentation was complete. The fermentation continued in the bottle: the still active fermenting agents transformed the sugar into alcohol and carbon dioxide. The carbon dioxide caused the champagne to fizz when the bottle was opened. The phenomenon was observed collectively and it is impossible to attribute it to one person. It is only in recent years that **Dom Pérignon** has been hailed as the person to discover champagne. Although he was known for his skilful blending of different grapes to enhance his wines, these were mostly red wines, and there is no proof that he took an interest in the bubbly wine from Champagne.

Chewing-gum (1869)

In 1848 an American, J. Curtis, marketed spruce resin for the first time. Spruce is a native tree of Maine, USA.

In 1860 spruce resin was abandoned in favour of chicle, a gumlike substance obtained from the sapodilla, a tree which grows in Yucatan. This resin was a popular chew among the Aztecs and was brought to Staten Island, New York by General Santa Anna, the Mexican who led the attack on the Alamo. He showed it to Thomas Adams, and Adams began selling this gum from 1871. It was not until 1875 that John Colgan came up with the idea of flavouring it. However, it was only in the 1890s that chewing-gum became truly widespread, thanks to William Wrigley.

Choc-ice (1922)

The first choc-ice was invented by an American from Iowa, **C. K. Nelson**. He called it an Eskimo-pie and patented it on **24 January 1922**.

Chocolate (1819)

A 23-year-old Swiss, **François-Louis Cailler**, made the first bars of chocolate at Vevey in 1819. Small-scale production of chocolate had begun in France and Italy after the Spaniards returned from South America with the recipe. At that time it was a drink prepared from roasted, crushed cocoa beans.

In **1879** another Swiss, **Rodolphe Lindt**, built a chocolate factory in Berne. In those days blocks of chocolate were hard and had to be crunched; they also left a gritty sensation in the mouth along with a bitter aftertaste. Even

---
THE SECRET OF THE PHARAOHS

A Scottish brewery, Scottish and Newcastle, is going to lend its expertise to a team of British archaeologists in search of the lost recipe of the beer drunk by the Pharaohs. During a three-year mission, the expedition consisting of archaeologists and expert brewers will unearth the ruins of Tutankhamen's royal brewery on the site of Tell-el-Amarna, and try to discover the secrets of this fermented drink, which must have been very different from our own beer as it contained dates and olive oil. They hope to recreate the flavour of the most popular brew in ancient Egypt.
---

when heated up, the chocolate remained thick and heavy. Because of this Lindt invented a machine that kneaded the chocolate for a long time; he then had the idea of adding cocoa butter to it. The chocolate we know today was born, and Lindt patented his invention in 1880.

Not suprisingly the Swiss are the biggest per capita consumers of chocolate in the world, eating 4.4kg *9lb 1loz* each per year – almost twice as much as the British. The USA, however, is the biggest chocolate-eating nation in the world.

Coca-Cola (1886)

Coca-Cola was invented in **1886** by **John Pemberton**, a 50-year-old chemist from Atlanta,

Without the invention of Rodolphe Lindt this spectacular chocolate stadium could not have been built.

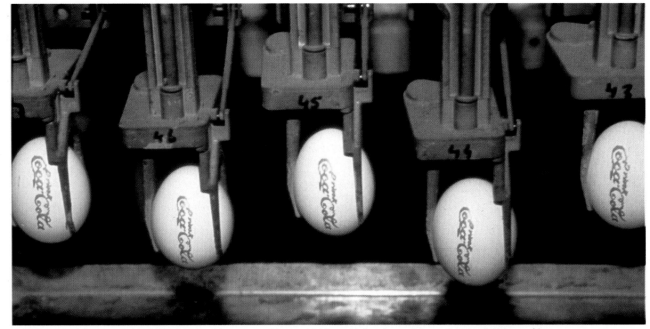

An Israeli firm has come up with an idea for advertising on eggs. The special ink used is harmless and does not come off during cooking.

Georgia. He decided to develop a soft drink that would be original and thirst-quenching. Working relentlessly in the back room of his 'drug store', he produced a mixture containing cola nut extract, sugar, a little caffeine, coca leaves with the cocaine removed and vegetable extracts. (The drink's exact composition is still a closely guarded secret.) A few months later, an assistant mistakenly served a customer Coca-Cola mixed with soda water: that proved to be the little touch that made the drink a success.

To market his new drink, Pemberton formed a partnership with Frank Robertson whose elegant handwriting was used for the Coca-Cola trademark.

In May 1985 'New' Coke was introduced and the old formula was retired. Coca-Cola drinkers were outraged and the original recipe was revived. Previously, in 1983, decaffeinated Coke and diet Coke had been launched.

Coca-Cola bottle (1913)

With the immense success of Coca-Cola, there followed many imitations. In July 1913 the company's managers realised that the only way to put an end to this was to give Coca-Cola a bottle that would be absolutely original. They entrusted the task to the glassmaker from Indiana, **C. S. Root**, who charged one of his assistants, Edward, to research the drink. Edward found an illustration of a cola nut which he copied. The design could not be used as it was as the bottle would not stand up. The base of the nut was therefore cut off. The technical director of the factory, Mr Samuelson, reproduced the truncated nut in glass and decorated it with vertical lines. The trademark on the bottle made the fortune of C. S. Root.

Cocoa powder (1828)

Cocoa powder was made for the first time by the Dutchman **Conraad Johannes van Houten** in Amsterdam in **1828**. He invented a way of obtaining a soluble cocoa powder which could be used to make a hot drink. Up to that time the only way to make it was by melting pieces of chocolate.

Coffee (15th century)

According to legend the stimulating qualities of coffee were discovered by a goat herder in the Yemen. He noticed that his herd would not sleep at night after eating the red fruit of the coffee bush. We know for a fact that coffee was drunk in Aden in 1420. It was adopted in Syria and Turkey and by 1615 coffee had reached Venice. Coffee houses became popular in the 18th century; perhaps the most famous is Edward Lloyd's in London where underwriters and merchants carried out much of their insurance business.

It is in the Scandinavian countries that the most coffee is drunk per head. In Britain some 2.5kg *5lb 8oz* of coffee are consumed by each person in a year.

Coffee grinder (1687)

The invention of the coffee grinder in **1687** contributed to the diffusion of this brand new drink. The electric coffee grinder was invented in 1937 by the Kitchen Aid division of the Hobart Manufacturing Co. of America. The first model sold for $12.75.

Coffee filter (1908)

In 1908 a German woman called **Melitta Bentz** wanted to improve the quality of the coffee for her family. She pierced holes in the bottom of a tin container, then cut out a disc from absorbent paper, which she placed in the bottom of the container. She placed it over the coffee pot, filled it with coffee and poured boiling water over it. The result was excellent, and that was how the Melitta coffee filter was born.

Instant coffee (1937)

The first attempts at the production and marketing of instant coffee took place in America in 1867, but with no great success.

It was the Swiss company **Nestlé** who gained a lion's share of the market by creating Nescafé in **1937**. Nowadays there are 100 different varieties of Nescafé in the world.

Espresso (1946)

Espresso coffee has been around since the late 19th century but it only became popular in Europe with the invention of the **Gaggia** coffee maker in **1946** in Italy.

Condensed milk (1858)

Although the Frenchman Nicolas Appert had the idea of condensing milk in 1827, the process was not applied industrially for another 30 years. It was not until **1858** that the American **Gail Borden** set up the first factory producing sweetened condensed milk in the United States.

In 1884 work by Meyenberg made it possible also to produce evaporated milk that contained no added sugar.

Corkscrew (17th century)

Towards the end of the **17th century**, the use of watertight corks made corkscrews indispensable. We do not know who invented the first ones, but in 1795 an Englishman called **Samuel Hershaw** developed the screw and nut corkscrew.

Croissant (1683)

The crescent roll was invented in **1683** in Vienna by the Pole **Kulyeziski**. The city had been under siege by an immense Turkish army led by Kara Mustafa. The famished Viennese were finally saved by Charles de Lorraine and the King of Poland, John III Sobieski. Kulyeziski, having taken a decisive part in the final victory, was given the stocks of coffee abandoned by the routed Turkish army and was authorised to open a cafe in Vienna. This he did, and to accompany his coffee, he had a baker make small milk bread rolls in the shape of crescents to commemorate the victory over the Turks. They were immediately successful.

Food processor (1947)

This kitchen appliance, destined to equip millions of kitchens throughout the world, has its roots in a **1947** design by the Englishman **Kenneth Wood**. Marketed as the Kenwood Chef, it was composed of a powerful and sturdy engine block to which a large number of accessories could be fitted: mixer, citrus squeezer, mincer, slicer and shredder, pasta and ravioli maker, food mill, can opener, etc. Its multiple uses allowed it single-handedly to replace a large number of small appliances.

Fork (6000 to 3000 BC)

Distant precursors of the modern fork have been unearthed at the diggings made at the site of Çatal-Hüyük in Turkey. It then seems to vanish, and the first indication of its 'reinvention' is its mention in certain inventories drawn up in the 14th century. It was probably brought to the West by the Italians. The 1307 inventory of Edward I mentions seven forks, including one in gold.

It was not until the first half of the 17th century that the fork reached English dining tables.

Freeze-dried food (1946)

In **1946–7** the American **E. W. Flosdorff** demonstrated that the process of freeze-drying, which was already known and used, could be applied, under proper conditions, to products such as coffee, orange juice, or meat.

Freeze-drying achieves dehydration through refrigeration: the water content solidifies faster than the other elements in the product and is eliminated in the form of ice.

Freeze-drying was invented by the Frenchmen Arsène d'Arsonval and F. Bordas in Paris, in 1906, and rediscovered by an American, Shackwell (1851–1940), in St Louis, Missouri, in 1909. The process was first applied medically.

It was not until 1955 that freeze-drying entered the food industry, where it was applied to Texas shrimps and Maryland crabs.

Goose liver (antiquity)

Although goose liver is a delicacy we most often associate with France (*foie gras*), the ancient Greeks enjoyed eating the livers of geese more than 2000 years ago.

In 52 BC, the Roman consul Metellus Pius Scipio had geese held in dark pens and force-fed with figs to obtain what he felt was a goose liver of perfect quality.

Ketchup (1876)

The ketchup we know today was invented by the American **Henry Heinz** in **1876**, but its origins go back to ancient times. The Chinese were probably the first to prepare a sauce called ketchup or *ke-tsiap*, a sort of brine marinade for fish or shellfish.

It was introduced into Europe at the end of the 17th century by the British, who had come across it in Malaysia, where it bore the name *ketchap*, and adapted it to the ingredients available in Britain. It was then taken to the United States by long-distance navigators from Maine, tomatoes were not introduced to the recipe until the 1790s.

To make his sculptures, the Argentine Luis Vicedo uses only table forks and spoons – eat your heart out Uri Geller!

KitKat (1937)

Britain's favourite chocolate bar (it has been the bestseller for several years) celebrated its jubilee year in 1987. It began life in 1935 as Chocolate Crisp, becoming KitKat two years later. **Rowntree** had to stop production during the war because of milk shortages and when the bar was relaunched in 1945 the familiar wrapper changed to a blue one to show that the chocolate was made without milk.

McDonald hamburgers (1948)

In 1940 two Americans, the brothers **Maurice** and **Richard McDonald**, set up a hamburger stand next to their cinema near Pasadena in California. In **1948** they had the idea of making it self-service, stressing the quality of the hamburgers served there.

By 1952 they were known throughout southern California, where they had established subsidiaries. Ray Kroc, a dealer in restaurant equipment, offered to sell franchises for them

The famous McDonald symbol has been slightly adapted for the Moscow market.

in the rest of the country. In 1962, when there were 200 establishments, Kroc bought the McDonalds' share of the business for $2.7 million. Today there are over 10300 McDonalds restaurants in 50 countries, including the USSR where, after 14 years' negotiation, one was opened in Moscow in 1990.

Margarine (1869)

Margarine was invented in **1869** by the Frenchman **Hippolyte Mège-Mouriès**, following a contest launched by Napoleon III to come up with a replacement for butter. An artificial butter that would be economical and would not go rancid represented an undeniable advantage when providing food for the army and navy.

Mège-Mouriès's method consisted in processing animal fat (essentially tallow) from which he obtained a paste of a colour and consistency close to butter and which did not have a disagreeable odour. He christened his product margarine because of its pearly colour (pearl is *margaron* in Greek). Later, thanks to improvements in Mège-Mouriès's process, margarine was made from vegetable fat.

Mars bar (1920)

The Mars bar was first sold in **1920** by the American **Frank Mars**. This famous bar is filled with caramel and soft nougat and coated with thick milk chocolate. Highly nutritious, it was given to the American GIs during the Second World War as part of their rations. In Britain, only KitKat sells better. Mars have recently expanded their range to include an ice cream Mars bar and a Mars bar drink. At the beginning of 1991 Mars bars were exported to the Soviet Union for the first time. Because only a few tonnes were sent, the numbers per person were limited to four each; even so, thousands queued up to have a taste of one of the West's most popular sweets.

Microwave oven (1945)

On **8 October 1945** the American **Percy Le Baron Spencer** applied for a patent for what was to be the microwave oven. He was following in the tracks of two Britons, Sir John Randall and Dr H. A. Boot, who developed an electronic tube which produces microwave energy – the magnetron. As they came up

An early advert for Mars bars – long one of the most popular sweets in the UK.

with their invention in 1940 it was put to military use in improving radar defences. Spencer, who was a physics engineer at Raytheon, one of the world leaders in radar equipment, noticed one day that the energy given off by the tubes used for radar produced heat.

This electromagnetic energy gave him the idea of putting a handful of maize in a paper bag and placing the bag within the field of the tube. The maize immediately burst, transforming itself into popcorn. He melted chocolate in the same way. Raytheon developed a cooking programme for microwaves and patented the first cooking apparatus of this type, the Radar Range. This machine had a power of 1600 watts. It was heavy, awkward and expensive and was originally intended for use in hospitals and military canteens. In 1952 the Tappan Company put the first household microwave oven on the market.

Microwave ovens, despite some scares about the way they cook food, remain one of the most popular domestic appliances and it is reckoned that by 1994 one in two European homes will have one.

Mustard (4th century)

In the footnotes of history we find the story of how the Gauls introduced the Romans to the mustard seed when they occupied Rome in the **4th century**. When these seeds were ground up with vinegar or wine must, the result was *mustum ardeo*, from which our name mustard comes. It was not until the Middle Ages that mustard found its way on to every table.

In the 13th century the town of Dijon first became famous for the quality of its mustards using verjuice, an extract of unripe grapes, to make this most sought-after condiment.

As centuries passed and tastes changed, mustard was flavoured in different ways: with vanilla in the 17th century, then with orange blossom or violet water, then, in the 19th century, with various spices or herbs like tarragon, chervil, chives, lemon or red fruit.

Non-stick pan (1954)

The non-stick pan was invented by the Frenchman **Marc Grégoire** purely by chance. Grégoire, a research engineer, was trying to perfect his fishing rods in **1954** when he discovered the processes which make it possible to encrust metal with Teflon. His patents were applied to kitchen utensils and with these he founded the Tefal company in 1956, which went on to produce its famous frying pan. Tefal is still the uncontested leader in non-stick utensils, having sold 25 million frying pans, casserole dishes, etc.

Teflon itself had been discovered by accident in 1938 by Roy Plunkett of Du Pont. It was both very slippery and impervious to corrosion. The name 'Teflon' comes from tetrafluoroethylene – Du Pont found many uses for it, but did not think to use it for cooking utensils.

The electric frying pan dates back to 1911, when it was launched by Westinghouse.

Ovaltine (1904)

In 1865 **Doctor George Wander** set up a laboratory in Berne, Switzerland, to manufacture concentrated barley malt. In **1904** Wander produced a healthy drink from the malt added to milk with cocoa, eggs and vitamins. He called it Ovomaltine. In 1909 a British factory was set up in King's Langley and the company applied to register the Ovomaltine trademark. A clerk wrongly transcribed it as Ovaltine – and the name stuck.

Plate (ancient times)

The plate was known to peoples of the ancient world, especially the Romans. But it disappeared during the Middle Ages and was replaced by bowls and wooden trenchers.

Plates reappeared in 1530, in silver, at the banquet celebrating the marriage of King Francis I of France (1494–1547) to Eleanor of Habsburg.

Refrigerator (1913)

The Domelre, manufactured in Chicago in **1913**, was the first functional household refrigerator. In 1918 the American **Nathaniel Wales** designed a device that was widely marketed under the name of Kelvinator. The Frigidaire trademark appeared one year later in 1919.

The Swedes Carl Munters and Balzar von Platen succeeded in constructing a silent and functional refrigerator. They filed their first patent in 1920, and developed a condenser device in 1929. Mass production began in 1931 with Electrolux, in Stockholm.

In 1926 the American company General Electric manufactured a hermetically sealed unit and in 1939 it introduced the first dual-temperature refrigerator. This allowed frozen foods to be kept in one compartment.

Refrigerated meat transport (1877)

In **1877** the Frenchman **Charles Tellier** (1828–1913), who had designed a method of

WEDGWOOD'S POTTERY REVOLUTION

When Josiah Wedgwood was born in 1730 pottery was still made in more or less the same way as it had been throughout the ages; those who wanted to produce up-market plates had to do them individually, as a result there could be differences in the colouring and the design. As part of a Staffordshire pottery family, Josiah was anxious to see if the process could be in any way improved.

While still very young Wedgwood began to experiment in ways to colour crockery, gradually making his efforts more scientific. His efforts so annoyed his family that he had to set up on his own in 1759. But soon after he discovered a process whereby he could colour plates in the same way each time. The designs were simple neo-classical white figures on a plain earthenware background. In 1765 Queen Charlotte requested a dinner set from him, and soon Europe's aristocracy followed suit. With improved manufacturing techniques he was able to sell large quantities of Wedgwood pottery and so when he died in 1795 he was a very rich man.

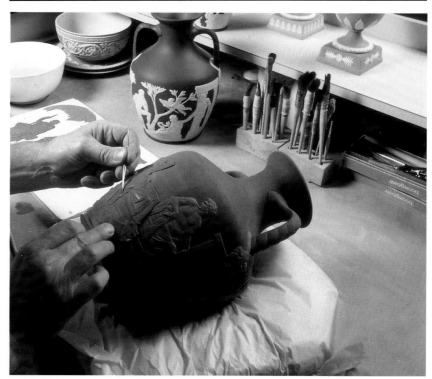

A craftsman works on the ornamentation of one of Wedgwood's famous Portland Vases – these traditional skills are highly valued.

meat preservation using dry cold, won an international competition for transporting meat between the Old World and the New.

The *Frigorifique*, a three-masted ship equipped with a steam engine, took 105 days to cover the 12000km *7456 miles* between Rouen and Buenos Aires. The carcasses of ten cows, 12 sheep and two calves were kept refrigerated in dry air and travelled very well. At about this time also the first meat transport by refrigerated wagon took place. It was developed by Gustavus F. Swift (1839–1903). Until then animals had to be transported on the hoof.

Deep-freezing (1924)

Industrial deep-freezing was launched by the American **Clarence Birdseye** in **1924**. He applied preservation techniques used by the Labrador Inuit, which he had observed in 1912 and 1915. In 1924 he set up the Freezing Company to deep-freeze up to 500 tonnes of fruit and vegetables a year. In 1929 he realised that the deep-freezing process

would have to be speeded up and invented a freezing machine with two plates, which chilled the product on both sides. Lastly, in 1935, he invented his multiple plate freezer, which is still used today.

Dehydration (1945)

The dehydration process, designed by the American **Howard** in **1945** and patented in 1949, put the finishing touch to freezing techniques. It made it possible to reduce the mass to be transported by about 50 percent.

Pre-cooked frozen meals (1945)

In **1945** the American **Maxson** was the first to offer pre-cooked frozen meals to airline passengers.

These were followed by 'TV dinners', which started to develop in a spectacular way in 1954. In the United States in 1960, 215 million dishes were prepared.

Fish fingers (1950s)

In the **1950s** Birdseye branched out into a new

REFRIGERATION

Name	Date	Characteristics
Water vapour refrigeration machine	1755	In this year the Scotsman William Cullen first obtained a little ice from water vapour in a vacuumed bell jar. In 1777 Gerald Nairne added a little sulphuric acid, which accelerated the process. In 1866 Edmond Carré took the process out of the experimental stage by developing a machine which was immediately successful, particularly for chilling carafes.
Compressed ether refrigeration machine	1805	A prototype was launched in Philadelphia (USA) by Oliver Evans. Its chief innovation lay in the introduction of a closed-cycle system. This process was patented in 1834 by the American Jacob Perkins. The first industrial machine was designed by a Scottish immigrant to Australia, James Harrison (patent granted in 1855).
Air refrigerating machine	1844	The principle of reducing air pressure was known as early as the 18th century. The American John Gorrie applied it in his machine in 1844. He was a doctor in Florida and invented this machine to relieve his patients. He obtained a British patent in 1850 but, strangely, his invention caused a scandal in the United States, where some people accused him of competing with God by using his machine to make ice at any time of year. Nevertheless after a great struggle he obtained his patent in 1851.
Absorption refrigerating machine	1859	In 1859 the Frenchman Ferdinand Carré, Edmond's brother (see above), patented a machine in which the fluid, having generated coldness, is absorbed by another substance rather than being drawn up by a compressor. This was the first absorption refrigerating machine. The absorption refrigerator was perfected in 1944 by the Swiss company Sibir.
Ammonia compressor refrigerating machine	1872	It was an American of Scottish origin, David Boyle, who obtained the first patent for a compressor using ammonia. But it was the German Karl von Linde who made it successful with two machines, developed in 1876 and 1877, which were soon on the market.
SO_2 compressor refrigerating machine	1874	In 1874 Raoul Pictet, a Swiss professor of physics in Geneva, used liquid sulphur dioxide (SO_2) in a system of refrigeration by compression. In 1876 Pictet's machine was used for London's first artificial skating rink.

area – small fillets of white fish coated in breadcrumbs. They were introduced in the UK in 1955 under two different names, but the one that caught on was fish fingers.

By the end of the decade millions of fish fingers, a new and tasty convenience food, were being sold. Now the British spend some £100 million on them each year.

Sandwich (1762)

John Montagu, fourth **Earl of Sandwich** (1718–92), is said to have invented the sandwich in **1762**. A devoted gambler, the earl one day refused to leave his gambling table for lunch. His cook prepared a small snack for him consisting of a piece of meat between two slices of buttered bread. The sandwich rapidly became very popular throughout the British Isles but did not spread to continental Europe until the following century.

Sugar (antiquity)

The extraction of cane sugar goes back to antiquity, and the plant was probably first cultivated in India: the Greeks and Romans referred to sugar as 'Indian salt' and 'honey of India'. The Christians probably brought it to the West during the Crusades. It has been proved that during the 12th century there were mills in Sicily that made 'honey canes'. Centuries ago the Chinese knew not only how to extract cane sugar but also how to refine it, an operation that was developed much later in the West.

Sugar beet (1812)

During the Continental System (Napoleon's

attempt to counteract British maritime power), he considered it of the utmost importance that France should be able to manufacture sugar, by extracting it from beet. On **2 January 1812** he was overjoyed to hear that the manufacturer **Benjamin Delessert** (1773–1847) had succeeded in doing this at his factory in Passy.

Napoleon went to Passy that very day and decided to establish imperial factories and to devote 600000 acres to sugar beet cultivation.

Delessert's predecessors were the German chemist Margraff, who started his work in 1747, and a German of French origins, Achard, who began in 1799. The juice was extracted by rupturing the cell walls of the root. But it was impure, people did not like the sugar and productivity was low. In 1864 the Frenchman Robert, a sugar manufacturer in Moravia, obtained the juice by diffusion, which did not require rupturing the cells.

Saccharine (1879)

Saccharine was discovered by **Constantin Fahlberg**, an American who was working under the direction of Professor Ira Remsen at Johns Hopkins University in Baltimore. He published the results of his work on **27 February 1879**. Recent studies seem to prove that saccharin can be hazardous to health but only if consumed in extremely large quantities.

Aspartam (1965)

Aspartam, the synthetic sweetener, has 200 times the sweetening power of sugar. It is a product of biotechnology and was discovered by scientists in the American **Searle Laboratory** in 1965. Although it has considerable sweetening power, it does not add calories or

cause dental caries, and has an excellent taste in foods and drinks.

In the United States its use has been permitted in foods since 1982 and it is also used in the UK, Germany and Switzerland.

Tea

Two different legends recount the discovery of tea. Shang Yeng was the Emperor of China around 2737 BC. As a health measure, he ordered his subjects to drink nothing but boiled water. One day, leaves from a nearby tree fell into his own simmering water and the Emperor was delighted by this new drink.

A horse for tea

The second legend is set circa AD 520. According to Japanese tradition, an Indian prince, Bodhidharma, who had become an ascetic, went to China to teach Zen Buddhism. To keep himself awake during long hours of meditation, he cut off his eyelids and threw them away. At the place where they fell there soon grew a bush. When the master's disciples came to meditate with him, they picked the leaves of this tree and made an infusion from them to keep themselves awake. It was a tea plant.

During the Ming dynasty in China, tea was used as money. A good horse would cost 68kg 150lb of tea.

Tinned food (1795)

In **1795** the Frenchman **Nicolas Appert** (1749–1841) invented a brilliant method for preserving food. *Appertisation* consisted of sterilising foodstuffs in hermetically sealed

DRINK HORNIMAN'S PURE TEA

"ALWAYS GOOD ALIKE"

The British have long had the reputation of being a nation of tea-drinkers.

General Electric Company of Schenectady, New York, in **1909**. The machine quite simply consisted of bare wires wound around mica strips.

The first prototype of the pop-up toaster that grills on both sides was developed by Charles Strite of Stillwater, Minnesota, and patented on 29 May 1919. They began to appear in the home from 1926.

Tonic water (1840)

In **1840** the British company **Schweppes**, founded by the German Jakob Schweppe, developed Indian tonic water. Schweppe had begun making soda water from distilled water charged with carbon dioxide in 1792.

Tonic water is a soda containing sugar and quinine. The idea of putting quinine in soda originated in the Indian Army as part of the fight against malaria.

Tupperware (1945)

The little airtight plastic boxes were the brainwave of the American **Earl W. Tupper**. He was a former chemist at Du Pont and invented Tupperware in **1945**. The particular feature of Tupperware is that items are not sold in the traditional way but through 'parties', and are guaranteed for ten years. Their ease of use and pleasant design brought them immediate popularity.

Vacuum flask (1892)

In **1892** the Scottish physicist and chemist **Sir James Dewar** (1842–1923) invented a thermal isolation device which made it possible to keep gases liquified. He did not patent the device, nor did he see its wider commercial application. Reinhold Burger, a German glass blower, cased the fragile vacuum flask in metal and eventually decided on calling it a Thermos flask. He patented it in 1903 and by 1906 the invention had crossed the Atlantic.

Whisk (1923)

In Racing (Wisconsin, USA) in 1910, Fred Osius, Chester A. Beach and L. H. Hamilton launched the first electric household motor compatible with both alternating and direct current. Drawing on this invention, **Air-O-Mix Inc.** of Wilmington (Delaware, USA) designed in **1923** the Whip-All, a portable whisk. Another first was the Mixmaster, from Sunbeam of Chicago. This was the first fixed whisk (like the present-day food processors) to be commercially successful: in 1930, the year it was put on the market, sales reached 60000.

Whisky (1494)

The first mention of a spirit made from malted barley dates from **1494**. The monk **John Cor** distilled it for his abbey.

Following the civil and religious wars which ravaged Scotland for centuries, the production of malted barley spirit, in other words whisky, remained secret until 1823, when a certain John Smith established an official distillery in the valley of Glenlivet.

Irish whiskey (5th century)

In the **5th century** Catholicism was very strong in Ireland. Monks were travelling

containers away from circulating air. This process was not yet that of tinning food and involved jars ▮ vered with five layers of cork.

Tin cans (1▮ ▮)

In 1810 Pi▮ ▮ Durand patented a metalled vessel for ▮ ▮serving food. The patent was bought fo▮ 1000 by the Englishmen **Bryan Donkin** a▮ **John Hall**, who combined Durand's pr▮ ▮rving process with Appert's. Tin cans we▮ ▮irst made in **1812** in a preserving factory ▮ ilt at Blue Anchor Lane, Bermondse▮ ▮ondon.

Tin can▮ opened by a key (1866)

On **2 October 1866**, the American **J. Osterhoudt** of New York invented a tin can with a key fixed onto the top. The key is simply loosened and then turned to open the can.

Baked beans (1880)

Perhaps the most famous canned food of all is baked beans. First produced in the US in **1880**, they were not brought to the UK until the beginning of this century and were not available nationwide until 1905. For many years they were imported into the UK, but in 1928 Heinz began to produce them here. Now Heinz alone sell over £100 million of baked beans every year in Britian.

Toaster (1909)

The first toasters were marketed by the

Europe and the Near East in all directions spreading the good word. Among them was Saint Patrick, who brought the first still and the art of distillation back from Egypt. From then on, as well as the Gospel, the Irish monks taught the art of distilling spirits. Using barley and pure water, they developed a spirit called *uisge beatha* ('water of life' in Gaelic), from which their cousins the Scots were the first to benefit.

In 1170 the Norman soldiers of Henry II, King of England and Duke of Normandy, discovered *uisge beatha*. They found the product excellent to drink but the name difficult to pronounce, so they changed it to whiskey. Historical documents dating from 1276 make Old Bushmills in Northern Ireland the oldest whiskey distillery in the world. It is still in operation today.

Bourbon (1789)

This alcohol, the American cousin of Scotch and Irish whiskies, was invented in 1789 by **Pastor Elijah Craig** in Bourbon County in northern Kentucky. The refinement of this whiskey, distilled from corn mash and malted barley, was carried out by Doctor James Crowe in Franklin County, Kentucky.

In the home

Aerosol (1926)

In 1926 the Norwegian **Erik Rotheim** invented the aerosol. He discovered that a product could be projected in a fine spray by introducing a gas or liquid into the container to create internal pressure.

On 22 August 1939 Julian S. Kahn from New York invented the disposable spraycan which could contain an aerosol. But this idea did not have its first commercial application until 1941. In that year two Americans, L. D. Goodhue and W. N. Sullivan, manufactured an insecticide in aerosol form.

Aerosols are now out of favour because of popular concern about the damage being done to the ozone layer by CFCs.

Air conditioning (1911)

The American **Willis Carrier** invented air conditioning in 1911. In 1902 he had studied the regulation of air humidity at a Brooklyn printing press. By 1904 this led him to devise an air-conditioning system whereby he modified a steam heater to accept cold water and circulate air. This system both cooled air and removed its humidity and is still in use today. Continuing his research, in 1911 Carrier devised an air humidity graph, that allowed him to make a rational estimate of air-conditioning requirements.

Artificial ventilation (1555)

Air conditioning can obviously be dated back to artificial ventilation and the person classically cited in relation to this is the mineralogist **Agricola**, who in 1555 described procedures for mine shaft ventilation.

We know that Leonardo da Vinci was interested in this problem too. But we must also remember the method of cooling by water evaporation in old Andalucian houses, where air entered after passing through vegetation and a fountain on the patio.

Early apparatus (1919)

In 1919 the first air-conditioned cinema opened in Chicago at the same time as Abraham and Straus, a large air-conditioned store in Brooklyn, New York.

The use of independent home air-conditioning systems was first foreseen in the United States in 1926 by H. H. Schutz and J. Q. Sherman. In 1931 they applied for a patent for an air conditioner to supplement windows.

Alarms and security devices

Anti-asphyxia alarm (1988)

In 1988 two American doctors **Kurt Shuler** and **Gerhard Schrauser**, horrified by the increasing number of accidents caused by carbon monoxide, developed a series of alarms using warning lights which come on when the level of CO in the air becomes dangerous. These are the world's first battery-operated alarms which can work anywhere.

Falcon Eye (1985)

The Falcon Eye, named after its inventor, the American **Bob Falconer**, is an automatic light which comes on when it detects a human presence, illuminating an area of up to 250m^2 2700sq ft, and switches off when the room is empty. Invented in 1985 and patented in 1988, this light is equipped with an infra-red detector adjusted to the frequencies of the human body. It cannot be activated accidentally by a pet or any other source of heat, and it only comes on if there is insufficient natural light. The Falcon Eye is a useful burglar deterrent, energy saver and aid for the handicapped as well as a general household convenience.

Securiscan (1987)

Securiscan is a new remote-controlled electronic system for the home which was launched by **Thomson** in 1987. Thanks to a tiny computer the size of a radio, you can switch on the central heating, the garden hose and household appliances. It also provides surveillance of the home and sends a telephone warning in the case of a breakdown, flood or fire, while speakers for relaying spoken messages and an alarm system make Securiscan a burglar deterrent.

Bleach (1789)

In 1789 the chemist **C. L. Berthollet** discovered the bleaching properties of eau de Javel, a mixture of lime, potash and water through which chlorine is passed. Charles Tennant, a Scottish chemist, transformed this liquid into powder, which was much more convenient. In the 19th century the pharmacist Antoine Labarraque (1777–1850) discovered its disinfectant properties and introduced it into hospitals.

Carpet-sweeper (1876)

The history of the mechanical sweeper starts at the end of the 17th century. In 1699 the Englishman Edmund Hemming invented a broom of this type to sweep the streets. Other Englishmen, James Hume in 1811 and Lucius Bigelow in 1858, can also be considered as

Robert Kennedy, a fervent follower of domotics – the application of information technology to the home – is able to use his telephone as a remote control to operate the door, hi-fi, air conditioning, etc. of his Arizona home.

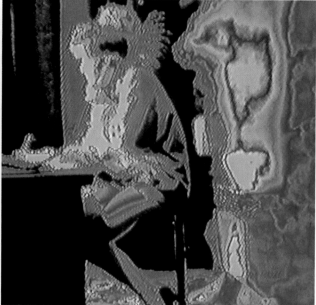

New technology developed by CETIAT makes it possible to photograph air movements. In the picture on the right the hot air from the convector heater can clearly be seen rising towards the ceiling.

creating forerunners of the carpet sweeper. The first efficient carpet-sweeper was invented by the American **Melville R. Bissell**, who patented it on **19 September 1876**. He was the owner of a porcelain shop in Grand Rapids (Michigan). Mr Bissell suffered from an allergy to the dust produced by the straw he used to pack his pots. To cure this, he designed a broom with a cylindrical brush which pushed the dust into a container. The local success of this device led Mr and Mrs Bissell to set up the Bissell Carpet Sweeper Company to market their product. Their name became synonymous with carpet-sweepers, much as Hoover is now linked with vacuum cleaners.

Detergent (1916)

The first synthetic detergent, Nikala, was invented in Germany in **1916** by two chemists, **H. Gunther** and **M. Hetzer**. It enabled water to penetrate fibres, but it could not itself remove dirt. There are brands of modern detergents that go back 60 or 70 years in some cases. The oldest, Lux flakes, was developed by the British manufacturer Unilever in 1921. Also from Unilever are Vim (1923), Persil (1932) and Omo (1952). The famous detergent Ariel was created in 1968 by Proctor & Gamble

(USA), who in 1982 created Vizir, the first machine-washing liquid.

Dishwasher (1886)

The first model of a mechanical dishwasher was developed between 1850 and 1865 in the United States. However, it was not until **1886** that **Josephine Cochrane** of Illinois, USA came up with an efficient design, albeit crude and cumbersome. Her main aim was to reduce the number of breakages of crockery by her servants, rather than as a labour-saving device.

The electrically powered dishwasher first appeared in 1912.

In 1932 an appropriate detergent, Calgon, was discovered. This facilitated the dishwasher's development.

The automatic dishwasher first appeared in 1940, also in the United States. It was not exported to Europe until about 1960.

Dry cleaning (1855)

The first dry cleaner's was founded in **1855** in Paris by the Frenchman **J.-B. Jolly**. He discovered the principle of dry cleaning accidentally when he tipped a bottle of turpentine over a dress. He noticed that the dress was not stained but, on the contrary, cleaned.

A German from Leipzig, Ludwig Anthelin, made a further step forward in 1897. He discovered the use of carbon tetrachloride, which is much less flammable. Unfortunately this product attacks the respiratory tracts, so it was replaced in 1918 by trichlorethylene.

Electric heater (1892)

The first electric heater was patented by the Englishmen **R. E. Bell Crompton** and **H. J. Dowsing** in 1892. They attached a wire to a cast iron plate and protected the whole with a layer of enamel.

In 1906 the American Albert Marsh from Lake County, Illinois invented an alloy of nickel and chrome which could be heated red hot without melting. This resistant alloy proved to be an ideal element for the construction of electrical heating apparatus.

Then in 1912 the Englishman C. R. Belling from Enfield in Middlesex perfected a refracting clay around which a nickel-chrome alloy wire could be wound. The same year he made the first Standard electric heaters.

Escalator (1892)

The escalator was born in 1892 from the combined efforts of the Americans **Jesse W. Reno**

CENTRAL HEATING

Type	Origins	History
Hot air	**antiquity**	Used in China from ancient times. It was also widely used by the Romans in thermal baths (hypocaust) and private houses. Hot air heating was mentioned by Seneca (1st century AD). It reappeared in the 19th century.
Steam heater	**18th century**	The first model was installed in a factory by the Scotsman James Watt.
Hot water heater	**1777**	This system was already known to the Romans. In 1899 the radiator made of assembled elements first appeared in the United States, but an earlier model had been made in France in 1777.

and **George H. Wheeler**. It was first given the name escalator by Charles D. Seeberger in 1899. The project for a mechanical stairway first gave rise to a moving slope, which proved rather dangerous. Reno perfected this slope by replacing it with rotating steps. He patented his invention on **15 March 1892**. Later he designed ribbed platforms that passed through the teeth of a comb fixed to the ridge of each step. The first public escalator was used at the 1900 Universal Exhibition in Paris, before being installed in the United States in Gimbel's Department Store in Philadelphia. From 1922 onwards Reno and Wheeler's escalator was installed in numerous shops and public offices. The first spiral escalator was put into operation in 1985 in a Japanese shop by the Mitsubishi Electric Corporation.

Fire extinguisher (1816)

In **1816 Captain George Manby** from Norfolk developed a fire extinguisher which worked using compressed air. The first fire extinguisher using a chemical base was invented in 1868 by the Frenchman François Carlier. His extinguisher contained bicarbonate of soda and water. A bottle filled with sulphuric acid was attached inside, near the cap. To use the extinguisher, one had to break the bottle with a needle, thus freeing the sulphuric acid. A chemical reaction then produced carbonic acid, which forced the water out and helped put out the fire.

In 1905 the Russian Alexander Laurent hit upon the idea of mixing a solution of aluminum sulphate and bicarbonate of soda with a stabilising agent. The bubbles so formed contained carbonic acid. They floated on oil, petrol, or paint, and prevented contact with the air, thus with oxygen.

Ironing

Origins (4th century)

The origins of the iron are very old. In the 4th century the Chinese were using a kind of receptacle with a brass shaft containing embers. In the West the ancestor of the iron was the 'smoother' made of wood, glass or marble. It was used cold until about the 15th century, since the use of starching gum meant it could not be heated.

The first mention of the iron does not appear until the 17th century. After this there were irons that were thrown on the fire, hollow irons filled with embers and lastly the classic laundry irons heated on stoves (19th century). Then other means of heating them were found, such as hot water, gas, or alcohol, until the first electric iron was perfected in 1882.

Electric iron (1882)

The electric iron was invented and patented by New Yorker **Henry W. Seeley** on **6 July 1882**. However, it could not be used at the time as homes were not then connected to an electricity supply. The first electric steam iron came out in 1926 from Eldec Company of New York.

Lift

Origins (1743)

The first known lift was built at Versailles in 1743 during the reign of Louis XV and was for use by the King himself. It was installed on the outside of the building, in a little courtyard, and enabled the monarch to go from his apartments (on the first floor) to those of his mistress, Mme de Châteauroux (on the second). Using a system of counterweights it was possible to move the lift without too much effort.

Mechanical lift (1829)

The first lift of this type was built in London, in the Coliseum in Regent's Park, in **1829**. It could take about ten passengers. The public were invited to go up into a replica of the dome of Saint Paul's cathedral to admire a panorama depicting London. It was thus more of an attraction than a real means of locomotion.

Otis lift (1857)

The first lift for public use was inaugurated on **23 March 1857** in New York. It was built by the American **Elisha Graves Otis** for R. V. Haughtwout & Co, a five-storey store on Broadway. E. G. Otis had already presented the first safety lift with a brake in 1852 in New York.

Hydraulic lift (1867)

The Frenchman **Léon Edoux** (1827–1910) installed two lifting devices using hydraulic

The first electric lift was built by Werner von Siemens for the Mannheim Industrial Exhibition.

		LIGHTING		
Type	Date	Inventor	Country	Characteristics
Oil lamp	1804	Aimé Argand	France	Argand was the true inventor of these lamps which take their French name from the Swiss pharmacist Antoine Quinquet. Argand made the first one in 1804 in England. Quinquet modified the chimney, which he made of crystal.
Safety lamp	1816	Sir Humphry Davy	UK	Invented for miners. In 1811 Davy had discovered the principle of the electric arc.
Arc lamp	1847	W. E. Staite	UK	After Davy's first model of an arc lamp, which remained at the experimental stage, Staite's lamp was the first really effective lamp. It was perfected in 1848 by another Englishman, W. Petrie.
Yablochkov's candle	1876	Pavel Niolayevich Yablochkov	Russia	An improved arc light. In 1872 Yablochkov was asked to light the Moscow–Kursk railway, on which the Tsar was to travel, so that any potential terrorists would be unable to take advantage of the dark. The insulating metal melted as it was used. Victoria Embankment in London became the first street in Britain to be permanently lit by electricity in 1878.
Incandescent lamp	1878–9	Thomas A. Edison Sir Joseph Swan	USA UK	After a series of court cases for patent violations, the two inventors joined forces in 1883. The incandescent lamp was based on heating a filament by an electric current in an evacuated glass chamber.
Neon tubes	1909	Georges Claude	France	The first tubes were used to light the Grand Palais on 3 December 1910. In 1912 Jacques Fonsèque used neon for the first advertising sign on the Boulevard Montmartre.
Tungsten filament	1910	William D. Coolidge	USA	Patented 30 December 1913.
Fluorescent tubes	1934	Arthur Compton	USA	Around 70 years' research into fluorescence, whereby gases glowed in the current, culminated in this light.
Litec bulb	1965	Donald Hollister	USA	Instead of a filament it has an electromagnet which draws the current through a built-in electronic device.
SL lamp	1980	Philips	Netherlands	Based on the same principle as the fluorescent tube. It can produce the same amount of light as an incandescent lamp using 25 percent of the energy and lasts five times as long.
Halogen lamp	1980	Philips	Netherlands	An incandescent lamp with a tungsten filament. Its gas atmosphere contains argon or krypton and a percentage of halogen.

pistons 21m *69ft* high at the Paris Exhibition in **1867**. He called them *ascenseurs*.

The lifts using hydraulic pistons, which became widespread in the United States after 1879, went 20 times faster than Otis' 1857 lift. Their development was held up by the difficulty of digging very deep foundations. Nevertheless in 1889 Edoux managed to build a lift that travelled 160m *525ft* up the Eiffel Tower.

Electric lift (1880)

The first electric lift was built by the German firm **Siemens & Halske**, for the Mannheim Industrial Exhibition in **1880**.

It reached a height of 22m *72ft* in 11 seconds. In one month it carried 8000 passengers to the top of an observation tower overlooking the exhibition.

The first electric lift to rise over 200m *656ft* was built in New York in 1908.

Today the fastest lift (600m *1968ft*/min) is in the Sunshine Building in Tokyo.

Lock (antiquity)

The oldest locks seem to have first appeared in ancient Egypt. These massive locks made of hard wood worked using combinations of cylindrical pins of different lengths, which

fitted into grooves cut in immobile components that acted as keys.

Safety locks

Safety locks date from the 18th century (the Englishman Robert Barron's throat lock in 1778, the pump lock by another Englishman Joseph Bramah in 1784). They were perfected in the 19th century, notably by Alexander Fichet (unhookable lock patented in 1829 and 1836), Charles-Louis Sterlin and Eugène Bricard (two bolted lock, 1829) and Linus Yale (pin lock, called the Yale lock, patented 6 May 1851, which was inspired by the ancient Egyptian locks).

The skeleton key was first displayed at the Chicago Exhibition in 1894 by Alfred and Jules Bricard.

Matches (1826)

The first primitive matches were developed at the end of the 17th century. They were simply small sticks of wood dipped in melted sulphur and were developed by the Irishman Robert Boyle (1627–91). They needed to touch something burning in order to catch light. The first real matches to light without contact with fire were invented by the Englishman **John Walker** in 1826 while he was working on developing a new explosive. He failed to see the commercial potential, but Samuel Jones did and set up a factory. These matches were foul-smelling and so Frenchman Charles Sauria and Austrian Stephen von Roemer independently came up with cleaner and more efficient matches based on phosphorus. The first factories were set up in Vienna in 1833.

The substance used (white phosphorus) was highly toxic for the workers and the product was dangerously inflammable, which led chemists to continue their research.

Red phosphorus

The discovery of red phosphorus in 1847 enabled the Swede Lundström to create so-called safety matches, which need to be struck against a special material. These new matches first gained recognition at the Universal Exhibition in Paris in 1855.

Sewing machine (1830)

In 1830 the Frenchman **Barthélémy Thimonnier** invented the first sewing machine to work in a regular and useful way. It already included all the elements of today's machines.

The following year Thimonnier set up a company in Paris making military uniforms. But he met with violent opposition from workers. Thimonnier had to return to his native town of Amplepuis and to his trade as a tailor.

In 1834, at the same time as the Frenchman was carrying out his research, an American, Walter Hunt, designed a machine with two threads and a shuttle. Twelve years later Elias Howe replaced the hook on this machine by a needle with a hole in it.

In 1845 Thimonnier and his new partner Magnin made a second application for a patent for a machine which could do 200 stitches a minute and then, on 5 August 1848, another application for a machine made of metal, the *couso-brodeur*, which could do chain stitch. A little earlier Thimonnier had applied for a British patent, which he almost immediately gave over to a Manchester company. In 1849 the Englishmen Morey and Johnson bought an American patent. The American machine had a hooked needle, like Thimonnier's. In 1851 the Great Exhibition was held in London. By an unbelievable stroke of bad luck, the *couso-brodeur* arrived in London two days after the judges had examined the exhibits.

The Singer (1851)

In 1851 the American **Isaac Singer** was the first to build and market a sewing machine for domestic use in Boston, Massachusetts. His

Thimonnier is seen here at work on the 1830 model of his sewing machine.

needle was taken from Howe's machine. Singer became far more famous than Thimonnier, who died a ruined man in 1857, after finally having the consolation of presenting his machine at the Universal Exhibition in Paris.

Vacuum cleaner (1901)

Hubert Cecil Booth designed and patented the first vacuum cleaner in London in 1901. His Vacuum Cleaning Company provided a cleaning service with uniformed employees.

A much lighter machine was developed by an American inventor, Murray Spangler. He sold the rights to his vacuum to William B. Hoover who launched the Hoover Model 'O' at the end of 1908. His device was much lighter than that of Booth and it was an immediate success. Its ability to suck up dust brought remarkable results, greatly simplified cleaning and even improved sanitary conditions.

Washing machine (19th century)

Replacing the steam boiler, which itself replaced the washtub of the Middle Ages, the washing machine appeared during the 19th century.

Composed of a wooden bin that was filled with soapy hot water, the first mechanical washing machines used heavy blades to stir the washing. This principle of tossing clothes inside a rotating cylinder still governs the operation of modern machines. One of them operated in 1830 in an English laundry. Around 1840 in France an industrial model with double sheathing, four compartments, and a draining plug was designed; it was driven by means of a crank.

Electric washing machine (1901)

The first electric washing machine was invented and developed by the American **Alva J. Fisher** in 1901.

It was not until the start of the Second World War that electric vertical-tub machines with built-in turbo-washers or with a vertical axle fitted with blades began to be mass produced in the United States. Horizontal drum machines appeared in 1960.

While the sophisticated modern women of October 1931 on the right demonstrate how to use the new labour-saving washing machine, the washerwomen on the left are made to show just how difficult the old ways were.

In the bathroom

Bath (antiquity)

The ancient Greeks and Romans used baths made of marble or of silver. In the Middle Ages people bathed in simple wooden tubs.

Ambroise Paré's bath

The ancestor of the individual bath with heated water is the steamroom designed by the French surgeon **Ambroise Paré** (c.1509–90) for hydrotherapeutic purposes in the second half of the 16th century. But it was another 200 years before this comfort became a normal part of life. In the 18th century metal baths (already in use in the preceding century) became more widespread. At the end of the 18th century a special varnish, developed by a Parisian craftsman called Clément, made it possible to varnish sheet metal and thus to manufacture bathtubs at an accessible price, which led to their quickly replacing the traditional wooden or marble tubs which had been used until then. It seems the first hotel to provide a bathroom for every room was the Mount Vernon Hotel, Cape May, New Jersey (USA) in 1853.

Bathroom scales (1910)

Scales for domestic use were invented in 1910 by a German company, **Jas Ravenol**. They were marketed under the name of Jaraso. The first American scale of this kind is attributed to J. M. Weber (patented in 1916). The first scale with a digital display was introduced by the

Hanson Scale Co. in 1964. In 1984 H. S. Ong, a native of Malaysia, designed a talking scale.

Eau de Cologne (1709)

The Italian **Farina** family are credited with creating eau de Cologne in Germany in 1709. It was an alcohol-based mixture blended with fresh-smelling products like mint oil.

Flushing system (1595)

As early as 1595 an English courtier, **Sir John Harington**, had invented a practical water-flushing system for cleaning toilets, but his invention did not end the reign of chamber pots, despite gaining favour with Queen Elizabeth.

It was not until 1775 that the British inventor **Alexander Cummings** patented a flushing system. In 1778 another Englishman, 30-year-old Joseph Bramah, invented the ball-valve-and-U-bend method still used today. But it was not until the end of the 19th century, with the advent of running water and modern plumbing, that the flushing system found its way into most homes.

Kleenex (1924)

The first disposable paper hankies were produced in 1924 by the **Kimberley-Clark Co.** of Neenah, Wisconsin (USA), under the name of Celluwipes. The product was later renamed Kleenex-'Kerchiefs and then shortened to Kleenex. Originally, however, the tissues had been used as face wipes for women.

Lipstick (17th century)

At the beginning of the **17th century**, women coloured their lips with a fairly harsh, slightly scented pomade, coloured with the juice of black grapes and alkanet (dyers bugloss).

Later, cerates, a kind of salve, were produced which had a base of wax and oil. The same principle is used in the manufacture of Rosat, a product used to prevent lips becoming sore and cracked.

In the 20th century, chemists came to the rescue of the cosmetologists. They succeeded in manufacturing sticks of rouge which were easily moulded and did not have any adverse effects on the lips or mouth.

Nivea cream (1911)

In 1911 a Hamburg chemist, **Paul Beiersdorf** (who also invented the sticking plaster in 1882), invented a skin cream. It was marketed by the company he set up in 1882. The cream, which was white as snow, was called Nivea.

Perfume

Perfume originated in the East where refined manners and a wealth of vegetation were both to be found. Initially wood and scented resins were burnt on altars, and then perfumes were put into dishes to increase the flavour of food or, failing that, to act as an aphrodisiac.

The perfume industry, which has been well developed in France since the 17th century as a result of the impetus given by Colbert, was transformed by chemical discoveries and, at

This group of French people are drawing up a record of the various types of perfumes.

the end of the 19th century, saw the introduction of synthetic products.

Dry perfume (1984)

The first dry perfume was invented in **1984** by **Franka Berger** of France who, from 1985, commercialised it under her own name in America and Japan where it was immediately successful.

In 1989 Franka Berger invented the first mousse perfume for the body.

Perfume-lighter (1988)

Following the success of their famous biros, lighters and razors, on **22 February 1988**, **Bic** brought out four perfumes presented in the form of a mini-spray. The container, designed by Joël Desgrippes, is not much bigger than a lighter and can be used 300 times.

Razor (12th century)

Obviously no one person can claim to have invented the razor. Man has always shaved, with seashells, shark's teeth and, later, bronze blades.

The razor, properly speaking, dates from the **12th century**. The steel razor was created in Sheffield in the 18th century.

Safety razor (1895)

In **1895** the American **King Camp Gillette** patented the safety or mechanical razor, whose distinguishing feature was its double-edged replaceable blades. He marketed his product through the company he founded in Boston in 1901 and the first razors went on sale in 1903. The Gillette Safety Razor Company has undergone steady expansion since then.

Gillette introduced the twin-blade GII in 1971 and the first swivel-head razor in 1975.

Electric shaver (1931)

The first electric shaver was developed by the American **Colonel Jacob Schick**. The first model was patented and marketed in **1931**. After a slow start, the electric shaver caught on and by the end of the 1930s he was selling millions every year.

The disposable razor (1975)

The disposable razor was invented in **1975** by the French company **Bic**, the famous biro manufacturers. The company was directed by Baron Bich, who was of the opinion that half a razor blade was sufficient for a shave and that with the saving made on the other half, it was possible to manufacture a handle.

Lubricating razor (1986)

Launched simultaneously in **1986** by **Schick** (Schick Pivot Plus) and **Gillette** (Contour Plus), this razor is designed with a blade containing a lubricating substance which gives a smoother shave without scraping the skin.

Soap (2500 BC)

For a very long time man had been aware of the cleansing properties of oily and fatty compounds, associated with vegetable ash. A form of soft soap, probably of a very indifferent quality, existed in Mesopotamia in **2500 BC**. It reached Rome and Gaul in the 4th century, *sapo* being a word of Gaulish origin.

From the 13th century onwards, it was known how to make a solid soap using such

BEGIN EARLY   SHAVE YOURSELF

Gillette Safety Razor
NO STROPPING NO HONING

Even babies could use Gillette's safety razor without risk, or so it would seem.

fatty raw materials as soot or oil and alkalis such as plant ash or, better still, ash from seaweed which contains sodium carbonate. Until the end of the 18th century, there was very little development in soap-making techniques, and it remained a rare and expensive commodity.

Marseilles soap came into being in 1791 with the invention of a new process for the manufacture of sodium carbonate by Nicholas Leblanc.

Toilet paper (1857)

Toilet paper was invented in America by **Joseph Cayetty** in **1857**, but for a long time it remained a luxury item. The Briton Walter Alcock in 1879 became the first to produce a toilet roll. Only by the end of the century did the product really catch on.

Toothbrush (15th century)

The toothbrush appears for the first time in a Chinese painting from the end of the **15th century**. It appeared in Europe in the 17th century.

The first nylon toothbrush was Doctor West's Miracle Tuft Toothbrush, manufactured by Du Pont in the United States in 1938.

The first patent for an electric toothbrush goes back to 1908, but they did not become popular until the 1930s.

Vaseline (1879)

Robert Cheseborough, an American chemist from Brooklyn, became worried by the growth of the petroleum industry, which was threatening his own sales of kerosene. So he visited the oilfields of Pennsylvania and there discovered a gummy residue which stuck to the drilling bits. The workers had found one use for it – it encouraged a cut or a burn to heal quickly, otherwise it was a complete nuisance to them and hindered their work.

Cheseborough took some samples of the paste back to his home. There he tried it out and, having confirmed its healing qualities, began to manufacture it, calling it Vaseline Petroleum Jelly. It quickly became enormously popular and soon was being used not only for medicinal purposes but also as a cleaning agent, an anti-rust device and so on. So, by the time he died in 1933, his product was in use the world over.

Clothes

Bikini (1946)

On **5 July 1946** the Frenchman **Louis Réard** presented an extremely daring two-piece in his swimwear collection. He called it the bikini because he considered it as explosive in its own way as the American atomic bomb which had been exploded four days earlier on the Pacific island of Bikini. The novelty was such that none of his professional models would wear it and Réard had to appeal for help to a dancer from the Casino in Paris, Micheline Bernardini. His creation was patented and, duly protected, the word bikini soon entered the dictionary.

Bra (antiquity)

There is proof that the bra existed in ancient Rome. It is depicted on ceramics where the female gymnasts wear the *strophium*, a sort of scarf wound over the breasts in order to provide support.

In 1805 a band of elastic material was worn below high-waisted muslin dresses to keep the bust firm. It crossed at the front and was fastened at the back of the neck. In 1889 Herminie Cadolle invented the bra as we know it, but it did not become widely used until the 1920s. In 1913 Mary Jacob of New York devised a backless bra to suit her ball gown. It was patented on 3 November 1914 and, after some early problems, soon became a success. According to current statistics, the average English woman buys three bras per year compared with 1.3 and five bought by her French and American counterparts.

Handkerchief (2nd century BC)

The handkerchief is thought to have appeared in Rome during the **2nd century BC**, but it did not become part of everyday life. It did not reappear until the 15th century in Italy where the distinction was made between the handkerchief used for the nose, which was slipped into the pocket, and the handkerchief used for the face, which was held in the hand. It reached France during the 16th century and was immediately adopted by the Court and actors, becoming as indispensable to tragedy as the fan can be to comedy. It became widely used during the 17th century.

Jeans (1850s)

Jeans were created around **1850** by **Oscar Levi Strauss** for pioneers of the Californian gold rush. These hard-wearing trousers were originally cut out of a blue cloth which served for tenting. This cloth had been imported from Nîmes, France's traditional production centre, where it was known as serge de Nîmes, hence the term denim. The famous copper studs first appeared on the pockets in 1873 to prevent splits down the seams caused by keeping tools in the pockets.

The earliest mention of the word *jean* dates from 1567 and appears to be a corrupt form of the word genoese, from Genoa. A twill cotton fabric was also manufactured in Genoa, where sailors wore pants made of this material. Denim is a heavy cotton cloth having an ecru woof and an indigo warp.

A selection of bikinis, 1949 style, create a great deal of attention at an industrial fair.

Macintosh (1823)

It was the Scotsman **Charles Macintosh** (1760–1843) who, in **1823**, was the first to succeed in producing a waterproof cloth that could be used to manufacture clothing. His cotton fabric, imbued with a mixture of rubber and turpentine, maintained its full flexibility. The Macintosh became *the* waterproofed overcoat worn by men during the 19th century.

Miniskirt (1965)

The miniskirt was created by the dress designer **Mary Quant** in her store, Bazaar, on King's Road, London in the spring of **1965**.

Almost simultaneously, the French fashion designer Courrèges was creating a line that was very architectural, quite short and futuristic. Wearing miniskirts, opaque tights and small helmets, fashionable women resembled astronauts. But this was a haute couture collection, whereas Mary Quant's skirts were enthusiastically taken up by a generation of young women.

Nylon stockings (1940)

The stocking market was revolutionised by the appearance of the first nylon in 1938. Nylon was developed by a team of researchers from the American company Du Pont led by **Doctor Wallace Carothers** (1896–1937), who committed suicide a year before nylon appeared. The potential for use as stockings was quickly seen and Du Pont prepared to launch the new fashion item on **15 May 1940**. The first nylon stockings reached Europe in 1945.

Pin (1817)

While pins have been made for thousands of years, it was not until **1817** that the American **Seth Hunt** informed the Patent Office of his

Nylon stockings revolutionised the fashion world in the 1940s.

invention of an automatic machine for manufacturing one-piece pins, with body, head and point. His machine began operation in 1824, when Samuel Wright filed a patent in England. England had been the home of the industrial pin since John Tilsby had founded the first large pin works in Gloucester in 1625.

Hunt's machine was improved in 1838 by the Englishmen Henry Shuttle Worth and Daniel Foote Taylor, from Birmingham. Their pin was less dangerous.

Safety pin (1849)

The invention of the modern safety pin is attributed to the American **Walter Hunt**, who developed it in **1849**. It appears that fibulas and brooches, used in ancient Crete to attach draped clothes, were made according to a related principle.

Pockets (16th century)

Surprisingly pockets are a rather late development in clothing. Prior to the **16th century**, if a man was carrying personal items, he would most usually place them in a codpiece at the front of his trousers. Towards 1600 these items became less popular and, instead, a small opening was made in the seam of a pair of trousers into which a pouch could be placed. Eventually this became a permanent fixture – and the pocket was invented.

ITEMS AND ACCESSORIES FROM ANTIQUITY

Objects	Origin	History
Button	3000 BC	An ancient invention found in the Indus Valley (3000 BC) and in Scotland (2000 BC). Only in the Middle Ages did the button come to be used with a buttonhole as a fastening device. Prior to that it was used simply for decoration.
Comb	prehistoric	Used as early as 8000 BC in Scandinavia. Used in ancient Egypt. The manufacture of tortoiseshell combs began in the United States in 1780.
Tie	ancient Rome	Of military origin (the Roman *focale*). Became more widely worn during the 17th century. The introduction of the fashion is attributed to either the Swedes c.1600 or the Croatian Army c.1668. In England the tie was popularised by Charles II in the 17th century and by Beau Brummel in the next.
Fan	antiquity	Lotus leaves in Egypt, peacock feathers in Rome. The folding fan appeared towards the end of the Middle Ages.
Mirror	ancient Egypt	Many mirrors have been discovered in the tombs of the pharaohs. The invention of the crystalline mirror is attributed to the Venetians during the 18th century.
Needle	prehistoric	Used in Egypt, Greece and Rome. By 1370 the German city of Nuremberg was an important centre for the manufacture of polished steel needles.
Stockings	ancient Rome	In the 16th century the strips of cloth used until then were replaced by knitted hose. The stocking trade revolutionised their manufacture at the end of the same century.

Press-stud (1886)

The press-stud was invented on **29 May 1886** by an industrialist from Grenoble in France, **Pierre-Albert Raymond**. The patent was requested in the name of the company Raymond & Guttin, the latter being the co-inventor. The metal press-stud was initially used as a fastener in the local glove industry.

Many imitations were produced worldwide, but the company always fought to protect its patent and won its case. It extended its products to the international level, and is still in existence today.

Rucksack (1936)

On **22 January 1936** the patent was issued for the first modern rucksack, an improved version of the Tyrolean rucksack developed by the company **Lafuma**. The main innovation was that the metal grid no longer protruded but was incorporated into the rucksack. This was the forerunner of all modern rucksacks.

Shoe (antiquity)

The museum in Romans, France, has a pair of Egyptian shoes made of papyrus, dating back to 4000 BC. But the shoe was undoubtedly invented much earlier, although the distinction between the right and left foot only dates from the middle of the 11th century. Until then, respectable footwear had to be made to measure.

The pump, which was originally a basic type of slipper for wearing indoors, appeared in the 16th century. Its popularity increased during the 18th century when it became extremely fashionable. From 1900 it played an important part in the emancipation of women by replacing the ankle boot and becoming a comfortable town shoe.

It was not until the 1890s that mass production of standard-sized shoes became possible and the Manfield Shoe Company of Northampton took the lead.

Screw-on button (1988)

The first button without thread, that doesn't have to be sewn on but which is screwed into place, was developed by the Swedish sculptor **Gudmar Olovson**. Presented at the Paris Trade Fair in **1988**, this ingenious device can be used on any kind of material. You merely screw the button into place, preferably near a buttonhole, and then open out the end of the screw and the button is firmly fixed. To remove it, you simply reverse the process!

Top hat (1797)

Although the French lay claim to having devised the top hat in 1796, the credit for creating it is usually given to a London milliner, **John Etherington**. On **15 January 1797** he emerged from his shop wearing a tall, hard, black hat. A crowd quickly gathered to have a look at this new item, and there was even some unrest. However, despite this controversial start, the hat was an immediate success.

Umbrella (2nd century BC)

It would seem that the umbrella was a Chinese invention from as early as the **2nd century BC**. However, some claim that umbrellas were used a thousand years previously in Egypt as sun shades. The Greeks and the Romans were both using them in the 1st century AD, but as a rain shield it was seen as a woman's item.

The umbrella was considered effeminate as recently as the mid 18th century, when the Englishman **Sir Jonas Hanway** began to popularise its usage for men. So, by the time of his death in 1786, they were often referred to as 'Hanways' and their future was assured.

Velcro (1948)

Velcro is a Swiss invention whose discovery dates from **1948**. Returning from a day's hunting, the engineer **Georges de Mestral** noticed that burdock seed heads clung to his clothing. Under the microscope he discovered that each of these heads was surrounded by minute hooks allowing them to catch onto fabrics. It then occurred to him to fix similar hooks on fabric strips which would cling together and serve as fasteners.

Eight years were needed to develop the basic product: two nylon strips, one of which contained thousands of small hooks, and the other even smaller loops. When the two strips were pressed together, they formed a quick and practical fastener. The invention was named Velcro (from the French *velours* velvet and *crochet* hook). It was patented worldwide in 1957.

Zipper (1893)

Around 1890, the American **Whitcomb Judson** devised a quick zipper system based on interlocking small teeth. The idea was ingenious

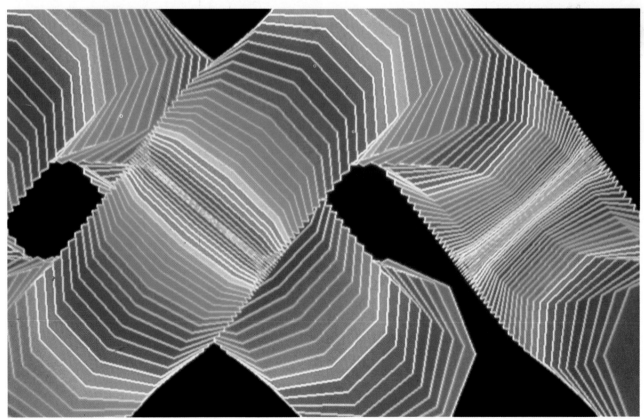

This is a numeric simulation of the path of two fibres in a traditional thread. Nowadays, natural fabrics such as cotton, wool and silk have been faced with much competition from acrylic fibres such as polyester and nylon.

but its practical application not simple. Judson filed his patent on **29 August 1893** and entered into partnership with a lawyer, Lewis Walker, to found a company.

In 1905 machines to manufacture zippers were in operation, but their products were far from perfect. It was not until 1912 that Judson's invention provided full satisfaction to its users: this was due to the improvements made by the Swede Gideon Sundback.

The American zipper was marketed by the Goodrich Company, which used it on snow boots.

At the hairdresser's

Hair colour (1909)

The first conclusive tests were carried out in **1909** by the French chemist **Eugène Schueller** based on the chemical paraphenylene-diamine. He founded a company which in 1910 became L'Oréal. In 1927 the hairdressing industry was revolutionised by the invention of Imédia, a dye which was manufactured from organic colouring agents and which offered a wide range of natural shades.

Hair dryer (1920)

The two earliest models appeared in Racine, Wisconsin (USA) in **1920**. They were the Race, made by the **Racine Universal Motor Co.**, and the Cyclone, made by **Hamilton Beach**. They were manual models.

In the winter of 1951 Sears, Roebuck & Co. marketed the Ann Barton, the first helmeted model for home use.

Hairstyle video (1988)

You can now see yourself on a screen with the hairstyle of your choice, without losing a single lock of hair. This has been made possible by the use of a video and a graphics sheet linked to a microcomputer, designed for use by professional hairstylists and beauticians and for beauty counselling. The Video-Look was invented in **1988** by **Alain Saulnier** of France.

Hair washer (1988)

A 24-year-old Japanese woman, **Fumiko Akutsu**, a factory worker for Mitsubishi, was responsible for the invention of a personal hair-washing machine for which she won first prize in a competition for new ideas run by Mitsubishi in **1988**.

It should be pointed out that many Japanese homes do not have bathrooms, showers or running hot water. This tiny machine has been extremely successful: 20 000 were sold in three months.

Hot air perm (1906)

On **8 October 1906 Nestle**, a German hairstylist living in London, demonstrated a new method of curling hair. He then went to live in the United States where his new invention, Permanent Waving, was extremely successful.

The set (c.1870)

The modern set was invented by **Lenthéric** of France around **1870**. The waves were no longer obtained by heating the hair with curling tongs, but by drying them with warm air. During the 1920s the Parisian hairstylist Rambaud realised the advantages of combining the techniques of the permanent wave and the set. After cutting and perming the hair, Rambaud rolled it and secured it with curling pins. It was then dried under a hot air drier.

The result was surprising. The hot air permanent applied on its own produced tight little curls which did have the advantage of not dropping out, but which were not particularly attractive. Rambaud had replaced it with a soft and loosely waving hairstyle.

Shampoo (1877)

The term *shampoo* originated in England in **1877**. It was derived from *champo*, a word in Hindi which means to massage or to knead.

Originally brewed by hairdressers, shampoos were made by boiling soft soap in soda water. But it was not until after the Second World War that shampoos came into general popular use.

Leisure

Beach-towel clamp (1989)

A beach towel spread on the sand is disturbed by the slightest gust of wind and every movement you make. **Christiane Caillat-**

The options open to people when they went to the hairdresser's in the mid 19th century (left) were much more limited than they are today (right), when spectacular creations such as these have become possible.

Thanks to developments in fibre optics and ultra-violet filters it is now possible for sun-lovers to have solar showers or, literally, to sun bathe.

FROM THE MOON TO THE SUN: THE INVENTION OF THE CALENDAR

The first calendars, going back to the Babylonians and the ancient Egyptians, were based on the lunar cycle of 29½ days. The months began with the full moon and had alternately 29 and 30 days. But the moon has little influence on the earth's flora and fauna, and the Egyptians, an agricultural people, soon abandoned the lunar calendar for one based on the solar year which determines the seasons and the harvest.

In the 8th century BC the Greeks also used a calendar made up of 12 lunar months. The astronomer Meton of Athens revised this calendar in the 5th century BC to bring it into line with the sun. Meton's calendar, both lunar and solar, was used for five centuries.

The Romans initially used a calendar based on ten lunar months, known as the calendar of Romulus, and it is from this calendar that we get the names of the months. Later king Numa Pompolius added two months to this calendar making 355 days in the year. The Romans looked to the priests to adjust the calendar from time to time to bring it back into line with the solar year and, at certain times, a street crier would be employed to announce the first day of each month. The situation remained confused for a long time, leading to Voltaire's remark: 'The Roman generals always won, but they didn't know the date of their victory.' It was Julius Caesar who finally revised the calendar in 45 BC on the advice of the Greek astronomer from Alexandria, Sosigenes. The new calendar, known as the Julian calendar, was independent of the moon and comprised months of 30 or 31 days and leap years, like the present calendar. Only one little correction had to be made to the Julian calendar, subtracting one day every 128 years, before it was in perfect harmony with the Sun. In 1582 Pope Gregory XIII decided to subtract in one go the ten days accumulated since the Roman era (so, in the space of one night, the date went from Thursday 4 to Friday 15 October 1582). The Gregorian calendar is so precise that it is only one day out every 3000 years.

Maillefer, a Swiss, has invented a clamp which holds the towel firmly in place on the ground. This is a single piece of plastic, consisting of a peg, which holds the towel, and a spike with a rough surface which is planted in the sand. This very useful accessory was patented in **1989**.

Cigarette (16th century)

The cigarette was invented by beggars in Sevilla, Spain, at the end of the **16th century**. They had the idea of rolling the tobacco salvaged from cigar butts inside a small cylinder of paper. Cigarette use spread to Portugal, Italy, England, and France.

The first commercial industrial cigarette factory opened in Havana in 1853. The average Briton smokes 2100 cigarettes a year.

Metal detector (1931)

Those who have scoured the beaches for treasure buried beneath the sand are quite familiar with these small instruments. They were invented in **1931** by the American **Gerhard Fisher**, and were originally intended for industrial and geological use. The chance discovery of some coins dating back to the American Civil War opened up a whole new dimension. Since then they have been continually improved. A new range was patented in 1985 by the Fischer Research Laboratory. They are light, easy to handle and capable of detecting any kind of precious metal on land and even in shallow water. The latest model, the 1280 X Aquanaut was designed for underwater treasure hunting and is operated by a battery which will last for up to 40 hours.

Sun-tan parasol (1984)

In **1984** the Englishman **John Sear** developed a sunshade which makes it possible to sunbathe without suntan oil, without sunglasses and with complete protection from the sun. It is made from Solmax, a filter screen invented in 1982 by another Englishman, J. A. Cuthbert. Tests have proved that this filter, in violet coloured plastic, will, as long as it retains its colour, exclude 90 percent of the sun's harmful rays while letting through 75 percent of the UVA rays which tan the skin. In this way it eliminates the risks of sunburn and sore and inflamed eyes.

DIY

Brace (15th century)

The forerunners of the brace, i.e. all tools used for piercing, existed in prehistoric times. The Egyptians used an instrument derived from the hand drill. The auger, which only dates back to the middle of the Bronze Age, found its final form during the Iron Age.

The screw auger, from which the brace was developed, seems to have been used in Scandinavia from the 11th to 13th century, mainly on the structures of river-going vessels. The brace, in the form that we know it, appeared in the first quarter of the **15th century**. The first known depiction of it is on the painting of the *Annunciation* by Robert Campin, Master of Flémalle.

Electric hand drill (1917)

After developing presses for postage stamps, machines for attaching boot buttons and machines for printing banknotes, two young American inventors, **S. Duncan Black** and **Alonso G. Decker** revolutionised popular DIY in **1917** by manufacturing the first rotary hand drill. Their portable drill weighed 11kg *24lb*. After the Second World War, much lighter and greatly improved hand drills enjoyed a rapid and widespread popularity, to the point of becoming a basic and indispensable item for all DIY enthusiasts.

Gas operated drill (1986)

This new wireless hand drill was invented in **1986** by the Japanese company **Tanaka Kogyo**. It has a two-stroke engine, a fuel tank and is completely safe to use, even in damp weather. The absence of electrical wiring makes it safe and easy to use.

The hammer (prehistory)

This is one of the oldest tools. A stone may have been the first hammer. The first decisive improvement was the addition of a handle. The stone axe hammer of the Neolithic Age already had a handle, as does the current hammer. However, stone was a fragile material. It was not until the Bronze Age that the metallic hammer made its appearance and its widespread uses became understood.

Nail (18th century)

The first machines to make nails date from the **18th century** (patents of the American **Ezekial Reed** in 1786 and the Englishman **Thomas Clifford** in 1790). However, the artisan's nail goes even further back in time, since the oldest known nails were found in Mesopotamia and date from approximately 3500 BC.

Plane (c.1200 BC)

The plane appeared during the Iron Age, around **1200 BC**. The earliest depictions we have date back to the Gallo–Roman era, in countries occupied or influenced by the Romans.

A variation of the plane, the trying-plane, is one of the earliest tools. The best preserved are those which were carefully worked, sculpted and polished, between the 16th and the 18th century.

A pouring lip for paint (1987)

The pouring lip was invented in **1987** by the American company **Spill Bill**, and makes life a lot easier for painters and DIY enthusiasts. It is made of flexible plastic and fits onto the rim of the paint tin once the lid has been removed. The paint can be poured easily and cleanly into another receptacle and the brush can be rested on it without running down the side of the tin. Once the paint is dry, it is easily removed from the lip.

Saw (antiquity)

The saw would appear to have been invented by the Egyptians during the Bronze Age, around 3500 BC to 1200 BC. Roman craftsmen produced a wide variety of saws, including the frame saw, which until the 14th century formed the basis for this type of equipment. The metal saw appeared in the 15th century.

Screwdriver (17th century)

This is a tool which has been continually developed since it was first used at the end of the **17th century**. The screw has become more important since the middle of the 19th century, with the development of machine tools. For a long time, producing screws was a laborious task since the grooves had to be filed by hand.

The Englishman **John Whitworth** was responsible for the standardisation of the thread in **1841**.

The first electric hand drill was built by the German Wilhelm Fein in 1895.

Vice (prehistory)

The earliest vice is considered, rightly, to have been the human jaw (paleolithic). The primitive object itself was made of wood. At the end of the Bronze Age (c.3500–c.1200 BC) the discovery of the screw completed an invention that has survived broadly unchanged to the present day. It was greatly simplified by the discovery of iron (c.1200 BC). Its evolution continued until the 12th century.

The first screw vices similar to ours seem to have appeared in the 14th century. They were perfected in the 16th and 17th centuries.

Commerce

Coins (7th century BC)

Coining, i.e. the affixing of an official mark to a gold ingot, was invented in the middle of the **7th century BC** in Asia Minor during the reign of Ardys, King of Lydia.

The coins were small ingots made of a mixture of gold and silver known as *electrum*, found in its natural state in the river which flowed through Sardis, the capital of Lydia. The name of the river, the Pactolus, later became synonymous with abundance and wealth.

The first coins to be made from this mixture were shaped like flattened pellets. On one side they bore a triangular or square hallmark and on the obverse side, an Assyrian-style lion whose nose was decorated with a sort of shining globe.

Bill of exchange (4th century BC)

In the **4th century BC** the Greeks invented the bill of exchange. Isocrates' (436–388 BC) *Discourse on Banking* bears witness; he refers to this means of payment allowing one to travel without taking along large sums of money.

Travellers handed over a sum of money to their local banker. In return, the banker gave them a letter. Upon presentation of this letter to a banker at the traveller's destination, the traveller would be given the money required.

The bill of exchange was the forerunner of the banknote.

Watermark (1282)

The translucent mark printed on a piece of paper, known as the watermark, appeared for the first time in Fabriano, Italy, in **1282**. The Italian word, *filigrana* or filigree, used originally to refer to a piece of delicate work in gold or silver. For centuries paper-makers used this method, known as the clear watermark, to mark their products.

Dark watermark

Towards the end of the 18th century the appearance of the watermark changed due to the introduction of a dark line, the dark watermark. Combined with the clear watermark, it provided increased protection.

Shaded watermark

Finally, by combining the raised or clear watermark with the sunk or dark watermark, an Englishman, **William Henry Smith**, invented the shaded watermark in **1848**. This transformed the art of the watermark by

making it possible to produce more complicated compositions with an almost unlimited fineness of detail and richness of half-tones.

Stock exchange (1450)

The stock exchange, that is, a place where financial transactions occur, was created about **1450**. Until then, merchants and bankers got together at fairs. In the middle of the 15th century, a family of Bruges bankers, the **Van de Bursens**, opened its house to these transactions. Over the entrance portal was a frontispiece depicting three engraved purses. Antwerp in turn opened an exchange in 1487. It soon became the largest in Europe. **Sir Thomas Gresham** (c.1519–79) founded the Royal Exchange in 1568, which became known as the Stock Exchange in 1773.

Banknotes (1658)

Originally, bankers at medieval fairs delivered registered receipts to their depositors. Then, in about 1587 in Venice, it became possible to transfer these receipts through the practice of endorsement. It was this endorsement that helped spread the use of paper money.

The first bank to issue banknotes was the **Riksbank** of Stockholm in **1658**. The Bank of England was founded in 1694.

Traveller's cheque (1891)

The traveller's cheque was invented in 1891 by **American Express**. The first cheque was counter-signed on **5 August 1891** and the system spread rapidly throughout Europe, contributing to the development of tourism and international exchanges.

Since 1985 traveller's cheques have existed in ECUs, the European Currency Unit.

Credit card (1950)

The first company to organise payment by credit card was founded by an American **Ralph Schneider** in 1950. The first 200 members of the Diners Club were able to dine on credit in 27 New York restaurants. The Bank of America was the first to introduce a bank credit card, the Bankamericard, in 1958.

In the UK, American Express was the first credit card and it became available on 10 September 1963. Barclaycard followed in 1966 and Access first appeared in 1972.

Biometry

It is currently (theoretically) possible to check the identity of a person without any risk of error by using techniques of biometry, based on the biological parameters of the human being, i.e. fingerprinting, retinal printing, voiceprinting, etc.

This type of technology is of interest in the areas of defence, the nuclear industry, banks, large companies, etc. The first operational biometric system was the EyeDentification 7.7.

Eye prints (1984)

After fingerprinting comes 'eye printing', launched in **September 1984** by the American company **Eye Dentify**. It is a rapid system of identification by a retinal image which sweeps the back of the eye and enables a more accurate identification than by the standard fingerprinting method. To date, a little over 400 EyeDentification System 7.5s have been installed, 280 of which are in the United States. This makes the company the world leader in biometric systems.

IDX 70 (1987)

The main competitor of the EyeDentification system is the IDX 70 produced by the American company **Identix**. This is a system for the identification of fingerprints, recorded on a memory card. The invention is based on a process known as global vision developed by researchers at the University of Berkeley and by the work of Rockwell for the FBI in 1962.

Identification by fingerprinting was invented by the English physiologist and cousin of Charles Darwin, **Sir Francis Galton** (1822–1911), in 1892.

The IRS (American tax inspectors) have all manner of technological weapons to help them. Here, a study is being made of the origin of an ink by using chromotography.

A British invention imported to Texas – cardboard policemen. When placed in shops these models have a remarkable deterrent effect, simply by reminding people that theft is a crime.

Jardinière, founded in Paris in **1824** by **Pierre Parissot**. His publicity and sales methods revolutionised commercial practice. He insisted that his merchandise was sold at 'a fixed price and for cash' whereas trade had always been based on two main principles: the negotiation of the price between the seller and the buyer, and buying on credit. Harper's Building, designed by the architect John B. Corlies, opened in New York in 1854, followed in 1858 by the Crystal Palace Bazaar, the first department store to be opened in London.

Safe (1844)

In **1844** the Frenchman **Alexandre Fichet**, a locksmith born in 1799, invented the first modern safe. Previously, strong boxes with secret compartments had been used; now they were also fireproof and more difficult to break into.

In 1829 he had already applied for a patent for a burglarproof lock of his own invention.

Mail order (1850)

Direct mail order sales date back to the 17th century. But it was not until about **1850**, when postal charges came down, that the practice became widespread. Mail order catalogues appeared simultaneously in France (Manufacture des Armes et Cycles of Saint-Etienne) and in the United States (Sears & Roebuck).

Supermarkets (1879)

The first shops of this type were born in the United States in **1879**. They were introduced into Britain in 1909. In those days, they had a plain and rather drab appearance, not at all like the flashy style that we know today. Tesco is the largest supermarket chain in Britain, with annual sales of about £5 billion.

Cash register (1879)

The cash register was invented by the American **James J. Ritty** on **4 November 1879**. He owned a saloon in Dayton, Ohio, and the constant quarrels with his customers exasperated him.

During a boat trip to Europe, he noticed a machine that registered the number of times a propeller turned. This machine triggered the idea for his cash register, which served both as a printing–adding machine and a till.

Car hire (1918)

Car hire was introduced in **1918** by a second-hand car dealer from Chicago. He hired out 12 vehicles. His company was bought in 1923 by the president of the yellow taxi cab company of Chicago, **John D. Hertz**, who renamed the unsteady business the Hertz Self-Drive System.

Supermarket trolleys (1937)

In Oklahoma City (USA), the owner of the Humpty Dumpty Store invented the first supermarket trolley on **4 June 1937**. He had noticed that his customers had trouble lugging all their purchases through the different departments. He converted folding chairs into carts: the feet were mounted on wheels, a basket replaced the seat, and the back served to push the vehicle.

Geometry of the hand (1987)

A device based on the evaluation of the geometry of the hand, known as the Palm Recognition System, has been developed by **Mitsubishi** and is used only in Japan.

Sign-on (1987)

The Sign-on system is based on the recognition of the dynamics of the signature, in other words the movement made during signing. It was brought onto the market by the English company **Alan Leibert Associates** in **1987**. Another, much earlier, British system was also based on the (non-dynamic) recognition of the signature. Verisign was developed in 1973 and marketed in 1982 by the Transaction Security Division of Analytical Instruments Ltd.

Disappearing cheques (1988)

Some American inventors (who carefully conceal their identities) developed cheques that self-destruct a short time after being cashed. They have cost the banks $70 000!

Scales (c.3500 BC)

In about **3500 BC**, the Egyptians weighed wheat and gold using scales which consisted of two pans suspended from a beam. The scales with unequal arms were invented in Italy, probably in Campania, c.300–200 BC.

Department stores (1824)

The first department store was the *Belle*

The latest in hi-tech supermarket trolleys made its debut in Hermosa Beach, California.

Chester Carlson invented the process of Xerography in 1938 when aged just 32.

Tele-shopping (1985)

The first television sales channels were introduced in the United States in **1985**. Viewers are invited to telephone their orders for items shown on their screens during various shows and games.

Anti-theft label (1988)

Metostop was invented by the Swedish company **Esselte** and has been responsible for a 70 percent reduction in the thefts carried out in department stores. It looks very ordinary and should, in theory, be able to protect all types of merchandise: books, records, cassettes, as well as alcohol and perfumes, products which until now have proved difficult to defend.

In the office

Carbon (1806)

Carbon paper, used to obtain several copies from one document, was invented by the Englishman **R. Wedgwood**, who patented it on **7 October 1806**. The process he described employed a thin sheet of paper saturated with ink and dried between sheets of blotting paper.

Photocopy (1903)

Photocopy refers to the process of rapid reproduction of a document by the instantaneous development of a photo negative. It was invented by the American **G. C. Beidler** in **1903**. Beidler, an office clerk, noticed the constant need for copies of documents, so he developed a machine for replacing laborious manual or typed copies and patented it in 1906. The first photocopy machine was marketed by the American company Rectigraph in 1907, but it was not until the 1960s that the photocopier became commonplace.

Xerography (1938)

On **22 October 1938** the American **Chester Carlson** (1906–68) produced the first xerographic image (from the Greek *xeros* meaning dry and *graphein* to write). He called the new process Xerography and patented it after several improvements had been made. Between 1939 and 1944, 20 companies refused his patents. In 1944 the Battelle Memorial Institute, a non-profit-making organisation based in Columbus, Ohio (USA), signed an agreement with Carlson and began to develop xerography.

In 1947 Battelle signed an agreement with a small photographic business, Haloid, which later became Xerox.

In 1959 the first photocopier, the Xerox 914, was brought onto the market.

For a long time Xerox has had no competition in the photocopying market, making $15 billion in 1987, but in the last few years its virtual monopoly has been threatened by the Japanese. Toshiba, for example, has machines which can produce a hundred copies per minute.

Colour photocopier (1973)

The Japanese company **Canon** developed the first colour photocopier which was brought out in Japan in **1973**.

This staircase is the result of a three-dimensional photocopy. The process was developed by a research group at CNRS in France. They hope that it will prove useful to architects and designers who need to see a model of the object they wish to build.

Laser colour copier (1986)

The laser colour copier, launched in **1986**, was also invented by **Canon**. It offers a good quality quadrichrome reproduction, i.e. in four colours, on ordinary paper. The image can be reproduced in several ways by enlargement, reduction, changing the dimensions.

Pocket photocopier (1986)

This tiny, extra-light photocopier, the KX Z40X, is an ideal size, barely 16cm *6.2in* long by 7cm *2.7in* wide. It was developed by **Panasonic** in **1986**. It can reproduce any kind of document and operates for up to 20 minutes. It has no wires, no batteries and can be recharged from a storage battery.

Paper clip (1900)

The paper clip, a metallic clip that allows one to attach sheets of paper together, was invented in **1900** by a Norwegian, **Johann Waaler**, who patented his invention in Germany.

'Post-it' notes (1981)

This invention has invaded our daily lives, in the office, at home, everywhere. It was invented purely by chance in 1970. **Doctor Spencer Sylver** of the American company 3M was involved in research on a completely different product when he discovered an adhesive which sticks without sticking. He sent samples of his discovery to other laboratories in the 3M group, but no use could be found for this surprising product.

It was not until ten years later that **Arthur Fry**, another research worker in the 3M group, found a use for what was to become the Post-it, again purely by chance. He was a member of a choir and was trying to find a way of marking the pages of his music book without damaging the paper. And this was why, in 1980, he put a thin layer of this famous 'unknown' adhesive onto the page markers of his score . . . and it worked! The little pastel coloured pieces of paper which stick, unstick and can be re-stuck at will, came into being. The name Post-it was invented in **1981**.

Scotch tape (1925)

An American, **Dick Drew**, invented adhesive tape in **1925**. Then a young assistant at the 3M laboratory at St Paul, Minnesota, Drew asked car manufacturers to test the first samples of waterproof adhesive paper. At that time, car-body builders had to paint cars in two tones. Paint was applied by spray gun, the difficult part was to separate the colours clearly and distinctly. Glued together newspapers were used, but it often happened that when the bands were removed, the fresh paint also came off. Drew studied the problem and, with the encouragement of management, sought a solution: adhesive masking tape. Five years later cellulose adhesive tape appeared.

The name Scotch tape arose because initially only the edges of it were self-adhesive. Car-body workers, who were asked to use it, suspected that this was done to save tape and money, rather than to make it easier to stick on and peel off. So they called it Scotch tape, maligning the reputation of the Scots.

Games and toys

Billiards (14th century)

The first billiard game took place in the **14th century**. It was played on the ground, a little like croquet. Henri de Vigne conceived and built the first billiard table for Louis XI, King of France 1461–83. However, it was only during the 19th century that the game began to develop in anything like its current form. Other versions have since evolved.

Snooker (1875)

The most likely inventor of the game is **Sir Neville F. F. Chamberlain**, who devised the game in India in **1875**. It did not reach Britain for about ten years. Until very recently it was largely a bar-room game, despite the popularising efforts of the 15-time world champion Joe Davis in the 1930s and 1940s. It was only in the 1980s, with the boom in television coverage thanks to stars like Steve Davis and Alex Higgins, that the game began to attract television audiences of over 10 million and sponsors that enabled top players to earn up to £500000 from match winnings alone in a season.

Pool (c.1890)

This version of billiards was invented in the United States in the **1890s**, and remains the most popular form of billiard game in that country – snooker and billiards having made little impact. In Britain, pool is very much confined to pubs and bars and it seems unlikely to break out of this environment for some while yet.

Bridge (1850)

Bridge grew out of whist and first appeared around **1850** in Istanbul. The game consists of a battle between two camps, hence the name 'Bridge', since each player is partnered by the player sitting opposite. Bridge has been and continues to be the object of many scientific studies.

The contract system, which evolved from a French game, was devised by Harold Vanderbilt in 1925 and enabled players to evaluate the strength of their hands. This form of the game rapidly became popular and soon international competitions were being held.

Chess (6th century)

The earliest mention of the game of chess is made by the Persian **Karnamak** (590–628). The game seems to have originated in northern India, around the year **500**, but the rules we use today were established in Europe around 1550. The 16 pieces, king, queen, bishop, knight, rook or castle and pawns, are arranged on a chequered board with 64 squares and manoeuvred against the opponent.

The expression 'checkmate' comes from a phonetic deformation of the Arabic phrase *al shâh mat*, which means 'the king is dead'.

Computer chess

In 1950 Claude Shannon set out the basics for programming games of strategy. In 1959 a computer programmed by the American Arthur Samuel played draughts. The first chess-playing microcomputer, the Chess Challenger 3, was built by **Fidelity Electronics**

Gary Kasparov regularly plays and beats computers at chess – but for how long? Here, he takes on 15-year-old chess prodigy Gata Kamsky in New York.

COMPUTER GAMES: A SUCCESS STORY

It was when he watched a demonstration of the first ever computer game that Nolan Bushnell became an enthusiast in the field that was to make his fortune. Developed by a research team from the MIT (Massachusetts Institute of Technology) at the beginning of the 1960s, the 'Space War' game required equipment which was so costly and cumbersome that it did not seem to have a commercial future.

As a young engineer with Ampex, Bushnell devoted all his spare time to developing a miniature version of the invention and incorporating it into a box similar to that of a pin-ball machine. With the benefit of recent developments in technology, he succeeded in 1971. His first game, the first commercial video game ever produced, was called 'Computer Space' and involved a battle between space ships and flying saucers. He sold barely 2000 copies.

Bushnell went on to produce another game the following year, 'Pong' (based on the principle of table tennis), which proved a huge success. The first copy of the game, installed in Andy Capp's Tavern in Sunnyvale, California, seized up only a few hours after it had been installed because it was completely jammed with coins! To improve the marketing of the game, Bushnell formed the company Atari, named after a term used in the traditional game Go. In 1974 100000 copies of 'Pong' were sold, but because the Japanese had successfully copied it, only 10000 of these were manufactured by Bushnell.

He continued to produce other games, while at the same time his company followed the lead of Magnavox, pioneers in the market for VDUs for computer games, and then moved into the fast-developing market in games programs for home computers. In 1982, at the height of his success, Bushnell sold Atari to Warner, making a personal profit of $15 million.

in the United States in the 1970s. Human supremacy is gradually being worn away, but we cannot yet predict when a computer will be a chess grand master.

Crosswords (1913)

The crossword game was invented in 1913 by an American journalist born in Liverpool: **Arthur Wynne**.

Wynne worked in the games department of the *New York World* and was always looking for new puzzles. He remembered a game from Victorian times which he had played with his grandfather called the Magic Square. By reconstructing the square, including black squares and adding a list of 32 definitions, he invented the crossword, the first of which appeared on **21 December 1913** in the *New York World*'s weekly supplement. His definitions were descriptive and very simple.

Crosswords did not reach Britain until 1924 when the *Sunday Express* became the first newspaper in the country to feature one.

Dolls (antiquity)

Dolls have been around almost as long as children. Originally they were made from wood, terracotta and, more rarely, wax and ivory. The ancient Greeks and Romans had dolls with moveable limbs. The torsos of Greek dolls were often made of burnt clay to which the limbs were attached by cords. The Romans were fond of rag dolls.

In 19th century Europe, Saxony produced most of the torsos for dolls which were made from papier-mâché. Nuremberg and London, among other cities, specialised in making porcelain dolls. These would be dressed in Paris before being sent as far afield as China.

Talking dolls (1820s)

The first talking dolls were created in the 1820s by the inventor of the metronome: **Johann Maelzel**. In around 1887 Thomas A. Edison (1847–1931), the inventor of the record player, adapted a phonograph with round discs to go inside a doll.

Barbie Doll (1958)

Barbie was created in **1958** by **Mattel**. Mattel had been founded by Elliot and Ruth Handler in 1945. They named the doll Barbie after their daughter. It was the first doll to have an adult's body and a whole wardrobe of miniature clothes. Ken, Barbie's boyfriend (named after the Handlers' son), appeared in 1961. In 1963 Barbie's friend Midge came on to the market followed by a younger sister, Skipper, and others have since been added to the range. Barbie has continued to follow fashion and is as popular as ever; in 1989 a Barbie doll was bought somewhere in the world every ten seconds.

Barbie's English competitor is Sindy who also has a boyfriend, called Paul, a wardrobe of clothes, and a fan club.

Dominoes (c.2450 BC)

In the National Museum of Baghdad (Iraq) there are objects made of bone dating from **c.2450 BC** that were found in Ur in Chaldea and that archaeologists think are similar to our dominoes. However, it was not until the 18th century that this game appeared in Europe, reaching Britain via France around 1795. The term domino comes from a similarity with the black garment of the same name worn by priests in winter over their white surplice. Dominoes were ebony on one side and ivory on the other.

Dungeons and Dragons (1973)

Dungeons and Dragons is the first modern role-play game and is the fruit of the imagination of an American travelling salesman, **Gary Gigax**.

Gigax was bored with wargames and so, with his friend Dave Arneson, designed a simulation game where the players would not be obliged to move pieces on a board. Each participant takes on a character. The universe Gigax created was inspired by the famous novel *The Lord of the Rings* by J. R. R. Tolkien.

Having perfected the rules of his game, Gigax tried in vain to sell it to the big games

companies of the United States. In the face of so many rejections, he became a part-time shoe mender before producing and selling his game himself in 1973. Today TSR Hobbies, of which he is Managing Director, is one of the most successful games producers.

Frisbee (1948)

The Frisbee was invented by students at Yale University (Connecticut) in 1947, who played with aluminium flan cases. These came from a Bridgeport baker, Joseph Frisbie, who was a regular supplier to the University. In 1948 a young American just out of the army, **Fred Morrisson**, applied for a patent for a similar disc in plastic. Later he granted the licence to the Californians Wham-O (inventors of the hula-hoop), who, having heard about the origins of the game, called it Frisbee.

Go (1000 BC)

Tradition has it that the game of go was invented 3000 years ago by the Chinese Emperor Yao to encourage his children to think logically. Go was introduced to Japan via Korea towards the mid 8th century, and it was in Japan that it had its greatest success. The object of the game is to capture one's opponent's territory.

Go was at its peak of popularity in the 17th century and a former Buddhist monk called Hon Inbosansa, a go champion, founded an official go academy in Edo (Tokyo).

Hula-hoop (1958)

The plastic hula-hoop was invented in **1958** by **Richard P. Knerr** and **Arthur K. 'Spud' Melvin**, who owned the Wham-O Manufacturing Company of San Gabriel, California. In six months, the inventors sold 20 million hula-hoops in the United States at $1.98 each, a turnover of about $40 million.

Jigsaw puzzle (c.1760)

The jigsaw puzzle, a picture glued on to some kind of backing and cut into irregular pieces which must then be reassembled, came into being simultaneously in France and in Britain around 1760. It was originally an educational toy. The Frenchman **Dumas** in 1762 began selling cut up maps which had then to be put back together. In Britain **John Spilbury** stuck a map of England on to a thin layer of mahogany. He cut the jigsaw along the borders between counties which were then sold separately. Spilbury died at the age of 29, without having made a success of his idea. In 1787 the Englishman William Darton produced a puzzle with portraits of all the English kings, from William the Conqueror to George III. The player had to know the order of succession off by heart to be able to do the jigsaw.

In 1789 Wallis simplified this game and produced a history of England in colour, which provided the model for all later puzzles that required more observation and patience.

Lego (1955)

The Lego bricks we know today first came on to the market in **1955**. They were designed after the Second World War by the Dane **Ole**

Singer Ronnie Carroll and cabaret artiste Jose Boulton try out the new craze of hula hooping.

Kirk Christiansen, a former carpenter who had retrained in toy manufacturing. He formed the name Lego from the Danish *leg godt*, which means 'to play well'.

The Lego World Cup took place for the first time in Billund, the town where its inventor was born, in August 1988. Some 175000 children from 14 different countries took part in the qualifying rounds. The Italians and the Japanese proved to be the best.

Meccano (1900)

Meccano was invented by the Englishman **Frank Hornby** in Liverpool in **1900**. Hornby started dreaming up wonderful inventions when he was a little boy. He made several unsuccessful attempts, then got married, settled down to work for a meat importing company and bring up his two sons. It was for them that he invented the toy Mechanics Made Easy which, in 1907, changed its name to Meccano. Hornby wanted a toy which would encourage children to build things rather than destroy them. Frank Hornby set to work and thought of the different elements needed to construct a crane. In the first stage he thought of making metal strips to similar formats with regularly spaced holes so that they could be assembled. Then he made nuts and bolts which would fit the holes and designed small pulleys. And then the idea took off.

Hornby was also the creator of the clockwork train set.

Model cars (19th century)

The first small model cars appeared at the same time as their life-size namesakes at the end of the last century. The first cars on a 1/45 scale were launched by the British company **Matchbox**, who became one of the world's leading firms in the toy car business.

Monopoly (1933)

Monopoly was invented in **1933** by the American **Charles Darrow** (1889–1967), who was unemployed during the great depression which followed the stockmarket crash of 1929. The game was soon very successful.

However, Monopoly was inspired by a game invented in 1904 by a young woman called Lizzie J. Magie. When the Parker company (Kenner-Parker Brothers) bought the rights to Monopoly from Darrow in 1935, they gave Mrs Magie $500.

Monopoly has been translated into 19 languages and has earned more than £700 million. At the end of 1988 the USSR finally permitted Monopoly to be sold within its borders thanks to a policy of *perestroika*.

Othello (1974)

Goro Hasegawa invented Othello in Japan in **1974**. This game of strategy, which pits two players against each other, consists not in eliminating an opponent's men by removing them from the board (as in chess or draughts), but in turning them over to take possession of them. Othello, which also exists in an electronic form, is the most widely played game in Japan after the game of go.

Pictionary (1986)

Many young inventors have emerged in the

A Lego man reads the newspaper at a toy fair held at Earl's Court in London.

games field over recent years and gone on to found their own companies and make a fortune.

One of these is the Canadian **Rob Angel**, who at the age of 29 created Pictionary, based on a game from his childhood. One player draws a word and the others have to guess what the word is. By the end of 1989 it was the bestselling board game in Britain, outstripping Trivial Pursuit.

Pinball (1930s)

The distant ancestor of pinball is the game of billiards described by Charles Dickens in 1836. The great economic crisis of 1929 and Prohibition favoured its development. In **1931** pinball went into mass production and soon acquired the features it still has today: in 1932 the tilt was invented by Harry Williams, and the Ballyhoo was launched by a young Chicago businessman, Richard T. Moloney; in 1933 the machines were electrified, while the Rockelite, created by the American company Bally, was the first to be brightened by luminous scores, and bumpers were invented in 1936.

Electric pinball machine (1938)

It was **Samuel Gensberg**, a Pole who emigrated to the United States at 18, who invented the first electric pinball machine around **1938**, called the Beamlight. The first modern pinball machines appeared in 1947, with Chicago Coin's Bermuda and H. Mabs' Humpty-Dumpty.

Poker (1000 BC)

Contrary to what one might think, poker was not created in Chicago at the time of Prohibition. The principle of the game first appeared 3000 years ago in another game called *As*, which was played in Persia. The role of pairs, threes, full houses and fours was already established, as was that of one of poker's essential elements: bluff.

The game was introduced into Europe by the Crusaders and developed in Spain under the name of *primero*. French versions of *primero*, called *bouillotte* ('kettle') and *brelan* ('threes'), were imported into Louisiana by French settlers. These games travelled up the Mississippi as the West was won and a new variety began to take over from the former types. Poker (so called because players 'poke' their opponents to make them flare up like a fire) was born.

Rubik's cube (1979)

In **1979** a Hungarian academic, **Erno Rubik**, invented a fiendish cube, of which more than 100 million have been sold throughout the world. This made him one of the few Hungarian multi-millionaires. With his royalties, Rubik set up a small design company in Hungary and funded a foundation for inventors. The idea of the cube was to make all nine squares that comprised each face of the cube the same colour, and to do this for each of the six faces.

In 1988 he launched the mind-blowing Rubik's clock. The trick is to use the knobs to set all the hands of 18 clocks to midnight when each knob controls several clocks at once.

The 1980s saw the growth in popularity of outdoor training games aiming to build team spirit.

Scrabble (1948)

In **1948 James Brunot** from Newton, Connecticut, patented the game of Scrabble. The source of his patent was a game called crisscross, in which players had to make up crosswords on a piece of cardboard using wooden letters. Criss-cross was invented in 1931 by Alfred M. Butts to keep himself amused after losing his job in the depression. It was not until Brunot came along that Butts saw the commercial potential. By 1953 over a million sets had been sold.

Snakes and ladders (17th century)

The oldest version known today is a carved wooden board of Venetian origin, dating from **1640**.

The Survival Game (1981)

The aim of this outdoor team game is to capture the enemy's flag and take it back to your camp. The players are armed with guns loaded with gelatine bullets which do not kill or hurt the victims but leave bright red marks. The game was invented in the United States in **1981** and caught on in England in 1984 when there are some 30 Survival Game sites currently in use. Some companies send their employees to play the game as a way of developing initiative and team spirit.

Tarot (1457)

No one knows who created tarot, or when and where it originated. In **1457** St Anthony, in his *Treatise on Theology*, makes the first known reference to tarot. In any case, tarot is considered the precursor of modern card games. No one knows either what the word means or what language it comes from. The Italians knew it by the name *tarocco*. Some say the origin of the word is Egyptian (*tar* meaning way and *ro* meaning royal); others claim it has its origins in Hebrew (a derivation of Torah, the Law). The letters mixed up give *rota*, which means wheel in Latin: hence the Wheel of Fortune.

Teddy bear (19th century)

The Americans, Germans and Russians all claim to be the inventors of the teddy bear.

Toys representing bears have long been made in Russia. Tsar Nicholas II gave a wooden bear to President Loubet of France at the time of the Franco–Russian Treaty of 1892.

According to other sources, while Theodore 'Teddy' Roosevelt was President of the United States (1901–9) his son had a little bear that he loved. When the bear died, the boy was so unhappy that a handyman had the idea of making a toy that looked like the bear for him. The President's son was also called Teddy, hence the name teddy bear.

A third version holds that in 1902 the German Richard Steiff designed the first teddy bear, with boot-button eyes and grey mohair fur. An American trader bought 3000 of them from him. These soft toys appeared dressed as pages at the wedding of Theodore Roosevelt's daughter hence the Teddy bear. Some of the Teddy bears made by Richard Steiff and his wife Margarete are now highly valuable and have been sold at auction for thousands of pounds.

There is a fourth version of the origin of the name 'Teddy', again involving Roosevelt. One day, while out hunting, he saw a young bear and refused to shoot it. The story caught the public imagination and a New York shopkeeper began to make stuffed toy bears and called them Teddy bears. Whatever the origins, by the First World War over a million were being sold every year.

Transformers (1980)

Within a decade of having been launched by the American company **Hasbro**, Transformers had become one of the world's bestselling toys. They are remarkably adaptable: one moment they are robots and then they can be reassembled as vehicles in a few seconds. And, with their hi-tech look, they have proved a great hit with many children.

Trivial Pursuit (1981)

Invented in **1981** by three young Canadians,

Chris and John Haney and Scott Abbott, this game tests general knowledge of geography, history, art and literature, sport, science and entertainment. From two to 36 players may take part at a time, but the game is usually played by six people. The game was a huge success in Canada and well over 50 million of them have been sold throughout the world. It was the bestselling board game in Britain in the 1980s.

Video games (1972)

The first video game was invented in 1972 by an American engineer who was then aged 28: **Nolan Bushnell**. The first two big successes were Space Invaders, launched on 16 June 1978 by the Japanese company Taito Corp., and Pac Man in 1983, the result of a collaboration between two companies, Namco (Japan) and Midway (USA).

Game Boy (1989)

This Walkman of the video game, developed by Nintendo, is completely autonomous. It is fitted with a small screen and ear plugs and takes game cassettes. Since it was brought onto the market, it has been extremely popular in the United States and Japan, and is now catching on in Britain.

The first portable electronic games were brought out by Nintendo in 1983 with Game and Watch. After a phenomenal start, the market subsided and Nintendo almost went bankrupt and were only saved by the VDUs.

VDUs for computer games (1985)

Microcomputers proved disappointing in the field of computer games. For this reason, Atari, Sega and Nintendo developed VDUs which were specially designed for video games. One of the leaders in the market, Nintendo, was founded in Kyoto, Japan in 1889 and originally specialised in manufacturing playing cards before undergoing an amazing transformation. Nintendo has manufactured games such as Dragon Quest, Super Mario and Zelda, among others. The company has four in-house design teams working in competition with independent inventors. In all

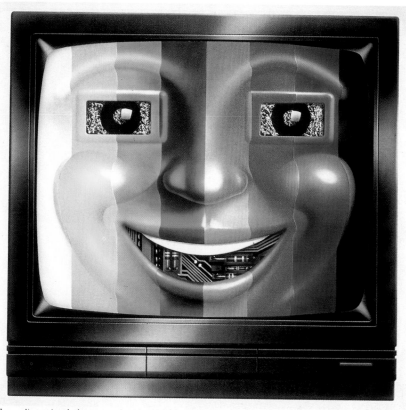

Three-dimensional glasses can be plugged into Sega games terminals. The field of video games has come a very long way since the days when Space Invaders ruled.

there were some 50 million Nintendo systems in homes worldwide by the end of 1990. Launched in Britain in 1988, by the end of 1991 it was expected that there would be 750 000 of them around the country.

Wargames (1780)

These are simulations of historical or entirely fictitious military conflicts. The contemporary form of the wargame was invented by **Helvig**, the Duke of Brunswick's master of pages, in **1780**. In 1837 von Moltke, the general in charge of the Prussian Army, made the play-

ing of wargames part of military training. After 1870 all nations followed this example. Then wargames were popularised in the United States in 1953 by Charles Roberts. The mass production of the game Tactics enabled him to set up the Avalon Hill company, which today dominates the wargames market.

Whist (1743)

This card game of British origin, the ancestor of bridge, was described for the first time in **1743** by **Edmund Hoyle**, in a treatise he wrote about it.

Sport

Athletics

In ancient Greece races and throwing competitions had pride of place in the Olympic Games. Modern athletics really began to develop in the mid 19th century in Great Britain. The first championships were organised in 1866 by the Amateur Athletic Club.

Fosbury flop (1968)

By his own account, the American **Richard Fosbury** created his famous highjump

technique almost involuntarily. When he could not manage to execute a western roll correctly, he started from a scissors jump and gradually developed the backwards jump which earned him an Olympic gold medal in Mexico in 1968 and a new Olympic record. Today he is a civil engineer in Idaho and designs mountain bike tracks.

Marathon (1896)

In the first of the modern Olympic Games, held in Athens in 1896, the marathon was won by a Greek shepherd, **Spiridon Louis**.

In so doing he emulated the feat of Phidippides, who ran from Marathon to Athens to announce Miltiades' victory over the Persians under Darius the Great, on 13 September 490 BC. Legend has it that the exhausted messenger died on arrival, after running 40km *24 miles* without stopping. In 1924 the distance he had run was fixed at 42.195km *26 miles 385 yd.*

Sports shoes (1868)

The **Candee Manufacturing Co.** in New Haven (USA) began making canvas sports

Michael Jordan promotes the sports shoe named after him – the Nike Air Jordan. Thanks to these inflatable shoes he can jump even higher.

shoes with rubber soles in **1868**. In 1920 the Dassler brothers, Adolf (Adi) and Rudolf, shoemakers in a small town near Nuremberg, Germany made their first sports shoes. Adi went on to invent running spikes, the studs under football boots and screw-on crampons. The company, Adidas, became one of the world leaders in leisure footwear and was recently taken over by the Frenchman Bernard Tapie.

Inflatable shoes (1990)

In **February 1990** the basketball player **Michael Jordan** launched the new Nike Air Jordan. These shoes were designed so that he could jump even higher to get closer to the net. The English firm Reebok has brought out The Pump which can be inflated with a little pump inserted into the tongue.

Ball games

American football (1880)

American football appeared at the end of the last century and is today played by millions in the United States. It was probably around 1870 at Harvard University that a type of football crossed with rugby was first played. The rules of American football were fixed in **1880** by **Walter Camp**. The first professional game was played in 1895. The highlight of the season, the Super Bowl, was first played in January 1967. In March 1991 London Monarchs played their first game in the new World League of American Football.

Badminton (1860s)

Badminton is descended from the ancient racket game of battledore and shuttlecock. Our version of the game is named after the Duke of Beaufort's country seat at **Badminton** in Gloucestershire where it was first played in the 1860s. It is said that one rainy day a cord was stretched across the hall for an indoor game of battledore, and modern badminton was created.

In 1893 the Badminton Association was formed in England, and the rules codified.

Baseball (1750)

According to legend, baseball was invented in **1839** by **Abner Doubleday** in New York (USA). It is doubtful that this is so.

The game actually has its origins in England where, around **1750**, it evolved from the children's game of rounders.

In 1845 Alexander Cartwright, one of the founders of the first baseball club, the Knickerbocker Club of New York, defined the rules of the game. He invented the diamond-shaped playing field. Up until then the game had been played on square or pentagonal fields. Although the game has a massive following in the States, it has never really caught on in Europe.

Basketball (1891)

Basketball is one of the few sports that did not come about as a result of a slow evolution. In **1891 James Naismith**, a professor at the

International YMCA College in Springfield, Massachusetts (USA) decided to develop a sport that could be played indoors, at night or in winter. He nailed two baskets to the opposite walls of a gym and set down the rules. The first game took place on **20 January 1892**. The teams were made up of seven players each and the game was played over three 20-minute periods. One of the most famous teams is the Harlem Globetrotters who, at one stage, were even the subject of a cartoon TV series.

Bowls (13th century)

Outdoor bowling has its origins in the Middle Ages, with some towns claiming to have had greens in the **13th century**. The most famous incident involving bowls concerns Sir Francis Drake who, on hearing that the Spanish Armada was approaching England, refused to abandon his game despite the fact that the country seemed to be on the point of being invaded.

The modern rules were devised by the Scotsman William Mitchell in the 1840s. There are two forms of bowls – crown green, which is played outdoors on grass, with the ground very gently sloping away from the central point; and indoor, where the target ball (the jack) has to be in line with the position of the players.

Cricket (1727)

Games using sticks and balls are ancient and the oldest sport of this type in Britain was known as knur and spell. This was of Norse origin and was played before the 11th century.

A primitive form of cricket was being played during the reign of Elizabeth I, but the rules were not codified until **1727**. In 1730 the first match was played in London at the Artillery Ground in Finsbury. By 1760 the prime exponents of the game were the members of the Hambledon Cricket Club who played on Broad Halfpenny Down in Hampshire. In 1787 Thomas Lord founded the Marylebone Cricket Club (MCC) which moved to its present site in St John's Wood in 1814.

Football (1848)

The antecedents of football can be traced back to ancient times, but it was not until the 19th century that anything resembling the modern game began to come into existence in the public schools and universities. In **1848** Cambridge University made the first attempt to codify the rules, while the term 'soccer' originates from a corrupted abbreviation of Association Football and was first coined in Oxford University by Charles Wreford Brown.

The Football Association was formed on 26 October 1863, but it was not until 17 April 1888 that the Football League was founded, the world's first national football league. Since those distant beginnings, football has grown into the world's most popular team game, with television audiences of hundreds of millions for the World Cup final.

Golf (15th century)

Golf was invented in Scotland and it gained such popularity there that King James II

Graham Gooch adds some more runs on the way to his 333 against India at Lord's in 1990. It was the sixth highest score in Test history.

Some 85 years after the first £1000 transfer, Paul Gascoigne was valued at over £8 million.

banned the sport in March 1457 as he felt that his subjects were wasting too much time playing the game. However, golf remained the national sport and Mary Queen of Scots was the first woman to play the game.

The first golf balls were made of leather stuffed with feathers. Balls made from gutta-percha appeared in the middle of the 19th century. They were superseded by the rubber-cored ball invented by the American Coburn Haskell in 1899.

Computer golf course (1979)

In **1979**, to make it possible to play golf in the city, the American companies **Optonics** and **Texas Instruments** developed a computer simulation of a golf course. The course unfolds on screen, depending on the ball's trajectory. Part. T. Golf recreates all the conditions encountered on a real course.

Hockey (1875)

Although there are early references to the game, it was not until the 1870s that the modern game began to develop. In **1875** the English Hockey Association was formed. Although the game started here, it is only recently that England's fortunes have revived, notably when the national team won the gold medal in the 1988 Olympics.

Rugby (1823)

Rugby was invented in **November 1823** by **William Webb Ellis**, a pupil at Rugby School. The story goes that during a fast-moving football match, he picked up the ball and ran

WHO INVENTED THE ASHES?

The most famous competition in cricket has its origins in 1882, after the Australians had beaten England in a Test match at The Oval in London on 28–29 August. It was not the first time that the countries had met (there had been eight Tests previously, and Australia had the better record), but the manner of the defeat was crucial. England, needing only 85 runs to win, had failed to do so by seven runs.

The humiliation was deeply felt among the cricketing public, who had thought that England would be invincible on home territory, and so an announcement was placed in the *Sporting Times*: 'In Affectionate Remembrance of English Cricket which died at The Oval on 29 August 1882, deeply lamented by a large circle of sorrowing friends and acquaintances. RIP. NB – The body will be cremated and the ashes taken to Australia.'

The phrase stuck, and since then competitions between the nations have been known as The Ashes. The Ashes trophy is a tiny urn that contains the ashes of a set of bails and, no matter who the 'holders' of The Ashes are, the trophy itself remains at Lord's.

Ellery Hanley is one of the greatest players of Rugby League since it was devised in 1895.

towards the opponents' goalposts clutching it to his chest. The new game using hands soon expanded, but the rules remained vague. In 1871 the Rugby Football Union was founded, which established the rules for the 15-player game.

In 1893 the Yorkshire Union proposed that payments to players should be allowed but were outvoted. However, just two years later, some northern clubs broke away to form Rugby League, in which payments were permitted, following a meeting on 29 August 1895 in Huddersfield. The most obvious difference between the two codes is that League teams have only 13 in their sides.

Skittles (antiquity)

We find the earliest mention of skittles in the *Odyssey*. At that time they were made of stone and square at the top.

In medieval Germany the skittle symbolised the devil who had to be knocked down. This is probably why Luther recommended playing skittles after church, giving each skittle the name of a sin. Since then a great number of variations on the game have been created in every country and region.

Tenpin bowling (1874)

Tenpin bowling is the modern form of skittles, whose rules were codified in 1874 in the United States. There is one important difference: the skittles are righted automatically.

Squash (1886)

Opinions differ as to the date that squash first appeared. Some say the game was devised at Harrow School in 1817, others 1830. According to the latter, squash was invented by two English gentlemen who were imprisoned for debt, and thought up the game so that they could get some exercise in prison.

Squash is a sport derived from tennis, and was not recognised in its own right until 1886. It differs from tennis in that it is an indoor game played in an enclosed space; rather than hitting the ball over a net, it is hit against the front wall with both players facing it. Both the ball and the racket are smaller than in tennis.

Table tennis (19th century)

Derived from a medieval game, like lawn tennis and badminton, table tennis developed in Britain in the second half of the 19th century.

The first known mention of table tennis is to be found in the catalogue of a sports equipment manufacturer, F. H. Ayres, dating from 1884. The oldest patent that has been traced dates from 1891. At about the same time (1890) the Englishman James Gibb brought the idea of celluloid balls from America. Another Englishman, M. Goode, invented rubber bats with small raised points on the surface (1924). As for the name Ping-Pong, it comes from the sound made by the ball and was patented around 1891 by John Jacques of Croydon.

Strangely, the earliest national championships took place not in England but in Hungary, in 1897.

Tennis (1874)

Tennis was invented in 1873 by **Major Walter C. Wingfield**, who patented the new game in **1874**. He introduced a certain number of rules borrowed from an Indian game, in particular the practice of playing on grass. Wingfield called his game *Sphairistikè*, a Greek word meaning 'ball game'. The word tennis comes from the French. In the earlier *jeu de paume* ('palm game'), the server cried *Tenez!* ('Here!') to warn the other player that play was about to start.

In 1875 the All-England Croquet Club decided to set aside one of its lawns for tennis. The game proved so popular that the club changed its name to the All-England Croquet and Tennis Club a year later. In 1877 the first Tennis Championship was held at Wimbledon.

Half-court tennis (1970s)

Half-court tennis was invented in Australia in the **1970s**. It is played in a smaller space (a third the size of a tennis court) with rackets of about 50cm *20in*, which have very short handles and are less tightly strung than normal tennis rackets. The balls used are the same size, but softer. The half-court method was promoted in Australia by players like Tony Roche and Allan Stone. From Australia, half-court spread to the United States and then Europe.

Volleyball (1895)

Volleyball was invented in **1895** by the American **William G. Morgan** at Holyoke, Massachusetts and first came to Europe during the First World War with the arrival of the American troops.

Cycling

Cycle races quickly followed the invention of the bike. The first race was held on **30 May 1868** in the Saint Cloud park in Paris over a distance of 1800m, *1 mile 209yd*. The race was won by an Englishman, James Moore, who also won the first town-to-town race between Paris and Rouen in 10h 40min.

Tour de France (1903)

The Tour de France, conceived by **Henri Desgranges**, took place for the first time on 1 July 1903. There were six stages and 20 out of the initial 60 runners completed the course. The first race was won by Maurice Garin. Henri Desgranges also devised the *maillot jaune*, the yellow shirt, introduced in 1919.

Mountain bike (1973)

In 1973 fans of sport, space and adventure in Marin County, California (USA), customised their road cycles so that they could take them on the nearby mountain slopes. Many of them became very skilful at this and soon the Canyon Gang was to be seen haring down the steepest slopes.

Gradually small-scale manufacturers began to build these machines, which were soon called mountain bikes. These bikes have become very popular, even in flat cities, so now up to 80 percent of all new bikes sold are of this kind.

High speed tricycles (1986)

On 11 May 1986 a human-powered machine (an enclosed cycle) broke the 29m *95ft* a second barrier, thereby winning the $18000 prize set up in 1984 by Du Pont. The winner was the Gold Rush, ridden by Fred Markham. The Gold Rush is an improvement on the Easy Racer, a widely sold bicycle, and was designed by **Gardner Martin**. It weighs 14kg *31lb*. It has an aluminium frame, kevlar streamlining, mylar brake discs, a lexan windscreen and spandex filled wheels.

Cycletouring (1896)

Cycletouring came into being in Italy. The first official route was from Rome to Naples and it was covered by nine cyclists in 1896. The first Audax certificates were created by Vito Pardo in 1898: they were awarded to cyclists capable of covering 200km *124 miles* between sunrise and sunset.

Swimming, sailing and watersports

Swimming

In all civilisations the origins of swimming are lost in the mists of time, but the first organised competitions started as recently as the 19th century: the first took place in London in 1837.

The Australians held a contest in 1846 (Sydney Championship) and soon afterwards organised the first world championships.

In August 1875 the British swimmer Captain Matthew Webb was the first to cross the English Channel, in 21h 45min.

Crawl (1902)

The indigenous peoples of the South Pacific swam the crawl. It was adapted by two Australians, **Syd** and **Charles Cavill**, who introduced it to Europe in 1902 and to the United States the following year.

Butterfly (1926)

This variant of breaststroke, which is very tiring but very fast, was developed by a German swimmer, **Eric Rademacher**, in 1926. The Americans used it in breaststroke races. It was banned before becoming an official stroke in its own right.

Water polo (1869)

Water polo is a combination of swimming and a ball game played in teams (11 players per side, seven of whom are in the water). It first appeared in Britain in 1869.

Rowing (antiquity)

Rowing's origins date back to antiquity. Virgil described a rowing race in the *Aeneid*. The Olympic sport of rowing is practised in more than 50 countries. One of the oldest races, held every year since 1829, is between coxed eights from the Universities of Oxford and Cambridge. The Henley Royal Regatta is the most famous meeting and has been held annually since 1839.

Canoe-Kayak (1865)

The canoe is descended from the hollowed-out tree trunk, a primitive form of boat used by the Native Americans of Canada, while the kayak was first used by the Eskimos. It differs from the canoe in that it has a watertight 'skirt' which is tightly attached round the waist, and two paddles are used. The British Royal Canoe Club was founded in 1865.

Rafting (c.1950)

Rafting is an American invention. At the end of the Second World War, the American Army Surplus bought small inflatable dinghies designed for disembarkation. Though flexible and easy to handle, they were also long, heavy and motorised and were used to carry groups of tourists through the gorges of the Grand Canyon. The sport developed when the inflatable dinghies were shortened and strengthened and the motor replaced by oars, so that these boats, now called rafts, could take the most impressive rapids.

Yachting (17th century)

Yachting, as a sport, was established in Britain in 1661 by **King Charles II**, who got a taste for navigation while he was in exile in Holland. He challenged his brother to a race that year between Greenwich and Gravesend, the winner taking £100.

Yachting, the sport of kings, then spread to the other European courts. Louis XIV of France had mini-ships built to sail on the great lake at Versailles, and ordered a Venetian gondola to be carried over the Alps for his use.

Yachting for pleasure also attracted the upper-middle classes of Cork City in Ireland. The Water Club was set up there in 1720 and its descendant, the Royal Cork Yacht Club, is the oldest yacht club in the world.

Centreboard (15th century)

At the end of the 15th century the Dutch began to equip their boats with lateral centreboards, two streamlined wooden surfaces which could be lifted for tacking. A few hundred years earlier, the Incas were equipping their rafts with *guaras*, or small centreboards which were stuck between two balsa trunks.

In 1774 in Boston, Massachusetts (then a British colony), a British officer, Lieutenant Schank, who had heard about the Inca system, built a dinghy with a vertical centreboard which ran right along the keel. In 1811 the American brothers Joshua, Henry and Jacob Swain applied for a patent for a pivoting centreboard without ballast which was immediately very successful in the United States.

It was an Englishman, Uffa Fox, who popularised the sliding centreboard, which was capable of remarkable speeds. In 1928 his Avenger won 52 out of 57 regattas. Since then, the hull shape of centreboard boats has changed little.

Fin keel (1840)

The complexity of centreboards and the space taken up by their shaft led boat builders to place fixed centreboards under

Alain Jacques, an engineer in fluid mechanics, decided to see if he could take his hang-glider and continue his flight underwater. He found that he could twist and turn as in the air.

CROSSINGS, REGATTAS AND RACES

Type	Date	Characteristics
Solo crossing	1601	The earliest unconfirmed example dates from 1601, when the Dutch surgeon Henry de Woogt asked for a permit to make a crossing from Vlessingen to London. In 1869 Empson Edward Middleton sailed solo around Britain on board a 7m *23ft* long yawl. The first person to sail solo across the Atlantic was Alfred Johnson in 1876. The first solo trip around the world was made by the American captain Joshua Slocum, from 1895–8. He did it despite the fact that he could not swim.
America's Cup	1851	This is the world's oldest sporting trophy (in any sport). It was during a regatta around the Isle of Wight on 22 August 1851 that the schooner *America* won the silver Cup. In 1983, after 132 years of American domination, the Cup was won by the Australians. In February 1987 the Cup was returned to the United States through the efforts of Dennis Conner on *Stars and Stripes*.
Solo transatlantic race	1891	The first solo transatlantic race left Boston on 17 June 1891. It was won by J. W. Lawlor in 45 days. Some 70 years later, in 1960, the first solo transatlantic race against the prevailing wind took place, from Plymouth (UK) to Newport (USA).
Atlantic record	1905	This competition was organised on the initiative of the Kaiser and was won by the American Charlie Barr and the schooner *Atlantic* (56-man crew). In 1917, when the winner donated his gold cup to the American war effort, it was discovered that the cup was not real gold! In 1988 the competition was won by Serge Madec, on board the 23m *75ft* catamaran *Jet Services*, in seven days, 6h 30min (New York to Lizard Point, UK).
Blue Ribband	1937	A symbolic trophy given to the fastest Atlantic crossing by passenger liner between Bishop Rocks (UK) and the Ambrose lighthouse (USA), a distance of 4727km *2938 miles*. It has been held by the *Normandie*, the *Queen Mary* (1938) and then the *United States* (1952), for a crossing of 35.59 knots in three days, 10h 40min. This record was beaten in 1986 by the British *Virgin Atlantic Challenger II*, owned by Richard Branson, in three days 8h. In June 1990 the *Hoverspeed Great Britain*, the biggest catamaran in the world at 76m *249ft*, completed the journey in three days, 7h 55min.

The SeaCat *Hoverspeed Great Britain gained the prestigious Blue Ribband for the fastest crossing of the Atlantic in June 1990. However, it now ploughs a much shorter route between England and France.*

Aimé Sauvage, the inventor of a new sport called Trial-Dog, runs nearly as much as the dogs. Other breeds than huskies can be used to pull the carriage.

their keels. These fixed centreboards made of strong sheet metal to ballast the boat, first appeared in Bermuda around **1840**.

At the end of the 1870s a type of boat called the Houari with a non-ballasted keel was developed in Marseilles. The bulb-shaped ballast at the end of the keel was invented by the Englishman E. Bentall on his 15.4m *50ft 9in* boat *Experiment*, which was launched in 1880.

But the first to make fin keels really effective was Nathanael Herreshof with his 1891 boat *Dilemma*. This sailing boat brought about a real revolution and was the forerunner of the modern monohulls.

Catamaran

The catamaran appeared several thousand years ago off the Coromandel Coast in India. The catamaran was basically a raft made with three tree trunks of different lengths. Its name comes from the Tamil word *kattumaram*: tied timber. The term is now applied only to boats that have two similar hulls. These derive more immediately from the huge canoes, each hewn from a single trunk and temporarily joined together, used by Polynesians from Tahiti and Hawaii to cross the ocean.

In 1662 the Englishman William Petty, having learnt of the Pacific style of sailing, built two catamarans and raced them successfully against single hulled yachts.

The first American catamaran was the *Double Trouble* built by John C. Stevens in 1820. Unfortunately, its name turned out to be prophetic.

The first person to come up with a seaworthy and manageable sporting catamaran was Nathanael G. Herreshof, who worked from 1876 to 1881 on the project.

The first modern high sea catamaran was launched from Hawaii in 1947 by Brown, Kumalae and Choy. It was called *Manu Kai* and measured 12m *39ft* in length, and was the first vessel to exceed 20 knots.

Hobie Cat (1968)

In **1968**, after many years of development, the first Hobie Cat appeared bearing the name of

its inventor, the American **Hobart L. Alter**. The Hobie 14 (*14ft*) is an ultralight craft, very strong and easy to handle. Its two highly streamlined asymmetrical hulls are joined by two metal poles and a trampoline. It is ideal for pleasure trips and for racing, as its light structure (fibreglass hulls, metal mast) allows it to reach high speeds. Some 200 000 of these exciting boats have already been sold.

Trimaran (1786)

The first boat with three hulls, derived from the Polynesian *latakoïs*, was built by the Scot **Patrick Miller** in **1786**. It was essentially a steam-propelled trimaran with a paddle wheel between each hull.

In 1868 the first inflatable boat to cross the Atlantic, the American sailing ship *Non-Pareil*, captained by John Mikes, had three hulls. This crossing was to prove the efficacy of 'tri-hulls' as rescue boats.

Around 1943 a Russian immigrant to the United States, Victor Tchechett, decided to improve ships with three hulls; he coined the word trimaran. It was not until the end of the 1960s, however, with the designs of Derek Kelsall, and especially those of the American Dick Newick, that trimarans were really refined.

Proa (1933)

It was **Nathanael Herreshof** who, around **1933**, had the idea of applying the techniques of craft with balancers used in the Pacific to pleasure craft. These sailing boats, which originated in Malaysia, are laterally asymmetrical.

While Herreshof was satisfied with making models, in 1970 Englishman Rod Macalpine-Downie designed a sailing boat with a balancing pole, the *Crossbow*, which reached a speed of 31.09 knots in 1975.

Marconi rigging (1921)

Around 1820 the 'leg of mutton' sail appeared in the Bermudas. Instead of being trapezoidal like the sails of the time, the sail was triangu-

lar. The English imported the design to Europe around 1880, and it became known as 'Bermuda rigging'. At the same time, it was determined that lengthening the sail influenced the boat's speed. In 1895 a small American yacht owned by William P. Stephens, the *Ethelwynn*, had a single-sail Bermuda-rigging mast, but the mast was shrouded to give it greater rigidity. This streamlined, shrouded rigging was called 'Marconi rigging' by analogy with the design of radio antennas. The first great yacht equipped with Marconi rigging was the *Nyria*, 34.2m *112ft*, designed by **Charles E. Nicholson** in 1921.

Waterproof ship's log (1989)

The idea is catching on: a ship's log that is resistant to bad weather and particularly water. But it took long years of research at **Sogetic** to develop a waterproof synthetic paper that could be written on in biro or pencil without problems. However, felt tips and fountain pens should not be used, as the paper does not absorb ink any more than it does water.

Shooting

Archery

Although the bow and arrow was invented in prehistoric times, the first sporting archery competitions took place at the end of the Roman Empire. In the Middle Ages the importance of the bow and arrow as a weapon gave rise to contests of skill, but archery did not really become a sport until the beginning of the 19th century. It became an Olympic sport in 1900.

Shooting (1814)

The origins of shooting as a sport go back to the institution of live pigeon shooting in Britain in **1814**. Clay-pigeon shooting was invented, again in Britain, in 1880.

Airborne sports

Hang-gliding (1948)

In **1948** the American **Francis Melvin Rogallo** designed a supple, flexible wing made of woven wire, covered with a silicon-based coating. His invention was taken up by various organisations, notably NASA, before being abandoned.

By 1964 increasingly efficient delta-shaped wings had appeared. That year Bill Moyes, an Australian engineer who had worked for NASA, designed a 4.5m² *48sq ft* delta wing. On 4 July 1969 Moyes' partner and compatriot Bill Bennett set off on water-skis pulled by a dinghy, then released himself from the dinghy and flew over the Statue of Liberty.

The autonomous take-off hang-glider which did not require another vehicle to pull it replaced the towed version thanks to the work of inventor Dave Kilbourne. Today hang-gliding has become an international sport.

Ultra-lights (1975)

In the 1970s the popularity of hang-gliding began to grow. But people who lived in flat

The paraplane is the smallest flying machine in the world, as it is little more than an engine, a harness and a parachute.

areas had to travel to be able to practise this sport. This is why hang-gliding fans thought of motorising the wings. In **1975** the first viable prototype ultra-lights appeared more or less simultaneously in Australia, France and the United States. The Americans Mauro, Mac-Cormack, Rotec and Chlurzaczik sold launching machines.

Advances are being made all the time: performance is improved and models become safer, but often more complex.

Parachute (1946)

The first parachute worthy of the name was patented in 1802, but parachuting as a sport did not appear until after 1945. World championships have been held since 1951. The sport is largely dominated by the Soviet Union, which holds almost all the world records. However, the record altitude for a jump is 25816m *84700ft* by Joseph Kittinger on 16 August 1960.

Paraplaning (1986)

This is the smallest plane in the world. The engine and propeller are mounted on a light frame and worn on the pilot's back. Take-off and landing are achieved with a running jump over a few metres and the maximum speed is 50km/h *31mph*. The first tests were carried out by a German para-jumper, **Bernd Gartig**, who wanted to be able to pursue his favourite sport on a flat surface.

Acrobatic kites (1989)

The Spyro-Jet, designed by two young men from Quebec, **Robin Parent** and **François Daigneault**, can be flown in most wind conditions, unlike ordinary kites. It can be controlled from the ground and made to perform all manner of acrobatic movements. An interest

in kites since early childhood, as well as some hang-gliding experience, influenced the inventors' decision to build a kite incorporating the latest developments in the field. It proved so successful that they were able to start up a business to manufacture them.

A Dutchman, Wouter Koster, uses a kite to pull him along the beach, rather as if he were water-skiing. He calls this sport stuntkiting.

Combat sports

Aikido (1925)

In **1925**, having been a major figure in martial arts, **Morihei Ueshiba** (1883–1969) invented a new fighting technique: aikido. The *aikidoka* gives fighting a spiritual significance beyond its utilitarian aspects, channelling the attacker's aggression and proving its uselessness. Ueshiba defined the aim of aikido thus: to destroy the attack, not the adversary.

Boxing (3000 BC)

Boxing is an ancient sport; a decorative fresco in Iraq dating from about **3000 BC** shows boxers with their fists wrapped in pieces of leather. In ancient Greece the gloves were adorned with pieces of iron and contests often ended in death.

In modern times the first great champion was James Figg (born in 1696), who opened the first boxing school on Tottenham Court Road in London in 1719. Another Englishman, Jack Broughton (1704–89), established the rules for fighting barefisted. He set the dimensions of the ring and prohibited blows below the belt.

The eighth Marquess of Queensberry and boxer Arthur Chambers drew up the rules that are used today: the wearing of gloves, the break after three-minute rounds, the ten-

second count for a floored boxer, etc. The first fight staged under these rules took place in Cincinnati, Ohio (USA) on 19 August 1885.

Power puncher (1988)

This piece of training equipment was invented by a Briton, **Graham Burton**, in order to develop the speed, power, precision and accuracy of a punch. Consisting of fixed wall bars and extremely powerful springs, it is both simple and efficient.

Fencing (1383)

The first fencing association was founded in Germany in **1383**. The Egyptians were already using visors and pointed swords for training exercises, but it was the Germans who made fencing into a sport. The bell which protects the hand was designed in 1510 by Gonzalo, a Cordovan captain in the Spanish Army.

Judo (1882)

Judo (which means 'gentle art' in Japanese) was invented in **1882** by **Jigoro Kano**. Born in 1860, Kano first devoted himself to jujitsu, but he was not very strong. He decided to compensate for this handicap by developing his body and spirit. Kano perfected a method of attack and defence that brought about victory by using suppleness rather than strength. Judo was immensely popular in Japan and then spread throughout the world. There are now more than 15 million judoists worldwide, including 500000 black belts.

Karate Do (1916)

Karate is based on the use of the human body's natural weapons.

It is said to have been first practised by Bodhidharma, a Buddhist monk who went to China from India in the 6th century. The combat technique was forgotten and not revived until the 16th century in Okinawa, Japan.

But it was on this island that the master **Gichin Funakoshi** (1869–1957) was born. He devoted his life to the development of his art and the first historic demonstration of the technique took place at Kyoto in 1916. At the time this method of combat was known by the name 'Okinawa Te'. Funakoshi gave it a more meaningful name: Karate, from *Kara* empty and *te* hands. He added the suffix *do* which means way.

The first world championship took place in Paris in 1970.

Sumo (200 BC)

Rice farmers were probably practising sumo around **200 BC**, and the sport's first grand patron was Emperor Suinin in 23 BC. Sumo continued under imperial patronage until 1185, but under the shoguns, public matches were banned. Sporting sumo was allowed again after 1600 and in 1684 Ikazuchi Gondaiya, a masterless *rikishi* (wrestler), proposed rules and techniques to control the sport. It was around this time that the hard clay ring or *dohyo* was introduced. In 1889 the Japanese Sumo Association was formed.

Wrestling (antiquity)

Weaponless combat sports are among the

oldest known to mankind. Wrestling was popular in ancient Egypt and Mesopotamia and was practised in India around 1500 BC. Indeed, it is mentioned in the epic Sanskrit poem *Mahabharata*.

Wrestling was a common pastime in ancient Greece and images of the sport were very popular. It was probably one of the first Olympic sports, and there are many references to wrestling in Europe in the Middle Ages.

Surfing and gliding

Funboard (1979)

The funboard was created by **Arnaud de Rosnay, Robby Naish, Matt Schweitzer** (son of the inventor of windsurfing) and **Mike Waltze**, a group of windsurfing fans who were hungry for ever greater exhilaration. They customised surfboards, making them lighter and smaller, and set off to tackle the enormous waves of the Hawaiian islands.

Ice yachting (1790)

In **1790** the American **Oliver Booth** put a sail and ice skates on a packing case. He travelled on the frozen surface of the Hudson in winter, at Poughkeepsie, where the first ice yachting club was set up. The largest ever ice yacht was 21m *69ft* long and carried 100m² *1070sq ft* of sail; the *Icicle* was built in 1870 for John E. Roosevelt of New York. In 1938, on the ice of Lake Winnebago (Wisconsin, USA), John D. Buckstaff reached the fastest speed of any wind-propelled machine: 230km/h *143mph*.

Jet-ski (1971)

In 1963 a Californian, **Clayton Jacobson**, designed a piece of equipment which combined the excitement and skills of motocross and waterskiing. He persisted with it and in **1971** approached Kawasaki. The company was enthusiastic about the idea and the first machines were brought out in 1973. In 1989, after 20 years of exclusive rights, the patent for the articulated arm moved into the public domain and opened the way for competition.

Morey-Boogie (1971)

The inventor of Morey-Boogie is the Californian **Tom Morey**. In **1971** he created a strange, wide, almost rectangular surfboard, which was also softer, to help prevent accidents without affecting performance. You use this board lying on your stomach and wearing flippers (you can try to stand up if you like!). It is an excellent way to approach waves even if you are not a seasoned surfer and the Morey-Boogie requires no less athleticism. For the last few years it has been an extraordinary craze in the United States.

Roller skating (1759)

In **1759** a Belgian manufacturer of musical instruments, **Joseph Merlin**, invented roller skates. Invited to a ball at Carlisle House in London, he had the idea of making a gliding entrance while playing the violin at the same time. Unfortunately, he had not thought about the problem of brakes and he crashed into the mirror at the end of the grand entrance, smashing it and his violin to pieces and seriously injuring himself.

In the sporting world the ice skater J. Garcin created roller skating at the beginning of the 19th century, at first simply for summer training. But by 1820 the first indoor rink had been built in London. In 1863 an American, James L. Plimpton of New York, patented the first roller skates with four wheels.

Sail train (1988)

In **November 1988** a 42-year-old engineer, **Christian Nau**, took his sail train across the highest railway in the world, the Altiplano in the Andes (altitude 4881m *16019ft*), going through 66 tunnels and over 59 bridges.

His train consists of three connected wagons with solid steel wheels and bird-like wings. His next project is to cross Australia.

Sand yachting (1910)

The sand yacht is both a sport and a means of transport. It was used in ancient times by the Egyptians, the Romans and the Chinese. In the 19th century workers on the Kansas Pacific Railway used sand yachts to supervise the railway line.

In **1910** the Belgians **Frank** and **Ben Dumont** launched the sport of sand yachting. Their machines were faster than the cars of the day. In 1925 the form of the contemporary sand yacht – two wheels at the back and one in front which does the steering – was set. In the Californian deserts one often sees large sand yachts doing speeds of more than 120km/h *74mph*.

Speed sail (1977)

Invented in **1977** by the French windsurfer

At the end of 1989 three Austrians decided to cross the Takla Makan Desert in China, one of the most forbidding places in the world, on skis! They were able to go much faster than the caravan of camels that carried their provisions.

Fred Beauchêne organised the first indoor windsurfing competition. A huge hall in Paris was transformed into a gigantic swimming pool measuring 70m 230ft by 32m 105ft, while aeroplane turbine engines produced storm force winds. The event was a great success.

Arnaud de Rosnay, the speed sail is a kind of land-borne windsurfboard on roller skates. It makes for a spectacular competitive sport, with the best reaching speeds up to 140km/h *86mph*. Since it was invented, the sport has become popular outside France, especially in the United States.

Surfing (1771)

Surfing probably first appeared in Hawaii. The earliest description of it was made in **1771** by the English navigator and explorer Captain James Cook (1728–79). However, surfing did not reach California until around 1900, and did not become popular until the beginning of the 1950s, under the influence of films and music (particularly the Beach Boys in the 1960s). Today surfing is a real institution in the United States, as important as baseball, American football, boxing and basketball.

Waterskiing (1922)

In **1922 Ralph Samuelson** invented waterskis. He loved snow skiing and wanted to have the same sensations in the summer. However, he never tried to develop or market the sport he had created.

In 1925 Fred Walker of Huntington, New York, who had seen Samuelson's skis, created and patented Akwa-skees. Nowadays some water skiers have achieved speeds of over 160km/h *100mph*.

Windsurfing (1958)

Windsurfing was invented by the Englishman **Peter Chilvers** in **1958**. But this Rolls-Royce mechanic was happy to sail around by himself and never exploited his invention commercially.

In 1964 American Newman Darby had the same idea and mounted a sail on a surfboard. Four years later two Californians, Jim Drake and Hoyle Schweitzer, who had never heard of their forerunners, also put a sail on a board so as to be able to sail in calm weather. But they added a keel, articulating joint and wishbone boom, thus giving the sailboard its definitive form.

Originally made of wood, the sailboard has become lighter and lighter thanks to the introduction of new materials that allow speeds of more than 50km/h *30mph* to be achieved.

Cataplanche (1988)

The cataplanche was brought onto the market in 1990. As its name implies, it is a combination of a *planche* (surfboard) and a catamaran. Patented by **Gilles Mariteau** in **1988**, it can equal the speed of a surfboard, but has a much greater degree of stability.

Winter sports

Artificial snow (1935)

In **1935** the first artificial ski slope, with a ski jump, was set up in Boston, Massachusetts. Then it was the turn of Madison Square Gardens in New York in 1936 and, three years later, Los Angeles.

Snow maker (1976)

The snow maker came into being by chance, more than 30 years ago in the United States. The story goes that an irrigation company was in the habit of using water sprays in very cold weather to prevent freezing. And one day the spray turned by chance into snow . . . The most important patent in this domain is that of

Armand Marius, on which today's snow makers are based.

Snowmax snow inducer (1988)

Snowmax is a protein produced by a subsidiary of **Kodak**. It considerably improves the efficiency of snow makers by raising the temperature at which the water crystallises into snow to approximately 5°C *41°F*. It was very useful during the Calgary Winter Olympics in 1988.

Bobsleigh (1890)

The history of the bobsleigh begins in **December 1890** when **Wilson Smith** had the idea of joining two toboggans together with slats in St Moritz. That same winter, the local blacksmith used the design of this prototype to build the first bobsleigh fitted with four iron runners.

Curling (1551)

This sport originated in Scotland where the earliest evidence for it dates from **1551**. The rules were fixed by the Grand Caledonian Curling Club in 1838.

Ice hockey (1855)

Some see ice hockey as the descendant of a game played by the Dutch on frozen canals in the 17th century. But the real birthplace of the sport was Canada, where several towns claim to have invented it. The modern rules were fixed at Kingston, Ontario, in **1855**. The Soviet Union has dominated the sport of late.

Tobogganing (1872)

From **1872** onwards, toboggan races were

organised in the Swiss resorts of Davos and St Moritz. The competitors lie on their stomachs on the skeleton toboggan, head forwards. In this position, they hurtle down icy slopes such as the Cresta Run at St Moritz. The run, opened in 1884, is 1212m *3977ft* long and descends 157m *515ft*. The average speed is 80km/h *50mph*, but tobogganers can reach maximum speeds of 150km/h *93mph*.

In the sport of lugeing the racers sit, rather than lie down. Competitions started at a similar time and the speeds reached are very marginally slower.

Ice skating (1742)

Ice skating has existed for centuries in northern Europe. At first, blades made of bone were fitted into wooden soles; but by the beginning of the 17th century these blades had become metallic. The world's first skating club was formed in Edinburgh in **1742**.

In the United States, in 1850, the first true skates appeared, with iron blades. Immediately after the European tour by the American Jackson Haines, the American-style skates were adopted worldwide. The first world figure skating championships took place in 1896 in St Petersburg, now Leningrad, USSR. The skaters can achieve speeds of up to 48km/h *30mph*.

Skiing

The origins of skiing are Nordic; it was a mode of transport for thousands of years. The great Vasa Race commemorates the feat of one of the kings of Sweden, who escaped from Denmark and reached the Dalecarlia forest on skis with his partisans in 1520.

In 1880 the Norwegian Sondre Nordheim had the idea of making the front of his skis curved.

In 1888 Fridtjof Nansen crossed Greenland from east to west in 39 days and published an account of his expedition. Reading this gave the Austrian Zderski the idea of shortening skis and giving them metal attachments to hold shoes. The first downhill race was held on 6 January 1911 at Arlberg in Austria and organised by Lord Roberts of Kandahar (1832–1914). It was another Briton, Arnold Lunn, who created the slalom in Murren in Switzerland.

Speed skiing (1860)

This sport first appeared in California, in the Sierra Mountains. In **1860** six skiers wearing skis 3m *9ft 9in* long hurled themselves forward much to the delight of those laying bets. At the end of the 19th century, the Norwegians were achieving speeds of over 100km/h *62mph*. In April 1988 the French skier Michael Prüfer reached the astounding speed of 233.741km/h *145.25mph*.

Artistic skiing (1950)

The origins of artistic skiing go back to the first dangerous jumps said to have been performed in 1807. In 1920 a German, Fritz Rauel, took figures from skating and adapted them to skiing. But it was in **1950** that a Swede, **Stein Eriksen**, fixed the rules of this sport. The first world cup was held in 1980.

Ski jump (1808)

The first known ski-jumper was **Olaf Rye**, who

Phil Huff and John Stanford, who developed the idea of Upski in the Rocky Mountains, are not planning to compete against the ski lifts.

For Bruno Gouvy and Patrick de Cayardon, snow surfing down Mont Blanc proved to be two of the most thrilling minutes of their lives. Sadly, Gouvy died in June 1990 while pursuing this sport.

is said to have jumped 9.5m *31ft* in **1808**. The first official record was held by Haugen in 1914, with 46.3m *151ft 11in*. The record is now well over 190m *623ft*.

Monoski (1973)

The monoski was invented by a surfer. American **Mike Doyle** was the uncontested king of water surfing in the 1950s. In 1972 he took up snow skiing. His idea was to find, on snow, the same sliding sensations that are found on water. He built the first single ski in **1973** in only a few hours.

This prototype was transparent and as wide as nearly three normal skis. A pair of standard bindings keep both feet parallel. When he first used it on slopes in Jackson Hole, Wyoming he wore a Hawaiian shirt!

Ski boots (1893)

The first ski boots appeared in **1893**. They were made of reindeer skin with the fur outside and were directly inspired by the Eskimo shoes brought back by the Norwegian arctic explorer, Fridtjof Nansen (1861–1930) from his Greenland crossing in 1888/9. Boots with hooks were developed by the Frenchman Martin in 1962, who sold his patent to the Swiss company Henke. The principle of the plastic shell was developed in 1968 by the American company Lange.

Safety bindings (1948)

In **1948**, after suffering two broken legs in the same year, a French engineer and ski fanatic, **Jean Beyl**, designed a safety binding and set up the Look company.

In 1966 the French firm Salomon launched the first safety heelpiece which releases

the heel on falling. The next year Salomon marketed the first elastic double pivoted toe-piece.

Motor sports

All terrain vehicle (ATV) (1967)

John Plessinger, a student at the University of Michigan, created in **1967** a motorised tricycle that was designed to cope with rough ground. The first models did not have any suspension but the centre of gravity was low which lent the vehicle greater stability.

Plessinger sold his patent in 1969 to Sperry Rand, who launched the Tri Cart. However, it was the Japanese company Honda who began marketing ATVs in 1973 and made them popular.

Drag racing (1930)

Drag racing first appeared in the United States in **1930**, before spreading to Britain and then to the other European countries. Drag races are competitions of pure acceleration, carried out over a distance of a quarter of a mile (402m), between two single-seaters. These cars are extremely light in relation to the power of their engines, which may easily be as much as 1000hp, enabling them to accelerate from 0 to 470km/h *292mph* in five seconds.

Formula 1 (1950)

The first World Championship Grand Prix took place at Silverstone on Saturday **13 May 1950**. It was won by an Italian, Giuseppe Farina in an Alfa Romeo Tipo 158. Formula 1 cars are single-seaters with up to 3000cc or

boosted 1500cc engines. Grand Prix races cover a minimum distance of 300km *186 miles* and a maximum of 320km *199 miles* within a time of two hours. Petrol tank capacity is limited to 220l *48 gal*.

Since 1988 turbos have been banned. Jackie Stewart is Britain's most successful racer, winning 27 Grand Prix.

Central engine (1955)

In **1955** the British builders **Cooper** took their Racer 500 as a basis to develop a sports car with a central Coventry Climax engine, the Cooper Type 60, which was adapted to Formula 1 and in which the driver Jack Brabham won the title of World Champion racing driver in 1959 and 1960. In 1961 Ferrari, Lotus and BRM adopted the central engine.

Cooper's invention revolutionised the manufacture of all competition cars (from Formula 1 to simple go-karts), which now all have central engines.

Direct fuel injection (1960)

In **1960** the German **Kugelfischer** perfected direct fuel injection using a mechanical pump. This system was adopted on all competition cars a few years later, but did not appear in mass-produced models until 1975. Lucas (UK) and Bosch (West Germany) did much to spread its use by developing electronic control.

Motorbike racing (1897)

The first motorbike race was held on **29 November 1897** at Richmond, Surrey round a 1.6km *1 mile* oval circuit. Tricycles were barred from competing and the race was won by Charles Jarrott.

The cars line up for the Shell-sponsored competition to find the vehicle which can travel the furthest on the least amount of fuel. Last year it was won by a car which managed 1291.5km on one litre of fuel (that is 3650mpg).

Jet motorbike (1985)

In 1985 **Douglas J. Malewicki**, a prolific Californian inventor, created the most powerful motorbike ever built. It is powered by a T58-GE-8E turbine helicopter engine from General Electric. Ridden by Bob Cornell, this bike reached 331km/h *206mph* over a quarter of a mile in North Carolina on 28 September 1985.

Rally driving (1907)

At the start of 1907 the French daily newspaper *Le Matin* gave out a formidable challenge: 'Are there any drivers prepared to go from Peking to Paris?'. The race left Peking on **10 June 1907** and the victorious *Italia*, driven by Prince Borghese, reached Paris on 11 August, having overcome unbelievable difficulties. The next year there was an even crazier race: New York to Paris via Alaska and Russia. It was won by the American car *Thomas Flyer*. In 1909 the Transcontinental (New York–Seattle) was won by a Ford.

Paris–Dakar (1979)

In **1979**, taking up (and perfecting) an idea from the creator of the Ivory Coast–Côte d'Azur race Jean-Claude Bertrand, the rally driver **Thierry Sabine** launched and organised the Paris–Dakar long distance race. In the first year there were 70 competitors.

Despite the accidental death of Thierry Sabine during the 1986 race, the Paris–Dakar has continued and remains the top race of its category.

Stock cars (1969)

Stock cars were developed in Europe after a special track was opened in the United States in **1969**. This is the 4.3km *2⅔ miles* Talladega ring, in which speeds of 320km/h *200mph* are regularly reached with bursts of up to 350km/h *217mph*. There are frequent stock car races in the United States, where the cars used are mass-produced models which have been customised at great expense in order to beat speed records. In Europe the cars are stripped to the bare essentials, the aim being chiefly to eliminate the other competitors by pushing them off the track.

Superkart (1985)

Superkart was created in **1985**. Go-karts now have bodies that improve their aerodynamics, driven by 250cc engines with gearboxes, and race on car racing tracks at more than 240km/h *149mph*.

Theme parks

Disneyland (1955)

This was the first modern theme park and is still the most popular. Mickey Mouse, one of

Large crowds are drawn to some polo matches, as here in the Cartier International between England and France in July 1990, which England won 6–5.

its heroes, celebrated his 60th birthday in 1989 and hasn't a wrinkle to show for it. The first Disneyland, near Los Angeles, was opened on **17 July 1955**. It was followed by Orlando Park in Florida, and a third was opened in Tokyo. Between them, the three parks draw 40 million visitors a year!

Eurodisneyland

This is by far the most ambitious of the current theme park projects. More than £1 billion have been invested in this park which covers an area of 1945 hectares *4806 acres* and hopes to attract 10 million visitors a year from 1992 onwards. It is no small investment for the Paris region which, with the help of Mickey Mouse, the pirate river and several spectacular scenic railways, is hoping to confirm its position as the European tourist capital.

Equestrianism

Horse racing (1400 BC)

Beginning about **1400 BC**, the ancient Hittites of Anatolia gave themselves up to frenzied horse racing. Horse racing became an Olympic sport in 648 BC. As for the English, they were already importing Arabian horses in Roman times, and their first race took place in AD 210 at Netherby in Cumbria. English horse racing in its modern form began in 1600 in Newmarket. Each horse carried a uniform weight of 63.5kg *140lb*.

English thoroughbreds (1680)

The English thoroughbred stock was created by a group of horsebreeders whose aim was to produce faster horses. They crossed selected English mares with Arabian stallions: the Byerley Turk born in 1680, the Darley Arabian born in 1702 and the Godolphin Arabian born in 1734. All English thoroughbreds are descended from these three stallions.

Polo (1869)

Polo, the name is Tibetan in origin, was imported to England from Bengal in **1869** by the 10th Hussars, who were based at Aldershot. This sport combines horseriding and play with a mallet and ball.

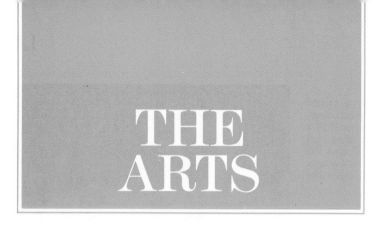

Music

Instruments

It is virtually impossible to retrace the origins of most musical instruments as they are often the result of a long evolution and of traditions whose roots go far back into the history of mankind.

On the other hand, the efforts made by instrument-makers to perfect and extend the possibilities of their instruments put them on a level with the greatest of inventors.

Traditional instruments

Percussion (prehistory)

Percussion instruments were undoubtedly the very first musical instruments to be created by man. Drums, tambourines, maracas, linga, cymbals and many others are used in folk music all over the world. The richness and colour of the sounds has often earned these instruments a place in symphonic orchestras. Many composers have written for percussion instruments: the glockenspiel was first used by Handel in 1783. Béla Bartók wrote for the celesta which had been invented in 1868; Saint-Saëns introduced the xylophone into the orchestra in the *Danse Macabre* in 1874; and Ravel the whip in his *Concerto en sol* in 1931.

Horn (prehistory)

The horn is undoubtedly one of the oldest of instruments. Hunters and warriors used primitive instruments carved from animals' horns. It is worth noting that the oliphant was originally made from an elephant's tusk. The horn was introduced into the orchestra in the 17th century, by which time it was made of metal. In **1815** the German **Stölzel** invented the chromatic valve horn, the only type used today.

This percussion instrument, invented by Michel Redolfi, is the first one of its kind ever made that can resonate properly underwater.

Flute (prehistory)

The origin of the flute lies in prehistory. In the Middle Ages a flute with a mouthpiece was generally used, and it was only from the 17th century that the transverse flute began to replace it. The change came about largely thanks to the Hotteterres, a family of flautists and instrument-makers living in Paris at the end of the 17th century. In **1832 Theobald Böhm** (1793–1881), flautist at the Chapel Royal in Munich, modified and improved the instrument (by covering the holes with keys), to such an extent that one can talk justifiably of a reinvention. It was at this time that wood was replaced by metal.

Harp (3000 BC)

The harp is one of the oldest of musical instruments, deriving from the primitive musical bow. It existed at the time of the Sumerians and of the Egyptians (3000 BC). The harp achieved its familiar form after various modifications which culminated in **1801** when the Frenchman **Sébastien Erard** put together the first double-action harps.

Oboe (2000 BC)

Instruments from the oboe family were played in Egypt around **2000 BC**. Like numerous instruments of this type, the oboe

It took 15 years of trial and error before Japanese master glass artist Sasaki Garasu perfected these crystal instruments.

derives from the double-reed aulos, whose invention the Greeks attributed to Minerva and even to Apollo. However, it was not until **Frédéric Triébert**'s refinements in the **19th century** that the oboe was perfected.

Trumpet (2nd millennium BC)

A bronze trumpet dating from the **2nd millennium BC** has been discovered in Egypt. The form, for a long time straight, was bent into an S-shape in the 15th century. The art of rolling the tube into a loop was discovered in the 16th century. The valve trumpet, which increased the instrument's chromatic capacities considerably, appeared around **1815**. The valve trumpet's invention is attributed to the German **Stölzel**.

Harpsichord (3rd century BC)

According to legend, the harpsichord derived from Archimedes' monochord (278–212 BC). The word harpsichord first appeared in 1631.

Organ (3rd century BC)

The earliest form of organ consisted of a large set of panpipes fitted with two pumps which forced air through the pipes. The air pressure was created by pumping water by hand which is why it was known as a hydraulic organ. It was developed by **Ctesibius** of Alexandria around **220 BC**.

The largest organ ever built is in Atlantic City, New Jersey, USA. Completed in 1930, it has 33 122 pipes and seven keyboards.

The smallest organ in the world was created in 1984 by a Strasbourg carpenter, Hubert Molard. The Lilliput organ is 28mm 1.1in wide and is played with a toothpick. It has a keyboard consisting of 23 keys, a pedal board of 12 pedals, a memory of 96 notes and a programme for eight pieces of music. Hubert Molard also invented the smallest musical computer in 1983.

Stave (10th century)

A proper musical stave was introduced into written music by the Italian monk **Guido** of Arezzo (c.990–c.1050). He advocated the use of four lines on which clefs and different colours provided the necessary reference points. Guido of Arezzo also invented the system known as solmisation, i.e. the naming of the notes of a scale by the sounds do, re, mi, fa, sol, la, si, which he devised from the first syllables of a Latin text.

Violin (17th century)

The violin evolved from medieval and Renaissance stringed bows. It was in **17th** and **18th century** Italy that the art of instrument-makers such as **N. Amati** and **Antonio Stradivari** (c.1644–1737) brought the violin to perfection. Stradivari and his family made more than 1100 instruments, half of which survive. It was he who also gave us the definitive form of the cello in 1680.

Clarinet (1700)

The German **Jean-Christophe Denner** invented the clarinet in Nuremburg around **1700**. However, its origins are ancient. After a series of modifications, the Böhm key system was applied to the clarinet and it reached its technical perfection.

Piano (1710)

The forerunner of the piano is the exchequer. But the inventor of the piano is the Italian **Bartolomeo Cristofori** who in 1698 created his first *cembalo a martelletti* (a clavichord with small hammers), and towards **1710** his first pianoforte. A number of improvements were later made: G. Silbermann perfected the system of hammers; J. A. Stein invented pedals (1789). But it is the Frenchman Sébastien Erard who, by inventing in 1822 the double escapement that allows a note to be repeated, can be considered the true creator of the modern piano.

Tuning-fork (1711)

The tuning-fork was invented in **1711** by the English instrument-maker **John Shore**.

Music box (1796)

The music box was probably invented in Geneva in **1796** by the watch-maker **A. Favre**. It uses a pin-studded drum originally found in mechanical chimes, which existed in the 14th century.

Barrel organ (1800)

This instrument, probably invented around **1800** by **Barberi**, was built to accompany wandering musicians.

Metronome (1816)

The invention of the metronome is attributed to the German **Johann Maelzel** (1772–1832), a friend of Beethoven. Maelzel's device created an exact tempo for the musician to follow.

Harmonica (1821)

The harmonica was invented in **1821** by the German **C. F. L. Buschmann**. He was searching for something that would allow him to tune a piano more easily. In 1857 the German organ-maker Mathias Hohner founded the first harmonica business.

Accordion (1829)

The accordion can claim a large number of ancestors, one of which is the Chinese sheng invented by a legendary queen, Nyu Wa, around 2500 BC. But we owe the invention of the accordion as we know it to the Austrian **Cyril Demian** who took out a patent on **6 May 1829**.

Saxophone (1846)

In his attempts to improve the bass clarinet a Belgian, **Adolphe Sax** (1814–94), invented a new instrument: the saxophone. Patented in **1846**, the saxophone first found success in military bands. It was later to become one of the leading instruments of the jazz era.

Digital sax (1988)

This saxophone, the D11-100, unveiled at the Las Vegas Electronics Exhibition at the beginning of **1988**, was developed by the Japanese company **Casio**. It is the first saxophone to be fitted with the MIDI interface (Musical Interface for Digital Instruments) and which can be connected to a synthesizer. Apart from producing the sound of the saxophone, the instrument can also reproduce the sounds of a trumpet, clarinet and flute.

Guitar (1850)

The origins of the guitar are much disputed. It takes its name from an Assyrian instrument of c.1000 BC called the *kettarah*, which had no neck, and it is supposed that the neck was added in the early years AD. After a long history the guitar, as we know it, was developed in about **1850** by the Spanish instrument-maker, **A. de Torres**. He concentrated particularly on enriching the tone, improving the upper soundboard and standardising the length of the strings.

Drum kit (1910)

The drum kit was born in New Orleans around 1910. After a long evolution it took on its familiar form around 1950.

Electric and electronic instruments

Electric organ (1930)

The American Thaddeus Cahill developed an electro-mechanical organ in 1895. However, the pioneers of the electric organ were the Frenchmen **Coupleux** and **Givelet** who,

around **1930**, invented an organ whose sound quality resembled that of the classical organ. Unfortunately, the number of oscillators used (about 80) made it rather unstable. In 1943 Constant Martin introduced an improved model.

Electro-magnetic organ (1935)

The inventor of the electro-magnetic organ was **Laurens Hammond** (1895–1973), a former clock-maker from Chicago, who had been ruined in the Great Depression. Around **1935** Hammond decided to convert the unused cogwheels he had in stock to make an organ in which the keys set in motion wheels that released electric currents. The organ had two keyboards, electric tone generation and a wide variety of tone colours.

Digital organ (1971)

It was the American company **Allen** who, in **1971**, took up **Ralph Deutsch**'s patent for the use of digital synthesis in musical instruments.

The Allen organ does not imitate the sound of an organ but faithfully recreates the sounds of numerous musical instruments from its memory bank. Some of the finest orchestras in the world now use this organ.

Electric guitar (1935)

The principle behind the electric guitar was found in the United States at the beginning of the 1920s. Lloyd Loar invented the first microphone to be specially adapted for the guitar between 1920 and 1924. If one excepts the electric Dobros (1930) and the Hawaiian electric guitars (Frying pan, 1931), the first solid frame electric guitar was created by the American **Rickenbacher** who, in **1935**, designed the Electro Vibrola Spanish Guitar, the body of which was made of bakelite.

It was not until 1947 that Paul Bigsby (the inventor of the vibrato system) designed the first modern electric guitar at the request of guitarist Merle Travis. A veritable industry

The film Young Einstein *has the inventor transforming his violin into an electric guitar.*

then began thanks to Leo Fender who, from 1948, marketed the Broadcaster and, from 1950, the Telecaster. The latter is still popular today in its quasi-original form.

Guitar synthesizer (1978)

In 1978 a collaboration between Swedish instrument-makers **Hagstrom** and American manufacturers **Ampeg** provided an opportunity to create a synthesizer based on a guitar. Modern technology has enabled synthesizers to be played using any guitar by means of the MIDI interface.

With the appearance of the SynthAxe in 1984 and the Steep in 1986, the British developed the idea of all-in-one instruments, i.e. guitars equipped with their own synthesizing generators.

Electric piano (1958)

The first instrument worthy of the name dates from 1958 when the American company, **Wurlitzer**, marketed one intended for use in music schools. It was very quickly adopted by the first rock musicians as it was easy to transport and had great potential for amplification. It was used for the recording of the Ray Charles classic 'What'd I Say?'.

In 1960 the German engineer Zacharias invented the Cembalet for the German company Hohner, an instrument which is inspired more by the harpsichord than the piano and which gave rise to the famous Clavinet as used by Stevie Wonder.

In 1963 the well-known Rhodes Fender piano made its appearance. Its particular tonal quality remains a feature of much modern music.

Electro-acoustic piano (1978)

As electronic techniques developed, so an increasing number of instruments came onto the market, but none was able to convey the skill of a musician. The desire for realism, both in touch and sound, led manufacturers to develop the electro-acoustic piano. This is a piano of almost traditional design in which the vibration of the strings is picked up by magnetic microphones. The first model to be widely used by professionals was the Yamaha CP70 which came onto the market in 1978.

Remote control piano (1991)

NHK, the Japanese national television network, has developed a process which enables viewers to reproduce a recording of their favourite performer on their own piano, transmitted by satellite via their television. It is of course necessary to adapt the piano so that it can receive and convert the numerical data of the sound. Once this has been done, the keys play on their own! At present, only the Yamaha U3A can be converted in this way, but conversions should become easier after 1991 with the launch of the Japanese television satellite.

Rhythm box (1965)

The organ-makers **Wurlitzer** developed an electro-mechanic automatic percussion system (Sideman), probably based on mechanical percussion, in 1965.

In 1970 at the Houston Fair, the American company Hammond revealed the first rhythm box to have automatic accompaniment. A few months later the Italian firm Farfisa unveiled its version, which they had been working on at the same time, and it was this one that remained one of the best-performing rhythm boxes for many years.

Numeric synthesis box (1981)

In 1981 the Englishman **Linn** patented a rhythm box using numeric synthesis. Thanks to the drop in price of electronic memories, the rhythm box became fully programmable and capable of reproducing the most complex rhythms.

Electronic drum kit (1980)

The British firm **Simmons** was the first to replace the skins on a drum kit with electronic sensors which were sensitive to pressure. The patent (1980) was soon taken up by other well-known names such as Roland, which brought out the Octopad, followed by Octopad II in 1990. With its special sound quality, the instrument, played with standard drum sticks, has become a supplement to, rather than a replacement for, the traditional drum kit.

Synthesizer (1965)

Despite a few earlier attempts, the history of sound synthesis (the creation of sounds from electric pulses) did not begin until the early 1950s, with experiments carried out at the University of Bonn. The first electronic music studio was set up in 1951 at a West German radio station. Through a complex assemblage of generators and filters, the composers created sounds which they put together manually afterwards on magnetic tapes. Because this was a very slow process, the American engineer **Robert Moog** (in collaboration with the composers Herbert A. Deutsch and Walter Carlos) had the idea of bringing together all the necessary equipment in one instrument. His research culminated in the Minimoog which became available in 1965, and that was when the word 'synthesizer' was first used.

The process used (subtractive synthesis) is still widely employed for many current instruments, and has been enhanced by sampling.

The introduction of information technology and the numeric processing of sound has led to the development of other techniques such as synthesis by frequency modulation (Yamaha, 1983) and additive synthesis.

Sampling (1980)

Based on the patent taken out by **Ralph Deutsch**, sampling marks a turning point in the history of electronic instruments. The process consists of transforming a natural sound, recorded with a traditional microphone, into numerical data (bits). Calculations can then be carried out on these data to play the same sound in different pitches, for example, mix it with others or use it as a basic note in a synthesizer. In practice, the sampler is usually made up of a central unit to which a keyboard is connected. Musicians use it mainly to imitate acoustic instruments or to create voice effects.

Although the first sampler was the Fairlight, the Japanese manufacturer Akai has since become established as the specialist in samplers for the consumer market with the S 612 (1985), the S 900 (1987) and most recently the S 100 (1989).

MIDI interface (1981)

In 1981, at the instigation of American synthesizer manufacturers, the MIDI interface (Musical Interface for Digital Instruments) was introduced. This made all synthesizers and their accessories (e.g. rhythm boxes) compatible, whatever their make or functioning method. One aspect of this system of intercommunication is that it has enabled the world of the synthesizer to be linked to that of the computer.

Electronic drumsticks (1986)

In 1986 the Japanese company **Casio** marketed the first electronic drumsticks. By striking any kind of surface, say a table, wall or saucepan, it is possible to obtain a similar sound to that produced by many percussion instruments. The drumsticks are connected to an electronic case.

An unusual instrumental duo push forward the boundaries of music by playing a motorbike – which model is best suited to this is hotly disputed by musicians.

Sound reproduction

Phonograph (1877)

Thomas Alva Edison (1847–1931) invented the phonograph on **12 August 1877** and patented it on 17 February 1878. The machine was a revolving drum with spiralled grooves around its circumference. It brought Edison worldwide fame, but the sound quality was mediocre and the cylinders did not last long. Edison preferred to move on to different lines of research and left the task of improving his machine to others. Two Americans, Chichester Bell (cousin of Alexander Graham Bell, the inventor of the telephone), and Charles Sumner Tainter took out a patent in 1886 for a piece of apparatus similar to the phonograph but which used wax cylinders. This was the graphophone.

Speaker (1877)

The first patents relating to the coil-driven speaker, which is virtually the only type in use today, date back to the 19th century. A patent was registered by **Ernst Wermer** for the German company Siemens on **14 December 1877**, and by the British physicist Sir Oliver Lodge on 27 April 1898. But at the time there was no electrical source that would have enabled the mechanism to operate.

In 1924 Chester W. Rice and Edward Kellogg, both of the American company General Electric, registered a patent for a voice coil speaker as well as constructing an amplifier capable of providing power of 1W for their device. The speaker, known as the Radiola Model 104, had a built-in amplifier and came onto the market the following year at a price of $250.

Ribbon speaker (1925)

The technique of the ribbon speaker was invented in **1925**. The standard cone was replaced by a very fine aluminium ribbon which was concertinaed and exposed to a magnetic field. The first models were brought out in America in the 1940s but in limited numbers. Today three American companies – Apogee Industries, Magnepan Inc. and VMPS – control their distribution.

Boxed-in loud-speakers (1958)

It was only later that someone had the idea of putting one or more speakers in a wooden or plaster case to form the loud-speakers we know today. In **1958** the French firm **Cabasse** built the first speakers with an incorporated amplifier.

Column speaker (1988)

This speaker was invented by a Swiss electronics engineer, **Walter Schupbach**, after 15 years of research. It is a single speaker which produces a stereo sound effect and, according to the most highly qualified specialists, makes it possible to achieve an authentic spatial reproduction of sound. It is placed in the centre of the room, either on the floor or suspended, and in this way gives an exact reproduction, on the horizontal as well as the vertical plane, of the position of the instruments (or other sources of sound) used during the recording. His invention came onto the market at the end of **1988**.

Gyrophone (1989)

The Gyrophone was launched at an exhibition in Geneva in **1989**. This electronic device for the distribution of sound was invented by a Lebanese, **Joseph Nicolas Maalouf**, and a Frenchman, **Philippe Sutter**. Gyrophony is a revolutionary concept in sound, which its inventors claim to be a fourth dimension of sound as it discloses the movement of music.

The listener becomes the central point of the sound which envelops and transports him. The first patents were registered in 1983 and the invention was first marketed in 1987. The process is proving extremely successful.

Record (1887)

In **1887 Emile Berliner**, a German living in America, came up with the idea of replacing the cylinder of the phonograph with thin discs of zinc covered with a layer of wax into which fine grooves were cut. Having invented the record he went on to develop the machine on which it could be played: the gramophone. The record did not replace the cylinder entirely and the two co-existed for many years.

In 1888 Berliner perfected a way of copying his records from matrices and on his return to Germany in 1898 he founded the Deutsche Grammophon Gesellschaft with his brother.

Tape recorder (1888)

The principle of the tape recorder was worked out theoretically in **1888** by the Englishman **Oberlin Smith**. Ten years later the 20-year-old Dane Valdemar Poulsen put the theory into practice. However, his presentation of the new machine at the 1900 Paris Exhibition did not raise much interest. It was not until 1935 that two German companies, AEG Telefunken and I. G. Farben, made a device based on Poulsen's principle with a plastic tape which ran at 7.6m *25ft* per second.

Lea Box (1985)

In **1985** a French engineer, **Louis Kanny**, developed a very sophisticated tape recorder: the Lea Box can read and record automatically and, among other things, is

The revolutionary design of the Technics SST-1 speakers is not aiming simply to shock – it is a fundamental part of the technological effort to create perfect sound.

voice-activated. The Lea Box has been on the market since January 1989.

In 1986 Philips brought out a small tape recorder which is sound-activated and which stops after four seconds' silence. It is ideal for recording enthusiasts and reporters.

Juke-box (1889)

The first juke-box (which worked with cylinders), was installed by the American **Louis Glas** at the Royal Palace in San Francisco on **23 November 1889**. It was followed by the public phonograph, the Automatic Entertainer produced by the Gabel Company in 1906, which offered a choice of music. Unfortunately, the sound quality was poor. The electric gramophone was introduced around 1925, and in 1926 a Swedish immigrant to the United States, J. P. Seeburg, invented the audiophone which offered a choice of eight records. It was not until 1950, and the introduction of machines that played 45s, that the juke-box became truly popular. The most famous juke-box of all is the Wurlitzer 1015; 56 000 of them were produced between 1946 and 1947.

Photographic sound recordings (1901)

The photographic recording of sound using a sensitised tape was developed simultaneously by the German **Ruhmer** and the English engineer **Duddell** in 1901. They had used the phenomenon of the singing arc which had been discovered in 1892 and studied by Thomson and Simon.

Microphone (1925)

In 1925 a team from the **Bell Laboratories**, directed by **Joseph Maxfield**, perfected an electrical system of recording. The microphone, by converting sounds into electric currents, replaced the huge horns that had been used until then. In the same year the first electrically engraved records were produced.

Pulse code modulation (1926)

Pulse code modulation appears to have been invented by **Paul Rainey** in 1926, reinvented in 1939 by the American inventor H. A. Reeves, and rediscovered during the Second World War by Bell Laboratories, USA, to fulfil the need for secrecy in telephone conversations. The process enables a continuous signal, such as a telephonic signal, to be sampled. The value of each sample is then quantified and converted by coding into a digital signal.

Magnetic recording tape (1928)

Magnetic recording tape was patented in 1928 by the German **Fritz Pfleumer**. Back in 1888 Oberlin Smith had already proposed using strips of fabric covered with iron filings.

AEG became interested in Pfleumer's invention; they concentrated on the development of the tape recorder and passed the work of improving the tape on to I. G. Farben. The first tests were carried out by the two firms in 1932 and in 1934 I.G. Farben was able to produce 50 000m *164 000ft* of tape.

Stereo record (1933)

The first stereophonic records were produced in Britain by **EMI** (Electric and Musical Industries) in 1933. The research, directed by the physicist **Alan Dower Blumlein**, culminated in the recording of stereo 78s. The work of Blumlein and EMI remained experimental until 1958 when the American company Audio Fidelity and the British companies Pye and Decca issued the first commercial stereo records thanks to numerous technical advances.

Long-playing record (1947)

Belgian René Snephvangers directed the CBS research team which in 1944 came up with the first 33rpm record. Snephvangers was a friend of Arturo Toscanini, the famous conductor, for whom he created a HiFi well before the term was invented. The long-playing record was perfected in America by **Peter Goldenmark** for CBS in 1947 to replace 78s. The patent was taken out under the initials LP (long-playing). The first recordings on a long-player were Mendelssohn's violin concerto, Tchaikovsky's *Fourth Symphony* and the musical *South Pacific*.

Tape cassette (1961)

It was in 1961 that the Dutch company **Philips** developed the first mini tape cassette which was 100mm *3.9in* long and designed for stereo and mono recordings. This cassette, along with the first cassette recorder, was unveiled in Berlin in 1963. Philips decided to allow manufacturers to use its patent free of charge so as to encourage the spread of the system throughout the world.

Dolby (1967)

The first noise reducer, designed to improve the signal/noise ratio, was the work of the American **Ray Dolby** in 1967. (Dolby had begun his career working on the tape recorder.) Dolby A was intended for professional use; a few years later, Dolby brought out a simplified system for general use called Dolby B. Dolby stereo, as used in the cinema, is produced from four sources which improve the sound quality and gives the audience a sense of depth and relief.

Micro cassette (1976)

The micro cassette, patented in 1976 by the Japanese company **Olympus**, is another type of audio cassette, smaller than the Philips mini cassette.

It operates at a greatly reduced speed and is mainly used in pocket tape recorders which act as audio notepads.

Pico cassette (1985)

In **April 1985** the Japanese company **JVC**, in conjunction with the American company **Dictaphone**, brought out a new format audio cassette, the pico cassette, and a new dictation machine based on the same model. The pico cassette contains a tape 2mm *0.08in* wide, and has a maximum recording time of one hour at a speed of 0.9cm *0.35in* per second.

Walkman (1979)

The Walkman is a portable, stereophonic cassette reading unit equipped with lightweight headphones. It was devised by **Akio Morita**, President of Sony, at Shibuara in **April 1979**.

Akio Morita shows off the wireless Walkman, available since 1988.

Morita, a keen golfer and music lover, wanted a lightweight and compact device which would allow him to pursue both his hobbies at the same time. The result was the Walkman. The first model was known as the TPS 12.

By 1988 30 million Walkmans had been sold worldwide.

Wireless Walkman (1988)

In **May 1988 Sony** brought onto the Japanese market the first wireless Walkman. It weighs 210g *7.4oz* and consists of a cassette player, a radio receiver and a micro transmitter which relays the selected programme to the headphones. The connection between the cassette player and the headphones is effected by radio frequency.

Compact disc (1979)

The compact disc was developed in **1979** by the Dutch company **Philips** and the Japanese company **Sony** under a joint licensing agreement. On this type of disc, a process of digital recording is used, rather than the analogue recording process used for the microgroove. The signal is coded in binary form, using the series 0 and 1. The conventional groove has therefore disappeared and has been replaced by millions of microcells known as pits: about 4 million per second. The compact disc has a diameter of 12cm *5in* and can hold up to an hour of music or sound on one side.

The sound is reproduced by a laser beam. The invention of the compact disc was the direct result of research carried out on the video disc, also invented by Philips.

The compact disc was first marketed in Europe in March 1983, and in 1987 nearly 29 million compact discs were sold in Britain alone. By 1989 sales figures had reached 48 million and the total market was valued at £265 million. In the space of a few years, the compact disc has enjoyed incredible success and its applications are many and varied.

From 1984 Matsushita and Philips brought out the prototypes of decoders which enabled fixed images, which had been stored on compact disc alongside an audio signal, to be viewed on a television. In 1985 the extensive storage capacity of the CD was applied to computers.

The latest CD players have the capability of running a disc at twice the normal speed, which makes it possible to record an hour-long disc onto a cassette in just 30 minutes. Both Trio-Kenwood and Sony have developed systems with this capacity.

CD single (1987)

The 45 is still very much alive! Since the beginning of **1987 Sony** and **Philips** have been marketing their latest invention, the CD single, the audio-digital equivalent of the microgroove 45. This new disc, which holds approximately 20 minutes' worth of music, was invented to supply a demand created primarily by young people. On a similar basis, Sony launched the Pocket Discman, an extra-light reader for the CD single, at the 1988 Music and Sound Exhibition.

Compact disc video (1987)

In **1987** there was a new development. The CDV, the compact disc video, was brought out by **Philips** and developed in conjunction with **Sony**. It enables video pictures to be shown on a television screen while laser quality sound is produced simultaneously on stereo. The new readers can reproduce both sound and picture. They will read standard compact discs, while the gold CDVs of the same format (ie 12cm *5in*) play pictures and sound for six minutes as well as 20 minutes of music, the 20cm *8in* CDVs offer 40 minutes of pictures and sound, and the 30cm *12in* CDVs last for a maximum of two hours, and give additional backing to films and operas. The CDV is one of the modern answers to the competition offered by DAT (Digital Audio Tape), an audio-digital cassette.

CD-Midi (1989)

In **June 1989** the Japanese company **JVC** brought out a new generation of compact disc, the CD-M, a piece of equipment which contains two types of information: MIDI data for the control of electronic instruments (for example, synthesizers and rhythm boxes), and graphic information related to the different instrumental functions including tempo, tone and so on. Each CD-M contains several pre-programmed musical works by professional artists.

Inserted into a special player, the CD-M reproduces the works on the connected instruments and the user can add or remove tracks, alter the tempo or adjust the tone at will.

Re-recordable CD (1991)

In 1989 **Sony** and **Taiyo Yuden** began working together to produce the CDR (R for recordable), to be launched soon, which can be recorded on once.

However, **Thomson** of West Germany had already begun work on a CD which could be wiped clean and re-recorded, the MOD (Magneto Optical Disc). In 1987 they won the German award for the best economic invention, but it is not expected to be marketed immediately. The American Tandy Corporation is also preparing to market a CD which can be wiped clean, re-recorded and will last almost indefinitely.

Digital audio tape (1987)

From 1980 several Japanese manufacturers researched the possibility of an audio cassette reader which used digital recordings (*Digital Audio Tape* or DAT) and offered a quality of sound equivalent to that of the compact disc.

There were two rival models: the JVC fixed-head S-DAT, and the R-DAT developed by Matsushita and Sony which had rotating

Invented by Philips and Sony, compact disc videos have been slow to catch on, but the market is beginning to grow.

heads and has since been adopted by the majority of manufacturers.

Aiwa was the first company to market the DAT in Japan in **February 1987**.

Personal cassette (1989)

This is an invention by Californian **Charles Garvin** which, with the help of a computer, enables you to record all your favourite songs on one cassette in less than five minutes. Using a catalogue of some 3000 or so titles, customers can listen, make their choice and then give the list to an assistant who makes the recording. The result is 90 minutes of personally selected music.

Compil Box (1989)

Patented in **1989** by the Swiss inventor **Pierre Schwab**, the Compil Box is a complete audio and video recording studio in a suitcase. Developed using Sony equipment, it works on a battery, a car cigarette lighter socket or standard electric current. It contains no less than two speakers, headphones, a TCD-D10 portable DAT, a CD player, a video Walkman, a camera input point, etc.

Musical composition and performance

Composition (17th century)

The Italian-born French composer **Jean Baptiste Lully** (1632–87) was superintendent of music at the court of Louis XIV (1638–1715), the Sun King. Lully insisted that the violinists play exactly what was written. He was thus the first composer in the modern sense of the word. Indeed, two identical manuscripts of the same work do not exist from the Middle Ages. Like jazz musicians, performers then would change the piece slightly every time they played.

Opera (1598)

In **1598** Jacopo Peri (1561–1633), court singer to the Medici family, presented the first dramatic entertainment with continuous music: *La Dafne*. It was performed at Carnival time at the Palazzo Corsi in Florence.

In 1660 Peri put to music a text by Ottavio Rinuccini (1563–1621), *Euridice*, which was performed at the marriage of Maria de' Medici to Henry IV of France at the Palazzo Pitti.

The first long work was **Claudio Monteverdi's** (1567–1643) *L'Orfeo*, which was performed in 1607.

Concert (1672)

The first paid concert was given before an audience of 42 people and organised in **1672** in London by an Englishman called **Bannister**.

Jazz (c.1914)

Profoundly influenced by the blues and the secular and spiritual songs of the American blacks, jazz was born around **1914** in New Orleans, Louisiana. The first jazz recording took place in 1917 on the other side of America in Chicago, by the Original Dixieland Jazz Band. Since then jazz has been through many changes of style from bebop to free jazz.

Blues (1860)

Blues, sung by the black slaves in the southern states of the USA, became known to a wider audience around the time of the American Civil War (1861–5) as it spread to the north of the country. The music owes its name to the fact that it uses many blue notes: the flattened third and seventh notes.

Dance

Tango (15th century)

A dance similar to the tango can be traced to

southern Spain at the beginning of the **15th century**, when the country was under Arab domination. Carried to Latin America, the initial rhythm of two beats in the bar underwent numerous changes and gave rise to dances like the Cuban habanera. The tango is characterised by its gliding steps and abrupt pauses with a duple rhythm.

Ballet (1581)

The first real ballet was the *Ballet comique de la reine* which was commissioned by **Catherine de' Medici** (1519–89) in **1581**.

The modern trappings of ballet appeared centuries later. It was not until about 1826 that Maria Taglioni began to dance on her points thanks largely to the developments in dance shoes. The tutu was designed by the painter Eugène Lamy for the performance of *La Sylphide* at the Paris Opera in 1832. The tutu was made from white muslin and reached mid-calf. The short, flared tutu was first worn by an Italian dancer, Virginie Zucchi, at the Imperial Theatre at St Petersburg in 1885. The name tutu derives from the childish French *cucu* meaning 'little bottom'.

Choreography (c.1671)

Charles Louis Beauchamps (1636–1719), who was the ballet master at the court of the Sun King (Louis XIV), invented a method of notation around **1671** that allowed dance steps to be recorded on paper.

Waltz (18th century)

The origins of this popular dance are obscure. However, it seems to have come from Bavaria at the end of the **18th century**. The name of the dance comes from *walzen*: Middle High German meaning 'to roll'.

The Austrians Johann Strauss (1804–49) and his son (1825–99) wrote many popular waltzes; the younger Strauss was known as the waltz king.

Photography

Origins

Photography results from the combination of two disciplines: optics and photo chemistry. Each followed separate paths through history: the former dating back to the middle of the 16th century, the latter to the beginning of the 18th century. Once they had come together, lenses and films progressed along parallel roads.

It was the Englishman Sir John Frederick William Herschel (1792–1871) who, in 1836, coined the word photography (from the Greek *photos* light and *graphein* to write) to describe the action of light on certain sensitive surfaces.

Camera obscura (16th century)

The Chinese probably knew the principle of the dark room – the *camera obscura* – as early as the 4th century BC. The Arab scholar Alhazen (965–1038) used it to observe solar eclipses and Leonardo da Vinci (1452–1519) described the phenomenon very clearly: a beam of light entering a darkened room through a small hole projects on the opposite wall the reverse image of the outside scene. The Venetian Daniele Barbaro (1513–70) in 1568 placed a lens over the hole and this gave a sharper image.

However, it seems to have been the Neapolitan dramatist and writer on natural magic

Gianbattista della Porta (1538–1615) who first advocated the use of the *camera obscura* to reproduce images (by drawing them).

In the 17th century several inventors including Johann Zahn and Athanase Kircher made portable 'dark rooms'.

Photographic lenses (1560)

When **Gerolamo Cardano** put a biconvex lens in front of the hole of a *camera obscura*, he invented the first photographic lens. But it was the French philosopher René Descartes (1596–1650) who laid the foundations of modern optics in *Dioptrics* (1637). The photographic lens corrects the distortion of the image that forms on the light-sensitive surface when the light has come through a simple lens.

The performance of the first photographic lens (single lens) was improved by a series of inventions: diaphragm (Barbaro, 1568), moveable mirror (Egnazio Danti, 1573), meniscus (Wollaston, 1812).

Chevalier's invention (the compound lens, 1840), improved by the Austrian J. Petzval, allowed for a larger aperture which meant a shorter exposure time and made daguerreotype portraits possible.

Birth of modern camera lenses

The rapid rectilinear lens (Thomas Dallmayer, Germany, 1865) gives a sharper picture, the aplanat (Dallmayer and Steinheil, 1866) does away with image distortion, and finally the anastigmatic lens (Doctor Schott, Germany, 1888) gives a sharp picture round the edges. H. D. Taylor's Triplet lens (Great Britain, 1893) was the first of a long series of rapid lenses such as Doctor Rudolph's Zeiss Planar (Germany, 1896) and the most famous of them all, the Zeiss Tessar from the same inventor (1902).

Diaphragm (1816)

The diaphragm regulates the amount of light passing through the objective lens. The iris diaphragm used in all modern cameras, and invented by **Nicéphore Niepce** (1765–1833) around **1816**, only came into general use around 1880.

The valve diaphragm was created in 1858 for rapid rectilinear lenses or doublets.

The automatic control of the diaphragm's aperture, according to the amount of light available, was the work of the Frenchman Alphonse Martin who patented his invention in 1939.

Wide angle lenses (1859)

Previously, the Englishman **Thomas Sutton**'s panoramic lenses (**1859**) covered a 120° field at f/12. To reduce refraction, the spaces between the lenses were filled with water.

The first wide angle lens was von Hoëgh's Hypergon in 1900. Robert Hill's disymetric objective lens (1924) gives an even wider field. The modern 'fish-eye' lenses were derived from it.

Telephoto lens (1891)

The telephoto lens is an objective lens in which the focal length is greater than the negative image's diagonal and thus produces an enlarged image of a distant object. The first one was used by **T. R. Dallmayer** in **1891**. Some telephoto lenses with a very long focal length use curved mirrors: they are the catadioptric telephoto lenses perfected by B. Schmidt in 1931.

Lens coating (1904)

Lens coating reduced reflections from the glass surfaces within the lens. In **1904 Taylor** patented a method for artificially tarnishing lenses. In 1935 Carl Zeiss patented a method of coating the lens surfaces with fluoride of magnesium.

Since 1945 all lenses have had coated surfaces, improving light transmission and contrast, and making it possible to produce multiple-element lenses.

This is one of Nicéphore Niepce's earliest heliographic prints, 'The Holy Family' of 1827. He developed the technique while trying to reproduce his son's drawings.

Zoom lenses (1945)

Zoom lenses are objective lenses with a variable focal length. In 1896 T. R. Dallmayer and J. S. Bergheim perfected a rudimentary lens of this type which can be considered the distant ancestor of the modern zoom lenses. The idea was taken up again in **1945** with **Frank Back**'s Zoomar (USA), a combination of two sets of mobile lenses. But it was with Roger Cuvillier's Pancinor (France, 1949) that the principle of the variable focal length was finally adopted.

The largest zoom lens in the world was built by the French company Angénieux in 1987: 3m long, × 300 focal length variation, germanium lenses. It was designed for the American Army's observations under infra-red light.

Space objective lenses (1962)

The first space photographs were taken on **3 October 1962** during the Mercury mission with a German **Carl Zeiss** objective lens (and a Swedish **Hasselblad** 500C camera). It was also a Carl Zeiss lens that recorded the first steps of the first man on the moon, Neil Armstrong, during the *Apollo 11* mission (16–24 July 1969). During the same period NASA also used the French Angénieux lenses, which can be used in extreme light conditions, to equip the *Ranger 7, 8, 9* missions. The Angénieux lenses also went on the first trip to the moon.

The most commonly used objective lenses are the 1.2/55mm outside and 1.4/35mm inside. NASA certainly puts photographic materials to the test and therefore acts as a gigantic laboratory which helps the progress of the photographic industry.

On the 1984 *Challenger* mission, pictures of an exceptional quality were taken at a speed of 28 000km/h *17 400mph* and without blur! In 1986 the space probe *Giotto*, after travelling 685 million km *426 million miles*, photographed the nucleus of Halley's comet for 45 minutes and sent back the pictures in eight minutes!

First light-sensitive surfaces (1727)

As early as **1727** the German physicist **Johann Heinrich Schulze** noticed that silver nitrate turned black when exposed to the light. In 1777, the Swedish chemist C. W. Scheele made an extensive study of the effect of light on paper with silver chloride. In 1802, the Englishman Thomas Wedgwood (son of Josiah Wedgwood, the potter) went further and obtained contact images on silver-nitrate coated paper of objects and drawings under glass. But as they were not fixed, these images disappeared when exposed to light.

Photography (1826)

The first attempts by the German J. W. Ritter and Englishmen Thomas Wedgwood and Humphry Davy between 1801 and 1802 to fix an image on light-sensitive paper in a *camera obscura* were unsuccessful.

A Frenchman, **Nicéphore Niepce**, was looking for a means of reproducing his son's drawings mechanically. Having thought about the effect of light on some chemicals, in 1816, after many unsuccessful attempts, he managed to capture a picture on silver-chloride coated paper, at the back of a *camera obscura*. But the image was negative and short-lived. He then tried a different process using Jew's pitch, which turns white and hardens when exposed to light. In 1822 he reproduced translucent pictures by contact on a pitch-covered plate. These 'heliographs' were the ancestors of photogravures. In **1826**, carrying on his research in the *camera obscura*, he captured on the same plate, after eight hours' exposure, the first positive image. Photography had been invented.

Daguerreotype (1835)

It was in **1835** that **Jacques Louis Mandé Daguerre** (1787–1851), Niepce's partner, perfected a new process to capture the image of an object on a me~~~~plate. In spite of its faults (it was fragile, co~~~~be reproduced only by rephotographing ~~~~d was reversed left to right), the dague~~~~ype produced a picture of an exceptional ~~~~lity for the time. On 19 August 1839 Arag~~~~ermanent secretary at the French Acad~~~~ of Science, revealed how daguerreotyp~~~~ere obtained. It was an immediate succe~~~~'Daguerreotypomania' spread like wildfir~~~~over the world: 500 000 plates were sold in Paris in 1846, and more than 3 million in the United States in 1853.

Photography on paper (1839)

The daguerreotype might be perfect from the artistic point of view, but on the technical side it was not the ancestor of contemporary photography. Modern photography has its roots in the work of two men who had no knowledge of the work of the other: the Englishman **William Henry Fox Talbot** (1800–77) and the Frenchman **Hippolyte Bayard** (1801–87).

As early as 1833 Talbot tried to fix on paper sensitised with silver chloride the image obtained at the back of a *camera obscura*. The following year, he obtained 'photogenic drawings': negative images of the objects placed on the paper. He fixed the images with cooking salt. Improving his technique in 1835

– after several hours' exposure and using a wooden box at the back of which he had placed some sensitised paper (a box his wife nicknamed the mousetrap) – he managed to obtain a faint negative image: the first negative on paper.

In 1839, when Daguerre's process was revealed, Talbot started his work again and discovered that by using this negative image as 'an object to be copied' he could obtain a positive image on sensitised paper. The negative/positive process had been discovered.

Positive images on paper (1839)

Also in 1839, in Paris, **Hippolyte Bayard** invented a process which enabled him to obtain positive images directly on paper. They were of such good quality that they were shown at the first photographic exhibition on **24 June 1839**. It is undeniable that these unique pictures, obtained after a 15-minute exposure, came before those of Daguerre. However, Arago asked Bayard not to reveal that fact so as to avoid upsetting Daguerre.

Calotype (1840)

In **1840** **William Henry Fox Talbot** revealed what Bayard had earlier discovered: that it was possible to make the latent negative image, formed on paper treated with silver iodide that had been subjected to strong light, appear by putting it in a developer. This process meant that a pose could be held for less than 30 seconds, but only Talbot dreamt of using the negative to obtain a positive image through contact. This development led photography into the era of endless reproduction. Talbot called it a Calotype from the Greek *kalos* meaning beauty.

Wet collodion plate (1851)

In 1849 the Frenchman Le Gray light-sensitised his negative materials with a collodion-based preparation, that is, one made of gun-cotton dissolved in ether. Nonetheless, it was the Englishman **Frederick Scott Archer** who first promoted the use of this process in **1851**.

Fifteen times faster than the daguerreotype, the wet-collodion process was a resounding success because of the quality of reproduction, and was adopted by all the great photographers including Roger Fenton and Matthew Brady.

Dry plates (1871)

In **1871** an English doctor, **Richard L. Maddox**, published the first description of a process using really efficient dry plates. Improved by Charles Harper Bennett in 1876, gelatine bromide plates revolutionised the world of photography. And suddenly, industry took over and quickly popularised photography.

In 1879 a young American amateur photographer, George Eastman (1854–1932), invented a machine that could produce dry plates in large quantities. On 1 January 1881 he founded the Eastman Dry Plate Company with Henry A. Strong, a horse-drawn carriage whip manufacturer. This small company, based in Rochester, New York, went through a spectacular expansion and is today universally known under the name of Kodak.

The Kodak camera (1888)

In 1888 the American **George Eastman** revolutionised the photographic market by creating a simple, light and cheap camera: the Kodak

A rare photograph of two important inventors: George Eastman (left) and Thomas Edison (right).

When Louis Armstrong flew into London in December 1956 to give a concert in aid of the Hungarian Relief Fund, it caught the imagination of the press, who came out in dazzling force – thanks to their flashing cameras.

camera. The small 82 × 95 × 165mm *3.2 × 3.7 × 6.5in* box, with its f/9 objective lens and a shutter with a 1/20 of a second speed, was a resounding success. It produced 100 round photos measuring 63mm *2.48in* in diameter. Once all the photos had been taken, the camera was sent back to the factory who took the film out, put a new one in, developed the photos and sent the whole lot back to its owner within ten days. 'You press the button, we do the rest!': the slogan was launched and 90 000 cameras were sold in the first year.

Why the name Kodak? Because it was short, easily remembered and could be pronounced throughout the world.

Celluloid roll film (1889)

The first celluloid roll film to be used commercially was developed by **Henri Reichenbach** for **George Eastman** and marketed in 1889. Already in 1884 Eastman and William H. Walker had invented a container for rolls of negative paper. In 1885 they developed the film Eastman America. Unlike negative paper, it was a thin film that used paper only as a temporary support for the emulsion. The paper was eliminated after development and a thin negative film remained, which was then mounted on glass for the production of prints.

Flash (1850)

Towards 1850 it was discovered that the combustion of magnesium wires produced an extremely brilliant light accompanied, however, by a thick cloud of white smoke. In 1887 Germans **Adolf Mietke** and **Johannes Gaedicke** invented flash powder (magnesium powder), an explosive mixture with a base of magnesium, potassium chlorate and antimony sulphate. This process won over photographers as a whole, despite the dangers involved in its use.

Flash bulbs (1929)

In 1925 **Paul Vierkotter** took out a patent for a new flash method whereby the inflammable mixture was contained in a vacuum lamp and set alight by means of an electric current.

But it was in 1929 that the first real flash bulb appeared, thanks to the German **Ostermeier** who perfected the system and created the Vacublitz bulb. This had the advantage of being both silent and smokeless. Today's flash cubes are miniaturised versions of the flash bulb.

Electronic flash (1931)

The principle goes back to the very beginning of photography. In 1851 Fox Talbot succeeded in obtaining an image of a newspaper fixed to a rotating wheel thanks to a spark supplied by means of a condenser battery.

In 1931 **Harold Edgerton** of the Massachusetts Institute of Technology (MIT) invented the electronic flash; the current accumulated at high voltage in a condenser explodes in a tube filled with rare gases.

Underwater photographic observations (1856)

The first underwater photograph was shown by **William Thompson** to the London Art Society in 1856. The photographic apparatus had been placed at the bottom of Weymouth Bay at a depth of 6m *20ft*. The lens, controlled from the surface, stayed open for ten minutes.

In 1889 the French zoology professor Louis Boutan took photos at a depth of 50m *164ft*. The photographs thus obtained were published in 1900 in an album which was the first of its kind.

In 1935 the Englishman William Beebe took photographs from the porthole of a bathyscape at a depth of 900m *2950ft*.

Ten years later an American, Maurice Ewing, developed an automatic underwater camera to photograph geological formations at depths between 400 and 700m *1310 and 2300ft*.

In addition to these purely photographic techniques, other means of looking at the sea depths have come into existence. One of the latest is the Sea Beam, from the French company Thomson, which takes radar images (viewed on a TV screen) with an apparatus mounted on a ship. This was used during the exploration of the wreck of the *Titanic*.

Photobooth (1924)

The photobooth is the invention of the Hungarian **Anatol Marco Josepho**, who registered his patent in Germany on 13 January 1924. The machine was marketed in England in 1928. The attendant was replaced by a coin slot in 1968 and in the same year colour was introduced.

Colour photography

First attempts (1840)

As soon as photography was invented the question of colour attracted inventors (coloured daguerreotypes, 1840; photographic glazes by Lafon de Carmasac in 1854).

In 1848 Edmond Becquerel (1820–91) managed to photograph colour prints but could not fix the images. It was **Gabriel Lippmann** who, in 1891, obtained the first direct colour pictures by the interferential process (the fixation of the luminous vibration traces). That success won its inventor the Nobel Prize for Physics in 1908. The only problem was that his work could only be seen at a certain angle and could not be copied.

Additive process (1855)

This process is based on the discovery made in 1855 by the Scottish physicist **James Clerk Maxwell** (1831–79). Any colour can be created by adding together the three fundamental colours, red, green and blue, in appropriate proportions.

Autochrome process (1903)

It was by applying the principles of additive colour synthesis that the **Lumière** brothers in 1903 perfected the autochrome plate process.

An autochrome dating from 1907 showing a woman in her garden. This process had only been developed some four years before by the Lumière brothers and was already achieving some spectacular results.

Each plate was sprinkled with a mixture of potato starch grains dyed green, red and blue. A single 9 × 12 plate carried nearly 90 million! This process remained popular until 1932 when it was replaced by Lumicolor and Filmcolor, also Lumière processes. It was subsequently abandoned altogether.

The autochrome technique produced some masterpieces which were very close to paintings in their texture and rich colours.

Subtractive synthesis (1869)

It is the process from which all modern colour photography processes are derived. The announcement of its discovery was marked by a dramatic turn of events: on **7 May 1869** two men, who knew nothing of each other's work, presented similar conclusions to the French Photographic Society. **Charles Cros** and **Louis Ducos du Hauron** (who had registered a patent in November 1868) had discovered trichromatic synthesis.

Modern films

Kodachrome (1935)

In 1911/12 the German chemist Rudolf Fischer discovered that dyes could be obtained by oxidation or coupling with other chemical substances. All modern colour films follow this general principle.

It was not until **1935** that subtractive colour synthesis found its first commercial application. Two American musicians, **Leopold Mannes** and **Leopold Godowsky**, with **Kodak**'s financial backing, invented Kodachrome.

Agfacolor (1936)

In **1936** the German company **Agfa**'s first reversal film, Agfacolor, came out. It had colour couplers present in the emulsion. Subtractive colour synthesis then spread all over the world and improvements were made in rapid succession: in 1939 the Agfacolor negative/positive film appeared, a process which was immediately used by Hitler's propaganda machine (e.g. in the making of prestige films such as the *Adventures of Baron Münchhausen* which created a sensation at the time).

In 1942 the United States' reply came in the shape of Kodacolor. The reversal and negative/positive processes continued to evolve in parallel: the former producing Ektachrome (1945), Anscochrome (1955) and Fujicolor (1948); the latter Ektacolor (1947) and Gevacolor. In 1949 a new generation of Kodacolor films and in 1953 of Agfacolor, applied a technique using colour 'masks' which gave better colour saturation.

In addition to its Kodacolor range, at the end of 1988 Kodak introduced the Ektar 25 and 1000, two types of negative films for print-

making, aimed at the amateur wanting very high quality pictures. These can only be used in 24 × 36 reflex cameras.

Polacolor (1963)

The announcement in 1963 by **Edwin H. Land** and his Polaroid Corporation that they had created a one-minute colour film, Polacolor, caused a sensation. Extremely sophisticated in its conception, this film allowed a colour print to be made on paper in only 60 seconds. The emulsion consisted of a negative part half the thickness of a hair, comprising nine distinct layers, and a positive part of four layers, as well as one last layer enclosing a capsule containing an alkaline solution which triggered off treatment. In total there were 14 layers in a single film!

In 1982 Polaroid launched a process for producing instant colour or black and white transparencies.

Contemporary colour emulsions

The perfecting of the renowned 'T' grain by **Kodak** in 1983 meant an amazing improvement in sensitivity. This grain makes it possible, among other things, to raise the sensitivity of Kodacolor negative films to ISO 1000. There is also a fantastic improvement for reversal films and the new Ektachrome comes with ISO 400, 600, 1600, even 3200, which makes it the most sensitive 'daylight' film to date. Other companies have researched the same areas: Agfa (use of structured twin crystals) and Fuji (double structure grain SG and Fujicolor that can be used at ISO 3200).

Films with enzymes (1987)

The biotechnological revolution has reached photography with the process perfected by **Canon**. The enzyme film uses amylase (an enzyme which attacks starch) emulsions on a mixture of starch and colour pigments. Light deactivates the enzyme. After reaction and drying, the black and white photo obtained is identical to standard film ones.

3-D

Stereoscopy (1838)

In **1838** the Englishman **Charles Wheatstone** made the first stereoscope, an apparatus which permitted geometric patterns to be seen in three dimensions. Each eye receives an image of the same object from a slightly different angle and the two images are synthesised by the brain. This gives us the illusion of three-dimensional perception.

In 1849 the Scottish physicist Sir David Brewster built a simple and practical stereoscope (a small closed box with two viewing holes) which, factory-produced by the Frenchman Dubosq, was all the rage in London at the Great Exhibition of 1851.

The stereoscopic revolution was all the more important as, because of the lenses' short focal length, exposure time was reduced to about a quarter of a second which made the first snapshots possible.

Anaglyphs (1891)

In **1891 Louis Ducos du Hauron** discovered a new process, anaglyphs, which consisted of superimposing two separate images of the same picture after dying one violet-blue and the other red and then looking at them through glasses with one lens each of the same two colours. Each eye saw only one of the images and the brain combined the two to give the illusion of a single three-dimensional picture.

Current cameras and processes

Automatic focus (1945)

The first automatic focus device appeared in **1945**. It was the Optar, invented by the German **Doctor Kaulmann**. However, the device was too bulky to be fitted on a camera. Automatic focus is now a common feature and the device is an integral part of the camera. There are various principles: the CCD (Charge-Coupled Device), the Sonar by Polaroid (which uses ultrasound), and a system exclusive to Minolta (1983) using an infra-red beam. Apart from the auto-focus cameras, the Minolta 7000 was the first reflex camera to use this system. The Minolta 9000 (1986) applies this automatic focusing system to all its range.

Compact auto-focus camera (1976)

The first compact auto-focus camera was the Japanese **Konica** in 1976. Since then, cameras

Two early coloured stereograph pictures of St Paul's (top) and Trafalgar Square (bottom). The technique was largely developed in the UK.

Mascher's 'Improved Stereoscope' was granted its patent in March 1853. After the Great Exhibition of 1851 stereoscopy was extremely popular.

have become more and more sophisticated, such as the Konica MR 70 or the Fuji TW 300.

The Konica A4, the smallest and lightest (193g *6.8oz*) automatic camera in the world, was voted the best compact camera in Europe for 1989–90. The Kanpai, the latest product in the Konica compact range, is voice-activated and has a stand with two legs.

Polaroid (1948)

In **November 1948** the American **Edwin Herbert Land** launched on the American market the first instant picture camera, the Polaroid 95. At the age of 28, Land had founded the Polaroid Corporation which specialised in the manufacture of sunglasses and polarising filters.

In 1947 Kodak had shown no interest in Land's invention. But, on seeing how popular Polaroid cameras were, in 1976 Kodak decided to launch their own instant picture cameras. However, Polaroid sued them for patent violation and after proceedings lasting ten years won the case in October 1985. This gave back to Polaroid exclusive use of the process and a minimum of $1 billion damages!

Edwin H. Land holds the second largest number of registered patents in the United States: 533.

Onyx (1987)

Onyx is the first transparent camera. A **Polaroid** invention which makes it possible to see the devices that operate the focus and allow a shutter speed of 50 milliseconds.

Magnetic photography (1981)

The first in this category came from the Japanese firm **Sony** which introduced its Mavica-Magnetic Video Camera on **24 August 1981**. This camera, which uses a magnetic disk, represents a revolutionary invention in photography: an electromagnetic system now replaces chemicals; it does not use a film, therefore there is no processing or printing as the pictures can be seen on a screen.

In 1984 Panasonic introduced a camera of this type, but that recorded colour pictures on a video floppy disk with a 50-frame capacity. Although they were the pioneers in this domain, Sony only marketed its Mavica (the Mavica MVC 1, a greatly improved version of the one introduced in 1981) at the end of 1988 in Japan.

First application (1984)

Making its debut at the Los Angeles Olympics in **July 1984** was a camera which looked like a 24 × 36 motorised reflex, the **Canon** Still Video System D413. It took magnetic colour photographs which were transmitted over the telephone to a newspaper and were viewed on a television monitor. The camera had interchangeable lenses and used a 4.7cm *1.85in* diameter disk which could hold 50 pictures.

Ion (1989)

This is the name given to the only magnetic camera on the European market. Produced by **Canon**, it is fitted with a fixed lens with a range of 1.2m *4ft* to infinity and a built-in flash. It can take up to 50 photographs on a magnetic floppy disk, which replaces the traditional roll of film.

Kodak disc-film (1982)

On **3 February 1982 Kodak** brought out a new type of photographic base: the disc-film. The flat plastic cartridge holds a disc-film which rotates round a hub in front of an exposure window which is behind the objective lens. Thicker than that of ordinary films, the base of the Kodacolor HR Disc film is made of Estar, a thick and rigid material.

DX coding (1984)

The 24 × 36 film cassettes have been coded since **1984**; initially perfected by **Kodak**, the coding system tells the camera the type of film used, its light sensitivity and the number of exposures. Absent-minded photographers (many devices have been geared to them!) will no longer run the risk of making dreadful mistakes. All the films on the market at present have such coding and most modern cameras are fitted with the system.

Quicksnap (1986)

In 1986 **Fuji** invented a negative colour film wrapped in a box which includes the lens and shutter. After the 24 pictures have been taken, the whole lot is sent to a laboratory for processing. No adjusting required, this film-camera is incredibly easy to use and should be made available from automatic dispensers. In 1987 it was Kodak's turn to put a camera of that type on the market, the Fling, which joined the Quicksnap, a second generation Fuji disposable camera. In 1988 Fuji brought out a Quicksnap with incorporated electronic flash.

In 1989 the Quicksnap telephoto lens was brought out. It enlarges the subject two and a half times compared with the standard Quicksnap lens, and provides improved long-distance photographic quality.

An infra-red photograph of a river seen through some trees. This picture was taken near to the village of Braco in Tayside, Scotland, and reveals the spectacular effects that can be achieved by this method.

Cinema

Origins (1654)

The ancestors of modern cinema are the magic lantern invented in **1654** by a German priest, **Athanase Kircher**, and the fantasmagoria developed by the Frenchman Gaspard Robert in 1798. These were both projection techniques with painted backgrounds mounted in front of a light source.

The Belgian Joseph Plateau demonstrated in 1828 the principle of the persistence of luminous images on the retina, thereby formulating the basis of cinema. He invented a *phénakistiscope* in 1832 that, for the first time, produced a moving image. A cardboard disc carried a sequence of pictures of a subject such as a dancer. As it revolved, the disc created the impression that the figure was moving.

The stroboscope, which worked on a similar principle, was invented by the Austrian Simon von Stampfer in 1833. It is used today to give the appearance of immobility or to slow down the image of something moving quickly. It has industrial applications but is also to be found in discos.

Pictures of movement (1878)

After years of work the English photographer **Eadweard Muybridge** succeeded in **1878** in demonstrating that a galloping horse does indeed lift all four legs completely off the ground. (The horse set off a series of cameras as it galloped along the track.)

Photographic gun (1882)

In 1882 the French scientist **Jules Marey** developed 'chronophotography' by constructing a repetitive-action 'photographic gun' that allowed him to take successive shots of a bird in flight. At the seashore in Naples, Marey chronophotographed the flight of seagulls. Peasants who saw him spoke about a crazy man armed with a gun who aimed at birds without ever shooting and seemed delighted to come back from hunting empty-handed.

Sound cine camera (1889)

The American **Thomas Edison**, in collaboration with **William Dickson**, found the solution to the problem of positioning of images by using perforated films, the forerunners of the modern 35mm films, which ensured that the film was correctly placed for each exposure. In **1889** he invented the first sound cine camera, which he patented in 1891. The shutter mechanism was connected to a gramophone, which made it possible to record the sound at the same time as the camera was filming. The films produced in this way were watched by viewers on an individual cine film viewer (patented in 1891).

Studio (1890)

W. K. L. Dickson, a collaborator of Thomas Edison, shot the first films for him in the world's first studio. It was more or less a shed lit by large windows and constructed on a

This is the Lumière cinematograph – the device that was to sp___ a multi-billion pound industry.

pivot. The whole thing turned, following the path of the sun; thus the scenes, played inside, received a constant flow of light. The first films shot in this studio were shown on the kinetoscope, a machine which contained an endless strip of film.

Movie projector (1894)

Credit must be given to the American **Le Roy** for having invented the first projector that brought together the essential elements of our current models. On **5 February 1894**, at 16 Beekman Street, New York, he publicly projected two of Thomas Edison's kinetoscope films.

Lumière cinematograph (1895)

On **13 February 1895** the **Lumière** brothers, **Louis** (1864–1948) and **Auguste** (1862–1954), took out a patent for 'a device for obtaining and ___wing chronophotographic prints'. They ___tised it the cinematograph.

The ___rst public showing was held on **28 December 1895** in Paris. This new form of entertainment attracted crowds, and its success led to the growth and development of the motion picture industry. One might add to the Lumière brothers' credit by mentioning that their films, which were the first moving picture films, had real artistic value: the very first, the entry of a train into the La Ciotat station, was taken at such an angle that the spectators were terrified.

Movie camera (1897)

The Frenchman **Charles Pathé** (1867–1957) broke down the Lumière brothers' cinematograph into two distinct elements, the camera and the projector, and made them independent.

Around 1904 camera speed was made

variable in order to allow speeded-up and slow-motion films. Sixteen images per second were used for ordinary shooting, but 24 per second were necessary for sound films.

Colour films (1900)

The first colour films were hand-painted, frame by frame. Then from 1900 **Méliès** and **Pathé** used a mechanical technique: the stencil. Despite the years, the few films that still exist from the era retain their fresh colour. Subsequently, progress in the development of moving film took place hand in hand with that of photography.

Technicolor (1881)

Technicolor had been imagined by the American **Warnake** in 1881, but it only appeared in 1917. This was in a two-colour film, *The Gulf Between* with Grace Darmond and Niles Welch. In 1932 a three-colour film, *Flowers and Trees*, was produced by Walt Disney.

The first full-length film shot in three-colour and in Technicolor was *Becky Sharp*, directed by Rouben Mamoulian in 1935.

The subtractive process is still used today, particularly for taking copies of films, because of the fine quality it produces.

Films with sound (1902)

Voices and music were added to Thomas Edison's films thanks to the kinetophone. In 1902 the Frenchmen **Baron** and **Gaumont** built an automatic electric synchronisation system using the phonograph and the projector, but the phonographs were not powerful enough. Sound amplification was a difficulty resolved in 1910 by the Frenchmen Decaux and Laudet for the Gaumont company. They modulated a flow of compressed air. In 1912 this process was used in Gaumont's large cinema in Paris.

Talkie (1927)

The first successful talkie was *The Jazz Singer*, an American film produced by **Warner Brothers** in 1927. Several of its sequences had sound added by means of 33rpm records.

Optical sound track (1929)

In 1929 the first truly talking film came out: *Hallelujah*, an American film produced by **Metro-Goldwyn-Mayer** and directed by **King Vidor**. On the film itself, next to the images, an optical soundtrack was engraved through photo-electric processes. This process had been demonstrated by Lee De Forest in 1923.

Slow motion (1904)

Two students of Jules Marey, the Frenchmen **Lucien Bull** and **Henri Nogues**, invented slow-motion filming in 1904. They understood that by shooting more frames per second than one normally would shoot, one obtains a longer film. Then, projecting this longer film at normal speed, events are seen to take place less rapidly than they do in reality. That is how slow motion works.

Colouring of the great classics (1986)

The Canadian **Wilson Markle**'s invention revolutionised the American world of cinema. This ex-NASA engineer has perfected a

A poster for a German version of the most famous Tarzan of them all – Johnny Weissmuller, the former Olympic swimming champion.

computer system which makes it possible to colour films shot in black and white. The main American television networks rushed out to buy film rights and have films coloured, ranging from Laurel and Hardy to John Huston's *Maltese Falcon* and *The Hunchback of Notre Dame*. In spite of protests from the traditionalists – headed by Woody Allen – this process, used by Vidcolor Inc. in Toronto and Color System Technologies in Los Angeles, appears to have a promising future.

Modern cameras

Steady Cam (1970)

Perfected by the American technician **Garrett Brown**, Steady Cam allows camera movements without a crane or dolly on rails. The camera is strapped onto the cameraman's body which means he needs only one hand to hold it. Thanks to a series of controls and balancing devices the cameraman is completely autonomous and can move about and even run. Dustin Hoffman's run in John Schlesinger's *Marathon Man* and the little boy's flight through the snowy maze in Stanley Kubrick's *The Shining* were filmed using a Steady Cam. Jim Muro's *Street Trash* of 1986 was filmed entirely by Steady Cam.

Sky Cam (1984)

Since then **Garrett Brown** has perfected two more revolutionary cameras: the Sky Cam

(first used in Alan Parker's *Birdy*, 1984), and more recently, the Cable Cam. These two cameras, fitted with video-relays, are fixed on cables stretched at very high altitudes and can glide along them at varying speeds. The result is an amazing sequence of shots that cannot be equalled even from a helicopter.

Shaky Cam (1982)

Devised by **Sam Raini**, a young American director, on the set of his film *Evil Dead*, the Shaky Cam is a motorised version of the Steady Cam. The camera is fitted on to a motorbike and protected from bumps by a system of shock absorbers. This allows for very smooth and fast runs at ground level. Raini used the Shaky Cam to give a vision of things from the point of view of a crawling creature crossing a forest at high speed and brushing against the trees.

Garrett Brown and the Steady Cam that he invented in 1970.

Special effects and make-up: inventors and inventions in the cinema

The first special effect in the history of cinema happened by accident: in 1896 the French film producer Georges Méliès (1861–1938), was filming the Place de l'Opéra in Paris when the film jammed for a minute in the camera. In the meantime, people and cars continued moving. When the film was projected, Méliès saw men change into women and a bus turn into a hearse. He re-used the technique in some of his subsequent films.

Single frame animation

This special effects technique, which is used to give the impression that inanimate objects are moving, originated at the end of the last century. The Frenchman Georges Méliès and the American production house Vitagraph (when they made the short film *Humpty Dumpty Circus* in 1897) were doubtless the first to attempt to make an object move by breaking up this motion into as many positions as there are frames to record.

In 1913 Willis O'Brien thought of filming a clay dinosaur with a wooden skeleton one frame at a time in *The Dinosaur and The Missing Link*. He had invented Stop Motion, a technique that he used again in 1933 in *King Kong*, this time using transparencies which enabled him to overlay the puppet on the real film.

Ray Harryhausen, Willis O'Brien's pupil, improved his techniques and obtained fabulous results in Don Chaffey's *Jason and the Argonauts* (1963) with the famous sequence of the fight with the skeletons; and in Gordon Hessler's *The Golden Voyage of Sinbad* (1973).

During the shooting of *Dragonslayer* in 1981, Denis Murren, a young American technician, introduced a new frame-by-frame animation technique: Go Motion. The puppets' movements were computer controlled which saved time and improved smoothness.

Painting in backgrounds

Introduced by the French film directors René Clair and Abel Gance at the beginning of the 1920s, this special effect consists of painting certain elements of the background on to a pane of glass which is then placed between the camera and the scene to be filmed. In 1943 the French director Henri Mahé invented Simplifilm, a process based on this technique, which he used in a long film entitled *Blondine*. Again, there were no artificial sets, but drawings and photographs were inserted in the camera between the lens and the actors.

Many American directors such as Spielberg (*Raiders of the Lost Ark*, 1981) and George Miller (*The Witches of Eastwick*, 1987) also use this technique, but in a more sophisticated manner. The two elements – the actual shot and the painting – are filmed separately in order to avoid an entire crew standing idle during the insertion and removal of the pane of glass. The painted elements are then inlaid into the actual shot by the technique of mask/counter mask (see below).

The Invisible Man

The inventor of *The Invisible Man* was John P. Fulton (1902–65). He created the special effects for *Frankenstein* in 1931 and two years later achieved real fame with his effects for *The Invisible Man*.

For some of the scenes in the film he used double, triple and even quadruple exposure (see the process of mask/counter mask below). He himself touched up several thousand frames by hand. However, for the famous scene where the invisible man smokes a cigarette (which moves around freely in mid-air), Fulton simply used transparent wires.

Mask/counter mask

Mask/counter mask is a major improvement on the technique introduced in 1898 in *The Corsican Brothers* by the English directors Williamson and G. A. Smith. They were the first to use the photographic principle of superimposing two images on a single exposure in the cinema. Mask/counter mask was launched by the master of special effects, John Fulton, in about 1930 (see above). The process is frequently used in scenes where the actor is confronted by his double, i.e. himself. The mask/counter mask is widely used in modern cinema, both in television and in major American productions such as Spielberg's *Indiana Jones and the Temple of Doom* (1984).

Jason's fight was filmed frame by frame in Jason and the Argonauts.

Breakfast cereal and tractor tyres

At the end of *Honey, I Shrunk the Kids* (1989), one of the children, only a few millimetres high, dives into a bowl of milk filled with breakfast cereal. It was therefore necessary to find a way of reproducing a scale model of the cereal. Greg Fonseca, a member of the special effects team, had the idea of using tractor tyres of over 3.5m *11ft* in diameter, coated with polyurethane foam. Balloons were inflated in the foam and then burst when it was dry to create the effect of the air pockets visible in real cereals. The tyres were cut into slices and immersed in a pool of 'milk'.

Make-up for monkeys . . .

The American, Rick Baker, born in 1950, is particularly well-known as a specialist in effects and make-up for monkeys. He created the mad gorilla in *Schlock* (1972) and also the apes for *Greystoke* (1983). He was the first to achieve a transformation on screen, in this case that of a man into a wolf in *An American Werewolf in London* (1981).

. . . and aliens

Carlo Rimbaldi, born in 1939, is considered one of the best make-up artists in the world. He created the tentacled monster in *Possession* (1981), the aliens in *Close Encounters of the Third Kind* (1977) and the giant gorilla in the remake of *King Kong* (1976). Carlo Rimbaldi also received the make-up Oscar for his creation of E.T. in the film of that name by Steven Spielberg (1982).

Rick Baker created this convincing creature in An American Werewolf in London.

Dead Ringers

The process of mask/counter mask was perfected in David Cronenberg's *Dead Ringers* (1988) in which Jeremy Irons plays the role of twin brothers.

For the confrontation scenes a computer-controlled camera recorded the first shot and then repeated exactly the same movement for a second shot. Meanwhile the actor had changed character and position so that, on screen, he is having a conversation with himself.

Blue screen

Discovered in the 1950s and put to magnificent use by the technician L. B. Abbott for the most famous crossing of the Red Sea in Cecil B. DeMille's *Ten Commandments* (1955), the blue screen principle is one of the most common principles of illusion in the cinema and in television (video shot). A subject filmed against a background of a special blue is isolated on a separate film so as to be inserted in a more complex scene. The blue is identified and eliminated in a laboratory process called 'separation'. This means that the subject, Superman for instance, will be on his own on a transparent film. He can then be overlaid on a shot of New York taken from a helicopter by the mask/counter mask process. The confrontation in one shot of the giant ectoplasms of *Ghostbusters* (Ivan Reitman, 1984) and the ghostbusters themselves was obtained using the same technique.

The most popular alien of all time – E.T.

Wide screens and 3-D

3-D (1937)

Starting as early as 1894, attempts were made in the direction of the 3-D cinema. Efforts at developing a lenticular system were very quickly abandoned, except in the Soviet Union, where experiments were tried out in the 1940s.

It was in the 1930s that the first commercial 3-D films were produced, in the form of shorts.

But it was the Polaroid system, based on the principle of light filtering, that sparked off the great epoch of the 3-D cinema. The first full-length film was released in Germany in 1937. The Gunzberg brothers imported into the United States their application of the process developed by Edwin H. Land which permitted producer Arch Oboler to shoot *Bwana* in 1952. The film was shot with two cameras; the two reels had to be projected by two machines that were strictly synchronised with each other. And, of course, the spectators had to wear Polaroid glasses. A good hundred films were produced in this way.

In 1966 Arch Oboler shot *The Bubble* with the use of a special lens, the polarisator. This device did away with the inconveniences of double projection.

Showscan (1983)

The result of several years' research by **Douglas Trumbull**, the special effects supervisor for Steven Spielberg's *Close Encounters of the Third Kind* (1977) and Ridley Scott's *Blade Runner* (1982), Showscan is a new process which gives the audience an almost tangible illusion of reality, a greatly increased three-dimensional impression.

It uses sophisticated equipment (70mm film, 60 frames/sec., Dolby stereo magnetic sound track). A demonstration film, made by Trumbull himself, is being shown at present in Disneyworld, Florida (USA). A network of appropriate cinemas is growing worldwide.

OMNIMAX cinema (1971)

It was a Canadian engineer **Graeme Ferguson** who, in **1971** in Toronto, invented the cinematographic process called OMNIMAX. This process uses large-size films, each frame being 70mm *2.76in* wide and 50mm *1.97in* high, with 15 perforations as opposed to the five used on a traditional 35mm film. The film moves horizontally, projected onto a semi-hemispherical screen by a special projector. The film is shot with a special camera. Ferguson is also the inventor of IMAX, a similar system but projected onto a flat screen. In 1967 Ferguson, with his partner Robert Kerr, shot his first multi-screen film, *Polar Life*. At present very few cinemas in the world can show OMNIMAX films: about 20 in all.

Pan-and-Scan (c.1980)

A process perfected by Warner Studios which allows the recentring of a 'big screen' film picture so that it takes up the whole area of the television screen. Pan-and-Scan (from *Panavision* and *Scanner*) is used by the video industry and television networks.

Holographic film (1985)

It was at the Franco-German research institute in Saint-Louis, France that the first convincing *cinéhologrammes* were made. Previously, they had been produced in the USSR (V. G. Komar, 1977) and in the United States (A. J. Decker, 1982).

The holographic cinema principle: to record on film the light reflected by an object or a person lit by laser and at the same time the light coming from the laser itself. From the meeting of the two lights a 3-D picture is born.

Holographic cinema is of particular interest in the study of four-dimensional physical phenomena. Several branches of industry are interested in it such as aeronautics, medicine, new materials' inventors, etc.

Underwater cinema

Origins

It was probably **Jacques-Yves Cousteau** who invented underwater cinema. However, before him, a few attempts had been made using some rule of thumb techniques: for instance, during the shooting of Buster Keaton's *The Navigator* (1926), in which there was an underwater scene. The cameraman had been lowered into the water in a glass cage but, as he breathed, the glass walls steamed up and he could not film through them any longer. The problem was remedied by filling the cage with blocks of ice.

Vanessa Paradis won a French Oscar, the César, for her performance in the film Noce Blanche. *In the UK she remains best-known for the record 'Joe le Taxi', which reached number three in the charts in 1988 around the time of her 15th birthday.*

The Silent World (1956)

It was **Jacques Cousteau**'s film *The Silent World*, produced in **1956**, that made him famous the world over. But he also has a lot of inventions to his credit: in 1952 the first underwater industrial television equipment with engineer André Laban and Thomson's co-operation; in 1954 a first 'sledge' for underwater photography using Professor Harold E. Edgerton's equipment; in 1955 the first 35mm underwater camera with Armand Davso. In that same year deep sea photography was also attempted, using Professor Edgerton's equipment; in 1956 the first survey of the well-known Rift Valley in the Atlantic Ocean; in 1957 final perfecting of the photographic 'sledges', called *troïkas*, to be used in deep waters; on 15 June the first undersea television programme in the Marseilles area in France, showing the *Calypso* team at work; in 1967 the first 16mm underwater camera with Armand Davso.

Cartoons

Origins (1908)

The forerunner of cartoons was Emile Reynaud's optical theatre of 1893. The scenery was projected behind the screen by a magic lantern, the characters painted on a white background and their successive positions transferred onto a perforated translucent strip. In **1908 J. Stuart Blackton** and **Emile Courtet**, known as Emile Cohl, invented film-strip cartoons. After them, the American Earl Hurd perfected, in 1914, a system which made it unnecessary to draw in the background each time.

Rotoscope (1915)

Invented by the **Fleischer** brothers, pioneers of the American cartoon who created *Betty Boop* and *Popeye*, the rotoscope is a technique which consists of filming a real actor and tracing this film so as to give the cartoon character the same ease of movement. The Fleischer brothers used that system in a feature-length cartoon which has remained famous: *Gulliver's Travels* (1939). The American Ralph Bakshi, a leader in cartoons for adults, used the technique again in his film *Fritz the Cat* (1970) as well as in *Lord of the Rings*. The rotoscopy principle is also used to make a 'mask' to hide unwanted elements such as the models' stands or even the technicians' heads showing behind miniature scenery. This indispensable process is still in use.

Cartoons by superimposition (c.1915)

We owe the first superimposition of cartoon characters on to live action films to the **Fleischer** brothers.

In *Out Inkle* (**1915**) a small cartoon character was seen coming out of a real inkwell and walking on Max Fleischer's drawing board. Due to the transparency and blue screen processes, the technique has continued to improve. Walt Disney productions were the first to extend the process to feature-length films. The most famous are: *The Three Caballeros* (1945) in which Donald Duck seduces a Mexican dancer; *Mary Poppins* (1964) and *Peter and Eliott the Dragon* (1987).

The technique, enhanced by the use of computer-controlled cameras, found its second wind in Bob Zemeckis's *Who Framed Roger Rabbit?* (1988), co-produced by Steven Spielberg and the Disney Studios. In it, actor Bob Hoskins does battle with a band of cartoon characters referred to as 'toons'.

Disney's Multiplane camera (1941)

It was in a short film starring Mickey Mouse, *The Little Whirlwind*, that **Disney Studios** tested a revolutionary camera: the Multiplane. Meant to re-establish the laws of perspective in cartoon films and allowing shots on several planes, the Multiplane camera has accentuated the realism of scenery and the three-dimensional impression.

Bambi (1942) was the first feature-length Disney cartoon to use Multiplane.

Nobel Prize-winners

Physics

1901 Röntgen, Wilhelm Conrad (1845–1923)   Germany
For the discovery of the remarkable rays subsequently
named after him.

1902 Lorentz, Hendrik Antoon (1853–1928)   Netherlands
Zeeman, Pieter (1865–1943)   Netherlands
For their researches into the influence of magnetism upon
radiation phenomena.

1903 Becquerel, Antoine Henri (1852–1908)   France
For his discovery of spontaneous radioactivity.
Curie, Pierre (1859–1906)   France
Curie, Marie, née Sklodowska (1867–1934)   France
For their joint researches on the radiation phenomena
discovered by Professor Henri Becquerel.

1904 Rayleigh, Lord (John William Strutt) (1842–1919)   UK
For his investigations of the densities of the most important
gases and for his discovery of argon.

1905 Lenard, Philipp Eduard Anton (1862–1947)   UK
For his work on cathode rays.

1906 Thomson, Sir Joseph John (1856–1940)   UK
For his theoretical and experimental investigations on the
conduction of electricity by gases.

1907 Michelson, Albert Abraham (1852–1931)   USA
For his optical precision instruments and the spectroscopic
and metrological investigations carried out with their aid.

1908 Lippmann, Gabriel (1845–1921)   France
For reproducing colours photographically based on the
phenomenon of interference.

1909 Marconi, Guglielmo (1874–1937)   Italy
Braun, Carl Ferdinand (1850–1918)   Germany
For their contributions to the development of wireless
telegraphy.

1910 Van Der Waals, Johannes D. (1837–1923)   Netherlands
For his work on the equation of state for gases and liquids.

1911 Wien, Wilhelm (1864–1928)   Germany
For his discoveries regarding the laws governing the
radiation of heat.

1912 Dalén, Nils Gustaf (1869–1937)   Sweden
For his invention of automatic regulators for use in
conjunction with gas accumulators for illuminating
lighthouses and buoys.

1913 Kamerlingh-Onnes, Heike (1853–1926)   Netherlands
For his investigations on the properties of matter at low
temperatures which led, *inter alia*, to the production of
liquid helium.

1914 Von Laue, Max (1879–1960)   Germany
For his discovery of the diffraction of X-rays by crystals.

1915 Bragg, Sir William Henry (1862–1942)   UK
Bragg, Sir William Lawrence (1890–1971)   UK
For their services in the analysis of crystal structure by
means of X-rays.

1917 Barkla, Charles Glover (1877–1944)   UK
For his discovery of the characteristic Röntgen radiation of
the elements.

1918 Planck, Max Karl Ernst Ludwig (1858–1947)   Germany
For his discovery of energy quanta.

1919 Stark, Johannes (1874–1957)   Germany
For his discovery of the Doppler effect in canal rays and
the splitting of spectral lines in electric fields.

1920 Guillaume, Charles Edouard (1861–1938)   Switzerland
For his discovery of anomalies in nickel steel alloys.

1921 Einstein, Albert (1879–1955)   Germany and Switzerland
For his discovery of the law of the photoelectric effect.

1922 Bohr, Niels (1885–1962)   Denmark
For his services in the investigation of the structure of atoms
and of the radiation emanating from them.

1923 Millikan, Robert Andrews (1868–1953)   USA
For his work on the elementary charge of electricity and on
the photoelectric effect.

1924 Siegbahn, Karl Manne Georg (1886–1978)   Sweden
For his discoveries and research in the field of X-ray
spectroscopy.

1925 Franck, James (1882–1964)   Germany
Hertz, Gustav (1887–1975)   Germany
For their discovery of the laws governing the impact of an
electron upon an atom.

1926 Perrin, Jean Baptiste (1870–1942)   France
For his work on the discontinuous structure of matter, and
especially for his discovery of sedimentation equilibrium.

1927 Compton, Arthur Holly (1892–1962)   USA
For his discovery of the effect named after him.
Wilson, Charles Thomson Rees (1869–1959)   UK
For his method of making the paths of electrically charged
particles visible by condensation of vapour.

1928 Richardson, Sir Owen Willans (1879–1959)   UK
For his work on the thermionic phenomenon and especially
for the discovery of the law named after him.

1929 De Broglie, Prince Louis-Victor (1892–1987)   France
For his discovery of the wave nature of electrons.

1930 Raman, Sir Chandrasekhara Venkata (1888–1970)   India
For his work on the scattering of light and for the discovery
of the effect named after him.

1932 Heisenberg, Werner (1901–1976)   Germany
For the creation of quantum mechanics, the application of
which has, *inter alia*, led to the discovery of the allotropic
forms of hydrogen.

1933 **Schrödinger, Erwin** (1887–1961) Austria
Dirac, Paul Adrien Maurice (1902–1984) UK
For the discovery of new productive forms of atomic theory.

1935 **Chadwick, Sir James** (1891–1974) UK
For the discovery of the neutron.

1936 **Hess, Victor Franz** (1883–1964) Austria
For his discovery of cosmic radiation.
Anderson, Carl David (1905–) USA
For his discovery of the positron.

1937 **Davisson, Clinton Joseph** (1881–1958) USA
Thomson, Sir George Paget (1892–1975) UK
For their experimental discovery of the diffraction of
electrons by crystals.

1938 **Fermi, Enrico** (1901–1954) Italy
For his demonstrations of the existence of new radioactive
elements produced by neutron irradiation, and for his
related discovery of nuclear reactions brought about by
slow neutrons.

1939 **Lawrence, Ernest Orlando** (1901–1958) USA
For the invention and development of the cyclotron and for
results obtained with it, especially with regard to artificial
radioactive elements.

1943 **Stern, Otto** (1888–1969) USA
For his contribution to the development of the molecular
ray method and his discovery of the magnetic moment of
the proton.

1944 **Rabi, Isidor Isaac** (1898–1988) USA
For his resonance method for recording the magnetic
properties of atomic nuclei.

1945 **Pauli, Wolfgang** (1900–1958) Austria
For the discovery of the Pauli Principle.

1946 **Bridgman, Percy Williams** (1882–1961) USA
For the invention of an apparatus to produce extremely
high pressures, and the discoveries made therewith in the
field of high pressure physics.

1947 **Appleton, Sir Edward Victor** (1892–1965) UK
For his investigations of the physics of the upper
atmosphere especially for the discovery of the so-called
Appleton layer.

1948 **Blackett, Lord Patrick Maynard Stuart** (1897–1974) UK
For his development of the Wilson cloud chamber method,
and his discoveries therewith in the fields of nuclear
physics and cosmic radiation.

1949 **Yukawa, Hideki** (1907–1981) Japan
For his prediction of the existence of mesons on the basis of
theoretical work on nuclear forces.

1950 **Powell, Cecil Frank** (1903–1969) UK
For his development of the photographic method of
studying nuclear processes and his discoveries regarding
mesons made with this method.

1951 **Cockcroft, Sir John Douglas** (1897–1967) UK
Walton, Ernest Thomas Sinton (1903–) Ireland
For their pioneer work on the transmutation of atomic
nuclei by artificially accelerated atomic particles.

1952 **Bloch, Felix** (1905–1983) USA
Purcell, Edward Mills (1912–) USA
For their development of new methods for nuclear
magnetic precision measurements and discoveries in
connection therewith.

1953 **Zernike, Frits (Frederik)** (1888–1966) Netherlands
For his demonstration of the phase contrast method,

especially for his invention of the phase contrast
microscope.

1954 **Born, Max** (1882–1970) UK
For his fundamental research in quantum mechanics,
especially for his statistical interpretation of the wave
function.
Bothe, Walther (1891–1957) W. Germany
For the coincidence method and his discoveries made
therewith.

1955 **Lamb, Willis Eugene** (1913–) USA
For his discoveries concerning the fine structure of the
hydrogen spectrum.
Kusch, Polykarp (1911–) USA
For his precision determination of the magnetic moment of
the electron.

1956 **Shockley, William** (1910–) USA
Bardeen, John (1908–) USA
Brattain, Walter Houser (1902–1987) USA
For their researches on semiconductors and their discovery
of the transistor effect.

1957 **Yang, Cheng Ning** (1922–) China
Lee, Tsung-Dao (1926–) China
For their penetrating investigation of the so-called parity
laws which has led to important discoveries regarding the
elementary particles.

1958 **Cerenkov, Pavel Aleksejvic** (1904–) USSR
Frank, Il'ja Michajlovic (1908–) USSR
Tamm, Igor Jevgen'evic (1895–1971) USSR
For the discovery and the interpretation of the Cerenkov
effect.

1959 **Segrè, Emilio Gino** (1905–1989) USA
Chamberlain, Owen (1920–) USA
For their discovery of the antiproton.

1960 **Glaser, Donald A.** (1926–) USA
For the invention of the bubble chamber.

1961 **Hofstadter, Robert** (1915–) USA
For his pioneering studies of electron scattering in atomic
nuclei and his discoveries concerning the structure of the
nucleons.
Mössbauer, Rudolf Ludvig (1929–) W. Germany
For his researches concerning the resonance absorption of
gamma radiation and his discovery of the effect which
bears his name.

1962 **Landau, Lev Davidovic** (1908–1968) USSR
For his pioneering theories for condensed matter,
especially liquid helium.

1963 **Wigner, Eugene P.** (1902–) USA
For his contributions to the theory of the atomic nucleus and
the elementary particles, particularly through the discovery
and application of fundamental symmetry principles.
Goeppert-Mayer, Maria (1906–1972) USA
Jensen, J. Hans D. (1907–1973) W. Germany
For their discoveries concerning nuclear shell structure.

1964 **Townes, Charles Hard** (1915–) USA
Basov, Nicolai Gennadievic (1922–) USSR
Prochorov, Aleksandre Mikhailovic (1916–) USSR
For fundamental work in the field of quantum electronics,
which has led to the construction of oscillators and
amplifiers based on the maser-laser principle.

1965 **Tomonaga, Sin-Itiro** (1906–1979) Japan
Schwinger, Julian (1918–) USA
Feynman, Richard P. (1918–1988) USA
For their fundamental work in quantum electrodynamics,
with deep-ploughing consequences for the physics of
elementary particles.

1966 **Kastler, Alfred** (1902–1984)   France
For the discovery and development of optical methods for
studying Hertzian resonances in atoms.

1967 **Bethe, Hans Albrecht** (1906–)   USA
For his contributions to the theory of nuclear reactions,
especially his discoveries concerning the energy
production in stars.

1968 **Alvarez, Luis W.** (1911–1988)   USA
For his decisive contributions to elementary particle
physics, in particular the discovery of a large number of
resonance states, made possible through his development
of the technique of using hydrogen bubble chamber and
data analysis.

1969 **Gell-Mann, Murray** (1929–)   USA
For his contributions and discoveries concerning the
classification of elementary particles and their interactions.

1970 **Alfvén, Hannes** (1908–)   Sweden
For fundamental work and discoveries in magneto-
hydrodynamics with fruitful applications in different parts of
plasma physics.
Néél, Louis (1904–)   France
For fundamental work and discoveries concerning
antiferromagnetism and ferrimagnetism which have led to
important applications in solid state physics.

1971 **Gabor, Dennis** (1900–1979)   UK
For his invention and development of the holographic
method.

1972 **Bardeen, John** (1908–)   USA
Cooper, Leon N. (1930–)   USA
Schrieffer, J. Robert (1931–)   USA
For their jointly developed theory of superconductivity,
usually called the BCS-theory.

1973 **Esaki, Leo** (1925–)   Japan
Giaever, Ivar (1929–)   USA
For their experimental discoveries regarding tunnelling
phenomena in semiconductors and superconductors,
respectively.
Josephson, Brian D. (1940–)   UK
For his theoretical predictions of the properties of a
supercurrent through a tunnel barrier, especially the
Josephson effects.

1974 **Ryle, Sir Martin** (1918–1984)   UK
Hewish, Antony (1924–)   UK
For their pioneering research in radio astrophysics: Ryle
for his observations and inventions of the aperture synthesis
technique, and Hewish for his decisive role in the
discovery of pulsars.

1975 **Bohr, Aage** (1922–)   Denmark
Mottelson, Ben (1926–)   Denmark
Rainwater, James (1917–1986)   USA
For the discovery of the connection between collective
motion and particle motion in atomic nuclei and the
development of the theory of the structure of the atomic
nucleus based on this connection.

1976 **Richter, Burton** (1931–)   USA
Ting, Samuel C. C. (1936–)   USA
For their pioneering work in the discovery of a heavy
elementary particle of a new kind.

1977 **Anderson, Philip W.** (1923–)   USA
Mott, Sir Nevill F. (1905–)   UK
Van Vleck, John H. (1899–1980)   USA
For their fundamental theoretical investigations of the
electronic structure of magnetic and disordered systems.

1978 **Kapitsa, Peter Leonidovitch** (1894–1984)   USSR
For his basic inventions and discoveries in the area of

low-temperature physics.
Penzias, Arno A. (1933–)   USA
Wilson, Robert W. (1936–)   USA
For their discovery of cosmic microwave background
radiation.

1979 **Glashow, Sheldon L.** (1932–)   USA
Salam, Abdus (1926–)   Pakistan
Weinberg, Steven (1933–)   USA
For their contributions to the theory of the unified weak and
electromagnetic interaction between elementary particles,
including *inter alia* the prediction of the weak neutral
current.

1980 **Cronin, James, W.** (1931–)   USA
Fitch, Val L. (1923–)   USA
For the discovery of violations of fundamental symmetry
principles in the decay of neutral K-mesons.

1981 **Bloembergen, Nicolaas** (1920–)   USA
Schawlow, Arthur L. (1921–)   USA
For their contribution to the development of laser
spectroscopy.
Siegbahn, Kai M. (1918–)   Sweden
For his contribution to the development of high-resolution
electron spectroscopy.

1982 **Wilson, Kenneth G.** (1936–)   USA
For his theory for critical phenomena in connection with
phase transitions.

1983 **Chandrasekhar, Subramanyan** (1910–)   USA
For his theoretical studies of the physical processes of
importance to the structure and evolution of the stars.
Fowler, William A. (1911–)   USA
For his theoretical and experimental studies of the nuclear
reactions of importance in the formation of the chemical
elements in the universe.

1984 **Rubbia, Carlo** (1934–)   Italy
Van Der Meer, Simon (1925–)   Netherlands
For their decisive contributions to the large project which
led to the discovery of the field particles W and Z,
communicators of weak interaction.

1985 **Von Klitzing, Klaus** (1943–)   W. Germany
For the discovery of the quantised Hall effect.

1986 **Ruska, Ernst** (1906–1988)   W. Germany
For his fundamental work in electron optics, and for the
design of the first electron microscope.
Binnig, Gerd (1947–)   W. Germany
Rohrer, Heinrich (1933–)   Switzerland
For their design of the scanning tunnelling microscope.

1987 **Bednorz, J. Georg** (1950–)   W. Germany
Müller, K. Alexander (1927–)   Switzerland
For their important breakthrough in the discovery of
superconductivity in ceramic materials.

1988 **Lederman, Leon M.** (1922–)   USA
Schwartz, Melvin (1932–)   USA
Steinberger, Jack (1921–)   USA
For the neutrino beam method and the demonstration of the
doublet structure of the leptons through the discovery of the
muon neutrino.

1989 **Ramsey, Norman F.** (1915–)   USA
For the invention of the separated oscillatory fields method
and its use in the hydrogen maser and other atomic clocks.
Dehmelt, Hans G. (1922–)   USA
Paul, Wolfgang (1913–)   W. Germany
For the development of the ion trap technique.

1990 **Friedman, Jerome I.** (1930–)   USA
Kendall, Henry W. (1926–)   USA
Taylor, Richard E. (1929–)   Canada

For their pioneering investigations concerning deep inelastic scattering of electrons on protons and bound neutrons, which have been of essential importance for the development of the quark model in particle physics.

Chemistry

1901 Van't Hoff, Jacobus Henricus (1852–1911)   Netherlands
For the discovery of the laws of chemical dynamics and osmotic pressure in solutions.

1902 Fischer, Hermann Emil (1852–1919)   Germany
For his work on sugar and purine syntheses.

1903 Arrhenius, Svante August (1859–1927)   Sweden
For his electrolytic theory of dissociation.

1904 Ramsay, Sir William (1852–1916)   UK
For the discovery of the inert gaseous elements in air, and his determination of their place in the periodic system.

1905 Von Baeyer, Johann Adolf (1835–1917)   Germany
For his services in the advancement of organic chemistry and the chemical industry, through his work on organic dyes and hydroaromatic compounds.

1906 Moissan, Henri (1852–1907)   France
For his investigation and isolation of the element fluorine, and for the adoption in the service of science of the electric furnace called after him.

1907 Buchner, Eduard (1860–1917)   Germany
For his biochemical researches and his discovery of cell-free fermentation.

1908 Rutherford, Lord Ernest (1871–1937)   UK
For his investigations into the disintegration of the elements, and the chemistry of radioactive substances.

1909 Ostwald, Wilhelm (1853–1932)   Germany
For his work on catalysis and for his investigations into the fundamental principles governing chemical equilibria and rates of reaction.

1910 Wallach, Otto (1847–1931)   Germany
For his services to organic chemistry and the chemical industry by his pioneer work in the field of alicyclic compounds.

1911 Curie, Marie, née Sklodowska (1867–1934)   France
For the discovery of the elements radium and polonium, by the isolation of radium and the study of the nature and compounds of this remarkable element.

1912 Grignard, Victor (1871–1935)   France
For the discovery of the so-called Grignard reagent, which in recent years has greatly advanced the progress of organic chemistry.
Sabatier, Paul (1854–1941)   France
For his method of hydrogenating organic compounds in the presence of finely disintegrated metals.

1913 Werner, Alfred (1866–1919)   Switzerland
For his work on the linkage of atoms in molecules by which he has opened up new fields of research especially in inorganic chemistry.

1914 Richards, Theodore William (1868–1928)   USA
For his accurate determinations of the atomic weight of a large number of chemical elements.

1915 Willstätter, Richard Martin (1872–1942)   Germany
For his researches on plant pigments, especially chlorophyll.

1918 Haber, Fritz (1868–1934)   Germany
For the synthesis of ammonia from its elements.

1920 Nernst, Walther Hermann (1864–1941)   Germany
For his work in thermochemistry.

1921 Soddy, Frederick (1877–1956)   UK
For his contributions to our knowledge of the chemistry of radioactive substances, and his investigations into the origin and nature of isotopes.

1922 Aston, Francis William (1877–1945)   UK
For his discovery, by means of his mass spectrograph, of isotopes, in a large number of non-radioactive elements, and for his enunciation of the whole-number rule.

1923 Pregl, Fritz (1869–1930)   Austria
For his invention of the method of micro-analysis of organic substances.

1925 Zsigmondy, Richard Adolf (1865–1929)   Germany
For his demonstration of the heterogenous nature of colloid solutions and for the methods he used, which have since become fundamental in modern colloid chemistry.

1926 Svedberg, The (Theodor) (1884–1971)   Sweden
For his work on disperse systems.

1927 Wieland, Heinrich Otto (1877–1957)   Germany
For his investigations of the constitution of the bile acids and related substances.

1928 Windaus, Adolf Otto Reinhold (1876–1959)   Germany
For his research into the constitution of the sterols and their connection with the vitamins.

1929 Harden, Sir Arthur (1865–1940)   UK
Von Euler-Chelpin, Hans (1873–1964)   Sweden
For their investigations on the fermentation of sugar and fermentative enzymes.

1930 Fischer, Hans (1881–1945)   Germany
For his researches into the constitution of haemin and chlorophyll and especially for his synthesis of haemin.

1931 Bosch, Carl (1874–1940)   Germany
Bergius, Friedrich (1884–1949)   Germany
For their contributions to the invention and development of chemical high pressure methods.

1932 Langmuir, Irving (1881–1957)   USA
For his discoveries and investigations in surface chemistry.

1934 Urey, Harold Clayton (1893–1981)   USA
For his discovery of heavy hydrogen.

1935 Joliot, Frédéric (1900–1958)   France
Joliot-Curie, Irène (1897–1956)   France
For their synthesis of new radioactive elements.

1936 Debye, Petrus Josephus W. (1894–1966)   Netherlands
For his contribution to our knowledge of molecular structure through his investigations on dipole moments and on the diffraction of X-rays and electrons in gases.

1937 Haworth, Sir Walter Norman (1883–1950)   UK
For his investigations on carbohydrates and vitamin C.
Karrer, Paul (1889–1971)   Switzerland
For his investigations on carotenoids, flavins and vitamins A and B2.

1938 Kuhn, Richard (1900–1967)   Germany
For his work on carotenoids and vitamins.

1939 Butenandt, Adolf Friedrich Johann (1903–)   Germany
For his work on sex hormones.
Ruzicka, Leopold (1887–1976)   Switzerland
For his work on polymethylenes and higher terpenes.

1943 De Hevesy, George (1885–1966)   Hungary
For his work on the use of isotopes as tracers in the study of
chemical processes.

1944 Hahn, Otto (1879–1968)   Germany
For his discovery of the fission of heavy nuclei.

1945 Virtanen, Artturi Ilmari (1895–1973)   Finland
For his research and inventions in agricultural and nutrition
chemistry, especially for his fodder preservation method.

1946 Sumner, James Batcheller (1887–1955)   USA
For his discovery that enzymes can be crystallised.
Northrop, John Howard (1891–1987)   USA
Stanley, Wendell Meredith (1904–1971)   USA
For their preparation of enzymes and virus proteins in a
pure form.

1947 Robinson, Sir Robert (1886–1975)   UK
For his investigations on plant products of biological
importance, especially the alkaloids.

1948 Tiselius, Arne Wilhelm Kaurin (1902–1971)   Sweden
For his research on electrophoresis and absorption
analysis, especially for his discoveries concerning the
complex nature of the serum proteins.

1949 Giauque, William Francis (1895–1982)   USA
For his contributions in the field of chemical
thermodynamics, particularly concerning the behaviour of
substances at extremely low temperatures.

1950 Diels, Otto (1876–1954)   W. Germany
Alder, Kurt (1902–1958)   W. Germany
For their discovery and development of the diene
synthesis.

1951 McMillan, Edwin Mattison (1907–)   USA
Seaborg, Glenn Theodore (1912–)   USA
For their discoveries in the chemistry of the transuranium
elements.

1952 Martin, Archer John Porter (1910–)   UK
Synge, Richard Laurence Millington (1914–)   UK
For their invention of partition chromatography.

1953 Staudinger, Hermann (1881–1965)   W. Germany
For his discoveries in the field of macromolecular
chemistry.

1954 Pauling, Linus Carl (1901–)   USA
For his research into the nature of the chemical bond and
its application to the elucidation of the structure of complex
substances.

1955 Du Vigneaud, Vincent (1901–1978)   USA
For his work on biochemically important sulphur
compounds, especially for the first synthesis of a
polypeptide hormone.

1956 Hinshel Wood, Sir Cyril Norman (1897–1967)   UK
Semenov, Nikolaj Nikolajevic (1896–1986)   USSR
For their researches into the mechanism of chemical
reactions.

1957 Todd, Lord Alexander (1907–)   UK
For his work on nucleotides and nucleotide co-enzymes.

1958 Sanger, Frederick (1918–)   UK
For his work on the structure of proteins, especially that of
insulin.

1959 Heyrovsky, Jaroslav (1890–1967)   Czechoslovakia
For his discovery and development of the polarographic
methods of analysis.

1960 Libby, Willard Frank (1908–1980)   USA
For his method to use carbon-14 for age determination in
archaeology and other branches of science.

1961 Calvin, Melvin (1911)   USA
For his research on the carbon dioxide assimilation in
plants.

1962 Perutz, Max Ferdinand (1914–)   UK
Kendrew, Sir John Cowdery (1917–)   UK
For their studies of the structures of globular proteins.

1963 Ziegler, Karl (1898–1973)   W. Germany
Natta, Giulio (1903–1979)   Italy
For their discoveries in the field of the chemistry and
technology of high polymers.

1964 Hodgkin, Dorothy Crowfoot (1910–)   UK
For her determinations by X-ray techniques of the
structures of important biochemical substances.

1965 Woodward, Robert Burns (1917–1979)   USA
For his outstanding achievements in the art of organic
synthesis.

1966 Mulliken, Robert S. (1896–1986)   USA
For his fundamental work concerning chemical bonds and
the electronic structure of molecules by the molecular
orbital method.

1967 Eigen, Manfred (1927–)   W. Germany
Norrish, Ronald George Wreyford (1897–1978)   UK
Porter, Sir George (1920–)   UK
For their studies of extremely fast chemical reactions,
effected by disturbing the equilibrium by means of very
short pulses of energy.

1968 Onsager, Lars (1903–1976)   USA
For the discovery of the reciprocal relations bearing his
name, which are fundamental for the thermodynamics of
irreversible processes.

1969 Barton, Sir Derek H. R. (1918–)   UK
Hassel, Odd (1897–1981)   Norway
For their contributions to the development of the concept of
conformation and its application in chemistry.

1970 Leloir, Luis F. (1906–)   Argentina
For his discovery of sugar nucleotides and their role in the
biosynthesis of carbohydrates.

1971 Herzberg, Gerhard (1904–)   Canada
For his contributions to the knowledge of electronic
structure and geometry of molecules, particularly free
radicals.

1972 Anfinsen, Christian B. (1916–)   USA
For his work on ribonuclease, especially concerning the
connection between the amino acid sequence and the
biologically active confirmation.
Moore, Stanford (1913–1982)   USA
Stein, William H. (1911–1980)   USA
For their contribution to the understanding of the
connection between chemical structure and catalytic
activity of the active centre of the ribonuclease molecule.

1973 Fischer, Ernst Otto (1918–)   W. Germany
Wilkinson, Sir Geoffrey (1921–)   UK
For their pioneering work, performed independently, on
the chemistry of the organo-metallic, so-called sandwich,
compounds.

1974 **Flory, Paul, J.** (1910–1985) USA
For his fundamental achievements in the physical chemistry of the macromolecules.

1975 **Cornforth, Sir John Warcup** (1917–) Australia and UK
For his work on the stereochemistry of enzyme-catalysed reactions.
Prelog, Vladimir (1906–) Switzerland
For his research into the stereochemistry of organic molecules and reactions.

1976 **Lipscomb, William N.** (1919–) USA
For his studies on the structure of boranes illuminating problems of chemical bonding.

1977 **Prigogine, Ilya** (1917–) Belgium
For his contributions to non-equilibrium thermodynamics, particularly the theory of dissipative structures.

1978 **Mitchell, Peter D.** (1920–) UK
For his contribution to the understanding of biological energy transfer through the formulation of the chemiosmotic theory.

1979 **Brown, Herbert C.** (1912–) USA
Wittig, Georg (1897–) W. Germany
For their development of the use of boron- and phosphorus-containing compounds, respectively, into important reagents in organic synthesis.

1980 **Berg, Paul** (1926–) USA
For his fundamental studies of the biochemistry of nucleic acids, with particular regard to recombinant-DNA.
Gilbert, Walter (1932–) USA
Sanger, Frederick (1918–) UK
For their contributions concerning the determination of base sequences in nucleic acids.

1981 **Fukui, Kenichi** (1918–) Japan
Hoffmann, Roald (1937–) USA
For their theories, developed independently, concerning the course of chemical reactions.

1982 **Klug, Aaron** (1926–) UK
For his development of crystallographic electron microscopy and his structural elucidation of biologically important nuclei acid-protein complexes.

1983 **Taube, Henry** (1915–) USA
For his work on the mechanisms of electron transfer reactions, especially in metal complexes.

1984 **Merrifield, Robert Bruce** (1921–) USA
For his development of methodology for chemical synthesis on a solid matrix.

1985 **Hauptman, Herbert A.** (1917–) USA
Karle, Jerome (1918–) USA
For their outstanding achievements in the development of direct methods for the determination of crystal structures.

1986 **Herschbach, Dudley R.** (1932–) USA
Lee, Yuan T. (1936–) USA
Polanyi, John C. (1929–) Canada
For their contributions concerning the dynamics of chemical elementary processes.

1987 **Cram, Donald J.** (1919–) USA
Lehn, Jean-Marie (1939–) France
Pedersen, Charles J. (1904–) USA
For their development and use of molecules with structure-specific interactions of high selectivity.

1988 **Deisenhofer, Johann** (1943–) W. Germany
Huber, Robert (1937–) W. Germany
Michel, Hartmut (1948–) W. Germany
For the determination of the 3-D structure of a photosynthetic reaction centre.

1989 **Altman, Sidney** (1939–) USA and Canada
Cech, Thomas R. (1947–) USA
For their discovery of catalytic properties of RNA.

1990 **Corey, Elias J.** (1928–) USA
For his development of the theory and methodology of organic synthesis.

Physiology or Medicine

1901 **Von Behring, Emil** (1854–1917) Germany
For his work on serum therapy, especially its application against diphtheria.

1902 **Ross, Sir Ronald** (1857–1932) UK
For his work on malaria, showing how it enters the organism.

1903 **Finsen, Niels Ryberg** (1860–1904) Denmark
For his treatment of diseases, especially lupus vulgaris, with concentrated light radiation.

1904 **Pavlov, Ivan Petrovic** (1849–1936) Russia
For his work on the physiology of digestion.

1905 **Koch, Robert** (1843–1910) Germany
For his investigations and discoveries in relation to tuberculosis.

1906 **Golgi, Camillo** (1843–1926) Italy
Ramon Y Cajal, Santiago (1852–1934) Spain
For their work on the structure of the nervous system.

1907 **Laveran, Charles Louis Alphonse** (1845–1922) France
For his work on the role played by protozoa in causing diseases.

1908 **Mecnikov, Ilja Il'jic** (1845–1916) Russia
Ehrlich, Paul (1854–1915) Germany
For their work on immunity.

1909 **Kocher, Emil Theodor** (1841–1917) Switzerland
For his work on the physiology, pathology and surgery of the thyroid gland.

1910 **Kossel, Albrecht** (1853–1927) Germany
For contributions to our knowledge of cell chemistry made through his work on proteins, including the nucleic substances.

1911 **Gullstrand, Allvar** (1862–1930) Sweden
For his work on the dioptrics of the eye.

1912 **Carrel, Alexis** (1873–1944) France
For his work on vascular suture and the transplantation of blood-vessels and organs.

1913 **Richet, Charles Robert** (1850–1935) France
For his work on anaphylaxis.

1914 **Bárány, Robert** (1876–1936) Austria
For his work on the physiology and pathology of the vestibular apparatus.

1919 **Bordet, Jules** (1870–1961) Belgium
For his discoveries relating to immunity.

1920 **Krogh, Schack August Steenberger** (1874–1949) Denmark
For his discovery of the capillary motor regulating mechanism.

1922 **Hill, Sir Archibald Vivian** (1886–1977)   UK
For his discovery relating to the production of heat in the muscle.
Meyerhof, Otto Fritz (1884–1951)   Germany
For his discovery of the fixed relationship between the consumption of oxygen and the metabolism of lactid acid in the muscle.

1923 **Banting, Sir Frederick Grant** (1891–1941)   Canada
Macleod, John James Richard (1876–1935)   Canada
For the discovery of insulin.

1924 **Einthoven, Willem** (1860–1927)   Netherlands
For his discovery of the mechanism of the electrocardiogram.

1926 **Fibiger, Johannes Andreas Grib** (1867–1928)   Denmark
For his discovery of the Spiroptera carcinoma.

1927 **Wagner-Jauregg, Julius** (1857–1940)   Austria
For his discovery of the therapeutic value of malaria inoculation in the treatment of dementia paralytica.

1928 **Nicolle, Charles Jules Henri** (1866–1936)   France
For his work on typhus.

1929 **Eijkman, Christiaan** (1858–1930)   Netherlands
For his discovery of the anti-neuritic vitamin.
Hopkins, Sir Frederick Gowland (1861–1947)   UK
For his discovery of the growth-stimulating vitamins.

1930 **Landsteiner, Karl** (1868–1943)   Austria
For his discovery of human blood groups.

1931 **Warburg, Otto Heinrich** (1883–1970)   Germany
For his discovery of the nature and mode of action of the respiratory enzyme.

1932 **Sherrington, Sir Charles Scott** (1857–1952)   UK
Adrian, Lord Edgar Douglas (1889–1977)   UK
For their discoveries regarding the functions of neurons.

1933 **Morgan, Thomas Hunt** (1866–1945)   USA
For his discoveries concerning the role played by the chromosome in heredity.

1934 **Whipple, George Hoyt** (1878–1976)   USA
Minot, George Richards (1885–1950)   USA
Murphy, William Parry (1892–1987)   USA
For their discoveries concerning liver therapy in cases of anaemia.

1935 **Spemann, Hans** (1869–1941)   Germany
For his discovery of the organiser effect in embryonic development.

1936 **Dale, Sir Henry Hallett** (1875–1968)   UK
Loewi, Otto (1873–1961)   Austria
For their discoveries relating to chemical transmission of nerve impulses.

1937 **Szent-Györgyi, Albert** (1893–1986)   Hungary
For his discoveries in connection with the biological combustion processes, with special reference to vitamin C and the catalysis of fumaric acid.

1938 **Heymans, Corneille Jean** (1892–1968)   Belgium
For the discovery of the role played by the sinus and aortic mechanisms in the regulation of respiration.

1939 **Domagk, Gerhard** (1895–1964)   Germany
For the discovery of the anti-bacterial effects of prontosil.

1943 **Dam, Henrik Carl Peter** (1895–1976)   Denmark
For his discovery of vitamin K.
Doisy, Edward Adelbert (1893–1986)   USA
For his discovery of the chemical nature of vitamin K.

1944 **Erlanger, Joseph** (1874–1965)   USA
Gasser, Herbert Spencer (1888–1963)   USA
For their discoveries relating to the highly differentiated functions of single nerve fibres.

1945 **Fleming, Sir Alexander** (1881–1955)   UK
Chain, Sir Ernst Boris (1906–1979)   UK
Florey, Lord Howard Walter (1898–1968)   UK
For the discovery of penicillin and its curative effect in various infectious diseases.

1946 **Muller, Hermann Joseph** (1890–1967)   USA
For the discovery of the production of mutations by means of X-ray irradiation.

1947 **Cori, Carl Ferdinand** (1896–1984)   USA
Cori, Gerty Theresa, née Radnitz (1896–1957)   USA
For their discovery of the course of the catalytic conversion of glycogen.
Houssay, Bernardo Alberto (1887–1971)   Argentina
For his discovery of the part played by the hormone of the anterior pituitary lobe in the metabolism of sugar.

1948 **Müller, Paul Hermann** (1899–1965)   Switzerland
For his discovery of the high efficiency of DDT as a contact poison against several arthropods.

1949 **Hess, Walter Rudolf** (1881–1973)   Switzerland
For his discovery of the functional organisation of the interbrain as a co-ordinator of the activities of the internal organs.
Moniz, Antonio Egas (1874–1955)   Portugal
For his discovery of the therapeutic value of leucotomy in certain psychoses.

1950 **Kendall, Edward Calvin** (1886–1972)   USA
Reichstein, Tadeus (1897–)   Switzerland
Hench, Philip Showalter (1896–1965)   USA
For their discoveries relating to the hormones of the adrenal cortex, their structure and biological effects.

1951 **Theiler, Max** (1899–1972)   South Africa
For his discoveries concerning yellow fever and how to combat it.

1952 **Waksman, Selman Abraham** (1888–1973)   USA
For his discovery of streptomycin, the first antibiotic effective against tuberculosis.

1953 **Krebs, Sir Hans Adolf** (1900–1981)   UK
For his discovery of the citric acid cycle.
Lipmann, Fritz Albert (1899–1986)   USA
For his discovery of co-enzyme A and its importance for intermediary metabolism.

1954 **Enders, John Franklin** (1897–1985)   USA
Weller, Thomas Huckle (1915–)   USA
Robbins, Frederick Chapman (1916–)   USA
For their discovery of the ability of poliomyelitis viruses to grow in cultures of various types of tissue.

1955 **Theorell, Axel Hugo Theodor** (1903–1982)   Sweden
For his discoveries concerning the nature and mode of action of oxidation enzymes.

1956 **Cournand, André Frédéric** (1895–1988)   USA
Forssmann, Werner (1904–1979)   W. Germany
Richards, Dickinson W. (1895–1973)   USA
For their discoveries concerning heart catherisation and pathological changes in the circulatory system.

1957 **Bovet, Daniel** (1907–)   Italy
For his discoveries relating to synthetic compounds that inhibit the action of certain body substances, and especially their action on the vascular system and the skeletal muscles.

1958 **Beadle, George Wells** (1903–) USA
Tatum, Edward Lawrie (1909–1975) USA
For their discovery that genes act by regulating definite chemical events.
Lederberg, Joshua (1925–) USA
For his discoveries concerning genetic recombination and the organisation of the genetic material of bacteria.

1959 **Ochoa, Severo** (1905–) USA
Kornberg, Arthur (1918–) USA
For their discovery of the mechanisms in the biological synthesis of ribonucleic acid and deoxiribonucleic acid.

1960 **Burnet, Sir Frank Macfarlane** (1899–1985) Australia
Medawar, Sir Peter Brian (1915–) UK
For discovery of acquired immunological tolerance.

1961 **Von Békésy, Georg** (1899–1972) USA
For his discoveries of the physical mechanism of stimulation within the cochlea.

1962 **Crick, Francis Harry Compton** (1916–) UK
Watson, James Dewey (1928) USA
Wilkins, Maurice Hugh Frederick (1916–) UK
For their discoveries concerning the molecular structure of nuclear acids and its significance for information transfer in living material.

1963 **Eccles, Sir John Carew** (1903–) Australia
Hodgkin, Sir Alan Lloyd (1914–) UK
Huxley, Sir Andrew Fielding (1917–) UK
For their discoveries concerning the ionic mechanisms involved in excitation and inhibition in the peripheral and central portions of the nerve cell membrane.

1964 **Bloch, Konrad** (1912–) USA
Lynen, Feodor (1911–1979) W. Germany
For their discoveries concerning the mechanism and regulation of the cholesterol and fatty acid metabolism.

1965 **Jacob, François** (1920–) France
Lwoff, André (1902–) France
Monod, Jacques (1910–1976) France
For their discoveries concerning genetic control of enzyme and virus synthesis.

1966 **Rous, Peyton** (1879–1970) USA
For his discovery of tumour-inducing viruses.
Huggins, Charles Brenton (1901–) USA
For his discoveries concerning hormonal treatment of prostatic cancer.

1967 **Granit, Ragnar** (1900–) Sweden
Hartline, Haldan Keffer (1903–1983) USA
Wald, George (1906–) USA
For their discoveries concerning the primary physiological and chemical visual processes in the eye.

1968 **Holley, Robert W.** (1922–) USA
Khorana, Har Gobind (1922–) USA
Nirenberg, Marshall W. (1927–) USA
For their interpretation of the genetic code and its function in protein synthesis.

1969 **Delbrück, Max** (1906–1981) USA
Hershey, Alfred D. (1908–) USA
Luria, Salvador E. (1912–) USA
For their discoveries concerning the replication mechanism and the genetic structure of viruses.

1970 **Katz, Sir Bernard** (1911–) UK
Von Euler, Ulf (1905–1983) Sweden
Axelrod, Julius (1912–) USA
For their discoveries concerning the humoral transmitters in the nerve terminals and the mechanism for their storage, release and inactivation.

1971 **Sutherland, Earl W. Jr.** (1915–1974) USA
For his discoveries concerning the mechanisms of the action of hormones.

1972 **Edelman, Gerald M.** (1929–) USA
Porter, Rodney R. (1917–1985) UK
For their discoveries concerning the chemical structure of antibodies.

1973 **Von Frisch, Karl** (1886–1982) W. Germany
Lorenz, Konrad (1903–1989) Austria
Tinbergen, Nikolaas (1907–) UK
For their discoveries concerning organisation and elicitation of individual and social behaviour patterns.

1974 **Claude, Albert** (1899–1983) Belgium
De Duve, Christian (1917–) Belgium
Palade, George E. (1912–) USA
For their discoveries concerning the structural and functional organisation of the cell.

1975 **Baltimore, David** (1938–) USA
Dulbecco, Renato (1914–) USA
Temin, Howard Martin (1934–) USA
For their discoveries concerning the interaction between tumour viruses and the genetic material of the cell.

1976 **Blumberg, Baruch S.** (1925–) USA
Gajdusek, D. Carleton (1923–) USA
For their discoveries concerning new mechanisms for the origin and dissemination of infectious diseases.

1977 **Guillemin, Roger** (1924–) USA
Schally, Andrew V. (1926–) USA
For their discoveries concerning the peptide hormone production of the brain.
Yalow, Rosalyn (1921–) USA
For the development of radio-immunoassays of peptide hormones.

1978 **Arber, Werner** (1929–) Switzerland
Nathans, Daniel (1928–) USA
Smith, Hamilton O. (1931–) USA
For the discovery of restriction enzymes and their application to problems of molecular genetics.

1979 **Cormack, Allan M.** (1924–) USA
Hounsfield, Sir Godfrey N. (1919–) UK
For the development of computer assisted tomography.

1980 **Benacerraf, Baruj** (1920–) USA
Dausset, Jean (1916–) France
Snell, George D. (1903–) USA
For their discoveries concerning genetically determined structures on the cell surface that regulate immunological reactions.

1981 **Sperry, Roger W.** (1913–) USA
For his discoveries concerning the functional specialisation of the cerebral hemispheres.
Hubel, David H. (1926–) USA
Wiesel, Torsten N. (1924–) Sweden
For their discoveries concerning information processing in the visual system.

1982 **Bergström, Sune K.** (1916–) Sweden
Samuelsson, Bengt I. (1934–) Sweden
Vane, Sir John R. (1927–) UK
For their discoveries concerning prostaglandins and related biologically active substances.

1983 **McClintock, Barbara** (1902–) USA
For her discovery of mobile genetic elements.

1984 **Jerne, Niels K.** (1911–)   Denmark
Köhler, Georges J. F. (1946–)   W. Germany
Milstein, César (1927–)   UK and Argentina
For theories concerning the specificity in development and control of the immune system and the discovery of the principle for production of monoclonal antibodies.

1985 **Brown, Michael S.** (1941–)   USA
Goldstein, Joseph L. (1940–)   USA
For their discoveries concerning the regulation of cholesterol metabolism.

1986 **Cohen, Stanley** (1922–)   USA
Levi-Montalcini, Rita (1909–)   Italy and USA
For their discoveries of growth factors.

1987 **Tonegawa, Susumu** (1939–)   Japan
For his discovery of the 'genetic principle for generation of antibody diversity'.

1988 **Black, Sir James W.** (1924–)   UK
Elion, Gertrude B. (1918–)   USA
Hitchings, George H. (1905–)   USA
For their discoveries of 'important principles for drug treatment'.

1989 **Bishop, Michael J.** (1936–)   USA
Varmus, Harold E. (1939–)   USA
For their discovery of the cellular origin of retroviral oncogenes.

1990 **Murray, Joseph E.** (1919–)   USA
Thomas, E. Donnall (1920–)   USA
For their discoveries concerning organ and cell transplantation in the treatment of human disease.

Index of inventors

Index of inventions

Picture credits

The publishers would like to thank the following for use of copyright material:

AFP/Dolby: 196;
Allsport: 251(Adrian Murrell);
ATOCHEM: 86;
Beugnet: 74t;
The Bridgeman Art Library: 167, 187t, 191t(Trinity College Dublin), 220;
Camera Press: 177;
Christophe L: 34, 35t&b, 264, 271, 277t, 279t&b, 280;
© Chrysler: 3;
Claus Ullrich: 188 t&b;
Bruce Coleman Ltd: 176b(Chris James), 178(Dr Echart Pott);
Colombe: 71t, 187b;
Colorsport: 251b, 261;
CNRI: 137t, 150, 153;
CNRS: 85(CROSI), 88(LND Farse), 101t&b(Tim), 103t(LAL), 109b(IJN Forest), 118t(IAP), 134(GPEC Imbert Noulin), 179(LND), 182(Kieffer), 218t(EDF), 238l(LPMT), 244(CPR Groos);
Dagli: 90, 91, 149, 180;
Decramer: 123t;
Deutsche Airbus: 60;
DGA ETCA: 207t;
Dimiglio: 30b;
Domani: 11;
Dorka: 113;
Elf Aquitaine: 172;
Environmental Picture Library: 70(M.Bond);
Ernoult: v, 22;
Ernoult Features: 7, 12b(Dingo), 26, 258(Dingo);
ESA: 116b, 119, 124, 125t, 201, 210;
Mary Evans Picture Library: 232;
CE Fein GmbH & Co: 241;
FOC: 130tl(Jacques);
Gamma: viiit, xt, 4, 8(Geeraerts), 9(Turner-Spooner), 15, 19, 28(Quemere), 29(Wada), 33(Guichard), 69t(Kurita), 115(Gaillarde), 118b(Gaillarde), 130cr(Tazzani), 132br(Kurita), 140t(Turner), 147t, 191b, 216t, 222(Baitel), 223t(Wollman), 230, 234, 240, 254, 257, 259t, 263;

Gamma Liaison: 5(Sander), 25, 50(Barr), 95(Kermani), 100, 103b, 121, 129c, 130tl&tr,cl&br, 131c, 132c, 139(Smart), 144(Remsberg), 146(Kermani), 157, 163, 164, 176c(Sander), 208, 229l&r, 242, 245(Allen), 250, 259b;
Greenpeace: 185r(Dorreboon);
John Hannavy Picture Collection; 275;
Holt Studios Ltd: ixt(Nigel Cattlin);
B. Howarth-Loomes: 273, 274t&b;
Hulton Picture Co: 18, 24, 38t, 47t, 73b, 92, 112(Bettman), 127t, 138, 148, 158, 183, 233, 235, 238r;
Illustrated London News: 204;
Imapress: 221;
INRA: 110(Digat), 111(Pelletier);
Institute of Agricultural History and Museum of English Rural Life, Reading: 160;
INTEL: 213;
Jerrican: 75, 217(Nieto), 219b, 248, 262;
Josse: 14, 57, 97, 193, 198r, 203, 276;
Landsat: 121;
Malaval: 219t;
The Mansell Collection: 56;
Marathon Shell: 260;
Mattel: xib;
Microsoft: 209;
National Maritime Museum: 179t;
National Motor Museum, Beaulieu: 1, 2;
Peter Newark's Western Americana: 31, 1981;
ONERA: vib, 30t, 65, 93;
Robert Opie Collection: 168, 224, 228, 234b;
Orbital: 63;
Oxford Scientific Films: 162b(Riccardo Villarosa);
Philips: 268;
Popperfoto: 20t(David McLellan) & b, 43, 47b(David McLellan) 127b, 143t, 149b, 181, 194, 195b, 200t, 237, 247t, 272;
Prohance: 215;
Pulsar: 12t;
QA Photos: 71b;
Rank Xerox: 243b;
David Redfern: xii, 83b;
Rex Features: vit, xit, 16b, 27, 36, 38b, 39, 42, 44, 53, 59t, 73t, 145, 159, 166t, 169t, 174, 223b, 243t, 247b, 265;

Gilles Rivet: 49;
Science Photo Library: viit(Phil Jude), viii(CNRI), ixb(Philip Plailly), xb(Ray Ellis), 16t, 66t&b, 69b, 74b, 75t, 81(Philip Hayson), 83t(Royal Greenwich Observatory), 86(J.L.Charmet), 98(J.L.Charmet), 102, 104(David Guyon), 105(Henri Schneebel), 107t(Jeremy Burgess), 107b, 109t(Francis Leroy), 114(Roger Ressmeyer), 116t(NASA), 123b(Roger Ressmeyer), 133, 135(Petit Format), 137b(Simon Fraser), 140b, 142(Van Bucher), 143l&r(Dr Robin Williams), 147b(Andrew McClenaghan), 151(Art Stein), 152(St Bartholomew's Hospital), 162t(Martin Bond), 165(Andrew McClenaghan), 173(Simon Fraser), 175(NASA), 176t(Hank Morgan), 184(Ron Church), 195t(Philip Plailly), 207b(David Parker), 212(Charles Falco);
Seigneury Conseil: 136;
SFP: 270;
Sipa Press: 10(Suu-Irogoyen), 155(Nicolas), 253;
SIRPA: 37, 40, 45;
Skuld Energie: 59b;
SODEL: 82(Crepin);
Solair: 23(Waker-Chemic, Germany);
Sony: 216b, 267;
Streetporter: 130bl, 132bl;
Studio X: 218b;
Technics: 266;
Texas Instruments; 214;
Eric Thornburn: 54;
Topham Picture Source: 205;
Usinor Sacilor: 78, 79;
Andrew Varley: 252;
T. Vidé Holotrane: 84(Lanceau);
Josiah Wedgwood & Sons Ltd: 225;
Zefa Picture Library: viib, 185l, 190, 239.

Cover: top, Science Photo Library, centre, Fischer, bottom left, Will McIntyre/Science Photo Library, bottom right, Roger Ressmeyer/Science Photo Library.

Stop press

Swimming with the sharks

The latest sport to take off in Australia is not for the faint-hearted. Every day many boats go out to sea, looking for sharks. When some are found, a group of divers go down to join them. Rather than swimming away, they follow the sharks around and even feed them! Those who enjoy this pastime say that there is nothing quite like the excitement of being so close to something that could easily kill them. So far, luckily, no one has died in this way. The legacy of *Jaws* has finally been overcome.

The Sry gene

In **May 1991** two British research teams led by **Dr Peter Goodfellow** at the Imperial Cancer Research Fund and **Dr Robin Lovell-Badge** at the National Institute for Medical Research announced the discovery of the fragment of DNA that makes the difference between men and women. Known as Sry, the sex-determining part of the Y-chromosome, this gene was injected into fertilised mouse eggs that would have developed into female mice, but some became male.

More research needs to be done so that the success rate can be improved and, at the moment, the males produced are sterile. This is not intended as a means of helping parents determine the sex of their children, but should help scientists to understand more about diseases caused by abnormal development.

Flycatcher

Alan Freeman of Rugby, Warwickshire, who is perhaps best-known for the solar-powered car which featured on the front cover of our first edition, has come up with many ingenious inventions over the years. His latest is a special flycatcher which he devised over the winter of **1990/91**. Shaped somewhat like a gun, all you have to do is point it at the fly or wasp, press a button and the insect is sucked into a transparent tube and trapped inside by a flap valve. The insect can then either be released outside or killed by a drop of disinfectant. In this way, nasty smear marks caused by squashed insects on walls or windows can be avoided.

Virtual Reality

Virtual Reality (VR) is the very latest form of computer simulator with which one can enter a world that has been created by a computer and interact with it. The basic requirements to create VR are: a powerful computer to provide the graphics and sound; a visor and helmet which give a 3-D view and stereo sound; and sensors in the helmet and glove that show you whereabouts you are in the simulation.

With VR one must wear a helmet which has a head-mounted display. In other words, the simulation is projected within the helmet and not on a screen, so the viewer can see and hear nothing else, as the sounds are also transmitted within the helmet. One must also wear a Dataglove (*see* Pg 215) and this will make the wearer's hand appear in the simulation. So, for example, one could pick up a computer graphic teapot. From being used only by such bodies as NASA and the US Air Force, VR systems could be for sale for domestic use in 1992 thanks to developments by companies like W Industries.

First Briton in space

On **18 May 1991**, at 1.50pm British time, **Helen Sharman**, a 27-year-old food scientist from Sheffield, took off on a Soyuz TM-12 rocket from Baikonur in the Soviet Union. She was the first Briton in space, and had been chosen from 13 000 original candidates who applied two years ago and had undergone an intensive 17-month training programme before lift-off. On Monday 20 May the Soyuz TM-12 docked at the orbital space station Mir to carry out some experiments.

Spectacles for the hard of hearing

The spectacles, developed by **Wim Soede** in the Netherlands, are designed to amplify only the sound that comes from directly in front. This enables the wearer to avoid the problem of normal hearing aids that they amplify everything. With having the microphones either above the eyes or along the arms, they are able to filter out much of the background noise.

Clothes that change colour in the heat

This new form of clothing has been developed by the English company **Merck**, who have long worked on liquid crystal materials. The colour changes because heat-sensitive chemicals have been added to an ink which is then printed onto a fabric. These 'thermochromic' clothes were first displayed at a London hotel in **May 1991**

The self-shearing sheep

Australian scientists have found a protein called an epidermal growth factor (EGF) which, when injected into sheep, will make them shed their wool in one go. The technique, developed by **Bill Panaretto**, works because the EGF stops the wool from growing for a day and weakens the link with the sheep's skin. To stop the sheep being bald, it is given a coat to hold the fleece in place for a few weeks. Then, when the farmer is ready to shear the sheep, he simply takes off the coat and the fleece falls off leaving behind only the stubble that has grown since the injection. By this method, it is hoped to greatly speed up the process of shearing and thus save on costs. There appear to be few, if any, after-effects except among pregnant ewes.

Ondansetron

After spending £100 million on developing the drug Ondansetron (trade name Zofran), **Glaxo** believe they could have found a substance which can improve the memories of middle-aged people to the level it was at six to eight years previously.

The drug is already used to treat nausea in people undergoing chemotherapy and could soon be used to relieve symptoms of anxiety. The first tests, carried out on over 200 American middle-aged patients, produced good results, announced in **June 1991**. If further trials prove successful, the drug could be on the market by 1995.